Entrevistas

An Introduction to Language and Culture

Rafael López, *Entendimiento universal*

ABOUT THE COVER ARTIST The work of Rafael López is a fusion of strong graphic style and magical symbolism. Growing up in Mexico City he was immersed by his architect parents in the rich cultural heritage and native color of street life. Influenced by Mexican muralists, **dichos** (*popular sayings*), and myths, he developed a bold, vital drawing style with roots in these traditions.

Trained as an illustrator at the Art Center College of Design, he finds inspiration in communicating concepts with an emotional twist. Recently Rafael completed two large murals in the downtown area of New York, and with his wife, Candice, coordinated the Urban Art Trail project in the East Village. Twelve city blocks plagued by blight and drug dealing were magically transformed with mosaics, sidewalk poetry, and the painting of traffic control boxes and electrical transformers.

Rafael López's studio is located in a 3,000 square foot industrial loft that was formerly the Tenth Avenue Car Garage in the 1930's. López renovated the downstairs space into an eclectic live/work area that houses his collections of folkloric art and fuel his work.

This cover painting, ***Entendimiento universal*** (*Universal Understanding*), symbolically shows the warm interaction of peoples and cultures, as well as their mutual understanding—which is the underlying premise of *Entrevistas*.

Entrevistas

An Introduction to Language and Culture

Second Edition

Robert L. Davis
University of Oregon

H. Jay Siskin
Cabrillo College

Alicia Ramos
Hunter College

Boston   Burr Ridge, IL   Dubuque, IA   Madison, WI   New York
San Francisco   St. Louis   Bangkok   Bogotá   Caracas   Kuala Lumpur
Lisbon   London   Madrid   Mexico City   Milan   Montreal   New Delhi
Santiago   Seoul   Singapore   Sydney   Taipei   Toronto

This is an book.

Entrevistas: An Introduction to Language and Culture

Published by McGraw-Hill Higher Education, an operating unit of The McGraw-Hill Companies, Inc., 1221 Avenue of the Americas, New York, NY 10020. Copyright © 2005, 2000 by The McGraw-Hill Companies, Inc. All rights reserved. No part of this publication may be reproduced or distributed in any form or by any means, or stored in a database or retrieval system, without the prior written consent of The McGraw-Hill Companies, Inc., including, but not limited to, in any network or other electronic storage or transmission, or broadcast for distance learning.

This book is printed on acid-free paper.

2 3 4 5 6 7 8 9 0   DOW / DOW   0 9 8 7 6 5 4

ISBN 0-07-255856-3 (Student Edition)
ISBN 0-07-255857-1 (Instructor's Edition)

Vice president/Editor-in-chief: *Emily G. Barrosse*
Publisher: *William R. Glass*
Senior sponsoring editor: *Christa Harris*
Development editor: *Allen J. Bernier*
Supplements development editor: *Fionnuala McEvoy*
Director of development: *Scott Tinetti*
Senior media producer: *Allison Hawco*
Executive marketing manager: *Nick Agnew*
Project manager: *David Sutton*
Senior production supervisor: *Rich DeVitto*
Senior designer: *Violeta Diaz*
Interior designer: *Mark Ong*
Cover designer: *Violeta Diaz*
Photo research coordinator: *Nora Agbayani*
Art editor: *Emma Ghiselli*
Compositor: *The GTS Companies/York, PA Campus*
Printer: *RR Donnelley*

Cover: Rafael López, *Entendimiento universal*

Because this page cannot legibly accommodate all the copyright notices, page C1 constitutes an extension of the copyright page.

Library of Congress Cataloging-in-Publication Data

Davis, Robert L. (Robert Lee), 1961-
    Entrevistas : an introduction to language and culture/Robert L. Davis, H. Jay Siskin, Alicia Ramos.— [2nd ed.]
       p. cm.
    Spanish and English.
    "This is an EBI book"—Verso t.p.
    Includes index.
    ISBN 0-07-255856-3 (student ed. : alk. paper) — ISBN 0-07-255857-1 (instructor's ed. : alk. paper)
    1. Spanish language—Textbooks for foreign speakers—English. I. Siskin, H. Jay. II. Ramos, Rosa Alicia. III. Title.

PC4129.E5D35 2004
468.2'4—dc22

                                                                2004040203

www.mhhe.com

Contents

Preface   **xiv**

    A Letter to the Student   xxvi

Para empezar   **1**

- What Is Culture?   2
- Culture or Cultures?   2
- Cultural Stereotypes   3
- **¡Adelante!**   3

Vocabulario

CAPÍTULO 1

Somos diferentes, somos iguales 4
Colombia

PARTE 1
Los saludos 6
El alfabeto español 8
El origen y la nacionalidad 10

Pronunciación y ortografía: **Vowels; Consonants 18**

PARTE 2
Los días y los números (1–31) 19
Las descripciones 20

CAPÍTULO 2

Los estudios 34
Costa Rica

PARTE 1
Los estudios universitarios 36
El horario 38
Preguntas para el estudiante típico 41

Pronunciación y ortografía: **Intonation in Questions; Spelling Conventions in Questions 49**

PARTE 2
En el aula 50
¿Dónde está? 51

CAPÍTULO 3

La familia 64
Ecuador

PARTE 1
La familia y los parientes 66
Los números y la edad 68

Pronunciación y ortografía: **Written Accents (I) 78**

PARTE 2
La familia en transición 79
Las actividades familiares 80

CAPÍTULO 4

La casa 92
España

PARTE 1
¿Dónde vives? 94
¿Qué haces en tu casa? 97

Pronunciación y ortografía: **ll and y; z 107**

PARTE 2
¿Qué hay en tu casa? 108

Entrevistas y cultura	Forma y función	Lectura y escritura
Entrevista 1: Jairo Bejarano Carrillo—Bogotá, Colombia 12 Análisis cultural: Greetings in Colombia 17	1.1 Subject Pronouns 14 1.2 The Verb **ser** 15	
Entrevista 2: Stella Amado Carvajal—Duitama, Colombia 22 Señas culturales: Colombian Pledge of Allegiance 28	1.3 Gender and Number Agreement 24 Definite and Indefinite Articles 24 Adjectives 25	Lectura: «Bailaremos lejos… » 29 Portafolio cultural 32
Entrevista 1: Silvana Quesada Nieto—San José, Costa Rica 42 Análisis cultural: Costa Rican Citizenry 48	2.1 Regular **-ar** Verbs; Negation 44 2.2 Question Formation 46	
Entrevista 2: Érika Claré Jiménez—San José, Costa Rica 53 Señas culturales: Ecotourism in Costa Rica 61	2.3 The Verb **ir; ir a** + Infinitive 55 2.4 The Verb **estar** 57	Lectura: «¿Cómo son las carreras que prefieren los jóvenes?» 59 Portafolio cultural 62
Entrevista 1: Cynthia Cevallos Mendoza—Quito, Ecuador 71 Análisis cultural: The Hispanic Family 77	3.1 Expressing Possession 73 3.2 Possessive Adjectives 75	
Entrevista 2: Gabriela Arteta Jácome—Guayaquil, Ecuador 82 Señas culturales: El monumento a la mitad del mundo 86	3.3 Regular **-er** and **-ir** Verbs 84 3.4 Irregular Verbs **dar, hacer, salir, ver** 84	Lectura: «Las familias en tiempos de crisis» 88 Portafolio cultural 90
Entrevista 1: María Benjumeda León—Cádiz, España 98 Señas culturales: Autonomous Regions of Spain 106 Análisis cultural: Spanish Neighbors 106	4.1 Demonstrative Adjectives 101 4.2 Stem-Changing Verbs (e → ie, o → ue) 103	
Entrevista 2: Elena de la Cruz Niggeman—Madrid, España 110	4.3 The Present Progressive 112 4.4 Affirmative Commands 114	Lectura: «Clasificados > Pisos» 116 Portafolio cultural 118

vii

¡A comer!   120
La República Dominicana y Venezuela

En el mercado 122
¿Cómo es la comida? ¿Cómo está
  el plato? 125

Pronunciación y ortografía: **Special Letter Combinations   134**

Las comidas del día 135
En el restaurante 136

Vivir bien   152
Bolivia

La hora exacta y aproximada 154
La rutina diaria 156
El estrés y la relajación 158

Pronunciación y ortografía: **Written Accents (II)   168**

El clima 169
¿Cómo te afecta el clima? 172

De compras   184
México

En el almacén 186
En la tienda 189

Pronunciación y ortografía: **Written Accents (III); Consonant + Vowel**
Combinations   202

En el mercado de artesanías 203

Ritmos de la vida   216
Puerto Rico

Los deportes 218
Los pasatiempos 220

Pronunciación y ortografía: ***l; r* and *rr*   231**

Fiestas y diversiones 232

Entrevistas y cultura	Forma y función	Lectura y escritura
Entrevista 1: Karina de Frías Otero—Santo Domingo, Rep. Dominicana 127 Análisis cultural: Eating in Venezuela 133	5.1 Speaking Impersonally **se** + Verb 129 5.2 **Por** and **para** 130	
Entrevista 2: Patricia Nevil Gallego—Caracas, Venezuela 139 Señas culturales: Simón Bolívar, el Libertador 149	5.3 Stem-Changing Verbs (**e → i**) 141 5.4 Direct Object Pronouns 142 The Personal **a** 144	Lectura: «La cocina en la República Dominicana» 146 Portafolio cultural 150
Entrevista 1: Güido Rivera Melgar—Santa Cruz, Bolivia 160 Señas culturales: La música indígena de Bolivia 159 Análisis cultural: Schedules in Bolivia 167	6.1 Reflexive Pronouns 162 6.2 **Saber** and **conocer** 165	

Entrevista 2: Mirtha Olmos Carballo—La Paz, Bolivia 175	6.3 Uses of **ser** and **estar** (Summary) 177
	    Uses of **estar** 177
	    Uses of **ser** 178
		Lectura: «La calidad de vida» 180
		Portafolio cultural 182

Entrevista 1: Minerva Rubio Andalón—México D.F., México 192
Análisis cultural: El mercado mexicano 200
	7.1 The Preterit 194
	    Forms of Regular Verbs 194
	    Basic Uses 194
	7.2 Indirect Objects and Pronouns 197	

Entrevista 2: Martín Delfín Lira—Zacatecas, México 206 Señas culturales: El Museo Nacional de Antropología 205	7.3 More About the Verb **gustar** 208 7.4 The Verb **quedar** 210	Lectura: «Mitiendita.mx» 212 Portafolio cultural 214
Entrevista 1: Mitch Ortega Caraballo—San Juan, Puerto Rico 223 Análisis cultural: Baseball in the Caribbean 230	8.1 Irregular Forms of the Preterit 225 8.2 Stem-Changing Verbs in the Preterit 228	
Entrevista 2: José Veliz Román—Ponce, Puerto Rico 234 Señas culturales: Roberto Clemente 243	8.3 Negative Words 236 8.4 Using Direct and Indirect Object Pronouns Together 237	Lectura: «Resoluciones para el año nuevo» 240 Portafolio cultural 243

Vocabulario

CAPÍTULO 9

Fiestas y tradiciones   246
Cuba

PARTE 1
La frecuencia 248
Las etapas de la vida 250

Pronunciación y ortografía: **Written Accents (IV)   259**

PARTE 2
¿Qué fiestas celebrabas de niño/a? 260
¿Cómo te sentías? 262

CAPÍTULO 10

Recorridos y recuerdos   274
Argentina

PARTE 1
Los medios de transporte 276
De viaje 277

Pronunciación y ortografía: ***b* and *v*   280**

PARTE 2
Destinos urbanos 291
La identidad regional 293

CAPÍTULO 11

Entre culturas   308
La frontera

PARTE 1
Para cruzar la frontera 310

Pronunciación y ortografía: ***d* and *g*   324**

PARTE 2
La identidad bicultural 325

CAPÍTULO 12

El trabajo   340
Chile

PARTE 1
El mundo del trabajo 342

Pronunciación y ortografía: **The Spanish *s* 352**

PARTE 2
¿Qué hago para buscar empleo? 353

Entrevistas y cultura	Forma y función	Lectura y escritura
Entrevista 1: Juan Oliva Orihuela—La Habana, Cuba 253 Análisis cultural: Cuban-Americans 258	9.1 The Imperfect 255 Forms 255 Basic Uses 255	
Entrevista 2: Eduardo Alemán Águila—La Habana, Cuba 264 Señas culturales: El picadillo 272	9.2 **Gustar** (Review) 266 **Gustar** with Actions (Verbs) 266 **Gustar** with Things (Nouns) 266 9.3 Other Verbs Like **gustar** 267	Lectura: «La madre, la cocina, la abuelita y los chicos» 269 Portafolio cultural 272
Entrevista 1: Nina Ibáñez—Buenos Aires, Argentina 281 Análisis cultural: Buenos Aires 289	10.1 Preterit vs. Imperfect 283 Narrating in the Past 284 Special Translations for the Preterit 284 10.2 More About the Present Participle 287	
Entrevista 2: Leticia Goenaga—Bahía Blanca, Argentina 296 Señas culturales: El tango argentino 305	10.3 The Present Perfect 298 10.4 **Lo** + Adjective 300	Lectura: «La guitarra» 302 Portafolio cultural 306
Entrevista 1: Yolanda Rodríguez Ávila—Tijuana, México 314 Análisis cultural: The Borderland 322	11.1 **Hace** + Time + **que** 317 11.2 **Por** and **para** (Summary) 318 Expressions with **por** 319 Uses of **por** 319 Uses of **para** 319	
Señas culturales: La *Tejano Music* 327 Entrevista 2: Érika Meza Román—Los Ángeles, California 328	11.3 Expressing Unexpected or Unplanned Actions 330 11.4 Adverbs 332	Lectura: «Culturas y generaciones» 335 Portafolio cultural 338
Entrevista 1: Susana Cid Hazard—Santiago de Chile 345 Análisis cultural: Women in Chile 351	12.1 Formal Commands 347	
Entrevista 2: Hernán Fuentes Estévez—Santiago de Chile 356 Señas culturales: La Isla de Pascua 362	12.2 Familiar Commands 358 12.3 Reciprocal Actions 361	Lectura: «Canción del minero» 363 Portafolio cultural 366

Vocabulario

CAPÍTULO 13

El mundo actual   368

El Salvador, Guatemala, Honduras,
Nicaragua y Panamá

PARTE 1

El periódico en línea 370
La comunicación electrónica 371
La televisión y el cine 372

Pronunciación y ortografía: ***p, t,* and *c/qu*   385**

PARTE 2

La política y la comunicación en
    Centroamérica 386

CAPÍTULO 14

**Grupos minoritarios y
mayoritarios   402**

Perú

PARTE 1

La sociedad peruana 404

Pronunciación y ortografía: ***m, n,* and *ñ*   416**

PARTE 2

Los problemas sociales 417

CAPÍTULO 15

**Conexiones y
comunidad   432**

Paraguay y Uruguay

PARTE 1

Las amistades 434

Pronunciación y ortografía: **Written Accents (Summary and Review)   447**

PARTE 2

Para formar pareja 448

Appendix A: Basic Pronunciation Guide   A1

Appendix B: Verb Charts   A3

Vocabularies   V1

Spanish-English Vocabulary   V1

English-Spanish Vocabulary   V40

Index   I1

Credits   C1

Entrevistas y cultura	Forma y función	Lectura y escritura
Entrevista 1: David Guzmán Arias— Tegucigalpa, Honduras 375 Análisis cultural: Newspapers in Central America 384	13.1 The Present Subjunctive 377 Introduction 377 Forms 377 13.2 Basic Uses of the Present Subjunctive 380 Criteria and Cues 380 Expressions of Volition 381	
Entrevista 2: Claudia Bautista Nichola— San Salvador, El Salvador 389 Señas culturales: Mayan Textiles 396	13.3 The Subjunctive with Expressions of Doubt 391 13.4 The Subjunctive with Expressions of Emotion 394	Lectura: «Sociedad civil nicaragüense irrumpe en la televisión con *Sexto sentido*» 397 Portafolio cultural 400
Entrevista 1: Sandra Montiel Nemes— Lima, Perú 407 Señas culturales: Machu Picchu 414 Análisis cultural: Peruvian Society 415	14.1 The Subjunctive with Noun Antecedents 409 14.2 Comparisons 411 Unequal Comparisons 411 Equal Comparisons 412	
Entrevista 2: Héctor Cabral Domínguez— Lima, Perú 419	14.3 The Future Tense 421 Forms 421 Uses 422 14.4 The Subjunctive with Future Actions 423	Lectura: «Testimonio de una mujer shipiba» 426 Portafolio cultural 430
Entrevista 1: Gustavo Camelot— Montevideo, Uruguay 437 Señas culturales: El mate 436 Análisis cultural: Contrasting Uruguay and Paraguay 445	15.1 The Conditional 439 Forms 439 Uses 439 15.2 Results and Consequences 442 **Si** Clauses 442 Forms of the Imperfect Subjunctive 442	
Entrevista 2: Wanda Solla—Montevideo, Uruguay 450	15.3 The Subjunctive (Summary) 452	Lectura: «Citas en el ciberespacio» 455 Portafolio cultural 458

Preface

Welcome to *Entrevistas: An Introduction to Language and Culture!* As technology offers increased opportunities for communication among people and nations, it has become even more crucial to provide students with the necessary tools for developing global communication and multicultural understanding. With these goals in mind, we are delighted to bring you the second edition of *Entrevistas,* an exciting introductory Spanish textbook that will help turn your classroom into a setting for engaging communicative interaction. Richly supported by print and multimedia supplements, including an integrated video and CD-ROM, *Entrevistas* will help you accomplish the following objectives:

- to promote the teaching of language in a cultural context

- to combat stereotypical perceptions of Hispanics that your students may hold

- to develop students' communicative language abilities while simultaneously providing them with clear and comprehensive grammatical coverage

Entrevistas: Highlighting the Cultural Context of Language

The title of the textbook closely reflects its goals and organization. Through interviews with native speakers from throughout the Spanish-speaking world (presented on video and in audio formats and integrated within the text), we have sought to highlight the cultural context of language. Troubled by some students' misunderstanding and lack of empathy for other cultures as part of language study, we critically examined the treatment of culture in first-year Spanish textbooks before setting pen to paper in *Entrevistas.* Although integrating language and culture was a common goal of these textbooks, culture often remained physically and symbolically separated from the remainder of the textbook. Furthermore, culture lacked an authentic voice: it was compartmentalized into high and low culture, at times diminished through show-and-tell pictures and artifacts or simplified through pedagogically contrived texts.

In *Entrevistas,* culture moves from the margins to the center. It drives the organization of each chapter and provides the context for communication. As students acquire the linguistic skills that are essential for effective interaction, they also begin to make connections between the native and target cultures. We believe that by listening to the daily rituals and the aspirations and concerns that these authentic voices communicate, students will modify stereotypes they may have and broaden their global cultural understanding.

How Does *Entrevistas* Help You and Your Students Attain These Goals?

A number of unique sections throughout each chapter will help you and your students in their study of Spanish language and culture. Here is a description of just some of these innovative sections.

- Maps, timelines, and demographic information in the chapter openers orient students to geographical, historical, and racial issues that represent cultural points of reference for native speakers.

- Interviews with native speakers, presented in audio and video formats, provide a point of departure for the development of listening strategies, contextualized grammar practice, thematic readings, process-writing activities, and cross-cultural comparisons.

- Excerpts from English-language guidebooks, travel narratives, and reference works in the **Análisis cultural** sections provide an "outsiders'" point of view; follow-up questions invite students to analyze critically the content and to compare it to the "insider" interviews.

- Cultural images in the **Señas culturales** sections highlight architecture, myth, folklore, ecology, music, and other artifacts that symbolize a country's national identity.

The *entrevistas:* What Are They?

As the name of the textbook suggests, interviews are the point of departure for students' exploration of the Spanish-speaking world. Each chapter contains two interviews that represent a synthesis of several dialogues with native speakers of a given country. From these exchanges, we distilled commonly represented information, themes, and opinions into an interview of appropriate length and level of difficulty for the beginning-level student. Although the language was modified for pedagogical goals, every effort was made to retain natural-sounding language and authentic cultural voices. These lively, engaging interviews invite students to share the lives, concerns, and aspirations of native Spanish speakers.

Culture as Content

Whereas culture is often relegated to the margins in many textbooks, in *Entrevistas* we have sought to restore culture to a central position in the language program. In doing so, we have related culture to broader instructional goals, making it a tool for the exploration of various disciplines, such as history, anthropology, and sociology. Culture also serves as a springboard for exercises emphasizing higher-order thinking skills, including analysis, hypothesis, and synthesis. In addition, we emphasize the importance of cultural (self-) awareness for the development of a

knowledgeable and socially responsible citizen in the global community.

Traditionally, a distinction has been made between "high C" (Olympian) culture—the artistic achievements, historical events, political institutions of a people—and "low c" (hearthstone) culture—everyday patterns of thinking and behavior. Nevertheless, these categories can and do overlap. To illustrate this point, is the tango an example of high or low culture? From its humble origins in the **barrios** of Buenos Aires, it has developed into a "high" art form, the subject of theater and film. And yet, going to a local bar to watch a tango performance may not qualify as a representation of Olympian culture.

As a further illustration, *Don Quijote* may be considered an exemplar of high culture, yet a portrait of Don Quijote and Sancho Panza on a wall hanging may not. Likewise, a performance of *Man of La Mancha* may not meet everyone's criteria for artistic achievement.

The difficulty in making the high/low distinction when defining culture leads us to another observation: culture is not monolithic. That is to say, cultural processes and products differ geographically within the same national entity; between generations, sexes, and races; between immigrants and native-born citizens, and so on. Culture is dynamic, changing rapidly through global communications, technological advances, political turmoil, as well as through other influences.

Despite this variation, we recognize that there exists significant congruence in belief and practice to bind a people together and to allow us to speak of a (national, regional, professional) culture. It is this ambiguity that makes the characterization of a culture so slippery.

Representing culture "authentically" in a textbook is a challenging proposition. No one person or text can express the multifaceted nature of culture. We have therefore decided to introduce a multiplicity of voices, calling on the experiences of native speakers in the **Entrevistas,** presenting the viewpoints of the print media in the **Lecturas,** identifying cultural icons in the **Señas culturales,** and exposing a cultural outsider's observations in the **Análisis culturales.**

An additional challenge in the teaching of culture is the lack of critical awareness on the part of some students: they may have never reflected on their own values, behaviors, and world views, and on what distinguishes them from other members of society. Furthermore, students may hold negative associations with linguistic and cultural diversity and therefore stubbornly cling to an ethnocentric point of view.

We have addressed the first problem by providing numerous exercises that encourage self-reflection and critical analysis. By reflecting on their own experiences and by sharing these experiences with others, students will become aware of the cultural diversity within their own classroom and, by extension, within the greater society.

Helping students develop empathy for other cultures is an important goal of *Entrevistas*. The interview format—an encounter between a non-native speaker and a native speaker—"opens up" the culture, explaining beliefs and behaviors. Throughout *Entrevistas,* we have attempted to avoid generalizations and stereotypes. Nevertheless, in order to avoid overly complex definitions/characterizations that might make it difficult to define/characterize national identity, we make references to **los norteamericanos, los colombianos,** and so on. We trust that the readers of *Entrevistas* will understand these terms in the spirit of cultural diversity—and unity.

A Word About Grammar

The unique approach to culture in *Entrevistas* is complemented by a comprehensive and practical coverage of grammatical structures. The following features characterize the treatment of grammar in *Entrevistas:*

- carefully sequenced grammar activities, moving from form-focused exercises to those that require a more creative use of language

- presentation and practice of linguistic items in contextualized, functional frames

- a focus on process strategies—both in the textbook and in the workbook—that encourages students to view listening, reading, and writing as active tasks, requiring meaningful interaction as well as high-order cognitive processing

- continuous attention to the development and reinforcement of linguistic accuracy and culturally appropriate behaviors

Entrevistas: In Step with the National Foreign Language Standards

In response to the *Goals 2000: Educate America Act,* the American Council on the Teaching of Foreign Languages (ACTFL) received funding to develop K–12 content standards for foreign language education. Working in collaboration with professional organizations such as the American Association of Teachers of Spanish and Portuguese (AATSP), among others,[1] ACTFL launched the National Standards in its 1996 volume, *Standards for Foreign Language Learning: Preparing for the 21st Century.* The Standards and their challenging vision of educational reform were embraced by government, business, and over fifty professional and state organizations.

The Standards are organized into five goal areas: Communication, Cultures, Connections, Comparisons, and Communities. These "five C's" are symbolized by five interlocking circles, representing the close interrelationship among these goals. Each includes two or three content standards that describe what students should know and be able to do as a result of their language study. The Standards differ from a skill-based paradigm, where listening, speaking, reading, and writing are divorced from content and communication. Rather, the Standards emphasize the four skills as instruments for acquiring cross-disciplinary knowledge, developing critical-thinking skills, and communicative strategies. Although the goals do not prescribe curriculum, they necessarily influence pedagogical approaches and performance outcomes.

More specifically, the Standards ask us to reconceptualize our approach to culture. As Phillips notes: "In spite of much lip service over the years, culture remained at the periphery of instruction, most frequently referred to as a fifth skill, a capsule, a cultural note at the bottom of a textbook page, or a Friday 'fun' activity . . . . Teachers taught the culture as they knew it; students learned items randomly, not as connected threads or themes. In most courses, no systemic process was visible that enabled students to observe cultural manifestations; to analyze the patterns of behavior; to hypothesize

---

[1] The other organizations included in this project were the American Association of Teachers of French (AATF) and the American Association of Teachers of German (AATG).

about origins, usage, or context; and to understand the perspectives of the people in the target cultures. In sum, most cultural content learned was fact or act in isolation from how it related to the values and attitudes of a person or a people."[2]

With its integrated, multifaced approach to culture, *Entrevistas* exemplifies the fresh spirit of the Standards. Culture is organized thematically by chapter. Within each chapter, however, students are exposed to a multiplicity of *products, processes,* and *perspectives.* From authentic interviews with native speakers, to artifacts symbolizing national identity, to "outsiders'" reflections on behaviors and institutions, *Entrevistas* provides sustained opportunities for hypothesis and analysis, inviting students to make connections between beliefs, behaviors, and cultural artifacts.

In addition to culture, *Entrevistas* reflects the four additional goal areas described in the National Standards. Through its presentation of functional language, role-play, small-group, and personalized activities, *Entrevistas* emphasizes *communication.* The documents, readings, and other exploratory activities help students make *connections* among discipline areas. Ample opportunities are provided for cross-cultural *comparisons* in the follow-up activities to the interviews and also in additional reading and listening exercises. Finally, Internet-based and experiential activities allow students to explore *communities.*

What's New to the Second Edition?

In addition to the all new design for the Second Edition, we have made the following changes in response to instructor feedback on the First Edition.

- There are thirty all new video interviews with native Spanish speakers from seventeen different countries from around the Spanish-speaking world. All are available on VHS videotape or digitally on the Interactive CD-ROM included with every new copy of the textbook.

- In response to reviewer comments, grammar explanations have been simplified or clarified to make it easier for students to understand some of the more complex grammar points of the Spanish language. Additionally, a new form-focused **Análisis estructural** activity that allows students to focus on the new grammar rules before moving on to the more communicative activities has been added to many grammar explanations.

- New readings have been selected for **Capítulos 3, 4, 5, 7, 10, 12, 13, 14,** and **15,** thus keeping content current and of interest to today's students.

- A new **Portafolio cultural** feature, which combines the **A ti te toca** and the **Portafolio cultural** from the First Edition textbook and *Manual de práctica* respectively, provides a combination composition **(Redacción)** and Internet cultural research and in-class presentation activity **(Exploración),** thus expanding on the four-skills approach of *Entrevistas.*

- **Capítulo 13,** with the new title **El mundo actual,** adds the topic of technologies such as cell phones, the Internet, and so on to the First Edition's general theme of **Los medios de comunicación.**

- There are some new names for First Edition features. The two **Entrevistas** sections in each chapter are now called **Entrevista 1** and **Entrevista 2, Se dice que...** sections are now **Análisis cultural,** and **Señas de identidad** have been renamed **Señas culturales.**

- Regional maps of the Spanish-speaking world and an English-Spanish dictionary have been added to the textbook.

- Finally, the activities, content, and themes have been revised and in some cases expanded to keep the textbook fresh and up-to-date.

---

[2] Phillips, June K., ed. 1999. *Foreign Language Standards: Linking Research, Theories, and Practices.* Lincolnwood, Ill.: NTC, p. 8.

A Guided Tour of *Entrevistas*

Chapter-Opening Pages

Each chapter begins with a list of cultural and grammatical objectives that preview goals and content. These pages also contain timelines that relate important historical, political, and cultural events in the United States, Canada, and the country or region of focus. Maps allow students to situate the homes of the native-speaker interviewees as well as geographic features that provide points of reference for that country's inhabitants. Demographic information emphasizes cultural and linguistic diversity.

Following the chapter-opening pages, each chapter is divided into two major sections: **Parte 1** and **Parte 2.** The contents of each **Parte** are easily distinguished by the unique border treatment along the outside edge of each page: red and orange for **Parte 1,** red and blue for **Parte 2.**

Vocabulario

Vocabulary is organized thematically and often presented visually through line drawings, photos, and realia wherever appropriate to illustrate culturally significant contrasts and similiarities. Students are given ample opportunity to practice new lexical items through form-focused and communicative activities.

Entrevista 1/2

Entrevista 1, the first of two native-speaker interviews recorded in audio and video formats, personalizes the cultural themes of the chapter, illustrates vocabulary usage in context, and previews grammatical structures. Biographical information and photos acquaint students with the speaker's immediate surroundings and cultural context.

The interview is introduced by **Antes de ver** activities, which facilitate comprehension by activating relevant vocabulary, grammar, and discourse items. As students watch the interview, they are given specific tasks to perform in the **¡Veamos!** section. Their comprehension is checked through **Después de ver** activities.

The second native-speaker interview can be found in **Parte 2** in the corresponding **Entrevista 2** section. At the end of each **Entrevista 2** section is a special **Piénsalo bien** activity that asks students to compare the two interviewees from the chapter.

Forma y función

An average of two grammar points are presented in this section, both of which are closely linked to the interview. Charts and bulleted lists facilitate self-study. Each grammar presentation is followed by a series of activities that emphasizes meaningful use of language. At the end of many grammar explanations there is a new **Análisis estructural** section with a form-focused activity designed to focus students' attention on the grammar rules before they attempt the more communicative activities.

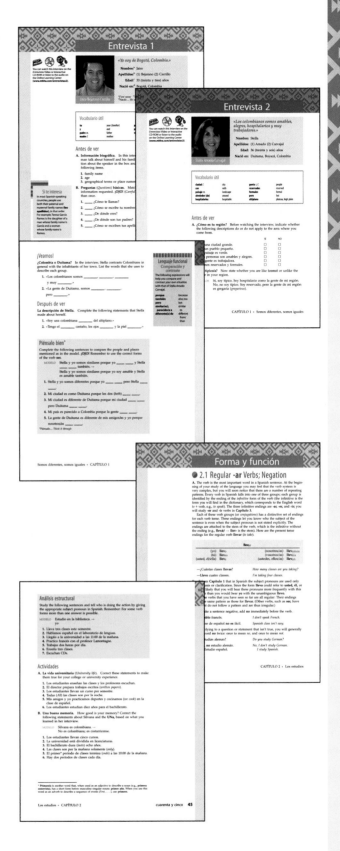

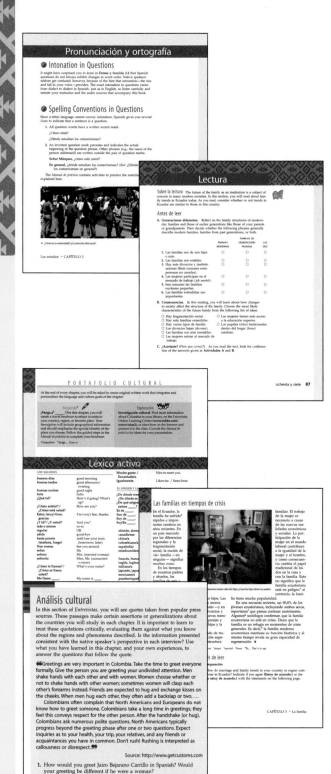

Pronunciación y ortografía

This section, which separates **Parte 1** from **Parte 2,** presents major spelling rules and pronunciation contrasts between English and Spanish. Listening, pronunciation, and writing activities are provided in the *Manual de práctica.*

Lectura

Parte 2 contains the same major sections as **Parte 1.** However, **Parte 2** also includes additional focus on reading and writing. The **Lectura** is an authentic text (journalistic or literary in nature) that is thematically linked to the chapter content. **Lectura** sections begin with **Antes de leer** activities that emphasize process strategies such as the activation of background knowledge, scanning for information, guessing from context, cognate recognition, and so on. **Después de leer** activities check comprehension.

Portafolio cultural

The final activity in the chapter has two parts: **Redacción** and **Exploración. Redacción** introduces a writing task that is thematically integrated into the chapter and invites students to synthesize vocabulary, grammatical structures, and cultural content. **Exploración** directs students to make use of the vast cultural resource that the Internet can be as well as other resources to explore the themes presented in the chapter. Process writing strategies that support the **Redacción** assignment and a list of key words for the **Exploración** component can be found in the *Manual de práctica.*

Additional Features

Análisis cultural

Students' knowledge of the Spanish-speaking world is often shaped by the media or the personal tales of tourists. These impressions are rarely challenged. It is the goal of the **Análisis cultural** section to provide a forum for critical analysis of these popular portrayals as presented in excerpts from English-language travel guides, travel narratives, and reference books. Students are invited to discuss these passages in light of what they have learned through the native-speaker interviews and readings.

We realize that instructors differ in their philosophies toward the use of English in the Spanish-language classroom. In this case, we believe that the opportunities for culture learning and the development of critical-thinking skills provide a strong rationale for this activity. Indeed, as students' linguistic skills develop, the language of the accompanying questions changes to Spanish.

Señas culturales

The flag, baseball, and apple pie. . . . These have been traditional American cultural icons, calling up historical, political, and emotive attachments to the nation. As American society becomes more diverse, these icons are perhaps less meaningful. Nevertheless, Americans can readily generate a list of people, places, events, or institutions that evoke their country and form part of its cultural mythology. In this section, we have asked native Spanish-speakers to do the same, and we have highlighted at least one symbol of cultural identity in this section. Students are then asked to analyze and reflect upon issues of personal, social, and national identity.

Lenguaje funcional

Functional language, that is to say, language used to carry out communicative tasks, such as requesting, inviting, agreeing, and refusing, is presented in this feature. Students are asked to practice language functions in context through role-play activities based on the theme of the chapter.

Si te interesa

This feature provides additional details to the cultural, lexical, and grammatical presentations in the chapter. Since linguistic rules and cultural behaviors may appear to be arbitrary or capricious to students, these explanations attempt to address the "hows" and "whys" of language systems. In addition, many students are genuinely interested in furthering their knowledge of culture and language. The **Si te interesa** explanations can provide a point of departure for their exploration.

New Media Supplements

There are some exciting new or updated media supplements for the Second Edition.

- The new *Video*, which is available to adoption institutions and also for student purchase, contains all of the new native-speaker interviews integrated in the **Entrevista** sections of each chapter. Students will have the opportunity to view speakers from diverse countries of the Spanish-speaking world while learning about their lives, their customs, and their culture. Each interview is separated into manageable segments that contain useful on-screen interview questions, providing structure to the interview and also helping to facilitate comprehension.

- The redesigned *Interactive CD-ROM*, available in both Windows and Macintosh formats and packaged with every new copy of the student textbook, offers an interactive language learning experience for the student. Through the CD-ROM's innovative and visually appealing activities, which include digital video versions of the new native-speaker interviews, students develop listening comprehension skills, refine their reading ability, reinforce their understanding of vocabulary and grammar, and explore the culture of the Spanish-speaking world.

- McGraw-Hill is proud to partner with **Quia**™ in the development of the new *Online Manual de práctica*. Carefully integrated with the textbook, this robust digital version of the printed *Manual de práctica* is easy for students to use and great for instructors who want to manage students' coursework online. Virtually identical in content to the print version, and also split into two volumes, the *Online Manual de práctica* contains the full audio program and provides students with automatic feedback and scoring of their work. A robust Instructor's Workstation contains an easy-to-use gradebook and class roster system that facilitates course management.

- The redesigned *Online Learning Center* (**www.mhhe.com/entrevistas2**) offers even more practice with the vocabulary and grammar presented in the textbook, audio files of the interviews, and sample links to various websites that students can use as a starting point to explore further the cultural themes presented in each chapter. Several additional resources including links to the *Instructor's Manual / Testing Program, Audioscript, Videoscript*, digital transparencies of some of the drawings and PowerPoint presentations of the grammar tables found in the textbook are available in the password-protected Instructor's Edition.

Premium Content on the *Online Learning Center*

If you have purchased a *new* copy of the Student Edition of *Entrevistas*, you have access to premium content on the *Online Learning Center* at **www.mhhe. com/entrevistas2.** This includes the complete audio program that supports the *Manual de práctica*. The card bound inside the front cover of this book provides a registration code to access the premium content. *This code is unique to each individual user.* Other study resources may be added to the premium content during the life of the edition of the book.

If you have purchased a *used* copy of the Student Edition of *Entrevistas* but would also like to have access to the premium content, you may purchase a registration code for a nominal fee. Please visit the *Online Learning Center* for more information.

If you are an instructor, you do not need a special registration code for premium content. Instructors have full access to all levels of content via the Instructor's Edition link on the homepage of the *Online Learning Center*. Please contact your local McGraw-Hill sales representative for your password to the Instructor's Edition.

Supplements

As a full-service publisher of quality educational products, McGraw-Hill does much more than just sell textbooks to your students. We create and publish an extensive array of print, video, and digital supplements to support instruction on your campus. Orders of new (versus used) textbooks help us to defray the cost of developing such supplements, which is substantial. Please consult your local McGraw-Hill representative to learn about the availability and restrictions of the supplements that accompany this second edition of *Entrevistas*.

For Instructors *and* Students

- The *Manual de práctica*, developed by the authors, with contributions by Sayo Murcia and Wayne Gottshall of the University of Oregon, follows the organization of the textbook and provides additional review and practice of vocabulary and grammatical structures. In addition, each chapter of the *Manual de práctica* begins with a review section (**Repaso y anticipación**) that recycles previously studied vocabulary and grammatical items in preparation for the current chapter's work. A **Portafolio cultural** at the end of each chapter is a selection of three activities that allows students to synthesize the material covered in the textbook chapter. Some tasks stress observation, analysis, and comparison of texts and realia; others focus on developing knowledge of content through web-based or library research; and still others provide students with free-writing tasks. Instructors may assign any number of these activities, which students may turn in with their *Manual* or assemble into a cultural portfolio to be collected and assessed at the end of the term. Volume 1 of this combination workbook / laboratory manual contains **Capítulos 1–8.** Volume 2 contains **Capítulos 9–15** with **Capítulo 8** in an appendix.

- The new *Online Manual de práctica,* produced in collaboration with **Quia™,** offers the same outstanding practice as the printed *Manual de práctica* with many additional advantages such as on-screen links to corresponding audio files, immediate feedback and scoring for students, and an easy-to-use gradebook and class roster system for instructors. Students should purchase the bifold sleeve, which contains a unique *Student Book Key* (passcode). Instructors should contact their local McGraw-Hill sales representative for an *Instructor Book Key.*

- The *Audio CD Program* that accompanies the *Manual de práctica* provides hours of focused listening practice and opportunities to develop pronunciation and speaking abilities. Included in the *Audio CD Program* is the *Textbook Audio CD* that contains audio versions of the new native-speaker interviews.

- The *Interactive CD-ROM* is available in a multiplatform format and offers students opportunities to practice the vocabulary, grammar, and cultural topics presented in the textbook, and to view the new native-speaker interviews, all in an engaging multimedia environment.

- The Student Edition of the *Online Learning Center* (www.mhhe.com/entrevistas2) provides even more practice with the vocabulary, grammar, and cultural topics presented in the textbook. It also contains audio-only versions of the native-speaker interviews. (Please see the section about premium content on the *Online Learning Center* presented earlier in this preface.) The Instructor's Edition contains resources to assist instructors in getting the most out of the *Entrevistas* program.

- The *Video* contains the thirty new interviews with native speakers from around the Spanish-speaking world.

- *Sin falta* is a new Spanish writing program that contains the following features: a word processor; a simple method for using accented characters; a bilingual Spanish-English dictionary with over 250,000 entries including slang, technical terms, idioms, and more; a complete online Spanish grammar reference; spelling and basic grammar check functions; automatic verb conjugations for thousands of verbs; correction of common beginners' errors; and sample letters for correspondence in Spanish.

- The *Ultralingua en español Spanish-English Dictionary on CD-ROM* is an interactive bilingual dictionary, available for purchase, offering additional opportunities for students to enrich their vocabulary and improve their Spanish.

For Instructors Only

- The annotated *Instructor's Edition* of the textbook contains numerous on-page teaching suggestions, informative notes, ideas for follow-up and expansion activities, and answers for activities whenever feasible.

- The *Instructor's Manual* portion of the combined *Instructor's Manual / Testing Program* provides sample syllabi and lesson plans, additional teaching techniques, supplementary exercises and activities, and the *Videoscript* of the new native-speaker interviews. The *Testing Program* offers three tests per chapter: two chapter tests updated from the First Edition and one new test for the Second Edition. The complete *Instructor's Manual / Testing Program* is available in electronic format on the new *Instructor's Resource CD-ROM*.

- The *Audioscript* is a complete transcript of the *Audio CD Program*.

- The new *Instructor's Resource CD-ROM* includes MSWord files of the *Instructor's Manual / Testing Program* and the *Videoscript* of the new native-speaker interviews, MSWord and Adobe PDF files of the *Audioscript*, as well as digital transparencies of some of the drawings and PowerPoint presentations of the grammar tables found in the textbook.

Acknowledgements

We would like to acknowledge the many individuals at McGraw-Hill who contributed to the Second Edition of *Entrevistas*. First, to Thalia Dorwick, former Vice President and Editor-in-Chief for her insightful feedback and encouragement of the *Entrevistas* program since its humble beginnings in 2000. We wish her the best in all her future endeavors. Many thanks are owed to William R. Glass, our Publisher, and to Christa Harris, our Sponsoring Editor, for their overall ideas, support, and work with the revision plan and the initial stages of this project. We would like to express our deep gratitude to Allen J. Bernier, our Development Editor, for his ideas and outstanding editorial and project management skills that ensured a polished manuscript and steady progress throughout the editorial process. We thank Laura Chastain (El Salvador), whose careful reading of the manuscript for details of style, clarity, and language added considerably to the quality of the final version. Many thanks are also due to Scott Tinetti, Director of Development, Fionnuala McEvoy, Supplements Development Editor, Allison Hawco, Senior Media Producer, Stacy Shearer and Daniela Reissmann, Editorial Assistants, and to freelance editors Pennie Nichols, Jane Johnson (*University of Texas at Austin*), and Julie Sellers (*University of Wyoming*) for their invaluable contributions to the editorial process of the textbook and various print and media supplements. Special thanks go to the entire production team at McGraw-Hill, especially to David Sutton, Emma Ghiselli, Nora Agbayani, Louis Swaim, Mel Valentín, and Rich DeVitto, as well as to Violeta Díaz for the wonderful new design of the Second Edition. We would like to thank Nick Agnew, Executive Marketing Manager, Terri Rowenhorst, Field Publisher, and the rest of the McGraw-Hill Marketing and Sales force for their enthusiastic and continued support and promotion of our program. Certainly there were many other individuals involved behind the scenes at McGraw-Hill, all of whom worked tirelessly on this project, and whom we also thank for their participation.

We would like to thank Jennifer Rodes, Diana Lee, Steven Grossman, and the entire staff at Klic Productions for their outstanding work in all stages of filming, editing, and producing the new video for this edition as well as to the thirty interviewees who participated in and contributed to this project. Their words, beliefs, and aspirations form the essence of the *Entrevistas* program: Eduardo Alemán Águila, Stella Amado Carvajal, Gabriela Arteta Jácome, Claudia Bautista Nichola, Jairo Bejarano Carrillo, María Benjumeda León, Héctor Cabral Domínguez, Gustavo Camelot, Cynthia Cevallos Mendoza, Susana Cid Hazard, Érika Claré Jiménez, Karina de Frías Otero, Elena de la Cruz Niggeman, Martín Delfín Lira, Hernán Fuentes Estévez, Leticia Goenaga, David Guzmán Arias, Nina Ibáñez, Érika Meza Román, Sandra Montiel Nemes, Patricia Nevil Gallego, Juan Oliva Orihuela, Mirtha Olmos Carballo, Mitch Ortega Caraballo, Silvana Quesada Nieto, Güido Rivera Melgar, Yolanda Rodríguez Ávila, Minerva Rubio Andalón, Wanda Solla, and José Veliz Román.

We extend a heartfelt thanks to the following individuals who reviewed the First Edition or participated in a preliminary survey or final review of the Second Edition. Their comments were indispensable in the development of this Second Edition. The appearance of their names does not necessarily constitute an endorsement of the program or its methodology.

First Edition Reviewers

- Franklin Attoun, *College of the Desert*
- Leslie Bary, *University of Louisiana—Lafayette*
- Carol A. Beresiwsky, *Kapiolani Community College*
- Luciana T. Castro, *Skyline College*
- Luis E. Latoja, *Columbus State Community College*
- Carmen Schlig, *Georgia State University*
- Domenico Sottile, *College of the Desert*
- Alice Susco Reyes, *Marywood University*
- Germán Torres, *Georgia State University*

Second Edition Survey Participants

- Kevin Beard, *Richland College*
- Melissa Bronfman, *Albright College*
- María Castro DeMoux, *US Naval Academy*
- June Chatterjee, *Contra Costa College*
- Martivon Galindo, *Holy Names College*
- Yolanda Hernández, *Community College of Southern Nevada*
- Linde Keil, *Kapiolani Community College*
- Andrea Kubiak, *College of the Desert*
- Kim Lowry, *Asbury College*
- Charles Merrill, *Mount Saint Mary's College*
- Marcie Rinka, *University of San Diego*

- Kristin Routt, *Eastern Illinois University*
- Eric Sakai, *Community College of Vermont*
- Sandra Uribe, *Northwest Vista College*

Second Edition Final Reviewers

- Marge Andrews, *Eastern Washington University*
- Andrea Bakorn, *North Harris Montgomery Community College*
- Alejandra Balestra, *University of New Mexico*
- Ron Cere, *Eastern Michigan University*
- Harriett Hamilton, *Northwest Arkansas Community College*
- Lora Looney, *University of Portland*
- Oscar Moreno, *Georgia State University*
- Maritza Salgueiro-Carlisle, *Bakersfield College*
- Angela Tavares-Sogocio, *Miami Dade Community College—Wolfson Campus*
- Theresa Zmurkewycz, *St. Joseph's University*

Finally, we are indebted to our families and friends who, through their support and understanding, have helped make this Second Edition of *Entrevistas* a reality: Frances and Jan Siskin, Ruby Lee, Mike Stafford, Caitlin Snyder, Dana Raymond, and Mrs. Rosa Ramos.

We dedicate this Second Edition to the loving memory of Gregory Trauth (1958–2000), Wayne Gottshall (1955–2002), and David Siskin (1914–2003).

A Letter to the Student

Dear Student:

Welcome to *Entrevistas,* an innovative program that introduces you to the Spanish language and the diverse cultures of the Spanish-speaking world. The title of the textbook reflects its goals and content: by watching interviews **(entrevistas)** with native speakers, interacting with your classmates, and exploring the community outside your classroom, you will learn not only the vocabulary and structures of the Spanish language but also gain insight into the thought patterns, behaviors, and traditions that form the basis for cultural understanding.

Throughout *Entrevistas* you will encounter numerous activities that ask you to analyze, reflect upon, and synthesize ideas expressed by a wide variety of speakers and writers. Indeed, your investigation of "foreign" cultures will lead to increased understanding of your own culture and empathy for those you might have considered "different." You'll have a chance to begin exploring some of these issues in the preliminary chapter, titled **Para empezar.** By the end of the course, you will know far more than just the grammar of the Spanish language. You will have discussed immigration patterns to the United States, minority populations in Peru, the Caribbean cuisine, housing in Spain, the indigenous languages of Paraguay, and many other topics of interest.

Learning a foreign language is an enriching undertaking. To make the most of your experience, you may need to develop specialized study strategies. Here are some principles to keep in mind:

- *Language is more than a set of grammar rules.* Although structural accuracy is an important component of communication, you must also learn how to communicate in a manner that is appropriate to the situation. Likewise, in addition to building a strong vocabulary, you will also need to learn ways of paraphrasing so that you will be able to communicate effectively when you don't know an expression or it has slipped your mind. Body language and gestures are also important communicative strategies.

- *Active language use is far more important than talking about language.* The ability to recite the rules of Spanish grammar does not guarantee that you

will actually be able to communicate in the language. Spend your time communicating in the language, creating messages, obtaining information, listening for details, and so on.

- *Don't be afraid to make errors!* Errors are a natural part of the language-learning process and are to be expected. Do not let fear of making an error prevent you from communicating. Even if your language is not perfect, your message may be understood. Of course, accurate use of language is an appropriate goal of language study. Pay careful attention to the models you have available: your instructor, the video, the audio program, and the other components of *Entrevistas.* If you are corrected, do not take it as a personal affront. Rather, use this feedback to check your understanding of the linguistic system and to improve your communication skills.

- *Language learning is a long-term process.* Therefore, you must have realistic expectations of your performance after one semester, one year, or several years of language study. Advanced proficiency is often best achieved after long periods of practice and residence in a country where the target language is spoken.

- *Be an active language learner.* Study models, look for patterns, and make informed guesses. If you do not entirely understand a passage, do not ask for a translation immediately. Make use of the language you already know: for example, words that look like English words or that may be related to other words you know in Spanish.

Throughout *Entrevistas,* you will learn other tips for refining your language-learning skills. Although language learning can be hard work (involving memorization and close attention to detail), your efforts will be rewarded with a deeper understanding of yourself and the global village of which you are a citizen. **¡Adelante!**

RLD
HJS
AR

Para empezar

▲ Un mural en La Pequeña Habana, Miami, los Estados Unidos

▲ Una mezquita (mosque) en Marbella, España

◀ Un artefacto maya en el Museo Nacional de Antropología, México, D.F. (Distrito Federal)

▲ Un festival folclórico en Coya, Perú

▲ El Museo Guggenheim en Bilbao, España

What Is Culture?

One of the main goals of this book is to familiarize you with the cultures of Spain and Spanish America. Definitions of the word *culture* can be long and complex. Moreover, culture may signify different things to different people.

A. Culture. What associations do you have with the word *culture*? Check all the boxes that apply, and add some other associations.

I associate the term *culture* with . . .

☐ folk dance and handicrafts.
☐ festivals (national, religious, and so on).
☐ shopping habits.
☐ religious beliefs.
☐ literature.
☐ gestures people use when speaking.

☐ people's reactions in different situations.
☐ masterpieces of art.
☐ how people conceptualize time.
☐ opera.
☐ the distance between people when they talk.
¿ ?

Discuss your answers in small groups and then compare them with the rest of the class. What are the most common associations with the word *culture*?

Culture or Cultures?

We often refer to "American culture," "Hispanic culture," "French culture," and so on, as if they were uniform and static. Instead, within each broadly defined national culture there are a number of different cultures, and aspects of a culture are always undergoing change. The following activity will help you focus on this concept of cultures-within-a-culture.

B. "Typical" characteristics

Paso (*Step*) **1.** Introduce yourself to your partner. Then, working together, write a couple of sentences describing a "typical" person from your country. When you are finished, read your descriptions aloud. Which characteristics are mentioned by different pairs of students? Overall, is there more uniformity or divergence in your responses?

Paso 2. Now answer the following questions by yourself.

1. Do you have your groceries put in a "sack" or in a "bag"? Do you put water in a "bucket" or in a "pail"?
2. Which of the following TV shows did you watch during your childhood: *Leave It to Beaver, The Brady Bunch, The Cosby Show,* MTV's *The Real World,* . . . ? (List two or three others.)
3. When you are addressing a group of people, which pronoun do you use: *you, y'all, you guys,* . . . ? Do you use different pronouns when talking to a group of adults or unknown persons than when talking to a group of friends or peers?

4. Which of the following holidays do you observe: Easter, Passover, Christmas, Hannukah, Ramadan, Kwanzaa, . . . ?
5. Which language(s) do you speak at home? Which language(s) do your parents/grandparents use with their parents or their friends?

Paso 3. Compare your answers to **Paso 2** with those of a partner, then with those of the rest of the class. What do your answers reveal about your age, where you grew up, your background, and so on? How similar are you to the "typical" person described in **Paso 1** and to other members of your class? How inclusive, then, is the term *culture*?

Cultural Stereotypes

You have seen that the "culture" of a given country may include a diversity of beliefs, celebrations, ethnic origins, and regional variations of speech/behavior. Yet people from within a country as well as from outside it often make general, sweeping statements about its inhabitants, such as "Americans are materialistic," "Germans are efficient," or "The French are romantic." These statements are called *stereotypes*: They are generalizations, often based on limited knowledge of a culture or a refusal to accept the validity of cultural differences. Although you may know some people of these nationalities who exhibit these traits, you can probably name many more who do not.

C. Dispelling stereotypes.   Answer the following questions.

1. What stereotypes have you heard about Hispanics? Which relate to overall "Hispanic culture" and which are more specific to a given nationality within the Spanish-speaking world?
2. How valid do you think these statements are? Can you represent a culture fairly without having spent an extended period of time living in it? Why or why not?
3. Do you know (or know of) some people from these countries? Explain how their own traits dispel the stereotypes about them.
4. Are all generalizations stereotypes? How do you know when one is and when one is not? Give some examples of both types of generalizations.

¡Adelante!ª

The activities you have just completed have prepared you for what you will learn throughout this text. Always keep your eyes, ears, heart, and mind open, and you will discover a whole new world. Good luck on this exciting journey!

ªOnward!

Somos diferentes, somos iguales

Colombia

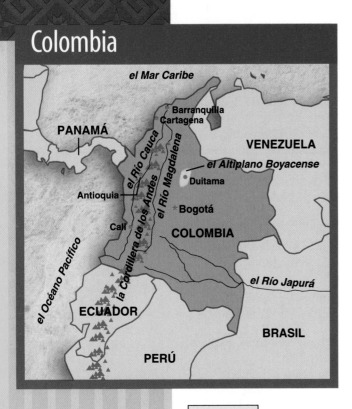

Cultura

◆ Formal vs. Familiar *You*

◆ Cultural Identity: **Ballet Folclórico de Antioquia**

◆ **Señas culturales:** Colombian Pledge of Allegiance

Lengua

◆ Greetings and Introductions

◆ The Spanish Alphabet

◆ Origin and Nationality

◆ Days of the Week; Numbers 1–31

◆ Adjectives of Description

◆ Subject Pronouns (1.1)

◆ The Verb **ser** (1.2)

◆ Gender and Number Agreement (1.3)

Colombia								
Calima, Muiscas, Quibaya, Sinú, Tayrona, and other Amerindian tribes	Arrival of first Europeans			First permanent European settlement in Santa Marta, Colombia	Conquest of interior begins; displacement of indigenous population			
until 1499	**1499**	**until 16th c.**	**1500–1600**	**1525**	**1534**	**1536**	**1600–1750**	**1608**
		Various indigenous tribes inhabit North America	Spanish exploration of North America		Jacques Cartier claims Canada for France		British colonies founded in North America	Quebec founded

Los Estados Unidos y el Canadá

Instantánea

ORIGEN DEL NOMBRE

Colombia: from *Christopher Columbus* (**Cristóbal Colón**)

POBLACIÓN

44.533.300

LENGUAS

Spanish (official), Chibcha, Arawakan (and other indigenous languages)

◀ La calle (*The Street*), *del artista colombiano Fernando Botero (1950–)*

For additional practice, check out the *Manual de práctica,* the Interactive CD-ROM, and the Online Learning Center (**www.mhhe.com/entrevistas2**)!

	Independence		Country named **República de Colombia**		Most violent of Colombia's civil wars breaks out		Gabriel García Márquez wins Nobel Prize	New constitution		Álvaro Uribe Vélez elected president
1776–1783	**1819**	**1846–1848**	**1866**	**1898**	**1952**	**1953**	**1982**	**1991**	**1994**	**2002**
American War of Independence		Mexican-American War		Spanish-American War	Puerto Rico becomes U.S. commonwealth		Canada cuts legal ties with Britain		U.S., Canada, Mexico sign NAFTA	

🔵 Los saludos[a]

1. *IRENE: ¡Hola, Marisa! ¿Qué tal?
MARISA: Bien, ¿y tú? ¿Cómo estás?
IRENE: Más o menos. Nos vemos, ¿eh?
MARISA: Sí, hasta luego.

2. SEÑORA MÁRQUEZ: Buenos días, señor Castillo.
¿Cómo está usted?
SEÑOR CASTILLO: Estoy bien, gracias. ¿Y usted,
señora Márquez?
SEÑORA MÁRQUEZ: Muy bien. Hasta mañana.
SEÑOR CASTILLO: Adiós.

3. HUMBERTO: ¿Cómo te llamas?
IRENE: Me llamo Irene.
HUMBERTO: Encantado. Yo me llamo Humberto.
IRENE: Encantada, Humberto.

4. SEÑOR CASTILLO: ¿Cómo se llama usted, señorita?
MARISA: Me llamo Marisa Cuéllar.
SEÑOR CASTILLO: Mucho gusto.
MARISA: Igualmente, señor Castillo.

buenas noches	good night
buenas tardes	good afternoon/evening
hasta pronto	until (see you) soon
regular	OK

---

[a] Los… *Greetings*
* 1. IRENE: Hi, Marisa! How's it going? MARISA: Fine, and you? How are you? IRENE: So-so. See you around, OK? MARISA: Yes, see you later.
2. SEÑORA MÁRQUEZ: Good morning, Mr. Castillo. How are you? SEÑOR CASTILLO: I'm fine, thank you. And you, Mrs. Márquez? SEÑORA MÁRQUEZ: Very well. See you tomorrow. SEÑOR CASTILLO: Good-bye.
3. HUMBERTO: What's your name? IRENE: My name is Irene. HUMBERTO: Nice to meet you. My name is Humberto. IRENE: Nice to meet you, Humberto.
4. SEÑOR CASTILLO: What is your name, miss? MARISA: My name is Marisa Cuéllar. SEÑOR CASTILLO: Pleased to meet you. MARISA: Likewise, Mr. Castillo.

Did you notice in the dialogues that "How are you?" and "What is your name?" were said in two different ways? This is because Spanish distinguishes between two levels of formality when addressing people directly. Dialogues 1 and 3 represent *familiar* speech: **¿Qué tal?, ¿y tú?, ¿Cómo estás?,** and **¿Cómo te llamas?** are used with people you know well, on a first-name basis. In dialogues 2 and 4, the expressions **¿Cómo está usted?, ¿y usted?,** and **¿Cómo se llama usted?** are formal expressions, used to address someone you do not know well, or someone with whom you have a formal relationship. You will learn more about this in **Forma y función 1.1.**

Actividades

A. ¿Formal o informal?

Paso 1. Say whether you would use the following expressions with a close friend or with someone you have just met.

1. Buenos días, señor.
2. Bien, gracias, ¿y tú?
3. ¿Cómo te llamas?
4. Adiós, señorita.
5. ¿Cómo estás?
6. ¡Hola, Ángela!
7. ¿Cómo está usted?
8. ¿Qué tal?

Paso 2. How would you say good-bye to the following people?

1. someone you will be seeing shortly
2. someone you will be seeing tomorrow
3. your instructor
4. your best friend

B. Diálogos incompletos. Complete the following dialogues.

1. —Hola, Antonio. ¿Qué tal?

   —_____, ¿y tú?

   —Más o menos.

2. —¿_____?

   —Me llamo Alicia.

   —_____.

   —Igualmente.

3. —¿_____?

   —Bien, gracias, ¿y usted?

   —_____.

4. —¡Buenas tardes, profesora!

   —_____, Irene. ¿Cómo estás?

   —Muy bien, ¿_____?

   —Estoy muy bien, gracias.

C. La hora (*time*) exacta. Which expression would you use at the following times of day? Choose from **buenos días, buenas tardes,** and **buenas noches.**

1. 9:30 A.M.
2. 2:00 P.M.
3. 12:00 (noon)
4. right before bed
5. 7:45 P.M.
6. 9:30 P.M.

Si te interesa[a]

The expressions **Buenos días, Buenas tardes,** and **Buenas noches** have slightly different connotations than their English counterparts. **Buenos días** is used up until the midday meal, which in Hispanic countries generally starts between 1:00 and 3:00 in the afternoon. **Buenas tardes** is used from the midday meal until the evening meal, usually around 8:00 P.M. (although sometimes as late as 10:00). **Buenas noches** is used only after the evening meal, or before going to bed.

[a]Si... *If you're interested*

 D. Entrevista: ¿Cómo te llamas?

Paso 1. Introduce yourself to several classmates. Ask their names and how they are doing. Then say good-bye.

Paso 2. Introduce yourself to your instructor. Ask how he/she is and answer his/her questions.

● El alfabeto español[a]

—¿Cómo se escribe **Bejarano**?   *How is **Bejarano** spelled?*

—Se escribe:
   be grande-e-jota-a-ere-a-ene-o.   *It's spelled,* b-e-j-a-r-a-n-o.

Letter*	Name of letter	Examples	Letter	Name of letter	Examples
a	a	Argentina, Andalucía	p	pe	Perú, Paraguay
			q	cu	Quito,
b	be[†]	Bolivia, Bariloche			Barranquilla
c	ce	Colombia, Ceuta	r	ere	Mérida, Caracas
d	de	Durango, Dinamarca	rr	erre, ere doble	Monterrey, Navarra
e	e	Ecuador, Europa	s	ese	El Salvador, Brasil
f	efe	Florida, Francia	t	te	Tampico, Toledo
g	ge	Guatemala, Gibraltar	u	u	Uruguay, Acapulco
h	hache	Honduras, Huelva	v	ve, uve[†]	Venezuela,
i	i	Ibiza, Iguazú			Valparaíso
j	jota	Jerez, Guadalajara	w	doble ve, ve doble,	Washington,
k	ka	Kansas, Katmandú		uve doble	Hawai
l	ele	Lima, León	x	equis	Extremadura,
m	eme	México, Montevideo			Oaxaca
			y	i griega	Guayaquil,
n	ene	Nicaragua, Panamá			Yucatán
			z	ceta (zeta)	Zaragoza,
ñ	eñe	España, Logroño			Cozumel
o	o	Orinoco, Bogotá			

---

[a] *Spanish*

* A basic guide to the pronunciation of Spanish letters appears in Appendix A, pp. A1–A2. Individual sounds will be practiced throughout *Entrevistas.*

[†] In some countries, the name **uve** is not used for the letter **v.** Since the names for the letters **b** and **v** (**be** and **ve,** respectively) are pronounced exactly alike, Spanish speakers use a variety of expressions to distinguish between the two. The letter **b** is often referred to as **"be de burro,"** **"be grande,"** or **"be larga,"** whereas the letter **v** is referred to as **"ve de vaca,"** **"ve chica,"** or **"ve corta."**

Actividades

A. El alfabeto. Listen to your instructor pronounce the names of the letters of the alphabet, then repeat them after him/her. What differences do you notice between the Spanish and English alphabets (number of letters, types of letters)?

B. Letras perdidas (*Missing letters*). Based on their English equivalents, can you guess which letters are missing from the following words? Spell out the entire word.

1. airport: ae__opuer__o
2. marvelous: __aravillo__o
3. university: u__i__ersidad
4. student: est__dian__e
5. professor: pro__es__r

C. Entrevista: ¿Cómo se escribe? Work with a partner to create short dialogues, using the following cues as a guide.

1. Introduce yourself to your partner, ask his/her name, and ask him/her to spell it for you.
2. Ask your partner how to say a word in Spanish, then ask him/her to spell it.

Si te interesa

Note that the letter **ñ** is a distinct letter from **n.** Until 1996, Spanish had two compound letters: **ch** (**che,** pronounced like the *ch* in the English word *cheerful*) and **ll** (**elle,** in most countries pronounced like the *y* in the English word *yes*). Spanish-language dictionaries alphabetized words with these letters in separate sections (**ch** after **c, ll** after **l**). But in 1996, the **Real Academia Española** (*Royal Spanish Academy,* a group of scholars in Spain that decides matters concerning the Spanish language) decreed that **ch** and **ll** should be sequences of two letters each. Accordingly, in dictionaries published after 1996, words beginning with **ch** now appear among the **c** words between those beginning with **ce** and those beginning with **ci.** Similarly, words beginning with **ll** are now found between words beginning with **li** and those beginning with **lo.** However, remember that **ch** and **ll** still retain their distinctive pronunciations.

⬤ El origen y la nacionalidad

Jorge es **colombiano.***
Luisa es **colombiana**
también.*

—Luisa, ¿**de dónde eres?**	*Luisa, where are you from? (familiar)*
—**Soy de** Cali. **Soy colombiana.**†	*I'm from Cali. I'm Colombian.*
—¿**De dónde es usted,** señor Castillo?	*Where are you from, Mr. Castillo? (formal)*
—**Soy de** Bogotá. **Soy colombiano** también.	*I'm from Bogotá. I'm Colombian, too.*
—¿**De dónde es** él/ella?	*Where is he/she from?*
—**Es de** Medellín.	*He/she is from Medellín.*
—¿**De qué origen es** el café?	*Where is the coffee from?*
—**Es de** Colombia.	*It's from Colombia. (It's Colombian.)*
(Es colombiano.)	

Soy/Es _____.   I am / He (She, It) is _____.

alemán, alemana	German	**francés, francesa**	French
canadiense	Canadian	**inglés, inglesa**	English
chino/a	Chinese	**italiano/a**	Italian
español(a)	Spanish	**japonés, japonesa**	Japanese
estadounidense	American (from the United States)	**mexicano/a**	Mexican
		puertorriqueño/a	Puerto Rican

Actividades

A. Productos internacionales

Paso 1. What nationality do you associate with the following products? Use the expression **Es un producto** + the masculine form of the adjective.

MODELO   el tango → Es un producto argentino.

1. el café (*coffee*)
2. el té (*tea*)
3. el vino (*wine*) Chianti
4. el automóvil Volkswagen
5. el arroz (*rice*)
6. la torta de manzana (*apple pie*)
7. el taco
8. la paella

---

* Spanish words may use different endings to describe males and females. For adjectives that have one form ending in **-o** and another ending in **-a**, use the form ending in **-o** to refer to males and the form ending in **-a** to refer to females. Adjectives with only one form can be used for males and females.
† Note that in Spanish, adjectives of nationality are *not* capitalized.

Paso 2. Ask your partner where the following international products are likely to originate. He/She will answer, choosing one of the countries given.

MODELO   el café (Colombia, Australia) →
          E1:* ¿De qué origen es el café?
          E2: El café es de Colombia.

1. el perfume (Francia, Canadá)   **4.** el sushi (México, Japón)
2. el chocolate (Rusia, Suiza)   **5.** el cigarro (Cuba, Italia)
3. la pizza (Italia, Bolivia)

▲ *Hay* (There is) *mucha diversidad en Colombia.*

B. Encuesta (*Survey*): **¿De qué origen es tu** (*your*) **familia?**   Find out the national origin of three or four of your classmates.

MODELOS   E1: ¿De qué origen es tu familia?
           E2: Mi (*My*) familia es colombiana. (Mi familia es de origen colombiano.)

           E1: ¿De dónde eres?
           E2: Soy de Colombia. (Soy colombiano/a.)

----

* **E** stands for **Estudiante** (*Student*). This abbreviation will be used throughout *Entrevistas.*

You can watch this interview on the *Entrevistas* Video or Interactive CD-ROM or listen to the audio on the Online Learning Center (**www.mhhe.com/entrevistas2**).

Jairo Bejarano Carrillo

«*Yo soy de Bogotá, Colombia.*»

Nombre:[a] Jairo

Apellidos:[b] (1) Bejarano (2) Carrillo

Edad:[c] 33 (treinta y tres) años

Nació en:[d] Bogotá, Colombia

[a]*First name* [b]*Family names* [c]*Age*
[d]*Nació… He was born in*

Vocabulario útil

tu	your (*familiar*)	**pueblos**	towns
y	and	**pequeños**	small
padre *m.*	father	**sus**	their
madre *f.*	mother		

Antes de ver

A. Información biográfica.   In this interview, you will hear a Colombian man talk about himself and his family. Study the biographical information about the speaker in the box and find the Spanish equivalents of the following items.

1. family name
2. age
3. geographical terms or place names

B. Preguntas (*Questions*) **básicas.**   Match each question with the type of information requested. **¡OJO!** (*Careful!*) Some answers are used more than once.

1. _____ ¿Cómo te llamas?
2. _____ ¿Cómo se escribe tu nombre?
3. _____ ¿De dónde eres?
4. _____ ¿De dónde son tus padres?
5. _____ ¿Cómo se escriben tus apellidos?

a. a person's origin
b. a person's name
c. the spelling of a person's name

Si te interesa

In most Spanish-speaking countries, people use both their paternal and maternal family names (**los apellidos),** in that order. For example, Teresa García Ramos is the daughter of a man whose family name is García and a woman whose family name is Ramos.

¡Veamos!

Respuestas (*Answers*).   Now, watch the interview and fill in the blanks with what Jairo says.

1. «Mi _____ ____ Jairo Bejarano Carrillo.»

2. «**Jairo** ____ _____: **jota-a-i-ere-o.**»

3. «Yo ____ de Bogotá, Colombia.»

4. «**Bejarano** se escribe con _____ **de burro.**»

5. «Mi padre y mi madre son _____, pero no _____ de Bogotá.»

6. «Son de pueblos pequeños. Sus _____ son de _____ español.»

Después de ver

¿Cierto o falso?   Indicate whether the following statements about Jairo's family are true (**cierto**) or false (**falso**). If you don't know, check the box in the column marked **No sé.** (*I don't know*).

	CIERTO	FALSO	NO SÉ.
1. El padre y la madre de Jairo son de Bogotá.	☐	☐	☐
2. Jairo es de Bogotá.	☐	☐	☐
3. Los apellidos de esta (*this*) persona son **Jairo** y **Bejarano.**	☐	☐	☐
4. El apellido **Bejarano** es de origen español.	☐	☐	☐
5. Jairo está bien.	☐	☐	☐

▲ *Bogotá es una ciudad grande.*

Somos diferentes, somos iguales • CAPÍTULO 1

1.1 Subject Pronouns

Subject pronouns (**Los pronombres de sujeto**) are the words that indicate the subject of the sentence—the person or thing performing the main action. Here are the subject pronouns in Spanish, with their English equivalents.

Singular		Plural	
yo	I	**nosotros/nosotras**	we
tú	you (*familiar*)	**vosotros/vosotras**	you all, you guys (*familiar*)
usted*	you (*formal*)	**ustedes***	you all (*formal*)
él	he	**ellos**	they (*masculine*)
ella	she	**ellas**	they (*feminine*)

Although English differentiates sex only in the third person singular (he/she), Spanish has a number of plural feminine forms as well: **nosotras**, **vosotras**, and **ellas** are used to refer to groups of women or girls.[†]

Spanish also distinguishes between two levels of formality when addressing a person directly (*you*). The familiar (informal) forms are used generally with a friend, a pet, an unknown person your own age in an informal social setting, and a family member. The formal forms are used to show respect to an elder or to an unknown person in a formal setting (job interviews, business establishments, with college professors, etc.). The exact distinctions in usage vary slightly from country to country, but the following table provides a general guide.

			Familiar	Formal
Spain		Singular	**tú**	usted
		Plural	**vosotros/as**	ustedes
Spanish America		Singular	**tú**	usted
		Plural	**ustedes**	ustedes

Si te interesa

The singular pronoun **vos** is used instead of **tú** in many countries. In *Entrevistas* you will only practice **tú** and its corresponding verb forms for familiar usage, but you will see the **vos** form in future chapters that focus on the countries in which it is frequently used.

---

* **Usted** and **ustedes** are abbreviated **Ud.** and **Uds.**, respectively. Note that the abbreviations are capitalized, but the long forms are not.
† The female forms of subject pronouns are used only when the *entire* group consists of women. If there is even one male in the group, the masculine form must be used.

Análisis estructural

Classify the following subject pronouns according to the categories given. In some cases, more than one category is possible.

	SINGULAR	PLURAL	MASCULINE	FEMININE	FAMILIAR	FORMAL
1. nosotras	☐	☐	☐	☐		
2. usted	☐	☐	☐	☐	☐	☐
3. tú	☐	☐	☐	☐	☐	☐
4. ellos	☐	☐	☐	☐		
5. ustedes	☐	☐	☐	☐	☐	☐
6. él	☐	☐	☐	☐		
7. yo	☐	☐	☐	☐		

Actividades

A. ¿Tú, usted, nosotros, vosotros o (or) ustedes? Which subject pronoun would you use to address the following people?

1. your instructor
2. you and a mixed group of friends
3. your parents
4. a friend
5. a mixed group of friends
6. the parents of your friends

B. Muchas personas. Which plural pronouns would you use to refer to the following groups of people?

1. tú y yo
2. él y yo
3. él y ella
4. usted y yo
5. usted y ella
6. él y tú

1.2 The Verb **ser**

In Spanish, there is a distinct verb form for most of the subject pronouns. The following table shows the present tense forms of the irregular verb **ser** (*to be*).

ser					
(yo)	**soy**	I am	(nosotros/as)	**somos**	we are
(tú)	**eres**	you (*fam. s.*) are	(vosotros/as)	**sois**	you (*fam. pl.*) are
(usted, él/ella)	**es**	you (*form. s.*) are, he/she is	(ustedes, ellos/as)	**son**	you (*form. pl.*) are, they (*m., f.*) are

One of the most common uses of the verb **ser** is to give the nationality or origin of people and things, in two different patterns. One way is to use the appropriate form of **ser** with an adjective of nationality.

Yo **soy española.** *I am Spanish.*

El señor Castillo **es colombiano.** *Mr. Castillo is Colombian.*

The other way is to use a form of **ser** with the preposition **de** (*from*).

¿**De** dónde **eres***?   *Where are you from?*

Soy* **de** Misisipí.   *I'm from Mississippi.*

¿**De** qué origen **es** el café?   *Where is the coffee from?*

Es* **de** Colombia.   *It's from Colombia.*

Análisis estructural

Which subject pronoun corresponds to the following verb forms? ¡**OJO**! Sometimes more than one pronoun is possible.

1. eres   **4.** soy
2. somos   **5.** es
3. son   **6.** sois

Actividades

A. Orígenes.   Use the following phrases to make complete sentences. ¡**OJO**! Be sure to use the correct form of the verb **ser.**

1. yo **/** ser **/** de España
2. mi amiga (*friend*) **/** ser **/** de Colombia
3. ¿de dónde **/** ser **/** tú?
4. y la profesora, ¿de dónde **/** ser?
5. nosotros **/** ser **/** de Bogotá
6. mi madre y mi padre **/** ser **/** de Bogotá

B. Personas famosas

Paso 1. Say in Spanish where the following famous people are from. Choose from these countries:

Inglaterra (*England*), España, los Estados Unidos (*United States*), México

1. la reina (*queen*) Isabel II
2. Enrique Iglesias
3. los príncipes (*princes*) Guillermo y Harry
4. el ex presidente Bill Clinton
5. Antonio Banderas
6. la artista Frida Kahlo

Paso 2. Work with a partner to name at least one well-known person from each of the following countries. Say where that person is from, then give his/her nationality.

MODELO   Alemania (*Germany*) →
                Boris Becker es de Alemania. (Él) Es alemán.

el Canadá   Francia   Puerto Rico
Chile   Italia   la República
China   Japón   Dominicana

---

* Since the verb form indicates the subject of the sentence, it is not always necessary to use subject pronouns in Spanish. They are generally used only for emphasis or for clarification.

C. Encuesta: ¿De dónde son tus compañeros/as de clase (*classmates*)**?**
Circulate among the members of your class to find out how many are
from Canada, the United States, Spanish America **(Hispanoamérica),**
Europe **(Europa),** Asia, Africa **(África),** and Australia. Then give a profile
of the class by completing the following sentences. **¡OJO!** Remember to
use the correct form of the verb **ser.**

La mayoría de la clase **/** ser de _____.

Pocos estudiantes (*Few students*) **/** ser de _____.

Ningún (*No, Not one*) estudiante **/** ser de _____.

Análisis cultural

In this section of *Entrevistas,* you will see quotes taken from popular press
sources. These passages make certain assertions or generalizations about
the countries you will study in each chapter. It is important to learn to
treat these quotations critically, evaluating them against what you know
about the regions and phenomena described. Is the information presented
consistent with the native speaker's perspective in each interview? Use
what you have learned in this chapter, and your own experiences, to
answer the questions that follow the quote.

❝Greetings are very important in Colombia. Take the time to greet everyone
formally. Give the person you are greeting your undivided attention. Men
shake hands with each other and with women. Women choose whether or
not to shake hands with other women; sometimes women will clasp each
other's forearms instead. Friends are expected to hug and exchange kisses on
the cheeks. When men hug each other, they often add a backslap or two. . . .

Colombians often complain that North Americans and Europeans do not
know how to greet someone. Colombians take a long time in greetings; they
feel this conveys respect for the other person. After the handshake (or hug),
Colombians ask numerous polite questions. North Americans typically
progress beyond the greeting phase after one or two questions. Expect
inquiries as to your health, your trip, your relatives, and any friends or
acquaintances you have in common. Don't rush! Rushing is interpreted as
callousness or disrespect.❞

Source: http://www.getcustoms.com

1. How would you greet Jairo Bejarano Carrillo in Spanish? Would
   your greeting be different if he were a woman?

2. Is the role of the greeting in Colombia similar to, or different from,
   the role of the greeting in your own country?

3. Give some examples of greetings you consider (im)polite.

4. What misunderstandings might arise from an inappropriate greeting
   in Colombia? Could a similar situation arise in your country?
   Explain.

Pronunciación y ortografía

This section focuses on various aspects of Spanish pronunciation and spelling **(ortografía).** It is important to pay close attention to these details. They will make your spoken Spanish comprehensible to native speakers and your spelling more accurate—something many Spanish speakers consider to be culturally important!

 Vowels

Spanish has five vowels—**a, e, i, o,** and **u**—and each is pronounced as a short, clear sound, whether in a stressed or an unstressed syllable.

Letter	Sound	Examples	Avoid English sounds
a	similar to *a* in *father*	**papá, casa**	schwa ("uh") sound: *a*bove
e	similar to *a* in *day*	**café, cerveza**	[ei] diphthong: m*a*ke; schwa sound: tel*e*phone
i	similar to *i* in *machine*	**imposible, días**	schwa sound: imposs*i*ble
o	similar to *o* in *go*	**todo, donde**	[ou] diphthong: g*o* [gou]; [a] sound: h*o*spital, d*o*ctor; schwa sound: aut*o*matic
u	similar to *oo* in *food*	**uso, música**	[yu] sound: *u*se

Consonants

Many Spanish consonants sound similar to their English counterparts, so you can probably read aloud the majority of Spanish words you have not heard before. A few consonants deserve special mention because their mispronunciation can seriously impede your listener's comprehension.

Letter	Sound	Examples	Avoid English sounds
j, ge, gi*	similar to English *h*, but stronger	**Tejas, general, gigante**	[j]: *j*ump
ll	similar to *y* in *yes*	**me llamo**	[l] sound: hi*ll*
h	always silent; *never* pronounced	**hola, horóscopo**	[h]: *h*elp
ñ	similar to *ny* in *canyon*	**señor, mañana**	[n] sound: *n*o

The *Manual de práctica* contains activities to practice the material explained in this section.

---

* The sound of the letter **g** before **a, o,** and **u** is similar to the *g* in *again:* **g**ato, **g**ota, **g**usto.

CAPÍTULO 1 • Somos diferentes, somos iguales

Vocabulario

Los días y los números (1–31)

octubre

lunes	martes	miércoles	jueves	viernes	sábado	domingo
primero 1 (uno)*	dos 2	tres 3	cuatro 4	cinco 5	seis 6	siete 7
ocho 8	nueve 9	diez 10	once 11	doce 12	trece 13	catorce 14
quince 15	dieciséis 16	diecisiete 17	dieciocho 18	diecinueve 19	veinte 20	veintiuno 21†
veintidós 22	veintitrés 23	veinticuatro 24	veinticinco 25	veintiséis 26	veintisiete 27	veintiocho 28
veintinueve 29	treinta 30	treinta y uno 31				

> **Si te interesa**
>
> Like adjectives of nationality, days of the week and months are not capitalized in Spanish: **Hoy es lunes, el trece de septiembre.** (*Today is Monday, September thirteenth.*)

Actividades

A. Asociaciones. What numbers do you associate with the following images? Give all the possibilities you can think of.

1.
2.
3.
4.
5.

---

* Whereas English uses ordinal numbers for dates (the second, the ninth, the twenty-fifth), Spanish uses cardinal numbers (**el dos, el nueve, el veinticinco**). The first day of the month, however, is generally expressed in Spanish by the ordinal **el primero** (*the first*). When counting, use **uno**.

† The numbers 16–19 and 21–29 can be written as one word, as shown, or as three separate words: **diez y seis, diez y siete,… ; veinte y uno, veinte y dos,…**

B. La temperatura. Read aloud the average temperatures for Bogotá, the capital of Colombia. (The temperatures are given in the Celsius scale; Fahrenheit equivalents are in parentheses.)

Mes	Temperatura
enero (*January*)	16° (grados) (61)
abril	17° (63)
agosto	14° (57)
noviembre	15° (59)

C. Fiestas importantes. Here are the dates of some important holidays in Colombia.

Paso 1. Read the dates aloud.

1. el Día de los Reyes Magos (*Epiphany*): el 6 de enero
2. el Día de San José (*St. Joseph's Day*): el 19 de marzo
3. el Día de la Independencia: el 20 de julio
4. el Día de la Hispanidad (la Raza): el 12 de octubre
5. el Día de la Inmaculada Concepción: el 8 de diciembre

Paso 2. Look at a calendar of the current year and say what day of the week each of these holidays falls on.

MODELO   el Día de los Reyes Magos → Es sábado, el seis de enero.

● Las descripciones

¿Cómo es/son _____? What is/are _____ like?

un muchacho **bajo**   un coche **grande**   una motocicleta **pequeña**

una muchacha **alta**   un gato **delgado**   un perro **gordo**

la piel (clara, morena, oscura)	(light, brown, dark) skin
el pelo (castaño, corto, largo, negro, rubio)	(brown, short, long, black, blond) hair
los ojos (azules, castaños, negros, verdes)	(blue, brown, black, green) eyes

alegre	happy	feo/a	ugly
amable	friendly	guapo/a	handsome, good-looking, pretty
antipático/a	unfriendly		
bonito/a	pretty	malo/a*	bad
bueno/a*	good	perezoso/a	lazy
encantador(a)	delightful, charming	trabajador(a)	hardworking

Actividades

A. ¿Quién es?   Write a description of yourself, using the model as a guide. Your instructor will collect the descriptions and read them aloud while the class tries to guess who each description refers to.

VOCABULARIO ÚTIL

también	also, too	**tengo**	I have

MODELO   Tengo el pelo rubio y los ojos azules. Soy alto, alegre y amable. También soy…

B. ¿Cómo eres?   Take turns with your partner asking questions to find out what he/she is like. Later, tell the class what you learned about your partner.

MODELO   E1: Jennifer, ¿eres perezosa?
E2: No, no soy perezosa. Soy muy trabajadora. (Sí, soy perezosa.) Y tú, Kevin, ¿eres perezoso?
E1: Sí, soy muy perezoso.
E1: (*To the class*): Jennifer no es perezosa. Es trabajadora.

Lenguaje funcional
Más sobre los adjetivos

At the beginning of this chapter you learned that adjectives in Spanish are marked by gender. In simple terms, this means using an **-o** ending when describing a male and an **-a** ending when describing a female. However, some adjectives don't follow this simplified rule. For example, **encantador** and **trabajador** are used to describe a male, whereas **encantadora** and **trabajadora** are used to describe a female. Adjectives with only one form like **alegre, amable,** and **grande** can describe either a male or a female.

---

* The adjectives **bueno/a** and **malo/a** shorten to **buen** and **mal**, respectively, before masculine singular nouns: **Él es un** *buen* **hombre, pero es** *mal* **padre.** (*He is a good man, but he is a bad father.*)

You can watch this interview on the *Entrevistas* Video or Interactive CD-ROM or listen to the audio on the Online Learning Center (**www.mhhe.com/entrevistas2**).

Stella Amado Carvajal

«*Los colombianos somos amables, alegres, hospitalarios y muy trabajadores.*»

Nombre: Stella

Apellidos: (1) Amado (2) Carvajal

Edad: 36 (treinta y seis) años

Nació en: Duitama, Boyacá, Colombia

Vocabulario útil

ciudad *f.*	city	**gente** *s. f.*	people
con	with	**reservados**	reserved
paisaje *m.*	landscape	**formales**	formal
alrededor (de)	around	**pero**	but
hospitalarios	hospitable	**altiplano**	plateau, high plain

Antes de ver

A. ¿Cómo es tu región? Before watching the interview, indicate whether the following descriptions do or do not apply to the area where you come from.

	SÍ	NO
1. Es una ciudad grande.	☐	☐
2. Es un pueblo pequeño.	☐	☐
3. El paisaje es verde.	☐	☐
4. Las personas son amables y alegres.	☐	☐
5. La gente es trabajadora.	☐	☐
6. Somos reservados y formales.	☐	☐

B. ¿Eres típico/a? Now state whether you are like (**como**) or unlike the people in your region.

MODELOS   Sí, soy típico. Soy hospitalario como la gente de mi región.
No, no soy típico. Soy reservado, pero la gente de mi región es gregaria (*gregarious*).

¡Veamos!

¿Colombia o Duitama?   In the interview, Stella contrasts Colombians in general with the inhabitants of her town. List the words that she uses to describe each group.

1. «Los colombianos somos _____, _____, _____

   y muy _____.»

2. «La gente de Duitama, somos _____, _____,

   pero _____.»

Después de ver

La descripción de Stella.   Complete the following statements that Stella made about herself.

1. «Soy una colombiana _____ del altiplano.»

2. «Tengo el _____ castaño, los ojos _____ y la piel _____.»

Lenguaje funcional
Comparación y contraste

The following expressions will help you compare and contrast your own situation with that of Stella Amado Carvajal.

porque	because
también	also, too
pero	but
similar(es),	similar
parecido/a a	to
diferente(s) de	different from/ than

Piénsalo bien[a]

Complete the following sentences to compare the people and places mentioned as in the model. **¡OJO!** Remember to use the correct forms of the verb **ser.**

MODELO   Stella y yo somos similares porque yo _____ _____ y Stella _____ _____ también. →

Stella y yo somos similares porque yo soy amable y Stella es amable también.

1. Stella y yo somos diferentes porque yo _____ _____ pero Stella _____

   _____.

2. Mi ciudad es como Duitama porque los dos (*both*) _____ _____.

3. Mi ciudad es diferente de Duitama porque mi ciudad _____ _____

   pero Duitama _____ _____.

4. Mi país es parecido a Colombia porque la gente _____ _____.

5. La gente de Duitama es diferente de mis amigos/as y yo porque

   nosotros/as _____ _____.

[a]Piénsalo... *Think it through*

1.3 Gender and Number Agreement
Definite and Indefinite Articles

In the interview, Stella Amado Carvajal used the following terms: **los colombianos, la gente, el pelo.** There are many ways to say *the* in Spanish due to the phenomenon called *agreement.* Just as in English, Spanish nouns can be singular or plural in *number,* but in Spanish every noun, even those that refer to nonliving things, also has an inherent *gender,* either masculine or feminine. All words associated with a noun (i.e., articles and adjectives) have to match, or *agree,* with the gender and number of the noun. Thus, there are four different forms of the definite article (*the*) and the indefinite articles (*a, an, some*)—masculine singular, masculine plural, feminine singular, and feminine plural—depending on the noun they appear with. These forms are shown in the following table.

	Singular		Plural	
Masculine	el **pueblo**	the town	los **pueblos**	the towns
Feminine	la **casa**	the house	las **casas**	the houses
Masculine	un* **pueblo**	a town	unos **pueblos**	some towns
Feminine	una **casa**	a house	unas **casas**	some houses

How do you know which form of the article to use with a noun? Here are a few guidelines.

1. Most nouns that end in **-o** are masculine, and most that end in **-a** are feminine:[†] **el pelo, la fiesta.**
2. Nouns that end in **-ción/-sión** and **-dad** are generally feminine: **la nación, la extensión, la identidad.**
3. Nouns that end in **-ista** are either masculine or feminine, depending on biological sex: **el artista** (male), **la artista** (female).

In general, grammatical gender is arbitrary and must be memorized for each new item. Biological sex can provide a good hint—**el padre, la madre**—but watch out for exceptions! In *Entrevistas* the singular definite article (**el** or **la**) is listed with every noun in the end-of-chapter vocabulary lists and in most lists within the chapter; get into the practice of memorizing the article along with the word. You also should consult a dictionary if you are not sure of the gender of a noun; look for the labels *masc. / n. m.* (noun, masculine) and *fem. / n. f.* (noun, feminine).

---

[*] Note that **uno** and numbers that end in **uno** (**veintiuno, treinta y uno,** and so on) become **un** before a masculine noun: **un pueblo, veintiún pueblos.**
[†] A few common exceptions are **la mano** (*hand*), **el día** (*day*), and **el mapa** (*map*).

Adjectives

Not only do articles change form to agree with nouns; adjectives must also agree with the nouns they modify. They can have up to four different forms: masculine singular, masculine plural, feminine singular, and feminine plural.

	Singular	Plural
Masculine	**El pueblo es pequeño.** The town is small.	**Los pueblos son pequeños.** The towns are small.
Feminine	**La ciudad es pequeña.** The city is small.	**Las ciudades son pequeñas.** The cities are small.

You will have to learn exactly what changes in form are required for each adjective, but there are three basic patterns.

Type 1: o/a/os/as	
El pueblo es típico. **La casa es típica.**	**Los pueblos son típicos.** **Las casas son típicas.**

The base form of Type 1 adjectives ends in **-o.** This type of adjective is indicated in vocabulary lists by **/a: típico/a.**

Type 2: —/—/(e)s/(e)s	
El pueblo es diferente. **La casa es diferente.**	**Los pueblos son diferentes.** **Las casas son diferentes.**
El pueblo es tradicional. **La casa es tradicional.**	**Los pueblos son tradicionales.** **Las casas son tradicionales.**
El hombre (*man*) **es optimista.** **La mujer** (*woman*) **es optimista.**	**Los hombres son optimistas.** **Las mujeres son optimistas.**

The base form of Type 2 adjectives ends in **-e, -ista,** or a consonant. Words that end in a vowel form their plural by adding **-s;** words that end in a consonant form their plurals by adding **-es.*** These adjectives have no special designation in vocabulary lists.

---

* Words that end in **-í** add **-es: israelíes.**

Type 3: —/a/es/as	
El pueblo es encantador.	Los pueblos son encantadores.
La casa es encantadora.	Las casas son encantadoras.
El hombre es inglés.	Los hombres son ingleses.
La mujer es inglesa.*	Las mujeres son inglesas.

The base form of Type 3 adjectives ends in a consonant, and the feminine singular ends in **-a.** Many adjectives of nationality fall into this group. This type of adjective is indicated in vocabulary lists by **(a): encantador(a).** If the adjective undergoes a spelling change in different forms, it is indicated in vocabulary lists with the entire feminine singular form: **inglés, inglesa; alemán, alemana.**

There are three more details you should know about using adjectives to describe things in Spanish.

1. When masculine and feminine nouns are mixed, the adjective must be in the masculine plural form: **El hombre y la mujer son colombianos.** The feminine plural form of the adjective is used only when *all* the nouns being described are feminine: **Las mujeres son colombianas.**
2. Unlike in English, most adjectives are placed *after* the nouns they describe.

    Es un pueblo **pequeño.**   *It's a small town.*

3. A few common adjectives often go before the noun—for example, **bueno** and **malo.** Like **uno,** these adjectives also have short forms before a masculine singular noun.

    un **buen** café   *a good cup of coffee*
    un **mal** café   *a bad cup of coffee*

Before plural nouns, however, they follow the normal pattern of agreement.

    buenos perros   *good dogs*
    malos perros   *bad dogs*

---

* Note that the accent on the **e** of the masculine singular form is dropped in all other forms. You will learn about this type of spelling change in **Capítulo 3.**

Análisis estructural

Tell which type of ending (1, 2, or 3) the following adjectives have. Then give the correct forms to agree with **un padre, una madre, unos amigos,** and **unas amigas** as shown in the model.

MODELO   español →
Type 3; un padre español, una madre española, unos amigos españoles, unas amigas españolas

1. alemán
2. generoso
3. sentimental

4. pesimista
5. trabajador

Actividades

A. Personas famosas.   Which of the following adjectives could describe the people listed below? Be sure to match adjective endings as well as their meanings to the people.

PERSONAS

1. _____ Hulk Hogan
2. _____ David Letterman y Jay Leno
3. _____ Madonna
4. _____ la reina Isabel II
5. _____ los Beatles
6. _____ Oprah Winfrey

ADJETIVOS

a. cómicos
b. controversial
c. grande
d. habladora (*talkative*)
e. inglesa
f. populares

B. Descripciones.   Complete the following sentences with logical adjectives from the options given. Make sure the adjective endings agree in gender and number with the nouns they describe.

1. Jairo Bejarano Carrillo es _____ (alto, colombiano, formal, hospitalario, moderno).

2. Los colombianos son _____ (alegre, amable, antipático, encantador, maravilloso, moreno, tradicional).

3. Los norteamericanos* somos _____ (alto, amable, antipático, informal, maravilloso, reservado, tradicional).

4. La gente de mi estado (*state*)/provincia es _____ (amable, encantador, hospitalario, moderno, moreno, reservado, serio, tradicional).

5. Las mujeres de mi familia son _____ (alegre, alto, maravilloso, moderno, reservado, rubio, típico).

---

* Although the term **norteamericano/a** can mean American (*from the United States*), *Canadian,* and even *Mexican,* since Mexico is a part of the North American continent, many Spanish speakers use it to mean only *American* (*from the United States*). Throughout *Entrevistas,* **norteamericano/a** will refer to people and things from *both* the United States and Canada. The terms **canadiense, estadounidense,** and **mexicano/a** will be used to specify *Canadian, American* (*from the United States*), and *Mexican,* respectively.

C. ¿Cómo son? Working in groups of three or four, look at the following photos and describe the people in them with as many adjectives as possible. In your opinion, where are these people from?

VOCABULARIO ÚTIL

el hombre	man
la mujer	woman
el/la niño/a	child
de la derecha/izquierda	on the right/left
en mi opinión,...	in my opinion, . . .

MODELO   El niño de la izquierda es bajo y moreno.

1.

2.

3.

Señas culturales

Here is the Colombian pledge of allegiance.

> Juro por Dios fidelidad a mi bandera y a mi patria, Colombia, de la cual es símbolo, una nación soberana e indivisible, regida por principios de libertad, orden y justicia para todos.

> *I swear by God loyalty to my flag and to my country, Colombia, of which it* [the flag] *is a symbol, a sovereign and indivisible nation, ruled by the principles of liberty, order, and justice for all.*

Paso 1. Compare the Spanish text with the English translation. Which Spanish words are equivalent to the following English words?

loyalty, symbol, sovereign, liberty, order

Paso 2. Compare the Colombian pledge of allegiance to the pledge of allegiance of your country. Which words or ideas do the two have in common?

Lectura

Sobre la lectura   The following advertisement from a Colombian magazine reveals several images that Colombians feel are essential to their national identity.

Antes de leer

The activities in the **Antes de leer** (*Before reading*) section will improve your comprehension of this reading. Following the strategies and tips in this section will also help boost your Spanish reading skills in general.

A. Los cognados.   Spanish words that are similar in form and meaning to English are called *cognates* **(cognados).** The ability to recognize cognates is an important skill that will greatly facilitate your reading speed and comprehension.

Paso 1. Guess the English meanings of the following Spanish words.

1. la civilización
2. la libertad
3. el paquete
4. desastroso
5. la idea

Paso 2. Now scan the advertisement for three more examples of cognates.

B. ¿Qué tipo de texto es?   In most cases, knowing what kind of text you are reading will help you guess many of the words you do not know—for example, an ad for air freshener might have words that mean *flower, sweet,* and so on. Look over the reading rapidly and answer the following questions.

1. What kind of text is this? Identify the text type.
   □ This is an announcement for a sporting event.
   □ This is an advertisement for clothing.
   □ This text publicizes cultural events.
2. What kinds of vocabulary and topics would you probably find in such a text? Give specific examples.

C. Imágenes de Colombia.   Based on what you have learned in this chapter and your general cultural knowledge, what objects or images do you associate with Colombia? Try to name at least three.

Bailaremos lejos...[a]

Colombia es más que[b] café, deportes[c] o bellos[d] paisajes; es por ejemplo, tradición popular. El Ballet Folclórico de Antioquia participará[e] en los más importantes festivales folclóricos de Norteamérica y Europa, llevando[f] la buena imagen de nuestro país.[g]

CANADÁ
2–3 de julio

E.E.U.U.
14–19 de julio

FRANCIA
27 de julio al 6 de sep.

ITALIA
23 de julio al
30 de agosto

BOGOTÁ
11–14 de junio
8 pm
Teatro de Colsubsidio
Roberto Arias Pérez
Boletería: Taquilla del Teatro
Informes y reservaciones
especiales tel. 6006000

CALI
28–30 de octubre
8 pm
Teatro Jorge Isaac
Boletería: Taquilla del Teatro

Ballet Folclórico
de Antioquia
presenta:
**COLOMBIA,
CULTURA
MILENARIA**

[a]Bailaremos... *We will dance far from home* [b]más... *more than* [c]*sports* [d]*beautiful*
[e]*will participate* [f]*presenting* [g]nuestro... *our country*

Después de leer

The activities in the **Después de leer** (*After reading*) section assess your comprehension of the reading and give you opportunities to express your own opinions and further your cultural knowledge.

A. ¿Comprendiste? (*Did you understand?*) Answer the following questions based on the advertisement.

1. In **Actividad C** of **Antes de leer** you identified images that you associate with Colombia. Which of them do Colombians associate with their own identity (i.e., what does the text reveal about Colombian identity)? What association(s) that you did not think of does the text suggest?

2. Will the **Ballet Folclórico de Antioquia** participate in small local festivals, national festivals, or international festivals? Which words from the ad indicate where they will perform?

3. On what days are the performances in Bogotá? How could you find out more information about these events?

4. Do you think that this cultural event will change the image of Colombia abroad? In what way(s)?

B. Tu «identidad cultural». Describe a new image for your country, state/province, city, or community by making up phrases in Spanish similar to those in the ad. Substitute the italicized words in the model with your own local details. If you need extra vocabulary, be sure to ask your instructor for it in Spanish with the phrase **¿Cómo se dice _____ en español?**

MODELO   New York City es más que *la Estatua de Libertad* y *el tráfico;* por ejemplo, es también *los teatros.*

VOCABULARIO ÚTIL

el arte (*pl.* **las artes**)	art(s)
la comida	food, cuisine
la danza / el baile	dance
la diversidad	diversity
el equipo de (béisbol, básquetbol, fútbol americano)	(baseball, basketball, football) team
el monumento	monument
la música	music
el parque	park
el restaurante	restaurant

At the end of every chapter, you will be asked to create original written work that integrates and personalizes the language and culture goals of the chapter.

Redacción[a]

¡Venga a[b] _____! For this chapter, you will create a travel brochure to attract tourists to your country, region, or favorite place. Your description will include geographical information and should emphasize the special identity of the place you choose. Follow the guided steps in the *Manual de práctica* to complete your brochure.

[a]*Composition*   [b]Venga... *Come to*

Exploración

Investigación cultural. Find more information about Colombia in your library, on the *Entrevistas* Online Learning Center (**www.mhhe.com/ entrevistas2),** or elsewhere on the Internet and present it to the class. Consult the *Manual de práctica* for ideas for your presentation.

Léxico activo

LOS SALUDOS

buenos días	good morning
buenas tardes	good afternoon/ evening
buenas noches	good night
hola	hello
¿Qué tal?	How's it going? What's up?
¿Cómo está(s)? / ¿Cómo está usted?	How are you?
Estoy (muy) bien, gracias.	I'm (very) fine, thanks.
¿Y tú? / ¿Y usted?	And you?
más o menos	so-so
regular	OK
adiós	good-bye
hasta pronto (mañana, luego)	until (see you) soon (tomorrow, later)
Nos vemos.	See you around.
señor	Mr.
señora	Mrs. (married woman)
señorita	Miss, Ms. (unmarried woman)
¿Cómo te llamas? / ¿Cómo se llama usted?	What's your name?
Me llamo ____.	My name is ____.

Mucho gusto. / Encantado/a.	Nice to meet you.
Igualmente.	Likewise. / Same here.

EL ORIGEN Y LA NACIONALIDAD

¿De dónde eres (tú)? / ¿De dónde es usted?	Where are you from?
¿De qué origen es/son ____?	What is/are ____'s/s' (national) origin(s)?
Es de ____.	He (She, It) is from ____.
Son de ____.	They are from ____.
Soy de ____.	I am from ____.
Soy/Es ____.	I am / He (She, It) is ____.
alemán, alemana	German
canadiense	Canadian
chino/a	Chinese
colombiano/a	Colombian
español(a)	Spanish
estadounidense	American (from the United States)
francés, francesa	French
inglés, inglesa	English
italiano/a	Italian
japonés, japonesa	Japanese
mexicano/a	Mexican
puertorriqueño/a	Puerto Rican

¿Cómo se dice _____ en español?	How do you say _____ in Spanish?
Se dice _____.	You say _____.
¿Cómo se escribe _____?	How do you spell _____?
Se escribe _____.	It's spelled _____.

LOS PRONOMBRES DE SUJETO

yo, tú, usted, él, ella, nosotros/as, vosotros/as, ustedes, ellos, ellas

LOS ARTÍCULOS

el/la/los/las	the
un(a)	a, an
unos/as	some

LOS VERBOS

ser (irreg.) (de)	to be (from)
Tengo _____.	I have _____.

LOS DÍAS

lunes, martes, miércoles, jueves, viernes, sábado, domingo

LOS NÚMEROS

uno, dos, tres, cuatro, cinco, seis, siete, ocho, nueve, diez, once, doce, trece, catorce, quince, dieciséis, diecisiete, dieciocho, diecinueve, veinte, veintiuno, veintidós, veintitrés, veinticuatro, veinticinco, veintiséis, veintisiete, veintiocho, veintinueve, treinta, treinta y uno

LAS DESCRIPCIONES

la piel (clara, morena, oscura)	(light, brown, dark) skin
el pelo (castaño, corto, largo, negro, rubio)	(brown, short, long, black, blond) hair
los ojos (azules, castaños, negros, verdes)	(blue, brown, black, green) eyes
alegre	happy
alto/a	tall
amable	friendly
antipático/a	unfriendly
bajo/a	short
bonito/a	pretty
buen, bueno/a	good
delgado/a	thin
encantador(a)	delightful, charming
feo/a	ugly
gordo/a	fat
grande	big, large
guapo/a	handsome, good-looking, pretty
mal, malo/a	bad
pequeño/a	little, small
perezoso/a	lazy
trabajador(a)	hard-working
¿Cómo es/son _____?	What is/are _____ like?

LENGUAJE FUNCIONAL

como	like
diferente (de)	different (from/than)
parecido/a (a)	similar (to)
pero	but
porque	because
sí	yes
similar (a)	similar (to)
también	also, too
y	and

2.

Los estudios

Costa Rica

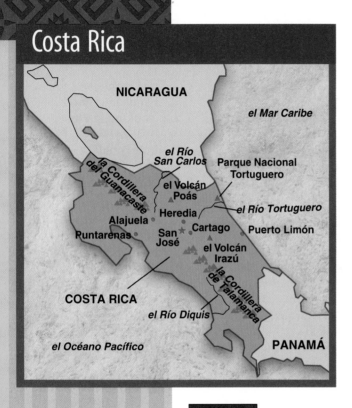

NICARAGUA

el Mar Caribe

el Río San Carlos

Parque Nacional Tortuguero

la Cordillera del Guanacaste

el Volcán Poás

Heredia

el Río Tortuguero

Alajuela

Cartago

Puerto Limón

Puntarenas

San José

el Volcán Irazú

la Cordillera de Talamanca

COSTA RICA

el Río Diquís

el Océano Pacífico

PANAMÁ

Cultura

◆ University Studies in the 21st Century

◆ Student Life and the Academic System in Costa Rica

◆ **Señas culturales:** Biodiversity

Lengua

◆ University Studies; University Life

◆ Question Words

◆ In the Classroom

◆ Prepositions

◆ Regular **-ar** Verbs; Negation (2.1)

◆ Question Formation (2.2)

◆ The Verb **ir; ir a** + Infinitive (2.3)

◆ The Verb **estar** (2.4)

Costa Rica

	Bribri, Talamanca, and other Amerindian groups	Columbus visits on fourth (final) voyage			Central America declares independence from Spain
until 16th c.	until 1502 1500–1600	1502 1534	1600–1750	1776–1783	1821
Various indigenous tribes inhabit North America	Spanish exploration of North America	Jacques Cartier claims Canada for France	British colonies founded in North America	American War of Independence	

Los Estados Unidos y el Canadá

Instantánea

ORIGEN DEL NOMBRE

Costa Rica (*Rich Coast*): Columbus (erroneously) believed the area to harbor great wealth in gold.

POBLACIÓN

4.148.500

LENGUAS

Spanish (official), Creole-English

◀ Atardecer Heredia, *del artista costarricense Crisanto Badilla (1941–   )*

For additional practice, check out the *Manual de práctica,* the Interactive CD-ROM, and the Online Learning Center **(www.mhhe.com/entrevistas2)**!

Central American Federation formed	Federation dissolves; Costa Rica becomes independent state	Costa Rica declares itself republic	New constitution; army dissolved				Óscar Arias elected president	Arias receives Nobel Peace Prize	
1823	**1838**	**1846–1848**	**1848**	**1898**	**1949**	**1952**	**1982**	**1986**	**1987**	**1994**
		Mexican-American War		Spanish-American War		Puerto Rico becomes U.S. commonwealth	Canada cuts legal ties with Britain			U.S., Canada, Mexico sign NAFTA

● Los estudios universitarios

Las facultades	Las clases y las carreras
Facultad de Arte y Arquitectura	el diseño la música
Facultad de Ciencias y Matemáticas	la biología la informática la química
Facultad de Ciencias Sociales	la antropología la psicología* la sociología
Facultad de Filosofía y Letras	la educación el español, el inglés, el francés la filosofía la literatura

Para describir las clases

aburrido/a	boring	**necesario/a**	necessary
difícil	difficult	**obligatorio/a**	obligatory, required
fácil	easy	**optativo/a**	elective, optional
importante	important	**práctico/a**	practical
interesante	interesting	**útil**	useful

Actividades

A. ¿Qué clase es?   Here are some typical quotes from different classes. Identify the course they come from.

1. «El año 1776 (mil setecientos setenta y seis) es el año de la independencia de los Estados Unidos.»
2. «La fórmula del agua es H_2O.»
3. «Los sonetos de Shakespeare son muy interesantes.»
4. «¡Hola! ¿Qué tal?»
5. «El diseño de la casa es muy importante… »

---

* **Psicología** and related words (e.g., **psicólogo/a**) are sometimes spelled without an initial p: **sicología, sicólogo/a.**

B. ¿Cómo es? Describe the following subjects and fields of study in complete sentences, using all the adjectives you think are appropriate.

MODELO   la historia → La historia es interesante y útil.

1. la geología
2. la física
3. el diseño
4. las lenguas

5. el cálculo
6. la informática
7. las ciencias sociales

C. Encuesta: ¿Qué clases te gustan?   Interview five classmates to find out which class(es) they like the most and why. Then report what you think the favorite class **(la clase favorita)** is at your school.

VOCABULARIO ÚTIL

¿por qué?   why?   **porque**   because

MODELO   E1: ¿Qué clases te gustan?
E2: Me gustan el español y la informática.
E1: ¿Por qué?
E2: (Porque) El español es interesante y la informática es muy práctica (útil).

Lenguaje funcional
Los gustos[a]

In your study of language you will soon learn that the way you express complex ideas in one language can be completely different from how you express the same ideas in your native language. The Spanish equivalent of to *like* is one such example. You will learn the complete pattern in **Capítulo 7.** For now, just use **me gusta(n) _____** to express your likes, and **no me gusta(n) _____** to express your dislikes. Use **me gusta** with singular nouns and with actions (verbs) and **me gustan** with plural nouns: **Me gusta la clase de historia. Me gusta estudiar** (*to study*). **Me gustan las clases de inglés y español.** To ask a friend about his/her likes, ask **¿Te gusta(n) _____?**

[a]*Likes*

UNIVERSIDAD DEL DISEÑO
acreditada por Conesup

Arquitectura y Arquitectura de Interiores
MAESTRÍA
proyecta las futuras maestrías en

**Arquitectura • Arquitectura Interior
Arquitectura Paisajista • Diseño Urbano
Diseño Industrial • Diseño Gráfico • Artes Visuales**

interesados comunicarse con la Universidad

COLEGIO LEONARDO DA VINCI
Universidad Autónoma de Centroamérica

MAESTRÍA ADMINISTRACIÓN INDUSTRIAL Msc.

Ventajas:
• Acreditación Internacional del título
• Enseñanza personalizada
• Conferencias y seminarios impartidos por especialistas internacionales
• Excelencia académica
• Acceso a intercambios y becas internacionales

Requisitos:
• Mínimo bachillerato en áreas técnicas afines
• Experiencia y cualidades gerenciales

OTRAS CARRERAS:
• ADMINISTRACIÓN DE NEGOCIOS • INGENIERÍA CIVIL
• INGENIERÍA INDUSTRIAL • RELACIONES PÚBLICAS

● El horario[a]

Las actividades

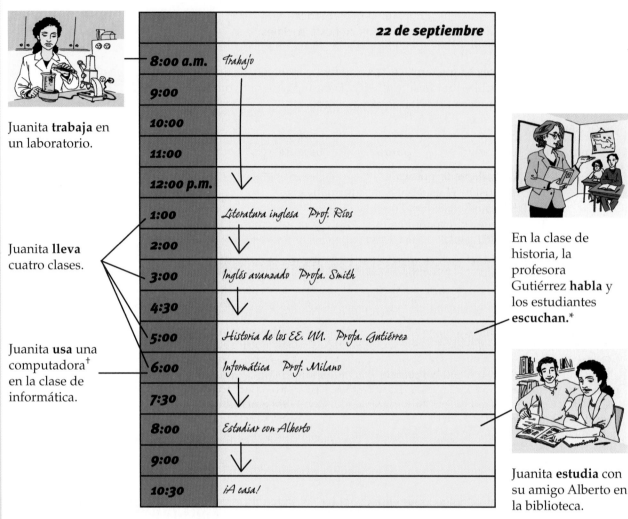

Juanita **trabaja** en un laboratorio.

Juanita **lleva** cuatro clases.

Juanita **usa** una computadora[†] en la clase de informática.

22 de septiembre

8:00 a.m.	Trabajo
9:00	
10:00	
11:00	
12:00 p.m.	
1:00	Literatura inglesa Prof. Ríos
2:00	
3:00	Inglés avanzado Profa. Smith
4:30	
5:00	Historia de los EE. UU. Profa. Gutiérrez
6:00	Informática Prof. Milano
7:30	
8:00	Estudiar con Alberto
9:00	
10:30	¡A casa!

En la clase de historia, la profesora Gutiérrez **habla** y los estudiantes **escuchan.***

Juanita **estudia** con su amigo Alberto en la biblioteca.

cenar	to eat dinner
desayunar	to eat breakfast
enseñar	to teach
entrar (en + *place*)	to enter (*a place*)
escuchar	to listen (to)
estar (*irreg.*)	to be (*location*)
estudiar	to study
hablar	to speak

---

[a] *schedule*
* Note that the verb **escuchar** means both *to listen* and *to listen to.* For example, **Juanita escucha música.** (*Juanita listens to music.*)
[†] In Spain, **la computadora** is called **el ordenador.**

ir (*irreg.*)	to go
llegar (a)	to arrive (at)
llevar	to take (*a class*); to carry
participar	to participate
practicar	to practice
regresar (a + *place***)**	to return (to *a place*)
trabajar	to work
usar	to use

¿A qué hora?

Juanita trabaja **por la mañana.**	*Juanita works in the morning.*
Llega a la universidad **a la una (1:00).**	*She arrives at the university at 1:00.*
Las clases son **por la tarde.**	*Classes are in the afternoon.*
Juanita entra en la clase de inglés avanzado **a las tres (3:00) de la tarde.**	*Juanita enters the advanced English class at 3:00 in the afternoon.*
La clase de informática es **de las seis (6:00) a las siete y media (7:30).**	*The computer class is from 6:00 to 7:30.*
Juanita regresa a casa **a las diez y media (10:30) de la noche.**	*Juanita returns home at 10:30 at night.*

Actividades

A. Actividades típicas. Choose the more logical verb in parentheses to say what these people do.

1. Los estudiantes (escuchan/enseñan) CDs en inglés.
2. El profesor Tomasa (enseña/habla) literatura y composición.
3. (Llego/Practico) a la universidad a las 10:00 de la mañana.
4. En la clase de español, (llevamos/hablamos) español con el profesor.
5. Alberto y Juanita (participan/estudian) en la biblioteca (*library*).
6. (Regresas/Participas) mucho en clase.

B. El horario de Juanita

Paso 1. Examine Juanita's schedule on page 38 to determine at what times she does the following things. Complete the sentences with the appropriate times.

1. Entra en la clase de literatura inglesa _____.

2. Estudia con Alberto _____.

3. Trabaja _____.

4. Llega a la clase de historia _____.

Paso 2. All of the following statements about Juanita's schedule are false. Look at the schedule to provide the correct information.

> MODELO   Juanita llega a la universidad a las 2:00 de la tarde. →
>   No, Juanita no llega a las 2:00 de la tarde. Llega a la 1:00.

1. Juanita lleva seis clases este año (*this year*).
2. Trabaja por la mañana y por la tarde.
3. Juanita enseña la clase de literatura inglesa.
4. Estudia dos horas por la tarde.
5. Juanita y Alberto trabajan en la biblioteca.
6. En la clase de historia los estudiantes practican el español.

 C. Entrevista: El horario.   Interview a classmate to find out when he/she has the following classes.

VOCABULARIO ÚTIL

los lunes (martes,...)	(on) Mondays (Tuesdays, . . .)
(No) Tengo	I (don't) have

> MODELO   la clase de matemáticas (cálculo, álgebra) →
>   E1: ¿A qué hora es la clase de matemáticas?
>   E2: Es a las 2:30 los lunes, miércoles y viernes.
>   (No tengo clase de matemáticas.)

1. la clase de literatura/composición
2. la clase de historia mundial (*world*)/europea
3. la clase de psicología (sociología, antropología)
4. la clase de arte (arquitectura, diseño)
5. la clase de informática
6. la clase de _____.

Si te interesa

There are many different words and expressions for talking about studies in Spanish, and some terms vary from country to country. You need not memorize them all, but you should recognize them when you see or hear them.

class (course): **la asignatura, la clase, el curso, la materia**
major: **la carrera, la especialización**
residence hall (dorm): **el colegio mayor** (*Sp.*), **la residencia (estudiantil/universitaria)**
to take classes: **cursar estudios, llevar clases/cursos, tomar clases/cursos**

● Preguntas para el estudiante típico

¿**Qué** estudias?	*What do you study?*
¿**Cuál** es tu clase favorita?	*What is your favorite class?*
¿**Cuáles** son tus clases este semestre?	*What are your classes (What classes are you taking) this semester?*
¿**Dónde** estudias?	*Where do you study?*
¿**Quién** es tu profesor(a)?	*Who is your instructor?*
¿**Quiénes** son tus amigos?	*Who are your friends?*
¿**Cómo** llegas a la universidad?	*How do you get to the university (campus)?*
¿**Cuándo** son los exámenes?	*When are the exams?*
¿**Cuánto** es la matrícula?	*How much is tuition?*
¿**Cuántas** horas trabajas por semana?	*How many hours do you work per week?*

Actividades

A. Minidiálogos incompletos.   Complete the following minidialogues with the necessary question words.

1. —¿_____ es la clase de español?
   —Es a las 10:00 de la mañana.

2. —¿De _____ eres?
   —Soy de Costa Rica.

3. —¿_____ estudia usted?
   —Estudio inglés.

4. —¿_____ es el profesor de historia?
   —Es el profesor García.

5. —¿_____ clases llevas?
   —Llevo cinco clases: tres por la mañana y dos por la tarde.

6. —¿_____ son ellas?
   —Son mis amigas Juana y Elisa.

7. —¿_____ son tus clases favoritas?
   —La clase de cálculo y la clase de física.

8. —¿_____ es la clase de física?
   —Es muy difícil, pero también es muy interesante.

B. Preguntas personales.   Prepare for an interview with the following celebrities by completing these questions in as many logical ways as possible.

1. Donald Trump, ¿_____ es su hotel favorito?

2. Señor presidente, ¿_____ descansa (*rest*) usted?

3. Sammy Sosa, ¿_____ horas practica usted el béisbol todos los días?

4. Madonna, ¿_____ es tu cantante (*singer*) favorito?

5. Stephen King, ¿_____ horas trabaja usted en su novela?

You can watch this interview on the *Entrevistas* Video or Interactive CD-ROM or listen to the audio on the Online Learning Center (**www.mhhe.com/entrevistas2**).

Silvana Quesada Nieto

«La universidad está dividida en facultades.»

Nombre: Silvana

Apellidos: (1) Quesada (2) Nieto

Edad: 45 (cuarenta y cinco) años

Nació en: San José, Costa Rica

Vocabulario útil

tica,* costarricense	Costa Rican	**puede ser**	it may be
tiene	has	**por**	per
quince mil	15,000	**llevar estudios**	take general studies /
está dividida en	is divided into	**generales**	liberal arts
entre otras	among others	**idioma** *m.*	language
depende de	it depends on	**el primero, el**	the first, the second
para	for	**segundo**	
cada	each	**un poquito más**	a little (bit) more

Antes de ver

Mi universidad. Answer the following questions based on the situation at your university.

1. ¿Cuántos años estudian los estudiantes para el bachillerato?
2. ¿Y para la licenciatura?
3. ¿Cuántos cursos llevan los estudiantes?
4. ¿Hay requisitos o clases obligatorias?
5. ¿Cuándo son las clases? (¿De qué hora a qué hora?)

---

* The term **tico/a** referring to people from Costa Rica is believed to have come from Costa Ricans' frequent use of the diminutive suffix **-ico/a: cafecico** (*little coffee*), **lugarcico** (*little place*), and so on.

CAPÍTULO 2 • Los estudios

¡Veamos!

A. La Universidad Nacional de Costa Rica en Heredia. Now watch the interview and answer the same questions from **Antes de ver** based on the situation where Silvana works.

B. Las facultades. Watch the interview again, if necessary, and indicate which schools and departments in the **Universidad Nacional de Costa Rica (la UNa)** Silvana mentions.

La Facultad de…

☐ Arte y Arquitectura   ☐ Ciencias y Letras   ☐ Educación
☐ Ciencias Sociales   ☐ Derecho (*Law*)   ☐ Filosofía

C. Las clases. Read through the following questions, watch the interview again, and fill in the blanks with the missing information according to what you hear.

1. « …los estudiantes están obligados a _____ estudios generales que consisten en una _____ de _____, una de letras y una de _____.»

2. «Hay tres períodos de clases: el primero en la mañana de _____ a _____ del día, el segundo en la tarde de _____ a _____ y el nocturno que es de _____ a _____ o un poquito más.»

Después de ver

Un país excepcional. Read the additional information provided by Silvana, and indicate what distinguishes Costa Rica from other countries in the Americas.

«Algo muy interesante es que Costa Rica es un país sin ejército.[a] En otros países, el gobierno[b] dedica mucho dinero[c] al ejército, pero en Costa Rica estos recursos[d] son para la educación. Es obvio que para los costarricenses la educación es muy importante.»

[a]sin… *without an army*   [b]*government*   [c]*money*   [d]*resources*

☐ Hay muchos estudiantes en las escuelas y universidades costarricenses.
☐ Las escuelas y universidades costarricenses tienen más dinero que en otros países.
☐ En general, los costarricenses son pacifistas.

● 2.1 Regular -ar Verbs; Negation

A. The verb is the most important word in a Spanish sentence. At the beginning of your study of the language you may feel that the verb system is very complex, but you will soon notice that there are a number of repeating patterns. Every verb in Spanish falls into one of three groups; each group is identified by the ending of the *infinitive* form of the verb (the infinitive is the form you will find in the dictionary, which corresponds to the English word *to* + verb, e.g., *to speak*). The three infinitive endings are **-ar, -er,** and **-ir;** you will study **-er** and **-ir** verbs in **Capítulo 3.**

Each of these verb groups (or *conjugations*) has a distinctive set of endings for each verb tense. These endings let you know who the subject of the sentence is even when the subject pronoun is not stated explicitly. The endings are attached to the stem of the verb, which is the infinitive without the ending (e.g., **llevar → llev-** is the stem). Here are the present tense endings for the regular verb **llevar** (*to take*).

llevar			
(yo)	**llevo**	(nosotros/as)	**llevamos**
(tú)	**llevas**	(vosotros/as)	**lleváis**
(usted, él/ella)	**lleva**	(ustedes, ellos/as)	**llevan**

—¿Cuántas clases **llevas**?	*How many classes are you taking?*
—**Llevo** cuatro classes.	*I'm taking four classes.*

Recall from **Capítulo 1** that in Spanish the subject pronouns are used only for emphasis or clarification. Since the form **lleva** could refer to **usted, él,** or **ella,** it is likely that you will hear these pronouns more frequently with this verb form than you would hear **yo** with the unambiguous **llevo.**

The **-ar** verbs that you have seen so far are all regular: Their endings follow the same pattern as those for **llevar.** (Other verbs, such as **ser,** have forms that do not follow a pattern and are thus irregular.)

B. To make a sentence negative, add **no** immediately before the verb.

No hablo francés.	*I don't speak French.*
La clase de español **no es** fácil.	*Spanish class isn't easy.*

When replying to a question or statement that isn't true, you will generally use the word **no** twice: once to mean *no,* and once to mean *not.*

—¿Estudias aleman?	*Do you study German?*
—**No, no** estudio alemán. Estudio español.	*No, I don't study German. I study Spanish.*

Análisis estructural

Study the following sentences and tell who is doing the action by giving the appropriate subject pronoun in Spanish. Remember: For some verb forms more than one answer is possible.

MODELO   Estudio en la biblioteca. →
            yo

1. Lleva tres clases este semestre.
2. Hablamos español en el laboratorio de lenguas.
3. Llegáis a la universidad a las 11:00 de la mañana.
4. Practico francés con el profesor Lamontagne.
5. Trabajas dos horas por día.
6. Enseña tres clases.
7. Escuchan CDs.

Actividades

A. La vida universitaria (*University life*).   Correct these statements to make them true for your college or university experience.

1. Los estudiantes enseñan las clases y los profesores escuchan.
2. El director prepara trabajos escritos (*written papers*).
3. Los estudiantes llevan un curso por semestre.
4. Todas (*All*) las clases son por la noche.
5. Mis amigos y yo practicamos deportes y cocinamos (*we cook*) en la clase de español.
6. Los estudiantes estudian diez años para el bachillerato.

B. Una buena memoria.   How good is your memory? Correct the following statements about Silvana and the **UNa,** based on what you learned in her interview.

MODELO   Silvana es colombiana. →
            No es colombiana; es costarricense.

1. Los estudiantes llevan cinco cursos.
2. La universidad está dividida en licenciaturas.
3. El bachillerato dura (*lasts*) ocho años.
4. Las clases son por la mañana solamente (*only*).
5. El primer* período de clases termina (*ends*) a las 10:00 de la mañana.
6. Hay dos períodos de clases cada día.

---

* **Primero/a** is another word that, when used as an adjective to describe a noun (e.g., **primera entrevista**), has a short form before masculine singular nouns: **primer año.** When you use this word as an adverb to describe a sequence of events (*First, . . .*), use **primero.**

C. **En esta universidad.** Use the following elements to create sentences that provide information on the college experience at your institution.

MODELO ellos **/** estudiar **/** francés →
Ellos estudian francés.

1. la profesora de psicología **/** enseñar **/** muchas clases
2. nosotros **/** hablar **/** español
3. yo **/** practicar español **/** en el laboratorio
4. mis amigos(as) y yo **/** cursar **/** cuatro materias por semestre/trimestre
5. los estudiantes **/** necesitar **/** libros de texto
6. ¿tu **/** trabajar **/** en la biblioteca?

⬤ 2.2 Question Formation

Asking questions is a very useful tool for learning about another culture. You have already heard and used a number of question words **(palabras interrogativas)** in Spanish. In general, questions with these words follow this pattern.

QUESTION WORD + VERB + SUBJECT + COMPLEMENT(S)
¿Cuándo   estudias   (tú)   en la biblioteca?

¿Qué estudias?	*What do you study?*
¿Cuál es tu clase favorita? / **¿Cuáles** son tus clases favoritas?	*What is your favorite class? / What are your favorite classes?*
¿Cómo llegas a la universidad?	*How do you get to the university?*

NOTES:

- The English term *what?* is expressed with **¿qué?** when a definition of a term is asked for (first example above) and as **¿cuál(es)?** in all other uses (second example). **¿Cuál(es)?** can also be translated as *Which one(s)?*
- **¿Cuánto?** can be used either as an adjective or as an adverb. As an adjective, it agrees with the noun it modifies **(-o/-a/-os/-as).** As an adverb, it does not change form: **¿Cuánto es la matrícula?**
- **¿Cómo?** usually means *How?* With the verb **ser,** however, it asks for a description: **¿Cómo es?** *What is he (she, it) like?*
- Spanish sentences cannot end in a preposition. Rather than dangle a preposition at the end of a sentence, you must place it before the question word, at the beginning of the question: **¿Con quién estudias?** *Who do you study with?*

In addition to the preceding questions, which use interrogative words to elicit information, Spanish has *yes/no* questions that require simply **sí** or **no** as the answer. You can form this type of question in two ways.

1. Use the same word order as you would for a statement, but with rising intonation at the end.

Statement   Muchos costarricenses estudian por la noche.

Question   ¿Muchos costarricenses estudian por la noche?

2. Invert the order of the subject and the verb; the intonation also changes to match the pattern in 1.

| | SUBJECT | VERB | |
| **Statement** | Muchos costarricenses | estudian | por la noche. |

| | VERB | SUBJECT | |
| **Question** | ¿Estudian | muchos costarricenses | por la noche? |

Actividades

A. La pregunta correspondiente.   Change the following sentences into questions, making the underlined phrase the answer.

MODELO   Estudio <u>en la biblioteca</u>. →
         ¿Dónde estudias?

1. El profesor llega a la oficina <u>a la 1:30</u>.
2. Ellos estudian <u>español</u> todos los días.
3. El laboratorio de biología dura <u>dos horas</u>.
4. Llego a la universidad <u>en autobús</u>.
5. Este semestre llevamos <u>cinco</u> clases.
6. Trabajamos <u>en un restaurante</u>.

B. Preguntas para Silvana.   Although Silvana has described some aspects of studying in Costa Rica, you are still curious about many details. Prepare a list of questions for her, using the following question words.

1. ¿Con quién _____?

2. ¿Cuál _____?

3. ¿Cuántos/as _____?

4. ¿Dónde _____?

5. ¿Qué _____?

C. Conversación con un estudiante nuevo / una estudiante nueva.   There is a new exchange student (your partner) in your class. Ask him/her questions to find out the following information at the top of p. 48.

VOCABULARIO ÚTIL

la clase más difícil/fácil	the most difficult/easiest class
en casa	at home
en un restaurante (una tienda, una oficina)	in a restaurant (a store, an office)
solo/a	alone

1. his/her **(tu)** favorite class
2. his/her most difficult class and easiest class
3. if he/she works and, if so, how many hours per week
4. where he/she studies and how many hours a day
5. whom he/she studies with

Análisis cultural

The following quote from an English-language source will add to your knowledge of cultural phenomena in Costa Rica. Is this information consistent with the native speaker's perspective in **Entrevista 1?** Use what you have learned in this chapter about Costa Rica, as well as your own experience, to answer the questions that follow the quote.

66Costa Rica has the most egalitarian citizenry in Central America. Although 10% of Costa Ricans still live in poverty, the country also has the largest middle class in the region. Costa Rica's political leaders have made serious attempts to break down class and economic barriers. Costa Rica also boasts the region's highest literacy rate at 93%. Despite the culture of egalitarianism, there is a wealthy upper class, and three-quarters of the presidents before 1970 descended from just three of the original colonizers of Costa Rica.99

Source: *The International Traveler's Guide to Doing Business in Latin America*

1. In general terms, how would you describe Costa Rican society?

2. Name the five Spanish-speaking countries that neighbor Costa Rica. How would you say Costa Rica compares to them in terms of education, social structure, and way of life?

3. How would you say Costa Rica compares to your own country in terms of education, social structure, and way of life?

4. What influence do you think a high literacy rate might have on various aspects of Costa Rican culture and society, for example, on health care, on participation in the political process, on demand for higher education, and so on?

5. In your opinion, does access to education help to break down social and economic barriers? What are the implications, therefore, for Costa Rica and other countries in Central America?

● Intonation in Questions

It might have surprised you to learn in **Forma y función 2.2** that Spanish questions do not always exhibit changes in word order. Native speakers seldom get confused, however, because of the hint that intonation—the rise and fall in your voice—provides. The exact intonation in questions varies from dialect to dialect in Spanish, just as in English, so listen carefully and imitate your instructor and the audio sources that accompany this book.

● Spelling Conventions in Questions

Since written language cannot convey intonation, Spanish gives you several clues to indicate that a sentence is a question.

1. All question words have a written accent mark.

    ¿**Có**mo estás?

    ¿**Dó**nde estudian los costarricenses?

2. An inverted question mark precedes and indicates the actual beginning of the question phrase. Other phrases (e.g., the name of the person addressed) are written outside the pair of question marks.

    Señor Márquez, ¿cómo está usted?

    En general, ¿dónde estudian los costarricenses? (*But:* ¿Dónde estudian los costarricenses en general?)

The *Manual de práctica* contains activities to practice the material explained here.

▲ *¿Cómo es tu universidad? ¿Es como ésta* (this one)?

● En el aula[a]

(no) hay	there is/are (not)
mucho/a (*adj.*)	many, a lot (of)
mucho (*adv.*)	a lot

Actividades

A. Entrevista: ¿Qué llevas en la mochila? Ask your partner questions to find out what he/she carries in his/her backpack every day. Then answer his/her questions.

B. ¿Qué hay en el aula? Say what there is in the drawing of the classroom, then what there is in your classroom. How do the two compare?

VOCABULARIO ÚTIL

las dos (aulas)	both (classrooms)
más/menos… que	more/less (fewer) . . . than

---

[a] *classroom*
* You might also hear **el pizarrón** and **la pizarra de tiza** for *chalkboard*.

¿Dónde está?

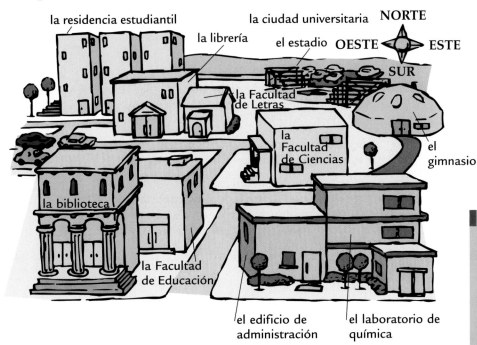

la residencia estudiantil   la ciudad universitaria   **NORTE**

la librería   el estadio   **OESTE**   **ESTE**

SUR

la Facultad de Letras

la Facultad de Ciencias

el gimnasio

la biblioteca

la Facultad de Educación

el edificio de administración

el laboratorio de química

Hay muchos edificios (*buildings*) **en** la ciudad universitaria.

El edificio de administración está **a la izquierda de**l laboratorio de química.

El gimnasio está **a la derecha de**l estadio.

La Facultad de Ciencias está **entre** la biblioteca y el estadio.

La librería (*bookstore*) está **al lado de** la Facultad de Letras.

La Facultad de Educación está **detrás de** la biblioteca.

dentro de	in, within, inside
enfrente de	in front of, facing
está	it is (located)

Lenguaje funcional
Contractions

When the prepositions **a** and **de** are followed by the definite article **el**, contractions are required.

a + **el** = **al** (*to the*)
de + **el** = **del** (*of, from the*)

The other definite articles (**la, los, las**) do not form this contraction: **a la, de los, a las,** and so on.

Actividades

A. La ciudad universitaria

Paso 1. Look at the map as your instructor reads several descriptions. Say whether each description is true (**cierto**) or false (**falso**).

Paso 2. Now your instructor will describe the location of a building on the map. Listen and say which building he/she is describing.

B. Nuestra (*our*) **universidad.** Work with a partner to create a map of your campus. Sketch a quick map and write sentences based on it.

VOCABULARIO ÚTIL

cerca de	near, close to
fuera de	outside of
lejos de	far from

C. ¿Adónde voy (*do I go*)**? ¿Dónde estoy** (*am I*)**?** Say where you are or are going, based on the clues. Use **estoy…** (*I am*) or **voy a** (*I'm going to*), as appropriate.

MODELO   Hay muchos libros. →
Estoy en la biblioteca.

1. Preparo un experimento científico.
2. Hay un partido (*game*) de béisbol muy importante esta tarde.
3. Necesito (*I need*) comprar los libros de texto.
4. Las clases son de las 2:00 a las 6:00 de la tarde. Ahora (*Now*) son las 6:30 de la tarde.
5. Tomo (*I'm taking*) un examen.
6. Hablo con los amigos.

D. ¿Adónde vas (*do you go*) **para… ?** Where do you go to do the following things?

MODELO   estudiar →
Voy a la biblioteca para estudiar.

1. tomar un café
2. practicar deportes
3. pagar (*to pay*) la matrícula
4. comprar libros
5. escuchar música
6. usar la computadora
7. comprar libros, cuadernos, etcétera
8. escuchar un concierto
9. dormir (*to sleep*)

▲ *Estos estudiantes charlan* (chat) *enfrente de la biblioteca de la Universidad de Costa Rica en San José.*

Érika Claré Jiménez

«No existen residencias en la universidad... »

Nombre: Érika

Apellidos: (1) Claré (2) Jiménez

Edad: 24 años

Nació en: San José, Costa Rica

You can watch this interview on the *Entrevistas* Video or Interactive CD-ROM or listen to the audio on the Online Learning Center (**www.mhhe.com/entrevistas2**).

Vocabulario útil

si	if	**la playa**	beach
por ejemplo	for example	**queda**	is located
lo cual quiere decir	which means	**como**	about, more or less
alquilan cuartos	(they) rent rooms	**chismear**	to gossip
varias opciones	various options	**con**	with
puestos de comida	food stands	**bares** *m.*	bars
está incluida	is included	**tomarnos un traguito**	to have a little drink
el tiempo libre	leisure (free) time	**de todo tipo**	of all kinds

Antes de ver

En mi universidad. The following questions appear in the interview you are about to watch. Make sure you understand each question and indicate which answers are true for you or typical for students at your university.

1. ¿Trabajas mientras (*while*) estudias?
   - ☐ Depende. Cuando tengo un horario flexible, trabajo y estudio.
   - ☐ Sí, trabajo y estudio.
   - ☐ Sólo estudio.
   - ☐ Trabajo todos los días. No estudio mucho.

2. ¿Dónde viven (*live*) los estudiantes?
   - ☐ en apartamentos, solos o con amigos
   - ☐ en casa, con la familia
   - ☐ Alquilan cuartos.
   - ☐ en residencias estudiantiles

3. ¿Dónde comen (*eat*) los estudiantes?
   - ☐ en «pulperías» o puestos de comida
   - ☐ en residencias estudiantiles
   - ☐ en cafés o cafeterías
   - ☐ en casa con la familia

4. ¿Y qué hacen Uds. (*do you do*) en el tiempo libre?
   - ☐ Vamos a la playa.
   - ☐ Vamos a conciertos para escuchar música.
   - ☐ Chismeamos con los amigos.
   - ☐ ¡No hay tiempo libre!

¡Veamos!

Según (*According to*) **Érika.**   Now as you watch the interview, supply the missing information about student life at the **Universidad de Costa Rica (UCR).**

1. «Si trabajás, necesitás un _____ flexible... y por ejemplo tomás _____ _____ al día,... »

2. « ...pero existen personas que alquilan _____ a estudiantes o también _____ con sus padres.»

3. «Hay varias opciones: ...pulperías... también _____ que son _____ para _____ _____, y si sos un estudiante... »

4. «Hay muchas cosas... Vamos a _____ _____, que queda a como _____ y media, vamos a _____ a chismear _____ _____ _____, y también... »

Después de ver

Érika y sus compañeros.   Choose the best answer to complete each statement, based on Érika's description of student life at her university.

1. Los estudiantes de la **UCR** viven _____.
   - ☐ en residencias fuera de la universidad
   - ☐ en cuartos que alquilan

2. Para comer, los estudiantes generalmente van _____.
   - ☐ a las pulperías
   - ☐ a casa

3. En su tiempo libre, los estudiantes _____.
   - ☐ practican deportes
   - ☐ van a conciertos

Piénsalo bien

Using the information you have collected so far, how would you compare the **UCR** to your university—**muy similar / algo** (*somewhat*) **similar / diferente / muy diferente?** Consider the following categories in your comparisons.

las actividades	la organización
los edificios e* instalaciones	el tamaño (*size*)
las horas de clase/trabajo por semana	la vida estudiantil

---

* The word **y** (*and*) changes to **e** before a word that begins with **i-** or **hi-**. This is done to facilitate pronunciation, similar to the way English uses *an* instead of *a* before words beginning with a vowel (e.g., *an apple*).

● 2.3 The Verb **ir; ir a** + Infinitive

A. Here are the present tense forms of the irregular verb **ir** (*to go*).

ir			
(yo)	**voy**	(nosotros/as)	**vamos**
(tú)	**vas**	(vosotros/as)	**vais**
(usted, él/ella)	**va**	(ustedes, ellos/as)	**van**

Although **ir** is irregular in all its forms, its present tense endings do resemble those of the **-ar** verbs you have studied in this chapter.

In general you can use the verb **ir** just as you do the English verb *to go*.

Los estudiantes **van** a la cafetería a la 1:00.	*Students go to the cafeteria at 1:00.*
Voy a la clase de biología a las 10:00.	*I go (I'm going) to biology class at 10:00.*
¿Adónde **vas** ahora?	*Where are you going (to) now?*

The verb **ir** implies motion *to* some place; note the special question word **¿adónde?** (*to where?*).

B. Use a form of **ir** + **a** + the infinitive form of a verb (*to be going to* [*do something*]) to refer to future actions. (There is also a future tense in Spanish, which you will study in **Capítulo 14.**)

Voy a estudiar en la biblioteca mañana.	*I'm going to study in the library tomorrow.*
¿Cuántas clases **vas a llevar** este semestre?	*How many classes are you going to take this semester?*
Vamos a mirar un video en la clase de español.	*We're going to see a video in Spanish class.*

Actividades

A. ¿Adónde van? The students in a dorm all have different schedules. Complete the sentences on the following page to tell where each goes on Monday mornings. (Bonus: Say what they do there using the expression **para** + *infinitive.*)

Los lunes por la mañana,…

MODELO   tú **/** a la libraría →
Los lunes por la mañana, tú vas a la libraría (para comprar un periódico).

1. Rafael **/** al gimnasio
2. nosotros **/** a la clase de español
3. tú y Marta **/** al laboratorio de lenguas
4. Elena y Juan José **/** a la Facultad de Letras
5. yo **/** a la biblioteca

B. **Preguntas.** How would you find out where the following people go to do the accompanying activities? Form the necessary questions. How do you think Silvana or Érika would answer your questions?

MODELO   los estudiantes **/** estudiar →
              ¿Adónde van los estudiantes para estudiar?

1. los estudiantes **/** sacar (*to check out*) libros
2. el profesor **/** preparar la clase
3. tú **/** tomar (*to take*) un examen
4. nosotros **/** escuchar música
5. ustedes **/** usar una computadora

C. **La próxima semana** (*Next week*).   What is your schedule going to be like next week? Say what you are going to be doing or where you will be on each of the days/times mentioned.

VOCABULARIO ÚTIL

la fiesta	party
la oficina del profesor / de la profesora	the professor's office
comer	to eat (lunch)
desayunar	to eat breakfast
tomar un café	to drink a cup of coffee

MODELO   el lunes a las 8:00 de la mañana →
              El lunes a las 8:00 de la mañana, voy a ir a la cafetería para hablar con los amigos.

1. el lunes a las 10:00 de la mañana
2. el martes a las 3:00 de la tarde
3. el miércoles a las 7:00 de la tarde
4. el jueves por la tarde
5. el viernes por la mañana
6. el sábado por la noche

D. **Los compañeros de estudio.**   Work with two or three classmates to arrange a common time to study by explaining your schedule.

VOCABULARIO ÚTIL

Es (im)posible.	It's (im)possible.
(No) Está bien.	It's (not) OK.
Me parece bien/mal.	That seems fine/bad to me.
¿Qué tal _____?	How about _____?

MODELO E1: ¿Cuándo vamos a estudiar? ¿Qué tal mañana a las 10:00?
E2: Está bien. Tengo tiempo libre.
E3: Es imposible. A las 10:00 voy a la clase de química.
E4: Y yo voy a hablar con mi profesor de español. ¿Qué tal... ?

● 2.4 The Verb **estar**

In **Capítulo 1** you saw several forms of the irregular verb **estar** (*to be*):
¿Cómo estás? Estoy bien, gracias. Here are all the present tense forms.

estar			
(yo)	**estoy**	(nosotros/as)	**estamos**
(tú)	**estás**	(vosotros/as)	**estáis**
(usted, él/ella)	**está**	(ustedes, ellos/as)	**están**

In addition to describing a person's health, **estar** is used to indicate the location of people and things.*

La Facultad de Educación **está** detrás de la biblioteca. | *The School of Education is behind the library.*

Las canchas de tenis **están** a la izquierda del estadio. | *The tennis courts are to the left of the stadium.*

Esta semana **estamos** en el laboratorio. | *This week we are in the lab.*

Si te interesa

Throughout *Entrevistas* you will study the different uses of **ser** and **estar,** which cannot be mastered in just one lesson, or even in one year! Both verbs can sometimes be translated as *to be* in English, but they are not interchangeable. Even when you can substitute one for the other in the same sentence, there is a definite change in meaning, usually in other words in the sentence. For example, the noun **la clase** can mean *the event of holding the class* or *the students who make up the class,* depending on whether it is used with **ser** or **estar.** Note the following contrast.

La clase **es** en el laboratorio. | *The class is (held) in the lab.*

La clase **está** en el laboratorio. | *The class (i.e., the students) is in the lab.*

In future lessons, you will see similar contrasts when **ser** and **estar** are combined with adjectives and other verb forms. For now, just pay close attention to the usage at hand.

---

* The location (and time) of events, however, is expressed with the verb **ser: La clase es en el aula 304** (*The class is* [*held*] *in room 304*); **La clase es a las 11:00** (*The class is at 11:00*).

Actividades

A. ¿Dónde está? How would you ask someone where to find the following buildings? Form the necessary questions.

1. la biblioteca
2. la Facultad de Química
3. las residencias estudiantiles
4. los restaurantes universitarios
5. el laboratorio de lenguas

B. ¿Qué edificio es? Describe the location of buildings on your campus, and have a partner guess which building you are talking about.

MODELO   E1: Es muy grande. Está detrás de la biblioteca.
             E2: ¿Es el estadio?

C. Encuesta: Tu horario

Paso 1. Ask five classmates where they generally are at the following times on a Monday.

MODELO   E1: ¿Dónde estás a las 3:00 de la tarde?
             E2: A las 3:00 de la tarde estoy en el trabajo.

1. a las 7:00 de la mañana
2. a las 10:00 de la mañana
3. a la 1:00 de la tarde
4. a las 4:30 de la tarde
5. a las 7:00 de la tarde
6. a las 11:00 de la noche
7. ¿ ?

Paso 2. Report the results of your questionnaire to the class.

▲ *¿Te gusta estudiar al aire libre (outside) como estas estudiantes de la Universidad de Costa Rica en San José?*

Lectura

Sobre la lectura The following reading profiles a few of the most popular undergraduate major fields among university students in Costa Rica. As you read it, try to determine which major has the broadest range of required courses.

Antes de leer

A. Consideraciones importantes. When choosing a major, people take many different considerations into account. Which of the following criteria were important to you in choosing your major (or which will be important, if you haven't decided yet)?

☐ mi aptitud (*ability*)
☐ el tamaño de la universidad
☐ la localización (*location*) de la universidad
☐ mi interés en la materia
☐ las asignaturas
☐ los requisitos

☐ los servicios de orientación para los estudiantes
☐ las tareas (*tasks*) profesionales
☐ otro(s) aspecto(s) del programa o de la universidad (¿cuál[es]?)

B. Las carreras y las asignaturas. Which classes **(asignaturas)** would probably be required for each of the following majors **(carreras)? ¡OJO!** In some cases, more than one answer may apply.

CARRERA

1. administración de empresas (*business*)
2. computación
3. educación
4. medicina

ASIGNATURA

a. análisis de algoritmos
b. biología
c. economía
d. física
e. matemáticas
f. pedagogía

¿Cómo son las carreras que prefieren[a] los jóvenes[b]?

Administración, computación, medicina y educación especial son las carreras favoritas en Costa Rica. ¿Qué aptitudes necesita[c] usted si desea[d] estudiar administración de empresas? ¿Qué asignaturas necesita cursar? Los servicios de orientación contestan[e] sus preguntas.

[a]*prefer* [b]*young people* [c]*do you need* [d]*you want* [e]*answer*

Administración de empresas

Asignaturas: contabilidad,[f] cálculo, economía

Tareas profesionales: planificar proyectos; organizar actividades; trabajar en grupo

Computación

Asignaturas: matemáticas para la computación, análisis de algoritmos

Tareas profesionales: trabajar con relaciones numéricas; interpretar información abstracta (no verbal); diseñar sistemas de información

Medicina

Asignaturas: física, biología, medicina

Tareas profesionales: analizar; diagnosticar; trabajar en equipo[g]

Educación

Asignaturas: relaciones interpersonales; psicología; pedagogía; diseño curricular

Tareas profesionales: hablar bien; enseñar; trabajar en equipo; diseñar actividades educativas

[f]*accounting* [g]en… *on/with a team*

Después de leer

A. El perfil de las personas. Indicate the field(s) you could enter if you had the following personality traits and interests.

	ADMINISTRACIÓN DE EMPRESAS	COMPUTACIÓN	MEDICINA	EDUCACIÓN
1. Me gusta trabajar solo/a.	☐	☐	☐	☐
2. Trabajo bien en equipos.	☐	☐	☐	☐
3. Soy bueno/a para los números.	☐	☐	☐	☐
4. Tengo aptitud no verbal.	☐	☐	☐	☐
5. Me gusta hablar con muchas personas.	☐	☐	☐	☐
6. Me gustan las ciencias.	☐	☐	☐	☐
7. Tengo aptitud analítica.	☐	☐	☐	☐
8. Soy muy creativo/a.	☐	☐	☐	☐

B. Las carreras en tu país. Do the observations on popular majors in Costa Rica apply to your country? Consider the following statements and decide if they are true for your country.

En mi país…

1. la educación es una carrera popular.
2. los estudiantes de administración de empresas estudian contabilidad.

3. la física es una asignatura de la carrera de medicina.
4. los doctores educan al público en asuntos (*matters*) de medicina.
5. los expertos en computación diseñan sistemas de información.
6. la planificación y la organización son aptitudes importantes para la administración de empresas.

Señas culturales

◀ *La selva costarricense es conocida por* (known for) *la diversidad de plantas y animales.*

El estudio de la flora y la fauna ▶
de la selva tropical es una carrera
importante y popular.

Costa Ricans take great pride in their country's biodiversity, striving to preserve natural habitats and indigenous species. Ecotourism brings many visitors to the country. Look at the map of Costa Rica at the beginning of this chapter and these photos. Given the country's location and topography, what kind of climate(s) would you expect to find there? What are some examples of flora and fauna you might encounter?

Redacción

Un mensaje a Costa Rica. For this chapter, you will write an e-mail to students at the **UNa (Universidad Nacional de Costa Rica)** in Heredia, describing your university, studies, and student life, and comparing them to what you know about Costa Rican universities. Follow the guided steps in the *Manual de práctica* to complete your message.

Exploración

Investigación cultural. Find more information about Costa Rica in your library, on the *Entrevistas* Online Learning Center **(www.mhhe.com/entrevistas2),** or elsewhere on the Internet and present it to the class. Consult the *Manual de práctica* for ideas for your presentation.

Léxico activo

LOS ESTUDIOS

la **antropología**	anthropology
la **arquitectura**	architecture
el **arte** (*pl.* las **artes**)	art
la **biología**	biology
la **carrera**	major; carreer
la **clase**	class
la **ciencia**	science
las **ciencias sociales**	social sciences
la **computación**	computer science
el **diseño**	design
la **educación**	education
el **español**	Spanish
la **filosofía**	philosophy
el **francés**	French
la **informática**	computer science
el **inglés**	English
las **letras**	arts, letters
la **literatura**	literature
las **matemáticas**	math(ematics)
la **música**	music
la **psicología**	psychology
la **química**	chemistry
la **sociología**	sociology

EN LA UNIVERSIDAD

el/la **amigo/a**	friend
el **aula** (*pl.* las **aulas**)	classroom

la **biblioteca**	library
la **cafetería**	cafeteria
la **ciudad universitaria**	campus
el **edificio de administración**	administration building
el **estadio**	stadium
la **facultad**	school, college
el **gimnasio**	gymnasium
el **horario**	schedule
el **laboratorio (de química, de lenguas)**	(chemistry, language) lab
la **librería**	bookstore
la **residencia (estudiantil/ universitaria)**	dormitory, residence hall

EN EL AULA

el **bolígrafo**	ballpoint pen
el **cuaderno**	notebook
el/la **estudiante**	student
el **lápiz** (*pl.* los **lápices**)	pencil
el **libro (de texto)**	(text)book
la **mochila**	backpack
la **pizarra**	chalkboard
el/la **profesor(a)**	teacher
el **pupitre**	desk
la **silla**	chair
la **tiza**	chalk

PALABRAS INTERROGATIVAS

¿(a)dónde?	(to) where?
¿cómo?	how?
¿cuál(es)?	what?, which?
¿cuándo?	when?
¿cuánto/a?	how much?
¿cuántos/as?	how many?
¿qué?	what?
¿quién(es)?	who?

¿CUÁNDO?

a la(s) _____	at _____ o'clock
a la(s) _____ y media	at _____:30 (at half past _____)
de la mañana (tarde, noche)	in the morning (in the afternoon/evening, at night) (*specific time*)
por la mañana (tarde, noche)	in the morning (in the afternoon/evening, at night) (*in general*)

¿DÓNDE ESTÁ?

a la derecha (de + *noun*)	to the right (of + *noun*)
a la izquierda (de + *noun*)	to the left (of + *noun*)
al lado (de + *noun*)	beside (+ *noun*)
dentro (de + *noun*)	in, within, inside (+ *noun*)
detrás (de + *noun*)	behind (+ *noun*)
en	in
enfrente (de + *noun*)	in front of, facing (+ *noun*)
entre	between; among

LOS VERBOS

cenar	to eat dinner
desayunar	to eat breakfast
enseñar	to teach
entrar (en + *place*)	to enter (*a place*)
escuchar	to listen (to)

estar (*irreg.*)	to be (*location*)
estudiar	to study
hablar	to speak
(no) hay	there is/are (not)
ir (*irreg.*)	to go
llegar (a)	to arrive (at)
llevar	to take (*a class*); to carry
participar	to participate
practicar	to practice
regresar	to return, go back
trabajar	to work
usar	to use

LOS ADJETIVOS

aburrido/a	boring
difícil	difficult
fácil	easy
importante	important
interesante	interesting
necesario/a	necessary
obligatorio/a	required
optativo/a	elective, optional
práctico/a	practical
útil	useful

PALABRAS ADICIONALES

a	to
con	with
mucho/a	much, a lot (of); *pl.* many, a lot (of)
no	no, not

LENGUAJE FUNCIONAL

al (*contraction of* **a** + **el**)	to the
del (*contraction of* **de** + **el**)	of/from the
para + *inf.*	in order to (*do something*)
(no) me gusta(n) _____	I (don't) like _____
(no) te gusta(n) _____	you (*fam.*) (don't) like _____

La familia

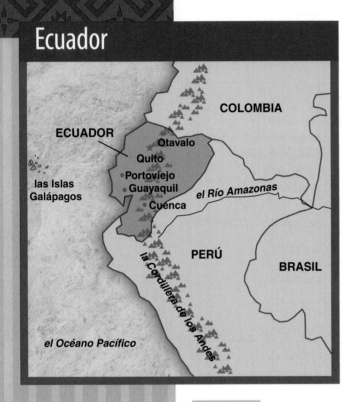

Ecuador

COLOMBIA

ECUADOR

Otavalo
Quito
Portoviejo
Guayaquil
Cuénca

las Islas
Galápagos

el Río Amazonas

la Cordillera de los Andes

PERÚ

BRASIL

el Océano Pacífico

Cultura

◆ The Makeup of Today's Families

◆ The Importance of Family Ties in Latin America

◆ **Señas culturales:** The **Mitad del Mundo** Monument

Lengua

◆ Describing Family Members and Relationships

◆ Numbers 32–105 and Expressing Age

◆ Family Activities

◆ Expressing Possession (3.1)

◆ Possessive Adjectives (3.2)

◆ Regular **-er** and **-ir** Verbs (3.3)

◆ Irregular Verbs: **dar, hacer, salir, ver** (3.4)

Ecuador	Caras, Quitus Duchicela, Cañari, and other Amerindian tribes	Incas become dominant among Amerindians	First Europeans land in Ecuador	Civil war in Incan Empire; Spanish conquest of Incas begins	Inca stronghold Quito conquered by Sebastián de Benalcázar	
	until 1438	**1438–1532 until 16th c.**	**1526 1500–1600**	**1532**	**1534**	**1600–1750**
Los Estados Unidos y el Canadá		Various indigenous tribes inhabit North America	Spanish exploration of North America		Jacques Cartier claims Canada for France	British colonies founded in North America

Instantánea

ORIGEN DEL NOMBRE

Ecuador: from the Spanish for *equator* **(la línea del ecuador),** which passes through Quito

POBLACIÓN

12.471.600

LENGUAS

Spanish (official), Quechua

▲ El matrimonio, *del artista ecuatoriano Daniel Chusin Vega*

For additional practice, check out the *Manual de práctica,* the Interactive CD-ROM, and the Online Learning Center **(www.mhhe.com/entrevistas2)**!

	Defeat of remaining Incas	Antonio José de Sucre, Ecuador's national hero, defeats main Spanish army	Independence from Spain		Invasion of Ecuador by Peru; Ecuador surrenders half of its territory			Oil exploration and export transform Ecuadorian economy	Ecuador and Peru continue fight over disputed border region	Ecuador adopts new constitution	Ecuador adopts U.S. dollar as official currency
1780–1783 **1776–1783**		**1822**	**1830**	**1846–1848**	**1898**	**1941**	**1952**	**1970–1979** **1982**	**1995** **1994**	**1997**	**2000**
American War of Independence				Mexican-American War	Spanish-American War		Puerto Rico becomes U.S. commonwealth	Canada cuts legal ties with Britain	U.S., Canada, Mexico sign NAFTA		

La familia y los parientes*

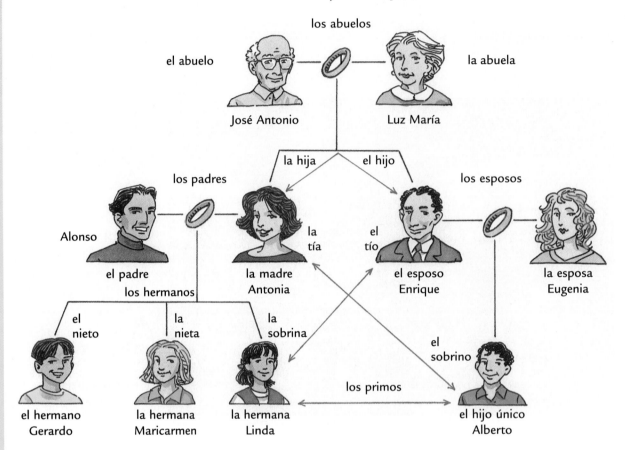

los abuelos

el abuelo — la abuela

José Antonio — Luz María

la hija — el hijo

los padres — los esposos

Alonso — la tía — el tío

el padre — la madre Antonia — el esposo Enrique — la esposa Eugenia

los hermanos

el nieto — la nieta — la sobrina — el sobrino

el hermano Gerardo — la hermana Maricarmen — la hermana Linda — el hijo único Alberto

los primos

Otros^a miembros de la familia

el/la cuñado/a	brother-in-law / sister-in-law
el gato	cat
el/la gemelo/a (los gemelos)	twin (twins)
la madrina	godmother
el/la niño/a (los niños)	child (children)
el padrino	godfather
el perro	dog
cariñoso/a	affectionate

estrecho/a	close
gregario/a	gregarious
junto/a	together
materno/a	maternal
paterno/a	paternal
poco/a	little; *pl.* few
solo/a	alone
unido/a	close-knit

---

[a] *Other*

* **El/La pariente** is a false cognate. It means *relative; parents* are **los padres.**

Actividades

A. ¿Quién es? Read the following statements and tell which family member each one describes.

1. Esta persona es la madre de mi madre.
2. Es la hija de mis tíos.
3. Es el hijo de mi abuelo paterno.
4. Es la esposa de mi cuñado.
5. Son los hermanos de mi madre.
6. Es el hijo de mi tío.
7. Es el hijo de mis padres (¡no yo!).

B. ¿Qué relación tienen (*do they have*)**?** Look at the family tree on page 66 and describe all the possible relationships for each of the following people.

> MODELO   Luz María →
> Luz María es la esposa de José Antonio, la madre de
> Antonia y…

1. Enrique
2. Gerardo
3. Maricarmen y Linda
4. José Antonio
5. Alberto
6. Antonia y Alonso

C. ¿Qué tipo de familia es?

Paso 1. Five Ecuadorians (**ecuatorianos**) describe their families. Give appropriate adjectives to describe each one, choosing from **grande, pequeño/a, nuclear,** and **extendido/a.**

> MODELO   Es una familia _____.

1. «Tengo sólo (*only*) un hermano.»
2. «En mi familia somos mi padre, mi madre, mi hermano mayor (*older*), mi hermana mayor, mi abuela y mi tía Alejandra.»
3. «Vivo (*I live*) solo.»
4. «Vivo con mi hermano y su esposa y los tres hijos de ellos.»
5. «Tengo dos hermanos y un perro.»

Paso 2. Now reread the descriptions and say whether each family described is similar to or different from your family. Give details to explain your answer.

> MODELO   La familia número tres es parecida a / diferente de mi familia
> porque en mi familia somos…

Si te interesa

In **Capítulo 1** you learned that most Spanish speakers use two last names (**apellidos**)—the first is the father's family name, and the second is the mother's. In some cases, the two names may be connected with the word **y:** María Andrade y Rojas. Married women often do not take their husband's family name, but this custom varies by region and country. If a woman does use her husband's last name, it is usually preceded by **de.** For example, when María Andrade y Rojas marries José Antonio Sabater Pérez, she may be known as María Andrade de Sabater, and people may address her as **la señora (de) Sabater.** Their children's last names are Sabater Andrade.

D. Entrevista. Interview a classmate to find out how many family members he/she has and what they are like. Then report your results to the class.

MODELO E1: ¿Cómo es tu familia?
E2: Es grande. Tengo tres hermanas, dos hermanos y dieciséis primos.
E1: Jaime tiene (*has*)…

VOCABULARIO ÚTIL

chico/a	small
las mascotas	pets
el/la primer(a) esposo/a	first husband/wife
el/la segundo/a esposo/a	second husband/wife

● Los números y la edad

To tell someone's age you need to know the numbers up to 100 (and sometimes higher). You have already learned numbers 1–31. Remember from **Capítulo 1** that the numbers 16–19 and 20–29 can be written as a single word (**dieciséis, veintidós**) or as three words (**diez y seis, veinte y dos**); be careful with the written accent marks! The numbers 31–99 are always written as three words.

30 **treinta**	39 **treinta y nueve**	48 **cuarenta y ocho**
31 **treinta y uno***	40 **cuarenta**	49 **cuarenta y nueve**
32 **treinta y dos**	41 **cuarenta y uno**	50 **cincuenta**
33 **treinta y tres**	42 **cuarenta y dos**	60 **sesenta**
34 **treinta y cuatro**	43 **cuarenta y tres**	70 **setenta**
35 **treinta y cinco**	44 **cuarenta y cuatro**	80 **ochenta**
36 **treinta y seis**	45 **cuarenta y cinco**	90 **noventa**
37 **treinta y siete**	46 **cuarenta y seis**	100 **cien**
38 **treinta y ocho**	47 **cuarenta y siete**	105 **ciento**[†] **cinco**

—¿Cuántos años tienes?
—Tengo 19 años.

—¿Qué edad tiene tu hija?
—Tiene 3 años y medio.

---

* Remember that **uno** becomes **un** before a masculine noun (**tengo** *un* **hermano,** but **sólo tengo** *uno*). Likewise, the compound form **veintiuno** is shortened to **veintiún** before masculine nouns like **años.**

[†] The number **cien** becomes **ciento** in the numbers 101–199 (**ciento uno, ciento dos,** and so on).

Soy **mayor que** mi hermana.

¿Sólo tiene 19 años? Es **menor que** yo.

I'm older than my sister.

She is only 19? She is younger than I (am).

Actividades

A. ¿Cuántos años tienen? How old are the following people?

Paso 1. Give complete sentences to tell their ages. Use the appropriate form of the verb **tener: (yo) tengo, él/ella tiene.** If you do not have one of the relatives listed, use a different family member instead.

1. yo
2. mi padre/madre
3. mi hermano/a _____

4. mi abuelo/a
5. mi tío/a _____
6. mi primo/a _____

Paso 2. Now say how the people above are relative to each other in age.

MODELO   Mi prima Mary tiene 35 años y mi hermano Samuel tiene 34. Mary es **mayor que** Samuel.

B. ¿Cuántos años tienen ahora? Read aloud the following people's date of birth. How old are they now? How old are they going to be in 2010?

VOCABULARIO ÚTIL

ahora	now
Nació en _____.	He/She was born in _____.
1967	**mil novecientos sesenta y siete**
2010	**dos mil diez**
Va a tener _____ años.	He/She is going to be _____ years old.

1. Ramiro González Moreno
   el 4 de diciembre de 1961

2. Pilar Herrera Cano
   el 25 de julio de 1979

3. Gregorio Redondo Haro
   el 12 de noviembre de 1992

4. Elena García Gallego
   el 31 de agosto de 1927

C. Encuesta: ¿Qué edad tienen tus compañeros/as de clase? Ask ten classmates how old they are. Then summarize the ages of those classmates, using the following statements.

La mayoría de la clase tiene _____.
La mayoría de la clase es mayor/menor de* _____ años.
Ningún estudiante es mayor/menor de _____ años.

D. La edad ideal. In your opinion, what is the ideal age for the following activities?

MODELO   casarse →
En mi opinión, la edad ideal para casarse (*get married*) es 25 años.

1. terminar los estudios universitarios
2. empezar a (*to begin to*) trabajar
3. tener hijos
4. comprar una casa
5. jubilarse (*to retire*)

E. ¿Quién es mayor/menor? Work with a partner to examine these photographs and guess how old the people are. Then compare their ages, using **mayor/menor que.**

VOCABULARIO ÚTIL

el hombre	man
joven (*pl.* **jóvenes**)	young (*person*)
la mujer	woman
viejo/a	old (*person*)

1.

2.

3.

---

* **De,** not **que,** is used with **mayor** and **menor** to talk about numbers or quantities.

CAPÍTULO 3 • La familia

Cynthia Cevallos Mendoza

«*Mi familia es mi papá y mi mamá…*
También tengo dos hermanos.»

Nombre: Cynthia

Apellidos: (1) Cevallos (2) Mendoza

Edad: 31 años

Nació en: Quito, Ecuador

You can watch this interview on the *Entrevistas* Video or Interactive CD-ROM or listen to the audio on the Online Learning Center (**www.mhhe.com/entrevistas2**).

Vocabulario útil

viene de	comes from	**te importa / me importa**	you care / I care
varones	males	**calor**	warmth, closeness
una relación muy unida	a very close relationship	**saber**	to know
a pesar de que	in spite of	**simplemente**	simply
hacer cosas	to do things		

Antes de ver

A. La familia nuclear de Cynthia.   Study this family tree and indicate the relationship of each member of the nuclear family to Cynthia.

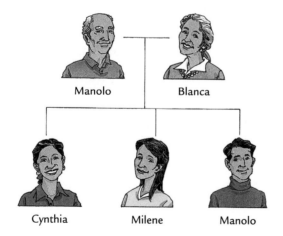

Manolo   Blanca

Cynthia   Milene   Manolo

B. **En la familia de Cynthia.**   Read the following statements and indicate whether they apply to a close-knit family or not. Then, as you watch, check which are true for Cynthia's family.

	SÍ	NO
1. Estamos siempre (*always*) en comunicación.	☐	☐
2. Cada uno (*Each one*) trabaja y estudia.	☐	☐
3. Tratamos de (*We try to*) hacer cosas juntos.	☐	☐
4. La vida familiar (*Family life*) es importante.	☐	☐
5. No somos cariñosos. No hay calor familiar.	☐	☐
6. Si tienes problemas, puedes contar con alguien (*you can count on someone*).	☐	☐

¡Veamos!

¿Qué edad tienen?   Watch the interview again and indicate the ages of Cynthia's family members on her family tree, when given. Complete the following sentences with as many possibilities as you can.

1. _____ es mayor que _____.

2. _____ es menor que _____.

Después de ver

A. **¿Cómo son los hermanos Cevallos?**   Based on what you know about Cynthia and her family, describe how you imagine Cynthia's relatives to be by completing the following sentences.

1. Los padres de Cynthia se llaman _____ y _____ y tienen _____ y

   _____ años respectivamente.

2. Milene tiene _____ y está _____.

3. Su hermano Manolo está _____, tiene _____ años y tiene un

   _____.

B. **Entrevista: ¿Cómo es tu familia?**   Now that you know a little bit about Cynthia's view of her family, what about your classmates' families? Use the following cues to form questions for a classmate, changing or adding any necessary words.

1. ¿quiénes / ser / los miembros de tu familia?
2. ¿ustedes / ser / una familia / unido?
3. cuando hay un problema, ¿tú / hablar / con la familia?
4. en tu opinión, ¿qué aspecto de la vida familiar / ser / más importante?
5. ¿tú / visitar / a los parientes / frecuentemente?

3.1 Expressing Possession

A. The verb **tener** (*to have*) is used to express possession, just like its English equivalent. You have already seen some forms of **tener** used to express age in Spanish.

Tengo 23 años.	*I am 23 years old.* (lit., *I have 23 years.*)
¿**Tienes** una familia grande?	*Do you have a large family?*

Here are all the present tense forms of the irregular verb **tener.** Note that some forms have an additional **e** → **ie** change in the stem.

tener			
(yo)	**tengo**	(nosotros/as)	**tenemos**
(tú)	**tienes**	(vosotros/as)	**tenéis**
(usted, él/ella)	**tiene**	(ustedes, ellos/as)	**tienen**

B. Another way to express possession in Spanish is by using the construction *noun* + **de** + *noun*. There is no suffix equivalent to English -'s/s'.

Roberto es **el hijo de una amiga.**	*Roberto is a friend's son.* (*Roberto is the son of a friend.*)

To ask about possession, use the question ¿**De quién es/son... ?**

—¿**De quién es** el libro?	*Whose book is it?* (lit., *Of whom is the book?*)
—**Es de** mi madre.	*It's my mother's.*
—¿**De quién son** los lápices?	*Whose pencils are they?*
—**Son del*** estudiante nuevo.	*They are the new student's.*

Actividades

A. Habla Cynthia Cevallos Mendoza. Form complete sentences that Cynthia might say about herself and her family.

1. yo **/** tener **/** dos hermanos
2. nosotros **/** tener **/** buenas relaciones
3. mi hermana Milene **/** tener **/** novio (*boyfriend*)
4. mis padres **/** no tener **/** muchos problemas de salud (*health*)
5. ¿tener **/** usted **/** una familia grande?

---

* Remember that the preposition **de** and the definite article **el** contract to form a single word: **del.**

B. Las posesiones

Paso 1. Use a form of **ser de** to match the objects on the left with their probable owners on the right. **¡OJO!** There are a number of possible combinations.

MODELO   La calculadora es del estudiante de matemáticas.

OBJETOS

1. el coche grande
2. los perros
3. la tetera (*teapot*)
4. la computadora
5. el diccionario inglés/español
6. la mochila
7. los libros en español
8. las bicicletas

PERSONAS

a. la persona rica (*rich*)
b. el/la estudiante de matemáticas
c. mi compañero/a de cuarto (*roommate*)
d. el jugador / la jugadora (*player*) de básquetbol
e. la reina de Inglaterra
f. nosotros en la clase de español
g. mis hermanos (primos, sobrinos)
h. el profesor / la profesora de español
i. el veterinario

Paso 2. Which of the objects mentioned in **Paso 1** do you own? Which don't you own? Use the verb **tener** to describe your possessions.

C. Consejos (*Advice*) prácticos.

The following letters were written to and by a family counselor. Fill in the blanks with the appropriate form of the verb **tener**.

Querida[a] *Consuelo:*

Yo ____ *un problema.* ____ *tres hermanos. Somos una familia grande. Mi hermano mayor* ____ *16 años y los gemelos* ____ *14 años. Soy la menor (* ____ *11 años) y la única hija de la familia. El problema es que mis hermanos creen que*[b] *mis padres me miman.*[c] *Ellos me atormentan*[d] *constantemente, y ¡no puedo más!*[e] *¿* ____ *usted una solución para mi problema?*

    Sinceramente,

    Lucrecia Quinteros Moral, Quito

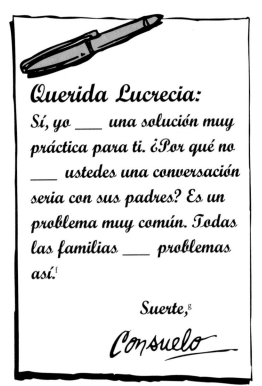

Querida Lucrecia:

Sí, yo ____ *una solución muy práctica para ti. ¿Por qué no* ____ *ustedes una conversación seria con sus padres? Es un problema muy común. Todas las familias* ____ *problemas así.*[f]

    Suerte,[g]

    Consuelo

[a]*Dear* [b]*creen... think that* [c]*me... spoil me* [d]*me... tease me* [e]¡*no... I can't take it anymore!*
[f]*like this* [g]*(Good) Luck*

D. Preguntas indiscretas.   What questions would you like to ask the following people about things they have (possessions, age, and so on)? Form complete questions using the appropriate forms of the verb **tener.**

MODELO   el presidente de los Estados Unidos →
             ¿Tiene usted momentos tranquilos en la vida?

VOCABULARIO ÚTIL

muchos admiradores	many fans
novio/a*	boyfriend/girlfriend
tiempo para descansar	time to rest

1. la primera dama de los Estados Unidos (la esposa del presidente)
2. tu actor favorito / actriz favorita
3. el presidente de Ecuador
4. un compañero / una compañera de clase
5. tu profesor(a) de español

3.2 Possessive Adjectives

Another way to express possession in Spanish is by using possessive adjectives.

Los adjetivos posesivos			
mi(s)	my	**nuestro**/a/os/as	our
tu(s)	your (*fam. s.*)	**vuestro**/a/os/as	your (*fam. pl.*)
su(s)	your (*form. s.*), his (her, its)	**su**(s)	your (*form. pl.*), their

These forms are used before nouns. Like all adjectives in Spanish, they agree with the noun they modify.

Mi familia es muy unida.	*My family is very close-knit.*
Nuestros padres son estrictos.	*Our parents are strict.*
Sus parientes son de Quito.	*His relatives are from Quito.*

Note that in the last example, **su(s)** could mean *his, her, its, your* (form. sing., pl.), or *their*, depending on the context. To avoid ambiguity in this situation, it is common to express possession with *definite article + noun + **de** + pronoun.*

Los parientes de él son de Quito.	*His relatives are from Quito.*
Los parientes de ellos son de Quito.	*Their relatives are from Quito.*
Los parientes de usted son de Quito, ¿no?	*Your relatives are from Quito, right?*

---

* Note that you do not use **un(a)** with most nouns following **tener,** unless you further describe them with adjectives: **Tengo novia** but **Tengo una novia muy guapa.**

Análisis estructural

Study the phrases below, comparing them to their English translations to make sure you have the correct meaning. In each case, what do you notice about gender/number agreement? What do Spanish possessive adjectives agree with, the *possessor* or the *thing possessed*?

1. **a.** mi hermano   *my brother*
   b. mi hermana   *my sister*
   c. mis hermanos   *my brothers (and sisters)*
   d. mis hermanas   *my sisters*
2. **a.** nuestro tío   *our uncle*
   b. nuestra tía   *our aunt*
   c. nuestros tíos   *our uncles (and aunts)*
   d. nuestras tías   *our aunts*
3. **a.** su hijo   *your (his, her, their) son*
   b. su hija   *your (his, her, their) daughter*
   c. sus hijos   *your (his, her, their) sons (and daughters)*
   d. sus hijas   *your (his, her, their) daughters*

Actividades

A. ¿De quién es?   Fill in the correct endings to tell whose family member(s) is/are mentioned.

1. m_____ madre
2. s_____ hermanos
3. nuestr_____ primos
4. t_____ hermana

5. vuestr_____ sobrina
6. m_____ tíos
7. s_____ hijos
8. nuestr_____ madrina

¿Cuántas generaciones ves en esta ▶
familia ecuatoriana?

B. Posesiones. Convert the following phrases into expressions with the possessive adjectives.

MODELO   el libro del profesor →
                su libro

1. la mochila de Raquel
2. los libros de mi padre
3. las nietas de doña Ana
4. el álbum de nosotros
5. los parientes de ellos
6. el hermano de Raúl y Federico

Análisis cultural

The following quote from an English-language source will add to your knowledge of the concept of "family" in the Hispanic world. Is this information consistent with the native speaker's perspective in **Entrevista 1**? Use what you have learned in this chapter, as well as your own experience, to answer the questions that follow the quote.

❝The family is considered the single most important institution in the social organization of Hispanics. It is through the family and its activities that all people relate to significant others in their lives and it is through the family that people communicate with the larger society. The family incorporates the idea of **la familia** (*the greater family*), which includes in addition to the immediate nuclear household, relatives that are traced on both the female and male sides. These include parents, grandparents, brothers and sisters, cousins, and to a certain extent any blood relatives that can be identified through the hierarchy of family surnames. This broad-ranging concept has important consequences for actual social and cultural behavior. It places individuals as well as nuclear families into a recognizable network of social relations within which mutual support and reciprocity occur.❞

Source: *The Hispanic Almanac: From Columbus to Corporate America*

1. What evidence have you found in this chapter to support the statement that the family is an important institution of social organization?

2. What Spanish terms have you learned to identify members of the nuclear household? the greater family?

3. What example have you seen of a "network of social relations within which mutual support and reciprocity occur"?

Pronunciación y ortografía

● Written Accents (I)

You have probably noticed an acute accent mark (´: **acento escrito**) on many of the Spanish words you have seen. This mark serves a number of purposes:

- to mark question words (**cuál, qué, quién,** and so on)
- to distinguish homophones (**tú** = *you,* **tu** = *your,* **sí** = *yes,* **si** = *if*)
- to indicate the stressed syllable on many words

This last purpose is a very important function of the accent mark. Not all words have a written mark to show you which syllable is stressed. Nonetheless, you can read and pronounce words without an accent mark with confidence if you keep in mind the following simple rules. Any deviation from these rules is *always* indicated by a written accent mark.

Rule	Examples	Exceptions
1. A word that ends in a *vowel* or the consonants *n* or *s* is stressed on the next-to-last syllable.	pa-**dre** tie-**nen** her-**ma**-nos	te-**lé**-fo-no, ca-**fé** va-**rón** in-**glés**
2. A word that ends in a *consonant* other than *n* or *s* is stressed on the last syllable.	es-pa-**ñol** ma-**yor**	**ú**-til a-**zú**-car

These rules explain why one form of a word may have a written accent mark and another form does not. For example, the noun **relación (re-la-ción)** is stressed on the last syllable even though it ends in the letter **n;** the accent mark shows that it is an exception to Rule 1. The plural **relaciones (re-la-cio-nes),** however, does not need a written accent: It ends in the letter **s** and is therefore stressed on the next-to-last syllable, in accordance with Rule 1.

The *Manual de práctica* contains activities to practice the material explained here.

La familia en transición

| Enrique Arteta Trujillo | Consuela Jácome Gómez | Julián Acevedo Moreno | Carmen Barrios Osorio |

| Alicìa Arteta Jácome | Enrique Arteta Jácome | **Gabriela Arteta Jácome** | Sandra Acevedo Barrios | Cristina Acevedo Barrios | Rafael Acevedo Barrios |

Los **padres** de Gabriela **están divorciados.**
Gabriela es **soltera.** No tiene **esposo.**
Su madre **está casada.** El segundo esposo de su madre es su **padrastro.**
(Gabriela no tiene **madrastra.**)
Su madre y su padrastro tienen tres hijos. Son los **hermanastros** de Gabriela.
Gabriela **vive** con su madre, su padrastro y sus hermanastros.

Actividades

A. ¿Quién es?   Read the following statements and tell which family member each one describes.

1. El hijo de mi padrastro es mi _____.

2. La hija de mi padrastro es mi _____.

3. La segunda esposa de mi padre es mi _____.

4. El segundo esposo de mi madre es mi _____.

5. La hermana de mi hermanastro es mi _____.

B. Una familia en transición.   Draw the family tree of a family you invent, including at least three of the details below. Describe the family to a partner to see if he/she can draw the tree as you created it. Use the verb **vive** (*he/she lives*) to describe who lives where and with whom.

- el hermanastro
- la madre soltera
- la segunda esposa

- La abuela murió (*died*) en _____.
- La hija nació en _____.

C. Encuesta: Las relaciones familiares. Take a class opinion poll on the following topics. How many students agree with the statements listed? How many disagree? When you ask your classmate, use the phrase **¿Crees que _____?** (*Do you think that _____?*).

En mi país…

1. no hay respeto para los ancianos (*elders*).
2. los hijos no respetan a los padres.
3. las relaciones familiares no son muy estrechas.
4. los padres no ayudan (*help*) a los hijos.
5. los abuelos miman a los nietos.
6. los padres maltratan (*mistreat*) a los hijos.
7. no hay una relación íntima entre los miembros de la familia.
8. los hijos no viven con los padres.

Si te interesa
The **a personal**

Note that when the objects of the verbs in **Actividad C** are human beings, they are preceded by the preposition **a** (e.g., **…respetan *a* los padres**). This is known as the **a personal** in Spanish, and there is no English equivalent for it. You will learn more about this feature of Spanish in **Capítulo 5.** For now, just remember to use it with expressions such as the ones in **Actividad C.**

● Las actividades familiares

Los padres de Gabriela **están jubilados:** no trabajan. Para **pasar el tiempo libre,** les gusta…

caminar en la playa.

comer con la familia.

discutir la política con sus amigos.

beber un refresco, una cerveza, vino	to drink a soft drink, a beer, wine	**leer novelas, el periódico, revistas**	to read novels, the newspaper, magazines
conversar	to chat	**mirar/ver la televisión**	to watch TV
descansar	to rest	**pasar tiempo con los hijos**	to spend time with the (one's) children
echar una siesta	to take a siesta (nap)		
escribir cartas	to write letters	**pasear**	to go for a walk
hacer crucigramas	to do crossword puzzles	**salir a bailar**	to go out dancing
		ver (visitar) a los parientes	to see (visit) the (one's) relatives
ir de compras	to go shopping		

Actividades

A. ¿Qué tipo de actividad es? Classify the verbs in the preceding list as actions that you enjoy doing alone or with other family members and as physical or mental activities. **¡OJO!** Some actions can fit into more than one category.

Actividades que hago (*I do*) solo/a	Actividades que hago en familia	Actividades físicas	Actividades mentales

B. ¿Qué te gusta hacer? Which of the following activities do you enjoy doing with family members and friends? Form complete sentences using elements from each column and any others you can think of. Remember: Even if you name two or more actions, use **gusta**, not **gustan**.

MODELO   Me gusta mirar la televisión con mi padre, pero no me gusta discutir la política con él.

Me gusta… No me gusta…	+	discutir la política pasear en el parque mirar la televisión salir a bailar ir al cine (*movies*) trabajar en el taller 　(*workshop*) visitar a mis parientes ir de compras practicar deportes tomar un café ¿ ?	+	con mi padre con mi madre con mis amigos/as con mi hermano/a con mi 　hermanastro/a con mis abuelos con mis tíos con mis primos solo/a con toda la familia ¿ ?

C.   Entrevista: En el tiempo libre

Paso 1. Interview a classmate to find out what he/she generally does in his/her leisure time.

MODELO   E1: ¿Qué te gusta hacer en tu tiempo libre?
　　　　　E2: Me gusta…

Paso 2. Find out what his/her plans are for different times in the future: **este fin de semana** (*this weekend*), **en el verano** (*summer*), **el sábado por la noche,** and so on.

MODELO   E1: ¿Qué vas a hacer este fin de semana?
　　　　　E2: Voy a…

Entrevista 2

You can watch this interview on the *Entrevistas* Video or Interactive CD-ROM or listen to the audio on the Online Learning Center (**www.mhhe.com/entrevistas2**).

Gabriela Arteta Jácome

«Pasamos muchos ratos agradables.»

Nombre: Gabriela

Apellidos: (1) Arteta (2) Jácome

Edad: 28 años

Nació en: Guayaquil, Ecuador

Vocabulario útil

a pesar de	in spite of	**la distancia**	the distance
misma sangre	same blood	**no nos separamos**	we don't become
ratos agradables	pleasant times/moments		separated (we
primordial	fundamental		stay close)
sentimos	we feel		

Antes de ver

A. Predicciones. Read Gabriela's quote and study the **Vocabulario útil.** Which of the following phrases do you think you might hear in this interview?

1. ☐ «Caminamos, salimos a pasear, comemos juntos… »
2. ☐ «Hay separación a causa de (*on account of*) la distancia.»
3. ☐ «Mis padres están divorciados.»
4. ☐ «Nuestra familia es muy unida.»
5. ☐ «Tenemos mucha comunicación.»

B. La información exacta. How do you think Gabriela will respond to the following questions in the interview?

1. ¿Cómo es tu familia?
   a. Vivo con _____.
   b. Mis padres están _____.
   c. Tengo dos hermanos y _____.
2. ¿Es una familia unida?
   ☐ Sí.   ☐ No.
3. ¿Pasan ustedes mucho tiempo juntos?
   Sí, nos gusta _____.

☐ caminar en la playa ☐ leer revistas
☐ comer juntos   ☐ mirar la televisión
☐ ir al cine   ☐ pasear

¡Veamos!

Comprobar y confirmar. Now watch the interview to see how well you predicted Gabriela's responses to the questions in **Actividad A** and **Actividad B.**

Después de ver

Gabriela y su familia. Read the following statements and indicate if they are true **(cierto)** or false **(falso),** based on what Gabriela says in her interview.

	CIERTO	FALSO
1. Gabriela no tiene buenas relaciones con sus hermanastros.	☐	☐
2. Para esta familia, es agradable salir, comer y hablar juntos.	☐	☐
3. En esta familia, el trabajo es primordial.	☐	☐
4. La distancia no es un problema para Gabriela y su familia.	☐	☐
5. Siempre conversan y están en comunicación.	☐	☐

Piénsalo bien

Paso 1. Based on the following chart, summarize what you know about Cynthia's and Gabriela's families.

	Tamaño	¿Unida o no?	Aspectos familiares importantes
La familia de Cynthia			
La familia de Gabriela			

Paso 2. Now write three sentences describing the way(s) in which your family is similar to or different from Cynthia's and Gabriela's families. Follow the models and give as many details as possible.

MODELOS **Al igual que** la familia de Cynthia, mi familia es grande. Somos… (Tengo…)

A diferencia de la familia de Cynthia, mi familia no es unida. Cada persona vive en un lugar diferente y no hablamos con mucha frecuencia.

Lenguaje funcional
Comparación y contraste

The following expressions are useful for comparing and contrasting.

al igual que	just like
a diferencia de	unlike
distinto/a de	different, distinct (from)

Also remember to use the other words you have learned so far for comparing and contrasting.

● 3.3 Regular **-er** and **-ir** Verbs

Regular verbs whose infinitives end in **-er** and **-ir** form their conjugations similar to regular **-ar** verbs: A set of regular endings is attached to the stem of the verb. Here are the present tense forms of the regular verbs **comer** (*to eat*) and **vivir** (*to live*).

comer			
(yo)	**com**o	(nosotros/as)	**com**emos
(tú)	**com**es	(vosotros/as)	**com**éis
(usted, él/ella)	**com**e	(ustedes, ellos/as)	**com**en

vivir			
(yo)	**viv**o	(nosotros/as)	**viv**imos
(tú)	**viv**es	(vosotros/as)	**viv**ís
(usted, él/ella)	**viv**e	(ustedes, ellos/as)	**viv**en

Other **-er** and **-ir** verbs that are regular in the present tense include: **beber, discutir, escribir,** and **leer.**

Siempre **discuto** la política con mi tío.

I always discuss politics with my uncle.

Mi abuelo **lee** el periódico todos los días.

My grandfather reads the newspaper every day.

● 3.4 Irregular Verbs: **dar,**[a] **hacer,**[b] **salir,**[c] **ver**[d]

These verbs have irregularities only in the **yo** form; otherwise, their forms follow the pattern for regular **-ar, -er,** and **-ir** verbs.

dar		hacer		salir		ver	
day	**da**mos	**ha**go	**hac**emos	**sal**go	**sal**imos	**ve**o	**ve**mos
das	**da**is*	**hac**es	**hac**éis	**sal**es	**sal**ís	**ve**s	**ve**is*
da	**da**n	**hac**e	**hac**en	**sal**e	**sal**en	**ve**	**ve**n

---

[a] *to give* [b] *to do; to make* [c] *to leave; to go out* [d] *to see*
* **Vosotros/as** forms that are only one syllable need no written accent mark.

Actividades

A. Con la familia. What activities do you do with different family members? Form complete sentences to describe with whom you do each of the following activities.

MODELO   Practico deportes con mi hermano.

- comer en restaurantes
- mirar la televisión
- escribir cartas a los parientes
- beber (una cerveza, un refresco, vino)
- ir al cine los sábados por la noche
- trabajar en el taller
- leer novelas (el periódico, revistas)
- discutir la política
- dar un paseo en el parque
- hacer crucigramas
- salir a bailar
- escuchar música
- hablar por teléfono

B. La vida en mi familia. Use the following cues to form complete sentences that describe family life. Which sentences are true for your family? Fix the other statements to make them true for you.

1. mis hermanos y yo / mirar la televisión / todos los días
2. yo siempre / hacer la cama (*bed*) / por la mañana
3. mi padre / hacer crucigramas / mientras desayuna
4. yo / ir al cine / los sábados / con mis amigos
5. mi abuela / vivir / con nosotros
6. mis padres / discutir la política durante la cena (*during supper*)
7. los hijos jóvenes / beber vino con la cena
8. nosotros / echar una siesta / a las 3:00 de la tarde
9. mi madre y yo / ver a mis abuelos (los padres de ella) / cada semana
10. mis abuelos / mimar / excesivamente a sus nietos

C. Un pariente parecido

Paso 1. Who in your family do you most/least resemble? First, jot down some relevant information, based on the following chart.

	Edad	Descripción física	Actividades favoritas
Yo			
Mi ____			

Paso 2. Now write three to five sentences comparing or contrasting yourself and the relative you chose, using the vocabulary you have learned. **¡OJO!** Be careful to distinguish the **yo, él/ella,** and **nosotros/as** verb forms.

MODELOS   Al igual que mi hermano, yo miro la televisión por la tarde.

Yo practico deportes, pero mi hermano lee novelas.

D. Entrevista: ¿Qué haces?

Paso 1. Using the list in **Actividad C** or other activities you have learned to say in Spanish, ask three different classmates what they do with their families and jot down their answers.

Paso 2. Now report your information to the class, summing up information when possible.

MODELOS   Jennifer mira la televisión con su abuelo, pero Raquel y Carlos miran la televisión con sus hermanos.

Jennifer y Carlos salen a comer con sus padres.

Señas culturales

El monumento a la mitad del mundo[a]

Ecuador means *equator* in English. The equator is the imaginary line that divides the northern and southern hemispheres of the Earth. European geographers visited the area in the 17th and 18th centuries to try to measure the exact circumference of the Earth, and today a monument in San Antonio de Pichincha (22 kilometers north of Quito), at latitude 0°0'0", commemorates their accomplishments.

The monument, which measures 30 meters tall and has a large metallic globe on top, is located in a replica of a colonial Spanish town called **Ciudad Mitad del Mundo.** The town also contains a church, a traditional plaza, a bull-fighting arena, parks, museums, restaurants, and shops, and on the solstices and equinoxes of every year, there are celebrations with music and dance performances.

The equator crosses many countries around the world, but Ecuadorians are particularly proud that their country bears the name of this geographical feature. What geographical features are important to your national and regional identity?

[a]Mitad... *Middle of the World*

Lectura

Sobre la lectura   The future of the family as an institution is a subject of concern in many modern societies. In this section, you will read about family trends in Ecuador today. As you read, consider whether or not trends in Ecuador are similar to those in this country.

Antes de leer

A. Generaciones diferentes.   Reflect on the family structures of modern-day families and those of earlier generations like those of your parents or grandparents. Then decide whether the following phrases generally describe modern families, families from past generations, or both.

	FAMILIAS MODERNAS	FAMILIAS DE GENERACIONES PASADAS	LAS DOS
1. Las familias son de seis hijos o más.	☐	☐	☐
2. Las familias son estables.	☐	☐	☐
3. Hay más divorcios y también uniones libres (uniones entre personas no casadas).	☐	☐	☐
4. Las mujeres participan en el mercado de trabajo (*job market*).	☐	☐	☐
5. Son comunes las familias nucleares pequeñas.	☐	☐	☐
6. Las familias extendidas son importantes.	☐	☐	☐

B. Consecuencias.   In this reading, you will learn about how changes in society affect the structure of the family. Choose the most likely characteristics of the future family from the following list of ideas.

☐ Hay fragmentación social.
☐ Hay más familias extendidas.
☐ Hay varios tipos de familia.
☐ Los divorcios bajan (*decrease*).
☐ Las familias son más inestables.
☐ Las mujeres entran al mercado de trabajo.

☐ Las mujeres tienen más acceso a la educación superior.
☐ Los papeles (*roles*) tradicionales dentro del hogar (*home*) cambian.

C. ¿Acertaste? (*Were you correct?*)   As you read the text, look for confirmation of the answers given in **Actividades A** and **B.**

Las familias en tiempos de crisis

En el Ecuador, la familia ha sufrido[a] rápidos e importantes cambios en años recientes. En un país marcado por las diferencias regionales y la fragmentación social, la noción de «la» familia —en singular— significa muchas cosas.

En los tiempos de nuestros padres y abuelos, las familias de seis o más hijos eran[b] las más típicas. En contraste, hoy en día,[c] es normal tener sólo dos o tres hijos. Las familias ahora son más pequeñas y menos estables. En los últimos[d] años en Quito —y en todo el país— cada día hay más divorcios y también más uniones libres. Las nuevas transformaciones afectan la vida de las parejas y también la relación entre padres e hijos y la conducta habitual de las familias.

La entrada de la mujer al mercado de trabajo y su mayor acceso a la educación superior modifican profundamente la estructura

▲ Estos padres ecuatorianos tienen sólo dos hijos. ¿Cuantos hijos tienen tus padres o tienes tú?

familiar. El trabajo de la mujer es necesario a causa de las nuevas realidades económicas y sociales. La participación de la mujer en el mundo laboral contribuye a la igualdad de la mujer y el hombre, y como consecuencia cambia el papel tradicional de los dos en la casa y con la familia. Esto no significa que la familia ecuatoriana está en peligro;[e] al contrario, la familia tiene mucha popularidad.

En una encuesta reciente, un 90,8% de los jóvenes ecuatorianos, incluyendo ambos sexos, reportaron[f] que piensa contraer matrimonio. Algunos[g] sociólogos confirman que la familia ecuatoriana no está en crisis. Dicen que la familia es un refugio en momentos de crisis generales. Es decir,[h] la familia moderna ecuatoriana mantiene su función histórica y al mismo tiempo revela su gran capacidad de regeneración. ■

[a]ha… *has suffered* [b]*were* [c]hoy… *nowadays* [d]*recent* [e]*danger* [f]*reported* [g]*Some* [h]Es… *That is to say*

Después de leer

A. La comparación

Paso 1. How do marriage and family trends in your country or region compare to those in Ecuador? Indicate if you agree (**Estoy de acuerdo.**) or disagree (**No estoy de acuerdo.**) with the statements on the following page.

En mi país o región…

	ESTOY DE ACUERDO.	NO ESTOY DE ACUERDO.
1. la noción de «la» familia puede ser ambigua.	☐	☐
2. la estructura familiar es inestable.	☐	☐
3. las uniones libres aumentan (*increase*).	☐	☐
4. las nuevas realidades económicas y sociales exigen (*demand*) el trabajo de la mujer.	☐	☐
5. los papeles tradicionales dentro del hogar se cambian.	☐	☐
6. muchos jóvenes piensan contraer matrimonio.	☐	☐

Paso 2. Now work with a partner and explain why you agree or disagree with the statements in **Paso 1,** adding your own observations to expand on each topic.

B. Mis opiniones

Paso 1. Choose the option that best reflects your opinion.

1. El matrimonio (es / no es) una institución en peligro de extinción.
2. Las familias (deben [*should*] / no deben) tener muchos hijos.
3. Una familia con un padre soltero o una madre soltera (es / no es) una opción aceptable.
4. La mujer (debe / no debe) trabajar.

Paso 2. Now work with a partner to explain your choices in **Paso 1,** adding your own observations to expand on each topic.

C. Encuesta y debate. Share your ideas from **Actividad A** and **Actividad B** with the rest of the class to see what the general consensus is on the family related topics presented in this **Lectura** section. Then answer the following questions.

1. ¿Están todos de acuerdo con tus opiniones, o hay una variedad de opiniones?
2. ¿Son las opiniones de la clase diferentes de o similares a lo que ya sabes de las familias en el mundo hispano?
3. ¿Qué piensa tu profesor(a) de la importancia de la familia en el mundo hispano, según sus propias experiencias con las culturas hispanas?
4. ¿Piensan otros hispanohablantes nativos igual que tu profesor(a)? Entrevista a un(a) hispanohablante en tu región para saber.

PORTAFOLIO CULTURAL

Redacción

Una carta a Ecuador. You are going to be an exchange student in Ecuador. Write a letter to your host family describing yourself, your family, and your leisure activities. Ask questions about the members of your host family and what they do in their leisure time. Follow the guided steps in the *Manual de práctica* to complete your letter.

Exploración

Investigación cultural. Find more information about Ecuador in your library, on the *Entrevistas* Online Learning Center **(www.mhhe.com/entrevistas2)**, or elsewhere on the Internet and present it to the class. Consult the *Manual de práctica* for ideas for your presentation.

Léxico activo

LOS MIEMBROS DE LA FAMILIA

el/la **abuelo/a** (los **abuelos**)	grandfather/grandmother (grandparents)
el/la **cuñado/a** (los **cuñados**)	brother-in-law/sister-in-law (siblings-in-law)
el/la **esposo/a** (los **esposos**)	husband/wife (spouses)
el **gato**	cat
el/la **gemelo/a** (los **gemelos**)	twin (twins)
el/la **hermanastro/a** (los **hermanastros**)	stepbrother/stepsister (stepsiblings)
el/la **hermano/a** (los **hermanos**)	brother/sister (siblings)
el/la **hijo/a** (los **hijos**)	son/daughter (children)
el/la **hijo/a único/a**	only child
el/la **nieto/a** (los **nietos**)	grandson/granddaughter (grandchildren)
el/la **niño/a** (los **niños**)	child (children)
el **padrastro** / la **madrastra**	stepfather/stepmother
el **padre** / la **madre** (los **padres**)	father/mother (parents)
el **padrino** / la **madrina**	godfather/godmother
el/la **pariente**	relative
el **perro**	dog
el/la **primo/a** (los **primos**)	cousin (cousins)
el/la **sobrino/a**	nephew/niece
el/la **tío/a**	uncle/aunt

LOS ADJETIVOS

cariñoso/a	affectionate
(estar) casado/a	(to be) married
(estar) divorciado/a	(to be) divorced
(estar) jubilado/a	to be retired
estrecho/a	close
gregario/a	gregarious
junto/a	together
materno/a	maternal
paterno/a	paternal
poco/a	little; few (*pl.*)
solo/a	alone
soltero/a	single, unmarried
unido/a	close-knit

LA EDAD

¿Cuántos años (tiene)? ¿Qué edad (tiene)?	How old (are you [*form.*] / is he/she)?
mayor (que)	older (than)
menor (que)	younger (than)
tener _____ años (y medio)	to be _____ (and a half) years old

LOS NÚMEROS

treinta, treinta y uno, treinta y dos, treinta y tres, treinta y cuatro, treinta y cinco, treinta y seis, treinta y siete, treinta y ocho, treinta y nueve, cuarenta, cuarenta y uno,… , cincuenta, sesenta, setenta, ochenta, noventa, cien, ciento cinco

¿De quién es (son) ____**?**	Whose is (are) ____?
mi(s)	my
tu(s)	your (*fam. s.*)
su(s)	his, her, its, their, your (*form. s., pl.*)
nuestro/a/os/as	our
vuestro/a/os/as	your (*fam. pl.*)

LOS VERBOS

beber (un refresco, una cerveza, vino)	to drink (a soft drink, a beer, wine)
comer	to eat
conversar	to chat
dar (*irreg.*) **un paseo**	to take a walk
descansar	to rest
discutir	to discuss; to argue
echar una siesta	to take a siesta (nap)
escribir (cartas)	to write (letters)
hacer (*irreg.*)	to do; to make
hacer crucigramas	to do crossword puzzles

ir de compras	to go shopping
leer (novelas, el periódico, revistas)	to read (novels, the newspaper, magazines)
mirar	to look (at)
mirar la televisión	to watch TV
pasar (el tiempo libre / tiempo con los hijos)	to spend (free time / time with the [one's] children)
pasear	to take a walk
salir (*irreg.*) **(a bailar)**	to go out (dancing)
tener (*irreg.*)	to have
ver (*irreg.*)	to see
ver la televisión	to watch TV
visitar	to visit
vivir	to live

LENGUAJE FUNCIONAL

a diferencia de	unlike
al igual que	just like
distinto/a (de)	different, distinct (from)

La casa

España

Cultura

◆ What Does Your House Reveal About Your Personality?

◆ Connection Between Housing and Where People Live

◆ **Señas culturales:** Nations Within a Nation

◆ Classified Ads for Housing

Lengua

◆ Parts of the House; Household Items

◆ Demonstrative Adjectives (4.1)

◆ Stem-Changing Verbs (**e → ie, o → ue**) (4.2)

◆ The Present Progressive (4.3)

◆ Affirmative Commands (4.4)

	España							
	Inhabited by Celts, Iberians, and Basques	Conquered by Romans; becomes part of Roman Empire	Moors enter Spain, subjugate country within a few years	Consolidation of Aragon and Castile through marriage of Ferdinand II and Isabella I	Moors defeated; Columbus makes his first voyage to America	Era of exploration and colonization		
	until 206 B.C.	206 B.C.	711	1469	1492	until 16th c.	16th c.	1500–1600	1534
Los Estados Unidos y el Canadá						Various indigenous tribes inhabit North America	Spanish exploration of North America	Jacques Cartier claims Canada for France

Instantánea

ORIGEN DEL NOMBRE

España: uncertain; probably from the ancient Carthaginian *Ispania*, "land of the rabbits" (The Carthaginians colonized what is now Spain before the Roman occupation.)

POBLACIÓN

41.547.400

LENGUAS

Spanish (official), co-official languages include Catalan in Catalonia, Basque in the Basque Country, Galician in Galicia and others.

◄ La Casa Milà (*1910*) *es un bloque de pisos* (apartment building) *en Barcelona, diseñado por el arquitecto catalán Antoni Gaudí (*1852–1926*).*

For additional practice, check out the *Manual de práctica,* the Interactive CD-ROM, and the Online Learning Center (**www.mhhe.com/entrevistas2**)!

1600–1750	1776–1783	1808–1814	1846–1848	1898	1936–1939	1952	1975	1982	1986	1994	1999
	War of Independence against Napoleon's troops			Spanish-American War	Civil War; Francisco Franco establishes dictatorship		Franco dies; Juan Carlos I de Borbón proclaimed king		Spain enters European Union		Spain adopts euro as new currency
British colonies founded in North America	American War of Independence		Mexican-American War	Spanish-American War		Puerto Rico becomes U.S. commonwealth		Canada cuts legal ties with Britain		U.S., Canada, Mexico sign NAFTA	

🌑 ¿Dónde vives?

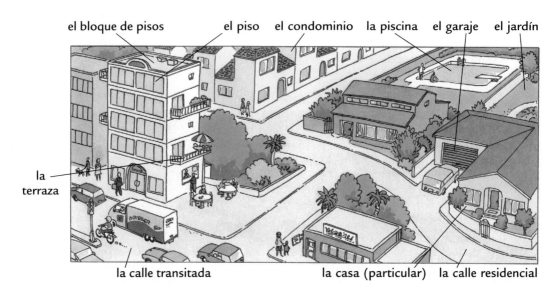

el bloque de pisos · el piso · el condominio · la piscina · el garaje · el jardín

la terraza

la calle transitada · la casa (particular) · la calle residencial

Este (*This*) bloque de pisos está en una calle transitada **del barrio** (*neighborhood*).

Esas (*Those*) casas están en **la ciudad.**

Aquel condominio (*That condominium over there*) está en **las afueras** (*outskirts, suburbs*).

el comedor	dining room
el dormitorio	bedroom
el pasillo	hallway
el pueblo	town
el/la vecino/a	neighbor
la zona residencial	residential zone/area

la habitación · la ventana · la habitación

el cuarto de baño

la cocina · el salón · el patio

la puerta

Si te interesa

Habitación and **cuarto** can refer specifically to a bedroom or to any room in general. **Dormitorio** always means *bedroom*.

Actividades

A. ¿Dónde están? Read the following quotes and tell in which room of a house each statement was probably made.

1. «Papá, ¿hay más patatas (*potatoes*)?»
2. «¡Estas flores (*flowers*) son muy bonitas!»
3. «Este coche no funciona.»
4. «¡Mira, éste es mi programa favorito!»
5. «Voy a leer una novela.»
6. «¡Buenos días, señor Atxaga! Pase. (*Come in.*)»

Si te interesa

You probably call the ground floor of a building the *first floor* and the floors above the *second floor, third floor,* and so on. In Spanish, however, the ground floor is called **la planta baja,** and the floor above it is called **la primera planta** or **el primer piso.** Above these are **la segunda planta / el segundo piso, la tercera (*third*) planta / el tercer piso,** and so on.

B. ¿Qué tipo(s) de persona(s) vive(n) aquí (*here*)? What kind of person(s) would probably live in each of the following places? Match the persons on the right with the dwellings on the left.

1. _____ un bloque de pisos en la calle principal de la ciudad
2. _____ una casa en el campo (*country*)
3. _____ un piso cerca de un parque
4. _____ un piso pequeño en el centro (*downtown*) de la ciudad
5. _____ un condominio en la playa (*beach*)

a. una pareja (*couple*) con hijos
b. un estudiante universitario soltero
c. una pareja sin hijos y con mucho dinero
d. una madre soltera con una hija
e. un granjero (*farmer*) y su familia

C. Entrevista: ¿Cómo es tu casa?

Paso 1. Write down questions you want to ask your partner about his/her house, apartment, or dorm room. Include questions about the number of rooms, kinds of rooms, location, garden, amenities, and so on.

VOCABULARIO ÚTIL

el desván	attic
la flor	flower
la planta	plant; floor of a building
el sótano	basement, cellar
estar a _____ manzanas de	to be _____ blocks from
estar pegado/a a (otros edificios / otras casas)	to be attached to (other buildings / other houses)
estar rodeado/a de	to be surrounded by

Paso 2. Interview your partner and take notes on his/her answers so that you can report back to the entire class.

D. La casa ideal. What is your dream house like? Where would it be? What amenities would it have? Describe the details to a partner, who will try to draw a floor plan as you speak.

MODELO   Mi casa ideal está en _____. Es _____, y tiene _____.
La cocina está al lado de _____. También hay _____.

E. La casa, la cultura

Paso 1. What does a living space say about the culture and lifestyle of its inhabitants? The following photographs represent typical houses in a suburb of a North American city, a traditional Mediterranean house in southern Spain, and a **piso** in a Spanish city. Study these images and make a list of the basic features of each construction. Also keep in mind the space surrounding the houses and what may or may not be present: parks, sidewalks, stores, streets and alleys, and so on.

MODELOS   La casa norteamericana es _____. Tiene _____.
La casa mediterránea es _____. Tiene _____.
El piso español es _____. Tiene _____.

▲ *Una casa norteamericana típica, Salinas Valley, California*

▲ *El interior de una casa en Córdoba, España*

▲ *Bloques de pisos en Elgoibar, Guipuzcoa, País Vasco, España*

Paso 2. What are the cultural implications of the housing features you mentioned in **Paso 1?** Decide which option on each of the following scales is more accurate for each type of house.

La casa es grande. ⟵⟶ El espacio es mínimo.
El coche es necesario. ⟵⟶ No es práctico tener coche.
La casa es un espacio íntimo ⟵⟶ Los amigos visitan mucho la para la familia. casa.
El diseño es moderno. ⟵⟶ El diseño es tradicional.
La construcción es económica. ⟵⟶ La construcción no es económica.
El clima determina el diseño ⟵⟶ El diseño no depende del clima. de la casa.
Hay más espacio común. ⟵⟶ Hay más espacio privado.
Hay mucho contacto con los ⟵⟶ Hay poco contacto con los vecinos. vecinos.

● ¿Qué haces en tu casa?

almorzar (ue)	to eat lunch	**preparar la comida**	to prepare the meal/food
cerrar (ie)	to close	**querer (ie)**	to want
charlar	to chat	**soler (ue)** + *inf.*	to be in the habit of / be accustomed to (*doing something*)
compartir	to share		
dormir (ue)	to sleep		
jugar (ue) a	to play (*a game*)	**soñar (ue) (con)**	to dream (*about*)
pensar (ie) (de/en)*	to think (of, about)	**volver (ue)**	to return (*to a place*), come back
poder (ue)	to be able to, can		
preferir (ie)	to prefer		

Actividades

A. Asociaciones.   What actions do you associate with each of these words and expressions? Use the verbs from the list or any others you know.

1. la cama
2. el fútbol
3. la cafetería universitaria
4. la habilidad
5. tres hermanos en una habitación
6. «(no) me gusta»

B. Tus actividades.   What activities do you usually do in each part of your house? Form complete sentences by linking the activities on the left with the parts of the house on the right. Also add some other activities and places. Then ask your partner questions about his/her activities at home.

MODELO   Me gusta dormir en mi dormitorio.
E1: ¿Sueles escuchar música en el salón?
E2: No. Suelo escuchar música en mi dormitorio.

ACTIVIDAD		PARTE DE LA CASA
almorzar		la cocina
dormir		el comedor
escuchar música		el dormitorio
estudiar		el garaje
jugar al béisbol	**+**	el jardín
leer		el patio
mirar la televisión		el salón
preparar la comida		la terraza
soñar con el futuro		¿ ?
tomar el sol (*to sunbathe*)		
¿ ?		

---

* To communicate the idea of *to think about* in Spanish, for example, if you want to ask someone's *opinion* about something, use the preposition **de** with a form of the verb **pensar.**
—¿Qué piensas **de** eso? (*What do you think about that?*)
—Pienso que es una buena idea. (*I think [that] it's a good idea.*)
In all other cases, use the preposition **en.**
—¿**En** qué estás pensando? (*What are you thinking about?*)
—Estoy pensando **en** mi novio. (*I'm thinking about my boyfriend.*)

You can watch this interview on the *Entrevistas* Video or Interactive CD-ROM or listen to the audio on the Online Learning Center (**www.mhhe.com/entrevistas2**).

María Benjumeda León

«Vivo en... un pueblo precioso.»

Nombre: María

Apellidos: (1) Benjumeda (2) León

Edad: 27 años

Nació en: Cádiz, España

Vocabulario útil

precioso	gorgeous	**andaluzas**	Andalusian
encima de una colina	on top of a hill	**la cómoda**	chest of drawers
viñas y olivos	vineyards and olive trees	**da a**	faces
macetas	flowerpots	**viuda**	widow
entrada	entrance, foyer	**de toda la vida**	lifelong
un espejo	a mirror	**la amistad**	friendship

Antes de ver

A. ¿Cómo es María?

Paso 1. Read the following sentences and make sure you understand what they mean.

1. «Vivo en Arcos de la Frontera... es un pueblo precioso... está encima de una colina y rodeado de viñas y de olivos.»
2. «Vivimos en una casa de vecinos... compartimos un patio muy bonito... hay muchas macetas y muchas plantas.»
3. «Hay un salón que da a la calle, cuatro dormitorios, una cocina pequeña y un comedor... »
4. «Los vecinos son vecinos de toda la vida, es como una familia,... »

Paso 2. Based on the quotes in **Paso 1,** choose the phrases that best complete a description of María's house.

1. María vive en _____.
   □ un pueblo
   □ el campo
2. Arcos de la Frontera es un lugar _____.
   □ bonito
   □ desagradable
3. María vive en _____.
   □ una casa particular
   □ un piso
4. La casa de María es _____.
   □ grande
   □ pequeña
5. Los vecinos de María _____.
   □ son simpáticos
   □ no hablan con ella

B. Las familias españolas. Based on what you already know about Spanish families, indicate whether you think the following statements are true **(cierto)** or false **(falso).**

	CIERTO	FALSO
1. La abuela típicamente vive con la familia.	□	□
2. Los hijos solteros viven con los padres.	□	□
3. Los parientes (primos, tíos, etcétera) no son muy unidos.	□	□
4. No hay mucho contacto con los vecinos.	□	□
5. Muchas familias tienen una casa particular.	□	□

¡Veamos!

A. Los cuartos. As you watch, indicate which household and city features María mentions in her interview.

□ la calle
□ la casa
□ la cocina
□ la colina
□ el comedor
□ la cómoda
□ el condominio
□ el cuarto de baño
□ el dormitorio
□ la entrada
□ el espejo
□ el garaje
□ el jardín
□ el pasillo
□ el patio
□ la piscina
□ el piso
□ la pueblo
□ el puerta
□ el salón
□ la terraza
□ los vecinos
□ la ventana

B. Dictado (*Dictation*). Watch María's interview again and fill in the blanks with her exact words, based on her responses to the first three questions.

Pregunta 1: ¿Dónde vives?

«Vivo en Arcos de la Frontera, que es un _____[1] _____[2] y que está encima de una _____[3] y _____[4] de viñas y de olivos.»

Pregunta 2: ¿Cómo es tu casa?

«Mi casa es _____[5] _____.[6] _____[7] en una casa de _____[8]... y compartimos un _____[9] muy _____[10] y también muy _____.[11] Y hay muchas _____[12] y muchas plantas.»

Pregunta 3: ¿Y el interior?

«¿El interior? Pues, tenemos una _____[13] muy grande, con un _____,[14] muy típico de las _____[15] andaluzas. Y la _____,[16]... Hay un _____[17] que da a la _____,[18] cuatro _____,[19] una cocina pequeña y un _____[20] pegado a la cocina, y todo eso da al patio.»

Después de ver

¿Una familia típica?   In which of the following ways does María think her family is a typical Spanish family? Indicate the ones you think apply, then cite details from the interview to support your selections. Use a separate sheet of paper.

1. el número de personas en la familia
2. la composición de la familia
3. la casa
4. el contenido (*contents*) de la casa
5. las relaciones con los vecinos

Algatocin (Provincia de Málaga), uno de los pueblos blancos de Andalucía, España ▶

CAPÍTULO 4 • La casa

● 4.1 Demonstrative Adjectives

A. Here are some additional descriptions of Arcos de la Frontera. Notice that the demonstrative adjectives precede the nouns they modify.

Esta casa está pegada a **ese** edificio.	*This house is attached to that building.*
Ese tipo de casa es muy típico en Andalucía.	*That type of house is very common in Andalusia.*
Aquellas tierras, en las afueras del pueblo, son de nuestros vecinos.	*Those lands, on the outskirts of the town, belong to our neighbors.*

Like all adjectives, demonstrative adjectives change form to agree in gender and number with the noun they modify. Here are all the forms.

Singular			Plural		
MASCULINE	FEMININE		MASCULINE	FEMININE	
este	**esta**	this	**estos**	**estas**	these
ese	**esa**	that	**esos**	**esas**	those
aquel	**aquella**	that (over there)	**aquellos**	**aquellas**	those (over there)

Notice that, unlike the two-way distinction made in English (*this/these, that/those*), Spanish has a third distinction: *that over there / those over there.* The following adverbs correspond to these distinctions and will help you figure out what person, place, or thing the speaker is indicating.

aquí (acá)	here
ahí	there
allí (allá)	(way) over there

The following illustration will help you visualize these positions, which are always relative to the position of the speaker and the listener.

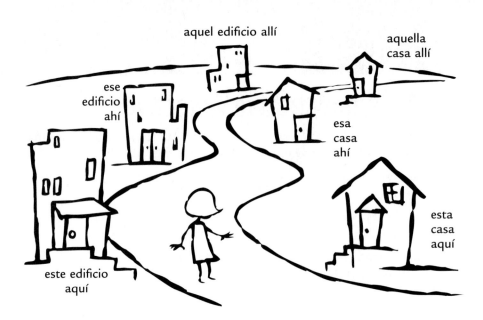

aquel edificio allí

aquella casa allí

ese edificio ahí

esa casa ahí

esta casa aquí

este edificio aquí

B. When it is clear what person or object the demonstrative adjective refers to, you can use it without the noun. In that case, it becomes a demonstrative pronoun and carries a written accent mark to distinguish it from the adjective used with a noun.* English often uses the word *one(s)* when no noun is present.

De todas las casas, me gusta **ésta,** pero no **aquéllas.**

Of all the houses, I like this one, but not those ones (over there).

C. To refer to a general idea or a group of things without a specific gender or number, use the forms of the demonstrative pronouns that end in **-o** (called neuter forms): **esto, eso, aquello.** These pronouns never carry a written accent mark.

Compartimos la luz, el agua y los sótanos. **Eso** es lo único que compartimos.

We share electricity, water, and the cellars. That (stuff) is the only thing that we share.

Todo **esto** es muy típico en las casas andaluzas.

All of this is common in Andalusian houses.

Análisis estructural

Compare the singular and plural endings of the masculine demonstrative adjectives **(este, ese, aquel)** with other adjectives you have studied (e.g., **grande, general**). What is unusual about the singular and plural masculine forms?

---

* You may see demonstrative pronouns without accents in some sources. However, throughout *Entrevistas,* we have retained this distinction as a matter of style.

Actividades

A. ¿Cuál es?   Change the definite articles (**el/la/los/las**) in the following phrases to the corresponding demonstrative adjectives. (Hint: The adverb will tell you which demonstrative to use.)

MODELO   el edificio (allí) → aquel edificio

1. las casas (ahí)
2. los jardines (aquí)
3. las plantas (allá)
4. los cuartos (allí)
5. la habitación (aquí)
6. el barrio (allá)
7. el piso (ahí)
8. la ventana (allí)

B. ¿Cuál es mejor?   Complete the following sentences with the appropriate demonstrative endings. Then say which place you would prefer to live in—1, 2, or 3—and why.

1. **a.** Est_____ casa tiene mucha luz ([*overhead*] *light*[*ing*]).
   b. Est_____ edificio de ocho plantas es muy moderno.
   c. Est_____ pisos son baratos (*inexpensive*).
   d. Est_____ barrio es fantástico para las familias con niños.
2. **a.** Es_____ habitaciones no tienen mucha luz.
   b. Es_____ bloque de pisos es muy antiguo (*old*).
   c. Es_____ cuartos son pequeños.
   d. Es_____ barrio tiene problemas económicos.
3. **a.** Aquel_____ casas tienen salones grandes.
   b. Aquel_____ edificios son muy elegantes.
   c. Aquel_____ piso no es muy barato.
   d. Aquel_____ zona es histórica.

C. Tus gustos.   Bring in a photograph of your house, your parent's house, or a house from a magazine. Working with three or four classmates, take turns telling which house each person prefers and why. When pointing out a specific house or feature, be sure to use the appropriate demonstrative.

MODELOS   Este piso me gusta porque _____. Ése no me gusta porque _____.

Esta terraza me gusta porque _____. Aquélla no me gusta porque _____.

● 4.2 Stem-Changing Verbs (e → ie, o → ue)

In **Capítulo 3** you saw that a small number of verbs have a slight irregularity in the **yo** form **(hago, salgo),** but otherwise follow the regular pattern of personal endings **(haces, hace,… ; sales, sale,…).** Several of the new verbs in this chapter have changes in their stems while the endings are perfectly regular. For these verbs, the stem vowels **-e-** and **-o-** in the infinitive change to **-ie-** and **-ue-**, respectively, in the forms in which the stress falls on the stem.

Prefiero esta casa.	*I prefer this house.*
¿**Duermes** bien la noche antes de un examen?	*Do you sleep well the night before an exam?*

Since the stress in the **nosotros/as** and **vosotros/as** forms does not fall on the stem vowel, these two forms do not undergo any stem change.

preferir (ie)			
(yo)	**prefiero**	(nosotros/as)	**preferimos**
(tú)	**prefieres**	(vosotros/as)	**preferís**
(usted, él/ella)	**prefiere**	(ustedes, ellos/as)	**prefieren**

dormir (ue)			
(yo)	**duermo**	(nosotros/as)	**dormimos**
(tú)	**duermes**	(vosotros/as)	**dormís**
(usted, él/ella)	**duerme**	(ustedes, ellos/as)	**duermen**

In *Entrevistas,* the verbs that have this type of stem change will be indicated by the symbols **(ie)** and **(ue)** after the infinitive. For example, **soñar (ue)** means that this verb is conjugated in the present tense as **sueño, sueñas, sueña, soñamos, soñáis, sueñan.**

Here are some other common verbs that have these stem changes. You should add these useful verbs and expressions to your active vocabulary.

almorzar (ue)	to eat lunch	**pensar (ie) (de/en)**	to think (of, about)
cerrar (ie)	to close	**poder (ue)**	to be able to, can
dormir (ue) la siesta	to take a siesta (nap)	**querer (ie)**	to want
entender (ie)	to understand	**soler (ue)** + *inf.*	to be in the habit of / be accustomed to (*doing something*)
jugar* (ue) (al béisbol, al baloncesto, al fútbol)	to play (baseball, basketball, soccer)		
		volver (ue)	to return (*to a place*), come back
merendar (ie)	to snack		

You may have noticed that, except for the irregular **yo** form, the verb **tener** is also a stem-changing verb: **tengo, tienes, tiene, tenemos, tenéis, tienen.**

Análisis estructural

Sometimes an **-ie-** stem-changing verb has more than one **-e-.** How do you know which **-e-** changes to **-ie-?** Tell which vowel is the stem-changing vowel in the preceding list of verbs. Then practice saying the **yo** and **nosotros/as** forms to hear the contrast in stress and stem vowels.

---

* **Jugar** is the only verb that has a **u → ue** stem change.

Actividades

A. Actividades domésticas. Combine the phrases to form complete sentences.

1. yo / cerrar las ventanas / cuando hace frío (*it's cold*)
2. los arquitectos / entender / el diseño de la casa
3. ustedes / dormir / la siesta en la terraza
4. Rafael y yo / jugar al fútbol en el jardín
5. tú / soler / estudiar en tu dormitorio, ¿no?
6. mi mamá / querer / decorar la casa para la fiesta
7. yo / no poder / comprar la casa ideal
8. mis hermanos y hermanas / almorzar en la cocina

B. Nosotros somos diferentes. A student made the following statements about his activities around the house. Respond to each one for yourself and a roommate (use the **nosotros/as** form) to state your preference for the actions mentioned.

MODELOS   Yo duermo en la terraza en el verano. →
Nosotros también dormimos en la terraza.

Pero nosotros dormimos en nuestras habitaciones.

1. Yo prefiero almorzar en la cocina.
2. Yo quiero mirar la televisión en el salón.
3. Yo puedo tomar el sol en la terraza por la tarde.
4. Yo vuelvo a casa para cenar.
5. Yo almuerzo a las 2:00 de la tarde.
6. Yo suelo dormir en el sofá.

C. Encuesta: ¿Qué sueles hacer?

Paso 1. Where do your classmates do the following activities? First, use the phrases below as cues to prepare interview questions. Then interview three different classmates and jot down their responses.

MODELO   ¿Dónde almuerzas en tu casa?

1. dormir
2. mirar la televisión
3. estudiar
4. jugar (al béisbol, al fútbol,...)
5. merendar
6. pensar en los problemas
7. hablar por teléfono
8. ¿ ?

Paso 2. Report your findings to the class, summarizing information when possible.

VOCABULARIO ÚTIL

los/las dos, tres,...	the two, three, . . . of them/us
tanto _____ como _____	both _____ and _____

Señas culturales

Catalunya

Galicia

Euskadi

Andalucía

Spain is divided into seventeen autonomous regions, similar to states or provinces in terms of their government and functioning. Here are the flags of four of these regions. Do you know what languages or dialects are spoken in each? Are there any areas in your country that have distinctive cultures (regional languages, food, music, dance, and so on)?

Análisis cultural

The following quote from an English-language source will add to your knowledge of cultural phenomena in Spain. Is this information consistent with the native speaker's perspective in **Entrevista 1?** Use what you have learned in this chapter about Spain, as well as your own experience, to answer the questions that follow the quote.

❝If you live in an apartment block in one of the larger cities and have Spanish neighbours, you will probably become close friends in due course. But, if you live in an urbanization,* it may be more difficult to make friends with the people occupying the other houses. However, in most instances, should there be any form of 'emergency,' no matter how minor, your Spanish neighbour will leap at the opportunity to help in any way possible.❞

Source: *Culture Shock! Spain*

1. Are any of these observations reflected in María's interview?
2. Do city dwellers in your country typically become well acquainted with their neighbors? Why or why not?
3. Do suburbanites in this country usually make friends with their neighbors?
4. Is the situation described similar to, or different from, your own experiences?
5. Why might it be more difficult to become acquainted with your neighbor if you live in an urbanization as opposed to an apartment building?

---

* In Spain, **una urbanización** is a modern housing development.

CAPÍTULO 4 • La casa

Pronunciación y ortografía

As you may have noticed in the interview with María, there are some pronunciation features that distinguish the Spanish spoken in Spain from other dialects of Spanish around the world. Here are two of these features.

ll and y

As you have heard in previous interviews, the letters **ll** and **y** are pronounced the same in most dialects. In parts of northern Spain and in some of the Andean regions of South America, however, the **ll** is pronounced more like the combination *-lli-* in the English word *million*. Since Mariá is from *southern* Spain, her **ll** resembles the South American pronunciation [y].

In all countries, the Spanish **y** (or **ll** pronounced like **y**) is generally stronger than the English *y*. Compare the pronunciation of English *yes* with a native speaker's pronunciation of **yeso** (*plaster*); the first sound of **yeso** may be so strong that it sounds like an English *j* or *zh*. A common mistake made by English speakers is to use a weak **y** in Spanish, failing to distinguish between words like **ahí** [aí] and **allí** [ayí]. You should be able to distinguish the [y] sound in the second word.

Note also that **ll** can never be written or pronounced at the end of a word in Spanish. That's why we say **aquel edificio,** but **aquella casa.** When you see a word-final **-ll,** it is probably a Catalonian name: **el Parque Güell, Sabadell, Carbonell.**

z

In most of the Spanish-speaking world, the letter **z** and the letter **c** in the combinations **ce** and **ci** are all pronounced just like the English *s*. (The Spanish letter **z** is *never* pronounced like the English *z* in *zip!*) One of the most recognizable features of standard Spanish from Spain, however, is the pronunciation of these letters like the English *th* in *think*. Not all Spaniards use this pronunciation, but even in regions where it is not common, as in Andalusia, it is completely recognized and understood. It is not used in Spanish America, however.

You may have noticed that the Spanish spelling system uses **z** before the hard vowels **a, e,** and **o,** and **c** before the soft vowels **i** and **e.** This gives rise to some tricky spelling changes when different endings are added to the same stem. Study the four forms of the adjective **andaluz:**

andaluz	andaluza
andaluces	andaluzas

In future chapters, you will see that some verb forms also alternate between **z** and **c,** depending on the vowel that follows.

The *Manual de práctica* contains activities to practice the material explained here.

● ¿Qué hay en tu casa?

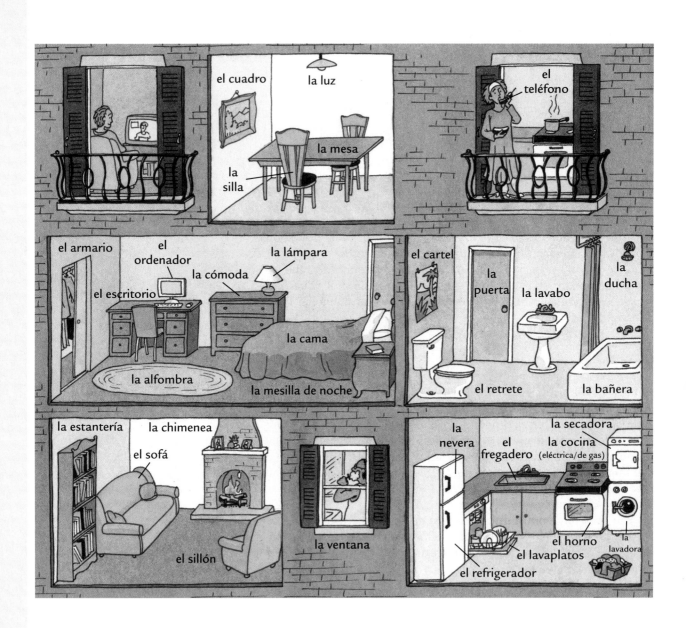

el cuadro la luz
la mesa
la silla
el teléfono

el armario
el ordenador la lámpara
el escritorio la cómoda
la cama
la alfombra la mesilla de noche

el cartel
la puerta la lavabo la ducha
el retrete la bañera

la estantería la chimenea
el sofá
la ventana
el sillón

la nevera la secadora
el fregadero la cocina (eléctrica/de gas)
el horno la lavadora
el lavaplatos
el refrigerador

¿Cómo es tu casa?

el ambiente		**feo/a**	ugly
el diseño		**humilde**	humble
el exterior		**(in)formal**	
el interior		**lujoso/a**	
el lujo	luxury	**moderno/a**	
la necesidad		**sencillo/a**	simple
		tradicional	
acogedor(a)	welcoming		
elegante		**por dentro**	on the inside
encantador(a)	delightful, charming	**por fuera**	on the outside

Actividades

A. Clasificaciones

Paso 1. Classify the household objects shown in the drawing on p. 108 into the following categories: **muebles** (*furniture*), **electrodomésticos** (*appliances*), **decoración**.

Paso 2. Now classify them as a luxury (**un lujo**) or a necessity (**una necesidad**).

B. Asociaciones.   What room do you associate with the following items?

1. la alfombra
2. el armario
3. la cama
4. la chimenea
5. la ducha
6. el refrigerador
7. la secadora
8. el sillón

C. La casa ideal.   What qualities do you consider positive in a house? Classify the following words and phrases as having positive or negative associations for you personally.

1. acogedor(a)
2. agradable
3. cómodo/a
4. elegante
5. encantador(a)
6. enorme
7. humilde
8. lujoso/a
9. sencillo/a

Compare your lists with those of your classmates. Are there any items common to all lists?

D. ¡Tu casa revela tu personalidad!   What does a house say about its owner? Work with a partner to say what these people might have in their houses.

MODELO   un profesor →
   Un profesor probablemente prefiere una casa con un estudio. Prefiere tener estanterías para sus libros y un ordenador en el escritorio.

1. una estudiante universitaria
2. un artista
3. un actor famoso
4. una presidenta de una empresa
5. un cocinero (*cook*)
6. una madre soltera con tres hijos

You can watch this interview on the *Entrevistas* Video or Interactive CD-ROM or listen to the audio on the Online Learning Center (**www.mhhe.com/entrevistas2**).

Elena de la Cruz Niggeman

«Paso la mayor parte del tiempo en mi cuarto.»

Nombre: Elena

Apellidos: (1) de la Cruz (2) Niggeman

Edad: 34 años

Nació en: Madrid, España

Vocabulario útil

al contrario de	in contrast to	**cuarto de servicio**	utility room
el parque	park	**la mayor parte del**	most of the time
octavo piso	eighth floor	**tiempo**	
una sala / el cuarto	family room, den	**me encanta**	I love it
de estar		**no te dice nada**	it's nothing to brag about (Lit.: it doesn't say anything to you)

Antes de ver

De costumbre.   Tell what room you normally do the following activities in.

1. Suelo mirar la televisión en…
2. Suelo desayunar en…
3. Suelo comer en…
4. Suelo estudiar en…
5. Durante el día, suelo echar una siesta en…
6. De noche, suelo dormir en…

¡Veamos!

¿Es normal o es un lujo?   First, indicate which of the following household features you consider to be *normal* in this country (**Yo: normal**). Then, as you watch Elena's interview, indicate which items seem to be a *luxury* for her (**Elena: un lujo**).

	YO: NORMAL	ELENA: UN LUJO

1. tener una casa particular ☐ ☐
2. tener tres dormitorios ☐ ☐
3. tener tres baños ☐ ☐
4. tener un salón para recibir visitas ☐ ☐
5. tener un cuarto de servicio ☐ ☐
6. ver la televisión en el salón ☐ ☐

Después de ver

Las preferencias de Elena.   Jot down where Elena does the following activities. If she did not mention an activity, write, "**Elena no dijo.**" (*Elena didn't say.*)

1. Duerme en…
2. Estudia en…
3. Ve la televisión en…
4. Charla con la familia en…

5. Desayuna en…
6. Cocina en…
7. Habla por teléfono en…

Piénsalo bien

Paso 1. Use each of the following words and phrases in sentences that refer either to María's house or to Elena's house. Your partner will add a sentence to compare or contrast an aspect of the other person's house.

MODELOS   E1: La casa de María está en un pueblo pequeño.
           E2: Pero la casa de Elena está en una ciudad grande.

           E1: La casa de María es grande.
           E2: La casa de Elena es grande también.

la abuela	compartir cosas	acogedor(a)
el bloque de pisos	tener muchas personas	grande
el campo	en casa	moderno/a
la ciudad	tener plantas	pequeño/a
el comedor	tener varios baños	típico/a
el lujo		tradicional
Madrid		
el patio		
el pueblo		
la sala de estar		
los vecinos		

Paso 2. Now try to answer the following questions, based on what you have learned in this chapter and on your own experiences.

1. ¿Qué elementos de la casa son comunes a todas las culturas? ¿Por qué?
2. ¿Qué elementos son exclusivos de una cultura en particular? ¿de tu propia (*own*) cultura?

🌑 4.3 The Present Progressive

Thus far in *Entrevistas*, you have seen and have been using only one simple present tense, the present indicative. It can be used to express the following types of actions.

HABITUAL	(Siempre) **Comemos** en la cocina.	*We (always) eat in the kitchen.*
ONGOING	**Comemos** en la cocina.	*We are eating in the kitchen.*
FUTURE	Mañana **comemos** con nuestra abuela.	*Tomorrow we (will) eat with our grandmother.*

To avoid ambiguity, you can add adverbs (**siempre, ahora, mañana,** and so on) to indicate the type of action. But Spanish has another present tense that specifies and emphasizes that the action is ongoing and in progress, the present progressive.

Está hablando con la vecina en este momento.	*She's talking to the neighbor right now.*
Estamos bebiendo café.	*We're drinking coffee.*
Estoy escribiendo una carta.	*I'm writing a letter.*

Thus the ongoing action **Comemos en la cocina** could also be expressed as **Estamos comiendo en la cocina.**

Unlike the simple, or one-word, verbs you have seen so far in Spanish, the progressive is a compound tense: It uses a form of the verb **estar** and the present participle, or **-ndo** form, of another verb. Present participles are formed in Spanish by adding **-ando** to the stem of an **-ar** verb and **-iendo** to the stem of an **-er** or **-ir** verb.

hablar: habl- + -ando = **hablando**

beber: beb- + -iendo = **bebiendo**

escribir: escrib- + -iendo = **escribiendo**

NOTES:

- The **-i-** of **-iendo** changes to **-y-** when it is between two vowels.

    leer: le- + -iendo = leyendo

    construir (*to build*):   constru- + -iendo = construyendo

- The **-o-** in **dormir (ue)** and **morir (ue)** (*to die*) changes to **-u-.**

    Está d**u**rmiendo.   *She's sleeping.*
    ¡Estoy m**u**riendo de celos!   *I'm dying of jealousy!*

Análisis estructural

First, read the following sentences in English. What types of action are described in each—habitual, future, or ongoing? Then compare the progressive verbs in English with their translations in Spanish, and answer this question: Is it possible to use the progressive in Spanish to describe future actions?

1. *We are painting* our living room next week. **Vamos a pintar...**
2. *She's leaving* for Santander tomorrow. **Sale para...**
3. *He's building* a new garage next summer. **Va a construir...**
4. *They're spending* next month in Barcelona. **Van a pasar...**
5. *I'm going* to see the neighbors at 3:00 this afternoon. **Voy a ver...**

Actividades

A. ¿Dónde están estas personas?   Say where these people probably are if they are doing the following activities.

1. «Estamos bebiendo café.»
2. «Estoy leyendo una revista.»
3. «Estamos mirando la televisión.»
4. «Están durmiendo.»
5. «Está almorzando.»
6. «Estoy escuchando al profesor.»

B. En este momento.   What are these people doing right now **(ahora mismo)?** Invent original sentences, combining elements from the following columns and adding other people and activities.

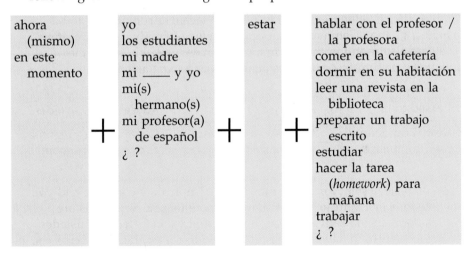

| ahora (mismo) en este momento | + | yo los estudiantes mi madre mi ____ y yo mi(s) hermano(s) mi profesor(a) de español ¿ ? | + | estar | + | hablar con el profesor / la profesora comer en la cafetería dormir en su habitación leer una revista en la biblioteca preparar un trabajo escrito estudiar hacer la tarea (*homework*) para mañana trabajar ¿ ? |

C. Entrevista: Un día típico. Ask a classmate what the following people are probably doing at different times of the day. Use the phrase **Digamos que es la / son las** (*Let's say that it's*) and choose a time of day as in the model.

MODELO   la madre →
E1: Digamos que son las 7:00 de la tarde, ¿qué está haciendo tu madre?
E2: Está preparando la cena.

1. el padre
2. los/las hermanos/as
3. el/la compañero/a de cuarto (piso, casa)
4. el/la profesor(a) de español
5. los vecinos

D. Excusas. Your parents want you to do the following household chores, but you are otherwise engaged. Tell them what prevents you from doing the chores. Use your imagination to create other chores and excuses!

MODELO   limpiar (*to clean*) el garaje →
Papá, no puedo limpiar el garaje ahora. Estoy escribiendo un trabajo muy importante para la clase.

1. lavar (*to wash*) los platos
2. limpiar tu cuarto
3. jugar con tu hermano menor
4. barrer (*to sweep*) el patio
5. ir al supermercado
6. ¿ ?

4.4 Affirmative Commands

"You're always telling me what to do!" the teenager complained to his parents. It's true: Commands can be a big part of family communication. They are also useful in the classroom; you have probably heard the following, or similar, commands related to classroom activities.

	Addressed to *tú*	**Addressed to *usted***	**Addressed to *ustedes***
Answer the question. *Write your name.*	**Contesta** la pregunta. **Escribe** tu nombre.	**Conteste** la pregunta. **Escriba** su nombre.	**Contesten** la pregunta. **Escriban** su nombre.

The complete system for commands in Spanish is quite complex, and you will study it in **Capítulo 12.** For now, just note that **tú** commands are like the present indicative **tú** form minus the final **-s. Usted** and **ustedes** commands seem to have the "wrong" vowel in the endings: **-ar** verbs end in **-e/-en,** and **-er/-ir** verbs end in **-a/-an.** (Actually, these endings are borrowed from another mood, the subjunctive, which you will learn in **Capítulo 13.**)

As mentioned in this chapter's **Pronunciación y ortografía** section, changing a verb's ending vowel can necessitate some spelling changes in the verb's stem consonant.

	Addressed to *tú*	Addressed to *usted*	Addressed to *ustedes*
Begin!	¡Empieza!	¡Empiece!	¡Empiecen!
Look for another one!	¡Busca otro!	¡Busque otro!	¡Busquen otro!
Pick one!	¡Escoge uno!	¡Escoja uno!	¡Escojan uno!

Most verbs that have irregularities in the **yo** form repeat these same irregularities in the **usted** and **ustedes** commands. The **tú** forms may be irregular, but in general they are close enough to the verb stem spelling to be easily recognized.

	Addressed to *tú*	Addressed to *usted*	Addressed to *ustedes*
Leave! Get out!	¡Sal!	¡Salga!	¡Salgan!
Hold (Have) this.	Ten esto.	Tenga esto.	Tengan esto.
Do your homework.	Haz la tarea.	Haga la tarea.	Hagan la tarea.

Affirmative **vosotros/as** commands never retain any of these irregularities. They are always formed quite simply by replacing the final **-r** of the infinitive with a **-d: hablar** → **hablad; comer** → **comed; escribir** → **escribid; salir** → **salid; tener** → **tened.** You probably have not heard many of these in class (unless your instructor is from Spain), but they are quite common in Spain.

Análisis estructural

These command forms are presented in this chapter to help you recognize them when you encounter them in readings and activity instructions (oral and written). Practice your recognition skills by stating the infinitive for each of the following commands and who each command is addressed to (**tú, usted, ustedes,** or **vosotros/as**).

1. mira
2. estudien
3. duerma
4. almorzad
5. cerrad
6. piensen
7. entiende
8. pregunten
9. escriba
10. sueña

Sobre la lectura If you plan to spend any time studying in a Spanish-speaking country, you should become familiar with ads for lodging **(alojamiento)**. This reading contains ads from two types of people from Spain: those who have a place to rent **(Se alquila)** and those looking for a place to rent **(Se busca).**

Antes de leer

A. Se busca. Imagine that you are spending next year in Spain and need housing. Which of the following items are a necessity **(una necesidad),** and which ones are a luxury **(un lujo)** that you could do without?

1. aire acondicionado
2. calefacción (*heating*)
3. cocina amueblada (*furnished*)
4. cuarto de baño
5. habitación individual (no compartida)
6. piscina
7. situación (*location*) excelente
8. vistas inmejorables (*unsurpassable*)

B. Se aquila. Now imagine that you are a landlord **(dueño/a)** in Spain and that you are renting out your own property. What kind of tenant(s) **(inquilino/a/os/as)** would you prefer? Choose from the following list and explain your choice(s).

☐ dos chicos/as de 21 años
☐ un(a) estudiante de posgrado (*graduate*)
☐ un(a) joven de aspecto *punk*
☐ una pareja de profesionales
☐ una pareja solvente (*debt-free*)
☐ una persona con tres gatos
☐ una persona sin referencias
☐ un(a) profesor(a) en paro (*unemployed*)

Clasificados > Pisos

Se alquila

A. Se aquila ático, barrio céntrico. Ático de 70 m^2,[a] 90 m^2 de terraza, 3 habitaciones, 1 baño, barbacoa, amplio comedor con chimeneas, soleado todo el día, vistas inmejorables, excelente situación. Alicia124 ✎

B. Se aquila piso de lujo en Madrid. Residencial con piscina, de 6 años, cocina totalmente amueblada, calefacción, 3 habitaciones, dos cuartos de baño. Roberto623 ✎

C. Aquilo piso nuevo, aire acondicionado. Piso nuevo, totalmente amueblado, 1 dormitorio, zonas comunes con piscina y pista de paddel.[b] Marusa34 ✎

Se busca

D. Se busca piso en Madrid. Pareja de profesionales necesita piso a partir del[c] 17 de septiembre, solventes y responsables, referencias. Guillermo45 ✎

E. Se busca habitación en piso compartido. Estudiante peruanoitaliano busca habitación en piso compartido a partir de octubre, máx.[d] 290 euros mensuales[e] incl. gastos.[f] Edgardo78 ✎

F. Buscamos dos habitaciones a compartir. Dos chicas buscan desesperadamente[g] un piso para compartir, preferiblemente amueblado, con cocina equipada. Tulia52 ✎

[a]metros cuadrados   [b]pista... racquetball court   [c]a... starting on the   [d]máximo   [e]monthly   [f]expenses   [g]desperately

Después de leer

A. ¿Cuál es?   Review the **Se alquila** ads and indicate which property/properties probably match the following descriptions.

1. _____ Es caro.

2. _____ Es grande.

3. _____ No está en el centro.

4. _____ Es nuevo.

5. _____ Es lujoso.

6. _____ Es ideal para una familia grande.

7. _____ Es ideal para una persona soltera o una pareja sin hijos.

B. Otras opiniones.   Indicate which **Se busca** ad(s) was/were probably written by people who match the following descriptions.

1. _____ Quiere(n) alquilar un piso / una habitación durante mucho tiempo.

2. _____ Es la persona más joven. / Son las personas más jóvenes.

3. _____ Es serio/a. / Son serios/as.

4. _____ No es/son muy exigente(s) (*demanding*).

5. _____ No tiene(n) mucho dinero.

6. _____ Tiene(n) una situación estable.

C. **Entrevista.** Make a list of questions that you would expect to hear in an interview between a landlord and a prospective tenant. Then form small groups. One student will play the role of the landlord. The other(s) will assume the role of the professional couple, the graduate student, or the young women looking for a place to live. At the end of the role play, the landlord will decide whether or not he/she is willing to rent out his/her property to the applicant(s).

D. **Anuncios locales.** Imagine that you are renting out the place where you currently live, and write an ad describing it in Spanish. Your instructor will then put several of the ads on the board and ask members of the class to choose a property and explain why they'd prefer to rent it.

PORTAFOLIO CULTURAL

Redacción

Un año en España. You are going to Spain to study for a year at the **Universidad de Sevilla,** and you'd like to offer your house to a Spanish student in exchange for a place to stay in Seville. Compose one ad in which you describe your lodging preferences for your future home in Seville and another ad describing your current home to a prospective tenant. Follow the guided steps in the *Manual de práctica* to complete your ads.

Exploración

Investigación cultural. Find more information about advertising and lodging in Spain in your library, on the *Entrevistas* Online Learning Center (**www.mhhe.com/entrevistas2**), or elsewhere on the Internet and present it to the class. Consult the *Manual de práctica* for ideas for your presentation.

Léxico activo

TIPOS DE CASAS

la **casa (particular)**	(private, single-family) house
el **condominio**	condominium
el **bloque de pisos**	apartment building
el **piso**	flat, apartment

¿DÓNDE ESTÁ TU CASA?

las **afueras**	outskirts; suburbs
la **calle transitada/ residencial**	busy/residential street
la **ciudad**	city
el **pueblo**	small town
la **zona residencial**	residential zone/area

LAS PARTES DE LA CASA

la **cocina**	kitchen
el **comedor**	dining room
el **cuarto**	(bed)room
el **cuarto de baño**	bathroom
el **dormitorio**	bedroom
el **garaje**	garage
la **habitación**	(bed)room
el **jardín**	garden
el **pasillo**	hallway
el **patio**	courtyard, patio
la **piscina**	swimming pool
el **salón**	living room
la **terraza**	terrace

este/a (éste/a)	this (this one)
estos/as (éstos/as)	these (these ones)
ese/a (ése/a)	that (that one)
esos/as (ésos/as)	those (those ones)
aquel, aquella (aquél, aquélla)	that _____ over there (that one over there)
aquellos/as (aquéllos/as)	those _____ over there (those ones over there)
esto	this (stuff)
eso	that (stuff)
aquello	that (stuff) over there
aquí (acá)	here
ahí	there
allí (allá)	over there

LOS VERBOS

almorzar (ue)	to eat lunch
cerrar (ie)	to close
charlar	to chat
compartir	to share
dormir (ue)	to sleep
entender (ie)	to understand
jugar (ue) (al béisbol, al baloncesto, al fútbol)	to play (baseball, basketball [Sp.], soccer)
pensar (ie) (de/en)	to think (of, about)
poder (ue)	to be able to, can
preferir (ie)	to prefer
preparar la comida	to prepare the meal/food
querer (ie)	to want
soler (ue) + inf.	to be in the habit of / be accustomed to (doing something)
soñar (ue) con	to dream about
volver (ue)	to return (to a place)

¿QUÉ HAY EN TU CASA?

la alfombra	rug, carpet
el armario	closet
la bañera	bathtub
la cama	bed
el cartel	poster
la chimenea	fireplace
la cocina (eléctrica / de gas)	(electric/gas) stove unit
la cómoda	dresser, chest of drawers
el cuadro	picture, painting
la ducha	shower
el escritorio	desk
la estantería	bookcase, shelving
el fregadero	sink (kitchen)
el horno	oven
la lámpara	lamp
el lavabo	sink (bathroom)
la lavadora	washing machine
el lavaplatos	dishwasher
la luz	(overhead) lamp; light(ing); electricity
la mesa	table
la mesilla de noche	night table
la nevera	freezer
el ordenador	computer (Sp.)
la puerta	door
el refrigerador	refrigerator
el retrete	toilet
la secadora	dryer
el sillón	armchair
el sofá	sofa
el teléfono	telephone
la ventana	window

Repaso: silla

¿CÓMO ES TU CASA?

el ambiente	ambience, atmosphere
el exterior	exterior
el interior	interior
el lujo	luxury
la necesidad	necessity
acogedor(a)	welcoming
elegante	elegant
encantador(a)	charming
humilde	humble
lujoso/a	luxurious
sencillo/a	simple
tradicional	traditional
por dentro	on the inside
por fuera	on the outside

Repaso: diseño, feo/a

¡A comer!ᵃ

La República Dominicana y Venezuela

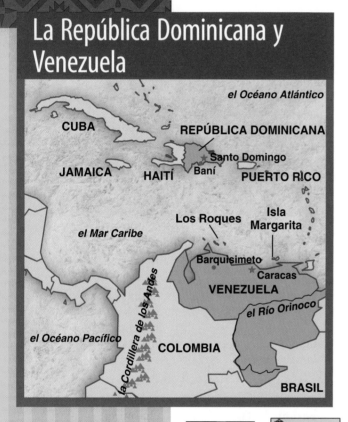

el Océano Atlántico

CUBA

REPÚBLICA DOMINICANA

JAMAICA HAITÍ Baní Santo Domingo

PUERTO RICO

Los Roques Isla Margarita

el Mar Caribe

Barquisimeto

Caracas

VENEZUELA

el Río Orinoco

el Océano Pacífico

la Cordillera de los Andes

COLOMBIA

BRASIL

la República Dominicana

Venezuela

Cultura

◆ Food in the Caribbean
◆ Food Names in Different Countries
◆ **Señas culturales:** Simón Bolívar, El Libertador (1783–1830)

Lengua

◆ Describing Foods, Meals, and Food Preparation
◆ Comparisons
◆ Speaking Impersonally: **se** + Verb (5.1)
◆ **Por** and **para** (5.2)
◆ Stem-Changing Verbs **(e → i)** (5.3)
◆ Direct Object Pronouns (5.4)

ᵃ ¡A... *Let's eat!*

La República Dominicana y Venezuela	Columbus visits island of Hispaniola	Santo Domingo founded on Hispaniola	Columbus reaches Venezuela		First Spanish mainland outpost established at Cumaná (Venezuela)		Caracas founded			Venezuelan independence from Spain
	1492	**1496**	**1498 until 16th c.**		**1523 1500–1600**		**1567 1534**	**1600–1750**		**1811 1776–1783**
Los Estados Unidos y el Canadá				Various indigenous tribes inhabit North America		Spanish exploration of North America	Jacques Cartier claims Canada for France	British colonies founded in North America		American War of Independence

Instantánea

ORIGEN DEL NOMBRE

La República Dominicana: from Santo Domingo, the name of the Spanish colony before independence

Venezuela (*Little Venice*): The many waterways reminded Spanish explorers of the Italian city famous for its canals.

POBLACIÓN

La República Dominicana: 9.219.800

Venezuela: 23.865.800

LENGUAS

La República Dominicana: Spanish (official), French-Creole

Venezuela: Spanish (official), various indigenous languages

▲ El mercado, *de la artista dominicana Celeste Woss y Gil (1891–1985)*

For additional practice, check out the *Manual de práctica,* the Interactive CD-ROM, and the Online Learning Center (**www.mhhe.com/entrevistas2**)!

Establishment of D.R.		Dictatorship of Rafael Leónides Trujillo in D.R.		Balaguer wins in free elections; U.S. and other foreign troops withdraw from D.R.	Venezuela nationalizes oil industry		Chávez attempts overthrow of Venezuelan gov't.		Chávez elected president of Venezuela	Chávez deposed, reinstated two days later
1844 1846–1848	1898	1930–1961 1952	1965	1966	1975	1982	1992	1994	1998	2002
	Mexican-American War	Spanish-American War	Puerto Rico becomes U.S. commonwealth	U.S. invades D.R.		Canada cuts legal ties with Britain		U.S., Canada, Mexico sign NAFTA		

● En el mercado

el café — coffee
la cerveza — beer
el mercado libre / del barrio — farmers'/ neighborhood market
la pescadería — fish market
el pescado — fish
el refresco — soft drink

el té — tea
el vegetal — vegetable
el vino — wine

cocinar — to cook
comprar — to buy
hacer la compra — to do the (grocery) shopping

Si te interesa

The names for shops in Spanish are easily recognizable by the suffix **-ería** attached to the name of the product sold. What do you think you could find in the following stores: **pastelería, taquería (México)?**

Actividades

A. Ingredientes para... Tell which dishes could contain the following food items. ¡OJO! There may be more than one answer for each item.

1. la banana
- ☐ una ensalada de fruta
- ☐ un sándwich
- ☐ la sopa
- ☐ un pastel

2. la papa
- ☐ la sopa
- ☐ una bebida
- ☐ una ensalada
- ☐ un pastel

3. el aguacate
- ☐ el flan (*type of custard with caramel on top*)
- ☐ un sándwich
- ☐ una pizza
- ☐ el guacamole

4. la piña
- ☐ un sándwich
- ☐ un pastel
- ☐ una ensalada de fruta
- ☐ una pizza

B. ¿Dónde compras... ? Imagine that you are living in the Dominican Republic or Venezuela. Where do you buy the following foods?

1. el salmón
2. el mango
3. el melón
4. el yogur
5. la pasta (los espaguetis)
6. el azúcar
7. las espinacas (*spinach*)
8. los frijoles
9. las especias (*spices*)
10. la mermelada

C. Dietas diferentes. Name at least three foods that each of the following people can or would be likely to eat and three that each cannot or would not eat.

(No) Come...
(No) Puede comer...

VOCABULARIO ÚTIL

el atún	tuna
el helado	ice cream
el tocino	bacon
una variedad de	a variety of

1. una persona vieja
2. un(a) atleta
3. un(a) modelo
4. un niño / una niña de 4 años
5. una persona diabética
6. una persona con el colesterol alto

D. Entrevista: ¿Quién en tu familia... ? Interview a classmate to find out who in his/her family does the following things. If nobody does them, say **Nadie...**

1. hacer la compra
2. cocinar/preparar la comida
3. comer todas las sobras (*leftovers*)
4. no comer carne
5. poner la mesa (*to set the table*)
6. no probar (ue) (*to taste, try*) nuevas comidas

Si te interesa

Just as there are regional variations in the terms used for some ideas in the English-speaking world, the words used for some concepts in Spanish can vary from one region to another. The words used to name foods are especially rich in variations. Here are some of the most common examples. Ask your instructor and other Spanish speakers what they call the food items presented in this chapter.

En México se dice...	En España la gente dice...	En la República Dominicana dicen...	En Venezuela se dice...	Los chilenos dicen...
batata (*sweet potato*)	batata	batata	ñame	batata
chícharos (*peas*)	guisantes	arvejas	arvejas	arvejas
durazno (*peach*)	melocotón	durazno	durazno	durazno
frijoles	alubias, judías	habichuelas	caraotas	porotos
jitomate	tomate	tomate	tomate	tomate
papa	patata	papa	papa	papa
papaya	papaya	lechosa	lechosa	mamón
plátano	plátano, banana	guineo	cambur	plátano
tamal	tamal	pastel	hallaca	tamal

CAPÍTULO 5 • ¡A comer!

¿Cómo es la comida? ¿Cómo está el plato[a]?

agrio/a	sour	**picante**	hot, spicy
amargo/a	bitter	**rico/a**	rich; delicious
crudo/a	raw	**sabroso/a**	tasty
delicioso/a	delicious	**salado/a**	salty
dulce	sweet	**seco/a**	dry
fresco/a	fresh	**tierno/a**	tender
frito/a	fried	**verde**	green, unripe
maduro/a	ripe	**viejo/a**	old, stale

Actividades

A. Asociaciones. What foods do you associate with the following adjectives? Form complete sentences.

1. rojo/a
2. amarillo/a (*yellow*)
3. verde
4. ácido/a
5. dulce
6. crudo/a
7. alcohólico/a
8. picante

B. Comparaciones. How do the following food products compare? Form complete sentences according to the model. (You may want to refer to the **Si te interesa** box on page 124 to recall what some of these food items are.)

MODELO   Las espinacas son como la lechuga, pero son más verdes.

PRODUCTOS

1. el melón / la lechosa
2. el salmón / el atún
3. el pollo / el pavo (*turkey*)
4. la langosta / el camarón
5. el limón / la naranja
6. el ñame / la papa

+

DESCRIPCIONES

agrio/a
barato/a
caro/a (*expensive*)
dulce
grande
tierno/a
¿ ?

Si te interesa

As you have seen, the verbs **ser** and **estar** both can be translated as *to be* but have different connotations. When describing food and dishes, use **ser** with adjectives to say what they are like in general: **Algunas manzanas son verdes.** (*Some apples are green [in color].*) Use **estar** with adjectives to say what some specific food or dish is like: **Estas manzanas están verdes.** (*These apples are green [unripe].*) By the same token, a food can be rich, as in high in fat and sugar—**El flan es rico**—or it can taste delicious: **¡Este flan está rico/delicioso!**

---

[a] (*prepared*) *dish*

Lenguaje funcional

No sé cómo se dice, pero es...

Circumlocution is talking around a word you do not know. A useful pattern for describing an unknown object is: **Es/Son** + *general description* + *specific description*. Can you guess what is being described in the following examples?

> **Es una fruta roja y dulce.**
> **Son hojas** (*leaves*) **verdes que comes en una ensalada. No es la lechuga.**

If you don't know the word for a general description of an object, such as **hojas** in the preceding example, you can use the word **cosa** (*thing*).

> **Son cosas verdes que comes en una ensalada. No es la lechuga.**

Another technique is to compare the unknown object to a known object, by using the pattern:

> **Es/Son como** + *known object* + **pero es/son más/menos** + *description*.
> **Son como la langosta pero son más pequeños.**

C. No sé cómo se dice, pero es... After reviewing the preceding **Lenguaje funcional,** think of a few food items and try describing them to a partner in Spanish without stating the name of the item.

D. Encuesta: ¿Cuáles son tus comidas favoritas y menos (*least*) **favoritas?** Interview three classmates to find out what their favorite foods are, how they like them prepared, and why. Also find out what food they like the least and why. Later, report the results of your interview to the class, summarizing information when possible.

VOCABULARIO ÚTIL

al horno	baked
cremoso/a	creamy
duro/a	hard
ligero/a	light
pesado/a	heavy
(no) saludable	(un)healthy
soso/a	bland, tasteless

Karina de Frías Otero

«*En los mercados... las frutas son más frescas.*»

Nombre: Karina

Apellidos: (1) de Frías (2) Otero

Edad: 29 años

Nació en: Santo Domingo, La República Dominicana

You can watch this interview on the *Entrevistas* Video or Interactive CD-ROM or listen to the audio on the Online Learning Center (**www.mhhe.com/entrevistas2**).

Vocabulario útil

enlatados	canned (foods)	**los cocos de agua**	coconuts
congelados	frozen (foods)	**el ñame**	yam
igualmente	likewise	**el plátano**	plantain
las venden	(they) sell them	**los molondrones**	okra
las cultivan	(they) grow them	**mezcla**	mixture
se ven	are seen	**sabores** *m.*	flavors
se encuentran	(that) are found	**la bandera**	flag
la chinola	sour orange	**tendrás**	you will have

Antes de ver

A. ¿El mercado o el supermercado? Read the following sentences and say whether each applies to a **mercado,** to a **supermercado,** or to both.

1. Las frutas y verduras son más frescas.
2. Hay más variedad de productos.
3. Está más cerca de la casa.
4. No tienes que (*you don't have to*) ir en carro.
5. Es más barato.
6. Es muy caro.

B. ¿Fruta o verdura? Classify each of the following food items as a fruit or a vegetable.

	FRUTA	VERDURA		FRUTA	VERDURA
el aguacate	☐	☐	la naranja	☐	☐
la chinola	☐	☐	el ñame	☐	☐
el guineo	☐	☐	la papa	☐	☐
la lechosa	☐	☐	la piña	☐	☐
la manzana	☐	☐	el tomate	☐	☐

¡Veamos!

¿Cuáles se mencionan? Now watch the interview and indicate which of the items from **Actividad B** of **Antes de ver** are mentioned.

Después de ver

A. ¿Adónde van? Watch the interview again to get the answers to the following questions.

1. ¿Adónde va Karina para hacer la compra?
2. ¿Adónde va la abuela de Karina? ¿Qué compra en cada lugar (*place*)?
3. ¿Quiénes venden en los mercados?
4. ¿Cómo es la comida en los mercados, en comparación con la del supermercado?

B. ¿Y tú? Answer the following questions for yourself. Afterward, compare your answers with Karina's. How are you and she similar? How are you different? What does this say about the similarities and differences between your culture and Dominican culture as described by Karina?

1. ¿Comes muchas frutas? ¿Y verduras?
2. ¿Cuál es tu fruta o verdura favorita? ¿La comes (*Do you eat it*) con mucha frecuencia?
3. ¿Tienes un plato favorito hecho (*made*) con frutas? ¿con verduras? ¿Qué contiene y cómo se llama?
4. ¿Hay una fruta o verdura «típica» de tu familia (región, cultura)?
5. ¿Hay nombres especiales para algunas comidas en tu familia (región, cultura), por ejemplo, *pop* vs. *soda* vs. *soft drink*?
6. En tu opinión, ¿cuáles son los elementos de la dieta norteamericana «típica»?
7. En tu opinión, ¿qué dieta es más saludable: la norteamericana o la dominicana? ¿Por qué?

▲ *Éste es un mercado libre de Caracas, Venezuela, ¿hay mercados libres donde tú vives?*

● 5.1 Speaking Impersonally: se + Verb

It's often useful to avoid having to say who is doing an action. In English, such impersonal descriptions use the passive voice (*is eaten, are seen, are bought*, and so on) or impersonal expressions like *you, people, they*, or *one*. In Spanish, the equivalent impersonal descriptions are formed with the **se** + *verb* construction, in which the verb is conjugated in the third-person singular or plural form, depending on the number of nouns you are referring to.

se + SINGULAR VERB + SINGULAR NOUN

Se come mucha lechosa.	*People eat (One eats, You eat) a lot of papaya.*
Se compra el pan en la panadería.	*People buy bread at the bakery. (One buys bread . . . , Bread is bought . . .)*

se + PLURAL VERB + PLURAL NOUN

Se ven muchas verduras frescas en los mercados.	*You see a lot of fresh vegetables at the markets. (A lot of vegetables are seen . . .)*
Se hacen los tamales al vapor.	*You make tamales by steaming (One makes . . . , Tamales are made . . .)*

If another verb, or series of verbs, follows the first verb, only the first verb is conjugated.

Se **puede comer** mariscos en el Caribe.	*One (People, You) can eat shellfish in the Caribbean.*
Se **debe bailar, tomar** el sol y **dormir** mucho en las vacaciones.	*One (People, You) should dance, sunbathe, and sleep a lot on vacation.*

Análisis estructural

In the following examples, first identify the **se** + *verb* construction, then the subject. Where can you place the subject of the sentence with respect to the verb—before or after? How would you render the sentences in English?

1. El almuerzo se come a la 1:00.
2. Se venden frutas frescas en los mercados libres.
3. Este pan se hace en la Panadería El Trigal.
4. ¿Se puede encontrar pescado en los mercados libres?
5. Los mariscos se comen con frecuencia en el Caribe.

Actividades

A. Los buenos modales.   What are considered good manners in your family? Say whether the following actions are acceptable or unacceptable in your family. Ask your instructor what customs apply in the Spanish-speaking countries he/she knows about.

	ES ACEPTABLE.	NO ES ACEPTABLE.
1. Se come el pollo con las manos.	☐	☐
2. Se come la fruta con las manos.	☐	☐
3. Se habla con la boca llena (*mouth full*).	☐	☐
4. Se bebe la leche directamente del envase (*container*).	☐	☐
5. Se bebe la cerveza directamente de la botella.	☐	☐
6. Se usan los dedos (*fingers*) para atrapar los guisantes en el plato.	☐	☐
7. Se divide el pan grande con las manos.	☐	☐
8. Se ponen los codos (*elbows*) en la mesa.	☐	☐
9. Se eructa (*burp*) en la mesa después de la comida.	☐	☐

B. Una rutina típica.   Use the passive **se** to make complete sentences about what is done on a typical trip to the open-air market.

1. escribir una lista de compras

2. sacar el dinero del banco

3. hablar con los vendedores (*sellers*) de productos

4. buscar los mejores (*best*) precios

5. pagar en efectivo (*cash*)

6. regresar a casa con las compras

C. De compras.   What is probably the best place to buy each of the following items in the Dominican Republic—a small shop or the supermarket? Complete the sentences with **se,** paying special attention to verb endings (third-person singular or plural).

MODELO   los guineos más frescos (*freshest*) →
Los guineos más frescos se compran en la frutería.

1. el arroz más barato

2. la lechuga más fresca

3. el melón más dulce

4. los espaguetis (secos)

5. el azúcar más barato

6. más variedad de latas de sopa

7. el aceite de oliva importado

8. los mariscos más ricos

● 5.2 **Por** and **para**

You may have noticed that there are two prepositions in Spanish that can be translated as *for* in English: **por** and **para.** The two are not interchangeable, so take note of the basic uses of each one as outlined in this section. You will encounter more uses of these prepositions as you continue your studies of Spanish.

Por

A. "through" space and time

Vas **por** el comedor. *You go through the dining room.*

Se comen cereales **por** la mañana. *They eat cereal in (during) the morning.*

B. length or duration of time

Vamos a Caracas **por** tres días. *We're going to Caracas for three days.*

C. fixed expressions

por ejemplo	*for example*
por eso	*for that reason, that's why*
por favor	*please*
por lo menos	*at least*

Para

A. purpose or goal

To express purpose, use **para** + *infinitive*. Note that the English equivalent is *in order to*.

Para encontrar las frutas más frescas, tienes que ir al mercado libre. *(In order) To find the freshest fruit, you have to go to the open-air market.*

B. recipient or destination

Estas lechosas son **para** mi abuela. *These papayas are for my grandmother.*

La carne es **para** la sopa. *The meat is for the soup.*

Mañana salimos **para** Caracas. *Tomorrow we are leaving for Caracas.*

Actividades

A. **¿Para qué?** Why must one do the following things? Choose the phrase that best completes each sentence.

VOCABULARIO ÚTIL

Debes + *inf.*	You should (*do something*).
Es necesario + *inf.*	It's necessary to (*do something*).
Tienes que + *inf.*	You have to (*do something*).

1. Se va a la frutería…
   □ para encontrar naranjas. □ para encontrar queso.
2. Debes ir a la carnicería…
   □ para comprar pollo. □ para comprar cambures.
3. Es necesario ir al mercado en carro…
   □ para llevar muchas compras. □ para llevar pocas cosas.
4. Tienes que ir al supermercado…
   □ para encontrar frutas enlatadas. □ para encontrar frutas baratas.

B. ¿Cómo se hace? How can one accomplish the tasks **(tareas)** on the left? Form complete sentences, combining expressions from both columns and adding any necessary words.

MODELO   Preparar una ensalada →
Para preparar una ensalada, se necesitan espinacas
o lechuga y…

TAREAS		ACCIONES
1. hacer tostadas		se necesita(n)…
2. comer la mejor pizza	**+**	se compra(n)…
3. ir al supermercado		se va a…
4. encontrar los productos más baratos		se _____(n)…

C. Vacaciones gastronómicas en Baní. Complete the following sentences with **por** or **para,** as appropriate.

1. Queremos ir a Baní _____ dos semanas.

2. La mejor ruta (*route*) pasa _____ San Cristóbal.

3. Pero la carretera (*highway*) está bloqueada. _____ eso vamos _____ una ruta alternativa.

4. _____ encontrar los buenos restaurantes allí, consultamos una guía (*guidebook*).

5. Vamos a buscar regalos (*gifts*) _____ toda la familia en los mercados.

6. _____ la mañana vamos a visitar lugares turísticos, y _____ la tarde queremos explorar las famosas dunas en la playa.

¿Te gusta cocinar tanto como (as ▶ much as) *esta mujer en Santo Domingo?*

Análisis cultural

The following quote from an English-language source will add to your knowledge of food and eating customs in the Caribbean, specifically in Venezuela. As you read this quote, compare the information about the Dominican Republic given by Karina in **Entrevista 1** with the ideas presented here. Then answer the questions that follow the quote.

❝Venezuela is a good place to eat. On the whole, food is good and relatively inexpensive. Apart from a variety of typical local dishes, there are plenty of Western cuisines available, including a dense array of gringo fast-food outlets. Spanish and Italian restaurants are particularly well represented, thanks to a sizeable migration from these two countries. There are also some good Chinese and Arab restaurants, mostly in the main cities. . . .

Espresso coffee is strong and excellent in Venezuela. It's served in **panaderías** (coffee shops-cum-bakeries), which are plentiful. Ask for **café negro** if you want it black, **café marrón** if you prefer half coffee, half milk, and **café con leche** if you like very milky coffee.

Fruit juices are readily available in restaurants, **fuentes de soda, fruterías, refresquerías,** and other eating outlets. Given the variety of fruit in the country, you have quite a choice. Juices come pure or watered down **(batidos),** or as milkshakes **(merengadas).**❞

Source: *Lonely Planet on a Shoestring: South America*

1. Based on the information about Caribbean food that you have studied so far in this chapter, do you feel that Venezuela is "a good place to eat"? Explain.

2. What dishes would you like to try there?

3. Which "gringo fast-food outlets" might the text be referring to?

4. Do you know of any other words for coffee drinks in the Spanish-speaking world? Ask your instructor or other Spanish speakers you may know about the names of the most common ones.

As you proceed through **Parte 2** of this chapter and watch **Entrevista 2,** make sure you reread the above quote to see if this information is consistent with what Patricia says about Venezuela.

● Special Letter Combinations

The Spanish spelling system is extremely regular in representing sounds. There are a few combinations you must be careful with, however, in order to pronounce and spell words correctly. Study how the following sounds are written.

1. The [k] sound is represented by **c** before **a, o,** and **u,** but by **qu** before the vowels **e** and **i:**

   carne   rico   cultura   queso   mantequilla

2. The [g] sound is spelled with **g** before **a, o,** and **u,** but with **gu** before the vowels **e** and **i:**

   gamba   jugo   agudo   hamburguesa   guisante

3. The [x] sound (like English *h* in *happy* but stronger) is normally represented by **j** before **a, o,** and **u,** but by **g** before the vowels **e** and **i.** However, there are many exceptions to this rule (e.g., **jinete, ají**), so be careful to remember the spelling of new words with this sound!

   jamón   viejo   jugo   vegetal   gigante

The *Manual de práctica* contains activities to practice the material explained here.

▲ *Las familias caraqueñas (de Caracas, Venezuela) suelen salir a comer con frecuencia.*

Las comidas del día

Restaurante La Gaviota: Menú del Día

Desayuno 7:00–10:00
Bs. 600
Tostadas con mantequilla
y mermelada
o
Arepas con mantequilla
Café o té

Merienda 4:00–6:00
Bs. 600–700
Sándwich de queso
o
Hamburguesa con queso
(+ Bs. 100)
Pastel de manzana
Café o té

Almuerzo 12:00–3:00
Bs. 3.000
Primer plato:
Espaguetis con salsa de
tomate y queso
Plato principal:
Bistec con verdura del día
y arepas
Postre:
Flan o fruta
Vino de la casa o agua
mineral

Cena 7:00–11:00
Bs. 2.500
Tortilla española
o
2 huevos al gusto
Ensalada mixta
o
Sopa de verduras
Pan o arepas

Carrera 5, Barquisimeto

En el Restaurante La Gaviota, **se desayuna** entre las 7:00 y las 10:00 de la mañana, **se merienda** de las 4:00 a las 6:00 de la tarde y **se cena** desde las 7:00 hasta las 11:00 de la noche. ¿A qué hora se puede almorzar?

El almuerzo es **más caro que** el desayuno.

La cena ofrece **menos comida que** el almuerzo.

De postre, se recomienda el flan: es **mejor que** el pastel de manzana (el pastel es **peor que** el flan).

En mi opinión, el pastel de manzana es **tan bueno como** el flan.

No hay **tanta** comida para el desayuno **como** para el almuerzo.

Este restaurante tiene los **mejores** precios: Son muy razonables.

Actividades

A. Lo mejor (*The best*) **de tu ciudad.** Where are the best and worst products in your city or town sold? Complete the following sentences with local information, then change the sentences to tell about the worst products, using **peor(es).**

VOCABULARIO ÚTIL

servir (i)   to serve   **vender**   to sell

1. Encuentro la mejor carne (los mejores mariscos) en _____.
2. Se venden los mejores ingredientes mexicanos (chinos, italianos,...)

   en _____.
3. Se sirve el mejor desayuno (almuerzo,...) en _____.
4. Se sirve la mejor pizza en _____.
5. ¡Las hamburguesas de _____ son las mejores del mundo!

B. **Tus gustos** (*tastes*).   Give your opinions on the following food items. Follow the model.

MODELO   la ensalada de frutas: la piña, el cambur →
En mi opinión, la piña es mejor que el cambur para una ensalada de frutas. (Me gusta más la piña que el cambur en una ensalada de frutas.)

1. el sándwich: el jamón, el aguacate
2. la sopa: las verduras, el pollo
3. la pizza: la piña, los champiñones
4. la hamburguesa: el queso, la cebolla
5. los espaguetis: la salsa de tomate, la salsa de queso

C. **Entrevista: ¿Qué comes?**   Use the verbs **almorzar, cenar, desayunar,** and **merendar** to find out what your partner's typical eating schedule is like. Also find out what he/she generally eats during each meal.

En el restaurante

Los señores (*Mr.* and *Mrs.*) Guzmán **tienen hambre** cuando llegan. **El mesero trae*** los menús.

El mesero **recomienda** los especiales del día.

La señora Guzmán **pide** el bistec y el señor Guzmán **pide** la carne de cerdo. **De beber,** piden **una copa** (*glass*) **de vino.**

---

* The verb **traer** (*to bring*) has an irregular **yo** form—**traigo**—but is otherwise conjugated like regular **-er** verbs: **traes, trae, traemos, traéis, traen.**

El mesero **sirve** la comida.

De postre, piden helado y **una taza de** café.

El mesero trae **la cuenta.**

algo	something	**nada de***	no, not any
algo de*	some	**ningún,† ninguna***	no, not any
algún,† alguna/os/as*	some	**un poco de**	a little (of)
nada	nothing		

Lenguaje funcional
¡No quiero comer nada!

When the expressions **nada** and **ninguno/a** follow a verb, you must place **no** before the verb as well. This would be considered a "double negative" and incorrect in English, but in Spanish it is never incorrect to include more than one negative in a sentence.

No tengo **ninguna** receta vegetariana.	*I don't have any vegetarian recipes.*
Este producto **no** contiene **ningún** ingrediente artificial.	*This product contains no artificial ingredients.*

Note also that the nouns described by the adjective **ningún, ninguna** must always be in the singular, not in the plural as in the English translations. You will learn more about negative sentences in **Capítulo 8.**

Actividades

A. Dietas especiales. Marcela has food allergies and needs to know each dish at the top of the next page contains to avoid having an allergic reaction. Use words of quantity (**algo [de], nada [de], algún, alguna/os/as, ningún, ninguna, mucho/a/os/as, un poco de, un trozo** (*piece/chunk*) **de,** and so on) to form complete sentences and tell Maricela what each of the dishes contains and doesn't contain. **¡OJO!** You can mention ingredients other than those listed.

---

* Use **algo de** and **nada de** before a noun that is used in a collective sense. Use **algún, alguna/os/as,** and **ningún, ninguna** before a noun that is *not* used in a collective sense.
  Esta salsa necesita **algo de** ajo, pero no necesita **nada de** sal. (*This sauce needs some garlic, but it doesn't need any salt.*)
  Quiero comprar **algunas** manzanas, pero no necesito **ninguna** naranja. (*I want to buy some apples, but I don't need any oranges.*)
† **Algún** and **ningún** are used before masculine singular nouns.

MODELO   una sopa de pollo: ajo, conservantes (*preservatives*), guisantes, pollo,... →
Esta sopa contiene mucho pollo, guisantes, algo de cebolla y un poco de ajo, pero no contiene nada de conservantes.

1. un pastel de chocolate: ajo, leche, huevos, carne,...
2. un plato de espaguetis: queso, sal, huevos crudos, piña,...
3. una ensalada: sal, tomates, lechuga, pastel,...
4. una salsa para carne: vino, pimienta, sopa, azúcar,...
5. un sándwich: jamón, champiñones, maíz, queso,...

B. Tu plato favorito.   Describe your favorite dish to a partner, including as many details about its ingredients and preparation as you can. Also provide adjectives to describe how it smells, tastes, feels, and so on. Your partner will try to guess what your favorite food is.

VOCABULARIO ÚTIL

añadir/agregar	to add
hornear	to bake
mechado/a	shredded
picar	to mince, chop
rellenar (de)	to stuff (with)
relleno/a (de)	stuffed (with)
un trozo de	a piece/chunk of
una cucharada de	a spoonful of
una pizca de	a pinch of

MODELO   E1: Mi plato favorito es un tipo de pastel sabroso con peperonis, queso, verduras y salsa de tomate. Se prepara en el horno.
E2: ¿Es la pizza?

C. Minidrama: En el restaurante.   Work in groups of three or four to act out a scene at a restaurant. One of you is the waiter/waitress **(el mesero / la mesera),** and the others are customers. The waiter should describe the daily specials, explain how things are prepared, find out what the customers want, and serve the meal. The customers should be ready to ask for details about how the foods and dishes are prepared, explain their likes and dislikes to the waiter, and make their food and drink requests.

Lenguaje funcional
En el restaurante

¿Qué desea(n) (de comer)?	What would you like (to eat)?
¿Qué recomienda (usted)?	What do you recommend?
¿Qué le(s) traigo (de entrada, de primer plato, de plato principal, de postre)?	What can I bring you (for appetizers, as the first course, for the main course, for dessert)?
¿Y de beber?	And to drink?
Me gustaría una ensalada.	I would like a salad.
¿Me trae la cuenta, por favor?	Could you please bring me the check?
¿Me pasa(s) la sal, por favor?	Could you pass the salt, please?

Patricia Nevil Gallego

« ...la arepa... es un plato que se come todos los días.»

Nombre: Patricia

Apellidos: (1) Nevil (2) Gallego

Edad: 36 años

Nació en: Caracas, Venezuela

You can watch this interview on the *Entrevistas* Video or Interactive CD-ROM or listen to the audio on the Online Learning Center (**www.mhhe.com/entrevistas2**).

Vocabulario útil

desmechada	shredded	**muchísimo**	very much
harina de maíz	corn flour	**hecha de masa**	made of dough
viene precocida	it comes precooked	**se envuelve**	it is wrapped
tibia	warm	**hoja**	leaf
pancitos	little rolls	**ya que**	since
lo que tú quieras	whatever you want	**quehaceres** *m.*	chores
Navidad *f.*	Christmas	**reposo**	rest

Antes de ver

Tus comidas. When do you typically eat the following meals? Are they light or heavy?

1. el desayuno: a eso de las _____; ☐ ligero ☐ pesado

2. el almuerzo: a eso de la(s) _____; ☐ ligero ☐ pesado

3. la cena: a eso de las _____; ☐ ligera ☐ pesada

¡Veamos!

A. Las comidas caribeñas. Indicate which ingredients the dishes on the following page contain, based on Patricia's description.

	PABELLÓN CRIOLLO	AREPAS	HALLACAS
agua	☐	☐	☐
arroz blanco	☐	☐	☐
azúcar	☐	☐	☐
carne	☐	☐	☐
condimentos	☐	☐	☐
frijoles	☐	☐	☐
harina de maíz	☐	☐	☐
leche	☐	☐	☐
maíz	☐	☐	☐
masa de maíz	☐	☐	☐
queso	☐	☐	☐

B. El horario de las comidas. Jot down at what time Venezuelans eat the following meals, according to Patricia.

1. el desayuno: entre las _____ y _____

2. el almuerzo: entre las _____ y _____

3. la cena: entre las _____ y _____

Después de ver

¿Cierto o falso?   Based on what you learned in the interview, indicate whether the following statements are true **(cierto)** or false **(falso).**

	CIERTO	FALSO
1. Las arepas se preparan en Navidad.	☐	☐
2. La hallaca es un postre.	☐	☐
3. Los venezolanos desayunan en el trabajo.	☐	☐
4. En Venezuela, se comienza a trabajar a las 9:00 de la mañana.	☐	☐
5. Hay un reposo entre las 12:00 y las 2:00 de la tarde.	☐	☐
6. La siesta es un lujo: Sólo las personas que no trabajan pueden echar una.	☐	☐

Piénsalo bien

Compare Caribbean eating customs with the customs in your country by answering the following questions.

1. ¿Quiénes comen alimentos más saludables, los caribeños o la gente de tu país? ¿Cuáles son algunos ejemplos?

2. ¿Cuáles son las ventajas (*advantages*) o desventajas de la siesta? Considera las siguientes ideas y otras más en tu respuesta.
- Reposar a mediodía (no) es saludable.
- (No) Es práctico. (No) Se pierde tiempo (*Time is [not] wasted*) si se vuelve a casa.
- (No) Permite mucho contacto con la familia.

3. Compara el horario caribeño de las comidas con el de tu país. ¿Cuál te gusta más? ¿Por qué?

Forma y función

5.3 Stem-Changing Verbs (e → i)

In **Capítulo 4** you saw two groups of verbs with stem changes: those that change their stem vowels from **e** to **ie** and those that change from **o** to **ue**. There is a third group of verbs that change the last stem vowel from **e** to **i** when that vowel is stressed.

Mi tío **dice** que **sirven** buenos mariscos aquí.	*My uncle says they serve good seafood (shellfish) here.*

Here is the conjugation of the verb **pedir** with the stressed vowel indicated.

pedir			
(yo)	**pido**	(nosotros/as)	**pedimos**
(tú)	**pides**	(vosotros/as)	**pedís**
(usted, él/ella)	**pide**	(ustedes, ellos/as)	**piden**

Here are some other verbs with this same stem change:

conseguir (i)	to get, obtain	**medir (i)**	to measure
decir (*irreg.*)*	to say, tell	**seguir (i)**	to follow
freír (i)	to fry	**servir (i)**	to serve

The present participle (used to form the present progressive, which you studied in **Capítulo 4**) of all these **e → i** stem-changing verbs also has **i** in the stem instead of **e**.

de**cir:**	diciendo	**s**e**rvir:**	sirviendo
pe**dir:**	pidiendo		

Están **sirviendo** la cena ahora.	*They are serving supper now.*

Actividades

A. Un anuncio publicitario. The following phrases were contributed by an ad agency to promote a new restaurant. Combine the phrases to form complete sentences, making the necessary changes and adding any necessary words.

1. nosotros / servir / vario / ensaladas
2. nuestros cocineros siempre / medir / los ingredientes con cuidado
3. un cliente: «yo / decir que / las pizzas aquí / ser / muy rico»
4. nosotros / preparar los platos / que usted / pedir
5. en este restaurante, sólo / servirse / los mariscos / más frescos

---

* **Decir** has an irregular **yo** form—**digo**—but is otherwise conjugated like other **e → i** stem-changing verbs: **dices, dice, decimos, decís, dicen.**

B. Costumbres diferentes. Complete the following sentences with the correct form of the indicated verb. Then say if the sentences are true for you.

1. Yo siempre (pedir) platos exóticos, pero mis padres (pedir) platos típicos de este país.

2. El mesero de mi restaurante favorito (servir) el café con el plato principal, pero algunos meseros lo (servir) (*serve it*) con el postre.

3. Algunos estudiantes (decir) que la cafetería universitaria no es buena, pero nosotros (decir) que la comida es excelente.

4. Un cocinero experto no (medir) los ingredientes, pero yo siempre los (medir) (*measure them*) con cuidado.

5. En mi familia, no se (freír) las verduras, pero los dominicanos (freír) los plátanos, las papas y los pimientos.

C. Conversación con el mesero / la mesera. Conjugate the verbs in the following dialogue. Then act it out with a partner, changing the details to suit your own preferences.

MESERO/A: ¿Qué desea de beber, señor(a)? ¿(Preferir) usted un refresco, una copa de vino, una cerveza, un vaso (*glass*) de agua,... ?

CLIENTE/A: (querer) una copa de vino, por favor.

MESERO/A: Muy bien. ¿(Servir: *yo*) la ensalada antes o después de la comida?

CLIENTE/A: Después, por favor. ¿Cuánto tarda (*How long [for]*) la langosta?

MESERO/A: Sólo 10 minutos.

CLIENTE/A: Entonces, (pedir: *yo*) langosta con la verdura del día.

MESERO/A: Muy bien, señor(a). (Traer: *yo*) el vino en seguida (*right away*).

5.4 Direct Object Pronouns

So far in your study of Spanish, you have learned to make sentences with the following pattern: *subject + verb + complement,* with the complement being any type of phrase that completes the sentence (a noun, a prepositional phrase, an adverb, and so on). In many cases, the complement is a *direct object* **(un complemento directo):** a noun (other than the subject) that receives the action of the verb and answers the questions *whom?* or *what?*

I eat *cereal* for breakfast.	*What* do I eat for breakfast? Cereal.
He sees *his family* on the weekends.	*Whom* does he see on the weekends? His family.

In English, you can replace the direct object (*cereal, his family*) with pronouns (*me, you, it, him/her, us, them*) when the objects or people you are referring to have already been mentioned. Pronouns that function in this way are known as *direct object pronouns*.

I eat *it* for breakfast.

He sees *them* on the weekends.

The same is true in Spanish: direct object pronouns **(los pronombres de complemento directo)** can replace direct object nouns in a sentence. Here are the direct object pronouns in Spanish:

Los pronombres de complemento directo			
me	me	**nos**	us
te	you (*fam. s.*)	**os**	you (*fam. pl.*)
lo/la	him/her, it (*m., f.*), you (*form. s., m., f.*)	**los/las**	them (*m., f.*), you (*form. pl. m., f.*)

NOTES:

- Although the pronouns **lo/la** and **los/las** can mean *it, him, her, you* (form. s.), and *them, you* (form. pl.) respectively, the context should make the meaning clear.

- The direct object pronoun is placed immediately before the conjugated verb.

  Su amiga **la** espera en la cafetería. *Her friend waits (is waiting) for her in the cafeteria.*

  Señorita Márquez, su amiga **la** espera en la cafetería. *Miss Márquez, your friend is waiting for you in the cafeteria.*

- When a conjugated verb combines with an infinitive, direct object pronouns can precede the conjugated verb or can be attached to the end of the infinitive.

  Tu madre **te** va a necesitar en la cocina. (Tu madre va a necesitar**te** en la cocina.) *Your mother is going to need you in the kitchen.*

- When a conjugated verb combines with a present participle, the direct object pronoun can precede the conjugated verb or be attached to the present participle. If it is attached, note that a written accent is needed to maintain the stress on the correct syllable.

  Lo estoy preparando ahora. (Estoy preparándo**lo** ahora.) *I'm preparing it now.*

The Personal **a**

If in a sentence there is a stated direct object (not a direct object pronoun) referring to a person, or to something considered as important as a person (such as the family pet), it must be preceded by the preposition **a.**

Veo **a** Juan	*I see John.*
Marta está caminando **al** perro.	*Marta is walking the (family) dog.*
Mi padre llama **a** mi hermano.	*My father is calling my brother.*

There is no direct translation for the personal **a** into English, but at least it will help you identify the object of a sentence.

Análisis estructural

Study the following sentences and identify the subject and the direct object, if there is one. Explain how you know which noun/pronoun is the subject and which is the object.

1. En ese restaurante el servicio es malo.
2. La mesera pone los utensilios en la mesa.
3. Mañana te llamamos nosotros.
4. El cocinero cambia (*changes*) los precios cada día.
5. Lo comen todos los domingos.

Actividades

A. Publicidad para un restaurante. Identify the direct object nouns in the following sentences. Then rewrite the sentences using direct object pronouns to replace the nouns.

MODELO   La mesera pone <u>la mesa</u> para cada cliente. →
         La mesera la pone para cada cliente.

1. Preparamos las arepas en el momento (*on the spot*).
2. Los clientes piden platos exóticos, y nosotros servimos estos platos.
3. Vamos a cambiar el menú la semana que viene (*next week*).
4. Los meseros traen las comidas y las bebidas rápidamente.
5. El cocinero está preparando la especialidad de la casa.

B. ¿Cómo lo preparas? Think of a favorite dish you know how to prepare and tell a partner how you prepare it. (Hint: Try not to choose anything too complicated.) Be careful with verb conjugations, and remember to use direct object pronouns whenever possible. Also, try to use what you learned earlier about circumlocution if you don't know a word. See the **Vocabulario útil** and the **modelo** on the following page.

aplastar	to mash, crush	**pelar**	to peel
batir	to beat, whip	**picar**	to mince, chop
cortar (en trozos)	to cut (into pieces/ chunks)	**rebanar**	to slice up
freír (i)	to fry	**después/luego**	next, then
hervir (ie)	to boil	**finalmente**	finally
lavar	to wash	**primero**	first
mezclar	to mix		

MODELO Para preparar un puré de papas (*mashed potatoes*), primero lavas las papas, las pelas, las cortas y las hierves por unos 30 minutos. Después, las aplastas con uno de esos utensilios que se usa para aplastar papas. Luego, _____.

C. Entrevista: ¿Qué comes? Interview a classmate to find out when he/she eats the following types of foods. To avoid repeating phrases, both of you should use direct object pronouns whenever possible.

MODELO la comida rápida →
  E1: ¿Cuándo comes la comida rápida? ¿Con quién la comes?
  E2: ¿La comida rápida? La como con mis amigos cuando estudiamos hasta muy tarde por la noche.

1. los ingredientes frescos
2. los platos congelados
3. la comida para llevar (*take-out*)
4. los platos exóticos o extranjeros (*foreign*)
5. ¿ ?

▲ *Estas mujeres venezolanas están preparando arepas.*

Sobre la lectura In this reading, you will find out more about Dominican cuisine and eating habits.

Antes de leer

A. ¿Qué comida para qué ocasion? In the reading, you will learn about dishes that Dominicans eat on certain special occasions. Before you read, tell what foods or meals *you* might serve in the following circumstances.

1. al mediodía
2. en la madrugada (*early morning hours*)
3. en reuniones familiares
4. en un buen encuentro (*get-together*) entre amigos
5. en una cena elegante
6. para calmar el hambre (*curb your hunger*)
7. para invitar al romance

B. Orígenes. What do you know of the origins of the ingredients used in Dominican cooking? Take this quiz. Your instructor will provide you with the correct answers later. Some of them might surprise you.

	DE ORIGEN AFRICANO	DE ORIGEN EUROPEO	DE ORIGEN INDÍGENA
el aguacate	☐	☐	☐
el arroz	☐	☐	☐
la carne de res	☐	☐	☐
el chocolate	☐	☐	☐
los guandules (*pigeon peas*)	☐	☐	☐
la ensalada verde	☐	☐	☐
las habichuelas	☐	☐	☐
la leche de coco	☐	☐	☐
el pan	☐	☐	☐
las papas	☐	☐	☐
el pescado	☐	☐	☐
el pollo	☐	☐	☐
las salchichas (*sausages*)	☐	☐	☐

C. Los platos dominicanos. As you read, make a list of ingredients for each of the dishes mentioned. Which dishes contain many food groups by themselves, and which are typically combined with other dishes?

La cocina en la República Dominicana
por Riamny Méndez

La comida dominicana combina la creatividad y el buen gusto.

Si la comida sirve para describir los pueblos,[a] puede afirmarse que los dominicanos son creativos por naturaleza y necesidad. Elementos nativos se mezclan con ingredientes de las culturas africana y europea para preparar las recetas más exquisitas.

La dieta dominicana diaria[b] está compuesta[c] a base de arroz. La cocción[d] del arroz está clasificada en tres categorías básicas: locrio, moro y asopao.

El locrio consiste en arroz cocinado con pollo, carne de res, pescado, salchichas o mariscos y algunas veces cocido[e] en leche de coco.

El moro es una mezcla de legumbres, vegetales o granos y en ocasiones también se le agrega[f] agua de coco.

El asopao se prepara de forma parecida al locrio, pero tiene una consistencia espesa[g] y se le suele agregar cerveza. Además de[h] servir para calmar el hambre del mediodía, es ideal para reuniones de amigos y familiares.

Los granos complementan esta dieta. Se cocinan cremas de guandules y habichuelas

▲ *Los granos son un elemento importante de la dieta dominicana.*

para acompañar el arroz blanco. El arroz blanco se elabora con agua, aceite y sal. Las carnes completan por lo general el plato más común en esta media isla: arroz, habichuela y carne. A este plato también se le conoce como «la bandera dominicana», y se consume al mediodía.

Los víveres,[i] como la yuca, el plátano y el ñame también ocupan un lugar importante en los hábitos alimenticios y regularmente se sirven en la cena, sancochados[j] y acompañados de huevos o embutidos.[k] Pero, con los víveres también se preparan platos para el almuerzo o destinados a ocasiones especiales. El rey de estas comidas es **el sancocho.** El sancocho se prepara a base de carnes, maíz, yuca, plátano y otros elementos. Se utiliza regularmente cuando hay encuentros familiares u otro tipo de celebraciones. El sancocho se sirve acompañado de arroz blanco y aguacate. Su preparación es una excelente excusa para armar un «can», como se conoce en buen dominicano a un buen encuentro entre amigos. Dicen que si se acompaña de unos tragos,[l] en una madrugada lluviosa[m] sabe[n] mucho mejor y hasta invita al romance. ■

[a]*peoples; nations* [b]*daily* [c]*composed* [d]*preparation* [e]*cocinado* [f]*se… is added* [g]*thick* [h]*Además… In addition to* [i]*staples* [j]*parboiled* [k]*salchichas* [l]*drinks* [m]*rainy* [n]*it tastes*

Después de leer

A. ¿Entendiste? (*Did you understand?*)   Answer the following questions based on the reading.

1. ¿Cuáles son las tres fuentes (*sources*) principales de la cocina dominicana?
2. ¿Cuál es el ingrediente más importante en la cocina dominicana?
3. ¿Se mencionan algunos platos vegetarianos típicos?
4. ¿Qué comidas se sirven en encuentros familiares o entre amigos?

B. Las comidas y el carácter nacional.   Can you draw a connection between the North American national character and popular dishes? Brainstorm a list of popular foods from this country and choose one of the following reasons for its popularity—or add other reasons you think of.

1. Éste es un país de inmigrantes con muchos platos étnicos.
2. A los norteamericanos les gustan las novedades, las innovaciones y la originalidad.
3. Los norteamericanos trabajan mucho y no tienen tiempo para cocinar grandes comidas.
4. ¿ ?

C. Nuestros platos.   Write a multiple-choice trivia quiz in Spanish in which you test the reader's knowledge about the ingredients, occasions for serving, origins, and so on, of the most popular dishes from this country that you mentioned in the preceding activity.

Simón Bolívar, el Libertador (1783–1830)

▲ Simón Bolívar se considera el padre de la independencia de varios países sudamericanos.

Simón Bolívar was a general and statesman who played a major role in the struggle for independence from Spain of several South American countries: Bolivia, New Granada (now Colombia and Panama), Ecuador, Peru, and Venezuela. He is called **"el Libertador"** and the "George Washington of South America."

Bolívar was born in Caracas, Venezuela, inherited a fortune at a young age, and traveled throughout Europe and the United States. When he returned to Latin America, he joined the fight for independence first in Venezuela, then later in New Granada and Ecuador. In 1819, he became the first president of the Republic of Colombia, which included modern day Colombia, Ecuador, and Panama. In spite of his strong belief in a democratic form of government, Bolívar later became dictator of Peru. In 1825, a section of that country became an independent state, Bolivia, named after the general.

There are monuments to Bolívar in many South American countries, and the Venezuelan currency, **bolívar,** is named after him. His ideas for the transition from a Spanish colony to a modern democratic society are still respected today.

Do you know of any other national heroes from Latin America? Who are the national heroes of your country? Who is honored on your currency or with important monuments?

▲ El Panteón Nacional en Caracas es un monumento construido en honor de Bolívar.

PORTAFOLIO CULTURAL

Redacción

Una reseña (*review*). Show what you have learned about foods and the culture surrounding them by writing a review of a restaurant you know well. Follow the guided steps in the *Manual de práctica* to complete your review.

Exploración

Investigación cultural. Find more information about the Spanish-speaking Caribbean in your library, on the *Entrevistas* Online Learning Center (**www.mhhe.com/entrevistas2**), or elsewhere on the Internet and present it to the class. Consult the *Manual de práctica* for ideas for your presentation.

Léxico activo

¿DÓNDE COMPRAR?

la **carnicería**	butcher's shop
la **frutería**	fruit store
el **mercado (libre / del barrio)**	(farmers'/neighborhood) market
la **panadería**	bakery
la **pescadería**	fish market
el **supermercado**	supermarket
la **verdulería**	vegetable store

LA COMIDA

el **aceite de oliva**	olive oil
el **aguacate**	avocado
el **ajo**	garlic
el **arroz**	rice
el **azúcar**	sugar
la **banana**	banana
el **bistec**	steak
el **camarón**	shrimp
el **cangrejo**	crab
la **carne (de res/vaca, de cerdo)**	meat (beef, pork)
la **cebolla**	onion
el **champiñón**	mushroom
la **ensalada**	salad
el **frijol**	bean
la **fruta**	fruit
el **huevo**	egg
el **jamón**	ham
la **langosta**	lobster
la **lechuga**	lettuce
el **limón**	lemon
el **maíz**	corn

la **mantequilla**	butter
la **manzana**	apple
el **marisco**	shellfish
la **naranja**	orange
el **pan**	bread
la **papa**	potato
el **pastel**	pastry; cake; pie
el **pescado**	fish
la **pimienta**	(black) pepper
el **pimiento rojo/verde**	red/green (bell) pepper
la **piña**	pineapple
el **plátano**, la **banana**	banana
el **pollo**	chicken
el **postre**	dessert
el **queso**	cheese
la **sal**	salt
el **sándwich**	sandwich
la **sopa**	soup
el **tomate**	tomato
la **tostada**	toast
la **uva**	grape
la **verdura**	vegetable
el **vegetal**	vegetable
la **zanahoria**	carrot

LAS BEBIDAS

el **agua** (*pl.* **las aguas**) (**mineral**)	(mineral) water
el **café**	coffee
la **leche**	milk
el **té**	tea

Repaso: cerveza, refresco, vino

CAPÍTULO 5 • ¡A comer!

LAS COMIDAS DEL DÍA

el **almuerzo**	lunch
el **desayuno**	breakfast
la **merienda**	(afternoon) snack

Repaso: cena

LAS COMPARACIONES

más/menos + *adj.* + **que**	more/less + *adj.* + than
mejor(es)/peor(es) que	better/worse than
el/la/los/las más/ menos + *adj.*	the most/least + *adj.*
el/la/los/las mejor(es)/ peor(es) + *noun*	the best/worst + *noun*
tan + *adj./adv.* + **como**	as + *adj./adv.* + as
tanto/a/os/as + *noun* + **como**	as much/many + *noun* + as

LOS ADJETIVOS

agrio/a	sour
amargo/a	bitter
barato/a	inexpensive, cheap
caro/a	expensive
crudo/a	raw
delicioso/a	delicious
dulce	sweet
fresco/a	fresh
frito/a	fried
maduro/a	ripe
picante	hot, spicy
rico/a	rich; delicious
sabroso/a	tasty
salado/a	salty
seco/a	dry
tierno/a	tender
verde	green, unripe
viejo/a	old, stale

LAS CANTIDADES

la **lata**	(tin) can

algo	something
algo de*	some
algún, alguna/os/as*	some
nada	nothing
nada de*	no, not any
ningún, ninguna*	no, not any

una **copa de vino**	a glass of wine
un **poco de**	a little (of)
una **taza (de)**	a cup (of)
un **vaso (de)**	a glass (of)

LOS VERBOS

cocinar	to cook
comprar	to buy
conseguir (i)	to get, obtain
decir (*irreg.*)	to say; to tell
desear	to want, desire
freír (i)	to fry
hacer la compra	to do the shopping
medir (i)	to measure
pedir (i)	to ask for, request
recomendar (ie)	to recommend
servir (i)	to serve
tener (mucha) hambre	to be (very) hungry
traer (*irreg.*)	to bring

Repaso: almorzar (ue), cenar, desayunar, merendar (ie)

EN EL RESTAURANTE

la **cuenta**	bill, check
el/la **mesero/a**	waiter/waitress
el **plato**	(prepared) dish

LOS PRONOMBRES DE COMPLEMENTO DIRECTO

me, te, lo/la, nos, os, los/las

LENGUAJE FUNCIONAL

¿Qué desea(n) (de comer)?	What would you like to eat?
¿Qué recomienda (usted)?	What do you recommend?
¿Qué le(s) traigo (de entrada, de primer plato, de plato principal, de postre)?	What can I bring you (as an appetizer, as a first course, as a main course, for dessert)?
¿Y de beber?	And to drink?
Me gustaría(n) _____.	I would like _____.
¿Me trae _____, por favor?	Could you bring me _____, please?
¿Me pasa(s) _____, por favor?	Could you pass (me) _____, please?

___

* See the footnotes on p. 137.

Vivir bien

Bolivia

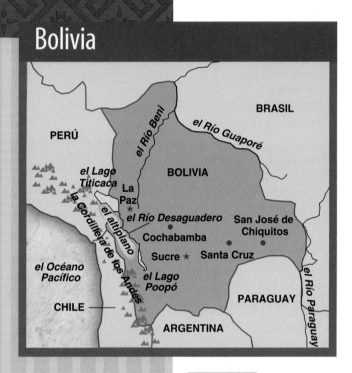

Cultura

◆ Quality of Life: Routines, Work, and Health

◆ Effect of Climate on Mood

◆ Traditional and Alternative Remedies

◆ **Señas culturales: La música indígena de Bolivia**

Lengua

◆ Telling Time

◆ Describing Your Daily Routine

◆ Describing the Weather

◆ Reflexive Pronouns (6.1)

◆ **Saber** and **conocer** (6.2)

◆ Uses of **ser** and **estar** (Summary) (6.3)

	Bolivia	Parte del Imperio inca	Los incas son vencidos por los españoles					Independencia de España
		hasta el siglo XVI	siglo XVI	1500–1600	1534	1600–1750	1776–1783	1825
	Los Estados Unidos y el Canadá	Varias tribus indígenas habitan en Norteamérica		Exploración española de Norteamérica	Jacques Cartier reclama para Francia el Canadá	Fundación de las colonias británicas en Norteamérica	Guerra de Independencia en los EE. UU.	

Instantánea

ORIGEN DEL NOMBRE

Bolivia: en honor de Simón Bolívar, «el Libertador» de Sudamérica

POBLACIÓN

8.676.000

LENGUAS

El español (oficial), el quechua, el aimara

For additional practice, check out the *Manual de práctica,* the Interactive CD-ROM, and the Online Learning Center (**www.mhhe.com/entrevistas2**)!

▲ *En Bolivia hay tiendas especializadas en remedios naturales. Las curanderas* (healers) *mantienen los conocimientos médicos de sus antepasados.*

	Guerra del Pacífico con Chile; Bolivia es derrotado		Guerra del Chaco con Paraguay		Poder devuelto al presidente electo Hernán Siles Suazo; reinstitución del gobierno civil	El aimara Víctor Hugo Cárdenas es elegido el primer vicepresidente indígena de Bolivia	Se establecen leyes para la privatización de la empresa y el mercado libre	Año de mucho conflicto social; bloqueo de transporte; la Guerra del Agua; muchos muertos	Representación indígena de casi el 30% en el parlamento
1846–1848	**1879–1884**	**1898**	**1932–1935**	**1952**	**1982**	**1993**	**1994**	**2001**	**2002**
Guerra Mexicano-Americana		Guerra Hispano-Americana		Puerto Rico se hace Estado Libre Asociado de los EE. UU.	El Canadá se separa legalmente de Inglaterra		Tratado de Libre Comercio entre los EE. UU., el Canadá y México		

La hora exacta y aproximada

Es la una en punto.

Son las siete y cuarto (quince).

Son las tres y media.

Es la una menos cuarto. (Faltan quince minutos para la una.)

a eso de la(s) _____	around _____
a medianoche	at midnight
a mediodía	at noon
a tiempo	on time
desde la(s) _____ **hasta la(s)** _____	from _____ until _____
tarde	late
temprano	early
Es la / Son las _____.	It's _____ (o'clock).
¿Qué hora es?	What time is it?
¿Tiene(s) la hora?	Do you have the time?

Lenguaje funcional
Las obligaciones

To talk about things that you have to do or should do, use the following expressions.

deber + _inf._	ought to, should (_do something_)
necesitar + _inf._	to need to (_do something_)
tener que + _inf._	to have to (_do something_)
hay que + _inf._	you (one) must (_do something_)
es necesario/importante + _inf._	it's necessary/important to (_do something_)
Es importante llegar a tiempo al trabajo.	_It's important to arrive at work on time._
Si sufres de estrés, **debes relajarte** más.	_If you are suffering from stress, you should (ought to) relax more._

Actividades

A. Los horarios bolivianos

Paso 1. Aquí se dan algunos horarios típicos en Bolivia. Léelos en voz alta (*aloud*).

1. Las oficinas gubernamentales abren (*open*) a eso de las 9:00 de la mañana.
2. El Museo de Etnografía y Folklore en La Paz está abierto (*open*) desde las 8:30 de la mañana hasta mediodía, y desde las 14:30 hasta las 18:30.
3. Los bancos cierran a mediodía para el almuerzo.
4. Las oficinas abren de nuevo (*again*) a las 2:00 y pico (*a little after*) de la tarde.
5. Algunos restaurantes abren a eso de las 8:00 de la mañana para el desayuno, y sirven la cena hasta las 10:00 de la noche.
6. En general, los negocios (*businesses*) se cierran como (*around*) a las 21:00.

Paso 2. ¿A qué hora abren y cierran estos lugares en tu ciudad/región? ¿Dónde se abren/cierran más tarde, más temprano, a la misma hora, etcétera?

B. Citas (*Appointments*) importantes.

La médico Arévalo tiene que ver a muchos pacientes esta semana. ¿A qué hora tiene que ver a las personas en la agenda?

MODELO   Raúl Martínez →
La médica tiene que ver al señor Martínez el lunes desde las 3:00 hasta las 4:00 de la tarde.

	lunes 21	martes 22	miércoles 23	jueves 24	viernes 25	sábado 26 domingo 27
08.00				Silvia Campos		
09.00		Amelia Milano 9.30				
10.00						
11.00				Violeta Donoso		
12.00			Francisco Pérez			
13.00						
14.00						
15.00	Raúl Martínez			gemelos Jiménez		
16.00	Javier Arenas					
17.00		Ezequiel Méndez				
18.00						

C. Tu horario de hoy. ¿Qué tienes que hacer hoy? ¿A qué hora? Da (*Give*) la hora exacta o aproximada, según el modelo.

MODELO   Tengo que ir al laboratorio de biología a las 3:00. Voy a estar allí hasta las 5:00 de la tarde. Después, necesito volver a casa para cocinar la cena…

D. Fijar una hora (*To set a time*).   Quieres hacer las siguientes (*following*) actividades con algunos compañeros / algunas compañeras de clase, pero es difícil fijar una hora. Trabajen en grupos de tres o cuatro estudiantes y traten de ponerse de acuerdo (*try to agree*) sobre cuándo van a reunirse (*get together*).

VOCABULARIO ÚTIL

Me parece bien/mal.	That seems fine/bad to me.
¿Qué tal (si) _____?	How about (if) _____?

1. almorzar juntos/as
2. ir al cine
3. estudiar juntos/as en la biblioteca
4. ¿ ?

🌑 La rutina diaria

Todos los días, Magdalena tiene que…

despertarse temprano.   **ducharse** y **vestirse.**   **acostarse** tarde.

afeitarse	to shave
bañarse	to bathe, take a bath
cepillarse los dientes	to brush one's teeth
dormirse* (ue)	to fall asleep
lavarse la cara (la espalda, las manos)	to wash one's face (back, hands)
levantarse	to get up
quedarse (en cama, en casa)	to stay (in bed, at home)

---

* Note the difference in meaning between **dormir** (*to sleep*) and **dormirse** (*to fall asleep*).

Actividades

A. ¿En qué orden? ¿En qué orden hace Magdalena las siguientes actividades, probablemente?

MODELOS   Prefiere _____ antes de _____.
           Le gusta _____ después de _____.

1. dormirse, despertarse, bañarse, afeitarse
2. levantarse, despertarse, hacer ejercicio, vestirse
3. ducharse, tomar una siesta, desayunar, cepillarse los dientes
4. vestirse, llegar a la universidad / al trabajo, acostarse, dar un paseo

B. ¿Una rutina saludable? Lee las siguientes descripciones e indica si cada persona lleva una vida saludable o no.

	SÍ	NO
1. María suele acostarse a las 10:30 y despertarse a las 6:30.	☐	☐
2. Juan Antonio suele levantarse a las 8:00. No desayuna, pero almuerza a las 2:00 de la tarde.	☐	☐
3. Carlos no hace mucho ejercicio. Le gusta quedarse en la cama mirando la televisión.	☐	☐
4. Gilberto no suele afeitarse los sábados.	☐	☐
5. A Olga le gusta cepillarse los dientes tres veces al día (*three times a day*).	☐	☐
6. Dolores suele acostarse tarde y dormirse en seguida.	☐	☐

C. La rutina diaria de Diego. ¿Qué tiene que hacer Diego los días de entresemana (*weekdays*)? Describe un día típico en su vida.

VOCABULARIO ÚTIL

la bata	robe	**ponerse**	to put on (*clothing*)
en seguida	right away	**tener prisa**	to be in a hurry

1.

2.

3.

4.

5.

6.

● El estrés y la relajación

divertirse (ie)	to enjoy oneself, have fun
hacer ejercicio (aeróbico)	to (do aerobic) exercise
reunirse (me reúno) con amigos	to get together with friends
seguir (i) / mantener* una rutina fija	to follow / to maintain a fixed (regular) routine
sufrir de ansiedad (estrés, insomnio)	to suffer from anxiety (stress, insomnia)
tomar un café (una cerveza, una copa)	to have coffee (a beer, a drink)
tomar una siesta	to take a siesta (nap)

Actividades

A. Tu modo de vida (*way of life*).   Haz una lista de actividades (de la sección anterior u† otras que conoces [*you are familiar with*]) que reducen el estrés y otra de actividades que lo aumentan.

B. ¿Lógico o ilógico?   Di si los siguientes consejos son lógicos o ilógicos. Si son ilógicos, sugiere (*suggest*) otros.

1. Si estás cansado/a (*tired*), tienes que cepillarte los dientes.
2. Si sufres de mucho estrés, tienes que divertirte más.
3. Si estás preocupado/a (*worried*), necesitas pasear.
4. Si tienes mucho sueño (*you're very sleepy*), debes ducharte con agua fría para despertarte.
5. Si duermes lo suficiente, es importante comer un almuerzo grande.

C. ¿Qué se debe hacer para... ?   Si una persona quiere lograr (*to attain*) las siguientes cosas, ¿qué debe hacer? Usa las expresiones de obligación que conoces y el **Vocabulario útil** para formar oraciones (*sentences*) completas.

MODELO   mantener el peso (*weight*) apropiado →
Para mantener el peso apropiado, hay que comer bien.

VOCABULARIO ÚTIL

dejar de + *inf.*	to stop (*doing something*)
empezar (ie) a + *inf.*	to begin to (*do something*)
respetar los horarios	to follow schedules

1. dormir bien
2. estar en buena forma (*shape*)
3. relajarse
4. no tener resfriado (*a cold*)
5. estar tranquilo/a
6. no tener caries (*cavities*)
7. llevar una vida saludable

---

* **Mantener** is conjugated like **tener: mantengo, mantienes, mantiene,...**
† **O** (*Or*) changes to **u** when it precedes words that begin with **o** or **ho.**

D. Señales (*Signs*) **de algo.** Completa las siguientes oraciones con información personal.

1. Estoy irritable cuando…
2. Cuando sufro de insomnio, tengo que…
3. Si no duermo lo suficiente,…
4. A veces (*Sometimes*) sufro de ansiedad cuando…
5. Tengo dolor de cabeza (*headache*) cuando…

E. Entrevista: Una vida saludable. Entrevista a un compañero / una compañera de clase para saber (*find out*) la siguiente información.

1. ¿Tienes mucho estrés en tu vida? ¿Qué haces para reducirlo? (Si no tienes mucho estrés, ¿qué haces para no tenerlo?)
2. En general, ¿llevas una vida agitada o tranquila? Explica.
3. ¿Prefieres seguir una rutina fija, o te gusta variar* (*to vary*) tus actividades? ¿Por qué?
4. ¿Pasas mucho tiempo en casa? ¿Qué haces allí?
5. ¿Haces mucho ejercicio? ¿Qué tipo(s) de ejercicio haces?
6. ¿Qué actividades haces con los amigos y cuáles haces solo/a? ¿Por qué?

Señas culturales

Éste es un fragmento de una canción (*song*) boliviana, en quechua y en español. ¿Qué emociones expresa?

Maypin kanki wawqeykuna, qapaq
pachamama Mayakuna, Inkakuna, pikuna
manan kaypiñachu

(¿Dónde están hermanos gloria de tierra,[a]
Los mayas, incas, todos aquéllos[b]
Que no están más?)

▲ *La música tradicional boliviana es popular dentro y fuera del país.*

[a]Madre Tierra (*Earth*)   [b]*those* (*peoples*)

---

* The verb **variar** is conjugated **varío, varías, varía, variamos, variáis, varían.** Note the written accents on all forms except **nosotros/as.**

You can watch this interview on the *Entrevistas* Video or Interactive CD-ROM or listen to the audio on the Online Learning Center (**www.mhhe.com/entrevistas2**).

Güido Rivera Melgar

«*Me levanto muy temprano, a eso de las 7:00…* »

Nombre: Güido

Apellidos: (1) Rivera (2) Melgar

Edad: 48 años

Nació en: Santa Cruz, Bolivia

Vocabulario útil

me levanto	I get up	**psicológicos**	psychological
me acuesto	I lie down	**la gente no planifica**	people don't plan
se respetan	they are respected/ followed	**Lo hace en el momento que se da.**	They (people) just do it when it comes up.
a la hora	on time	**la incertidumbre**	uncertainty
retrasada	behind schedule, late	**que uno se preocupe**	that one worries
reuniones f.	meetings, appointments	**por tanto**	therefore
solucionar	to solve		

Antes de ver

A. ¿Lógico o no? Di si es lógico o no hacer las siguientes actividades a la hora indicada. Si no es lógico, di a qué hora(s) tú sueles hacer cada actividad.

1. Me acuesto a las 11:30 de la mañana.
2. Ceno a las 4:00 de la tarde.
3. Almuerzo a mediodía.
4. Desayuno a las 7:00 de la mañana.
5. Salgo para la universidad a las 8:15 de la noche.

B. Actividades que relajan (*that relax*). Indica las actividades de la lista (en la siguiente página) que haces tú para relajarte. Después, ve la entrevista e indica las actividades que menciona Güido.

	YO	GÜIDO
1. tomar una siesta	☐	☐
2. hacer ejercicio / practicar deportes	☐	☐
3. pasear	☐	☐
4. reunirse con amigos	☐	☐
5. leer	☐	☐
6. mirar la televisión	☐	☐
7. escuchar música / la radio	☐	☐

¡Veamos!

¿A qué hora?   Mientras ves la entrevista, completa la siguiente tabla con la información necesaria. Si Güido no da una hora exacta, indica la hora aproximada (**a eso de las 7:00, después del desayuno,** etcétera).

Actividad	Hora
se levanta	**1.**
desayuna	**2.**
3.	a las 8:00
4.	a mediodía
toma una siesta	**5.**
regresa al trabajo	**6.**
7.	hasta las 6:00
8.	a eso de las 8:00
sale con los amigos	**9.**

Después de ver

Rutinas comparadas.   Ahora compara tu rutina diaria con la rutina de Güido.

MODELOS   Me levanto más temprano que Güido.

No tomo una siesta porque…

6.1 Reflexive Pronouns

In **Capítulo 5** you learned that many verbs in Spanish take a direct object, which may be a noun or a direct object pronoun. (Remember that when the direct object is a specific person, the **a personal** is used.)

El padre mira el coche.   *The father is looking at the car.*

El padre mira **al** hijo.   *The father is looking at his son.*

But what if the object of the verb is the same person as the subject? In English we show this relationship by using the pronouns *-self/-selves.*

I hit *myself* by accident.

They saw *themselves* on TV.

To show that the subject and direct object are the same, Spanish uses a special set of pronouns called *reflexive pronouns.*

Margarita **se mira** en el espejo.   *Margarita looks at herself in the mirror.*

Here are the forms using the verb **mirarse** (*to look at oneself* [*in a mirror*]).

mirarse			
(yo) **me miro**	I look at myself	(nosotros/as)	we look at
(tú) **te miras**	you (*fam. s.*)	**nos miramos**	ourselves
	look at yourself	(vosotros/as)	you (*fam. pl.*) look
(usted) **se mira**	you (*form. s.*)	**os miráis**	at yourselves
	look at yourself	(ustedes) **se miran**	you (*form. pl.*)
(él/ella) **se mira**	he (she, it) looks at		look at yourselves
	himself (herself,	(ellos/as) **se miran**	they look at
	itself)		themselves

These pronouns differ from direct object pronouns only in the third-person singular and plural. The infinitive includes the reflexive pronoun **se** to show which verbs are reflexive.

Reflexive verbs are used much more commonly in Spanish than in English, and at first it may not be obvious to you why certain Spanish verbs need a reflexive pronoun. For instance, in English we say *I bathe* (*take a bath*), with the understanding that it is ourselves we are bathing. In Spanish, however, this verb is always reflexive **(me baño)** unless the action is *not* being performed on oneself: **Yo baño al niño** (*I bathe the child* [*give the child a bath*]). At this point in your language study, it is best for you simply to memorize the verbs that can appear with reflexives and their meanings, rather than attempt to analyze each occurrence.

Análisis estructural

¿Dónde van los pronombres reflexivos en las siguientes oraciones: antes o después de los verbos? ¿Se aplican las mismas reglas (*rules*) a los pronombres de complemento directo o son diferentes? Explica.

1. José se ducha por la mañana.
2. Su hermana va a reunirse con los amigos a las 8:00.
3. Miguelito, tú te vas a acostar temprano esta noche.
4. Mi padre está duchándose ahora.
5. El padre de José no quiere levantarse tarde mañana.
6. Ellos se pueden dormir con la televisión a todo volumen (*on high*).
7. Para relajarme, yo trabajo en el jardín.
8. Me estoy mirando en el espejo.

Actividades

A. **¿Muchos o pocos?** ¿Quiénes hacen estas actividades —una o más personas? Convierte las oraciones plurales en singulares y viceversa.

1. Me relajo cuando doy un paseo.
2. Nos acostamos a las 10:00.
3. Mis primos se reúnen con amigos en ese café.
4. Te levantas temprano, ¿verdad?
5. Alberto no se despierta si no pone el despertador (*he doesn't set the alarm clock*).

B. Rutinas diferentes. Conjuga los verbos para formar oraciones completas con las siguientes expresiones.

1. Mi compañero (levantarse) a eso de las 6:00, pero yo no (levantarse) hasta las 8:30.
2. Juana, ¿a qué hora (acostarse)?
3. Los estudiantes (dormirse) leyendo en la biblioteca.
4. Yo no (afeitarse) todos los días.
5. Nosotros (divertirse) mucho los fines de semana.
6. El profesor siempre (vestirse) con elegancia.

C. Polos opuestos. Dolores y Teresa son hermanas, pero llevan vidas muy diferentes: Dolores es organizada, puntual e higiénica, pero ¡Teresa es un desastre! Usa las siguientes frases para formar oraciones completas sobre Dolores y Teresa. **¡OJO!** No todos los verbos son reflexivos.

MODELO   bañarse/ducharse con frecuencia →
Dolores probablemente se baña con frecuencia, pero Teresa no se baña regularmente.

1. hacer la cama todas las mañanas
2. preocuparse por (*to worry about*) la higiene
3. siempre vestirse con ropa limpia (*clean*)
4. mantener todas las cosas en su lugar
5. cepillarse los dientes después de cada comida
6. lavar los platos después de cocinar
7. lavarse las manos con jabón (*soap*) antibacterial

D. Encuesta: ¿A qué hora?

Paso 1. Hazles (*Pose*) preguntas a cinco compañeros, usando las siguientes expresiones u otras que conoces, para saber algo de su rutina diaria.

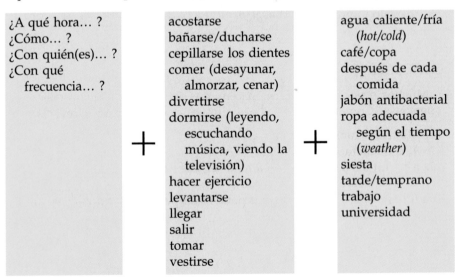

¿A qué hora... ?	acostarse	agua caliente/fría
¿Cómo... ?	bañarse/ducharse	(*hot/cold*)
¿Con quién(es)... ?	cepillarse los dientes	café/copa
¿Con qué frecuencia... ?	comer (desayunar, almorzar, cenar)	después de cada comida
	divertirse	jabón antibacterial
	dormirse (leyendo, escuchando música, viendo la televisión)	ropa adecuada según el tiempo (*weather*)
	hacer ejercicio	siesta
	levantarse	tarde/temprano
	llegar	trabajo
	salir	universidad
	tomar	
	vestirse	

Paso 2. Trabaja con el resto de la clase para hacer un resumen (*summary*) de la información. En general, ¿qué tipo de vida lleva la clase: (no) saludable, relajada/tranquila, estresada/frenética (*frantic*)?

6.2 **Saber** and **conocer**

Spanish has two verbs that can be translated in English as *to know*: **saber** (*to know facts and information*) and **conocer** (*to know [be familiar with] a person, place, or thing*). Both are regular in the present tense, except for the **yo** forms.*

saber		conocer (zc)	
sé	sabemos	conozco	conocemos
sabes	sabéis	conoces	conocéis
sabe	saben	conoce	conocen

The key to choosing the correct verb, **saber** or **conocer,** lies in *what* is known.

1. **saber** + *noun,* **saber** + **que,** or **saber** + *question word* all mean *to know facts and information*

¿**Sabes el nombre** de esta medicina?	*Do you know the name of this medicine?*
No **saben que** la oficina cierra a las 2:00.	*They don't know (that) the office closes at 2:00.*
No **sé cómo**† se llama ese doctor.	*I don't know what that doctor's name is.*

2. **saber** + *infinitive* = to know how to (*do something*)

No **saben reducir** el estrés.	*They don't know how to reduce their stress.*

3. **conocer** + **a** + *name/person* = to know, be familiar with, a person

¿**Conoces al doctor Guzmán?**	*Do you know Dr. Guzmán?*
Ellos no **conocen a mi familia.**	*They don't know my family.*

4. **conocer** + *places* or *things* = to be familiar with a place or thing

Conocemos una buena clínica en Sucre.	*We know a good clinic in Sucre.*
No **conozco ese tratamiento.**	*I'm not familiar with that treatment.*
¿**Conoces La Paz?**	*Do you know (Are you familiar with) La Paz?*

---

* Other Spanish verbs, such as **reducir** (*to reduce*), have the same **yo** form irregularity as **conocer: reduzco.** In *Entrevistas* they will be indicated by **(zc).**
† Note that the question word has a written accent mark, just as it does in normal questions.

Análisis estructural

¿Qué verbo se usa para formar preguntas sobre (*about*) las siguientes cosas?

¿Sabes...
¿Conoces...

1. a mi amigo boliviano?
2. que Bolivia tiene dos capitales: La Paz y Sucre?
3. dónde está Cochabamba?
4. el apellido del presidente de Bolivia?
5. llevar una vida saludable?
6. la fecha de la independencia de Bolivia?
7. resolver los problemas entre amigos?
8. un buen lugar para tomar un café?

Actividades

A. La Paz, Bolivia. Eres turista en La Paz y necesitas información. Completa las preguntas con la forma apropiada de **saber** o **conocer.**

1. Disculpe (*Excuse me*), señor. ¿_____ usted a qué hora abre este banco?
2. ¿_____ ustedes un restaurante chino en este barrio?
3. ¿_____ usted en qué año se construyó (*was built*) la catedral?
4. Perdone, señora, pero ¿_____ usted al dueño (*owner*) de este hotel?
5. ¿_____ ustedes llegar a la estación de trenes?

B. ¿Tienen buena memoria? Usando los eventos mencionados en la línea cronológica de las primeras páginas (*pages*) de este capítulo (págs. 152–153), pregúntales a tres o cuatro compañeros de clase si recuerdan los diferentes hechos (*facts*). **¡OJO!** Tus compañeros de clase no deben ver el libro.

MODELOS ¿Sabes el nombre de... ?

¿Sabes dónde está... ?

¿Sabes en qué año... ?

C. Entrevista: ¿Qué sabes de la salud? Entrevista a un compañero / una compañera de clase para saber si él/ella sabe cuidarse (*take care of himself/herself*) bien.

1. ¿Conoces técnicas para relajarte cuando estás estresado/a?
2. ¿Sabes dónde está el hospital más cercano (*nearest*)?
3. ¿Sabes preparar comidas saludables?
4. ¿Conoces buenos remedios para las enfermedades (*illnesses*) más comunes?
5. ¿Sabes si tienes reacciones alérgicas a alguna medicina?

Análisis cultural

La siguiente cita tomada de una fuente escrita en inglés para anglohablantes (*English speakers*) va a aumentar tus conocimientos sobre algunos fenómenos culturales en Bolivia. ¿Es consistente esta información con la perspectiva de Güido de la **Entrevista 1?** Usa lo que has aprendido (*have learned*) en este capítulo sobre Bolivia, más (*plus*) tu propia experiencia, para contestar las preguntas que siguen la cita.

❝[In] Bolivia, the concept of time has taken hold only superficially. Time-related terminology does exist but its interpretation isn't necessarily what visitors might expect. For example, **mañana,** *tomorrow,* could mean almost anytime in the indefinite future. In many places—particularly government offices—*come back tomorrow* is the equivalent of *go away and don't bother me with your problems.*

Bolivians invited to lunch on a Tuesday might arrive on a Wednesday and, by their understanding of time, may regard themselves as only a little late. You should not adopt local habits to this extent, but arriving a bit late is normal. If you're invited to a party at, say, 8:00 P.M. and you turn up at 9:00 P.M., you're likely to be the first guest to arrive . . . .**❞**

Source: *Bolivia: Lonely Planet Travel Survival Kit,* Third Edition

1. ¿Qué piensas tú del concepto del tiempo en Bolivia? ¿Crees que es una exageración?

2. ¿En qué se diferencia la opinión de este autor de lo que (*what*) dice Güido? En tu opinión, ¿quién es más creíble (*believable*)? ¿Por qué?

3. ¿Te gusta ser el primero / la primera en llegar a una fiesta? ¿Por qué sí o por qué no? Si no llegas a tiempo, ¿cuánto tiempo más tarde llegas? ¿Distingues entre ocasiones formales e informales?

Pronunciación y ortografía

● Written Accents (II)

As you saw in **Capítulo 3** (p. 78), the written accent mark in Spanish serves a number of purposes. This section expands on the basic uses presented earlier.

1. A written accent mark can distinguish two words that are otherwise spelled the same.

tu	*your*	**tú**	*you* (fam. s.)
el	*the* (m. s.)	**él**	*he*
si	*if*	**sí**	*yes*
te	*you* (object pron.)	**té**	*tea*
se	*himself, herself,* . . .	**sé**	*I know*
solo	*alone* (m. s.)	**sólo**	*only*
como	*like, as*	**¿cómo?**	*how?*
que	*that, who*	**¿qué?**	*what?*

   Dice **que** está enfermo. *He says that he is sick.*

   No sé **qué** pedir. *I don't know what to order.*

2. The accent mark also helps clarify syllabication and the pronunciation of certain vowel combinations. In Spanish, the vowels **a, e,** and **o** are considered "strong" vowels. Two adjacent strong vowels always belong to separate syllables.

   a-<u>ho</u>-ra (= [a-<u>o</u>-ra])   le-<u>er</u>   te-<u>a</u>-tro

   The other vowels, **i** and **u,** are "weak": They can be joined with an adjacent vowel to make a combination called a diphthong, in which the two vowel letters belong to the same syllable.

   bue-no   **cie**-rro   **cui**-da-do   Ma-**rio**   res-**tau**-ran-te

   In some words, however, the **i** or **u** is pronounced as a separate syllable. As you would expect, these exceptions are indicated with a written accent mark.

   grú-a   Ma-rí-a   re-ú-no   va-rí-o

The *Manual de práctica* contains activities to practice the material explained here.

● El clima

Los meses del año

enero	febrero	marzo	abril
1 2 3 4 5 6	1 2 3	1 2 3	1 2 3 4 5 6 7
7 8 9 10 11 12 13	4 5 6 7 8 9 10	4 5 6 7 8 9 10	8 9 10 11 12 13 14
14 15 16 17 18 19 20	11 12 13 14 15 16 17	11 12 13 14 15 16 17	15 16 17 18 19 20 21
21 22 23 24 25 26 27	18 19 20 21 22 23 24	18 19 20 21 22 23 24	22 23 24 25 26 27 28
28 29 30 31	25 26 27 28	25 26 27 28 29 30 31	29 30

mayo	junio	julio	agosto
1 2 3 4 5	1 2	1 2 3 4 5 6 7	1 2 3 4
6 7 8 9 10 11 12	3 4 5 6 7 8 9	8 9 10 11 12 13 14	5 6 7 8 9 10 11
13 14 15 16 17 18 19	10 11 12 13 14 15 16	15 16 17 18 19 20 21	12 13 14 15 16 17 18
20 21 22 23 24 25 26	17 18 19 20 21 22 23	22 23 24 25 26 27 28	19 20 21 22 23 24 25
27 28 29 30 31	24 25 26 27 28 29 30	29 30 31	26 27 28 29 30 31

septiembre	octubre	noviembre	diciembre
1	1 2 3 4 5 6	1 2 3	1
2 3 4 5 6 7 8	7 8 9 10 11 12 13	4 5 6 7 8 9 10	2 3 4 5 6 7 8
9 10 11 12 13 14 15	14 15 16 17 18 19 20	11 12 13 14 15 16 17	9 10 11 12 13 14 15
16 17 18 19 20 21 22	21 22 23 24 25 26 27	18 19 20 21 22 23 24	16 17 18 19 20 21 22
23 24 25 26 27 28 29	28 29 30 31	25 26 27 28 29 30	23 24 25 26 27 28 29
30			30 31

Las estaciones[a] del año

el invierno	winter	**el verano**	summer
la primavera	spring	**el otoño**	fall, autumn

¿Qué tiempo hace?

Hace frío.

Hace calor.

Hace viento.

---

[a] *seasons*

Está nublado.   Llueve.   Nieva.

hace buen/mal tiempo   it's nice/bad out(side)
hace fresco   it's cool
hace sol   it's sunny

Actividades

A. Las estaciones: norte y sur (*south*).   ¿En qué estación (estaciones) del año caen (*fall*) los siguientes meses en Norteamérica? ¿Y en Bolivia, en el hemisferio sur?

1. abril
2. agosto
3. diciembre
4. enero
5. junio
6. octubre

B. Climas diferentes.   ¿Qué tiempo asocias con los siguientes lugares?

VOCABULARIO ÚTIL

el cambio de temperatura	change in temperature
la tormenta	storm
está húmedo	it's humid (damp)
está seco	it's dry
hay hielo	it's icy
hay niebla	it's foggy

1. la selva (*jungle*) tropical
2. el desierto
3. el altiplano boliviano
4. el noroeste (*northwest*) de los Estados Unidos
5. el Mar Mediterráneo
6. la Siberia (en Rusia)
7. las montañas
8. la playa

C. Eres meteorólogo/a.   Usa la información de la siguiente tabla para describir el tiempo que hace en las diferentes regiones de Bolivia. Después haz comparaciones y contrastes entre las ciudades.

MODELOS   Hoy (*Today*) hace frío en La Paz, pero hace fresco en Cochabamba.

Está más húmedo en San José de Chiquitos que en Santa Cruz.

El tiempo: 14 de enero

Ciudad	Grados centígrados	Humedad
Cochabamba	19°	59% (por ciento)
La Paz	11°	54%
San José de Chiquitos	30°	92%
Sucre	12°	87%
Santa Cruz	27°	62%

Si te interesa

In most countries of the world, temperatures are measured in Celsius. The formula to convert from Celsius to Fahrenheit is somewhat complicated if you are unfamiliar with it; to get used to degrees Celsius it is best to memorize just a few common temperatures as points of reference.

	Celsius	Fahrenheit
boiling point of water	100°	212°
normal body temperature	37°	98.6°
good beach weather	32°	90°
average room temperature	22°	72°
freezing point of water	0°	32°

D. Entrevista: La mejor estación

Paso 1. ¿Cuál es la mejor estación del año para hacer las siguientes actividades? ¿Y el mes (los meses)? Pregúntale a (*Ask*) tu compañero/a para saber su opinión.

1. esquiar (yo esquío)
2. nadar (*to swim*)
3. caminar en las montañas
4. merendar en el parque
5. ver los colores variados de los árboles (*trees*)
6. plantar productos agrícolas

Paso 2. Ahora, pregúntale a tu compañero/a cuál es su estación favorita / mes favorito y qué hace durante ese período.

¿Cómo te afecta el clima?

La salud física y mental

Está aburrido.

Están tristes.

Está enferma.

estar cansado/a   to be tired
estar contento/a   to be happy
estar enojado/a   to be angry

Enfermedades y remedios
Estoy muy enfermo.

Tengo dolor de cabeza.

También **me duelen** las orejas.

Me duele la nariz; está congestionada.

Tengo fiebre.

Tengo **la garganta** inflamada.

Tengo que **tomar** mucha **medicina.**

sentirse (ie) bien/mal	to feel good/bad
tener gripe / resfrío (un resfriado)*	to have the flu / a cold

---

* Related expressions are **resfriarse (me resfrío)** (*to catch a cold*) and **estar resfriado/a** and **tener catarro** (*to have a cold*).

Actividades

A. El clima y la salud. ¿Qué relación existe entre el clima y los problemas médicos? Indica qué lugares geográficos, estaciones o condiciones meteorológicas se asocian con las siguientes enfermedades.

1. la malaria
2. el resfrío
3. la piel seca
4. la gripe
5. la alergia al polen
6. la deshidratación
7. la fiebre

B. ¿Cómo te sientes?

Paso 1. ¿Qué expresión describe tu estado mental en las siguientes situaciones?

VOCABULARIO ÚTIL

estoy irritado/a	I'm irritated, annoyed
estoy nervioso/a	I'm nervous
estoy preocupado/a	I'm worried

1. en la clase de _____
2. en un embotellamiento de tráfico (*traffic jam*)
3. en el consultorio (*doctor's office*)
4. en una larga cola (*long line*)
5. durante un examen
6. cuando nieva o llueve mucho

Paso 2. ¿Cómo te sientes hoy? ¿Por qué?

C. ¿Qué haces? ¿Qué actividades asocias con tus diferentes estados físicos y mentales? Usa los siguientes elementos u otros que conoces para formar oraciones completas.

MODELO   Cuando estoy enojado, me gusta hacer mucho ejercicio.

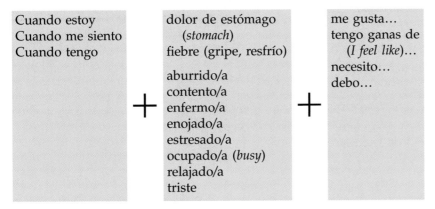

Cuando estoy
Cuando me siento
Cuando tengo

$+$

dolor de estómago (*stomach*)
fiebre (gripe, resfrío)

aburrido/a
contento/a
enfermo/a
enojado/a
estresado/a
ocupado/a (*busy*)
relajado/a
triste

$+$

me gusta...
tengo ganas de (*I feel like*)...
necesito...
debo...

D. Encuesta: Tus remedios personales. ¿Cuáles son los mejores remedios cuando tienes un resfriado? Pregúntales a cinco compañeros/as de clase para saber los remedios más comunes. (Ve el modelo en la siguiente página.)

MODELO   ir a ver al médico →
¿Vas a ver al médico cuando tienes un resfriado?

1. guardar (quedarse en) cama
2. tomar sopa de pollo
3. tomar muchos líquidos
4. tomar aspirinas, antibióticos u otras medicinas
5. ¿ ?

E. Minidrama: ¿Cuáles son sus síntomas?   Tienes algún problema y necesitas hablar con el doctor / la doctora. Con tu compañero/a de clase, inventen un diálogo entre un(a) paciente y su doctor(a). El doctor / La doctora debe usar expresiones de obligación para dar sus recomendaciones.

VOCABULARIO ÚTIL

el corazón	heart
la infección	infection
el jarabe (para la tos)	(cough) syrup
el pulmón	lung
estornudar	to sneeze
respirar	to breathe
tener el brazo roto (la pierna rota)	to have a broken arm (broken leg)
toser	to cough

Lenguaje funcional
En el consultorio

Abra la boca.	Open your mouth.
Saque la lengua.	Stick out your tongue.
Diga: «aaaa».	Say, "ahhh."
Vamos a ver.	Let's see.
¿Qué tiene hoy? / **¿Qué le pasa?**	What's wrong?
Tiene la garganta inflamada.	Your throat is inflamed (red).
Debe descansar más.	You should get more rest.
Tiene que descansar más.	You have to get more rest.

Mirtha Olmos Carballo

«*El clima en La Paz es bien*[a] *frío.*
Estamos rodeados de[b] *montañas.*»

Nombre: Mirtha

Apellidos: (1) Olmos (2) Carballo

Edad: 37 años

Nació en: La Paz, Bolivia

[a]muy [b]rodeados... *surrounded by*

You can watch this interview on the *Entrevistas* Video or Interactive CD-ROM or listen to the audio on the Online Learning Center (**www.mhhe.com/entrevistas2**).

Vocabulario útil

altura	altitude	**te cura**	cures you
ropa ligera	light clothing	**el farmacéutico me receta**	the pharmacist prescribes for me
de pronto	suddenly		
¿Cómo se curan _____?	How are _____ cured?	**la gente campesina**	people who live in rural areas
se tratan	they treat themselves	**de vez en cuando**	once in a while
la gente se cuida por sí misma	people take care of themselves on their own	**te falta**	you lack
		antes de reanudar	before resuming

Antes de ver

Los remedios naturales. Di si las siguientes oraciones son ciertas o falsas, según tu experiencia.

	CIERTO	FALSO
1. Los remedios naturales son eficaces (*effective*).	☐	☐
2. Los remedios naturales son muy caros.	☐	☐
3. Los remedios naturales saben mal.	☐	☐
4. Los remedios naturales no se encuentran (*can't be found*) fácilmente en mi ciudad/región.	☐	☐
5. El efecto de los remedios naturales es más lento (*slow*) que el efecto de las medicinas farmacéuticas (*pharmaceutical*).	☐	☐

¡Veamos!

En La Paz. Lee las siguientes preguntas para asegurar (*make sure*) que las entiendes. Después, ve la entrevista y escoge (*choose*) las respuestas apropiadas.

1. ¿Cuál es la enfermedad más común en La Paz?
   □ el dolor de cabeza   □ el resfriado   □ la malaria
2. ¿Qué oración describe mejor el clima de La Paz?
   □ Hace frío.   □ No hace sol.   □ La temperatura no cambia.
   □ Hace viento.   □ Llueve.
3. Según Mirtha, ¿por qué no van muchas personas a ver al médico cuando están resfriadas?
   □ No tienen suficiente dinero.
   □ Los tratamientos (*treatments*) no son eficaces.
   □ Creen que pueden curarse solos (*cure themselves*).
4. ¿Qué hace Mirtha cuando tiene gripe?
   □ Va a ver al médico.
   □ Se queda en casa y toma pastillas (*pills*).
   □ A veces va a la farmacia para hablar con el farmacéutico.

Después de ver

La medicina natural. ¿Por qué crees que la gente campesina prefiere tomar medicinas naturales? Indica cuál(es) de las siguientes posibilidades explica(n) este fenómeno.

□ Los hospitales en las ciudades son muy caros.
□ Las recetas farmacéuticas no son eficaces para ellos.
□ Los médicos no recetan medicinas naturales.
□ Los remedios naturales son parte importante de la cultura indígena.
□ Los campesinos no quieren o no pueden participar en el sistema nacional de salud.
□ ¿ ?

Piénsalo bien

Un amigo va a viajar (*travel*) a Bolivia y quiere hacer las siguientes actividades. ¿Qué consejos le das (*do you give him*)?

MODELOS «Soy atleta y quiero correr tres millas (*miles*) cada día.» →
Es importante acostumbrarte a (*to get used to*) la altura.

Es mejor…

(No) Debes…

1. «Quiero probar todos los platos exóticos del país.»
2. «Quiero ir a bailar a las discotecas hasta las 3:00 de la mañana.»
3. «Quiero pasar todo el día afuera (*outside*), haciendo actividades físicas.»
4. «Si me pongo enfermo, no quiero ir a ver al médico.»

6.3 Uses of **ser** and **estar** (Summary)

So far you have learned two Spanish verbs that can be translated as *to be:* **ser** and **estar.** Here is a summary of the most frequent uses of each verb.

Uses of **estar**

You have already learned various uses of the verb **estar.**

1. To talk about health.

   ¿Cómo **estás**?   *How are you?*

   Estoy bien, gracias.   *I'm fine, thanks.*

2. To express location of people and objects.

   Estamos en el hospital.   *We are in (at) the hospital.*

3. To express actions currently in progress.

   Está lloviendo.   *It's raining.*

Estar can also be used with adjectives to describe a variety of states that are in some way a change from the normal state of the subject, or to describe things that do not really have a normal way of being.

Julieta **está** nerviosa hoy.	*Julieta is (acting) nervous today.* (The use of **estar** represents a change from her normal, calm state of being.)
Ellos **están** estresados.*	*They are stressed.* (They are normally *relaxed* people.)
Este plato **está** rico.	*This dish is (tastes) delicious.* (The food in front of me tastes great, even though sometimes the recipe doesn't turn out well.)
El café **está** caliente.	*The coffee is hot.* (I just made it; it could get cold.)

---

* Note that many adjectives that end in **-ado** or **-ido** are related to verbs; for example, the adjective **relajado/a** comes from the verb **relajar.** This form is called the *past participle* of the verb, and you will study it in **Capítulo 10.** For now, just be sure not to confuse these adjectives with the *present participle*—the form of the verb that ends in **-ndo.**

Estoy **preparando** la cena.	*I'm preparing dinner.*
Estoy **preparado** para el examen.	*I'm prepared for the exam.*

Uses of **ser**

Here are the uses of **ser** you have already seen.

1. To express definition, occupation, or nationality, or otherwise equate the subject of the sentence with the word(s) following the verb.

Soy médico.*	*I'm a doctor.*
Las enfermeras **son** bolivianas.	*The nurses are Bolivian.*
Esta medicina **es** un nuevo tratamiento para la malaria.	*This drug is a new treatment for malaria.*

2. To express origin, composition, or possession.

Somos de Cochabamba.	*We're from Cochabamba.*
Los instrumentos **son de** madera.	*The instruments are (made of) wood.*
Son de María Luz.	*They belong to María Luz.*

3. To tell time.

Son las 8:20.	*It's 8:20.*

4. To indicate the time and location of events (*to take place* in English).

La operación va a **ser** en este hospital.	*The operation is going to be (take place) in this hospital.*
La reunión **es** a las 9:00.	*The meeting is (takes place) at 9:00.*

Whereas **estar** + *adjective* describes a change from the norm, **ser** + *adjective* expresses the normal condition of the subject. Compare the following examples of **ser** with the examples of **estar** you saw previously.

Julieta **es** nerviosa.	*Julieta is nervous.* (She's a nervous person.)
Este plato **es** rico.	*This dish is delicious.* (In general, I like this recipe.)
El hielo **es** frío.	*Ice is cold.* (By definition, it's a cold substance.)

Actividades

A. **Cambios de humor** (*mood*).   Completa las oraciones con información personal.

1. Normalmente soy _____, pero cuando llueve estoy _____.
2. En el invierno, frecuentemente estoy _____.
3. En el verano, siempre estoy _____.
4. Los fines de semana, normalmente estoy _____.
5. Los lunes por la mañana son _____, y yo generalmente estoy _____.

---

* Note that indefinite articles (**un, una**) are used with occupations only when modified by adjectives: **Es médico** (*He's a doctor*) but **Es un buen médico** (*He's a good doctor*).

B. Tus reacciones. ¿Cómo reaccionas en situaciones extraordinarias? Primero describe tus características mentales y físicas normales. Después, establece (*establish*) un contraste con tu estado mental o físico en una situación dada (*given*). Usa adjetivos de la lista.

MODELO   Normalmente soy tranquila, pero cuando tengo problemas de salud, estoy estresada y nerviosa.

ser	**estar**
aburrido/a (*bored*)	aburrido/a (*boring*)
delgado/a	contento/a
enfermo/a	delgado/a
feliz (*happy*)	enfermo/a
gordo/a	estresado/a
guapo/a	feliz
nervioso/a	gordo/a
sano/a (*healthy*)	guapo/a
tranquilo/a	irritado/a
triste	nervioso/a
	tranquilo/a
	triste

C. Casos específicos. Lee las siguientes situaciones y completa las descripciones con la forma apropiada de **ser** o **estar,** según la situación. Explica por qué se usa cada verbo.

1. Juan José no suele enfermarse (*get sick*), pero esta semana no se siente bien. Él _____ enfermo.

2. Mis abuelos _____ sufriendo de mucho estrés porque no tienen suficiente dinero para pagar sus gastos (*expenses*) médicos.

3. Desde muy joven, Rosalía tiene una infección crónica. Ella _____ enferma.

4. Yo no _____ seguro (*sure*), pero creo que mis padres _____ en el hospital hoy con mi hermana.

5. Después de cursar siete años de estudios, los estudiantes de medicina en Bolivia _____ preparados para ejercer (*practice*) su profesión.

D. Encuesta: Los males y problemas médicos. Hazles las siguientes preguntas a cinco compañeros. Luego, resume (*summarize*) las respuestas para presentarlas a la clase.

1. ¿Cómo son los servicios médicos en tu ciudad (región, universidad)? (bueno, malo, moderno, viejo, ineficaz, profesional, barato, caro, etcétera)
2. ¿Cuándo están abiertas las clínicas en tu ciudad (región, universidad)? ¿Son accesibles a toda hora, o es necesario hacer una cita?
3. ¿Es necesario tener seguro (*insurance*) médico para ir al hospital?
4. En tu opinión, ¿deben ser gratis (*free*) los servicios médicos en tu ciudad (región, país)? ¿Por qué sí o por qué no?
5. ¿Qué haces para prevenir (*prevent*) las enfermedades?
6. ¿En qué circunstancias vas al consultorio? ¿Qué haces si tu enfermedad no es muy grave (*serious*)?

Sobre la lectura Todo el mundo desea una alta calidad (*quality*) de vida, pero no todos están de acuerdo en qué consiste. En la siguiente lectura, la autora define varios elementos indispensable para tener buena calidad de vida y los aplica a la realidad boliviana. Mientras lees, determina las maneras (*ways*) en que la autora parece satisfecha (*satisfied*) o no satisfecha con la calidad de vida en su país.

Antes de leer

A. La calidad de vida. ¿En qué consiste la calidad de vida? Di si son importantes para ti los siguientes factores en la calidad de vida, utilizando una escala de 0 a 5 (0 = no es importante; 5 = es indispensable).

1. la salud personal y el acceso al cuidado médico
2. un buen trabajo y un buen sueldo (*wage*)
3. la familia y el hogar
4. los amigos y la vida social
5. el clima
6. una casa cómoda (*comfortable*)
7. vacaciones largas o frecuentes
8. la seguridad (*security*) y el orden públicos
9. la estabilidad política
10. los servicios tecnológicos (el teléfono, las computadoras, la electricidad, el agua corriente [*running*], etcétera)
11. los servicios municipales (el transporte público, la limpieza [*cleanliness*] de las calles, etcétera)
12. ¿ ?

B. ¿Qué tipo de problema es? Usando la lista de la **Actividad A** como una lista de categorías, di a qué categoría corresponden los siguientes problemas. **¡OJO!** Se puede aplicar algunos problemas a más de una categoría.

MODELO los atentados (*attacks*) terroristas →
Los atentados terroristas son un problema de estabilidad política.

1. las bandas (*gangs*) armadas de delincuentes
2. el calor intolerable
3. los huracanes o tornados
4. las inundaciones (*floods*)
5. los inviernos gélidos (muy, muy fríos)
6. la casa rodeada de basura (*garbage*)
7. música a todo volumen de los vecinos
8. el agua se corta (*is shut off*)
9. el miedo a los coches bomba (*fear of car bombs*)
10. los terremotos (*earthquakes*)

La calidad de vida

por Lupe Andrade Salmón

Debemos reconocer[a] que nosotros, en Bolivia, gozamos de[b] ventajas que en muchos otros países no tienen. El clima en general es benigno.[c] No nos atacan huracanes ni[d] tornados, ni terremotos ni inundaciones. En casi[e] todo el territorio boliviano, no debemos sobrevivir[f] inviernos gélidos ni veranos de intolerable calor.

▲ La Paz, Bolivia es la capital más alta del mundo. Está a unos 3.600m (casi 12.000 pies) sobre el nivel del mar.

ciento de los residentes de La Paz y casi el 50 por ciento de los bolivianos); si la electricidad no llega, no es constante, o se interrumpe;[k] si su teléfono no funciona o se corta; si no tiene acceso a transporte público confiable[l] que lo lleve hasta el trabajo (o hasta el pueblo más cercano, si usted vive en el campo); si su casa está rodeada de

Adicionalmente, somos un pueblo pacífico: podemos caminar en paz[g] por las calles, convivir[h] en relativa armonía, y dirigirnos hacia[i] la escuela o el trabajo sin miedo a coches bomba, atentados terroristas o bandas armadas de delincuentes. ¿Qué necesitamos para mejorar[j] nuestra calidad de vida y ser felices?

Pues en este tema influyen muchos factores. Si usted se levanta por la mañana y no tiene agua para bañarse (como más del 30 por

basura, su calidad de vida sufre.

Es el Municipio que influye directamente en la calidad de vida ciudadana,[m] y es directamente responsable por ella. Sin embargo, el Municipio no es una persona, sino[n] el total de recursos y fuerzas[o] ciudadanos. Para mejorar la calidad de vida, debemos exigir mayor calidad de las autoridades, pero también tenemos que mejorar la calidad de nuestro compromiso[p] con la ciudad en que vivimos. ■

[a]*recognize* [b]gozamos... *we enjoy* [c]*mild, benign* [d]*(n)or* [e]*almost* [f]*survive* [g]*peace* [h]*live together* [i]dirigirnos... *head toward, go to* [j]*improve* [k]se... *is cut off* [l]*reliable* [m]*urban, pertaining to a city* [n]*but rather* [o]*strengths* [p]*commitment*

Después de leer

A. Vivir en Bolivia. En esta lectura la autora analiza las ventajas y algunos problemas de vivir en Bolivia. Apunta (*Jot down*) por lo menos tres de las ventajas y tres de los problemas que se mencionan.

B. ¡Qué mala calidad de vida! Primero, indica las situaciones que afectan la calidad de vida, según la lectura. Después, escoge las tres que más afectan —negativamente— la calidad de vida en tu ciudad. (Hay más situaciones en la página 182.)

☐ No hay suficiente agua para bañarse.
☐ No llega —o se interrumpe— la electricidad.
☐ El teléfono no funciona o se corta la comunicación.
☐ El transporte público es irregular, no es confiable.
☐ Las calles están llenas de basura.
☐ Hay mucho ruido (*noise*) en las calles.

☐ El aire está muy contaminado (*polluted*) a causa de las industrias.
☐ Las calles están congestionadas.
☐ Hay mucha delincuencia e inseguridad ciudadana.

C. **Un tema que se repite.** Ve de nuevo las entrevistas de Güido y Mirtha. Según ellos y esta lectura, ¿cuáles son las causas principales del estrés en la vida boliviana?

☐ un ritmo duro (*difficult*) de trabajo
☐ los problemas familiares
☐ los problemas de salud
☐ la incertidumbre del trabajo
☐ la inestabilidad de los servicios básicos
☐ los problemas con los vecinos

D. **Minidrama: «¿Tiene usted una queja (*complaint*)?»** Imagina que en la estación de radio local hay un programa en el que el público puede llamar (*call*) y expresar sus quejas. Tú decides llamar para quejarte (*complain*) de la calidad de vida en tu comunidad: la cosa absolutamente más irritante para ti. Tu compañero/a es el entrevistador / la entrevistadora y debe sugerir cosas que tú puedes hacer para resolver el problema.

PORTAFOLIO CULTURAL

Redacción

Consejos. Un estudiante boliviano quiere estudiar en tu universidad por un año. Escríbele una carta en la que describes los horarios típicos, el clima y los problemas de salud más comunes de tu ciudad (región, país). Sigue los pasos en el *Manual de práctica* para completar tu carta.

Exploración

Investigación cultural. Busca más información sobre Bolivia en la biblioteca, en el *Entrevistas Online Learning Center* (**www.mhhe.com/ entrevistas2**) o en otros sitios del Internet y preséntala a la clase. El *Manual de práctica* contiene más ideas para tu presentación.

Léxico activo

LA HORA

a eso de la(s) _____	around _____
a medianoche	at midnight
a mediodía	at noon
a tiempo	on time
desde la(s) _____ **hasta la(s)** _____	from _____ until _____
en punto	on the dot
menos cuarto/quince	a quarter / fifteen minutes to
tarde	late
temprano	early

y cuarto/media	a quarter / half past
y quince	fifteen minutes past
Es la / Son las _____.	It's _____ (o'clock).
Falta(n) _____ (minuto[s]) para la(s) _____.	It's _____ (minute[s]) to _____.
¿Qué hora es?	What time is it?
¿Tiene(s) la hora?	Do you have the time?

LAS OBLIGACIONES

deber + *inf.*	ought to, should (*do something*)

necesitar + *inf.*	to need to (*do something*)
tener que + *inf.*	to have to (*do something*)
es necesario/ importante + *inf.*	it's necessary/important to (*do something*)
hay que + *inf.*	you (one) must (*do something*)

LA VIDA DIARIA

acostarse (ue)	to go to bed
afeitarse	to shave
bañarse	to bathe, take a bath
cepillarse los dientes	to brush one's teeth
despertarse (ie)	to wake up
dormirse (ue)	to fall asleep
ducharse	to shower, take a shower
lavarse la cara (la espalda, las manos)	to wash one's face (back, hands)
levantarse	to get up
quedarse (en cama, en casa)	to stay, remain (in bed, at home)
vestirse (i)	to dress, get dressed

EL ESTRÉS Y LA RELAJACIÓN

conocer (zc)	to know, be familiar with (*someone, some place, something*)
divertirse (ie)	to enjoy oneself, have fun
hacer ejercicio (aeróbico)	to (do aerobic) exercise
reunirse (me reúno) con amigos	to get together with friends
saber (*irreg.*)	to know (*facts, information*); to find out (*about something*)
saber + *inf.*	to know how to (*do something*)
seguir (i) / mantener (*irreg.*) una rutina fija	to follow / to maintain a fixed (regular) routine
sufrir de ansiedad (estrés, insomnio)	to suffer from anxiety (stress, insomnia)
tomar un café (una cerveza, una copa)	to have coffee (a beer, a drink)
tomar una siesta	to take a siesta (nap)

LOS MESES DEL AÑO

enero, febrero, marzo, abril, mayo, junio, julio, agosto, septiembre, octubre, noviembre, diciembre

LAS ESTACIONES DEL AÑO

el invierno	winter
la primavera	spring
el verano	summer
el otoño	fall

¿QUÉ TIEMPO HACE?

está nublado	it's cloudy
hace buen/mal tiempo	it's nice/bad out(side)
hace calor/frío	it's hot/cold
hace fresco	it's cool
hace sol	it's sunny
hace viento	it's windy
llueve	it's raining
nieva	it's snowing

LA SALUD FÍSICA Y MENTAL

estar aburrido/a	to be bored
estar cansado/a	to be tired
estar contento/a	to be happy
estar enfermo/a	to be sick
estar enojado/a	to be angry
estar triste	to be sad

ENFERMEDADES Y REMEDIOS

la garganta	throat
sentirse (ie) bien/mal	to feel good/bad
tener dolor de cabeza (fiebre, gripe, resfrío / un resfriado)	to have a headache (a fever, the flu, a cold)
tomar medicina	to take medicine
me/te duele(n) _____	my/your _____ hurt(s)

EN EL CONSULTORIO

el consultorio	doctor's office
el/la médico	doctor
Abra la boca.	Open your (*form. s.*) mouth.
Diga: «aaaa».	Say, "ahhh."
¿Qué tiene hoy? / ¿Qué le pasa?	What's wrong?
Saque la lengua.	Stick out your (*form. s.*) tongue.
Tiene la garganta inflamada.	Your (*form. s.*) throat is inflamed (red).
Debe / Tiene que descansar más.	You (*form. s.*) must / have to get more rest.
Vamos a ver.	Let's see.

De compras

México

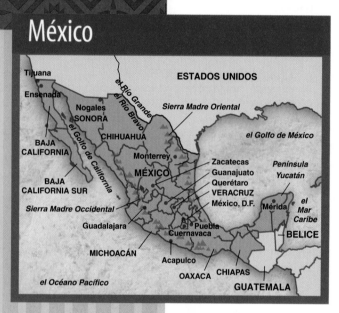

ESTADOS UNIDOS

Tijuana
Ensenada
Nogales
SONORA
CHIHUAHUA
el Río Grande
el Río Bravo
Sierra Madre Oriental
BAJA CALIFORNIA
el Golfo de California
Monterrey
MÉXICO
el Golfo de México
BAJA CALIFORNIA SUR
Sierra Madre Occidental
Zacatecas
Guanajuato
Querétaro
VERACRUZ
México, D.F.
Península Yucatán
Mérida
el Mar Caribe
Guadalajara
Cuernavaca
Puebla
MICHOACÁN
Acapulco
OAXACA
CHIAPAS
GUATEMALA
BELICE
el Océano Pacífico

Cultura

◆ Shopping and the Art of Bargaining

◆ Mexican Markets

◆ Shopping online

◆ **Señas culturales: El Museo Nacional de Antropología**

Lengua

◆ Clothing and Shopping

◆ Handcrafts and Outdoor Markets

◆ Numbers 100–9,999

◆ The Preterit (7.1)

◆ Indirect Objects and Pronouns (7.2)

◆ More About the Verb **gustar** (7.3)

◆ The Verb **quedar** (7.4)

México	Los aztecas, mayas, zapotecas y otras civilizaciones indígenas		Conquista del Imperio azteca por el español Hernán Cortés			
	hasta el siglo XVI	**1500–1600**	**1519–1521**	**1534**	**1600–1750**	**1776–1783**
Los Estados Unidos y el Canadá	Varias tribus indígenas habitan en Norteamérica	Exploración española de Norteamérica		Jacques Cartier reclama para Francia el Canadá	Fundación de las colonias británicas en Norteamérica	Guerra de Independencia en los EE. UU.

Instantánea

ORIGEN DEL NOMBRE

México: de los mexicas, un grupo indígena que habitaba (*lived*) en México antes de la llegada (*arrival*) de los españoles

POBLACIÓN

101.457.200

LENGUAS

El español (oficial), el náhuatl y otras lenguas indígenas

▲ Cargador de flores (*Flower Carrier*), *del artista mexicano Diego Rivera* (1886–1957)

For additional practice, check out the *Manual de práctica,* the Interactive CD-ROM, and the Online Learning Center (**www.mhhe.com/entrevistas2**)!

Independencia de España		Ocupación francesa; Batalla de Puebla (5 de mayo)	Benito Juárez, político y patriota indígena, es reelecto a la presidencia		Revolución Mexicana			Rebelión zapatista en Chiapas	Crisis económica causada por corrupción y escándalo en el sistema bancario	Vicente Fox es elegido el primer presidente no priísta desde 1910
1821	**1846–1848**	**1863**	**1867**	**1898**	**1910–1917**	**1952**	**1982**	**1994**	**1998–1999**	**2000**
	Guerra Mexicano-Americana			Guerra Hispano-Americana		Puerto Rico se hace Estado Libre Asociado de los EE. UU.	El Canadá se separa legalmente de Inglaterra	Tratado de Libre Comercio entre los EE. UU., el Canadá y México		

En el almacén[a]

La ropa

el impermeable   el reloj   la camisa   la chaqueta   el suéter

el abrigo

los calcetines

los (pantalones) vaqueros

los pantalones   los zapatos   la corbata

la ropa interior   el cinturón

el sombrero

la blusa

la falda

la camiseta

las medias

la bolsa	purse
las botas	boots
la cartera	wallet
los pantalones cortos	shorts
el traje (de baño)	(bathing) suit
el vestido	dress
los zapatos de tenis	tennis shoes
llevar	to wear (*clothing*)
ponerse (*irreg.*)	to put on (*clothing*)
regalarle	to give (*something to someone*) as a gift
es/son de	it is / they are (made of)
algodón	cotton
cuero	leather
lana	wool
seda	silk

[a]*department store*

Los colores

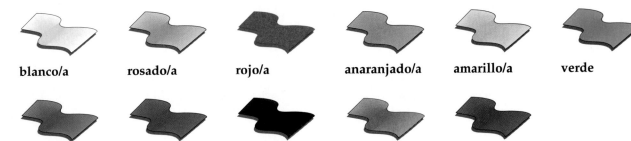

blanco/a   **rosado/a**   **rojo/a**   **anaranjado/a**   **amarillo/a**   **verde**

azul   **morado/a**   **negro/a**   **gris**   **pardo/a**

La joyería[a]

el anillo (de diamantes)	(diamond) ring
el arete	earring
el collar (de plata)	(silver) necklace
el pendiente	earring; pendant
la pulsera (de oro)	(gold) bracelet

Actividades

A. ¿Qué prenda es?   Tu profesor(a) va a describir varias prendas de ropa (*articles of clothing*). Adivina (*Guess*) qué prenda describe.

VOCABULARIO ÚTIL

cargar	to carry
cubrir	to cover
de nailon	(made of) nylon
una clase de	a type of

B. ¿De qué material es?   ¿Qué material(es) asocias con los siguientes artículos? Forma oraciones completas.

MODELO   los pantalones →
Los pantalones son de algodón o de lana.

VOCABULARIO ÚTIL

la mezclilla	denim
la pana	corduroy
el poliéster	polyester
el nailon	nylon

1. el anillo
2. la pulsera
3. las medias
4. la camisa
5. el suéter

6. el abrigo
7. los calcetines
8. los vaqueros
9. la cartera

---

[a]*jewelry*

De compras • CAPÍTULO 7

C. **¿Qué te pones?** ¿Qué ropa y otros artículos te pones en las siguientes situaciones?

MODELO Para _____ me pongo _____.

VOCABULARIO ÚTIL

la gorra	cap
el pijama	pajamas
el saco	sport coat
los zapatos de tacón alto	high-heeled shoes

1. la cama
2. la clase de español
3. un concierto de música clásica
4. una entrevista de trabajo
5. una fiesta con amigos
6. los sábados por la mañana en casa

D. **¿Qué ropa llevan?** Describe la ropa que llevan las personas en las siguientes fotos. ¿Adónde va cada persona, probablemente?

MODELO La mujer a la derecha lleva _____. Probablemente va a _____ para _____.

1.
Los indígenas mexicanos llevan ropa tradicional y también ropa moderna.

2.
Estudiantes mexicanos de Querétaro

3.
De vacaciones en el centro de México

E. **El regalo perfecto.** ¿Qué tipo de cosas les regalas a las siguientes personas? Compara tus ideas con las de un compañero / una compañera de clase.

1. a tus abuelos (hijos, nietos, padres)
2. a un compañero / una compañera
3. a tus hermanos (primos, sobrinos)
4. a tu mejor amigo/a
5. a tu novio/a (esposo/a)
6. a tu profesor(a) de español

● En la tienda

el probador
la caja
el dependiente
la dependienta
el cliente
la cliente
el mostrador

el centro comercial	shopping center, mall
el descuento	discount
la ganga	bargain
la rebaja	reduction
la tienda (especializada)	(specialty) store, shop
cambiar (por)	to exchange (for)
devolver (ue)	to return (*something*)
mostrarle (ue)	to show (*something to someone*)
probarse (ue)	to try on
quedarle bien/mal	to fit well/poorly
quedarle grande / pequeño/a	to be too large/small
quitarse	to take off (clothing)

Si te interesa

In **Capítulo 5** you saw that the names of many specialty shops are formed by adding the suffix **-ería** to the word that describes the store's main product (sometimes with changes to the root word).

carne → carnicería
fruta → frutería

What do you think you can find in each of the following shops?

una florería
una perfumería
una zapatería

Actividades

A. Definiciones. Lee las siguientes definiciones y di a qué se refieren (*they refer*).

1. Es la persona que trabaja en una tienda.
2. Es una reducción en el precio (*price*) de un artículo en una tienda.
3. Es una persona que compra en un almacén o una tienda.
4. Es el lugar donde se exhiben anillos, aretes, collares y pulseras.
5. Es un grupo de tiendas modernas en el mismo lugar.
6. Es el lugar donde se prueba la ropa.
7. Es lo que haces en un mercado para conseguir los precios más baratos.

B. ¿Qué están diciendo? Lee las siguientes oraciones y di a qué dibujo corresponde cada una.

1. _____ ¡Me queda muy grande!
2. _____ Me quedan pequeñas.
3. _____ ¿Me muestra éste, por favor?
4. _____ Tienes que quitarte éstos para ponerte los otros.
5. _____ Quiero cambiar éste por uno de ésos.

a.

b.

c.

d.

e.

C. Diálogo: En la tienda. Representa un diálogo entre un dependiente / una dependienta (tu compañero/a de clase) y un(a) cliente (tú). Tú buscas (*are looking for*) los siguientes artículos en un almacén grande.

1. zapatos de tenis
2. un traje o vestido para una ocasión especial
3. un regalo para un amigo / una amiga

Lenguaje funcional
En la zapatería

D:[a]	**¿En qué puedo servirle?**	How may I help you?
C:[b]	**Busco zapatos elegantes para una boda.**	I'm looking for elegant shoes for a wedding.
D:	**¿Qué tal éstos aquí?**	How about these (ones) here?
C:	**Me gustan mucho.**	I like them a lot.
D:	**¿Qué número* lleva?**	What size do you wear?
C:	**Llevo el veintisiete.**	I wear size 27.
D:	**Aquí los tiene.**	Here you go.
C:	**¿Cuánto cuestan?**	How much do they cost?
D:	**Cuestan cuatrocientos pesos.**	They cost 400 pesos.
C:	**¿Aceptan tarjetas de crédito?**	Do you take credit cards?
D:	**Sí, por supuesto.**	Yes, of course.
C:	**Bueno, me los llevo.**	OK, I'll take them.

[a]Dependiente/a   [b]Cliente

Si te interesa
Los números de zapato en México

En México, se usan dos sistemas de números de zapato. Existe un sistema de «números» que *no* corresponde ni al sistema norteamericano ni al sistema europeo. Pero también existe un sistema basada en la largura[a] en centímetros del pie de la persona. La siguiente tabla muestra las conversiones aproximadas de algunos números de zapato.

Sistema	Números de zapato										
mexicano											
números	4	4,5	5	5,5	6	6,5	7	7,5	9	10	11
centímetros	24	24,5	25	25	25,5	25,5	26	26,5	27,5	28	28,5
norteamericano											
mujeres	7	7,5	8	8,5	9	9,5	10	10,5	12	13	14
hombres	5,5	6	6,5	7	7,5	8	8,5	9	10,5	11,5	12,5
europeo	37,5	38	38,5	39	40	41	42	43	43,5	44	44,5

[a]*length*

---

* Se dice **número** para los zapatos y **talla** para la ropa.

You can watch this interview on the *Entrevistas* Video or Interactive CD-ROM or listen to the audio on the Online Learning Center (**www.mhhe.com/entrevistas2**).

Minerva Rubio Andalón

«El tianguis es un mercado sobre ruedas.»

Nombre: Minerva

Apellidos: (1) Rubio (2) Andalón

Edad: 34 años

Nació en: México, D.F., México

Vocabulario útil

¿Adónde fuiste?	Where did you go?	**huaraches** *m.*	traditional Mexican sandals
pude	I was able		
considerable [accesible]	reasonable	**los necesitaba**	she needed them
		¿Qué le regalaste... ?	What did you give her as gift . . . ?
un mercado sobre ruedas	a market on wheels		
colonia	neighborhood	**Navidades** *f.*	Christmas (Holiday) season
se mueve	it moves	**le regalé...**	I gave her . . .
un llavero	a key chain	**una muñeca**	doll
¿Qué compraste... ?	What did you buy . . . ?	**un carro a control remoto**	a remote control car
encontré	I found		

Antes de ver

A. ¿En el centro comercial o en el tianguis? Minerva va a hablar de las compras que hizo ayer en el centro comercial y en el tianguis. Lee las siguientes oraciones e indica cuáles probablemente se aplican a un centro comercial y cuáles a un tianguis.

	CENTRO COMERCIAL	TIANGUIS
1. «Primero fui a un… »	☐	☐
2. « …las cosas son un poco más caras.»	☐	☐
3. «Mi lugar favorito es… »	☐	☐
4. « …pude encontrar el regalo perfecto… »	☐	☐
5. « …puedes encontrar cosas muy interesantes.»	☐	☐
6. « …puedes encontrar… todo lo que necesitas en un mismo lugar.»	☐	☐

Si te interesa

In this interview Minerva talks about **el tianguis,** an open-air market similar to **un mercado de barrio** commonly found in Mexico. Look at the photo (p. 193) of one **tianguis.** How would you describe it? What types of items do you think can be bought there? How is it different from **un centro comercial**? Are there any similarities?

B. Ayer, no hoy. En esta entrevista, vas a oír (*hear*) las formas del pasado de algunos verbos. Mira los siguientes verbos en el presente y el pasado (en la forma de **yo**) mientras tu profesor(a) los pronuncia en voz alta. Después, combina las formas del pasado con los complementos apropiados para formar oraciones lógicas completas.

PRESENTE	PASADO		COMPLEMENTOS
busco	busqué		muy buenos zapatos
compro	compré		ropa
hago	hice		a un centro comercial
decido	decidí	**+**	un collar y una pulsera
encuentro	encontré		a diferentes lugares
regalo	regalé		mi actividad favorita
voy	fui		ir a otro lugar
			un(a) _____ para _____

MODELO   Ayer busqué un collar y una pulsera.

¡Veamos!

¿Acertaste? (*Were you right?*) Mientras ves la entrevista, compara tus respuestas de la **Actividad B** de **Antes de ver** con lo que dice Minerva. ¿Acertaste bien?

Después de ver

¿Qué compró? (*What did she buy?*) A continuación (*Following*) hay una lista de los miembros de la familia de Minerva y otra lista de lo que compró. Ve de nuevo la entrevista e indica qué compró Minerva para cada persona. ¿Compró Minerva algo para sí misma?

LA FAMILIA

1. _____ su hija
2. _____ su hermana
3. _____ su sobrina
4. _____ su sobrino

LAS COMPRAS

a. una muñeca
b. huaraches
c. un carro electrónico
d. una pulsera

▲ *Disculpe, ¿a cuánto* (how much) *son las pulseras?* (*En un tianguis en México D.F.*)

🌑 7.1 The Preterit

So far in your study of Spanish you have spoken only about the present (using present tense verb forms) and the future (using present tense verb forms or **ir** + **a** + *infinitive*). However, you have seen a number of past tense verb forms: **compré** (*I bought*), **decidí** (*I decided*), **nació** (*he/she was born*), and so on. These are *preterit* forms of the verbs **comprar, decidir,** and **nacer (zc).** The preterit is one of two tenses used to express actions in the past; you will learn about the other, the imperfect, in **Capítulo 9.**

Forms of Regular Verbs

Here are the regular preterit forms of **-ar, -er,** and **-ir** verbs.

	llevar	**devolver (ue)**	**recibir**
(yo)	**llevé**	**devolví**	**recibí**
(tú)	**llevaste**	**devolviste**	**recibiste**
(usted, él/ella)	**llevó**	**devolvió**	**recibió**
(nosotros/as)	**llevamos**	**devolvimos**	**recibimos**
(vosotros/as)	**llevasteis**	**devolvisteis**	**recibisteis**
(ustedes, ellos/as)	**llevaron**	**devolvieron**	**recibieron**

NOTES:

- The endings for **-er** and **-ir** verbs are identical in all persons.
- **-Ar** and **-er** verbs that have **ie** and **ue** stem changes in their present tense forms do not show these changes in the preterit. (You will study a different change in **-ir** verbs in **Capítulo 8.**)
- You will learn about other types of spelling changes in **Pronunciación y ortografía;** for now, just focus on recognizing and producing the correct sound.

Basic Uses

The differences in meaning between the two past tenses in Spanish—the preterit and the imperfect—are subtle; learning to distinguish between the two can be a long-term enterprise for English speakers. There is no single verb form in English that corresponds exactly to the preterit in Spanish. However, all the uses of the preterit share one important element: They focus on completed actions.

Compré estas botas en el almacén ayer.	*I bought these boots yesterday.*
Devolví esa camisa a la tienda el fin de semana pasado.	*I returned that shirt to the store last weekend.*

Specifically, the preterit is used in three main situations.

1. To narrate a series of completed actions in the past: Each action in the series is completed before the next happens; each must end before the next begins. Transition words, such as **primero, después, luego, por fin,** and so on, help signal this use of the preterit.

Primero el dependiente me **mostró** un vestido verde, pero **luego decidí** comprar una falda azul.	*First the clerk showed me a green dress, but later I decided to buy a blue skirt.*

2. To express completed actions that lasted for a precise period of time, with a definite start and/or finish: Note the use of phrases that indicate an exact time period.

Tardamos media hora en llegar.	*It took us half an hour to get there.*
Estudié por tres horas.	*I studied for three hours.*
Se quedó con nosotros **todo el verano.**	*He stayed with us all summer long.*

3. To mark the beginning of a new state or condition: Some verbs like **conocer, poder, saber,** and others usually express states, as opposed to action verbs like **bailar, comer, salir,** and so on. When such state verbs are used in the preterit, they refer to the moment when the state or condition began and thus have a special translation into English.*

Yo **conocí** a tus padres anoche.	*I met (started to know) your parents last night.*

Análisis estructural

Varias personas hicieron (*did*) las siguientes actividades ayer, y repiten las mismas acciones hoy. Cambia los verbos en el pretérito por la forma correspondiente del presente.

1. Salí a un centro comercial.
2. Bebieron café y refrescos en una cafetería.
3. Tomaste una copa con tus amigos.
4. Visitó a sus abuelos en Guadalajara.
5. Comimos en un restaurante elegante.
6. Le escribiste una carta a un amigo canadiense.
7. Encontró una ganga increíble en el almacén.
8. Jugó al básquetbol.
9. Almorcé en la cafetería estudiantil.
10. Prepararon una cena magnífica.

---

* You will learn about more irregular translations of the preterit in **Capítulo 10.**

Actividades

A. En el tianguis. Conjuga los verbos entre paréntesis en el pretérito para describir qué pasó un día en el tianguis.

1. El vendedor de flores (abrir) su puesto a las 6:00 de la mañana.
2. Los panaderos (sacar) los panes del horno.
3. Mi madre y yo (llegar) a las 7:30.
4. Nosotros (ver) muchos colores y muchos productos diferentes.
5. Mis amigos (hablar) con un vendedor de CDs.
6. Tú (encontrar) una ganga en un puesto de ropa.
7. Dos personas (regatear) con el hombre, pero éste no (rebajar) mucho los precios.
8. Yo (comprar) un periódico y lo (leer) en un puesto de tacos.

B. Fuera de lo normal. Cambia los verbos en el presente por el pretérito para completar las oraciones.

1. Normalmente compro ropa en el centro comercial, pero ayer la _____ en el tianguis.

2. En general, mi prima lleva ropa de moda (*fashionable*), pero anoche (*last night*) _____ un vestido muy viejo.

3. Siempre buscamos regalos baratos, pero ayer _____ un regalo muy especial para una ocasión importante.

4. En general, tú no devuelves las cosas defectuosas a las tiendas, pero la semana pasada _____ varias prendas, ¿verdad (*right*)?

5. Normalmente yo no me pruebo las prendas en la tienda, pero el otro día me _____ ese traje.

6. Ellos no suelen recibir regalos de sus nietos, pero la Navidad pasada _____ un sillón para el salón.

C. De compras. Escribe cinco o seis oraciones para describir la última vez que fuiste de compras, usando el pretérito de los siguientes verbos. Organiza la narración con palabras de transición como **primero, después, luego, finalmente,** etcétera.

cenar	ir (yo fui)	tomar un café
comer un pastel	mostrar	ver (yo vi) a un
comprar	pagar (yo pagué) con	amigo / una
decidir	cheque (efectivo,	amiga
desayunar	tarjeta de crédito)	¿ ?
encontrar	probarse	
hacer (yo hice)	salir	

D. Entrevista: ¿Y tú? Usando los verbos de la **Actividad C,** pregúntale a un compañero / una compañera sobre la última vez que él/ella fue (*went*) de compras.

MODELO   E1: ¿Qué compraste?
          E2: Compré muchas cosas: pantalones, zapatos,…

 7.2 Indirect Objects and Pronouns

You already know that Spanish, like English, uses a special set of pronouns to replace the direct object (the *who?* or *what?* associated with a verb) when that object has been explicitly or implicitly referred to. Unlike English, however, Spanish uses a different set of pronouns to express the *indirect object* of the verb, which tells *to whom* or *for whom* the action of the verb is performed.

SUBJECT	VERB	INDIRECT OBJECT	DIRECT OBJECT	
		(*to whom?*)	(*what?*)	
I	gave	*my mother*	*a datebook*	for her birthday.

Here are the indirect object pronouns in Spanish.

Los pronombres de complemento indirecto			
me	to/for me	**nos**	to/for us
te	to/for you (*fam.*)	**os**	to/for you (*fam. pl.*)
le	to/for him (her, you) (*form.*)	**les**	to/for them/you (*form. pl.*)

Indirect object pronouns differ from direct object pronouns only in the third-person forms **(le, les).**

Like direct object pronouns, indirect object pronouns can precede a conjugated verb or be attached to the end of an infinitive or present participle (the **-ndo** form of the verb). Remember that when a pronoun is attached to a present participle, a written accent must be added to the participle to maintain the stress on the correct syllable.

Él **me** regaló una agenda.	*He gave me a datebook.*
Te va a regalar (Va a regalar**te**) un CD.	*He is going to give you a CD.*
La profesora **le** está explicando (está explic**á**ndo**le**) la gramática a una estudiante.	*The professor is explaining the grammar to a student.*

For clarity or emphasis, indirect object nouns and pronouns can be accompanied by a prepositional phrase (**a mí, a él,** and so on) that repeats the same person as the indirect object noun or pronoun. Note the special forms **a mí** (with accent, to distinguish it from the possessive **mi**) and **a ti** (no accent mark).

A mí me regaló un libro.	*He gave me a book.*
A mi hermano le compré un CD.	*I bought my brother a CD.*

Since **le** and **les** can refer to so many different people (*him, her, it, you* [form.], and *you* [pl.] and *they*), these two pronouns are almost always used in conjunction with a prepositional phrase.

Los padres **les** regalaron **a sus hijos** un estéreo nuevo.	*The parents gave their children a new stereo.*
El dependiente **le** mostró un vestido elegante **a la cliente.**	*The salesperson showed the customer an elegant dress.*
¿**A quién le** vas a regalar ese anillo?	*Who are you going to give that ring to?*

Many verbs that are useful for talking about shopping and gift giving take indirect objects. **¡OJO!** Many of these verbs also take direct objects— you *buy* something (direct) for someone (indirect), *show* something (direct) to someone (indirect), *ask* something (direct) of someone (indirect), and so on. Here is a list of some common verbs that take indirect objects.

comprar	to buy	hacer una	to ask/pose a
dar	to give	pregunta	question
enseñar	to teach	mostrar (ue)	to show
enviar (yo envío)	to send	ofrecer (zc)	to offer
escribir	to write	preguntar	to ask
explicar	to explain	preparar	to prepare
hablar	to speak;	regalar	to give as a gift
	to talk	vender	to sell

Análisis estructural

Identifica los sujetos (S), complementos directos (CD) y complementos indirectos (CI) en las siguientes oraciones. Cuando hay una frase preposicional, conecta las dos partes del complemento indirecto como en el modelo.

MODELO   El dependiente <u>le</u> mostró <u>un vestido elegante</u> a la cliente.
　　　　　　　 S　　 CI　　　　　　 CD　　　　　 CI

1. El profesor les ofreció a los estudiantes puntos (*points*) extra en el examen.
2. Nuestros padres siempre nos dan dinero para los cumpleaños.
3. La profesora me explicó la respuesta.
4. El vendedor les imprimió un recibo (*printed a receipt*) a los clientes.
5. A los mejores clientes les preparamos un plato especial.

Actividades

A. ¡Qué detalle! (*How thoughtful!*)   La palabra **detalle** significa *detail* en inglés, pero también quiere decir **un gesto considerado** (*a considerate act*) en español. Contesta las siguientes preguntas. Luego, calcula tu puntaje (*points earned*) y compara tus resultados con la escala (*scale*) para saber si eres una persona **con mucho detalle** o no.

	NUNCA	A VECES	SIEMPRE
1. ¿Les escribes a tus amigos?	☐	☐	☐
2. ¿Les explicas las tareas a tus compañeros de clase cuando tienen dificultades?	☐	☐	☐
3. ¿Recuerdas las fechas de los cumpleaños de tus parientes y amigos?	☐	☐	☐
4. ¿Les envías regalos a tus abuelos (hijos, padres)? ¿A tus primos y tíos?	☐	☐	☐
5. ¿Envías tarjetas personalizadas con los regalos?	☐	☐	☐
6. ¿Les compras flores a tus amigos en ocasiones especiales?	☐	☐	☐

PUNTAJE

Cada respuesta **siempre** = 2 puntos.
Cada respuesta **a veces** = 1 punto.
Cada respuesta **nunca** = 0 puntos.

ESCALA

9–12 puntos: Eres una persona con mucho detalle. ¡Qué bien!

5–8 puntos: No está mal. Eres bastante considerado/a.

0–4 puntos: Casi nunca piensas en los demás. ¡Eres un desastre como amigo!

B. Un día en Querétaro.   Usa los siguientes elementos para formar oraciones completas. **¡OJO!** Los verbos se conjugan en el pretérito.

1. tú **/** comprar **/** regalos **/** a tus amigos
2. nosotros **/** hacer **/** algunas preguntas **/** a los vendedores del tianguis
3. yo **/** escribir **/** una tarjeta postal **/** a ti **/** desde Querétaro
4. los tacos del tianguis **/** parecer **/** a mí **/** estupendos
5. ellos **/** enviar **/** a mi hermano y a mí **/** paquetes para nuestro negocio
6. el vendedor de frutas **/** mostrar **/** las papayas **/** a ustedes

C. ¿A quién?   Usando las siguientes frases, forma oraciones completas para describir las cosas que hiciste para diferentes personas. **¡OJO!** Tienes que añadir los pronombres de complemento indirecto.

MODELO   Le compré a mi papá un reloj nuevo. (A mi papá le compré un reloj nuevo.)

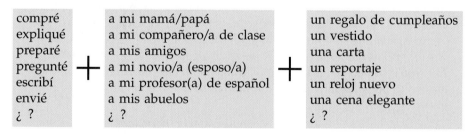

compré
expliqué
preparé
pregunté
escribí
envié
¿ ?

+

a mi mamá/papá
a mi compañero/a de clase
a mis amigos
a mi novio/a (esposo/a)
a mi profesor(a) de español
a mis abuelos
¿ ?

+

un regalo de cumpleaños
un vestido
una carta
un reportaje
un reloj nuevo
una cena elegante
¿ ?

D. Entrevista: Los regalos.   Entrevista a un compañero / una compañera de clase para saber la siguiente información sobre los regalos. Después, ustedes deben comparar los resultados con los del resto de la clase.

1. ¿Qué les regalaste a tus padres (abuelos, hijos) para su cumpleaños (aniversario)?

2. ¿Qué te regalaron tus amigos recientemente?

3. ¿Sueles comprarles regalos a tus compañeros/as de clase? ¿a tus profesores? ¿Por qué sí o por qué no?

4. ¿Cuánto pagas por regalos para las ocasiones especiales: la Navidad, el Januká, el cumpleaños, el bar/bat mitzvah, el aniversario, la graduación, etcétera?

5. En tu cultura, ¿es aceptable abrir un regalo delante de (*in front of*) la persona que te dio (*gave*) ese regalo?

E. Opiniones sobre los regalos. Completa las siguientes oraciones con las expresiones de la derecha (u otras que conoces) para indicar tus opiniones.

1. Cuando una persona que no conozco bien me regala algo,...

2. Si un amigo / una amiga me regala algo muy caro,...

3. Si un amigo / una amiga o mi familia se olvida de (*forgets about*) mi cumpleaños,...

+

(no) me siento triste.
(no) me gusta.
(no) tengo que comprarle un regalo también.
(no) me avergüenza (*embarrass*).
(no) me importa mucho.

Análisis cultural

Las siguientes citas tomadas de fuentes escritas en inglés para anglohablantes van a aumentar tus conocimientos sobre algunos fenómenos culturales en México. ¿Es consistente esta información con la perspectiva de Minerva de la **Entrevista 1?** Usa lo que has aprendido en este capítulo sobre México, más tu propia experiencia, para contestar las preguntas que siguen las citas.

❝One of the main shopping venues in Mexico is **el mercado,** the market. Virtually every town and city has at least one, sometimes housed in a centrally located **Mercado Municipal** building provided by city government. Market stalls are rented by vendors hawking everything from fresh meat to furniture, while sidewalk vendors cluster along the surrounding streets. Large cities feature several daily markets scattered around the city.

Smaller village communities may contain only an open space or plaza where vendors gather one day a week or on weekends. An open-air market of this type is sometimes called by its Nahautl name, **tianguis.** Even if you're not looking to buy, Mexican markets are worth a stroll for color and ambience alone.❞

Source: *Mexico Handbook,* Second Edition

❝Bargaining will stretch your money even farther. It comes with the territory in Mexico and needn't be a hassle. On the contrary, if done with humor and moderation, bargaining can be an enjoyable path to encountering Mexican people and gaining their respect, and even friendship.

The local crafts market is where bargaining is most intense. For starters, try offering half the asking price. From there on, it's all psychology: you have to content yourself with not having to have the item. Otherwise, you're sunk; the vendor will probably sense your need and stand fast. After a few minutes of good-humored bantering, ask for **el último precio** (the "final price"), which, if it's close, you may have a bargain.**99**

Source: *Pacific Mexico Handbook,* Third Edition

1. ¿Dónde están los mercados que se describen en la primera cita? ¿Qué cosas se venden allí? ¿Hay mercados así en tu ciudad/región?

2. ¿Quiénes hacen sus compras en estos mercados, principalmente?

3. Según la primera cita, ¿por qué es bueno ir a los mercados en México?

4. Según la segunda cita, ¿por qué es bueno regatear en México? ¿Cómo se regatea con los vendedores mexicanos? ¿Cómo se termina el regateo?

5. ¿Te gusta esta costumbre? ¿Por qué sí o por qué no? ¿Qué ventajas y desventajas tiene?

6. ¿En qué lugares o situaciones es aceptable regatear en tu ciudad/región? ¿Dónde no es aceptable nunca?

◀ *¿Qué tipos de productos se venden en esta tienda de Toluca, México? ¿Cómo son los productos, probablemente?*

De compras • CAPÍTULO 7

This section examines two important aspects of the Spanish spelling system that affect how verb forms are written in the preterit.

● Written Accents (III)

If you are not yet convinced of the importance of written accent marks in Spanish, learning the preterit forms of verbs should do the trick. Confusion would ensue if a reader saw **compro** (the present tense **yo** form) instead of **compró** (the preterit, **usted/él/ella** form). The two forms sound different to the ear, and in writing the accent mark is essential to distinguish them.

Remember that in words that end in a vowel, the stress normally falls on the second-to-last syllable. The preterit endings **-é, -í, -ó,** and **-ió** must, therefore, have a written accent to show that they deviate from the expected pattern of pronunciation.

Verb forms of only one syllable do not need this accent mark in the **yo** and **usted/él/ella** forms of the preterit: **vi, vio** (from **ver**).

● Consonant + Vowel Combinations

The vowels **e** and **i** affect the pronunciation of certain consonants that precede them. Since these two vowels are common in preterit endings, spelling changes occur when writing some preterit forms in order to preserve the sound of the verb stem. For example, the [k] sound in **buscar** is spelled with the letter **c** in the infinitive and in the present tense: **busco, buscas,** and so on. In the **yo** form of the preterit, however, the verb undergoes a spelling change, **busqué,** to retain the [k] sound of the verb stem. Without the spelling change, the word would be incorrectly written as **buscé** and would be pronounced with an [s] sound rather than a [k] sound.

Similar changes occur in verbs that have infinitives ending in **-zar (z → c)** and **-gar (g → gu).**

Infinitivo	Presente	Pretérito
bus**c**ar	yo bus**c**o	yo bus**qué**
comen**z**ar	yo comien**z**o	yo comen**cé**
lle**g**ar	yo lle**g**o	yo lle**gué**

These preterit verb forms with spelling changes are not really irregular; they are the *only* way to maintain the sound of the verb stem. From now on in *Entrevistas*, verbs with these preterit spelling changes will be indicated in vocabulary lists with **(qu), (gu),** and **(c).** Verbs that have both stem and spelling changes will be indicated as follows: **comenzar (ie) (c), negar (ie) (gu),** and so on.

The *Manual de práctica* contains activities to practice the material presented here.

En el mercado de artesanías[a]

▲ ¿Te gustan las artesanías que están vendiendo estas mujeres en Toluca, México?
¿Por qué sí o por qué no?

Me gusta ir de compras al **mercado de artesanías.** Allí **se venden** muchas cosas hechas por[b] los indígenas. La mayoría **está hecha a mano,**[c] y todas las cosas son de alta **calidad.** Es decir, **están hechas muy bien.** No suelen **costar** mucho, y puedes **regatear** para conseguir un precio mejor. Generalmente, los vendedores no aceptan tarjetas de crédito; tienes que **pagar** en efectivo.

¿Cuánto cuesta?

100 **cien***	500 **quinientos/as**[†]	1.000 **mil**[‡]
105 **ciento cinco***	600 **seiscientos/as**	2.000 **dos mil**
200 **doscientos/as***	700 **setecientos/as**[†]	3.849 **tres mil ochocientos**
300 **trescientos/as**	800 **ochocientos/as**	**cuarenta y nueve**[§]
400 **cuatrocientos/as**	900 **novecientos/as**[†]	

---

[a]mercado... *handicrafts market*   [b]hechas... *made by*   [c]a... *by hand*

* Remember that **cien** becomes **ciento** in the numbers 101–199. 200–900 agree in gender with the nouns they describe: **doscientas casas.**

[†] Note the irregular forms **quinientos, setecientos,** and **novecientos.**

[‡] Use a period to separate thousands and hundreds, and a comma to indicate decimals (e.g., 3.512,95).

[§] Use the connector **y** only between tens and ones.

Actividades

A. ¿Cuánto cuestan?

Paso 1. ¿Cuánto cuestan los siguientes artículos en pesos (*Mexican currency*)?

1. la muñeca de trapo (*rag*)   **2.** los objetos de plata   **3.** el sarape   **4.** la vasija de barro (*clay pot*)   **5.** los alebrijes (animales de madera)

Paso 2. ¿Cuánto cuestan los mismos artículos en tu región, típicamente? Usa la tasa de cambio actual (*current exchange rate*) entre pesos y la divisa (*currency*) de tu país para comparar los precios en tu región con los precios mexicanos.

B. Diferentes lugares de compras.
¿Dónde encuentras los siguientes artículos, en **el mercado de artesanías,** en **el centro comercial** o en **ambos lugares?** Clasifica los artículos según tu experiencia y añade otros.

1. una muñeca de trapo
2. un recipiente de barro
3. una cerámica
4. un sarape
5. una escultura (*sculpture*)
6. una máscara (*mask*)
7. un bastón (*walking stick; cane*)
8. un juguete (*toy*)
9. una guayabera (*short-sleeved, embroidered cotton shirt*)
10. un espejo
11. una alfombra
12. un anillo de plata
13. ropa de última moda (*the latest fashions*)
14. unos zapatos

C. Entrevista: A comprar regalos.
Estás en un mercado de artesanías con un compañero / una compañera. Pregúntale qué les compra a las siguientes personas. Él/Ella tiene que explicar el porqué (*why*) de sus respuestas.

MODELO   E1: ¿Qué le compras a tu padre?
                E2: Le compro alebrijes porque le gusta el arte popular.

1. tus padres (amigos)
2. tu mejor amigo/a
3. tu profesor(a) de español
4. un compañero / una compañera de clase
5. los padres de tu novio/a (esposo/a, mejor amigo/a)
6. tus abuelos (tíos)

D. Un lugar para reunirse

Paso 1. En México, es muy común reunirse en los parques y los mercados públicos. Lee las siguientes oraciones y di si estas actividades son comunes en el lugar donde tú vives.

1. Los adolescentes pasean con sus amigos en el parque.
2. Los niños comen helados y dulces (*candy*) en la calle.
3. Las señoras mayores chismean (*gossip*) de las familias en el mercado.
4. Los hombres discuten deportes y política en la cantina de la esquina.
5. Los jóvenes van al centro comercial sólo para comprar, no para reunirse.

Paso 2. Entrevista a un compañero / una compañera de clase para saber la siguiente información.

1. ¿Dónde ocurren tus encuentros sociales principales (en las fiestas en casa, en el centro comercial, etcétera)? ¿Por qué te gusta reunirte con tus amigos/as en ese lugar?
2. Cuando te reúnes con tus amigos/as o con tu familia, ¿qué temas prefieren comentar (*to discuss*)?

Señas culturales

▲ En el Museo de Antropología (Ciudad de México) hay una maqueta (*mock up*) de Tenochtitlán, la antigua capital de los aztecas.

El Museo Nacional de Antropología se fundó en 1825. El edificio actual fue terminado[a] en 1964 por el arquitecto Pedro Ramírez Vázquez.

Además de la colección de objetos antropológicos, el museo contiene una biblioteca, un archivo de películas, auditorios públicos y una escuela que organiza conferencias y cursillos.[b]

En tu región/país, ¿hay un museo nacional que exhiba objetos de valor[c] histórico o cultural? ¿Qué contiene? ¿Qué debe contener, en tu opinión?

[a]fue... *was completed*   [b]*short courses; seminars*   [c]*value*

You can watch this interview on the *Entrevistas* Video or Interactive CD-ROM or listen to the audio on the Online Learning Center (**www.mhhe.com/entrevistas2**).

Martín Delfín Lira

« *...hay una cosa que se llama sarape, ... Hay otra cosa que son platos pintados a mano.*[a] »

Nombre: Martín

Apellidos: (1) Delfín (2) Lira

Edad: 38 años

Nació en: Zacatecas, México

[a]platos... *hand-painted plates*

Vocabulario útil

lo que necesites	whatever you may need	**zonas turísticas**	tourist areas
medallas	medals	**no se relaciona**	does not interact
para detenérselo	to hold it back		

Antes de ver

¿Dónde compras?   Lee las siguientes oraciones e indica qué comercio (*business*) en tu ciudad se describe. **¡OJO!** Algunas oraciones pueden describir más de un tipo de comercio.

- **a.** el supermercado
- **b.** el centro comercial
- **c.** el centro (*downtown*)
- **d.** el *farmers' market*

1. _____ Tiene de todo.

2. _____ Tiene los precios más bajos.

3. _____ Hay comerciantes (*businesspeople*) individuales.

4. _____ Hay tiendas especializadas.

5. _____ Hay productos hechos por artistas regionales.

6. _____ Hay prendas de ropa.

7. _____ A los extranjeros les gusta ir de compras allí.

¡Veamos!

¿Y en México?   Ahora ve la entrevista de Martín e indica qué tipo de comercio en México se describe.

	CENTRO COMERCIAL	MERCADO DE ARTESANÍAS
1. Se encuentra en las zonas turísticas.	☐	☐
2. Se venden sarapes.	☐	☐
3. Parece que estás en este país.	☐	☐
4. Se venden medallas.	☐	☐
5. La gente va a comprar, no a relacionarse con otros.	☐	☐
6. Se venden productos hechos por los indígenas.	☐	☐

Después de ver

Las costumbres (*customs, habits*)

Paso 1. Lee las siguientes oraciones sobre las costumbres. ¿Cuáles son ciertas para ti? Después, ve la entrevista otra vez e indica cuáles son ciertas para los mexicanos, según Martín.

	YO	LOS MEXICANOS
1. Suelo comprar artesanía local.	☐	☐
2. Suelo reunirme con mis amigos/as en el centro comercial.	☐	☐
3. Voy al centro comercial solamente para comprar.	☐	☐

Paso 2. Ahora compara tus respuestas del **Paso 1** con lo que dijo (*said*) Martín sobre los mexicanos.

MODELOS   Yo suelo… pero los mexicanos…

Yo voy… y los mexicanos también…

Yo no suelo… y los mexicanos no suelen hacerlo tampoco (*either*).

Piénsalo bien

Compara los comentarios de los mexicanos de este capítulo con los de Karina del **Capítulo 5.** Usa las siguientes preguntas como guía (*guide*).

1. ¿Son similares los mercados de México a los de la República Dominicana?
2. ¿Qué tienen en común?
3. ¿En qué se diferencian?

7.3 More About the Verb **gustar**

In **Capítulo 2,** you learned to ask and answer basic questions about likes and dislikes using the patterns **me gusta(n)** and **te gusta(n).**

—¿**Te gustan** estos zapatos?	*Do you like these shoes?*
—Sí, **me gustan** mucho.	*Yes, I like them a lot.*

Here are the patterns for expressing other people's preferences in the present tense.

Usos de *gustar* en el presente	
(A mí) **Me gusta regatear.**	I like to haggle over prices.
(A ti) **Te gustan las muñecas.**	You (*fam.*) like dolls.
(A usted) **Le gusta la música latina.**	You (*form.*) like Latin music.
(A él/ella) **Le gusta comprar regalos.**	He/She likes buying gifts.
(A nosotros/as) **Nos gustan las gangas.**	We like bargains.
(A vosotros/as) **Os gusta el mercado.**	You (*fam. pl. Sp.*) like the market.
(A ustedes) **Les gusta el centro comercial.**	You (*form. pl. Sp.*) like the mall.
(A ellos/as) **Les gusta la última moda.**	They like the latest fashion.

NOTES:

- Pay special attention to the word before **gusta(n)** in the preceding examples. You should recognize these as the indirect object pronouns **(me, te, le, nos, os, les).** Don't confuse them with the reflexive pronouns **(me, te, se, nos, os, se),** because you should *never* use **se** in a **gustar** construction.

- As you saw in **Parte 1** of this chapter, you can clarify or emphasize indirect objects with prepositional phrases (**a mí, a él, a nosotros,** and so on).

- In this construction, nouns (the things you like) must be preceded by the appropriate definite article **(el/la/los/las)** when you are describing likes or dislikes in general.

- You can express a preference between two items by adding **más que** to a sentence with **gustar.**

Me gusta el mercado **más que** el centro comercial.	*I like the market more than the mall.*

Análisis estructural

Completa las siguientes oraciones con el elemento que falta (*is missing*): una forma del verbo **gustar,** un pronombre de complemento indirecto o una frase preposicional con **a.**

1. A Ramón _____ gusta ir de compras al tianguis.
2. _____ no me gustan los artículos importados.
3. A mis padres les _____ la ropa informal.
4. A nosotros _____ gusta reunirnos con amigos en el centro comercial.
5. ¿_____ te gusta esta chaqueta?
6. A Silvia le _____ las muñecas de trapo del mercado de artesanías.

Actividades

A. ¿A quién le gusta? Combina las expresiones de ambas columnas, y otras que conoces, para describir los posibles gustos de las siguientes personas. **¡OJO!** Tienes que añadir los pronombres de complemento indirecto.

MODELO   A mi padre le gustan las camisas de algodón.

¿A QUIÉN?

1. a mí
2. a mi madre
3. al líder de este país
4. a los comerciantes
5. a Luis Miguel*
6. a los estudiantes de esta universidad

¿QUÉ?

los trajes elegantes
la música latina
discutir la política
llevar ropa informal
las prendas más modernas
¿ ?

Si te interesa

Gustar does not mean *to like,* even though sentences with **gustar** are often translated with this English verb.

Me gustan   *I like*
   las fiestas.   *parties.*

Its meaning is closer to the phrase *to be pleasing to.* Thus, the *object* of an English sentence (the thing someone likes, in this case, *parties*) is actually the *subject* of a Spanish sentence (*Parties are pleasing to me.*). Do not be confused by the fact that subjects often are placed *after* the verb in Spanish (as in a sentence such as **Llamó Teresa.** = *Teresa called.*). Even though the plural noun **las fiestas** appears after the verb **gustan,** we know that it is really the subject of the sentence because the verb suffix **-n** shows plural agreement. The pronoun **me,** of course, is an indirect object pronoun that indicates who is pleased.

Lenguaje funcional
Todos los gustos

Just like English, Spanish has expressions to indicate varying degrees of like and dislike. The following expressions can be used to indicate strong likes and dislikes.

¡Me encanta ese sombrero!	*I love that hat!*
¡No me gusta para nada!	*I don't like it at all!*

Note that **encanta(n)** is used mostly with *things,* not *people.* For *people,* use **querer (ie).**

Te **quiero** mucho.	*I love you a lot.*

---

* Luis Miguel is a popular contemporary Mexican singer.

B. Minidrama: En busca de regalos. Tu amigo/a quiere comprarle un regalo a su mejor amigo/a, pero no sabe qué regalarle. Tú eres dependiente/a en un almacén y le haces preguntas para ayudarlo/la (*help him/her*).

Paso 1. Escribe cinco preguntas para saber qué tipo de música, películas, libros, etcétera, prefiere el amigo / la amiga de tu compañero/a. Pídele más vocabulario a tu profesor(a) si es necesario.

MODELO ¿A tu amigo le gusta la música clásica?

VOCABULARIO ÚTIL

el/la cantante	singer
el/la escritor(a)	writer
los libros intelectuales/prácticos	intellectual/practical books
la música clásica/rock	classical/rock music
las novelas románticas	romance novels
las películas de acción/terror	action/horror films

Paso 2. Representa la situación con tu compañero/a. Al final, el/la «cliente» debe escoger el regalo perfecto.

Paso 3. Cambien papeles (*Switch roles*), tomen dos minutos para prepararse y actúen (*act out*) el drama otra vez.

● 7.4 The Verb **quedar**

The verb **quedar** has many translations in English and is found in several different sentence patterns. Here are the most common.

1. In **Capítulo 6,** you saw that **quedar,** when used with a reflexive pronoun **(quedarse),** means *to stay, remain.*

Me quedo en casa los viernes.	*I stay at home on Fridays.*
Los comerciantes **se quedan** en su quiosco todo el día.	*The merchants stay in their kiosks all day.*

2. In this chapter, you have used **quedar** like **gustar,** with indirect object pronouns, to mean *to fit.* **Quedarle** can also mean *to have left, have remaining;* context will make it clear which meaning is intended. As with **gustar,** only the third-person verb forms are used in this way; note the singular-plural agreement between the verb and the subject.

Esta chaqueta **me queda** bien.	*This jacket fits me well / looks good on me.*
Sólo **me quedan** trescientos pesos.	*I have only 300 pesos left.*

3. **Quedar** by itself can be used instead of **estar** to express location.

El cine **queda** al lado del tianguis.	*The movie theater is next to the market.*

Análisis estructural

¿Qué tipo de pronombre se usa en las siguientes oraciones: pronombre de complemento indirecto o pronombre reflexivo?

1. Yo *me* quedé con mis amigos en Guanajuato.
2. Esos zapatos *le* quedan pequeños.
3. No *me* queda más dinero.
4. *Nos* quedamos en casa toda la noche.
5. ¿*Te* quedan bien esas botas?

Actividades

A. La ropa apropiada. Usa las siguientes frases, y añade los pronombres necesarios, para hacer oraciones completas. Luego, di cuáles de las oraciones son ciertas, en tu opinión.

1. a las modelos / quedar / bien / las minifaldas
2. a los comerciantes / quedar / ridículo / los pantalones cortos
3. a mí / quedar / mal / los vaqueros
4. a nosotros / quedar / perfecto / la ropa mexicana
5. al profesor (a la profesora) de español / quedar / bien / la ropa elegante

B. ¿Le queda bien? Di qué ropa les queda bien y qué ropa les queda mal a las siguientes personas.

MODELO a mi padre →
A mi padre le quedan bien los pantalones cortos, pero le quedan mal los vaqueros.

1. a mi madre
2. a mi mejor amigo/a
3. a las personas altas
4. a la gente joven
5. a los mayores
6. al profesor (a la profesora) de español

◀ *¿Te gustan las botas? Las botas son populares, especialmente en el norte de México donde hay mucha influencia ranchera.*

Lectura

 Sobre la lectura En esta lectura vas a leer las opiniones de algunos usuarios (*users*) de un sitio de subastas (*auction site*), *Mitiendita.mx*. Luego, vas a comparar las experiencias de estos usuarios mexicanos con tus propias experiencias haciendo compras en línea.

Antes de leer

A. Vender y comprar en línea. Usando los siguientes comentarios y tus propias experiencias de hacer compras en línea, di cuáles son algunas ventajas y desventajas de vender y comprar en línea.

VENTAJAS

☐ Los precios son bajos.
☐ Siempre encuentro lo que busco.
☐ Tiene una gran selección de productos.
☐ El diseño del sitio es muy bueno.
☐ Los productos llegan rápido.
☐ Es económico vender y comprar.

DESVENTAJAS

☐ Tienes que investigar antes de comprar.
☐ Algunos vendedores no son confiables.
☐ No encuentro nada bueno.
☐ El sistema de seguridad es malo.
☐ El producto nunca llega.

B. Opiniones. *Mitiendita.mx* utiliza un sistema de sonrisas (*smiles*) para evaluar las experiencias de los usuarios: Cinco sonrisas indican la mejor experiencia y una es la peor. Indica cuántas sonrisas corresponden a los siguientes comentarios, en tu opinión.

	☺	☺ ☺	☺ ☺ ☺	☺ ☺ ☺ ☺	☺ ☺ ☺ ☺ ☺
1. «Es un fraude.»	☐	☐	☐	☐	☐
2. «Su sistema de venta y compra es excelente.»	☐	☐	☐	☐	☐
3. «No me puedo quejar.»	☐	☐	☐	☐	☐
4. «¡Es algo increíble!»	☐	☐	☐	☐	☐
5. «Puede ser mucho mejor.»	☐	☐	☐	☐	☐
6. «Más o menos… »	☐	☐	☐	☐	☐
7. «¡Son ladrones (*thieves*)!	☐	☐	☐	☐	☐

Después de leer

A. ¡Verifica! Revisa tus respuestas de la **Actividad A** de **Antes de leer.** ¿Corresponden a las sonrisas que indicaron los usuarios? ¿Qué puntaje le das tú al sitio *Mitiendita.mx*, basándote en (*based on*) los comentarios de los usuarios?

·········· Mitiendita.mx ··········

¡Es un fraude!
Por: <u>Roberto</u> (10-IX-2003)
Puntaje: ☺
Lo bueno[a]: No encontré nada bueno.
Lo malo[b]: Su sistema de seguridad es malísimo.
El año pasado mi hermano compró una laptop en Mitiendita.mx y nunca nos llegó nada de nada. Pagamos 4.000 pesos (la mitad del precio) pero nunca llegó. ¡Son ladrones!

· · · · · · · · ·

¡Realmente EXCELENTE!
Por: <u>Joaquín</u> (13-XI-2003)
Puntaje: ☺ ☺ ☺ ☺ ☺
Lo bueno: Todo es excelente.
Lo malo: Nada. ¡Todo es excelente!
En mi opinión su sistema de venta y compra es excelente. Además tiene excelente promoción y siempre encuentras lo que buscas a un precio magnífico. Todos los días visito Mitiendita.mx. ¡Es algo increíble! ¡Completamente recomendable!

· · · · · · · · ·

¡No me puedo quejar!
Por: <u>Alicia</u> (12-X-2003)
Puntaje: ☺ ☺ ☺ ☺
Lo bueno: Es económico vender y comprar allí.
Lo malo: Tienes que investigar antes de comprar.
Mitiendita.mx es un excelente lugar para vender y comprar. Compré allí CDs de animé y figuras de acción y me va de maravilla.[c] No me puedo quejar. Al comprar, tienes que ver la reputación del usuario, éste puede tener una calificación alta y aun así no ser confiable. En resumen, Mitiendita.mx es el mejor de los sitios de subastas aquí en México.

· · · · · · · · ·

Más o menos...
Por: <u>Iris</u> (05-X-2003)
Puntaje: ☺ ☺ ☺
Lo bueno: Es fácil de usar. Siempre encuentras lo que buscas.
Lo malo: Debes saber con quién tratas.[d]
Tiene una gran cantidad de productos, tiene precios muy bajos y las ofertas normalmente empiezan desde un peso. Este sitio es recomendable para personas que buscan *comics* porque tiene una gran cantidad y a un buen precio. Y algunas veces *comics* muy viejos a un buen precio. Pero hay que prestar atención[e] porque en algunos casos los vendedores no son confiables. Debes saber con quién tratas.

· · · · · · · · ·

Puede ser mucho mejor.
Por: <u>Pascual</u> (03-IV-2003)
Puntaje: ☺ ☺
Lo bueno: Muy poco.
Lo malo: No puedes encontrar lo que buscas.
Yo no sé por qué dicen que el sitio es muy bueno, cuando no tiene muchas cosas que ver. Si buscas algo, encuentras muy pocas cosas, así que no te dan oportunidad de escoger. Además, no encuentras fácilmente los precios de los productos.

[a]Lo... *The good* (thing)   [b]Lo... *The bad* (thing)   [c]me... *it's working great for me*   [d]con... *whom you're dealing with*   [e]prestar... *pay attention*

B. Evaluaciones. Usa la siguiente tabla para evaluar la opinión de cada usuario sobre las siguientes categorías del servicio de *Mitiendita.mx*.

5 = Le encanta.   0 = No le gusta para nada.   ND = No dice.

Categoría	Roberto	Joaquín	Alicia	Iris	Pascual
Seguridad					
Precios					
Cantidad					
Selección de productos					
Agentes					

C. Experiencias personales. Cuenta a la clase tu experiencia con una compra reciente que hiciste. ¿Adónde fuiste? ¿Qué encontraste? ¿Les recomiendas la tienda (el mercado, el sitio, etcétera) a otras personas? ¿Por qué sí o por qué no?

PORTAFOLIO CULTURAL

Redacción

Una guía de compras. Diseña una guía de compras de tu ciudad para turistas. ¿Cuáles son los lugares más interesantes? ¿Dónde se consiguen los mejores precios? ¿Qué productos especiales se ofrecen? Sigue los pasos en el *Manual de práctica* para completar tu guía.

Exploración

Investigación cultural. Busca más información sobre México en la biblioteca, en el *Entrevistas Online Learning Center* (**www.mhhe.com/ entrevistas2**) o en otros sitios del Internet y preséntala a la clase. El *Manual de práctica* contiene más ideas para tu presentación.

Léxico activo

LA ROPA

el **abrigo**	overcoat
la **blusa**	blouse
la **bolsa**	purse
las **botas**	boots
los **calcetines**	socks
la **camisa**	shirt
la **camiseta**	T-shirt
la **cartera**	wallet
la **chaqueta**	jacket
el **cinturón**	belt
la **corbata**	tie
la **falda**	skirt
el **impermeable**	raincoat

las **medias**	stockings
los **pantalones**	pants
los **pantalones cortos**	shorts
los **(pantalones) vaqueros**	jeans
el **reloj**	watch
la **ropa interior**	underwear
el **sombrero**	hat
el **suéter**	sweater
el **traje (de baño)**	(bathing) suit
el **vestido**	dress
los **zapatos (de tenis)**	(tennis) shoes

LOS COLORES

amarillo/a	yellow
anaranjado/a	orange
blanco/a	white
gris	gray
morado/a	purple
pardo/a	brown
rosado/a	pink

Repaso: azul, negro/a, rojo/a, verde

LOS MATERIALES

es/son de	it's / they are (made of)
algodón	cotton
cuero	leather
lana	wool
seda	silk

LA JOYERÍA

el anillo (de diamantes)	(diamond) ring
el arete	earring
el collar (de plata)	(silver) necklace
el pendiente	earring; pendant
la pulsera (de oro)	(gold) bracelet

EN EL ALMACÉN / LA TIENDA

el almacén	department store
la caja	cash register; check-out
el centro comercial	shopping center, mall
el/la cliente	customer
el/la dependiente/a	salesperson
el descuento	discount
la ganga	bargain
el mostrador	display counter
el precio	price
el probador	dressing room
la rebaja	reduction
la tienda (especializada)	(specialty) store, shop
cambiar (por)	to exchange (for)
devolver (ue)	to return (something)
llevar	to wear (clothing)
mostrarle (ue)	to show (something to someone)
ponerse (irreg.)	to put on, wear
probarse (ue)	to try on
quedar	to be (located)
quedarle bien/mal	to fit well/poorly

quedarle grande/ pequeño/a	to be too large/small
quitarse	to take off
regalarle	to give (something to someone) as a gift

EN EL MERCADO DE ARTESANÍAS

la calidad	quality
el mercado de artesanías	handicrafts market
costar (ue)	to cost
estar hecho/a a mano	to be made by hand
estar hecho/a bien/mal	to be well/poorly made
pagar (gu)	to pay
regatear	to bargain

Repaso: en efectivo

¿CUÁNTO CUESTA?*

doscientos, trescientos, cuatrocientos, quinientos, seiscientos, setecientos, ochocientos, novecientos, mil, dos mil

Repaso: cien, ciento cinco

EN LA ZAPATERÍA

¿En qué puedo servirle?	How may I help you?
Busco _____.	I'm looking for _____.
¿Qué tal éste/a/os/as aquí?	How about this (one) / these (ones) here?
Me gusta(n) mucho.	I like it/them a lot.
¿Qué número/talla lleva?	What's size (shoes/ clothing) do you wear?
Llevo _____.	I wear _____.
Aquí lo/la/los/las tiene.	Here you go.
¿Cuánto cuesta(n)?	How much does it / do they cost?
Cuesta(n) _____.	It costs / They cost _____.
¿Aceptan tarjetas de crédito?	Do you take credit cards?
Sí, por supuesto.	Yes, of course.
Bueno, me lo/la/los/ las llevo.	OK, I'll take it/them.

TODOS LOS GUSTOS

encantarle	to love (a thing)
querer (ie)	to love (someone)
¡No me gusta(n) para nada!	I don't like it/them at all!

---

*See the footnotes on p. 203.

Ritmos de la vida

Puerto Rico

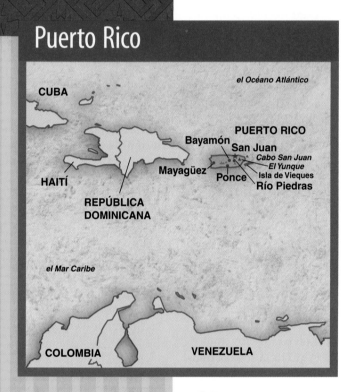

el Océano Atlántico

CUBA

PUERTO RICO
Bayamón
San Juan
Cabo San Juan
El Yunque
Mayagüez
Isla de Vieques
Ponce
Río Piedras

HAITÍ

REPÚBLICA
DOMINICANA

el Mar Caribe

COLOMBIA   VENEZUELA

Cultura

◆ Sports in Puerto Rico

◆ Your Social Circle

◆ New Year's Resolutions

◆ **Señas culturales:** Roberto Clemente

Lengua

◆ Sports; Fun and Pastimes

◆ Irregular Forms of the Preterit (8.1)

◆ Stem-Changing Verbs in the Preterit (8.2)

◆ Negative Words (8.3)

◆ Using Direct and Indirect Object Pronouns
Together (8.4)

Puerto Rico		Las tribus indígenas arauaca y caribe habitan en la isla	Llegada de Cristóbal Colón					Economía basada en las plantaciones cede paso a la exportación de los productos cultivados en ellas	
	hasta el siglo XVI	hasta 1493	1493	1500–1600	1534	1600–1750	1776–1783	1830
Los Estados Unidos y el Canadá		Varias tribus indígenas habitan en Norteamérica		Exploración española de Norteamérica	Jacques Cartier reclama para Francia el Canadá	Fundación de las colonias británicas en Norteamérica	Guerra de Independencia en los EE. UU.	

Instantánea

ORIGEN DEL NOMBRE

Puerto Rico (*Rich Port*): Los españoles llamaron la isla así por su esperanza (*hope*) no realizada de encontrar allí metales preciosos como el oro y la plata.

POBLACIÓN

3.949.200

LENGUAS

El español y el inglés (oficiales)

◀ *El fútbol es el deporte más popular de Hispanoamérica y en otras partes del mundo también. Aquí se ve un partido entre dos universidades puertorriqueñas.*

For additional practice, check out the *Manual de práctica,* the Interactive CD-ROM, and the Online Learning Center (**www.mhhe.com/entrevistas2**)!

	Guerra Hispano-Americana; Puerto Rico se convierte en territorio de los EE. UU.	Se les concede la nacionalidad estadounidense a los puertorriqueños	Puerto Rico se hace Estado Libre Asociado de los EE. UU.			Por tercera vez la mayoría puertorriqueña vota en contra de la unión total a los Estados Unidos		Se protestan los bombardeos y ejercicios militares por la Marina estadounidense en la Isla de Vieques
1846–1848	**1898**	**1917**	**1952**	**1982**		**1994**	**1998**	**1999**
Guerra Mexicano-Americana	Guerra Hispano-Americana			El Canadá se separa legalmente de Inglaterra		Tratado de Libre Comercio entre los EE. UU., el Canadá y México		

● Los deportes

¿Qué deportes practicas?

acampar

andar en bicicleta

bucear

correr

escalar montañas

esquiar

esquiar (en al agua)

hacer artes marciales

jugar al baloncesto/ básquetbol

jugar al béisbol

jugar al fútbol americano

jugar al fútbol

jugar al golf

jugar al tenis

jugar al voleibol

nadar

levantar pesas

montar a caballo

patinar sobre hielo

surfear

el/la aficionado/a	fan	la natación	swimming
el ciclismo	cycling	el partido	game, match
el/la deportista	sports-minded person	ganar	to win
el equipo	team	perder (ie)	to lose
la equitación	horseback riding	practicar (qu) un deporte	to practice a sport
el esquí	skiing; ski		
el/la jugador(a)	player		

Actividades

A. ¿Qué deporte?   ¿Qué deporte(s) se describe(n) en cada oración?

1. Este deporte se juega al aire libre (*outside*).
2. Este deporte se juega dentro de un edificio.
3. Para practicar este deporte, hay que tener una pelota (*ball*).
4. Este deporte se practica en el invierno.
5. Este deporte se practica en el verano.

B. Lugares ideales.   A muchos deportistas les gusta ir a los siguientes lugares para practicar su deporte. ¿Qué deporte(s) se practica(n) en cada lugar?

1. las montañas
2. la playa
3. el gimnasio
4. el estadio
5. la piscina
6. un parque nacional

C. Deportistas famosos.   ¿Qué deporte asocias con las siguientes personas? Forma oraciones completas. Si no sabes a qué deporte juega alguna persona, pregúntaselo a tu profesor(a).

VOCABULARIO ÚTIL

el/la boxeador(a)	boxer
el boxeo	boxing

1. Shaquille O'Neal
2. Sammy Sosa
3. Beatriz «Gigi» Fernández
4. Pelé
5. José Canseco
6. Kristi Yamaguchi
7. Marcelo Ríos
8. Carlos Ortiz
9. Picabo Street
10. Juan «Chi Chi» Rodríguez
11. Tiger Woods
12. Dan Marino

D. Entrevista: Deportes y aficionados

Paso 1. Entrevista a un compañero / una compañera para saber la siguiente información.

1. ¿Eres aficionado/a a algún deporte? ¿Cuál?
2. ¿Cuál es tu equipo favorito? ¿Por qué?
3. ¿Con qué frecuencia vas a ver partidos? ¿Cuántos miras por televisión o escuchas por radio?
4. ¿Quién es tu jugador favorito / jugadora favorita? ¿Por qué te gusta?

Paso 2. Ahora pregúntale a tu compañero/a sobre la última vez que fue a un partido de su deporte favorito (u otro deporte). Usa las siguientes preguntas como guía y añade otras.

1. ¿Cuándo fue la última vez que fuiste a un partido de... ? (Fui...)
2. ¿Quiénes jugaron?
3. ¿Quiénes ganaron/perdieron? ¿O terminaron en empate (*did they tie*)?
4. ¿Cuántas personas asistieron (*attended*), aproximadamente?
5. Además de ver el partido, ¿qué más hiciste (*did you do*) allí?

● Los pasatiempos[a]

Hoy tengo tiempo libre. **Tengo ganas de...**

jugar a los naipes.

cantar.

pintar.

coleccionar (estampillas/monedas)	to collect (stamps/coins)
contar (ue) chistes	to tell jokes
coser	to sew
dibujar	to draw
escribir cuentos/poesía	to write stories/poetry
ir al cine/teatro	to go to the movies/theater
jugar (ue) (gu) al ajedrez	to play chess
al billar	billiards (pool)
a los videojuegos	video games
tejer	to knit
ver una película	to watch a film

---

[a]*pastimes*

Actividades

A. Asociaciones. ¿Qué pasatiempos asocias con los siguientes grupos de personas?

1. los mayores
2. los estudiantes de la escuela secundaria (*high school*)
3. los niños
4. los hombres
5. las mujeres
6. las personas que viven en la ciudad
7. las personas muy inteligentes

B. Gustos → Actividades. ¿Qué pasatiempo(s) probablemente les gusta(n) a las siguientes personas?

MODELO   EMILIO: «Creo que las plantas son muy interesantes.» →
A Emilio le gusta trabajar en el jardín.

1. MARÍA: «Me gusta la música latina.»
2. ALBERTO: «Me fascinan los objetos de otras culturas.»
3. YO: «Tengo un gran sentido (*sense*) del humor.»
4. EL PADRE DE EMILIO: «Me gustan los deportes, pero no estoy en buenas condiciones físicas.»
5. TÚ: «Quiero probar estas recetas caribeñas; ¡probablemente están riquísimas!»
6. BEATRIZ Y MARCOS: «Para nosotros es importante expresar los sentimientos (*feelings*) de forma literaria.»

C. Con qué frecuencia? Di con qué frecuencia haces las siguientes actividades cada semana. Si no haces alguna actividad, explica por qué no la haces. Puedes añadir otras actividades que te gustan.

MODELO   hacer ejercicio aeróbico →
No hago ejercicio aeróbico porque nunca tengo ganas de hacerlo. Prefiero levantar pesas.

ACTIVIDADES	FRECUENCIA	RAZÓN PARA NO HACERLO
1. cocinar	todos los días	Es aburrido para mí.
2. ir al cine	_____ veces a la semana	No me gusta.
3. jugar a los videojuegos	una vez por semana	No sé hacerlo bien.
4. tejer	de vez en cuando	No soy bueno/a para _____.
5. ver un partido de fútbol americano	raras veces (*rarely*)	No tengo tiempo para _____.
6. ¿ ?	nunca	No tengo ganas de _____.
		¿ ?

(con los símbolos **+** entre las columnas)

Para hacer una invitación

¿Por qué no vamos al cine?	*Why don't we go to the movies?*
¿Qué tal si vamos al cine?	*How about if we go to the movies?*
¿Te gustaría ir al cine conmigo?	*Would you like to go to the movies with me?*

Para (no) aceptar la invitación

¡Qué buena idea! ¡Vamos!	*What a good idea! Let's go!*
¡Qué chévere!	*Cool! Great! (Carib.)*
Este... (no) me parece muy interesante.	*Uh... that seems (doesn't seem) very interesting.*
No, no me gustaría eso.	*No, I wouldn't like that.*
Pues, la verdad es que no me interesa mucho.	*Well, actually, that doesn't sound that interesting.*

D. ¿Qué hacemos?   Estás aburrido/a y no sabes qué hacer. Habla con tu compañero/a, quien te va a hacer sugerencias.

MODELO   E1: Estoy aburrido. No tengo nada que hacer.
E2: ¿Te gustaría ir al cine conmigo?
E1: La verdad es que no tengo ganas de ver películas.
E2: Pues, ¿por qué no vamos por un café?

▲ *A estas personas de Rincón, Puerto Rico, les gusta surfear cuando (whenever) pueden.*

Entrevista 1

Mitch Ortega Caraballo

«*El deporte nacional de Puerto Rico,... es la pelota.*»

Nombre: Mitch

Apellidos: (1) Ortega (2) Caraballo

Edad: 29 años

Nació en: San Juan, Puerto Rico

You can watch this interview on the *Entrevistas* Video or Interactive CD-ROM or listen to the audio on the Online Learning Center (**www.mhhe.com/entrevistas2**).

Vocabulario útil

correr a caballo	**montar a caballo**	**ídolo**	idol
el bosque	forest	**Cepeda**	Orlando Cepeda
lo más bonito	the most beautiful thing	**destacan**	(they) stand out
barbacoas	barbecues	**nunca hemos**	we've never
mantenerme en forma	to keep myself in shape	**aprendido**	learned
precioso	gorgeous	**tampoco nos ha**	(it) hasn't caught on
la caída del sol	sunset	**llegado**	(here) either
la pelota	baseball (*P. R.*)	**colegio**	high school
los niñitos desde jovencitos	little kids from a very young age	**lo juguemos**	we may play it

Antes de ver

A. Deportes posibles. Mira el mapa de Puerto Rico al principio de este capítulo. ¿Cómo es su clima y su geografía? ¿Qué deportes se pueden practicar allí?

CLIMA Y GEOGRAFÍA

- ☐ el mar
- ☐ las montañas
- ☐ hace calor
- ☐ hace frío
- ☐ nieva
- ¿ ?

DEPORTES POSIBLES

- ☐ bucear
- ☐ escalar montañas
- ☐ esquiar
- ☐ hacer *snow*
- ☐ patinar
- ☐ surfear
- ¿ ?

B. En la escuela primaria. En la escuela primaria donde estudiaste, ¿a qué pasatiempos y deportes se dedicaban los chicos (*did the boys devote themselves*)? ¿Y las chicas? Prepara una lista para los chicos y otra para las chicas.

¡Veamos!

A. Los pasatiempos de Mitch. Ve la entrevista y apunta los pasatiempos que Mitch dice que le gustan.

B. Los deportes en Puerto Rico. Ve de nuevo la entrevista y apunta los deportes que son populares en Puerto Rico, según Mitch.

Después de ver

A. Comparación con Mitch. Revisa (*Review*) tus datos de **¡Veamos!** y contesta las siguientes preguntas.

1. ¿Qué tipos de pasatiempos le gustan a Mitch?
2. En tú opinión, ¿son importantes los pasatiempos en la vida de Mitch?
3. ¿Tienes los mismos pasatiempos que Mitch? ¿Cuáles tienes y cuáles no? ¿Qué otros pasatiempos tienes que él no menciona?
4. ¿Te gustan los pasatiempos de Mitch? ¿Por qué sí o por qué no?

B. ¿Entendiste? Contesta las siguientes preguntas.

1. ¿Cómo le dicen al béisbol en Puerto Rico? ¿Cómo le dicen al fútbol?
2. ¿Por qué cree Mitch que el béisbol es el deporte más importante en Puerto Rico?
3. ¿Es Mitch un fanático del béisbol? Si no, ¿qué deportes prefiere?
4. Además del béisbol, ¿qué otros deportes son populares en Puerto Rico, según Mitch?

¿Y a ti qué te gusta hacer ▶
en tu tiempo libre? ¿Te gusta
andar en bicicleta?

Forma y función

8.1 Irregular Forms of the Preterit

A. In **Capítulo 7** you learned how to form the preterit of regular verbs: A special set of endings is added to the stem of the verb (**hablar** → **habl-** + **-é, -aste, -ó, -amos, -asteis, -aron**). Many Spanish verbs, however, have irregular forms in the preterit. You have already seen and heard some of these forms: For example, **fui** (from **ser**) and **hizo** (from **hacer**). Here are the irregular preterit forms for the verbs **dar, hacer, ir,** and **ser.**

dar		hacer		ir/ser	
di	dimos	hice	hicimos	fui	fuimos
diste	disteis	hiciste	hicisteis	fuiste	fuisteis
dio	dieron	hizo	hicieron	fue	fueron

NOTES:

- **Hizo** is spelled with a **z** to maintain the stem sound before **-o**.
- **Ir** and **ser** have identical forms in the preterit. Context will make the meaning clear.
- None of the irregular preterit forms carries an accent mark in the **yo** or **usted/él/ella** forms. They have a different stress pattern than the regular preterit forms you learned in **Capítulo 7**.
- The preterit endings for **dar** are the same as those for regular **-er/-ir** verbs, except that the accent marks are not needed.

B. The following verbs form the preterit by attaching a set of irregular endings to irregular stems. The endings are similar to those for **hacer: -e, -iste, -o, -imos, -isteis, -ieron.** (See the notes on the next page.)

Infinitivo	Raíz	Conjugaciones
andar	anduv-	anduve, anduviste, anduvo, anduvimos, anduvisteis, anduvieron
poder	pud-	pude, pudiste, pudo, pudimos, pudisteis, pudieron
poner	pus-	puse, pusiste, puso, pusimos, pusisteis, pusieron
saber	sup-	supe, supiste, supo, supimos, supisteis, supieron
tener	tuv-	tuve, tuviste, tuvo, tuvimos, tuvisteis, tuvieron
estar	estuv-	estuve, estuviste, estuvo, estuvimos, estuvisteis, estuvieron
querer	quis-	quise, quisiste, quiso, quisimos, quisisteis, quisieron
venir (*to come*)	vin-	vine, viniste, vino, vinimos, vinisteis, vinieron
decir	dij-	dije, dijiste, dijo, dijimos, dijisteis, dijeron
traer	traj-	traje, trajiste, trajo, trajimos, trajisteis, trajeron
reducir	reduj-	reduje, redujiste, redujo, redujimos, redujisteis, redujeron

NOTES:

- The preterit of **saber** refers to the moment when someone *began to know* something, in other words, when one *found out* or *discovered* something.

...y en ese momento, **supe** la verdad.	*. . . and at that moment, I discovered the truth.*

- The preterit of **querer** used affirmatively means that someone *wanted* to do something *and acted* on it, in other words, one *tried* to do it. When used negatively, the preterit of **querer** means that someone *refused* to do something.

Quise ir al cine anoche, pero no pude porque mi carro se descompuso.	*I tried to go to the movies last night, but I couldn't because my car broke down.*
Al principio Francisco dijo que me ayudaría, pero al final **no quiso** hacerlo.	*At first Francisco said (that) he'd help me, but in the end he refused to do it.*

- Verbs with a stem-final **-j** drop the **-i-** of the **-ieron** ending: **decir** → **dijeron, reducir** → **redujeron, traer** → **trajeron.**

- Other verbs derived from the verbs in the preceding table maintain the same irregularities as their parent verb.

  posponer (like **poner**) → **pospuse, pospusimos, pospuso,...**

  mantener (like **tener**) → **mantuve, mantuviste, mantuvo,...**

  contradecir (like **decir**) → **contradije, contradijiste, contradijo,...**

  Similarly, verbs whose infinitive ends in **-ducir** are conjugated like **reducir.**

  conducir → **conduje, condujiste, condujo,...**

  producir → **produje, produjiste, produjo,...**

- The preterit of **hay** is **hubo** (*there was / there were*).

Análisis estructural

¿Quién hizo las siguientes acciones? Di cuál es el sujeto posible / cuáles son los sujetos posibles del verbo.

1. Fue a la playa ayer.
2. Le dije: «No, gracias.»
3. ¿Dónde pusieron las raquetas de tenis?
4. ¿Viniste a mi casa ayer?
5. Anduvo en bicicleta por el centro.
6. No pude ir al cine anoche.
7. Dimos un paseo por el parque.
8. Hiciste mucho ejercicio aeróbico por la tarde, ¿verdad?

Actividades

A. Las noticias deportivas (*Sports news*).   Las siguientes noticias no están correctas porque los hechos que reportan tuvieron lugar (*took place*) ayer, no hoy. Cambia los verbos subrayados (*underlined*) del presente al pretérito.

VOCABULARIO ÚTIL

el/la entrenador(a)	coach
el esfuerzo	effort
la huelga	strike
la liga	league
la selección	national soccer team
la temporada	season
ganarle a	to defeat
no poder con	to be unable to handle

1. Alemania <u>quiere</u> ganarle a Brasil en los finales, pero no <u>puede</u> hacerlo.
2. Los Padres <u>atraen</u> a tres de los mejores jugadores de la Liga.
3. Huelga en la Liga <u>pone</u> en peligro el futuro de la pelota.
4. «<u>Hacemos</u> un esfuerzo, pero no <u>podemos</u> con Italia», <u>dice</u> el entrenador de la selección española.
5. La Liga <u>reduce</u> el número de equipos de catorce a doce en la temporada 2002.

B. Entrevista: ¿Qué hiciste?   Pregúntale a un compañero / una compañera de clase qué hizo para divertirse en las siguientes ocasiones. Luego, compara los resultados de la entrevista con los del resto de la clase. ¿Quién tiene las actividades más variadas?

MODELO   anoche →
          E1: ¿Qué hiciste anoche?
          E2: Fui al cine con mi compañero de cuarto.

1. el fin de semana pasado
2. el verano pasado
3. durante las últimas vacaciones
4. esta mañana
5. ¿ ?

C. La historia de una pasión.   ¿Tienes algún pasatiempo favorito? ¿Desde (*Since*) cuándo te dedicas a él? Cuenta a la clase cómo empezó tu interés, usando las siguientes frases para guiar tu narración.

VOCABULARIO ÚTIL

cometer un error   to make a mistake

Pasatiempo: _____

1. yo **/** empezar a [*infinitivo*] **/** a los _____ años
2. [*persona*] **/** ayudarme **/** a empezar
3. yo **/** tener que comprar [*cosa(s)*] **/** para practicar este pasatiempo
4. [*persona*] **/** darme **/** [*cosa(s)*]
5. ser (difícil/fácil) al principio
6. al principio, yo **/** cometer (muchos/pocos) errores

8.2 Stem-Changing Verbs in the Preterit

In **Capítulo 7,** you learned that **-ar** and **-er** verbs whose stems change in the present do not have this stem change in the preterit.

contar (ue)				
PRESENTE			PRETÉRITO	
cuento	contamos		conté	contamos
cuentas	contáis		contaste	contasteis
cuenta	cuentan		contó	contaron

However, **-ir** verbs that have stem changes in the present also undergo a stem change in the preterit: In the third-person forms, the **-e-** and **-o-** of the stems change to **-i-** and **-u-,** respectively. The regular preterit **-ir** endings (**-ió, -ieron**) are then added to the stem.

servir (i, i)				
PRESENTE			PRETÉRITO	
sirvo	servimos		serví	servimos
sirves	servís		serviste	servisteis
sirve	sirven		sirvió	sirvieron

dormir (ue, u)				
PRESENTE			PRETÉRITO	
duermo	dormimos		dormí	dormimos
duermes	dormís		dormiste	dormisteis
duerme	duermen		durmió	durmieron

From here on, verbs that have stem changes in both the present and the preterit will be listed as follows: **servir (i, i); dormir (ue, u).** The first vowel indicates the present tense stem change and the second indicates the preterit stem change, as shown in the preceding tables.

Análisis estructural

Completa la siguiente tabla con las formas indicadas de los verbos. **¡OJO!** Cuidado con los verbos que tienen *dos* cambios diferentes.

Infinitivo	Presente: yo	Pretérito: yo	Presente: él	Pretérito: él
divertirse (ie, i)				
morir (ue, u)				
pedir (i, i)				
perder (ie)				
sentir (ie, i)				
vestirse (i, i)				
volver (ue)				

Actividades

A. Un sábado divertido. Usa los siguientes elementos para contar lo que pasó un sábado reciente.

1. mis hermanos y yo **/** decidir **/** hacer algo divertido
2. mi hermano **/** sugerir (ie, i) (*to suggest*) **/** el lugar perfecto: ¡el lago!
3. mi padre **/** conseguirnos* **/** una canoa para usar en el lago
4. camino (*on the way*) al lago **/** nosotros **/** pararnos (*to stop*) **/** en un restaurante
5. todos **/** pedir **/** el plato del día
6. el mesero **/** servirnos* **/** una trucha (*trout*) local exquisita
7. nosotros **/** comer **/** demasiado y **/** sentirse **/** muy cansados
8. mis hermanos y yo **/** decidir **/** no ir al lago, y **/** volver a casa

B. Encuesta: ¿Quién lo hizo? ¿Quién de tu clase hizo las siguientes actividades la semana pasada? Pregúntales a tus compañeros/as hasta encontrar a por lo menos una persona que hizo cada actividad.

> MODELO   E1: La semana pasada, ¿te dormiste durante una clase?
> E2: Sí, me dormí durante la clase de biología.

1. vestirse con la misma ropa que la noche anterior
2. pedirle puntos extra a un profesor / una profesora
3. sentirse deprimido/a a causa de las notas
4. preferir no ir a una clase
5. divertirse mucho en una clase

C. Entrevista: La semana pasada. Hazle las siguientes preguntas a un compañero / una compañera de clase para saber más sobre sus actividades la semana pasada.

1. ¿Cuánto tiempo dedicaste a tus pasatiempos la semana pasada? ¿Cuánto tiempo dedicaste al trabajo? ¿Y a los estudios?
2. ¿En qué ocasión te divertiste más durante la semana pasada? ¿Qué pasó?
3. ¿Saliste recientemente? ¿Qué hiciste? ¿Conociste a otras personas, cenaste en algún restaurante, hablaste con amigos, bailaste, hiciste algo más?

---

* ¡OJO! In this sentence, **nos** is not the subject. It is an indirect object.

Análisis cultural

La siguiente cita tomada de una fuente escrita en inglés para anglohablantes va a aumentar tus conocimientos sobre algunos fenómenos culturales del béisbol hispanoamericano. ¿Es consistente esta información con la perspectiva de Mitch de la **Entrevista 1?** Usa lo que has aprendido en este capítulo sobre Puerto Rico, más tu propia experiencia, para contestar las preguntas que siguen la cita.

❝Although many sportswriters in the United States have considered the presence of ballplayers from Latin America to be an 'influx,' as if baseball were a uniquely American sport being invaded by outsiders, the truth of the matter is that baseball in Spanish-speaking countries has not only had a parallel development to baseball in the United States, but it has been intertwined with American baseball almost from the beginning of the game itself. The professional Cuban Baseball League **(Liga de Béisbol Profesional Cubana)** was founded in 1878, just seven years after the National Baseball Association was founded in the United States. But, reportedly, Cuban baseball goes back to 1866, when sailors from an American ship in Matanzas harbor invited Cubans to play the game; they built a baseball diamond together at Palmar del Junco and began playing while the ship remained in harbor. By 1874 Cuban teams had developed and were playing each other regularly.

By 1891 seventy-five teams were active on the island. From that time on, Cuban baseball—and later, Mexican and Puerto Rican baseball—has served baseball in the United States in various ways: as a training ground for the majors . . . ; as wintering and spring training grounds for the majors; and [until desegregation] as permanent homes for players from the U.S. Negro Leagues. . . .❞

Source: The Hispanic Almanac: From Columbus to Corporate America

1. ¿Conoces a algunos jugadores de béisbol hispanos que juegan para un equipo de las Grandes Ligas (*Major Leagues*) de Norteamérica? ¿De qué países son?

2. ¿Conoces a algunos atletas norteamericanos que juegan en otros países? ¿A qué deportes se dedican?

3. Considerando el intercambio (*exchange*) entre jugadores norteamericanos e hispanoamericanos que existe, ¿crees que haya (*there are*) deportes nacionales? ¿En qué consiste el concepto de **un deporte nacional?** ¿Puedes dar algunos ejemplos del deporte nacional de algunos países?

4. En tu opinión, ¿es positivo o negativo el intercambio de talento deportivo de un país a otro? Explica tu respuesta.

l

In English, there are two sounds associated with the letter *l*, depending on where the sound occurs in the word. You can distinguish the two by contrasting the syllable-initial "light" [l] of *lazy* with the syllable-final "dark" [l] of *hill*.

One of the features that makes a person's accent in Spanish more native-like is the articulation of the [l] sound. Spanish uses only the "light" [l] sound, so English speakers have to be very careful to avoid the "dark" [l] in syllable-final position in Spanish.

Listen as your instructor pronounces the following pairs of words, focusing on the different [l] sounds in the syllable-final position.

ENGLISH	SPANISH		ENGLISH	SPANISH
hotel	hotel		goal	gol
mall	mal		dell	del

 **r and rr**

The *single flap* and the *trill* are two sounds of the Spanish language often referred to as "**r** sounds." The single flap is made by touching the roof of the mouth with the tongue only once. This produces a sound similar to what American English speakers think of as the *t* or *d* sound in the words *butter* or *ladder*. In Spanish, the single flap is always represented by the letter **r**: ca<u>r</u>o, ve<u>r</u>de, habla<u>r</u>.

The trill is made by touching the tongue to the roof of the mouth several times in rapid succession. The trill is represented by **rr** between vowels (ca<u>rr</u>o, guita<u>rr</u>a) and by a single **r** at the beginning of a word (<u>R</u>oberto, <u>r</u>ojo) or after **n** or **l** (En<u>r</u>ique, al<u>r</u>ededor).

Note how the single flap / trill distinction can sometimes change the meaning of words.

caro	*expensive*		carro	*car*
pero	*but*		perro	*dog*
varios	*several*		barrios	*neighborhoods*

The *Manual de práctica* contains exercises to practice the materials explained here.

Si te interesa

In Puerto Rico, many speakers convert the syllable-final single flap sound into an [l] sound, resulting in pronouncing words such as **verde, puerto,** and **hablar** as if they were spelled **"velde," "puelto,"** and **"hablal."**

The trill in Puerto Rico is sometimes pronounced like a strong **j** of other dialects of Spanish (**José, jueves, jugar). Thus,** words like **carro, Enrique,** and **rico** may be pronounced as if they were spelled **"cajo," "Enjique,"** and **"jico."**

Fiestas y diversiones

En la discoteca

tocar (qu) música

bailar separados

sacar (qu) a alguien a bailar

bailar pegados

charlar con amigos

el baile	dance	**estar tranquilo/a**	to be calm
		molestar	to bother
encontrarse (ue)	to be in the mood	**tener prisa**	to be in a hurry
en ambiente		**pasarla bien**	to have a good time
estar en su punto	to be at one's best		
estar relajado/a	to be relaxed		

En la fiesta

el anfitrión /	host(ess)	**conocer (zc) a otras**	to meet / get to know
la anfitriona		**personas**	new people
la bebida (alcohólica)	(alcoholic) drink	**encontrarse (ue)**	to get together/meet
el humo	smoke	**con amigos**	with friends
el/la invitado/a	guest	**estar borracho/a**	to be drunk
el refresco	soft drink	**fumar**	to smoke
el ruido	noise	**tomar**	to drink

Actividades

A. Definiciones. ¿A qué se refieren las siguientes descripciones? **¡OJO!** En algunos casos hay más de una posibilidad.

1. cuando una persona bebe demasiado
2. un lugar para escuchar música y bailar
3. lo que se sirve en un bar
4. la persona que da una fiesta o cena
5. un sinónimo de *divertirse*
6. tener poco tiempo para hacer algo
7. reunirse con amigos
8. sentirse cómodo/a
9. algo que molesta a las personas que no fuman
10. cosas que hacer en una fiesta

B. ¿Qué tipo de persona es? Di si las siguientes oraciones corresponden a una persona diurna, es decir, una persona que funciona mejor durante el día, o a una persona nocturna.

1. «Estoy en mi punto a la 1:00 de la mañana.»
2. «Me levanto a las 6:00 de la mañana.»
3. «A mí me encantan las fiestas donde se baila hasta medianoche.»
4. «Yo me encuentro en ambiente a eso de las 11:00 de la noche.»
5. «Yo prefiero practicar deportes por la mañana.»
6. «A mí me gusta salir por la mañana; suelo quedarme en casa por la tarde.»

C. Una fiesta reciente. Describe los siguientes aspectos de una fiesta a la que (*that*) asististe recientemente.

1. ¿Quién fue el anfitrión / la anfitriona?
2. ¿Quiénes fueron los invitados?
3. ¿Qué sirvieron de beber y de comer?
4. ¿Qué tipo(s) de música tocaron? (por ejemplo, música rock, música clásica, salsa, merengue, tango, jazz, rap)
5. ¿Quiénes bailaron?
6. ¿La pasaron bien los invitados? ¿Por qué sí o por qué no?

D. Entrevista: Las diversiones. Habla con un compañero / una compañera de clase para saber la siguiente información.

1. Los fines de semana, ¿prefieres quedarte en casa o salir? ¿Qué haces?
2. ¿Qué haces para divertirte con tus amigos? ¿con tu familia? ¿Hay una diferencia entre los tipos de actividades que haces con los amigos y los que haces con la familia?
3. En general, ¿eres una persona relajada o siempre tienes prisa? Explica tu respuesta.
4. ¿En qué momento(s) del día estás en tu punto? ¿Cuándo te sientes cansado/a?

You can watch this interview on the *Entrevistas* Video or Interactive CD-ROM or listen to the audio on the Online Learning Center (**www.mhhe.com/entrevistas2**).

José Veliz Román

«Estas fiestas... terminan cuando terminan. No hay prisa... »

Nombre: José

Apellidos: (1) Veliz (2) Román

Edad: 27 años

Nació en: Ponce, Puerto Rico

Vocabulario útil

me encuentro	I feel	**disfrutar**	to have fun
amistades *f.*	friends	**reírnos**	to laugh
la pasamos increíble	we had an incredible time	**uno se siente a gusto**	one feels relaxed, happy

Antes de ver

¿Para qué (*For what purpose*) **sales?**   Primero, contesta las siguientes preguntas. Después, ve la entrevista de José e indica sus respuestas a las mismas preguntas. ¿Cómo se comparan las respuestas de José con las tuyas?

	YO	JOSÉ
1. ¿Para qué sales de noche?		
para bailar	☐	☐
para conocer a otras personas	☐	☐
para contar chistes	☐	☐
para hablar	☐	☐
para molestar a la gente	☐	☐
para tomar	☐	☐
2. Cuando sales, ¿adónde vas?		
a un bar	☐	☐
a una discoteca	☐	☐
a casa de amigos	☐	☐
a un lugar público (un parque, un estadio, etcétera)	☐	☐
¿ ?	☐	☐
3. ¿A qué hora estás en tu punto?		
a la(s)	____	____

¡Veamos!

La noche de José. Apunta tres cosas que José hizo anoche para divertirse.

Después de ver

¿En Puerto Rico o los Estados Unidos? Según José, ¿en qué país son ciertas las siguientes afirmaciones?

	PUERTO RICO	LOS ESTADOS UNIDOS
1. La gente llega a una fiesta y se va cuando quiere.	☐	☐
2. La gente disfruta tomando.	☐	☐
3. La gente sale principalmente para tomar.	☐	☐
4. La gente sale principalmente para conocer a otras personas o para pasarla bien.	☐	☐

Piénsalo bien

Contesta las siguientes preguntas.

1. ¿Estás de acuerdo con los comentarios de José sobre los norteamericanos? ¿Te describen a ti personalmente o describen a la gente que tú conoces?
2. ¿Coinciden o contrastan las costumbres sociales de Puerto Rico con las de Bolivia, según Güido Rivera Melgar de la **Entrevista 1** del **Capítulo 6?**
3. ¿Sueles llegar a tiempo a las fiestas, o siempre llegas tarde? Explica tu respuesta.
4. ¿Cuándo te vas de una fiesta?
   - ☐ cuando se acaban (*run out*) las bebidas
   - ☐ cuando el anfitrión / la anfitriona apaga (*turns off*) la música
   - ☐ cuando el anfitrión / la anfitriona empieza a dar señales de fatiga
   - ☐ ¿ ?
5. En Puerto Rico no es común que un anfitrión / una anfitriona les diga (*says*) a los invitados: «Ya es tarde, me tengo que acostar». En tu opinión, ¿son descorteses (*impolite*) los invitados que se quedan en una fiesta hasta muy tarde? ¿Por qué sí o por qué no?

● 8.3 Negative Words

"More is better" is certainly the rule in using negative words in Spanish. Unlike standard English, which forbids more than one negative word in a sentence ("I don't have *any*," instead of *none*), Spanish actually *requires* that a negative sentence contain negative words throughout.

El anfitrión **nunca jamás** le dice a **nadie** a qué hora tiene que irse **ni** a qué hora tiene que llegar.	*The host never ever says to anybody when they have to leave or when they have to arrive.*

In **Capítulo 5** you learned the word **nada** (*nothing*) and the adjective **ningún/ninguna** (*no, not any*). Here are the other most commonly used negative words in Spanish.

jamás	never	**ninguno/a**	none, not any
nadie	nobody, no one	**nunca**	never
ni _____	neither _____	**tampoco**	neither, not
ni _____	nor _____		either

Note that both **nunca** and **jamás** mean *never*. When used together **(nunca jamás)**, the repetition implies the stronger meaning *never ever*.

If a negative word is placed *after* the verb in a sentence, there must be a negative word *before* the verb as well. In most cases this first negative word is simply **no.** Study the following examples, paying close attention to the different possibilities for the position of negative words with respect to the verb (underlined).

Nada le <u>gusta</u> a él. A él **no** le <u>gusta</u> **nada.**	*He doesn't like anything.*
Nunca <u>salimos</u> a bailar. **No** <u>salimos</u> a bailar **nunca.** **No** <u>salimos</u> **nunca** a bailar.	*We never go out dancing.*
Ni tú **ni** yo <u>podemos salir</u> esta noche. **No** <u>podemos salir</u> esta noche **ni** tú **ni** yo.	*Neither you nor I can go out tonight.*
Tampoco <u>salen</u> ellos. Ellos **no** <u>salen</u> **tampoco.**	*They aren't going out either.*
Mi amiga **nunca** <u>habla</u> con **nadie** en las fiestas. Mi amiga **no** <u>habla</u> con **nadie nunca** en las fiestas.	*My friend never talks to anybody at parties.*

Remember from **Capítulo 5** that the adjective **ningún/ninguna,** as well as the corresponding pronoun **ninguno/a,** are only used in the singular.

No hay **ningún** estudiante puertorriqueño en mi clase.	*There are no (not any) Puerto Rican students in my class. (There is not a single Puerto Rican student . . . .)*
Nunca tenemos **ninguna** bebida alcohólica en nuestras fiestas.	*We never have any alcoholic drinks at our parties.*
¿CDs? **No** tengo **ninguno.**	*CDs? I don't have any.*

Actividades

A. ¡Me equivoqué! (*I was wrong!*)   Las siguientes oraciones están completamente equivocadas (*wrong*). Conviértelas en oraciones negativas, cambiando las frases subrayadas y haciendo los otros cambios necesarios.

1. <u>Siempre</u> escucho la música clásica.
2. En ese club, puedes comprar <u>bebidas alcohólicas</u> en la barra (*bar*).
3. Tienen <u>alguna</u> marca (*brand*) de cerveza importada aquí.
4. En las discotecas, los chicos <u>siempre</u> sacan a Elena a bailar.
5. Me gusta la música rock, <u>y</u> me encanta la salsa.
6. Para las fiestas en mi casa, <u>alguien siempre</u> trae CDs de salsa.
7. Yo tengo una colección de CDs <u>también</u>.
8. Los invitados a mi casa <u>siempre</u> traen algo de tomar.

B. Los consejos.   Los señores Ramírez siempre se preocupan mucho por la seguridad (*safety*) de sus hijos. ¿Qué les dicen los padres a sus hijos cuando éstos (*the latter*) salen con amigos? Usa palabras negativas para formar oraciones completas, según el modelo.

MODELO   tomar algo en los bares →
¡Ustedes no deben tomar nada en los bares!

1. ir a algún club de baile
2. fumar
3. usar alguna droga
4. perder algo importante
5. hablar con una persona desconocida (*unknown*) en la calle
6. ¿ ?

C. La fiesta ideal.   En tu opinión, ¿cómo es la fiesta ideal? Termina las siguientes oraciones para describir una fiesta exitosa (*successful*).

1. El anfitrión nunca…
2. Los invitados siempre…
3. Nadie debe…
4. Una cosa que nunca se hace es…
5. Tampoco se…

● 8.4 Using Direct and Indirect Object Pronouns Together

You have already learned how to use direct and indirect object nouns and pronouns individually in a sentence, but some verbs require both at the same time: For example, you can give something (direct object) to someone (indirect object). When both a direct and an indirect object pronoun occur in the same sentence, the indirect object pronoun (IO) *always* precedes the direct object pronoun (DO).

¿Este CD de salsa? Un amigo
me lo dio.
IO DO

*This salsa CD? A friend gave it
to me.*

¿Te compro este CD? —No,
gracias, mi novio va a
comprár**melo.**
    IO DO

*Shall I buy you this CD?
—No, thanks, my boyfriend
is going to buy it for me.*

¿Los pasos del chachachá?
La profesora está
enseñándo**noslos** ahora.
        IO DO

*The steps for the cha-cha-cha?
The teacher is showing them
to us now.*

NOTES:

- When two object pronouns are attached to the end of an infinitive or an **-ndo** form, a written accent must be added to the verb to maintain the original stress pattern of the infinitive (e.g., **comprármelo, enseñándonoslos**).
- When both the direct and the indirect object pronouns are in the third person (that is, if they both begin with the letter **l**), the indirect object pronoun **le/les** becomes **se**.

IO   DO   IO DO
Le diste **el regalo.**   →   **Se lo** diste.
You gave him the gift.   →   *You gave it to him.*

Since this **se** can indicate many different referents (*to him, to her, to it, to you* [form. s., pl.], *to them*), it usually requires a prepositional phrase to clarify who the indirect object is.

Se lo diste **a tu hermano.**   *You gave it to your brother.*

Se lo diste **a él.**   *You gave it to him.*

Se lo diste **a tus primos.**   *You gave it to your cousins.*

Si te interesa

Why do **le** and **les** change to **se** when they precede a direct object pronoun beginning with **l**? Contrary to popular belief, it is not because the sequence of sounds **le lo** is hard to say: There are a number of Spanish words like **paralelo** that discount this idea. The real reason is that in medieval Spanish (before the year 1500), a sentence such as "You gave it to him" was rendered as **Gelo diste**, with the **g** pronounced like the *s* in English *treasure*. In the course of the language's development, Spanish speakers began to confuse the old sound of **ge** with the [s] sound, leading to the modern version **Se lo diste.**

Análisis estructural

Identifica los complementos directos e indirectos en las siguientes oraciones.

1. Our teacher showed us a video on the history of salsa music.
2. In this video, a musician explained the origin of the term **salsa** to the audience.
3. The same musician performed a concert for us later that week at our school.
4. Our class sent him a thank-you note after his visit.
5. We wrote the note to him in Spanish, since he was from Puerto Rico.

Actividades

A. ¿Quién le dio qué a quién? Primero, identifica el sujeto y los complementos directos e indirectos en estas oraciones. Después, di a qué y a quién se refieren los pronombres, escogiendo entre las siguientes posibilidades.

PERSONAS	COSAS
a mí	el CD
a nosotros	la raqueta de tenis
a ella	los esquíes
a ustedes	las cartas de póquer
a ti	

1. Me los dio mi padre.
2. Se las enviaron los abuelos.
3. La profesora nos lo enseñó.
4. El entrenador me la reparó.
5. ¿Te las regaló un amigo?

B. En una fiesta. Escribe de nuevo las siguientes oraciones, sustituyendo los objetos directos e indirectos por los pronombres correspondientes.

1. La anfitriona nos enseñó los bailes nuevos.
2. Un amigo me trajo esta cerveza.
3. El anfitrión de la fiesta le ofreció el refresco a Daniel.
4. Un grupo de músicos nos cantaron estas canciones.
5. Nosotros les dimos las gracias a los anfitriones al irnos de la fiesta.

C. Otra gente. ¿Te gusta conocer a otra gente cuando sales? Contesta las siguientes preguntas sobre el tema (*topic*). **¡OJO!** Ten cuidado (*Be careful*) con los pronombres de complemento directo e indirecto.

1. ¿Qué les dices a los chicos / las chicas que quieres conocer?
2. ¿A quién le compras bebidas?
3. ¿A quién le das tu número de teléfono?
4. ¿Sueles sacar a bailar a gente que no conoces, o sólo bailas con amigos/as?

Sobre la lectura La sociedad moderna ofrece muchas conveniencias que facilitan el trabajo y —en teoría— nos dan más tiempo libre. Pero en realidad, el comentario «¡No tengo tiempo!» es muy común, y muchas personas hacen resoluciones de año nuevo para mejorar su manera de organizar su tiempo y su vida. En esta lectura se presentan las resoluciones que tomaron algunos puertorriqueños famosos. Mientras lees, decide si hay temas que se repiten en las metas (*goals*) y expectativas (*expectations*) de estas personas, y si las aspiraciones de ellos son similares a las tuyas.

Antes de leer

A. Mis resoluciones para este año. ¿Tomaste algunas resoluciones para este año? Si contestas afirmativamente, apunta las resoluciones que tomaste. Si contestas negativamente, explica por qué no tomaste ninguna resolución.

MODELOS Tomé las siguientes resoluciones:…

No tomé ninguna resolución porque…

B. ¿Qué revelan mis resoluciones? ¿Qué revelan tus resoluciones —o falta (*lack*) de resoluciones— de tus valores, metas, gustos y deseos? Analiza lo que escribiste en la **Actividad A** con la ayuda (*help*) de las siguientes preguntas.

1. ¿Valoras (*Do you value*) más a la familia y los amigos o valoras más el trabajo?

2. ¿Tienes metas flexibles o concretas?

3. ¿Prefieres ganar mucho dinero o prefieres ayudar a los demás?

4. ¿Estás satisfecho/a con tu vida o deseas experimentar (*experience*) algo nuevo?

C. El regalo que yo quiero. ¿Cuál es el regalo que más deseas en este momento? ¿Por qué? En una hoja de papel aparte (*separate piece of paper*) escribe tu nombre, la cosa que deseas y la razón por la que (*why*) la deseas. Después, entrégasela a tu profesor(a). Él/Ella va a leer los deseos sin mencionar los nombres, ¡y la clase tiene que adivinar de quién es cada deseo!

D. Inferencias. A veces, cuando leemos, no entendemos todas las palabras o la sintaxis de una frase u oración. Pero muchas veces podemos sacar algunas conclusiones. Usa tus conocimientos generales y el tema de esta lectura para escoger la mejor conclusión o interpretación de cada oración.

1. «El regalo ideal para mí sería (*would be*) no oír tantas noticias negativas.»
a. La persona es reportera de televisión o de un periódico.
b. La persona se lleva (*gets along*) muy mal con su familia.

2. «El regalo ideal para mí es un par (*pair*) de esquíes para no tener que alquilarlos más.»
   a. A esta persona le gusta gastar dinero.
   b. Esta persona esquía con frecuencia.
3. «Mi resolución de año nuevo es no hacer más resoluciones.»
   a. Esta persona no quiere tomar resoluciones que no va a cumplir (*fulfill*).
   b. Esta persona está deprimida.
4. «Quisiera (*I would like*) tarjetas de peloteros (jugadores de pelota) con las figuras de Luis Rodríguez Olmo, Jaime Almendro y Jackie Robinson.»
   a. Es un(a) deportista profesional.
   b. Es aficionado/a a los deportes.

Resoluciones para el año nuevo

Un año nuevo significa[a] nuevos retos,[b] metas y objetivos para alcanzar[c] prosperidad en todos los aspectos de la vida. A continuación se presentan algunas personalidades de Puerto Rico. Hablan de su regalo ideal, cómo van a despedir[d] este año y sus resoluciones para el próximo.[e]

▲ *German Wilkins, Carmen Jovet y Felix Trinidad*

Carmen Dominicci

«Como resolución, comenzar estudios de historia y literatura comparada. El regalo ideal para mí sería no oír tantas noticias negativas y no ver tanta criminalidad. Pienso despedir el año con mi hijo y mi familia en tranquilidad y paz, haciendo una reflexión sobre este año y el próximo.»

Carmen Jovet

«Mis resoluciones son: volver a lo que pesaba[f] cuando tenía[g] 18 años, levantarme antes de que salga el sol,[h] acostarme más temprano, completar todos los días mi rutina de ejercicios, sentarme[i] a comer, sacar tiempo para descansar, aprender a decir que no, trabajar menos y dedicar más tiempo a mi familia. El regalo ideal para mí es un par de esquíes para no tener que alquilarlos más. En despedida de año quiero romper[j] la dieta y cocinar los platos típicos para compartirlos con mi familia.»

Manny Manuel

«Me gustaría expandir mi carrera. Como regalo ideal deseo salud. A nivel personal, crecer[k] como ser humano. Despido el año trabajando. Pero siempre trato de compartir ese momento con mi familia.»

Jacobo Morales

«Mi resolución de año nuevo es no hacer más resoluciones. Como regalo ideal quisiera un guante[l] de pelotero color marrón[m] oscuro y tarjetas de peloteros con las figuras de Luis Rodríguez Olmo, Jaime Almendro y Jackie Robinson. Despido el año como siempre: en familia, con los mismos villancicos,[n] los besos y abrazos, las risas,[o] las nostalgias y la intimidad que provoca el pensar que ha pasado[p] un año más.» ■

[a]*means* [b]*challenges* [c]*attain* [d]*say good-bye to* [e]*next (year)* [f]*I used to weigh* [g]*I was* [h]*antes... before the sun rises* [i]*sit down* [j]*to break (ignore)* [k]*to grow* [l]*glove* [m]*brown* [n]*Christmas carols* [o]*besos... kisses and hugs, laughs* [p]*ha... has passed*

Después de leer

A. ¿Qué quieren? Indica en la columna apropiada los deseos de las personas de la lectura. **¡OJO!** Es posible indicar más de una persona para algunos de los deseos.

	C. DOMENICCI	C. JOVET	M. MANUEL	J. MORALES
Las resoluciones				
1. leer y estudiar	☐	☐	☐	☐
2. cuidar su estado físico	☐	☐	☐	☐
3. cuidar su salud	☐	☐	☐	☐
4. trabajar más/menos	☐	☐	☐	☐
El regalo que desean				
1. buenas noticias	☐	☐	☐	☐
2. equipo deportivo	☐	☐	☐	☐
3. salud	☐	☐	☐	☐
Planes para el fin de año				
1. estar con la familia	☐	☐	☐	☐
2. comer	☐	☐	☐	☐
3. pensar	☐	☐	☐	☐
4. trabajar	☐	☐	☐	☐

B. ¿Cómo son? ¿Qué puedes deducir acerca de estas personalidades puertorriqueñas? Empareja (*Match*) las siguientes cualidades con una de las personas de la lectura. Después, escribe las frases de la lectura que sirven como evidencia.

MODELO   cariñoso/a / familiar →
Parece que Carmen Dominicci es cariñosa porque dijo: «Pienso despedir el año con mi hijo y mi familia en tranquilidad... »

1. profesional
2. deportista/atleta
3. intelectual
4. ambicioso/a
5. hogareño/a (*family oriented*)

C. ¿Qué pasó después? Esta lectura se escribió hace algunos años (*some years ago*). En tu opinión, ¿cumplieron las personas sus resoluciones? Inventa las historias de lo que pasó en la vida de estos puertorriqueños al año siguiente. Ten en cuenta (*Keep in mind*) la profesión, la situación familiar y otros detalles de cada persona.

MODELO   Al año siguiente, Carmen Jovet nunca completó su rutina de ejercicios, ni aprendió a decir que no. Tampoco recibió los esquíes, pero sí, dedicó más tiempo a su familia.

Roberto Clemente fue el primer atleta hispanoamericano elegido[a] al Pasillo de los Famosos[b] de las Grandes Ligas de béisbol. Además de ser famoso por su récord en el béisbol, Clemente era[c] también reconocido por sus proyectos humanitarios. Murió trágicamente joven en 1972 durante una misión humanitaria: su pequeño avión,[d] destinado a llevar medicamentos y comida a Nicaragua, un país devastado por un desastre reciente, chocó[e] durante el despegue.[f]

En 1998, muchos de los mejores artistas musicales de Puerto Rico se reunieron para hacerle un homenaje[g] a Clemente. Ésta es la cubierta[h] del CD que crearon.

¿Hay en este país algún deportista (u otra figura famosa) cuya carrera fue truncada[i] por un accidente? ¿Qué pasó? ¿Cómo le han hecho[j] homenaje a esta figura?

[a]*elected* [b]*Pasillo... Hall of Fame* [c]*was* [d]*airplane* [e]*crashed* [f]*takeoff* [g]*hacerle... pay homage* [h]*cover* [i]*cut short* [j]*le... have they paid*

PORTAFOLIO CULTURAL

Redacción

Querido diario. Mantener un diario nos permite recordar los mejores momentos de la vida. Describe las tres ocasiones más importantes de tu vida, momentos en los que más te divertiste. Sigue los pasos en el *Manual de práctica* para completar tu diario.

Exploración

Investigación cultural. Busca más información sobre Puerto Rico en la biblioteca, en el *Entrevistas* Online Learning Center **(www.mhhe. com/entrevistas2)** o en otros sitios del Internet y preséntala a la clase. El *Manual de práctica* contiene más ideas para tu presentación.

Léxico activo

LOS DEPORTES

el/la **aficionado/a**	fan
el **básquetbol**	basketball
el **ciclismo**	cycling
el/la **deportista**	sports-minded person
el **equipo**	team
la **equitación**	horseback riding
el **esquí**	skiing; ski
el **fútbol americano**	football
el **golf**	golf
el/la **jugador(a)**	player
la **natación**	swimming
el **partido**	game
el **tenis**	tennis
el **voleibol**	volleyball

Repaso: el baloncesto, el béisbol, el fútbol;
  jugar (ue) (gu) a

acampar	to camp
andar (*irreg.*) **en bicicleta**	to ride a bicycle
bucear	to snorkle
correr	to run
escalar montañas	to go mountain climbing
esquiar (esquío) (en el agua)	to (water) ski
ganar	to win
hacer artes marciales	to practice martial arts
levantar pesas	to lift weights
montar a caballo	to go horseback riding
nadar	to swim
patinar (sobre hielo)	to (ice) skate
perder (ie)	to lose
practicar (qu) un deporte	to practice a sport
surfear	to surf

LOS PASATIEMPOS

cantar	to sing
coleccionar (estampillas/ monedas)	to collect (stamps/coins)
contar (ue) chistes	to tell jokes
coser	to sew
dibujar	to draw
escribir cuentos/poesía	to write stories/poetry

ir al cine/teatro	to go to the movies/ theater
jugar (ue) (gu) al ajedrez	to play chess
jugar (ue) (gu) al billar	to play billiards (pool)
jugar (ue) (gu) a los naipes	to play cards
jugar (ue) (gu) a los videojuegos	to play video games
pintar	to paint
tejer	to knit
tener ganas de + *inf.*	to feel like (*doing something*)
ver una película	to watch a film

FIESTAS Y DIVERSIONES

el **anfitrión** / la **anfitriona**	host(ess)
el **baile**	dance
la **bebida (alcohólica)**	(alcoholic) drink
la **discoteca**	discotheque
el **humo**	smoke
el/la **invitado/a**	guest
el **ruido**	noise
bailar (pegados/ separados)	to dance (close/apart)
charlar con amigos	to chat with friends
conocer (zc) a otras personas	to meet / get to know new people
encontrarse (ue) con amigos	to get together (meet) with friends
encontrarse (ue) en ambiente	to be in the mood
estar borracho/a	to be drunk
estar en su punto	to be at one's best
estar relajado/a	to be relaxed
estar tranquilo/a	to be calm
fumar	to smoke
molestar	to bother
pasarla bien	to have a good time
sacar (qu) a alguien a bailar	to ask someone to dance
tener prisa	to be in a hurry
tocar (qu) música	to play music
tomar	to drink

Repaso: el refresco

jamás	never, not ever
nadie	nobody, not anybody
ni _____ ni _____	neither _____ nor _____
ninguno/a	none, not any
nunca	never, not ever
tampoco	neither, not either

Repaso: ningún, ninguna

PARA HACER/ACEPTAR UNA INVITACIÓN

¿Por qué no (nosotros/as) _____?	Why don't (*we do something*)?
¿Qué tal si (nosotros/as) _____?	How about if (*we do something*)?
¿Te gustaría + *inf*.?	Would you like to (*do something*)?
¡Qué buena idea! ¡Vamos!	What a good idea! Let's go!
¡Qué chévere!	Cool! Great! (*Carib.*)
Este… (no) me parece muy interesante.	Uh . . . that seems (doesn't seem) very interesting.
No, no me gustaría eso.	No, I wouldn't like that.
Pues, la verdad es que _____.	Well, actually _____.

CAPÍTULO

9

Fiestas y tradiciones

Cuba

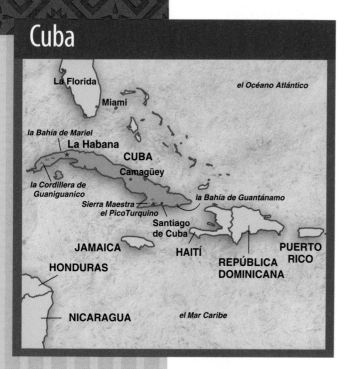

la Florida
el Océano Atlántico
Miami
la Bahía de Mariel
La Habana
CUBA
Camagüey
la Cordillera de Guaniguanico
Sierra Maestra
el PicoTurquino
Santiago de Cuba
la Bahía de Guantánamo
JAMAICA
HAITÍ
PUERTO RICO
HONDURAS
REPÚBLICA DOMINICANA
NICARAGUA
el Mar Caribe

Cultura

- ◆ Childhood Memories
- ◆ Family Traditions
- ◆ What Does It Mean to Be Cuban Outside of Cuba?
- ◆ **Señas culturales: Receta para el picadillo**

Lengua

- ◆ Expressing Frequency
- ◆ Stages of Life
- ◆ Holidays and Traditions
- ◆ The Imperfect (9.1)
- ◆ **Gustar** (Review) (9.2)
- ◆ Other Verbs like **gustar** (9.3)

	Cuba							
		Las tribus indígenas ciboney y taína habitan en la isla	Llegada de Cristóbal Colón	Fundación de Baracoa, la primera ciudad colonial española				Guerra Hispano-Americana; Cuba es república independien bajo la protección de los EE. UU.
	hasta el siglo XVI	hasta 1493	1493	1500–1600	1511	1534	1600–1750	1776–1783	1846–1848	1898

Cuba

hasta el siglo XVI	hasta 1493	1493	1500–1600	1511	1534	1600–1750	1776–1783	1846–1848	1898
Varias tribus indígenas habitan en Norteamérica			Exploración española de Norteamérica		Jacques Cartier reclama para Francia el Canadá	Fundación de las colonias británicas en Norteamérica	Guerra de Independencia en los EE. UU.	Guerra Mexicano-Americana	

Los Estados Unidos y el Canadá

Instantánea

ORIGEN DEL NOMBRE

Cuba: de *Cobai* o *Cubanacan*,
nombres indígenas

POBLACIÓN

11.822.800

LENGUAS

El español (oficial)

◀ *Peregrinos* (Pilgrims) *cubanos
visitan el convento de San Lázaro.*

For additional practice, check
out the *Manual de práctica,* the
Interactive CD-ROM, and the
Online Learning Center
(**www.mhhe.com/entrevistas2**)!

El Sargento Fulgencio Batista derroca al presidente y establece una dictadura	Batista abandona el poder; Fidel Castro toma el poder	Los EE. UU. rompen relaciones con Cuba	Inmigración masiva de cubanos a los EE. UU.	Caída de regímenes comunistas en Europa ocasiona severa crisis económica en Cuba	Regreso a Cuba de Elián González bajo protestas de cubanoamericanos	Diplomáticos cubanos son expulsados de Washington D.C. bajo sospecha de espionaje
1933	1952 1959	1961	1980 1982	1993	1994 2000	2002
	Puerto Rico se hace Estado Libre Asociado de los EE. UU.		El Canadá se separa legalmente de Inglaterra		Tratado de Libre Comercio entre los EE. UU., el Canadá y México	

La frecuencia

Los Ramírez **siempre** (*always*) sirven pavo en las fiestas familiares. **A menudo** (*Often*) su hijo casado participa en estas celebraciones, pero **a veces** las pasa en casa de sus suegros (*in-laws*).

Los Fischer son vegetarianos; nunca comen carne. **Casi siempre** comen arroz con vegetales. También comen *tofu* **con frecuencia.**

cada año/mes	each year/month
casi nunca	almost never
raras veces	rarely
todas las noches	every night
todos los días	every day

Actividades

A. ¿Con qué frecuencia? ¿Con qué frecuencia haces las siguientes cosas en tus fiestas y celebraciones? Indica las respuestas apropiadas. Usa la siguiente escala:

6 = siempre
5 = casi siempre
4 = a menudo (con frecuencia)
3 = a veces
2 = casi nunca
1 = nunca jamás

1. _____ Toco (*I play*) la guitarra / otro instrumento musical.

2. _____ Bailo con amigos o parientes.

3. _____ Escucho música tradicional o folclórica.

4. _____ Canto.

5. _____ Voy a la iglesia (*church*) / al templo / a la sinagoga / a la mezquita,…

6. _____ Visito a mis abuelos u otros parientes.

7. _____ Hablo por teléfono con mis padres / otros parientes.

8. _____ Les envío regalos a mis amigos o parientes.

B. En general. Combina frases de ambas columnas para decir con qué frecuencia haces las siguientes actividades. También añade otras frases.

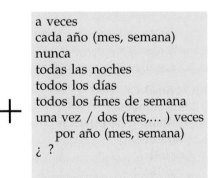

almorzar/cenar con la familia
ayudar a personas mayores / niños
estudiar
ir a fiestas
ir al dentista
practicar deportes / hacer ejercicio
salir a bailar
trabajar
ver películas
ver un partido de béisbol
    (fútbol, etcétera)
¿ ?

+

a veces
cada año (mes, semana)
nunca
todas las noches
todos los días
todos los fines de semana
una vez / dos (tres,…) veces
    por año (mes, semana)
¿ ?

C. Entrevista: ¿Y tú? Usa las ideas de las **Actividades A** y **B** para preguntarle a un compañero / una compañera con qué frecuencia hace esas actividades en sus fiestas y celebraciones familiares.

MODELO   E1: ¿Con qué frecuencia tocas la guitarra en tus fiestas familiares?
          E2: Nunca toco la guitarra.
          E1: ¿Tocas otro instrumento musical?
          E2: Yo no, pero a veces mi hermana toca el piano.

Las etapas[a] de la vida

la adolescencia

la infancia

la niñez

la edad adulta

la vejez

el/la adolescente	adolescent
el/la adulto/a	adult
el/la anciano/a (el/la viejo/a)*	elderly person
el/la bebé	baby
el/la joven (*pl.* jóvenes)	young person
el/la niño/a	child
la persona mayor	older person
estar deprimido/a	to be/feel depressed
emocionado/a	moved
fatal	awful
molesto/a	annoyed
orgulloso/a	proud
ser confiado/a	to be trusting
emocionado/a	emotional
(in)feliz (*pl.* [in]felices)	(un)happy
inocente[†]	naive, inexperienced
molesto/a	annoying
orgulloso/a	proud
rebelde	rebellious
respetuoso/a	respectful
sabio/a	wise
sensato/a	sensible
sensible[†]	sensitive, caring

---

[a]*stages*

* As nouns, **anciano/a** and **viejo/a** are used interchangeably to refer to people. As an adjective, however, **anciano/a** is used solely to describe people **(una mujer anciana)**, whereas **viejo/a** can describe things as well **(un hombre viejo; una guitarra vieja).**

[†] **Inocente** and **sensible** are false cognates: They look like English words but have different meanings.

Actividades

A. ¿Cuánto duran las etapas? ¿Entre qué edades queda cada etapa de la vida? Da tu opinión, siguiendo el modelo.

MODELO la infancia →
La infancia dura desde el nacimiento (*birth*) hasta los 24 meses.

VOCABULARIO ÚTIL

la muerte death

1. la niñez
2. la adolescencia
3. la edad adulta
4. la vejez

B. Lo bueno y lo malo. Clasifica los adjetivos del vocabulario de la página anterior en características positivas y negativas. También añade otros adjetivos. ¿Puedes explicar el porqué de tus clasificaciones?

Características positivas	Características negativas

C. Características de las edades. ¿Qué características asocias con las diferentes etapas de la vida? Completa las oraciones de manera lógica, usando los adjetivos de la **Actividad B** y los siguientes cognados. Después, compara tus respuestas con las de tus compañeros/as de clase. ¿Están todos de acuerdo?

VOCABULARIO ÚTIL

ser arrogante, conformista, conservador(a), creativo/a, curioso/a, egoísta, extrovertido/a, horrible, impresionable, (in)flexible, introvertido/a, (ir)responsable, nervioso/a, nostálgico/a, optimista, pesimista, tenso/a, tímido/a, vulnerable

estar desilusionado/a, frustrado/a, interesado/a en, irritado/a, nervioso/a, tenso/a

1. Durante la infancia, los bebés a veces / casi siempre…
2. En la niñez, los niños suelen/siempre…
3. En la adolescencia, con frecuencia / raras veces los jóvenes…
4. Los adultos a menudo / casi nunca…
5. En la vejez, las personas mayores siempre / a veces…

D. Los recuerdos (*memories*). Contesta estas preguntas sobre lo que hacías (*you used to do*) en diferentes etapas de la vida. Sigue el modelo. **¡OJO!** Los verbos están en el **imperfecto,** una forma verbal del pasado que significa *used to* or *would* + (*action*) en inglés. Vas a estudiarlo en más detalle en **Forma y función 9.1.**

MODELO De (*As a*) bebé, ¿llorabas (*did you cry*) con frecuencia? →
No. (No, de bebé, casi nunca lloraba.)

1. De bebé,...
   ¿dormías toda la noche?
   ¿gritabas (*did you scream*) mucho?
   ¿andabas en bicicleta todos los días?
   ¿estabas enfermo/a frecuentemente?
2. De niño/a,...
   ¿estabas aburrido/a a veces?
   ¿almorzabas con tus amigos todos los días?
   ¿venías a la universidad todas las semanas?
   ¿leías novelas románticas con frecuencia?
3. De joven/adolescente,...
   ¿te sentabas a la mesa para comer todas las comidas?
   ¿pasabas mucho tiempo con tus amigos/parientes?
   ¿hacías ejercicio tres o más veces por semana?
   ¿paseabas en el parque con mucha frecuencia?

▲ *De niño/a, ¿celebraban ocasiones especiales en tu familia, como esta familia cubanoamericana? ¿Todavía lo hacen ustedes?*

Juan Oliva Orihuela

« ...en la familia había la costumbre de hacer música diaria... »

Nombre: Juan

Apellidos: (1) Oliva (2) Orihuela

Edad: 41 años

Nació en: La Habana, Cuba

You can watch this interview on the *Entrevistas* Video or Interactive CD-ROM or listen to the audio on the Online Learning Center (**www.mhhe.com/entrevistas2**).

Vocabulario útil

en aquella época	in those days	**las herramientas**	tools
en 1800 tantos	in 1800 something	**un día casual**	no particular occasion
mayormente	mainly	**antes de yo haber**	before I was born
buenos consejos	good advice	**nacido**	
utilizar	to use	**pregones** *m.*	street vendors' calls
mi diario vivir	my daily living	**la venta**	the sale
que no fuera	other than cooking	**el viandero**	meat and grocery vendor
cocinar		**viandas**	cuts of meat
fabricaban	made	**el manicero**	peanut vendor
contrabajos	double bass	**a través de**	through

Si te interesa

The suffix **-ero/a** can be added to some word roots to indicate a person who does the action. Thus, a **pregonero/a** is one who calls out **un pregón;** a **pordiosero/a** is a beggar, from the expression **Déme algo, por Dios** (*Give me something, for* [*the love of*] *God*). What do you think these people do?

  dominguero/a,
  mesero/a,
  zapatero/a

Antes de ver

A. Los instrumentos. Juan viene de una familia que fabricaba instrumentos musicales en La Habana Vieja, y siempre tenía muchos en la casa. ¿Cuáles de los siguientes instrumentos musicales cubanos conoces tú? Busca rápidamente en el Internet fotos y descripciones de los que no conoces y preséntalas a la clase.

1. el bongó
2. las claves
3. el güiro
4. las maracas
5. el piano
6. el tambor

B. Describir el pasado. Juan va a describir su niñez usando formas del imperfecto, un tiempo verbal que vas a estudiar en **Forma y función 9.1.** Empareja las oraciones subrayadas del imperfecto con el infinitivo correspondiente.

ORACIONES

1. _____ Vivíamos en La Habana Vieja.
2. _____ La ciudad era alegre, festiva.
3. _____ Ella cantaba pregones.
4. _____ Pasaba mucho tiempo con mi familia.
5. _____ Fabricaban instrumentos musicales.
6. _____ Teníamos buenos amigos.
7. _____ Jugábamos pelota.
8. _____ El viandero vendía viandas, vegetales, plátanos y papas.

INFINITIVOS

a. cantar
b. fabricar
c. jugar
d. pasar
e. ser
f. tener
g. vender
h. vivir

C. Predicciones. Basándote en lo que has aprendido y visto (*you have learned and seen*) hasta ahora en esta sección, apunta dos o tres de los temas que Juan probablemente va a mencionar en la entrevista.

¡Veamos!

Los detalles. Mientras ves la entrevista, escoge la palabra o frase que mejor completa cada oración.

1. La Habana Vieja era _____.
   a. alegre   **b.** grande   **c.** triste
2. Juan pasaba mucho tiempo con la familia en _____.
   a. la calle   **b.** la cocina   **c.** la sala
3. A las 12:00, todos _____.
   a. limpiaban   **b.** salían a comer   **c.** tocaban música
4. Juan y sus parientes tocaban muchos instrumentos musicales, excepto _____.
   a. la guitarra   **b.** el piano   **c.** el saxofón

Después de ver

Reflexión. Contesta las siguientes preguntas.

1. ¿Crees que la familia de Juan se mudaba (*moved*) con frecuencia, o crees que vivió en el mismo lugar por muchos años? ¿Cómo lo sabes?
2. En tu opinión, ¿quién era la figura más importante en la familia de Juan? ¿Por qué?
3. Durante su niñez, ¿era muy importante la familia extendida para Juan? ¿Cómo lo sabes?
4. En tu propia niñez, ¿pasabas tu tiempo libre con la familia como Juan? ¿Por qué sí o por qué no?

9.1 The Imperfect

In **Capítulo 7,** you learned that the *preterit* is used to express completed actions in various contexts. In this section, you will learn about another past tense called the *imperfect.*

Forms

Here are the regular imperfect forms of **-ar, -er,** and **-ir** verbs.

	hablar	**conocer**	**vivir**
(yo)	habl**aba**	conoc**ía**	viv**ía**
(tú)	habl**abas**	conoc**ías**	viv**ías**
(usted, él/ella)	habl**aba**	conoc**ía**	viv**ía**
(nosotros/as)	habl**ábamos**	conoc**íamos**	viv**íamos**
(vosotros/as)	habl**abais**	conoc**íais**	viv**íais**
(ustedes, ellos/as)	habl**aban**	conoc**ían**	viv**ían**

NOTES:

- The imperfect endings for **-er** and **-ir** verbs are the same.
- The **yo** and **usted/él/ella** endings are identical in all verbs.

Only three verbs are irregular in the imperfect: **ser, ir,** and **ver.**

	ser	**ir**	**ver**
(yo)	era	iba	veía
(tú)	eras	ibas	veías
(usted, él/ella)	era	iba	veía
(nosotros/as)	éramos	íbamos	veíamos
(vosotros/as)	erais	ibais	veíais
(ustedes, ellos/as)	eran	iban	veían

Basic Uses

The imperfect can be translated into English in different ways. In this section, you will learn about three basic uses of the imperfect. You will study additional uses in later chapters, especially when a comparison between the imperfect and preterit is presented.

1. *To describe in the past without focusing on completed actions:* The imperfect is used to describe past actions or states, but unlike the

preterit, the imperfect does not convey that the actions were ever completed. It simply describes the way things were or the way they were done in the past. Consider the following statement by Juan from **Entrevista 1.**

La Habana Vieja **era** alegre,… un lugar donde se **bailaba,** se **cantaba** y se **reunían** muchas familias.	*Old Havana was happy, . . . a place where people danced, sang, and (where) many families got together.*

2. *To express habitual actions in the past:* The descriptive power of the imperfect also allows the speaker to refer to actions that people *used to* or *would* do as a matter of habit. Much of Juan's explanation of what life in Cuba *used to* be like falls into this category.

Un tío mío **llegaba** y **tomaba** una guitarra,…	*An uncle of mine used to (would) arrive and used to (would) take a guitar, . . .*
Los vecinos… **pasaban** y **entraban,**… y **comenzaba** esta gran fiesta…	*The neighbors . . . used to (would) pass by and come in, . . . and this big party used to (would) start up . . .*

3. *To express age and tell time in the past:* Since someone's age or the time of day is always descriptive information with respect to other actions, they *always* appear in the imperfect when they are in the past. Note, however, that other actions within a sentence will be in the preterit if they refer to completed actions.

Cuando yo **tenía** 20 años, mi familia se **mudó** a los Estados Unidos.	*When I was 20 years old, my family moved to the United States.*
Eran las 2:00 de la tarde cuando **pasó** el pregonero.	*It was 2:00 P.M. when the vendor passed by.*

Actividades

A. **La niñez de Juan.** Conjuga los verbos indicados, usando el imperfecto para describir la niñez de Juan. Luego, indica si las oraciones son ciertas o falsas.

	CIERTO	FALSO
1. Juan (vivir) en la Habana Vieja.	☐	☐
2. En La Habana, la música no (ser) muy importante.	☐	☐
3. En la familia de Juan, (haber) muchos músicos.	☐	☐
4. Ellos (tocar) y (cantar) raras veces.	☐	☐
5. La madre de Juan (tener) que correr.	☐	☐
6. Juan siempre (participar) cuando la familia (bailar).	☐	☐
7. Probablemente Juan (ver) a todos los vecinos del barrio todos los días.	☐	☐
8. Probablemente los niños (divertirse) con los pregoneros del barrio.	☐	☐

B. Los niños de hoy. Compara las actividades de los niños de hoy con las de tu propia niñez, completando las siguientes oraciones. Usa los modelos como guía.

MODELOS (no) mirar mucho la televisión →
Los niños de hoy miran mucho la televisión, y de niño yo también miraba mucho la televisión.

Los niños de hoy miran mucho la televisión, pero de niña yo no miraba la televisión.

1. (no) practicar muchos deportes
2. (no) jugar al fútbol
3. (no) comer alimentos naturales
4. (no) vestirse bien
5. (no) obedecer (*to obey*) a sus padres / las personas mayores
6. (no) pasar mucho tiempo en las guarderías (*day care centers*)

C. Entrevista: Tu niñez

Paso 1. Escoge uno de los siguientes temas acerca de tu niñez y escribe una lista de acciones (verbos en el infinitivo) que la describan.

- tu rutina diaria
- las vacaciones de verano
- una tradición familiar

Paso 2. Busca un compañero / una compañera que tenga (*has*) el mismo tema que tú. Convierte tu lista de infinitivos en preguntas para entrevistarlo/la; quieres saber si de niño/a tenía experiencias parecidas. **¡OJO!** ¡Cuidado con las formas del imperfecto!

MODELO ir a la iglesia con la familia →
¿Ibas a la iglesia con tu familia?

Paso 3. Presenta un resumen de tu entrevista a la clase, señalando (*pointing out*) las semejanzas (*similarities*) y las diferencias entre tú y tu compañero/a.

MODELOS Jack y yo íbamos a la iglesia con nuestra familia.

Jack iba a la iglesia con su familia, pero yo no.

D. Retrato personal. Escoge dos de las siguientes edades y escribe un párrafo en que compares esas diferentes etapas de tu vida. Las expresiones de la derecha te pueden servir de modelo. **¡OJO!** ¡Cuidado con los verbos en el presente y en el imperfecto!

Edades	Temas posibles	Expresiones
a los 5 años	familia y amigos	Tengo/Tenía…
a los 10 años	características personales	Yo soy/era una persona…
a los 15 años	gustos y disgustos	Me gusta(n)/gustaba(n)…
a los 18 años	creencias (*beliefs*)	Creo/Creía que…
ahora	aspiraciones	Quiero/Quería…

MODELO A los 10 años, yo era una persona tímida, pero ahora soy más extrovertida.

Análisis cultural

Juan, el primer entrevistado (*interviewee*) de este capítulo, nació y se crió en Cuba y emigró a los Estados Unidos de adolescente. La siguiente cita tomada de una fuente escrita en inglés para anglohablantes trata el tema de la vida de los cubanos en Cuba y de los cubanos que viven en los Estados Unidos. ¿Es consistente esta información con lo que dijo Juan? Usa lo que has aprendido en este capítulo sobre Cuba y los cubanoamericanos, más tu propia experiencia, para contestar las preguntas que siguen las citas.

66 Before 1959, when Fidel Castro took power in Cuba, about 35,000 Cubans lived in the United States, mainly in Florida and New York. Cuban immigration increased dramatically after this date, with over 250,000 people being airlifted to the United States between 1966 and 1973. In 1980, nearly half this number were 'boatlifted' from Mariel Harbor. Today, over 1,000,000 Cubans reside in the U.S., the majority in Florida. . . .

The extended family is generally a transitory household arrangement for recent immigrants, providing help and support for new arrivals. Hispanics in the United States favor the nuclear household over the extended family. . . .

While the children of Hispanic immigrants initially behave in traditional ways, the educational system and increasing exposure to North American culture often turn them toward more American models of behavior. Children often become intermediaries between their parents and the outside world, serving as linguistic and cultural interpreters. . . . 99

Source: *The Hispanic Almanac: From Columbus to Corporate America*

1. ¿En qué año, más o menos, crees que emigró Juan a los Estados Unidos? ¿Tiene el perfil (*profile*) de un inmigrante reciente, según la definición de la cita? ¿Por qué sí o por qué no?

2. Las personas que salen de su país por razones políticas frecuentemente quieren volver a su país tan pronto como (*as soon as*) posible. ¿Cómo les afecta la idea de una vuelta (*return*) rápida? ¿Crees que quieran adaptarse al nuevo país, o mantener las costumbres de su país de origen?

3. Cuántos años llevan los cubanos en los Estados Unidos desde 1959? ¿Cuántas generaciones han nacido (*have been born*) en los Estados Unidos? ¿Crees que los nietos de los primeros inmigrantes se sientan (*feel*) más cubanos que estadounidenses o viceversa? Explica.

Written Accents (IV)

As you have seen, many forms of the imperfect require the use of a written accent. Do you know why? You can review the rules for the written accent **(el acento escrito)** in **Capítulos 3, 6,** and **7,** but the ones relevant for these verb forms are repeated here.

1. **Bailábamos:** This word is called **una palabra esdrújula,** which means that it is stressed on the antepenultimate syllable, or third syllable from the end: **bai-lá-ba-mos.** All words with this stress pattern must bear a written accent in Spanish (e.g., **católico, gramática, único.**).

2. **Vivía:** This verb has a written accent to show that the **i** and the **a** are pronounced as separate syllables **(vi-ví-a).** Normally the combination of the weak vowel **i** with a strong vowel such as **a** forms a diphthong, meaning that the two vowel sounds are pronounced as one syllable: **previa (pre-via,** which is pronounced more or less like the *-b ya* of the phrase *grab ya*).

The *Manual de práctica* contains activities to practice the material presented here.

▲ *Según Juan, los pregoneros son personas que se dedican a la venta popular de diferentes productos, como este vendedor de granizados* (small snow cones) *en La Habana, Cuba.*

¿Qué fiestas celebrabas de niño/a?

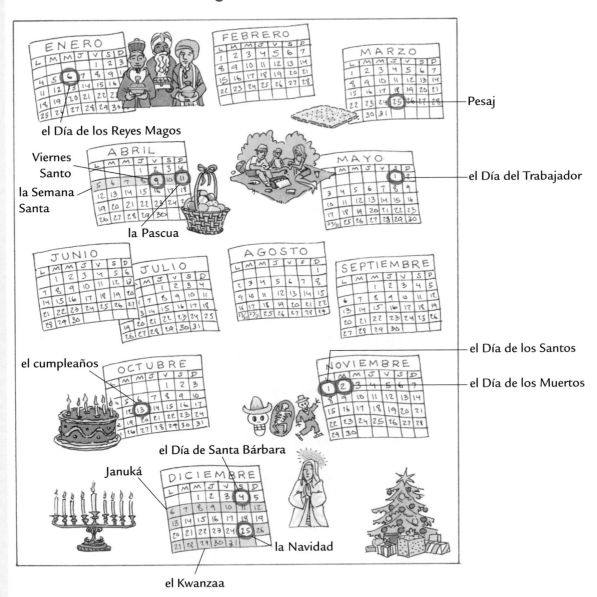

el Día de los Reyes Magos

Pesaj

Viernes Santo

la Semana Santa

la Pascua

el Día del Trabajador

el cumpleaños

el Día de los Santos

el Día de los Muertos

el Día de Santa Bárbara

Januká

la Navidad

el Kwanzaa

el barmitzvah / la batmitzvah	bar/bat mitzvah
la confirmación	confirmation
el Día de (Acción de) Gracias	Thanksgiving
el (día del) santo	saint's day
la primera comunión	first communion
la quinceañera	girl's fifteenth birthday party
celebrar	to celebrate
recordar (ue)	to remember

Actividades

A. El año actual. Mira un calendario del año corriente. ¿En qué fecha se celebran las siguientes fiestas? No olvides (*Don't forget*) indicar el día de la semana y/o del mes. También busca otras fiestas que se celebran en tu familia.

> MODELO   tu cumpleaños →
> Este año, mi cumpleaños es el lunes, el 4 de abril.

1. la Pascua
2. Januká
3. la Semana Santa
4. el Día de Acción de Gracias
5. el Día de la Independencia (de tu país)
6. ¿ ?

B. Asociaciones. ¿Qué fiesta(s) y emociones asocias con las siguientes palabras? Usa las palabras de la lista del vocabulario más las del siguiente **Vocabulario útil.**

VOCABULARIO ÚTIL

el Día de la Madre	Mother's Day
el Día del Padre	Father's Day
el Día de los Enamorados (de San Valentín)	Valentine's Day

1. regalos
2. sorpresa (*surprise*)
3. familia
4. viaje (*trip*)
5. flores
6. pastel o dulces
7. comida especial
8. amigos
9. novio/a
10. gobierno

C. Las fiestas hispanas. Describe lo que está pasando en las fotos en la siguiente página que son de dos fiestas diferentes que se celebran en el mundo hispano. Después, compáralas con tus propias celebraciones de ocasiones parecidas.

Si te interesa

Saint Barbara is an important Cuban patron saint. Note that May 1 is the *international* Labor Day, which most countries celebrate (the U.S. celebration on the first Monday of September is unique). Halloween is not generally celebrated in Hispanic countries; instead, the first of November (All Saints' Day) and the second of November (All Souls' Day) are celebrated as religious and family holidays.

1.

▲ *Una familia celebra el santo de una niña en Buenos Aires.*

2.

▲ *En esta procesión de Semana Santa en Antigua, Guatemala, muchos hombres llevan una carroza (float) con la imagen de Jesucristo.*

D. Entrevista: Las fiestas en tu vida. ¿Qué fiestas celebrabas de niño/a? ¿Cómo las celebrabas? ¿Qué comías en esas ocasiones? Trabajando con un compañero / una compañera de clase, describan por lo menos una fiesta que celebraban de niño/a que todavía celebran ahora y las semejanzas y diferencias entre las celebraciones del pasado y las de ahora.

● ¿Cómo te sentías?

llorar

¡Ja, ja, ja!

reírse (i, i)*

sonreír (i, i)†

---

* In the present, the verb **reírse** is conjugated: **me río, te ríes, se ríe, nos reímos, os reís, se ríen.** In the preterit, it's conjugated: **me reí, te reíste, se rió, nos reímos, os reísteis, se rieron.** Note the position of the written accents in each tense.

† The verb **sonreír** is conjugated like the verb **reírse** in all tenses but with the prefix **son-** and without the reflexive pronouns: *present* = **sonrío, sonríes, sonríe,…** ; *preterit* = **sonreí, sonreíste, sonrió,…**

ponerle (*irreg.*) + *adj.* **a alguien**   to make someone (feel) + *adj.*
sentirse (ie, i) + *adj., adv.*   to feel + *adj., adv.*

aburrido/a	enojado/a	optimista
alegre	frustrado/a	orgulloso/a
cansado/a	(in)feliz	pesimista
cariñoso/a	interesado/a	respetuoso/a
confiado/a	intimidado/a	tenso/a
deprimido/a	irritado/a	tímido/a
desilusionado/a	molesto/a	triste
emocionado/a	nervioso/a	unido/a

bien	fatal	mal
estupendo	horrible	maravilloso
fantástico		

A. La idea exacta. Trabajando con un compañero / una compañera, usa las siguientes preguntas para verificar el significado (*meaning*) de las palabras de la lista anterior (*preceding*).

1. ¿Qué palabras son sinónimas? ¿Cuáles son opuestas?
2. En tu opinión, ¿cuáles representan emociones positivas? ¿Cuáles representan emociones negativas?

B. Reacciones. ¿Qué emociones asocias con las siguientes ocasiones? Sigue el modelo.

MODELO   Las fiestas de despedida (*good-bye*) →
            Las fiestas de despedida me ponen triste y deprimido y lloro mucho.

1. la boda de un amigo / una amiga
2. las disputas familiares
3. las fiestas de cumpleaños
4. el Januká (el Kwanzaa, la Navidad)
5. la muerte de algún pariente
6. las reuniones familiares
7. las vacaciones en familia
8. ¿ ?

▲ *De niño/a, ¿salías el 31 de octubre para pedir caramelos en tu barrio como estos niños cubanoamericanos en Miami?*

You can watch this interview on the *Entrevistas* Video or Interactive CD-ROM or listen to the audio on the Online Learning Center (**www.mhhe.com/entrevistas2**).

Eduardo Alemán Águila

« *...recuerdo muchas fiestas, pero la fiesta de Fin de Año*[a] *en especial,*[b]*...* »

Nombre: Eduardo

Apellidos: (1) Alemán (2) Águila

Edad: 34 años

Nació en: La Habana, Cuba

[a]Fin... *New Year's Eve* [b]en... *in particular*

Vocabulario útil

en la cual	in which	**recogiendo caramelos**	picking up candies
sobre todo	above all	**las carrozas**	floats
traía un cerdo	(he) would (used to) bring a pig	**devota**	devout
		todo tipo de rituales	all types of rituals
asábamos	we would (used to) roast	**una ceiba**	silkwood tree
los cuales duraban	which would (used to) last	**le dábamos vueltas al árbol**	we'd go around the tree
hasta altas horas de la noche	until all hours (of the night)	**buena suerte**	good luck
alegría	joy		

Antes de ver

A. ¿Tradición religiosa o superstición? Empareja las siguientes descripciones con el tipo de tradición que describe.

DESCRIPCIONES

1. _____ ...fiestas de tambores, personas cantando y ofreciendo todo tipo de rituales.
2. _____ Íbamos a visitar un árbol, una ceiba, y dábamos vueltas alrededor de él. Esto traía buena suerte.
3. _____ Mi abuelo traía un cerdo y lo asábamos. Luego, todos nos sentábamos a la mesa a comerlo.
4. _____ Las personas se iban a la calle a bailar, y toda la ciudad estaba llena de alegría. Los niños nos divertíamos mucho recogiendo caramelos que caían de las carrozas.

TRADICIONES

a. una fiesta familiar
b. una fiesta pública en las calles
c. una celebración de santería (religión mixta de tradiciones católicas y africanas)
d. una práctica supersticiosa

B. Fiestas a lo largo (*throughout*) **del año.** Eduardo va a hablar de dos fiestas que tenían lugar en Cuba durante dos estaciones diferentes: el Fin de Año y los carnavales de julio y agosto. Usando la siguiente tabla como modelo, compara una celebración de Fin de Año y otra celebración del verano (el 4 de Julio, el Día del Trabajador, una fiesta local, etcétera) tal y como se celebraban en tu familia o en tu ciudad/región cuando eras niño/a. Para cada celebración, apunta los siguientes datos: las actividades que hacías tú, con quién(es) las hacías y dónde las hacías.

Celebración	Yo	Eduardo
Fin de Año		
(nombre de la celebración de verano)		

¡Veamos!

¿Qué dijo? Teniendo en cuenta tus apuntes de la **Actividad B** de **Antes de ver,** ve la entrevista y apunta lo que dice Eduardo sobre la fiesta de Fin de Año y los carnavales de julio y agosto.

Después de ver

¿Entendiste? Contesta las siguientes preguntas.

1. ¿Vivía Eduardo en una ciudad, un pueblo o en el campo? ¿Cómo lo sabes?
2. ¿Eran iguales todas las familias del edificio donde vivía Eduardo? ¿En qué se diferenciaban?
3. ¿Cómo eran los carnavales en La Habana? ¿Cuánto tiempo duraban? ¿Qué hacía la gente? ¿Cómo se ponía?
4. ¿Qué edades participaban en la tradición de dar vueltas alrededor de la ceiba?

Piénsalo bien

Comparaciones. Contesta las siguientes preguntas.

1. ¿Qué papel hacía la familia extendida durante la niñez de Eduardo?
2. En tu opinión, ¿cómo fue la niñez de Eduardo en general: alegre, triste, aburrida, interesante, etcétera?
3. ¿Qué elementos tienen en común las celebraciones o costumbres que mencionó Eduardo y las que mencionó Juan?
4. ¿Cómo se comparan las celebraciones y costumbres de tu niñez con las de Juan y Eduardo? Puedes usar la siguiente fórmula como modelo. Incluye el mayor número de detalles que puedas (*that you can*).

Las celebraciones de mi niñez eran	iguales a más o menos como (muy) diferentes de	las cubanas porque…

● 9.2 Gustar (Review)

You have already learned to use expressions with **gustar** when expressing likes and dislikes. In this section you will review these constructions and learn more details about the sentence patterns in which this verb appears.

Gustar with Actions (Verbs)

When talking about actions that you or others prefer, use a form of **gustar** with the *infinitive* form of the verb(s) (even if the English translation uses an *-ing* form of the verb). Note that, regardless of the number of actions (verbs) listed, the form of **gustar** does not change.

Me **gusta** preparar la cena.	*I like making supper.*
Nos **gusta** reunirnos a menudo.	*We like to get together often.*
Te **gusta** cantar y bailar.	*You like to sing and dance.*

The imperfect of **gusta** is **gustaba.**

De niño te **gustaba** tocar la guitarra en las fiestas familiares.	*As a child you used to like to play the guitar at family parties.*

Gustar with Things (Nouns)

When verbs like **gustar** are used with things (as opposed to actions), the ending of the verb changes to reflect the quantity—singular or plural—of the thing(s) liked.

A mí me gust**an las fiestas** de sorpresa, pero a mis padres les gust**a** más **una cena** elegante.	*I like surprise parties, but my parents prefer* (lit., *like more*) *a fancy dinner.*
Nos gust**a el regalo** de la abuela.	*We like our grandmother's gift.*
¿Te gust**an las fotos** de tu niñez?	*Do you like the pictures from your childhood?*

The imperfect of **gustan** is **gustaban.**

Me gustab**an** mucho **las fiestas** que daban mis padres.	*I really used to like the parties my parents gave* (used to give).

9.3 Other Verbs like **gustar**

Other verbs that use the same sentence pattern as **gustar** are useful for expressing positive and negative reactions. You have already learned some of these verbs; make sure you know the meaning of all of them.

Reacción positiva		Reacción negativa	
caer (*irreg.*)* **bien**	to like (*someone*)	**caer mal**	to dislike (*someone*)
encantar	to delight, charm	**disgustar**	to annoy, offend, upset
fascinar	to fascinate	**irritar**	to irritate
gustar	to be pleasing	**molestar**	to bother, annoy
importar	to matter, be important	**no importar**	not to matter, be unimportant
interesar	to interest	**aburrir**	to bore

NOTE:

- **Gustar** is generally used to express likes for things and actions.
- To express likes and dislikes for people, use **caerle bien/mal.**

   Me cae bien mi tío Alejandro, pero **me caen mal** mis primas.

   I like my Uncle Alejandro, but I don't care for my cousins.

- All these "other verbs like **gustar**" require the same agreements between subject (the thing that fascinates, interests, is pleasing, and so on) and verb and between the indirect object pronoun (**me, te, le, nos, os, les**) and any stated indirect object (**a mí, a ti, a usted/él/ella,...**).

   A ustedes les **fascinan** las películas de horror, ¿verdad?

   You (pl.) are fascinated by horror films, right?

   A mi madre no le **interesan** para nada.

   My mother isn't interested in them at all.

Actividades

A. Entrevista: La fiesta ideal

Paso 1. ¿Cuáles de las siguientes oraciones expresan tus ideas sobre lo que debe ocurrir en tu fiesta ideal?

☐ Me fascinan las comidas elegantes.
☐ Me importa tener allí a muchos amigos.
☐ Me encanta recibir regalos.
☐ Me irritan los juegos como *Charades*.
☐ Me importa invitar a mis padres.
☐ Me disgusta tomar bebidas alcohólicas.
☐ Me gusta incluir a personas de todas las edades (niños y adultos).
☐ Me caen mal los que se ponen borrachos.

---

* The verb **caer** is irregular in the present only in the **yo** form: **caigo, caes, cae,...** In the preterit, the third-person forms resemble those of **leer (leyó, leyeron): cayó, cayeron.**

Paso 2. Convierte las oraciones del **Paso 1** en preguntas y habla con un compañero / una compañera para comparar tu fiesta ideal con la suya (*his/hers*). Al final, prepara un resumen para la clase de las semejanzas y diferencias.

> MODELO   E1: Paula, ¿te gusta cantar y bailar en tus fiestas?
> E2: Sí, me gusta.
> E1: (*a la clase*): A Paula le gusta cantar y bailar en sus fiestas;
> también le gusta(n)…

B. Las fiestas de Armando.   Usa las siguientes frases para escribir oraciones completas (en el imperfecto) sobre las fiestas de Armando, un cubanoamericano de Miami. Luego, indica si las oraciones son ciertas o falsas, según lo que has aprendido en este capítulo.

	CIERTO	FALSO
1. Armando **/** gustar **/** *Halloween*	☐	☐
2. Armando y los otros niños **/** encantar **/** salir con sus padres en *Halloween*	☐	☐
3. Armando **/** caer mal **/** su abuela	☐	☐
4. los niños del barrio **/** no importar **/** recibir muchos caramelos	☐	☐
5. Armando **/** molestar **/** reunirse con su familia en Nochebuena (*Christmas Eve*)	☐	☐
6. Armando **/** encantar **/** cantar y bailar con su familia	☐	☐

C. ¿Qué opinas (*do you think*)**?**

Paso 1. Las fiestas y tradiciones familiares tienen aspectos positivos y negativos. Escribe tu opinión sobre cada tema de la lista, usando los verbos **gustar, encantar, irritar, molestar,** etcétera. ¿Puedes añadir otros detalles a la lista?

> MODELO   los besos de la abuela u otro pariente →
> Me irritan los besos de mi abuela. ¡Ya no soy bebé!

1. los regalos de parientes que no conoces muy bien
2. los platos típicos de tu familia (menciona platos específicos)
3. tener a toda la familia reunida
4. presentar a tu novio/a (esposo/a) a la familia
5. viajar a casa de los parientes
6. cenar/comer muy fuerte
7. cantar (mirar la televisión, escuchar la radio, etcétera) todos juntos
8. ¿ ?

Paso 2. Ahora compara tus respuestas con las de dos o tres compañeros/as de clase. ¿Qué cosas son positivas para la mayoría? ¿Cuáles son generalmente negativas?

Lectura

Sobre la lectura

La palabra **reliquia** (*heirloom*) generalmente implica joyería preciosa, antigüedades (*antiques*), obras de arte (*works of art*) y otros símbolos materiales de la riqueza (*wealth*). Esta lectura revela una reliquia más humilde e intangible: el amor (*love*) por la cocina. ¿Es raro (*peculiar*) el amor que tiene esta familia por la comida? Mientras lees, busca la respuesta del narrador antes de decidir por ti mismo/a.

Antes de leer

A. En familia. ¿Hay en tu familia alguna costumbre que sea (*is*) común a todos los miembros? ¿Tienes una actitud positiva o negativa hacia (*toward*) esta costumbre? Trabajando en grupos de tres o cuatro personas, descríbeles esta parte de tu historia familiar a tus compañeros/as. No te olvides de mencionar tu actitud.

MODELO   En mi familia, todos tenemos…
                        todos sabemos…
                        a todos nos gusta(n)…

B. Encuesta: Las familias y la cocina. ¿Tiene cada familia una actitud especial hacia la cocina? Para descubrirla, haz una encuesta en la clase, usando las siguientes preguntas. Después, habla con tus compañeros/as de clase sobre las observaciones que todos hicieron, para decidir si la clase en general tiene amor por la cocina o no.

1. ¿Quién cocina en tu familia?
   a. mi padre   **b.** mi madre   **c.** los hijos   **d.** otra(s) persona(s): _____
2. ¿Por qué cocina(n)?
   a. le(s) gusta   **b.** por obligación   **c.** otra razón: _____
3. ¿Qué cocina(n)?
   a. platos sencillos   **c.** comida comercialmente preparada
   b. platos especiales   **d.** otro tipo de comida: _____
4. ¿Cómo aprendió/aprendieron a cocinar?
   a. siguiendo recetas (*recipes*)   **c.** de algún miembro de la familia
   b. en la escuela/universidad   **d.** de otra manera: _____
       o un curso de cocina
5. ¿Al resto de la familia le gustan las comidas que se preparan y se comen en casa?
   a. sí   **b.** no   **c.** a veces

La madre, la cocina, la abuelita y los chicos
por Enrique Fernández

En un principio, era mi abuela materna. Mi madre y mi tía recuerdan cómo ella preparaba ciertos platos e intentan[a] hacerlos de memoria. Como ven, mi árbol genealógico es gastronómico y yo cocino.

Mi madre y yo llevamos una conversación constante sobre cocina. La mayor parte de la familia piensa que ella cocina mejor que yo, pero ella dice que no es cierto. Nos desvivimos[b] con falsa modestia, al reconocer que cada quien[c] tiene el don.[d] Entonces, volvemos a los libros de recetas, en busca de algo nuevo con qué impresionar a la familia y, más importante aún,[e] el uno al otro.[f]

▲ Así se preparan los tostones (plátano frito) en Cuba.

A veces me pregunto si no debemos compartir algo más que la cocina. ¿Es la conversación constante sobre la preparación de alimentos una forma de evadir algún problema familiar grave? ¡Qué va![g] El tema me une a mi madre y a mi abuela, que permanece[h] viva en la memoria de los dos cada vez que tratamos de cocinar «como lo hacía mami», como dice mi propia madre. Y mis hijos también cocinan.

Si alguien preguntara[i] si mi madre y yo nos queremos, responderíamos[j] que «sí, por supuesto». Pero, no nos distraigan[k] ahora con preguntas tontas,[l] porque estamos muy ocupados cocinando. ■

[a]*they try* [b]*Nos... We outdo ourselves* [c]*cada... each one* [d]*gift (talent)* [e]*más... even more important* [f]*el... each other* [g]*¡Qué... No way!* [h]*remains* [i]*were to ask* [j]*we would reply* [k]*no... don't distract us* [l]*foolish*

Después de leer

A. ¿Entendiste?   Contesta las siguientes preguntas con información de la lectura.

1. ¿Quiénes cocinan los platos de la abuela?
2. ¿Cómo se conservan las recetas de la abuela?
3. Según la opinión general en la familia, ¿quién cocina mejor? ¿Está de acuerdo la madre del narrador?
4. ¿Qué hacen el narrador y su madre para impresionar a la familia?
5. ¿Heredaron (*Inherited*) los hijos del narrador el don de cocinar?
6. ¿Se quieren la madre y el narrador? ¿Hay cariño o tensión entre ellos? ¿Cómo lo sabes?

B. ¿Cómo es esta familia?

Paso 1. Los primeros dos párrafos de la lectura nos presentan a la familia y su amor por la cocina. Apunta algunos detalles y frases que dan evidencia de la normalidad o peculiaridad de esta familia.

Paso 2. Ahora examina de nuevo los últimos dos párrafos para encontrar la opinión del narrador acerca de su familia. ¿Es el don de cocinar un síntoma de salud o de enfermedad mental? Apoya (*Support*) tu respuesta con la evidencia que se da en el texto.

C. Enrique Fernández, su familia y la cocina. En tu opinión, ¿cómo contestaría (*would answer*) el narrador las preguntas de la encuesta en **Antes de leer, Actividad B?** Contéstalas desde la perspectiva de Enrique Fernández. Después, compara tus respuestas con las del resto de la clase y di si la experiencia de Enrique Fernández es similar a la de la clase en general o si es diferente.

D. Conexiones familiares. ¿Cómo se establecen conexiones entre las generaciones en tu familia? Contesta las siguientes preguntas, pensando en ejemplos concretos. Prepárate para contar algunas anécdotas a la clase para ilustrar tus respuestas.

En mi familia…	SÍ	NO
1. los hijos tienden a (*tend*) seguir las mismas inclinaciones que sus padres y a adoptar sus gustos, pasatiempos, etcétera.	☐	☐
2. los hijos tienden a seguir la misma profesión u oficio (*trade*) que sus padres.	☐	☐
3. los padres usan los pasatiempos para enseñarles valores importantes a los hijos.	☐	☐
4. las actividades compartidas que implican diversión (pasatiempos, deportes, etcétera) establecen una conexión importante entre las generaciones.	☐	☐
5. las personas no se comunican hablándose directamente, sino participando juntas en actividades como cocinar, practicar deportes y otros pasatiempos.	☐	☐
6. existen rivalidades entre miembros de la familia en cuanto a (*with regard to*) la cocina, los deportes, etcétera.	☐	☐

E. Debate. El amor por la cocina es una inclinación de la familia Fernández a lo largo de varias generaciones. En tu opinión, ¿son innatas las inclinaciones y las vocaciones en general, son aprendidas de la cultura en que vive uno o son una combinación de los dos? Para responder, completa *una* de las siguientes oraciones, basándote en tu propia experiencia y en la lectura.

1. Yo creo que el amor de algunas familias por la cocina es innato porque…

2. En mi opinión, el amor por la cocina es algo aprendido porque…

Tu profesor(a) va a dividir la clase en dos partes, según su posición, para tener un debate sobre el tema.

Picadillo

Para hacer 4 porciones

1 cebolla mediana, picada[a]
1 diente de ajo finamente picado
1 libra[b] de carne molida[c] de res, extra magra[d]
1/4 de taza de jerez[e] (optativo)
1/2 cucharadita[f] de comino[g]
1/2 cucharadita de orégano
1/8 cucharadita de sal
Una pizca[h] de pimiento rojo molido
1/4 taza de pasas de uva[i]
1 taza de piña en cubos, fresca o envasada[j]
1 tarro[k] de 16 onzas de tomates en trozos
1 pimiento verde mediano, picado
1/4 de pimiento rojo, picado

Tamaño de cada porción: 1 1/2 tazas

En una sartén,[l] a fuego mediano, dore[m] la carne molida, la cebolla y el ajo hasta que la cebolla esté blanda,[n] la carne haya perdido[o] su color rosado y el líquido que suelta la carne salga claro.[p] Escurra[q] toda la grasa que suelte. Agregue los demás ingredientes, excepto los pimientos picados. Cocine suavemente durante 5 minutos. Agregue los pimientos y cocine hasta que se calienten[r] un poco. Sírvase con arroz y pan

El picadillo es un plato que se come especialmente en las fiestas. Es popular en Cuba, la República Dominicana y Puerto Rico. Esta receta es una de las muchas variaciones posibles.

[a]*diced* [b]*pound* [c]*ground* [d]*lean* [e]*sherry*
[f]*teaspoon* [g]*cumin* [h]*pinch* [i]*pasas… raisins*
[j]*canned* [k]*jar* [l]*frying pan* [m]*brown*
[n]*esté… is soft* [o]*haya… has lost*
[p]*que… that comes from the meat runs clear*
[q]*Drain* [r]*se… they become warm*

PORTAFOLIO CULTURAL

Redacción

Un retrato (*portrait*) escrito. Vas a crear un retrato escrito de tu profesor(a) o de otro adulto no de tu familia, incluyendo detalles y recuerdos personales de su niñez. Sigue los pasos en el *Manual de práctica* para completar el retrato.

Exploración

Investigación cultural. Busca más información sobre Cuba o los cubanoamericanos en los Estados Unidos en la biblioteca, en el *Entrevistas* Online Learning Center (**www.mhhe.com/entrevistas2**) o en otros sitios del Internet y preséntala a la clase. El *Manual de práctica* contiene más ideas para tu presentación.

Léxico activo

LA FRECUENCIA

a menudo	frequently
a veces	sometimes
cada año/mes	each year/month
casi nunca	almost never
casi siempre	almost always
con frecuencia	frequently
raras veces	rarely
siempre	always
todas las noches	every night
todos los días	every day

la **adolescencia**	adolescence
el/la **adolescente**	adolescent, teenager
el/la **adulto/a**	adult
el/la **anciano/a**	elderly person
el/la **bebé**	baby
la **edad adulta**	adulthood
la **infancia**	infancy
el/la **joven** (*pl.* **jóvenes**)	young person
la **niñez**	childhood
la **persona mayor**	older person
la **vejez**	old age
el/la **viejo/a**	elderly person
confiado/a	trusting
deprimido/a	depressed
emocionado/a	emotional; moved
fatal	awful
(in)feliz (*pl.* **[in]felices**)	(un)happy
inocente	naive, inexperienced
molesto/a	annoying; annoyed
orgulloso/a	proud
rebelde	rebellious
respetuoso/a	respectful
sabio/a	wise
sensato/a	sensible
sensible	sensitive, caring

Repaso: el/la niño/a

LAS FIESTAS

el **barmitzvah** / la **batmitzvah**	bar/bat mitzvah
la **confirmación**	confirmation
el **cumpleaños**	birthday
el **Día de (Acción de) Gracias**	Thanksgiving
el **Día de los Muertos**	All Souls' Day (November 2)
el **Día de los Reyes Magos**	Epiphany (January 6)
el **Día de los Santos**	All Saints' Day (November 1)
el **Día de Santa Bárbara**	Saint Barbara's feast day (December 4)
el **(día del) santo**	saint's day
el **Día del Trabajador**	Labor Day (May 1)
Januká	Hanukkah
el **Kwanzaa**	Kwanzaa (December 26–January 1)
la **Navidad**	Christmas (December 25)

la **Pascua**	Easter
Pesaj	Passover
la **primera comunión**	first communion
la **quinceañera**	girl's fifteenth birthday party
la **Semana Santa**	Holy Week
el **Viernes Santo**	Good Friday
celebrar	to celebrate
recordar (ue)	to remember

¿CÓMO TE SENTÍAS?

llorar	to cry
ponerle (*irreg.*) + *adj.* a alguien	to make someone (feel) + *adj.*
reírse (i, i)	to laugh
sentirse (ie, i) + *adj., adv.*	to feel + *adj., adv.*
sonreír (i, i)	to smile
desilusionado/a	disillusioned, deceived
frustrado/a	frustrated
interesado/a	interested
intimidado/a	intimidated
irritado/a	irritated
nervioso/a	nervous
optimista *m., f.*	optimistic
pesimista *m., f.*	pessimistic
tenso/a	stressed
tímido/a	shy
estupendo *adv.*	stupendous
fantástico *adv.*	fantastic
horrible *adv.*	horrible, terrible
maravilloso *adv.*	marvelous

Repaso: (*adjectives*) **aburrido/a, alegre, cansado/a, cariñoso/a, confiado/a, deprimido/a, emocionado/a, enojado/a, orgulloso/a, respetuoso/a, triste, unido/a;** (*adverbs*) **bien, mal**

VERBOS COMO *GUSTAR*

aburrirle	to bore (*someone*)
caerle (*irreg.*) **bien/mal**	to (dis)like (*someone*)
disgustarle	not to be pleasing to (*someone*)
fascinarle	to fascinate (*someone*)
gustarle	to be pleasing to (*someone*)
importarle	to matter / be important to (*someone*)
interesarle	to interest (*someone*)
irritarle	to irritate (*someone*)
molestarle	to bother/annoy (*someone*)

Recorridos[a]
y recuerdos

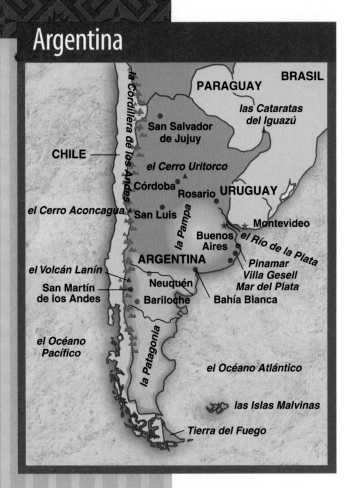

Argentina

PARAGUAY

BRASIL

la Cordillera de los Andes

las Cataratas del Iguazú

San Salvador de Jujuy

CHILE

el Cerro Uritorco

Córdoba

Rosario

URUGUAY

el Cerro Aconcagua

San Luis

la Pampa

Montevideo

Buenos Aires

el Río de la Plata

ARGENTINA

el Volcán Lanín

Neuquén

Pinamar
Villa Gesell
Mar del Plata

San Martín de los Andes

Bariloche

Bahía Blanca

el Océano Pacífico

la Patagonia

el Océano Atlántico

las Islas Malvinas

Tierra del Fuego

Cultura

◆ Traveling Through Argentina

◆ Vacation Spots and Types of Vacations

◆ **Señas culturales: El tango argentino**

Lengua

◆ Means of Transportation; Traveling

◆ Popular Travel Destinations

◆ National Symbols

◆ Preterit vs. Imperfect (10.1)

◆ More About the Present Participle (10.2)

◆ The Present Perfect (10.3)

◆ **Lo** + Adjective (10.4)

[a]*Travels*

Argentina					Fundación de Buenos Aires				Independencia de Argentina		Dictadura de Juan Manuel de Rosas	
	hasta el siglo XVI	**1500– 1600**	**1534**	**1536**	**1600– 1750**		**1776– 1783**	**1816**		**1835– 1852**	**1846– 1848**
Los Estados Unidos y el Canadá	Varias tribus indígenas habitan en Norteamérica	Exploración española de Norteamérica	Jacques Cartier reclama para Francia el Canadá		Fundación de las colonias británicas en Norteamérica		Guerra de Independencia en los EE. UU.				Guerra Mexicano-Americana

Instantánea

ORIGEN DEL NOMBRE

Argentina: del latín *argentum* (plata) (De allí también, tomó su nombre el Río de la Plata.)

POBLACIÓN

36.993.000

LENGUAS

El español (oficial), el italiano, lenguas indígenas

▲ *Otro puerto, del artista argentino Alejandro Xul Solar (1887–1963)*

For additional practice, check out the *Manual de práctica,* the Interactive CD-ROM, and the Online Learning Center **(www.mhhe.com/entrevistas2)**!

Inmigración masiva de europeos	Gobierno de Juan Perón		Guerra de las Islas Malvinas	Tratado de MERCOSUR entre Argentina, Brasil, Paraguay y Uruguay		Ciudadanos argentinos pueden visitar las Malvinas por primera vez desde la guerra	Crisis económica y política provoca varios cambios de presidente
1898	**los años 40–50**	**1946– 1955** / **1952**	**1982**	**1991**	**1994**	**1999**	**2001– 2002**
Guerra Hispano- Americana		Puerto Rico se hace Estado Libre Asociado de los EE. UU.	El Canadá se separa legalmente de Inglaterra		Tratado de Libre Comercio entre los EE. UU., el Canadá y México		

● Los medios de transporte

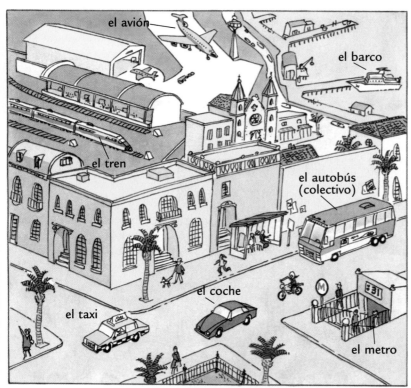

el centro	downtown; city center
la estación del metro* / de trenes	subway/train station
la parada de autobuses/taxis	bus stop / taxi stand
caminar	to walk
conducir (*irreg.*)[†]	to drive
ir a pie	to go on foot, walk
ir en autobús (avión, tren,...)	to go by bus (plane, train, . . .)
manejar	to drive

Actividades

A. Asociaciones. ¿Qué medio(s) de transporte asocias con las siguientes palabras y expresiones?

1. rápido
2. lento
3. entre ciudades
4. dentro de la ciudad
5. caro
6. barato
7. el agua
8. el aire

B. ¿Cómo llegas? ¿Qué medio(s) de transporte usas para llegar a los siguientes destinos (*destinations*)?

MODELO   ir al centro →
Cuando voy al centro, voy en taxi. (Voy en taxi para ir al centro.)

---

* In Argentina **el metro** is usually referred to as **el subte,** from **subterráneo** (*underground*).
[†] In the present, **conducir** is irregular in the **yo** form only: **conduzco.** In the preterit, it is completely irregular: **conduje, condujiste, condujo,...**

1. ir de tu casa a la universidad (o viceversa)
2. ir a la estación de trenes
3. ir de compras
4. ir de vacaciones
5. visitar a tus amigos/as en tu barrio
6. visitar a tus abuelos u otros parientes
7. ir a la parada de autobuses

C. ¿Cuál es mejor? ¿Cuáles son las ventajas y las desventajas de los diferentes medios de transporte? Trabaja con tres o cuatro compañeros/as para apuntar sus ideas al respecto. Luego, van a exponer sus ideas a la clase.

De viaje

En la agencia de viajes   En el aeropuerto   la maleta

la aduana	customs
el/la pasajero/a	passenger
abordar un avión (barco, tren)	to board a plane (ship, train)
bajar de un autobús (coche, taxi)	to get off a bus (out of a car/taxi)
cancelar una reserva	to cancel a reservation
confirmar una reserva	to book, confirm a reservation
desbordar un avión (barco, tren)	to get off a plane (ship, train)
estar de vacaciones	to be on vacation
estar de viaje	to be on a trip
hacer una excursión	to go on an excursion/outing

hacer un viaje	to take a trip
ir de vacaciones	to go on vacation
ir de viaje	to go on a trip
parar en	to stop (over) in
perder (ie) un autobús (barco, tren, vuelo)	to miss a bus (ship, train, flight)
perderse (ie)	to get lost
reconfirmar	to reconfirm a reservation
subir a un autobús (coche, taxi)	to get on a bus (in a car/taxi)
viajar	to travel
de ida	one-way
de ida y vuelta	round-trip

Los destinos más populares

¡Vení a Argentina y conocé algunas de sus riquezas naturales!

La Playa Pinamar

Mirá el **paisaje**[a] rústico y tranquilo, la **sierra**[b] cerca de Córdoba y las bellas **playas** del **Océano** Atlántico: Pinamar, Villa, Gesell, Mar del Plata.

Las Cataratas del Iguazú

Disfrutá las **Cataratas** del Iguazú, las más grandes del país, la famosa **llanura**[c] de la Pampa y el **desierto** de la Patagonia.

El Cerro Aconcagua

Contemplá la majestad del **Volcán** Lanín o del Cerro Aconcagua, el **pico**[d] más alto de la **Cordillera**[e] de los Andes (6.960m).

También hay que conocer la **selva**[f] y los **lagos**[g] y **bosques**[h] de San Martín de los Andes.

¡No lo pienses más,[i] vení ya!
¡Argentina te espera!

[a]*landscape* [b]*mountain range* [c]*flatlands, prairie* [d]*mountain peak* [e]*mountain range* [f]*jungle* [g]*lakes* [h]*forests* [i]*No… Don't wait (think about it) any longer*

el campo	country(side)	el río	river
la montaña	mountain	el salto	waterfall

CAPÍTULO 10 • Recorridos y recuerdos

Actividades

A. Definiciones. ¿A qué cosa, persona o acción se refieren las siguientes descripciones?

1. Cuando viajas de un país a otro, generalmente necesitas pasar por este lugar.
2. Es la persona que organiza tu viaje.
3. Es el viaje en avión.
4. Es la persona que viaja en avión, barco, tren, etcétera.
5. Es la acción de esperar un servicio con muchas otras personas, por ejemplo, en el banco.
6. Es un boleto que te permite ir a un lugar y después volver.
7. Es el conjunto (*collection*) de todas las maletas que llevas en un viaje.
8. Es la lista de las fechas y los lugares de un viaje.
9. Este tipo de viaje se puede hacer sobre la marcha (*off the cuff*), sin planearlo.
10. Es lo que muchos estudiantes hacen durante el descanso (*break*) de primavera.

B. El orden correcto. Juan Alberto vive en Buenos Aires. La semana pasada fue en autobús a ver a su tío en Córdoba. Pon las siguientes acciones en orden cronológico para describir su viaje.

a. _____ bajar del autobús en Córdoba
b. _____ comprar el boleto
c. _____ disfrutar del (*to enjoy the*) viaje en autobús
d. _____ hacer cola en la estación
e. _____ llegar a la estación de autobuses
f. _____ parar unos minutos en Rosario
g. _____ subir al autobús en Buenos Aires
h. _____ ir en taxi a la estación de autobuses

C. Descripciones. ¿Cómo describes los siguientes lugares? Usa las palabras de la lista y añade otras que conoces.

LUGARES	DESCRIPCIONES
1. _____ un pueblo de Nueva Inglaterra	a. mucho calor/frío
2. _____ el Desierto Sahara	b. pintoresco/a (*picturesque*)
3. _____ Buenos Aires	c. húmedo/a
4. _____ la selva amazónica	d. tranquilo/a
5. _____ las Montañas Rocosas en Colorado	e. rústico/a
6. _____ la Antártida	f. enorme
7. _____ las Cataratas del Niágara	g. cosmopolita
8. _____ la Cordillera de los Andes	h. seco/a
9. _____ el Lago Superior	i. ¿ ?

D. Una postal (*postcard*). Imagina que tú y un compañero / una compañera de clase están en uno de los destinos anunciados en el folleto (*brochure*) turístico de la página 278. Trabaja con tu compañero/a para escribirle una postal a tu profesor(a) de español que incluya la siguiente información:

- una descripción de lo que se ve en el destino
- las actividades posibles
- por qué les gusta el destino

E. Entrevista: Preferencias. Entrevista a un compañero / una compañera de clase para saber qué le gusta hacer cuando va de viaje.

1. ¿Cómo prefieres viajar? ¿Por qué? ¿Qué haces en camino (*en route*)?
2. ¿Te gusta viajar solo/a o con amigos o parientes?
3. ¿Te gusta acampar en las montañas? ¿Por qué sí o por qué no?
4. ¿Conoces buenos restaurantes y hoteles en los lugares que visitas?
5. ¿Planeas los viajes con mucho tiempo y cuidado, o te gusta tomar decisiones espontáneas?
6. ¿Te gusta hacer excursiones organizadas, o prefieres preparar tu propio itinerario?
7. ¿Siempre vas a los mismos lugares, o escoges nuevos destinos?
8. ¿Qué actividades haces cuando vas de vacaciones?

F. Un viaje reciente. Cuéntale a un compañero / una compañera de clase los detalles de un viaje reciente que hiciste. Usa las siguientes preguntas como guía.

- ¿Adónde fuiste?
- ¿Con quién(es) viajaste?
- ¿Cómo fuiste?
- ¿En qué época (*time*) del año viajaste?
- ¿Qué actividades hiciste en el viaje?

- ¿Dónde te alojaste (*did you stay*)?
- ¿Qué te pareció el lugar?
- ¿La pasaste bien, en general?
- ¿Por qué sí o por qué no?

¿Hiciste tu último viaje en avión ▶ *como estas personas en Buenos Aires, o usaste otro medio de transporte?*

CAPÍTULO 10 • Recorridos y recuerdos

Nina Ibáñez

«*En el verano el destino más común son las playas del Atlántico,...* »

Nombre: Nina

Apellido: Ibáñez*

Edad: 32 años

Nació en: Buenos Aires, Argentina

You can watch this interview on the *Entrevistas* Video or Interactive CD-ROM or listen to the audio on the Online Learning Center (**www.mhhe.com/entrevistas2**).

Vocabulario útil

otros eligen	others choose	**la cumbre**	summit
países (*m.*) **limítrofes**	bordering countries	**agarramos**	we grabbed
en medio de	in the middle of	**clavada en**	driven into
la última vez	the last time	**firmada**	signed
nieves eternas	eternal (permanent) snow	**recorrerlo**	to travel through
un guía	guide (*person*)	**jungla**	jungle
un buen equipo	a good set of equipment	**pradera**	meadowland
la punta	tip; top	**un montón de**	a lot of
un refugio	way station	**pingüinos**	penguins
la subida	climb	**una especie protegida**	protected species
atravesar (ie)	to cross		

Antes de ver

A. Destinos argentinos. Busca los siguientes lugares en el mapa de Argentina al principio de este capítulo. ¿Cuál es la geografía de cada lugar? (Por ejemplo, ¿está al lado del océano? ¿Queda muy alto en las montañas? Etcétera.) ¿Cuál es la atracción turística de estos lugares, probablemente? ¿En qué época del año es la temporada alta (la época de más actividad turística)?

1. Bariloche
2. las Cataratas del Iguazú
3. Mar del Plata
4. la Patagonia
5. San Martín de los Andes
6. Villa Gesell

---

* In Argentina, many people do not use two family names.

B. Los viajes de Nina. Nina va a hablar de dos viajes que hizo en Argentina. Revisa las siguientes oraciones que vienen de su entrevista.

1. «Viví _____ en la Patagonia, en Neuquén, en un _____ que se llama San Martín de los Andes,... »

2. «Queda en medio de _____ rodeado por el Lago Lácar... »

3. «Fui hace más o menos _____ a la Patagonia, otra vez adonde vivía.»

4. «Y fue muy _____ porque fuimos a escalar el _____, que es un volcán de nieves eternas,... »

5. «Éramos _____ personas y sólo _____ llegamos a la punta... Nos llevó _____ días enteros subir y bajar.»

6. « ...por suerte hay un refugio a mitad de la subida donde pudimos _____ y _____ antes de atravesar la zona de hielo,... »

¡Veamos!

A. Los viajes de Nina. Completa las oraciones de la **Actividad B** de **Antes de ver,** según lo que dice Nina.

B. La diversidad natural de Argentina. ¿Qué rasgos geográficos menciona Nina en su entrevista? Ve la entrevista de nuevo si es necesario e indica los rasgos que menciona.

☐ el bosque   ☐ la jungla   ☐ la playa
☐ las cataratas   ☐ el lago   ☐ la pradera
☐ la cordillera   ☐ la montaña   ☐ el río
☐ el desierto   ☐ el océano   ☐ el valle
☐ el glaciar   ☐ la pampa   ☐ el volcán

Después de ver

¿Qué pasó? Pon las siguientes oraciones en orden cronológico, según lo que cuenta Nina. Puedes ver la entrevista otra vez si es necesario.

a. _____ A la mitad pudimos comer y dormir.

b. _____ Agarramos la bandera argentina que estaba en la cumbre.

c. _____ Atravesamos la zona del hielo.

d. _____ Dejamos otra bandera con nuestras firmas.

e. _____ Empezamos la subida con un guía especializado.

Forma y función

10.1 Preterit vs. Imperfect

In previous chapters, you learned the forms and a few uses of the two past tenses in Spanish—the *preterit* and the *imperfect*. Here is a summary of those uses. The key expressions on the right can often tip you off to the various uses, but in the end the determining factor for choosing preterit or imperfect is the meaning you are trying to convey.

Preterit		
USES	EXAMPLES	KEY EXPRESSIONS
completed action in the past	**Fuimos a la playa durante las vacaciones de verano.**	**anoche/ayer** **de repente** (*suddenly*) **el año/mes pasado** **una vez, dos veces,…**
completed actions in a series	**Abordé el avión, me senté y entonces ¡cancelaron el vuelo!**	**primero,…** **después,…** **luego,…** **finalmente / por fin**
actions completed within a specified quantity of time	**Nos quedamos allí (por) tres días. Vivimos en Argentina (por) dos años.**	**(por) _____ años/días**

Imperfect		
USES	EXAMPLES	KEY EXPRESSIONS
description without focusing on completed actions	**Me gustaba mucho visitar a mis abuelos en Miami. Su casa era un lugar perfecto para jugar.**	
habitual actions in the past	**Siempre íbamos a la playa durante las vacaciones de verano.**	**cuando era niño/a** **siempre** **todos los días**
telling time and age in the past	**Tenía 13 años en 1993. Eran las 5:00 en punto de la tarde.**	

Narrating in the Past

The difference between the preterit and imperfect is especially important when telling a story in the past.

1. The background description of what things were like as the story unfolds is given in the *imperfect*; it is important to note that none of the activities expressed by verbs in the imperfect happens before or after the others in a sequence—they are all true simultaneously.

El lago **estaba** a 2.000 metros sobre el nivel del mar,... **había** un refugio por allí,... **hacía** mucho frío.	*The lake was 2,000 meters above sea level, . . . there was a way station around there, . . . it was very cold.*

2. The events that move the story along are recounted in the *preterit*—one action is completed before another happens.

Agarramos otra bandera argentina, la **firmamos** y la **dejamos** ahí.	*We grabbed another Argentine flag, signed it, and left it there.*

3. Both tenses can appear in the same sentence. Often when this occurs, the *imperfect* refers to an action that was in progress when another action (in the *preterit*) interrupted. Note that this "action in progress" use of the imperfect translates into English as *was/were (doing something)*.

Esperábamos al guía cuando **empezó** a nevar.	*We were waiting for the guide when it began to snow.*

Special Translations for the Preterit

In **Capítulo 8,** you learned that some state verbs like **querer** and **saber** have special translations when used in the preterit. The following list contains other verbs with special translations. When these verbs are used in the imperfect, they convey the expected past tense translation into English.*

Infinitive	Imperfect Preterit	Translations
conocer	conocía conocí	I was familiar with (I knew) I became familiar with for the first time (I met)
poder	podía pude	I could / was able to I could and did (I managed to / accomplished)
no poder	no podía no pude	I couldn't / wasn't able to I couldn't and didn't (I failed)
querer	quería quise	I wanted I wanted and acted on that desire (I tried)

---

* Only the **yo** forms are listed here, but these special translations apply to all persons of the verb: **Lo conocimos en Córdoba.** (*We met him in Córdoba.*)

Infinitive	Imperfect Preterit	Translations
no querer	no quería	I didn't want
	no quise	I didn't want and didn't act on that desire (I refused)
saber	sabía	I knew (*a fact*)
	supe	I knew (*a fact*) for the first time (I found out)
tener que + *inf.*	tenía que	I had to (*do something*) (I had the obligation)
	tuve que	I had to and did (*do something*)

Análisis estructural

Estudia los verbos de las siguientes oraciones en inglés. Di si cada verbo subrayado requiere el pretérito o el imperfecto en español.

1. Last winter I <u>went</u> to Argentina with my family.
2. When we <u>arrived</u> in Buenos Aires, it <u>was</u> summer there; it <u>was</u> warm and sunny.
3. We immediately <u>got</u> on a bus and <u>spent</u> several hours en route to Córdoba.
4. My mother <u>was looking</u> at all the quaint little shops and my father <u>was admiring</u> the colonial architecture when a policeman <u>rushed</u> toward us.
5. My mother <u>was</u> scared to death, because she <u>didn't know</u> much Spanish.
6. Finally, we <u>realized</u> what was happening: my little brother had dropped his passport on the bus, and the policeman <u>was returning</u> it.
7. My parents <u>thanked</u> the policeman, and they <u>tried</u> to buy him a coffee, but he <u>said</u> he <u>was</u> on duty.

Actividades

A. Un viaje a las Pampas. Cambia los verbos subrayados del presente al pasado. ¡Cuidado con los usos del pretérito y del imperfecto!

Un día <u>decidimos</u>[1] irnos de la ciudad. Buenos Aires <u>tiene</u>[2] demasiado tráfico y <u>hace</u>[3] un calor insoportable. Nos <u>ponemos</u>[4] de acuerdo: ¡Todos <u>queremos</u>[5] ir a las Pampas! <u>Subimos</u>[6] al coche y dentro de una hora <u>estamos</u>[7] en el campo. El paisaje <u>es</u>[8] muy diferente: todo <u>es</u>[9] plano[a] y no <u>hay</u>[10] muchos árboles. ¡Pero sí <u>hay</u>[11] vacas[b]! Finalmente <u>llegamos</u>[12] a una estancia.[c] <u>Es</u>[13] una estancia en funcionamento, pero <u>admiten</u>[14] turistas para mostrar la vida tradicional de las Pampas. No <u>conocemos</u>[15] a ningún gaucho,[d] pero <u>podemos</u>[16] comer unas carnes exquisitas y empanadas excelentes. Mientras mis amigos <u>montan</u>[17] a caballo, <u>hablo</u>[18] con el dueño de la estancia. <u>Es</u>[19] un hombre muy amable, y nos <u>invita</u>[20] a volver al fin de semana siguiente para una fiesta especial.

[a]*flat*   [b]*cows*   [c]*ranch*   [d]*Argentine cowboy*

B. Una anécdota personal. La abuela de Nina cuenta la siguiente anécdota de un incidente único respecto al tango. Complétala con la forma apropiada del pretérito o del imperfecto de los verbos entre paréntesis.

Cuando yo (ser)[1] más joven, todos los amigos de mis padres (ir)[2] a los clubs a bailar tango. A mi madre especialmente le (gustar)[3] la música y la letra[a] de los tangos. Una noche, ella (ir)[4] a un club del barrio para bailar con otras parejas, pero sin mi padre, quien a veces (trabajar)[5] por la noche. Por casualidad,[b] esa noche el famoso cantante Carlos Gardel (estar)[6] en el club. Mi madre (bailar)[7] por muchas horas con sus amigos esa noche, y a todos les (encantar)[8] la música. Cuando mi madre (volver)[9] a casa, le (contar)[10] a mi padre lo que había pasado[c] en el club. ¡Él no lo (creer)[11]!

Muchos años después, mi madre (morirse)[12] y mi padre (tener)[13] que revisar todos sus efectos personales. En el bolsillo[d] de un viejo vestido (encontrar)[14] una foto del cantante en que se había escrito[e]: «Vos[f] bailás divinamente. Carlos Gardel».

[a]*lyrics*   [b]*Por… By chance*   [c]*había… had happened*   [d]*pocket*   [e]*se… had been written*   [f]*You*

C. Entrevista: Un viaje

Paso 1. Escribe una lista de preguntas generales que usarías (*you would use*) para saber los siguientes detalles de un viaje.

> MODELO   el lugar → ¿Adónde fuiste? ¿Qué lugares visitaste?...

- el tiempo
- los medios de transporte
- las personas que iban en el grupo
- la duración del viaje
- las actividades principales
- un incidente inolvidable (*unforgettable*)

Paso 2. Entrevista a un compañero / una compañera de clase para saber más de un viaje determinado que hizo. Mientras habla, lo/la vas a interrumpir para pedirle más detalles.

> MODELO   E1: ...y allí conocí a mi novia.
> E2: ¿Ah, sí? ¿Qué hacía ella? ¿Con quién estaba?

VOCABULARIO ÚTIL

¿Ah, sí?	Oh really?
Cuéntame más.	Tell me more.
¿De veras?	Really?
¡No me lo puedo creer!	That's unbelievable!
¿Qué pasó después?	What happened next?

10.2 More About the Present Participle

You have already seen that the present participle (**-ndo** form) of a verb can be used with **estar** to form the present progressive tense: **Estoy haciendo cola** (*I am waiting in line*). The present participle can also be combined with other verbs and tenses to add shades of meaning to the main verb, usually describing how the subject carries out the main action. English generally uses the *-ing* form of the verb or another word to express the equivalent idea.

Nos **fuimos corriendo** cuando oímos la explosión.	*We took off running when we heard the explosion.*
Vamos a **seguir subiendo** hasta llegar a la cumbre.	*We're going to keep going up until we get to the top.*
Ella siempre **iba cantando** a la escuela.	*She always used to go to school singing (along the way).*
Consigues los mejores precios **hablando** directamente con el agente de viajes.	*You get the best prices (by) talking directly to the travel agent.*

To name an action as the subject of a sentence, or with a form of **ser,** Spanish uses the *infinitive,* not the present participle.

Conseguir un billete barato no **es** fácil.	*Getting a cheap ticket isn't easy.*
Mi actividad favorita **es acampar.**	*My favorite activity is camping.*
No me gusta **esquiar.**	*I don't like skiing.*

Actividades

A. ¿Cómo ahorro (*do I save*) **dinero?**   Usa expresiones de cada columna para formar oraciones completas que describan diferentes aspectos de un viaje barato.

A

1. _____ Se consigue la mejor tasa de cambio…
2. _____ Uno llega más rápido…
3. _____ No se paga comisión…
4. _____ Uno recibe descuentos especiales…
5. _____ Se evitan (*One avoids*) muchos problemas…
6. _____ Se gasta (*One spends*) poco dinero en la comida…
7. _____ Se paga menos por alojamiento…

B

a. cambiando el dinero en una casa de cambio (*moneychanger*).
b. comiendo en restaurantes de comida rápida.
c. confirmando las reservas con antelación (*in advance*).
d. haciendo reservas en el Internet.
e. viajando en avión.
f. viajando en grupo.
g. viviendo con una familia.
h. quedándose en hostales.

B. Actividades durante un viaje.   Completa las siguientes oraciones para describir lo que pasó durante un viaje de vacaciones. **¡OJO!** Tienes que conjugar el primer verbo entre paréntesis en el tiempo (*tense*) y la persona apropiados; para el segundo verbo, usa la forma de **-ndo.**

1. El verano pasado, nosotros (ir + acampar) por los Andes.
2. Queríamos estar en un campamento, pero (terminar + alojarse) en un hostal.
3. Durante el viaje, mi hermano constantemente (ir + buscar) regalos.
4. Yo intenté interrumpir al guía una vez, pero él (seguir + hablar).
5. Cuando por fin era hora de (*time to*) bajar de la montaña, nosotros (bajar + esquiar).

Análisis cultural

La siguiente cita tomada de una fuente escrita en inglés para anglohablantes va a aumentar tus conocimientos sobre algunos fenómenos culturales en Argentina. ¿Es consistente esta información con la perspectiva de Nina de la **Entrevista 1?** Usa lo que has aprendido en este capítulo sobre Argentina, más tu propia experiencia, para contestar las preguntas que siguen la cita.

❝Buenos Aires, the 'Paris of the Americas,' dominates Argentina's political and cultural life as much as, well, Paris dominates France. Buenos Aires is the capital, the largest city, the industrial and economic center, and the cultural heart of Argentina.

Nevertheless, there is more to Argentina than Buenos Aires—even though many foreign businesspeople never have the need to step outside its city limits. Some must-see areas include Patagonia, Iguazú, and Tierra del Fuego.❞

Source: *The International Traveler's Guide to Doing Business in Latin America*

1. Usando la información de esta cita y tus conocimientos de tu propio país, completa la siguiente tabla.

2. ¿Hay una ciudad en tu país que predomine (*dominates*) en el país al igual que Buenos Aires predomina en Argentina?

3. Busca la Patagonia, las Cataratas del Iguazú y Tierra del Fuego en el mapa al principio del capítulo. ¿Por qué se consideran lugares imprescindibles (*must-see places*) para los turistas?

4. En tu opinión, ¿qué lugares son imprescindibles para los turistas que visitan tu país? Explica cuál es la atracción de cada lugar que mencionas: ¿Son lugares históricos, de geografía impresionante, famosos por la alta tecnología,… ?

	Argentina	Mi país
la capital política		
la ciudad más grande		
la capital industrial		
la capital económica		
la capital cultural		

Pronunciación y ortografía

● b and v

The Spanish spelling system uses both the letters **b** and **v** to represent the same sounds. Thus, **vaca** (*cow*) and **baca** (*luggage rack on a car*) sound exactly the same.

Even though the letters **b** and **v** represent the same sounds, there are actually two different [b] sounds in Spanish, depending on the surrounding sounds.

The "hard" [b] occurs after a pause or after the letters **m** and **n.** It is also called the *stop* [b], because the flow of air out of the mouth is completely stopped by closing the upper and lower lips. Listen to your instructor's pronunciation of the following words and phrases and observe how his/her upper and lower lips close completely when pronouncing the letters **b** and **v.**

ambos	Buenos Aires	vaca
baca	cambio	vacaciones
bailando	invierno	viajando

The "soft" [b] occurs everywhere else (between vowels and after consonants other than **m** and **n**). It is also known as the *fricative* [b], because the flow of air out of the mouth is *not* completely stopped. That is, the upper and lower lips come close to touching but they don't actually close completely, creating friction in the airstream. Listen to your instructor's pronunciation of the following words and phrases and observe his/her upper and lower lips as he/she pronounces the letters **b** and **v.**

a Buenos Aires	¿Cuándo te vas?	las vacaciones
acabo	el viernes	lavar
al banco	las bases	

¡OJO! Resist the temptation to use the English [v] sound when you see the letter **v** in Spanish!

The *Manual de práctica* contains activities to practice these Spanish sounds.

Vocabulario

● Destinos urbanos

La plaza es un lugar de encuentro en la ciudad; ¡las personas van allí para ver y ser vistas (*be seen*)!

En **los quioscos** se venden periódicos, revistas, caramelos y otras necesidades.

Las catedrales en toda Sudamérica son destinos turísticos populares.

la autopista	super highway, interstate	**el museo**	museum
el ayuntamiento	city/town hall	**el puerto**	port
el banco	bank	**el teatro**	theater
el centro	downtown	**la oficina de correos**	post office
el monumento	monument	**la telefónica**	telephone company office

Actividades

A. ¿Adónde vas para... ? En la ciudad, ¿adónde vas para hacer las siguientes cosas?

1. aprender (*to learn*) algo
2. cambiar dinero
3. comprar estampillas
4. comprar un periódico o una revista
5. esperar el colectivo
6. llamar a parientes en otros países
7. obtener documentos oficiales
8. sentarse a mirar pasar a la gente
9. tomar fotos* turísticas
10. ver dramas

B. Los sitios que frecuento. ¿Con qué frecuencia vas a estos lugares (en la siguiente página) en tu ciudad? ¿Y cuando estás de viaje en otro lugar?

---

* **La foto** is an abbreviation for **la fotografía.** Thus, **las fotos turísticas.** Another word abbreviated in this manner is **la motocicleta: la moto.**

Paso 1. Usa la siguiente escala para indicar la frecuencia.

4 = voy muy a menudo   2 = no voy mucho
3 = voy a veces   1 = no voy nunca

1. _____ al ayuntamiento   7. _____ al hotel
2. _____ al banco   8. _____ a la iglesia o catedral
3. _____ al cementerio   9. _____ al museo
4. _____ a la estación de trenes 10. _____ a la oficina de correo
5. _____ al estadio   11. _____ a la piscina
6. _____ a la farmacia   12. _____ al teatro

Paso 2. ¿Qué haces en cada sitio?

C. ¿Cómo es tu ciudad? Describe tu ciudad, contestando las siguientes preguntas.

1. ¿Cómo es el centro? ¿Qué edificios hay y qué servicios ofrecen?
2. ¿Cuáles son los barrios más interesantes de la ciudad? ¿En qué se diferencian los unos de los otros?
3. ¿Hay suburbios o urbanizaciones? ¿Cómo son?
4. ¿Cuál es el transporte más común dentro de cada barrio de la ciudad o entre los barrios?
5. ¿Hay mucho tráfico y muchos embotellamientos? ¿Qué lugares se deben evitar? ¿A qué hora(s)?
6. ¿Hay monumentos famosos? ¿A quién(es)?
7. ¿Hay aeropuerto? ¿Dónde está en relación al centro?

Para orientarse[a] en la ciudad

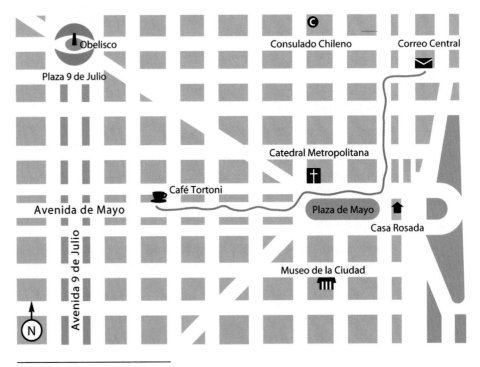

[a]Para... *Getting around* (lit. *Orienting oneself*)

—Disculpe señora, ¿cómo llego al Café Tortini?

—A ver. Estamos en el Correo Central. Usted **cruza** la calle, camina **una cuadra hacia el oeste, dobla a la izquierda** y **sigue derecho** otras tres cuadras hasta llegar[a] a la Plaza de Mayo. Allí, usted **dobla a la derecha** y sigue caminando hasta llegar al extremo oeste de la Plaza, donde va a ver el comienzo[b] de la Avenida de Mayo. Usted camina tres cuadras por esa avenida, y allí en la cuarta cuadra, **a mano derecha,** está el Café Tortini.

[a]hasta… *until arriving*   [b]*beginning*

Actividad

Dibujar un plano (*city map*)

Paso 1. Descríbele la orientación básica de tu ciudad a un compañero / una compañera de clase, quien va a dibujar un plano. Las siguientes expresiones, más las preposiciones que conoces, pueden ser útiles.

- La calle principal va de norte a sur / de este a oeste.
- La calle Elm cruza la calle principal en el centro.
- Hay un barrio en el norte que se llama _____.
- El ayuntamiento está en el centro de la plaza _____.
- Está enfrente / al lado de _____.

Paso 2. Ahora van a indicar cómo se llega a un lugar en su ciudad, según el modelo.

MODELO   E1: ¿Cómo llego (al ayuntamiento, al museo arqueológico,…)?
　　　　　E2: Primero cruzas la plaza, y después doblas a la derecha. Sigues derecho dos cuadras, y allí está el/la_____.

● La identidad regional

▲ *Buenos Aires es una de las capitales más grandes y cosmopolitas de Hispanoamérica.*

▲ *Bahía Blanca no es tan grande como Buenos Aires y no sufre de tantos problemas urbanos como la contaminación (pollution), por ejemplo.*

Por un lado,[a] Buenos Aires es el corazón de la identidad argentina, **por otro lado,**[b] es un centro internacional que **se parece** más a[c] París que a otras ciudades de Argentina como Bahía Blanca. De esta manera, Buenos Aires y Bahía Blanca **se diferencian** culturalmente, pero se diferencian en términos físicos también. Por ejemplo, Buenos Aires es **más grande que** Bahía Blanca, y de hecho,[d] Buenos Aires es **la ciudad más grande de** Argentina. **Mientras que** en Buenos Aires hay mucha industria, Bahía Blanca se mantiene del campo y de la agricultura. Buenos Aires es cosmopolita. **En cambio,**[e] Bahía Blanca tiene un ambiente más provincial. Pero, **al igual que** Buenos Aires, Bahía Blanca tiene problemas urbanos.

[a]Por... *On one hand*   [b]por... *on the other (hand)*   [c]se.... *more closely resembles*   [d]de... *in fact*
[e]En... *In contrast*

Actividades

A. Dos regiones diferentes

Paso 1. Describe la ciudad/región donde naciste, usando las siguientes categorías.

Categoría	Ejemplos
Ubicación (*Location*)	cerca del océano, en el interior del país, en las montañas, etcétera
Tamaño	grande, pequeña, más/menos grande que _____, etcétera
Carácter	cosmopolita, rural, urbana; la gente es abierta/cerrada; etcétera
Trabajos principales	agricultura, artesanías, industria, negocios, tecnología, turismo, etcétera

Paso 2. Compara tu descripción con la de un compañero / una compañera de clase que nació en otra región u otro país. ¿En qué se diferencian los dos lugares? ¿En qué se parecen? ¿Qué características comparten ambos lugares con el resto de este país?

MODELOS   Al igual que _____, mi ciudad es...

Mi ciudad se parece a _____ en que...

A diferencia de _____, mi ciudad no es...

Mi ciudad se diferencia de _____ en que...

Mi ciudad es más/menos _____ que _____.

B. Rural frente a (*versus*) **urbano.** ¿En qué se diferencian los habitantes de una ciudad grande de los de una comunidad rural o pequeña? Di cuáles de las siguientes características asocias, **en términos generales,** con los habitantes de cada tipo de comunidad, según tu propia experiencia. Añade otras ideas que se te ocurran (*that come to mind*).

MODELO   En términos generales, los habitantes de una ciudad grande ganan un salario más alto.

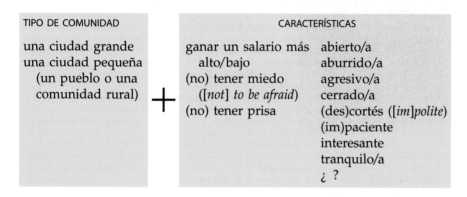

TIPO DE COMUNIDAD		CARACTERÍSTICAS
una ciudad grande una ciudad pequeña (un pueblo o una comunidad rural)	ganar un salario más alto/bajo (no) tener miedo ([*not*] *to be afraid*) (no) tener prisa	abierto/a aburrido/a agresivo/a cerrado/a (des)cortés ([*im*]*polite*) (im)paciente interesante tranquilo/a ¿ ?

C. Los símbolos.   Los símbolos regionales o nacionales son una parte importante de la identidad cultural. Da algunos ejemplos de símbolos regionales o nacionales de tu país y explica lo que representan. Añade otras ideas. ¿Son universales estos símbolos, o sólo tienen asociaciones para un grupo determinado?

MODELOS   En mi país, los colores rojo, blanco y azul representan la libertad.

Para algunas personas de mi país el águila (*eagle*) es un símbolo del honor.

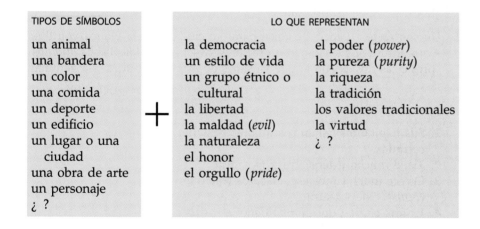

TIPOS DE SÍMBOLOS		LO QUE REPRESENTAN	
un animal una bandera un color una comida un deporte un edificio un lugar o una ciudad una obra de arte un personaje ¿ ?		la democracia un estilo de vida un grupo étnico o cultural la libertad la maldad (*evil*) la naturaleza el honor el orgullo (*pride*)	el poder (*power*) la pureza (*purity*) la riqueza la tradición los valores tradicionales la virtud ¿ ?

You can watch this interview on the *Entrevistas* Video or Interactive CD-ROM or listen to the audio on the Online Learning Center (**www.mhhe.com/entrevistas2**).

Leticia Goenaga

«Mi ciudad es una ciudad con costumbres bastante cerradas, muy provincial,... »

Nombre: Leticia

Apellido: Goenaga

Edad: 28 años

Nació en: Bahía Blanca, Argentina

Vocabulario útil

en ese sentido	in that sense	**asado**	Argentine grilled beef
tránsito	traffic	**recipiente** *m.*	container
anteriormente	previously	**se le agrega**	one adds
siglo [XX]	[twentieth] century	**bombilla**	straw
vagando por	wandering around	**hirviendo**	boiling
anchos	wide	**amarga**	bitter
surge	comes		

Antes de ver

A. Los rivales.   ¿Existe rivalidad entre tu ciudad y otra ciudad del país? ¿Por qué existe esta rivalidad?

B. Un contraste.   Leticia va a comparar su ciudad, Bahía Blanca, con Buenos Aires. Indica si las siguientes oraciones describen Bahía Blanca, Buenos Aires o las dos, según lo que ya sabes de estas dos ciudades argentinas.

	BAHÍA BLANCA	BUENOS AIRES	LAS DOS
1. Sus habitantes tienen costumbres bastante cerradas.	☐	☐	☐
2. Tiene mucha extensión (*surface area*).	☐	☐	☐
3. Ofrece muchísimos espectáculos (*entertainment events*), cine y teatro.	☐	☐	☐
4. Es una ciudad que se mantiene (*earns its livelihood*) del campo.	☐	☐	☐
5. Es una ciudad cosmopolita con grandes edificios.	☐	☐	☐
6. Es una ciudad de pocos habitantes.	☐	☐	☐
7. Es una ciudad más tranquila, más provincial, más reposada (*calm*).	☐	☐	☐

C. Los vaqueros (*cowboys*).   Leticia va a hablar de los gauchos (*Argentine cowboys*). Al igual que los vaqueros en Norteamérica, los gauchos cuidaban el ganado (*livestock*) y son un símbolo nacional muy importante en Argentina. Lee las siguientes oraciones e indica cuáles pueden aplicarse a los vaqueros norteamericanos del pasado.

1. ☐ Vivían en el campo.
2. ☐ Vivían en la ciudad pero trabajaban en el campo.
3. ☐ Andaban libremente (*freely*) por el campo.
4. ☐ Eran los dueños de las tierras que trabajaban.
5. ☐ Vivían de día en día (*from day to day, hand to mouth*).
6. ☐ La revolución industrial puso fin a su estilo de vida.
7. ☐ Existen todavía en este siglo.
8. ☐ No existen actualmente, pero tienen una importancia simbólica.
9. ☐ Llevaban ropa especial.
10. ☐ Algunas comidas típicas surgen de ellos.

¡Veamos!

¿Acertaste?   Ahora, ve la entrevista de Leticia y compara lo que ella dice sobre Bahía Blanca y Buenos Aires con tus respuestas a la **Actividad B** de **Antes de ver.**

Después de ver

Los gauchos y los vaqueros.   Ve la entrevista de nuevo y di qué oraciones de la **Actividad C** de **Antes de ver** se aplican también a los gauchos argentinos.

Piénsalo bien

¿En qué se diferencian los símbolos nacionales argentinos de los de tu país? ¿Hay símbolos comunes a ambos países? ¿Representan los mismos valores? Explica tus respuestas.

10.3 The Present Perfect

Many Argentines recognize that the present day rivalry between Buenos Aires and other cities in Argentina has its roots in the past.

Buenos Aires siempre **ha tenido** más contacto con el exterior.

Buenos Aires has always had more contact with foreign countries.

Los recursos siempre se **han concentrado** en Buenos Aires.

Resources have always been concentrated in Buenos Aires.

The verb forms used to express this temporal relationship are in the *present perfect* tense. This tense is formed by combining present tense forms of the auxiliary verb **haber** (*to have*) with the past participle of the main verb. Here are the present perfect conjugations of the regular verbs **hablar, comer,** and **vivir.**

	haber		Past participle
(yo)	**he**		
(tú)	**has**		
(usted, él/ella)	**ha**		hablado
		+	comido
(nosotros/as)	**hemos**		vivido
(vosotros/as)	**habéis**		
(ustedes, ellos/as)	**han**		

The *past participle* of a verb is formed by adding the endings **-ado** (for **-ar** verbs) and **-ido** (for **-er/-ir** verbs) to the verb stem; thus, **hablar** → **hablado; comer** → **comido; vivir** → **vivido.*** You have also seen some examples of irregular past participles. Here are the most common ones.

abrir:	abierto	morir:	muerto
decir:	dicho	poner:	puesto
descubrir:	descubierto	romper:	roto
escribir:	escrito	ver:	visto
hacer:	hecho	volver:	vuelto

---

* If the verb stem ends with a strong vowel (**a, e, o**), you must add a written accent mark to the **-ido** ending: **leer** → **leído; creer** → **creído; caer** → **caído; oír** → **oído; sonreír** → **sonreídoi;** and so on.

If an action that began in the past is still continuing into the present, Spanish cannot use the present perfect tense as English does. Since the action is still ongoing, Spanish simply uses the present tense in the pattern: **Hace** + *time period* + **que** + *present tense.*

Hace dos horas **que** te **espero.**	*I've been waiting for you for two hours.* (I'm still waiting.)

To pose a question of this type, use the pattern: **¿Cuánto tiempo hace que** + *present tense***?**

¿Cuánto tiempo **hace que estudias** español?	*How long have you been studying Spanish?*

NOTES:

- When used as part of the present perfect tense, the past participle never changes its form; it always ends in **-o,** no matter what the gender of the subject is.
- The expression **ha habido,** just like its present tense counterpart **hay,** is invariable whether referring to a singular or a plural subject.

Ha habido mucho tráfico esta tarde.	*There has been a lot of traffic this afternoon.*
Ha habido muchos embotellamientos como resultado.	*There have been a lot of traffic jams as a result.*

Análisis estructural

En las siguientes oraciones, di cuáles son los dos elementos del presente perfecto: la forma de **haber** y el participio pasado. ¿Dónde se colocan (*are located*) (1) los complementos pronominales, (2) los adverbios y (3) las palabras negativas **no/nunca** respecto al presente perfecto? ¿Van **antes de, después de** o **entre** los dos elementos de este tiempo verbal?

1. ¿Has visto a María recientemente? —No, no la he visto.
2. Todavía no nos hemos acostumbrado a los horarios diferentes en Argentina.
3. Nunca hemos estado en Bariloche.
4. El interior del país siempre ha sido una zona agrícola.
5. ¿Los billetes? No los he comprado todavía.

Actividades

A. ¿Siempre ha sido así?

Paso 1. Forma oraciones completas con las siguientes expresiones para expresar algunos aspectos de una ciudad. Usa el presente perfecto y recuerda hacer los cambios necesarios.

MODELO los habitantes / tener un buen nivel de vida →
Los habitantes siempre han tenido un buen nivel de vida.

1. los ciudadanos **/** asistir regularmente a los espectáculos patrios (*patriotic*)
2. los residentes **/** participar activamente en el gobierno
3. las escuelas **/** ser bueno
4. la población **/** ser bastante estable
5. los gobernantes **/** representar los intereses de los ciudadanos
6. el tráfico **/** circular sin problemas
7. haber suficientes actividades y trabajos para los jóvenes

Paso 2. Di si cada oración del **Paso 1** se aplica a tu ciudad o a la ciudad donde estudias. ¿Qué otros aspectos de tu ciudad siempre han sido así?

B. Cambios recientes. Usando las ideas de la **Actividad A** u otras ideas que se te ocurran, cuenta a la clase qué cosas importantes han cambiado recientemente en tu ciudad.

MODELOS Mi pueblo es muy pequeño, pero recientemente hemos tenido más tráfico.

Han puesto nuevos semáforos (*traffic lights*) en todas las calles.

C. Tus experiencias. De las siguientes acciones asociadas con los viajes, ¿cuáles has hecho tú y cuáles nunca has hecho?

MODELO viajar solo/a al extranjero (*abroad*) →
Yo (nunca) he viajado sola al extranjero.

1. vivir en otro país
2. perder el pasaporte o el dinero
3. visitar más de cinco países en un solo viaje
4. hacer deportes nuevos
5. comer platos exóticos
6. ver monumentos históricos impresionantes
7. ver paisajes increíbles
8. conocer a personas importantes
9. hacer nuevas amistades duraderas

D. Preguntas. Comenta los siguientes temas con dos o tres compañeros/as de clase.

1. Tradicionalmente, ¿cuáles han sido los valores más importantes de las zonas rurales de tu país (la religión, el uso de los recursos naturales, los trabajos disponibles [*available*], las relaciones familiares, etcétera)? ¿Cómo se comparan con el estilo de vida de las zonas urbanas o suburbanas?
2. ¿Qué símbolos nacionales siempre han sido importantes para ti o para tu familia? ¿Por qué? ¿Qué representan?

● 10.4 **Lo** + Adjective

A popular belief in Argentina is that *everything positive and good* (**lo positivo, lo bueno**) about the country comes from the gauchos. This construction (**lo** + *m. s. adj.*) is quite common in Spanish for expressing a general quality;

it allows an adjective to act as a subject or an object noun in the sentence and is translated into English as *the _____ thing, the _____ part,* or *what's _____.* The expression **todo lo _____** is equivalent to *all/everything that's _____.*

Se supone que **todo lo positivo** viene de los gauchos.

People believe that everything that's positive comes from the gauchos.

Lo bueno de esa ciudad son los museos.

The good part (The good thing, What's good) about that city are the museums.

En los años 50, destruyeron **lo bonito** de la ciudad y nos dejaron con **lo feo.**

In the 1950s, they tore down the pretty part of the city and left us with the ugly things.

Análisis estructural

En las siguientes oraciones, ¿qué función tiene la expresión **lo** + adjetivo: es el sujeto o el complemento? ¿Cómo se dicen estas expresiones en inglés?

1. <u>Lo horrible de nuestro viaje</u> fue el accidente.
2. Los agentes de viaje guardan <u>lo mejor</u> para sus clientes favoritos.
3. <u>Lo peor de ese hotel</u> son los cuartos de baño.
4. <u>Lo histórico de mi ciudad</u> se remonta al (*dates back to the*) siglo XIX.
5. Vimos <u>lo más interesante de Argentina</u> en nuestro viaje.

Actividades

A. Detalles. Completa las siguientes oraciones con información de tu ciudad/región.

1. Lo más antiguo de mi ciudad es/son _____; se remonta(n) al siglo _____ / a los años _____.

2. Para experimentar lo cultural de mi región, hay que ir a / visitar _____.

3. Lo más moderno de mi región se encuentra en _____.

4. Todo lo positivo de mi región se concentra en _____.

B. Aspectos de tu ciudad. ¿Cómo son los siguientes aspectos de tu ciudad? Haz oraciones completas, según tus opiniones.

1. lo bonito
2. lo mejor
3. lo triste
4. lo curioso
5. lo irónico
6. lo más interesante

C. En contraste. Usando las características de la **Actividad B,** compara tu ciudad con otra que conoces en este país.

MODELO   Lo bonito de mi ciudad es/son _____, pero lo bonito de _____ es/son _____.

Sobre la lectura Como nos dijo Leticia, la tradición gauchesca es la fuente de muchos símbolos importantes para la identidad argentina: el gaucho mismo, la vida solitaria de las pampas. Otro aspecto importante es la música gauchesca. En esta lectura, vas a leer una leyenda (*legend*) sobre los orígenes del instrumento musical más importante para el gaucho: la guitarra.

Antes de leer

▲ La noche, *del argentino Fernando Romero Carranza (1935–)*

A. Representaciones del gaucho. En el cuadro (*painting*) a la izquierda se ve un gaucho con su caballo. Describe la escena, usando las siguientes preguntas como guía.

1. ¿Cómo es el paisaje? ¿Qué ves en el cuadro? Usa el vocabulario que has aprendido en este capítulo (**el bosque, las montañas, la pradera,** etcétera).
2. Según tu descripción, ¿qué región de Argentina es, probablemente? Consulta el mapa al principio del capítulo si es necesario.
3. ¿Qué o quién acompaña al gaucho? ¿Cómo podemos describir su estilo de vida y su personalidad? ¿Es alegre, gregario, solitario, triste, etcétera?

B. ¿Quién es? En esta leyenda hay tres personajes: **Hilario,** un gaucho; **Rosa,** su mujer; y **Amuray,** un cacique (*chief*) indígena. La historia es bastante simple, y como en muchas leyendas, los personajes son estereotipados. Es fácil adivinar qué va a pasar. Primero, estudia las siguientes frases e indica si cada una representa una acción o una descripción. Luego, indica a quién se refiere, probablemente: a Hilario, a Rosa o a Amuray. **¡OJO!** Es posible indicar a más de una persona.

	¿ACCIÓN O DESCRIPCIÓN?	HILARIO	ROSA	AMURAY
1. arrancar (*to steal away*) a la mujer	_____	☐	☐	☐
2. estar desesperado/a (*desperate*)	_____	☐	☐	☐
3. estar triste	_____	☐	☐	☐
4. luchar (*to struggle*)	_____	☐	☐	☐
5. perseguir (*to pursue*) a Amuray	_____	☐	☐	☐
6. raptar (*to kidnap*) a Rosa	_____	☐	☐	☐
7. recuperar (*to regain*) a Rosa	_____	☐	☐	☐
8. ser lindo/a y gracioso/a (*attractive*)	_____	☐	☐	☐
9. ser rencoroso/a (*bitter*) y vengativo/a (*vengeful*)	_____	☐	☐	☐
10. tener celos (*to be jealous*)	_____	☐	☐	☐

C. Narrar una historia. En esta narración se usan el pretérito y el imperfecto. Primero, revisa los usos más importantes de las dos formas verbales y lee las siguientes oraciones tomadas de la lectura. Luego, di si cada verbo subrayado se ha conjugado en el pretérito o el imperfecto y di qué uso de ese tiempo verbal representa.

Pretérito	Imperfecto
una acción terminada	una acción en progreso
una acción en secuencia (una detrás de otra)	una acción habitual
	una descripción en el pasado

1. Hilario <u>vivía</u> en su rancho, lejos de toda población indígena. <u>Tenía</u> la soledad como compañera.
2. Un día <u>conoció</u> a Rosa, la joven más linda y graciosa del pueblo cercano.
3. Amuray, el cacique de una tribu indígena, <u>estaba</u> enamorado de Rosa, pero el indio <u>vio</u> que la mujer de sus sueños <u>amaba</u> a otro.
4. Hilario <u>persiguió</u> a Amuray… Finalmente… <u>mató</u> al cacique y <u>pudo</u> arrancar a Rosa de sus brazos.

D. Al leer la leyenda. Mientras lees la leyenda, compara tus respuestas a la **Actividad B** con lo que lees en la lectura. ¿Acertaste?

La guitarra

Hilario vivía en su rancho, lejos de toda población indígena. Tenía la soledad[a] como compañera. Pasó muchas auroras y crepúsculos[b] melancólicos; aquel gaucho solitario no oía más que la música grave[c] del bosque, la quietud de la llanura y la tristeza del campo con su horizonte de cielo y tierra. De vez en cuando pasaba por los pueblos lejanos esperando encontrar a la compañera de sus sueños. Aquélla que se une[d] a la vida del hombre para compartir sus esfuerzos, sus luchas y esperanzas. Aquélla que se busca como consuelo, como fuerza.[e]

▲ *Un cantor gaucho (anónimo)*

Un día conoció a Rosa, la joven más linda y graciosa del pueblo cercano. De repente las noches oscuras del gaucho se volvieron claras,[f] iluminadas por los ojos de la mujer amada.

Hilario vivía feliz con su compañera en el rancho en medio del bosque silencioso. La vida se transformó: Las mañanas se volvieron soñadoras,[g] y el viento corría suavemente en las noches, en constante diálogo con las hojas del bosque. Pero como toda cosa buena en la vida, no podía durar. Una mañana Hilario dejó sola a Rosa para ir a un pueblo cercano. Se

[a]*loneliness* [b]auroras… *sunrises and sunsets* [c]*low* [d]se… *joins* [e]como… *for consolation, for strength* [f]se… *became bright* [g]*dreamlike*

despidieron con un beso sin intuir[h] que esa mañana luminosa iba a ser la última.

Amuray, el cacique de una tribu indígena, estaba enamorado de Rosa, pero el indio vio que la mujer de sus sueños amaba a otro. Amuray, rencoroso y vengativo, resolvió raptar a Rosa y buscaba continuamente la ocasión de hacerlo. La ausencia de Hilario ese día le dio la oportunidad que deseaba. Por la tarde el gaucho regresó y encontró vacío el rancho. En el patio había señales frescas de una lucha desesperada y las huellas[i] de un caballo. Hilario persiguió a Amuray, y al alcanzarlo,[j] la lucha fue feroz. Finalmente el valiente gaucho mató al cacique y pudo arrancar a Rosa de los brazos del indio muerto. Pero no recuperó nada más que un cuerpo sin vida —Rosa había muerto[k] durante la lucha. Desesperado, Hilario tomó el cuerpo de Rosa entre sus brazos, mientras lloraba y llamaba su nombre. Llegó la noche con mucha tristeza. Hilario se durmió con la cabeza inclinada sobre la cara de su amada Rosa. Lo despertó el son[l] de una música de notas misteriosas, e Hilario encontró en sus brazos una caja[m] con forma de mujer en lugar del cuerpo de su compañera. Con este instrumento cantó durante su vida el recuerdo de su amada. Por eso la guitarra servirá[n] siempre para acompañar penas[o] y sentimientos. ■

[h]sin... *without foreseeing* [i]*hoof prints* [j]al... *upon catching up to him* [k]había... *had died* [l]*sound* [m]*box* [n]*will serve* [o]*sorrows*

Después de leer

A. ¿Entendiste?   Contesta las siguientes preguntas, según la leyenda.

1. Al principio de la historia, ¿dónde vivía Hilario? ¿con quién vivía?
2. ¿Qué hizo para cambiar su vida solitaria?
3. ¿Por qué raptó Amuray a Rosa?
4. ¿Quién mató a quién en la lucha?
5. ¿Cómo reaccionó Hilario a la muerte de Rosa?
6. ¿En qué se parece la guitarra a la mujer?

B. Una representación teatral (*stage play*).   Ahora, tienes que hacer una representación teatral de esta leyenda. Contesta las siguientes preguntas para preparar la escenificación.

1. Divide la leyenda en escenas e inventa un título para cada escena.
2. ¿Qué accesorios (*props*) se necesitan para cada escena?
3. ¿Qué tipo de persona debe hacer el papel de cada personaje? Da una descripción física y psicológica.
4. ¿Qué emociones debe representar cada personaje en cada escena?

C. La naturaleza y las emociones.   Lee de nuevo la leyenda y di qué relación existe entre la naturaleza y las emociones de Hilario durante las siguientes épocas de su vida.

Época de la vida de Hilario	Relación entre la naturaleza y las emociones de Hilario
antes de conocer a Rosa	
el día en que conoció a Rosa	
mientras vivieron juntos	
después de la muerte de Rosa	

D. Estereotipos. Los personajes de las leyendas suelen representar los valores o prejuicios (*prejudices*) de una cultura. ¿Qué podemos inferir de la cultura que creó esta leyenda? Escoge descripciones de cada personaje y cita ejemplos concretos de la leyenda para apoyar tus respuestas.

PERSONAJE

CÓMO SE REPRESENTA

1. _____ Hilario, el gaucho
2. _____ Rosa, la mujer
3. _____ Amuray, el indígena

a. activo/a en la narración
b. pasivo/a en la narración
c. bueno/a
d. malo/a
e. con características positivas
f. con características negativas

E. El verdadero origen de la guitarra. Esta leyenda explica el origen de la guitarra de manera creativa, pero, ¿es verdadera? Presenta tus respuestas a las siguientes preguntas y tu leyenda (para el número 4) a la clase.

1. ¿Cuál es el verdadero origen de la guitarra? Busca su historia en la biblioteca o el Internet.
2. ¿Qué simboliza la guitarra para el gaucho, según esta historia? ¿Qué función tiene en su vida?
3. ¿Por qué crees que se inventó esta leyenda?
4. Inventa una leyenda corta para un objeto de mucho valor para ti. ¡Cuidado con el uso del pretérito y del imperfecto!

Señas culturales

▲ *Carlos Gardel (1890–1935)*

El tango es una forma de baile y de música que tiene sus orígenes en los arrabales[a] de Buenos Aires a principios del siglo XX. El desarrollo[b] del tango fue influenciado por la canción folclórica autóctona[c] y también por los estilos musicales traídos a Argentina por los inmigrantes españoles, italianos y alemanes. Típicamente se toca con guitarras, violines y el bandoneón, un tipo de acordeón. Carlos Gardel fue el intérprete más famoso del tango tradicional. Astor Piazzola ofrece una interpretación más moderna.

Aquí hay unas estrofas[d] de dos tangos. ¿Qué emociones expresan? ¿Hay alguna forma de música popular en inglés que exprese sentimientos parecidos?

[a]*slums* [b]*development* [c]*autochtonous, native* [d]*stanzas*

(*sigue*)

«Canción de Buenos Aires»	«Adiós, pampa mía»
de M. Romero, A. Maizani y O. Cufaro	de I. Pelay, F. Canaro y M. Mores

Buenos Aires, cuando lejos me vi
sólo hallaba[e] consuelo
en las notas de un tango dulzón[f]
que lloraba el bandoneón;
Buenos Aires, suspirando[g] por ti,
bajo el sol de otros cielos,
cuánto lloró mi corazón
escuchando tu nostálgica canción.

Adiós, pampa mía... Me voy,
me voy a tierras extrañas.[h]
Adiós, caminos que he recorrido;
ríos, montes y cañadas,[i]
tapera[j] done[k] he nacido.
Si no volvemos a vernos,
tierra querida,
quiero que sepas[l]
que al irme dejo la vida.
¡Adiós!

[e]I found [f]sweet [g]yearning [h]foreign; strange [i]montes... mountains and canyons [j]shack
[k]donde (forma coloquial) [l]que... you to know

PORTAFOLIO CULTURAL

Redacción

Saludos desde Argentina. Imagina que estás de vacaciones en Argentina y quieres escribirles algunas postales a tus amigos y parientes. Inventa un itinerario y contesta las siguientes preguntas en tus postales: ¿Qué excursiones has hecho? ¿Qué cosas has visto y hecho? ¿A quiénes has conocido? Sigue los pasos en el *Manual de Práctica* para completar tus postales.

Exploración

Investigación cultural. Busca más información sobre Argentina en la biblioteca, en el *Entrevistas* Online Learning Center (**www.mhhe.com/entrevistas2**) o en otros sitios del Internet y preséntala a la clase. El *Manual de práctica* contiene más ideas para tu presentación.

Léxico activo

DESTINOS URBANOS

el **aeropuerto**	airport
la **agencia de viajes**	travel agency
la **autopista**	super highway, interstate
el **ayuntamiento**	city/town hall
el **banco**	bank
la **catedral**	cathedral
el **centro**	downtown
la **estación del metro /** de trenes	metro/train station
el **monumento**	monument
el **museo**	museum
la **oficina de correos**	post office
la **parada de** autobuses/taxis	bus stop / taxi stand
la **plaza**	square, plaza
el **puerto**	port
el **quiosco**	kiosk
el **teatro**	theater
la **telefónica**	telephone company office

LOS DESTINOS MÁS POPULARES

el **bosque**	forest
el **campo**	country(side)
las **cataratas**	(water)falls

el **cerro**	mount(ain)	el **boleto (de ida / de**	(one-way, round-trip)
la **cordillera**	mountain range	**ida y vuelta)**	ticket (*Span. Am.*)
el **desierto**	desert	el **itinerario**	itinerary
el **lago**	lake	la **maleta**	suitcase
la **llanura**	flatland, prairie	el/la **pasajero/a**	passenger
el **mar**	sea	el **vuelo**	flight
el **océano**	ocean		
el **paisaje**	landscape	**abordar un avión**	to board a plane
el **pico**	(mountain) peak	**(barco, tren)**	(ship, train)
la **playa**	beach	**bajar de un autobús**	to get off a bus (out of
el **río**	river	**(coche, taxi)**	a car/taxi)
el **salto**	waterfall	**cancelar**	to cancel
la **selva**	jungle	**confirmar**	to book, confirm
la **sierra**	mountain range	**desbordar un avión**	to get off a plane
el **volcán**	volcano	**(barco, tren)**	(ship, train)
		facturar el equipaje	to check luggage
Repaso: la montaña		**hacer una excursión**	to go on an outing/

COMPARACIÓN Y CONTRASTE

			excursion
diferenciarse	to be different,	**hacer un viaje**	to take a trip
	distinguish oneself	**estar de vacaciones**	to be on vacation
parecerse (zc) a	to resemble	**estar de viaje**	to be on a trip
en cambio	on the other hand, in	**ir de vacaciones**	to go on vacation
	contrast	**ir de viaje**	to go on a trip
mientras que	while	**parar en**	to stop (over) in
por un lado _____ por	on one hand _____ on	**perder (ie) un autobús**	to miss a bus (ship, train,
otro (lado) _____	the other (hand) _____	**(barco, tren, vuelo)**	flight)
		perderse (ie)	to get lost
Repaso: al igual que, el/la (+ *noun* +) **más/menos +**		**reconfirmar**	to reconfirm
adj. + **de, más/menos que**		**subir a un autobús**	to get on a bus (in a
		(coche, taxi)	car/taxi)
		viajar	to travel

LOS MEDIOS DE TRANSPORTE

PARA ORIENTARSE EN LA CIUDAD

el **autobús**	bus	la **cuadra**	(city) block
el **avión**	airplane		
el **barco**	ship, boat	**cruzar (c)**	to cross
el **coche**	car	**doblar a la derecha/**	to turn right/left
el **colectivo**	bus	**izquierda**	
el **metro**	subway	**seguir (i, i) derecho**	to continue straight
el **taxi**	taxi		ahead
el **tren**	train		
		a mano derecha/	on the right/left
caminar	to walk	**izquierda**	
conducir (*irreg.*)	to drive	**hacia el norte (sur,**	to the north (south, east,
ir a pie	to go on foot, walk	**este, oeste)**	west)
ir en autobús,	to go by bus, airplane,		
avión, tren,…	train, . . .	**Repaso: la calle**	
manejar	to drive		

DE VIAJE

la **aduana**	customs
el **billete (de ida /**	(one-way, round-trip)
de ida y vuelta)	ticket (*Sp.*)

Entre culturas

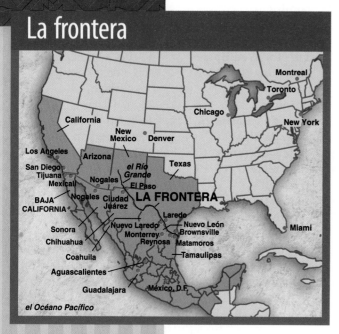

La frontera

Cultura

◆ Where Is the Border: in the Southwestern United States or in Your Own City?

◆ Maintaining Contact with Your Country of Origin

◆ **Señas culturales: La** *Tejano music*

Lengua

◆ Crossing the Border; Expressing Emotions

◆ Bicultural Identity

◆ **Hace** + Time + **que** (11.1)

◆ **Por** and **para** (Summary) (11.2)

◆ Expressing Unexpected or Unplanned Actions (11.3)

◆ Adverbs (11.4)

La frontera						Lucha por la independencia de Tejas	Tratado de Guadalupe Hidalgo pone fin a la Guerra Mexicano-Americana
	hasta el siglo XVI	**1500–1600**	**1534**	**1600–1750**	**1776–1783**	**1835–1836**	**1848**
Los Estados Unidos y el Canadá	Varias tribus indígenas habitan en Norteamérica	Exploración española de Norteamérica	Jacques Cartier reclama para Francia el Canadá	Fundación de las colonias británicas en Norteamérica	Guerra de Independencia en los EE. UU.		

Instantánea

Población hispana en los EE. UU.

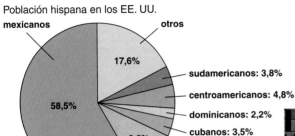

- **mexicanos** 58,5%
- **otros** 17,6%
- sudamericanos: 3,8%
- centroamericanos: 4,8%
- dominicanos: 2,2%
- cubanos: 3,5%
- **puertorriqueños** 9,6%

 www

For additional practice, check out the *Manual de práctica*, the Interactive CD-ROM, and the Online Learning Center (**www.mhhe.com/entrevistas2**)!

Población hispana como porcentaje de la población total de cada estado

Total nacional: el 12,5%

- el 25% o más
- del 12,5% al 24,9%
- del 6% al 12,4%
- menos del 6%

Este mural mexicoamericano se ▶ encuentra en el barrio de la Misión en San Francisco, California.

Compra Gadsden fija la frontera entre México y los EE. UU.	La Revolución Mexicana: éxodo masivo de mexicanos	La expansión de la economía estadounidense motiva mucha inmigración desde México	Millones de puertorriqueños se trasladan a los EE. UU.	La revolución encabezada por Fidel Castro en Cuba provoca un éxodo masivo	125.000 cubanos llegan en botes a los EE. UU.		Los EE. UU. aprueban una nueva ley de inmigración		
1853 **1898**	**1910–1917**	**los años 20**	**a partir de 1945** **1952** **1959**		**1980** **1982**		**1994** **1996**		
Guerra Hispano-Americana			Puerto Rico se hace Estado Libre Asociado de los EE. UU.		El Canadá se separa legalmente de Inglaterra	Tratado de Libre Comercio entre los EE. UU., el Canadá y México			

🔴 Para cruzar la frontera

Pasé el día en Tijuana

Un día decidimos pasar el día en Tijuana. Fuimos hasta **la frontera** en el tranvía de San Diego.

Hablamos con **un agente de inmigración.** Le mostramos nuestros **documentos** (el pasaporte, la visa) y cruzamos la frontera.

Como muchas otras ciudades, Tijuana tiene **partes** bonitas y otras partes feas.

Vimos mucha **influencia** norteamericana. **Se me hace** (Me parece) que Tijuana es **una mezcla** de dos culturas.

A la vuelta,ª nos **detuvieron*** en la aduana, pero finalmente nos **dejaron pasar.**

el extranjero	abroad
renovar (ue)	to renew
revisar	to check, inspect

ªA... *Upon returning*
* **Detener** (*To stop, detain*) is conjugated in all tenses like **tener.**

La inmigración

¿Por qué vienen los inmigrantes?

- Por **razones** económicas, políticas o sociales.
- Para **escapar de la pobreza**[a] cuando **no les va bien**[b] en su país.
- Para **buscar** más oportunidades de trabajo.
- Para trabajar en **las cosechas.**[c]
- Para visitar a parientes que **nacieron** en este país.
- Para **tener éxito**[d] en los negocios.

¿Cómo vienen?

- Algunas personas **ahorran** suficiente dinero para pagarle a un «**coyote**», quien **las ayuda a** pasar la frontera. No quieren **correr el riesgo** de **perderse** en el desierto.
- Otras personas vienen con los documentos necesarios (pasaporte o visa).
- Muchas personas **tienen la intención de** volver a su **país de origen.**

¿Qué es una persona «**(i)legal**»?

- **Los indocumentados** son las personas que entran en el país sin documentos oficiales.
- **Los ciudadanos** de un país son los que **tienen la ciudadanía.**
- **Las leyes**[e] han cambiado mucho en los últimos años. A veces los agentes **discriminan** a los mexicanos que quieren entrar en los Estados Unidos. Dejan pasar a algunas personas, pero a otras las **mandan de regreso**[f] a México.

[a]*poverty* [b]*no… things aren't going well for them* [c]*harvests*
[d]*tener… to be successful* [e]*laws* [f]*mandan… deportan*

▲ *Esta joven mexicoamericana de Los Ángeles, California, protesta en contra de las leyes de inmigración.*

¿Cómo se sienten los inmigrantes?

estar ansioso/a (por)	to be anxious (about)
estar entre dos culturas	to be (caught) between two cultures
ser trabajador(a)	to be hardworking
tener esperanza	to have hope, be hopeful
tener expectativas	to have expectations
tener miedo	to be afraid
tener suerte	to be lucky
vivir con la incertidumbre	to live with uncertainty

Actividades

A. Unas vacaciones en el extranjero.   Una familia salió de su país en auto para pasar las vacaciones en el extranjero. Pon sus acciones en orden cronológico.

_____ Fuimos hasta la frontera en coche.

_____ Los agentes nos revisaron las maletas.

_____ Metimos (*We put*) el equipaje en el coche.

_____ Nos dejaron pasar la frontera.

_____ Nos detuvieron en la aduana.

_____ Nos pidieron los pasaportes.

_____ Preparamos los documentos y renovamos los pasaportes.

B. Con la ayuda del coyote.   ¿Cómo sería (*would it be*) cruzar la frontera entre México y los Estados Unidos con la ayuda de un coyote? Para imaginar la experiencia, escoge la oración que probablemente describe mejor lo que pasa.

1. Viajas de noche. / Viajas de día.
2. Cruzas la frontera en una ciudad. / La cruzas en el desierto.
3. Necesitas mucho dinero. / Necesitas poco dinero.
4. Cruzar con un coyote es peligroso. / No es nada peligroso.
5. Tienes miedo. / No estás ansioso/a.
6. Si te descubren, vas a la cárcel (*jail*) o te regresan. / Si te descubren, no pasa nada.

C. ¿Quién tiene más éxito? Lee las siguientes frases y determina qué inmigrantes tienen más probabilidad de éxito en este país. Explica el porqué de tus respuestas.

1. una persona que tiene documentos legales
2. una mujer que quiere pasar sola
3. una persona con suficiente dinero para contratar a un coyote
4. una persona que habla un poquito de inglés
5. una persona que se viste bien
6. una persona de piel blanca

D. Tus viajes. ¿Has viajado al extranjero alguna vez (*ever*)? Contesta las siguientes preguntas sobre la experiencia de cruzar una frontera nacional.

1. ¿Te fue difícil cruzar la frontera?
2. ¿Qué documentos tuviste que mostrarle al / a la agente de inmigración?
3. ¿Te revisaron las maletas?
4. A la vuelta, ¿qué documentos te pidieron?
5. ¿Tuviste algún problema? Explica.

E. Entrevista: El origen. Hazle las siguientes preguntas a un compañero / una compañera de clase para saber más de la historia de su familia.

1. ¿De dónde eres?
2. ¿De dónde son tus padres? (¿Dónde nacieron?)
3. ¿De dónde son (¿Dónde nacieron) tus abuelos maternos y paternos? Si son de otro país, ¿cómo llegaron aquí?
4. ¿Por qué vinieron a este país (para estudiar, por razones económicas, por razones religiosas, por razones políticas, para evitar la persecución, etcétera)?
5. ¿Sabes dónde se conocieron (*met each other*) tus padres? Y tus abuelos, ¿cómo se conocieron?

Si te interesa

By now you should have noticed that Spanish has a number of idioms that use **tener** + *noun* where English uses the verb *to be* + *adjective*.

tener...	to be ...	tener...	to be ...
_____ años	_____ years old	**miedo**	afraid
celos	jealous	**prisa**	in a hurry
éxito	successful	**sed** (*f.*)	thirsty
hambre (*f.*)	hungry	**suerte** (*f.*)	lucky

Note that the English adjectives use an adverb like *really* or *very* to enhance the description. However, since the word after **tener** is a noun in Spanish, its modifier must be the adjective **mucho/a**.

Tuve **mucho** miedo.   *I was really afraid.*

Hemos tenido **mucha** suerte.   *We've been very lucky.*

You can watch this interview on the *Entrevistas* Video or Interactive CD-ROM or listen to the audio on the Online Learning Center (**www.mhhe.com/entrevistas2**).

Yolanda Rodríguez Ávila

« *...tuvimos suerte de que alguien nos encontró y pudimos cruzar.*»

Nombre: Yolanda

Apellidos: (1) Rodríguez (2) Ávila

Edad: 29 años

Nació en: Tijuana, México

Vocabulario útil

moverse (ue)	**mudarse**	**no tiene nada que**	it has nothing to
se puede decir	one might say	**ver con**	do with
que tengan	that they have	**por un decir**	in a manner of speaking
nos tardó	it took us	**estancada**	stuck
en verdad	truthfully		

Antes de ver

A. ¿Qué sabes de México? ¿Sabes dónde están los siguientes lugares mexicanos? Usando el mapa al princípio del capítulo, describe la ubicación (*location*) de los siguientes lugares. Puedes emplear estas expresiones y otras que conoces.

> es un estado / una ciudad que está cerca de...
> en el centro de...
> en la frontera con...
> entre... y...
> al norte/sur/este/oeste de...
> ¿ ?

1. la Ciudad de México
2. Guadalajara
3. Tijuana
4. Ciudad Juárez
5. Chihuahua
6. Monterrey

B. Tu ciudad. Yolanda va a hablar de la ciudad fronteriza de Tijuana, México. Indica cuáles de las siguientes oraciones pueden aplicarse a **tu** ciudad.

	SÍ	NO
1. Es sucia (*dirty*).	☐	☐
2. Tiene partes que son bonitas.	☐	☐
3. Es una mezcla de culturas diferentes.	☐	☐
4. Es representativa de la región / del país.	☐	☐
5. Está cerca de la frontera.	☐	☐
6. Se hablan lenguas diferentes.	☐	☐
7. Hay pobreza.	☐	☐

¡Veamos!

A. Cruzar no es fácil. Yolanda va a contar cómo cruzaron la frontera diferentes miembros de su familia. Primero, lee las siguientes oraciones. Luego, mientras ves la entrevista, indica a quién se refiere cada oración: a Yolanda, a sus padres o a todos.

	A YOLANDA	A SUS PADRES	A TODOS
1. Necesitaba(n) trabajar.	☐	☐	☐
2. Cruzó/Cruzaron con la ayuda de un coyote.	☐	☐	☐
3. Vino/Vinieron sin documentos.	☐	☐	☐
4. Pasó/Pasaron por las montañas.	☐	☐	☐
5. Se perdió/perdieron en el desierto.	☐	☐	☐
6. Tuvo/Tuvieron suerte de encontrar ayuda.	☐	☐	☐

B. Dictado. Completa los siguientes trozos de la entrevista con lo que dice Yolanda.

«[Mis padres] _____^{1} cruzados por un _____^{2} por las _____.^{3} Un

_____^{4} es la persona que se especializa, se puede decir, en _____^{5}

a gente a través de las _____,^{6} y esto puede _____^{7} entre _____^{8}

o _____^{9} días, dependiendo de la _____^{10} que tengan en cruzar.»

«En mi caso concreto, yo _____^{11} con el grupo de gente que venía,

que éramos como unas _____^{12} personas. Y nos perdimos en medio

del _____.^{13} Y fue muy duro porque no teníamos _____,^{14} no

teníamos _____,^{15} y no me encontraba bien físicamente. Fue muy

_____,^{16} y pues tuvimos suerte de que alguien nos encontró y

pudimos cruzar. Nos tardó más o menos como _____^{17} días.»

Después de ver

A. Un retrato de Tijuana. Indica si las siguientes oraciones sobre Tijuana son ciertas o falsas, según lo que dice Yolanda.

	CIERTO	FALSO
1. Es como el resto de México.	☐	☐
2. Es pobre y no hay mucho trabajo.	☐	☐
3. También es sucia.	☐	☐
4. Todo el mundo está de paso, nadie se queda a vivir allí.	☐	☐
5. Está cerca de la frontera.	☐	☐
6. Es representativa del país.	☐	☐

B. ¿A quién le fue bien? ¿Quién pasó la frontera más fácilmente, Yolanda o sus padres? Apoya tu respuesta con información de la entrevista.

C. Lugares importantes. Contesta las siguientes preguntas.

1. ¿Por qué son importantes los siguientes lugares en la vida de Yolanda?

   - Aguascalientes
   - Los Ángeles
   - Tijuana

2. ¿Qué lugares tienen una importancia similar para tu familia? ¿Por qué?

▲ *¿Qué aspecto de Tijuana representa para ti esta foto? ¿Crees que sea* (it is) *así todo México, o sólo en algunos lugares?*

11.1 **Hace** + Time + **que**

In **Capítulo 10**, you saw the construction **hace** + *time* + **que** + *present tense verb* to express how long an action or state has been in effect.

Hace 30 años que viven en California.

They've lived (been living) in California for 30 years.

The **hace** + *time* + **que** construction can be used with a past tense (usually the preterit) to express the equivalent of English *ago*. The *preterit* is used because the action was *completed* in the past and is no longer in effect.

Hace 30 años que cruzaron la frontera.

Thirty years ago, they crossed the border.

NOTES:

- You can also use the **hace** + *time* + **que** + *preterit verb* construction at the end of sentence, but in this case the **que** is not used.

  Cruzaron la frontera **hace 30 años.**

  They crossed the border 30 years ago.

- When asking a question about how long something has been going on or how long ago something happened, use the construction: **¿Cuánto tiempo hace que** + *verb…* **?***

  ¿Cuánto tiempo hace que viven en California?

  How long have they lived (been living) in California?

  ¿Hace cuánto tiempo que cruzaron la frontera?

  How long ago did they cross the border?

Análisis estructural

Lee las oraciones de la izquierda e indica la traducción correcta en inglés, a la derecha.

1. _____ Hace un año que estudio aquí.
2. _____ Hace un año que estudié aquí.

a. I have been studying here for a year.
b. I studied here a year ago.

3. _____ Hace una hora que te espero.
4. _____ Te esperaba hace una hora.

a. I have been waiting for you for an hour.
b. An hour ago, I was waiting for you.

5. _____ Te llamé hace dos días.
6. _____ Hace dos días que te llamo.

a. I have been calling you for two days.
b. I called you two days ago.

---

* In colloquial speech, this construction may be changed to: **¿Hace cuánto tiempo que** + *verb…* **?**

7. _____ Hace muchos años que los inmigrantes vinieron aquí.

a. Immigrants have been coming here for many years.

8. _____ Hace muchos años que los inmigrantes vienen aquí.

b. Immigrants came here many years ago.

9. _____ Tuvimos problemas económicos en México hace varios años.

a. We have had economic problems in Mexico for several years.

10. _____ Hace varios años que tenemos problemas económicos en México.

b. Several years ago we had economic problems in Mexico.

Actividades

A. Hechos históricos. Usando la información de las primeras dos páginas de este capítulo, contesta las siguientes preguntas sobre la historia fronteriza de los Estados Unidos.

1. ¿Cuánto tiempo hace que se puso fin a la Revolución Mexicana?
2. ¿Cuánto tiempo hace que Puerto Rico es Estado Libre Asociado de los Estados Unidos?
3. ¿Cuánto tiempo hace que empezó la revolución de Castro en Cuba?
4. ¿Cuánto tiempo hace que se inició la nueva ley de inmigración?
5. ¿Cuánto tiempo hace que se efectúa (*has been in effect*) el Tratado de Libre Comercio?

B. Entrevista: ¿Cuánto tiempo hace? Entrevista a un compañero / una compañera de clase para saber cuánto tiempo hace que hizo las siguientes cosas. También puedes añadir preguntas originales.

1. visitar a sus padres
2. ver a los amigos de la escuela secundaria
3. aprender algo sobre México
4. salir a comer con los amigos
5. hacer preguntas en la clase de español
6. ¿ ?

● 11.2 **Por** and **para** (Summary)

In your study of Spanish so far, you have learned many expressions with the prepositions **por** and **para.** Both words sometimes can be translated into English as *for,* but by no means do they have the same meaning. The following is a summary of their uses (some of which you have already learned), although for beginning students of Spanish it is probably best to memorize these two prepositions in the most common expressions in which they are used.

Expressions with **por**

Por eso llegamos tan tarde.	*That's why we arrived so late.*
Traigo mis documentos, **por si acaso.**	*I'll bring my papers, just in case.*
Gracias por el regalo.	*Thanks for the gift.*
Gracias por ayudarme anoche.	*Thanks for helping me last night.*
¿Me puede decir la hora, **por favor**?	*Could you please tell me what time it is?*
¡Por supuesto!	*Of course!*
Sólo el 12 **por ciento** de los inmigrantes es de ese país.	*Only 12 percent of the immigrants are from that country.*

Uses of **por**

1. with places, to express movement *through* or *around*

Pasamos **por** San Diego.	*We went (passed) through San Diego.*
Muchos inmigrantes viven **por** aquí.	*Lots of immigrants live around here.*

2. with time, to express *duration*

Nos detuvieron **por** tres horas en la frontera.	*They held us for three hours at the border.*

3. with an infinitive, to express *reason, motive,* or *means*

Fuimos a California **por** no tener trabajo en México.	*We went to California because we had no work in Mexico.*

4. with people or other nouns, to express *for* in the sense of *on behalf of, because of*

La madre de Yolanda lo hizo **por** su hija.	*Yolanda's mother did it on behalf of her daughter.*
Inmigraron **por** razones económicas.	*They immigrated because of (for) economic reasons.*

Uses of **para**

1. with places, to express *destination*

Mañana salimos **para** Ciudad Juárez.	*Tomorrow we're leaving for Ciudad Juárez.*

2. with time expressions, to express *deadlines*

Este trabajo es **para** mañana.	*This job is for tomorrow.*

3. with an infinitive, to express *purpose*

Voy a Arizona **para** trabajar.	*I'm going to Arizona (in order) to work.*

4. with people or other nouns, to express *recipient* or *standard of comparison*

¿Ese regalo es **para** mí?	*That present is for me?*
Es muy trabajador **para** un niño tan joven.	*He's very hardworking for such a young child.*

NOTES:

- When you give a motive or means with a noun, use **por** to mean *because of*. When a conjugated verb follows, use **porque** to mean *because*.

No fuimos con el coyote **por** el peligro.	*We didn't go with the coyote because of the danger.*
No fuimos con el coyote **porque** era muy peligroso.	*We didn't go with the coyote because it was very dangerous.*

- The distinction between *motives* (expressed with **por**) and *purposes* (expressed with **para**) is subtle. Think of motives as preexisting conditions, and purposes as future goals.

Los peregrinos dejaron Inglaterra **por** razones religiosas.	*The pilgrims left England for (because of) religious reasons. (reasons already existed in England)*
Vinieron a América **para** empezar una nueva vida.	*They came to America (in order) to start a new life. (future plans)*

- With the impersonal expressions **es difícil, es fácil, es necesario,** and so forth, use an infinitive alone (not with **para**) to express the action that is difficult, easy, necessary, and so on.

Es difícil cruzar la frontera sin coyote.	*It's hard to cross the border without a coyote.*
No siempre **es fácil conseguir** trabajo en los Estados Unidos.	*It's not always easy to get work in the United States.*

Actividades

A. Los motivos. Completa con **por** o **porque** las siguientes oraciones sobre la deportación de Mariluz, una estudiante mexicana de secundaria que vive sin documentos en los Estados Unidos con sus padres.

1. El director de la escuela llegó a la clase _____ Mariluz.

2. Al principio, ella estaba contenta _____ pensó que iba a salir de la clase con sus padres.

3. La madre de Mariluz lloraba _____ tener que separarse de su hija.

4. Mariluz no quería dejar su escuela _____ le gustaba.

5. Los padres de Mariluz querían regresar a su casa _____ dinero y ropa.

6. Los agentes deportaron a la familia de Mariluz _____ sus padres no tenían los documentos necesarios.

B. En el consulado (*consulate*). Un agente del consulado les da las siguientes instrucciones a dos personas que quieren conseguir una visa. Complétalas con **para** o **por**.

1. Ustedes necesitan pruebas (*proof*) de identificación _____ empezar el proceso.

2. Estos documentos son _____ el agente Ramírez.

3. Tienen que llegar al consulado _____ la próxima semana.

4. Los necesitamos _____ expedir (*issue*) la visa.

5. Normalmente guardamos los documentos _____ tres días, y luego se los devolvemos con la visa.

6. _____ un ciudadano norteamericano, el proceso es fácil.

C. Los titulares (*headlines*). Completa con **por** o **para** estos titulares sobre los indocumentados.

1. Familiares preocupados _____ inmigrantes deportados

2. Congreso aprueba (*passes*) nuevas leyes _____ inmigrantes procedentes (*originating from*) de México

3. Gobierno mexicano obligado a establecer condiciones de deportación _____ los indocumentados

4. El INS (Servicio de Inmigración y Naturalización) deporta a 30 mil mexicanos _____ Tijuana y Ciudad Juárez este año

5. Activistas demandan actitud más vigorosa _____ defender derechos de indocumentados

6. Indocumentados necesarios _____ el funcionamiento de servicios _____ toda la ciudad

D. La Visa Láser. Lee la descripción de la Visa Láser, un documento del INS de los Estados Unidos, y contesta las siguientes preguntas.

1. ¿Para quiénes es este documento?
2. ¿Por qué motivos se solicita (*apply for*) una Visa Láser?
3. ¿Por cuántos años es válida?
4. ¿Qué medidas de seguridad contiene? ¿Para qué sirven?

¿Qué es la Visa Láser?

- La Visa Láser es una visa combinada (B1/B2, de negocios y turismo) y una Tarjeta de Cruce Fronterizo (Border Crossing Card o BCC; también conocida como «mica» o «pasaporte fronterizo»).

- Se expide[a] a los ciudadanos mexicanos que viajen a los Estados Unidos por cuestiones[b] de turismo, negocios o compras.

- Su tamaño es el de una tarjeta de crédito, por lo que puede llevarse fácilmente en la cartera.

- Contiene datos, fotografía y huella digital[c] del portador;[d] la información será codificada[e] digitalmente en la tarjeta, de manera que[f] puede ser leída por un rayo láser. Contiene medidas[g] adicionales de seguridad para evitar[h] su falsificación, y puede ser leída electrónicamente.

- Tiene una validez de 10 años.

[a]Se... *It is issued*   [b]*issues, reasons*   [c]huella... *digital fingerprint*   [d]*bearer*   [e]será... *will be coded*   [f]de... *so that*   [g]*measures*   [h]*avoid*

Lenguaje funcional
Combining Ideas

You should have noticed by now in your study of Spanish that learning new vocabulary is not just learning translations; you must also learn how to combine the new items in meaningful phrases. Here is a summary of some tips on combining ideas.

PREPOSITION + INFINITIVE

The only verb form that can follow a preposition in Spanish is the *infinitive*. (Don't use the **-ndo** form the way English uses the *-ing* form.)

Después **de revisar** los pasaportes,...	*After checking the passports,...*
Sin saber la verdad,...	*Without knowing the truth,...*

CONJUGATED VERB + INFINITIVE

Remember that you can only conjugate the first verb in a clause. Some verbs can be followed immediately by an infinitive.

Quiero volver a México.	*I want to go back to Mexico.*
Debes renovar tu pasaporte.	*You should renew your passport.*

CONJUGATED VERB + PREPOSITION + INFINITIVE

Some verbs must be followed by a preposition before an infinitive.

Trata **de** esconder sus raíces.	*She tries to hide her roots.*
Me ayuda **a** mantener nuestras costumbres.	*It helps me preserve our customs.*

CONJUGATED VERB + **-NDO** FORM

Some verbs can be followed by the **-ndo** form.

Están dejando pasar a muchos inmigrantes en estos días.	*They're letting many immigrants pass through these days.*
Siguen hablando español en casa.	*They still speak Spanish at home.*

Análisis cultural

La siguiente cita tomada de una fuente escrita en inglés para anglohablantes va a aumentar tus conocimientos sobre algunos fenómenos culturales relacionados con la inmigración. ¿Es consistente esta información con la perspectiva de Yolanda de la **Entrevista 1?** Usa lo que has aprendido en este capítulo sobre la inmigración, más tu propia experiencia, para contestar las preguntas que siguen la cita.

66Time and distance have different values for Latino immigrants than for the European newcomers of long ago because they can visit home for the weekend or phone a loved one whenever they feel the urge to hear a familiar voice. . . .

The Statue of Liberty stands as a symbol of the European migration because it represents a terminus. There is no terminus for Latino immigrants. Latino immigrants pass through borders. Then they create barrios that are borderlands. At a time of quick and ready travel, the borderland can be anywhere. This holds for all immigrants today, but the ambiguities are most intense for Latinos because of the proximity of their homelands. The barrios are borderlands not because foreigners live in them, not because they are filled with exotic smells and voices. Instead, they are borderlands because of a constant traffic of goods and people, a give-and-take, a constant hybridization.

The human traffic between the United States and the Latin American countries that send it immigrants, especially Mexico, has achieved a size and speed unimaginable a few years ago. So many people in these countries are so closely linked and move back and forth so much that they create transnational spaces. These are not cactus-strewn deserts somewhere out in the Southwest, but chunks of American cities where national identities and geographic boundaries lose their relevance. These are barrios where Latinos invent new kinds of music and new identities and where a new generation of Americans is trying to define itself while living in a constant state of transition.**99**

Source: *Strangers Among Us: How Latino Immigration Is Transforming America*

1. ¿En qué ciudades o regiones estadounidenses hay poblaciones hispanas grandes? ¿Dónde se encuentran, en la frontera con México o por todas partes (*everywhere*)? ¿Cómo se compara esta tendencia con la de otros grupos de inmigrantes del pasado, por ejemplo, alemanes, irlandeses, italianos, noruegos, suecos, etcétera?

2. Los autores hablan de «*transnational spaces*» (espacios transnacionales). ¿Qué quieren decir con esto? ¿Cuáles son las características de esos espacios? ¿Conoces tú —personalmente o a través de lecturas, películas, etcétera— algún lugar que se pueda considerar un espacio transnacional? Si dices que sí, ¿cuáles son las peculiaridades que notas en esos espacios?

3. En la **Entrevista 1,** Yolanda habla de Tijuana como un lugar distinto al resto de México. ¿Crees que Tijuana se pueda considerar un espacio transnacional en México? Explica tu respuesta.

4. ¿Qué ejemplos de música u otras expresiones artísticas creadas por inmigrantes hispanos a los Estados Unidos conoces? ¿Tienen estas expresiones artísticas características especiales, diferentes a las demás de su género (*genre*)? Explica tu respuesta.

Pronunciación y ortografía

● d and g

In **Capítulo 10,** you learned that there are two variants, "hard" and "soft," of the Spanish [b] sound, depending on where the letters **b** or **v** occur in a word or phrase. The same is true for the letters **d** and **g.**

Both hard sounds are also called *stops,* because the flow of air out of the mouth is completely stopped. For the hard [d], the tip of the tongue touches the back side of the top front teeth. To produce the hard [g], which is similar to the [g] in English *go,* the tongue touches the soft palate (the rear portion of the roof of the mouth). Listen to your instructor pronounce the following words and phrases. Note that all hard sounds occur after a pause or after the letter **n.** The hard [d] also occurs after the letter **l.**

angustia	tengo	aldea	derecha
Guadalajara	un grupo	conducir	un director

The soft sounds occur everywhere else—between vowels and after consonants other than **n** (and other than **l** for [đ]). They are also known as *fricatives,* because the flow of air out of the mouth is *not* completely stopped. For the soft [đ], the tip of the tongue goes between the front teeth and produces a sound similar to the **th** in English *they.* To produce the soft [g], the tongue nears the back of the soft palate as if pronouncing the hard [g], but the flow of air is not completely stopped. Listen to your instructor pronounce the following words and phrases.

aduana	agua
catedral	seguir
a la derecha	a Guadalajara

¡OJO! Remember that the letter **g** followed by **e** or **i** has neither a hard nor soft **g** sound; it has the same sound as **j (jota): agente, Villa <u>G</u>esell, re<u>g</u>ión.**

The *Manual de práctica* has activities to practice the material explained in this section.

● La identidad bicultural

▲ *Gloria, 39 años, Los Ángeles*

▲ *Armando, 45 años, Miami*

Soy **bicultural,** pero **me identifico** más con la cultura norteamericana. Algunas personas quieren **esconder**[a] sus **raíces** mexicanas, pero yo estoy orgullosa de mis orígenes. Vivir entre dos culturas implica muchos **conflictos culturales.** Por ejemplo, en la escuela los maestros no nos **dejaban** hablar español. Mis padres tenían **valores** y expectativas diferentes para los chicos y para las chicas.

[a]*hide*

Para mí, ser bicultural significa **ser consciente de** mis orígenes, **aprender** de la cultura mexicana y **preservar**la y ser **bilingüe,** es decir, no **olvidar** el español ni **las costumbres** de mis padres y abuelos.

el conflicto generacional	generational conflict
la lengua nativa	native language
ser próspero/a	to be prosperous
tratar de mantener las costumbres	to try to maintain one's (native, traditional) customs

▲ ¿Hay escuelas o programas bilingües en la región donde vives?

Actividades

A. La identidad bicultural. ¿Con qué cultura se identifican los siguientes norteamericanos, probablemente?

> MODELO Esta persona se identifica más con la cultura sueca [*Swedish*].

1. «Mis antepasados (*ancestors*) son de Italia, pero no sé de dónde, exactamente.»
2. «Mis padres son de origen mexicano, pero nunca me hablaban en español.»
3. «Soy de Corea, y no hablo bien el inglés.»
4. «Mis abuelos vinieron de Suecia (*Sweden*), y todavía comemos ludefisk y otros platos típicos en las fiestas.»
5. «En mi casa, celebramos las posadas navideñas,* comemos tortillas más que pan y vamos a clases de español después de la escuela.»
6. «Mis antepasados son de Irlanda, pero no mantenemos ninguna costumbre de allí.»

B. Vivir entre dos culturas. Las siguientes citas vienen de la revista bilingüe *Latina.* Complétalas con las palabras apropiadas de la lista. **¡OJO!** No se usan todas las expresiones.

abuelos, conflictos, culturas, fiestas, flexible, identidad, por ciento, rebelión

1. «Más del 30 _____ de los latinos inmigrantes entre los 25 y los 34 años se casan con personas no latinas. Las latinas que se han casado con hombres de otras razas (*races*) dicen que sus familias se han enriquecido (*have been enriched*) con dos _____ distintas.»
2. «Aprender el español es parte importante de la _____ cultural.»
3. «Hay que exponer (*expose*) a los niños a personas como los _____, que pueden enseñarles a sentir la cultura.»
4. «Una pareja bicultural debe llegar a un acuerdo acerca de la crianza (*raising*) de los hijos y ser _____ en sus actitudes.»
5. «Si hay un asunto que afecta a la familia, como la celebración de ciertas _____, se debe discutir entre todos, incluidos a los niños.»

 C. Encuesta: Los orígenes de tu familia. Hazles las siguientes preguntas a cinco compañeros/as de clase para saber más de su historia familiar. Después, presenta sus respuestas al resto de la clase.

1. ¿De qué origen étnico o nacional es tu familia?
2. ¿Cuánto tiempo hace que llegaron tus antepasados a este país?
3. ¿Por qué vinieron, originalmente?
4. ¿Se mantienen muchas costumbres de su país nativo? ¿Cuáles?
5. ¿Hablas el idioma original de tu familia, o conoces por lo menos algunas expresiones?

---

* **Las posadas** son fiestas mexicanas que se celebran antes de la Navidad.

6. ¿Te identificas con el origen de tu familia, o te sientes más bien norteamericano/a? ¿Por qué?
7. ¿Tienes conflictos culturales o generacionales con tus padres o abuelos? ¿Qué soluciones han encontrado ustedes?

Señas culturales

KXTQ 93.7 FM, Lubbock, Texas

1.	Fantasía	Mazzizo
2.	Quisiera Decirte	Bobby Pulido
3.	Cuántas Veces	Mazz
4.	Duele	Elida Y Avante
5.	Pido	La Mafia
6.	Mi Chatita	Michael Salgado
7.	Porque	Eddie González
8.	Todo Por Ti	Fama
9.	Amor Maldito	Intocable
10.	Mira Juanita	Little Joe

KNUW 95.3 FM, Silver City, New Mexico

1.	Amor Maldito	Intocable
2.	Pido	La Mafia
3.	Los Albañiles	Emilio
4.	Hombres Y Mujeres	Jay Pérez
5.	Te Quiero Y Te Amo	David Lee Garza
6.	Fantasía	Mazzizo
7.	Mujer Sin Alma	Eddie González
8.	Casas De Madera	Ramón Ayala
9.	Tú Eres	Ram Herrera
10.	Candy Boy	Amber Rose

LA LEY 94.1 FM, San Antonio, Texas

1.	Gira La Rueda	Chon Arauza Y La Furia Colombiana
2.	Sobreviviré	Priscila Y Sus Balas De Plata
3.	Esperanza	Enrique Iglesias
4.	Fantasía	Mazzizo
5.	Quiero Ser	Los Ángeles Azules
6.	Hotel Corazón	Los Tucanes De Tijuana
7.	Cómo Te Recuerdo	Los Tigres Del Norte
8.	Ritmo De Colombia	Tony Molina Y Su Grupo Kumbe
9.	El Privilegio De Amar	Mijares
10.	Directo Al Corazón	Pepe Aguilar

KGBC 1540 AM, Galveston, Texas

1.	La Papaya	Rubén Vela
2.	Pido	La Mafia
3.	Sólo Una Patada	Ramón Ayala
4.	Te Voy A Dar Mi Corazón	Gustavo Y La Buena Vida
5.	Chatita	Michael Salgado
6.	Kranke	Albert Zamora Y Talento
7.	Cuando Tú Me Quieras	Los Palominos
8.	Quisiera Decirte	Bobby Pulido
9.	La Otra Parte Del Amor	Límite
10.	Porque	Eddie González

La *Tejano Music* es un estilo de música único cuyos sonidos[a] y letras reflejan las emociones, el orgullo y la experiencia multicultural de la vida mexicoamericana. Esta música es una mezcla de rock, *country, rhythm and blues* y jazz. También se caracteriza por el acordeón y la guitarra de doce cuerdas.[b]

Aunque esta música se originó en los años 70 entre los conjuntos musicales[c] del sur de Tejas, el nombre no tomó raíz hasta 1980, a partir del[d] concurso[e] internacional *Los premios[f] de música tejana.* Desde entonces, la *Tejano Music* ha alcanzado una popularidad y visibilidad que rebasa[g] todas las fronteras geográficas y culturales.

El músico David Lee Garza es el líder del grupo de música tejana Los Musicales. Revisa la lista de la revista *Planet Tejano.* ¿Goza de mucha popularidad este músico? ¿Reconoces otras canciones o a otros músicos?

[a]*cuyos… whose sounds* [b]*strings* [c]*conjuntos… bands* [d]*a… después del* [e]*competition* [f]*awards* [g]*surpasses*

Entrevista 2

You can watch this interview on the *Entrevistas* Video or Interactive CD-ROM or listen to the audio on the Online Learning Center (**www.mhhe.com/entrevistas2**).

Érika Meza Román

«*Yo diría que soy mexicoamericana porque soy en parte de las dos culturas.*»

Nombre: Érika

Apellidos: (1) Meza (2) Román

Edad: 22 años

Nació en: Los Ángeles, California

Vocabulario útil

lavar los trastes	to wash the dishes	**ha madurado**	she has matured
damas y chambelanes	young ladies and gentlemen	**ha crecido**	she has grown up
todo lo que le han brindado	all they have given her	**me hubiera gustado**	I would have liked

---

Antes de ver

A. La identidad de Érika. En esta entrevista, Érika va a hablar de su identidad de mexicoamericana. En tu opinión, ¿cuáles de las siguientes oraciones probablemente describen esta identidad?

1. ☐ Soy bilingüe.
2. ☐ Mi papá es americano y mi mamá es mexicana.
3. ☐ Siento que me han criado en las dos culturas.
4. ☐ De joven, creo que era más fácil tener una familia bicultural.
5. ☐ Mis padres no pudieron darme una fiesta de quince años.

B. Los motivos. Contesta las siguientes preguntas.

1. Cuando eras adolescente, ¿qué cosas no te dejaban hacer tus padres?
2. ¿Por qué no te dejaban hacer esas cosas? En tu opinión, ¿eran válidos sus motivos? ¿Los comprendes (*do you understand*) ahora?
3. ¿Fueron tus conflictos con tus padres conflictos culturales o solamente diferencias generacionales?

¡Veamos!

¿Acertaste? Vuelve a la **Actividad A** de **Antes de ver** y di qué oraciones son consistentes con lo que dice Érika sobre su identidad mexicoamericana.

Después de ver

A. ¿Qué dijo? Primero, lee las siguientes oraciones incompletas de la entrevista con Érika. Ve de nuevo la entrevista y completa las oraciones con la información que falta.

1. Érika se siente _____ porque es de las dos culturas.
2. Sus padres son muy _____. No la dejan _____ y no la dejan _____.
3. Su hermano siempre _____, pero Érika tenía que _____.
4. Los quince años se celebran con _____. Siempre hay _____, _____, _____, _____ y _____.
5. La quinceañera les da _____ a _____ por todo lo que le han brindado a ella. Los padres le dan _____ a _____ porque su hija ha madurado.

B. Comparaciones. Compara tu adolescencia con la de Érika, contestando las siguientes preguntas.

1. ¿Eran tus padres más estrictos que los padres de Érika o menos estrictos?
2. ¿Trataban (*Treated*) tus padres a los chicos igual que a las chicas? ¿Qué pasó en la familia de Érika?

Piénsalo bien

Lee el siguiente fragmento de un artículo de la revista *Latina* y contesta las preguntas que lo siguen.

La crianza de antes y la de ahora

por Leila Cobo-Hanlon

En una época, bastaba[a] que Mamá levantara una ceja[b] o que Papá frunciera el ceño[c] para disciplinar a un hijo.

Los tiempos han cambiado. Las latinas que fueron criadas[d] con mucha disciplina, bien sea[e] en Estados Unidos o en América Latina, ahora tienen hijos a quienes deben criar de manera distinta. Sus hijos, influenciados por los valores de la cultura dominante, se resisten a la crianza autoritaria. A su vez,[f] muchos padres modernos buscan tener con sus hijos una relación más informal que la que ellos tuvieron con sus padres, para poder lograr un mayor nivel de intimidad.

La ausencia de la familia extendida hace que todos tengan que esforzarse más[g] por construir una red de apoyo.[h] Los latinos tienen la carga[i] adicional de lograr que sus hijos incorporen a su personalidad, dos idiomas y dos culturas.

Pero no hay que desalentarse,[j] pues hasta[k] en los momentos más difíciles, la insistencia de los padres en comer todos juntos, en asistir a la iglesia los domingos, en hablar español en casa y en reunir a toda la familia, sirve para mantener la unión de ésta.[l]

1. ¿Está de acuerdo este artículo con lo que dijo Érika con respecto a los conflictos con sus padres?
2. ¿Qué conflictos pueden ocurrir si una madre hispana autoritaria trata de disciplinar a sus hijos «americanizados» de manera tradicional?
3. ¿Qué soluciones se ofrecen en este artículo para mantener la unión de la familia hispana en los Estados Unidos? ¿Crees que sean eficaces? ¿Puedes añadir otras soluciones?

[a]*it was sufficient* [b]*levantara... raised an eyebrow* [c]*frunciera... wrinkled his brow* [d]*fueron... were raised* [e]*bien... whether* [f]*A... In turn* [g]*hace... makes it so that everyone has to work harder* [h]*red... support network* [i]*burden* [j]*get discouraged* [k]*even* [l]*la familia*

● 11.3 Expressing Unexpected or Unplanned Actions

In **Capítulo 5,** you saw that the pronoun **se** can be used with third-person verb forms to express impersonal actions (that is, actions with no specified subject or "doer").

Se olvidan esas costumbres fácilmente.

> *Those customs are easily forgotten.*
>
> *People forget those customs easily.*
>
> *One forgets those customs easily.*

You have also seen, in **Capítulo 6,** that the indirect object pronouns **me, te, le, nos, os,** and **les** can indicate who is affected by an action (the beneficiary or "victim").

Mis padres **me** compraron una muñeca para la Navidad.

My parents bought (for) me a doll for Christmas.

A mi hermano **le** regalaron una bicicleta.

They gave my brother a bicycle.

If these two structures are combined, what would the meaning be? An action without a specified "doer" plus the indirect object naming the "victim" of the action creates the perfect way to express unplanned or unexpected events that have repercussions for a person.

A los jóvenes **se les pierde** el español.

Young people are losing their Spanish.

Se pierde el español tells us that the ability to speak Spanish is being lost, and **a los jóvenes (les)** indicates who is affected by this action. One could say **Los jóvenes pierden su español,** but this sentence might imply that they are doing it willingly or consciously (with **los jóvenes** as the subject, they are the "doers" of the action).

This structure typically follows a pattern and is commonly used with the verbs listed.

a + **Noun or Pronoun**	*se* +	**Indirect Object Pronoun**	**Verb (Third-Person Singular or Plural)**	**Subject**
1. A los jóvenes	se	les	pierde	la lengua.
2. A mí	se	me	olvidan	las costumbres.
3. A nosotros	se	nos	cayeron	los documentos.
4. A ti	se	te	venció	la visa.
5. A ella	se	le	rompió	el brazo.

The nuances of meaning in these sentences are often difficult to translate into colloquial English. Compare their literal meanings and colloquial English translations in the following table.

Literal Meaning	Closest Colloquial English Translation
1. The language is being lost; young people are the ones most affected.	*Young people are losing the language.*
2. The customs are being forgotten; I am the one who is affected by this loss.	*The customs are slipping away from me.*
3. The documents fell; we were the ones holding them.	*We (inadvertently) dropped the documents.*
4. The visa expired; you are the person who is affected.	*Your visa expired.*
5. The arm got broken; she is the one who suffered because of it.	*She broke her arm.*

Análisis estructural

Lee las oraciones e identifica los siguientes elementos: el sujeto, el verbo y el pronombre de complemento indirecto. Después, traduce (*translate*) las oraciones al inglés.

1. A los jóvenes se les olvidan las costumbres de sus antepasados.
2. En la aduana, se me cayó la mochila.
3. A mí se me venció la visa, y tuve que volver a México.
4. A Julia se le rompieron las maletas, y se le cayó toda la ropa.
5. A nosotros se nos perdieron los pasaportes; por lo tanto (*therefore*), no pudimos cruzar la frontera.

Actividades

A. **Contratiempos** (*Mishaps*) **en Tijuana.**   Forma oraciones completas para describir un viaje de San Diego a Tijuana. **¡OJO!** Tienes que añadir **se** + un pronombre de complemento indirecto y conjugar el verbo entre paréntesis en el pretérito.

1. ayer (ocurrir) (mí) la idea de pasar el día en Tijuana
2. cuando llegué a la estación del tranvía (perder) el boleto y tuve que comprar otro
3. (olvidar) llevar los documentos pero cuando llegué a la frontera el agente me dejó pasar
4. en Tijuana comí demasiado en mi restaurante favorito y ¡(romper) el pantalón!
5. después, fui a comprar un pantalón nuevo, pero rumbo (*on the way*) a la tienda, (extraviar) (perder) la cartera con todo mi dinero; por eso, tuve que volver con un alfiler (*pin*) en el pantalón
6. de vuelta, traté de explicarle al agente por qué no traía documentos, y en ese momento, ¡(caer) el pantalón!

B. Un día fatal. Cuéntale a un compañero / una compañera la historia de lo que te pasó en *una* de las siguientes situaciones.

1. Se te rompió algo importante.
2. Se te perdió algo importante.
3. Se te olvidó algo importante.

11.4 Adverbs

Adverbs are important function words that can be used with adjectives (and other adverbs) to enhance descriptions, or with verbs to tell how actions are carried out. You have already seen and used many adverbs in your study of Spanish:

Ella habla inglés **muy** bien.	*She speaks English very well.*
El autobús **siempre** llega **tarde.**	*The bus always arrives late.*

Here are some other common adverbs whose meanings you should know.

WITH ADJECTIVES OR OTHER ADVERBS

El problema es **bastante** complicado.	*The problem is rather complicated.*
Llegan a ser **súper** ricos aquí.	*They become super rich here.*
El agente de inmigración habló **demasiado rápidamente.**	*The immigration agent spoke too quickly.*

WITH VERBS

Quizá(s) no vamos.	*Perhaps we won't go.*
Sólo (Solamente) fuimos a Ciudad Juárez.	*We only went to Ciudad Juárez.*

NOTES:

• The **-s** of **quizá(s)** is optional; either word is correct.
• **Solo/a** without an accent is an adjective and means *alone* or *lonely;* with an accent, **sólo,** it is the shortened form of the adverb **solamente** (*only*) and is invariable in form.

Prepositional phrases (*preposition + noun* or *infinitive*) can often serve the same function as adverbs.

El tranvía llegó **a tiempo.**	*The streetcar arrived on time.*
Mi papá vino para acá **antes de llegar mi mamá.**	*My father came here before my mother arrived.*
Te voy a llamar **después de terminar** la tarea.	*I'm going to call you after I finish the homework.*

Just as we add *-ly* to many adjectives in English, most Spanish adjectives can be turned into a related adverb by adding the suffix **-mente** to the feminine form of the adjective (if there is one).

físico (*m.*) → física (*f.*) → físicamente *physical* (adjective) →
                physically (adverb)

cultural (*m., f.*) → culturalmente *cultural* (adjective) →
                culturally (adverb)

Note that these words are really compounds: They have two stressed syllables, maintaining the original stress (and the written accent) of the adjective: **fí-si-ca-men-te, cul-tu-ral-men-te.** When two **-mente** adverbs are used together, the first one does not take the suffix in standard Spanish, but rather it appears as just the feminine adjective form. You may hear native speakers break this rule in informal speech.

Física y **culturalmente** se *Physically and culturally, it*
 parece a una ciudad   *resembles a North American*
 norteamericana.   *city.* (standard Spanish)

Físicamente y **culturalmente** se *Physically and culturally, it*
 parece…   *resembles . . .* (informal
             speech)

Finally, when placing adverbs in a sentence, remember that in Spanish—unlike in English—*nothing* can intervene between the two parts of the present perfect. (See **Capítulo 10.**)

¿**Has pasado** la frontera en *Have you recently crossed the*
 Matamoros **recientemente**? *border at Matamoros?*

Actividades

A. ¿Cómo se hace? Forma los adverbios de los siguientes adjetivos. Después, empareja cada adverbio de la izquierda con el término opuesto de la derecha.

1. _____ agitado   **a.** ansioso
2. _____ detenido (*thorough, slow*) **b.** difícil
3. _____ fácil   **c.** inmediato
4. _____ feliz   **d.** lento
5. _____ rápido   **e.** tranquilo
6. _____ paciente   **f.** triste

B. Las experiencias de un inmigrante. Rogelio Sánchez, originario del estado mexicano de Durango, viajó a los Estados Unidos recientemente para trabajar en una compañía internacional. Completa las siguientes oraciones que describen su viaje con adverbios en **-mente.** Usa los siguientes adjetivos para formar adverbios.

alegre, ansioso, claro (*clear*), detenido, final, triste, triunfal

1. Después de muchos años de duro trabajo, Rogelio _____ ahorró el dinero necesario para el viaje.

2. Se despidió _____ de su familia en Durango, y subió al autobús con destino al norte.

3. Pasó la noche en el autobús _____, pensando en la incertidumbre de su nueva vida.

4. Durante el viaje, un hombre que frecuentemente cruzaba la frontera le explicó _____ lo que pasaría (*would happen*) en la frontera.

5. En El Paso, un agente le revisó _____ los documentos. ¡Rogelio pensaba que nunca lo dejaría (*he would let*) pasar!

6. Pasó la frontera _____, con los brazos arriba al estilo de Rocky Balboa.

7. _____ empezó su nueva vida en su país adoptivo.

C. **La historia de una familia inmigrante.** Escoge de la lista los adverbios apropiados para completar la narración. **¡OJO!** No se usan todos los adverbios.

bastante, demasiado, inmediatamente, muy, pacientemente, rápidamente, sólo, tranquilamente

Mis padres llegaron a los Estados Unidos en el año 1945, _____^{1} después de la Segunda Guerra Mundial (*World War II*). La vida en México era _____^{2} difícil y ellos soñaban con algo mejor para sus hijos. En los Estados Unidos mi padre y mis tíos encontraron trabajo _____^{3} en los campos y en las fábricas. No ganaban mucho dinero; su sueldo _____^{4} les permitían comer y dormir. Pero eran buenos trabajadores y _____^{5} consiguieron vivir más _____.^{6}

Un cruce de frontera entre los Estados Unidos y México ▶

Lectura

Sobre la lectura En casi toda cultura se encuentra una «brecha (*gap*) generacional», una etapa del desarrollo adolescente. Entre los hijos de inmigrantes a los Estados Unidos, las diferencias culturales entre adolescentes y sus padres pueden abrir esta brecha más aún. Mientras lees esta lectura, decide si las conductas que se describen son propias (*specific*) a la brecha generacional de los hispanos en los Estados Unidos, o si pueden existir también en otros contextos culturales.

Antes de leer

A. Los jóvenes de hoy. ¿Cuáles de las siguientes conductas crees que describan a los jóvenes típicos de hoy?

☐ Fuman cigarrillos.
☐ Se visten mal, según sus padres.
☐ No les gusta estudiar.
☐ Son esclavos (*slaves*) de la moda.
☐ Son independientes.
☐ Se maquillan mucho.

☐ Llevan tatuajes (*tattoos*).
☐ Se perforan (*pierce*) varias partes del cuerpo.
☐ Vuelven tarde a casa —o no regresan.
☐ Comen comidas especiales, no las que preparan sus padres.

B. Los valores de los jóvenes de hoy. De la siguiente lista, ¿qué cosas valoran los jóvenes de hoy? ¿Hay otros valores?

☐ los amigos
☐ la creatividad
☐ la familia
☐ la herencia (*heritage*) cultural

☐ la independencia/autonomía
☐ la nacionalidad
☐ ¿ ?

Culturas y generaciones

por Carmen Juri

Un caso anónimo Tu hija de 15 años de edad llega a casa dos horas después de la hora en que debe. Apesta a[a] cigarrillo, su ropa la cubre escasamente[b] y tiene los ojos delineados[c] con negro oscuro. Logras ver uno de sus muslos[d] y ves un tatuaje. Además, tiene la lengua perforada con un anillo, y te dice: «Por cierto, Mamá, voy a dejar[e] los estudios.»

En términos generales Si bien es cierto que los conflictos entre las generaciones son normales, todo se complica cuando la cultura de los padres es diferente a la de los hijos. «Por lo general, los adolescentes luchan por su independencia, y sus padres por mantener la integridad familiar. Eso lleva al choque[f]», dice Sergio Aisenberg, un psicoterapeuta argentino.

Casos concretos Tal es el caso de Giselle Arriaga, una joven de 17 años. Sus padres aún[g] no lo saben, pero ella desea perforarse el ombligo,[h] la lengua y la nariz, y está a punto de[i] tatuarse en una pierna. ¿Por qué? «Porque está de moda. Además, mi cuerpo es mío», dice Arriaga.

▲ ¿Hay conflictos entre lo que crees tú y lo que creen tus padres/hijos?

En ese aspecto, Belén Arriaga no entiende a su hija ni a los jóvenes de hoy en día. Giselle no quiere regresar a casa antes de las 11:00 de la noche. «No soy una rebelde, pero pienso que si hay algo que quiero hacer, ¿por qué no hacerlo?», dice la joven Arriaga.

¿Son latinos o no?

Según Aisenberg, otra forma de rebeldía[j] de los jóvenes latinos consiste en negarse[k] a hablar español o a comer ciertos platos típicos, porque se sienten «norteamericanos» y no de la nacionalidad de los padres.

Sylvia Balderrama, directora de servicios psicológicos de Vassar College, dice que si los padres insisten en mantener su herencia cultural de manera estricta en el hogar, producirán[l] más rebeldía.

Para concluir «Investigaciones recientes muestran que los jóvenes adolescentes con mejor conducta son aquellos que [...] lograron negociar algunos aspectos y obtuvieron su autonomía», dice Aisenberg. ∎

[a]Apesta… *She reeks of* [b]*la… barely covers her* [c]*outlined* [d]*thighs* [e]*to drop* [f]*clash* [g]*yet* [h]*belly button* [i]*está… she is on the verge of* [j]*rebellion* [k]*refusing* [l]*they will cause*

Después de leer

A. ¿A quién se refiere? La lectura menciona a varias personas. Indica con qué personas se asocian las siguientes afirmaciones. ¡OJO! Una afirmación puede aplicarse a más de una persona.

1. _____ Llega tarde.
2. _____ Se viste mal.
3. _____ Le gustan los tatuajes.
4. _____ Opina que la lucha por la independencia de los adolescentes está en conflicto con el deseo de la integridad familiar (de los padres).
5. _____ Quiere perforarse muchas partes del cuerpo.
6. _____ Es esclava de la moda.
7. _____ No entiende a los jóvenes.
8. _____ Si quiere hacer algo, lo hace.
9. _____ Dice que los jóvenes latinos quieren sentirse «norteamericanos».
10. _____ Cree que mucha disciplina en el hogar produce más rebeldía en los jóvenes.
11. _____ Opina que un(a) joven bien equilibrado/a (*balanced*) sabe negociar su disciplina con sus padres.

a. una chica de 15 años
b. Sergio Aisenberg, un psicoterapeuta
c. Giselle Arriaga, 17 años
d. Belén Arriaga, la madre de Giselle
e. Sylvia Balderrama, psicóloga de Vassar College

B. La rebeldía de los jóvenes latinos. Apunta tres formas de rebeldía entre los jóvenes latinos que se presentan en la lectura.

C. Yo también tuve conflictos. ¿Eras tú como los jóvenes de la lectura? ¿Tuviste conflictos intergeneracionales? ¿Cómo los expresabas? Completa las siguientes oraciones con una breve explicación.

MODELO   Yo (también/no) fumaba porque… →
Yo no fumaba porque quería ser como mis padres: ellos no fumaban.

1. Yo (también/no) me vestía mal porque…
2. Yo (también/no) regresaba a casa tarde porque…
3. Yo (también/no) me maquillaba mucho porque…
4. Yo (también no) era mal(a) estudiante porque…
5. Yo (también/no) respetaba la cultura de mi familia porque…

D. ¿Qué dice Érika? Usando la información de la entrevista con Érika, contesta las siguientes preguntas.

1. ¿Qué problemas o conflictos tenía Érika con sus padres cuando era adolescente?
2. En tu opinión, ¿se identifica Érika con los adolescentes mencionados en la lectura? ¿Por qué sí o por qué no?
3. ¿Se siente Érika más hispana o más estadounidense? ¿Cómo lo sabes?

E. Minidrama: Diálogos entre padres e hijos. Imagina *una* de las siguientes confrontaciones entre padres e hijos. Trabaja con un compañero / una compañera de clase para preparar un diálogo y luego presentarlo ante la clase.

1. La hija le anuncia a su madre que va a dejar el colegio. La madre protesta.
2. El padre y el hijo pelean (*fight*) porque el hijo rompe una de las reglas del hogar: no fumar en la casa.
3. La madre confronta a su hija de 15 años porque no regresa a casa los viernes ni los sábados.
4. La madre y el hijo pelean porque el hijo no quiere comer la comida que su madre prepara, siguiendo las recetas de su abuela.
5. La madre y la hija pelean porque a la madre le molestan los tatuajes y las perforaciones que se hace la hija.
6. El padre y el hijo están en conflicto: El padre quiere celebrar las fiestas hispanas —el Día de los Muertos, el Día de los Reyes Magos, etcétera— con toda la familia, hablando español y comiendo los platos típicos. En cambio, el hijo sólo prefiere estar con sus amigos anglohablantes.

PORTAFOLIO CULTURAL

Redacción

Una carta. ¿Qué pueden hacer los padres cuando los hijos no comparten los mismos valores culturales que ellos? Vas a contestar la carta de una madre preocupada por la «americanización» de sus hijos. Puedes usar tu propia experiencia para darle consejos. Sigue los pasos en el *Manual de práctica* para completar tu respuesta.

Exploración

Investigación cultural. Busca más información sobre la frontera y los hispanos en este país en la biblioteca, en el *Entrevistas* Online Learning Center (**www.mhhe.com/entrevistas2**) o en otros sitios del Internet y preséntala a la clase. El *Manual de práctica* contiene más ideas para tu presentación.

Léxico activo

LA INMIGRACIÓN

el/la **agente de inmigración**	immigration agent
el/la **ciudadano/a**	citizen
el **conflicto cultural**	cultural conflict
la **cosecha**	harvest
el **coyote**	*smuggler of illegal immigrants*
el **documento**	document
el **extranjero**	abroad

la **frontera**	border
el/la **indocumentado/a**	undocumented person
la **influencia**	influence
la **ley**	law
la **mezcla**	mixture
el **país de origen**	country of origin
la **pobreza**	poverty
la **razón**	reason
ahorrar	to save
ayudar	to help

buscar (qu)	to look for
correr el riesgo	to run the risk
dejarle pasar	to allow (*someone*) to pass
deportar	to deport
detener (*irreg.*)	to stop, detain
discriminar	to discriminate
escapar (de)	to escape (from)
estar ansioso/a (por)	to be anxious (about)
estar entre dos culturas	to be (caught) between two cultures
irle bien/mal	to go well/poorly for (*someone*)
mandar de regreso	to deport
preservar	to preserve
renovar (ue)	to renew
revisar	to check, inspect
ser próspero/a	to be prosperous
tener esperanza	to have hope, be hopeful
tener éxito	to be successful
tener expectativas	to have expectations
tener la ciudadanía	to have citizenship
tener la intención de + *inf.*	to intend to (*do something*)
tener miedo	to be afraid
tener suerte	to be lucky
vivir con la incertidumbre	to live with uncertainty
(i)legal	(il)legal

Repaso: perderse (ie), ser trabajador(a)

LOS ADVERBIOS

antes de + *inf.*	before (*doing something*)
bastante	rather, very
demasiado	too (much)
después de + *inf.*	after (*doing something*)
quizá(s)	perhaps
sólo (solamente)	only

suficiente	sufficient, enough
súper	super

LA IDENTIDAD BICULTURAL

el **conflicto cultural/ generacional**	cultural/generational conflict
la **costumbre**	custom
la **lengua nativa**	native language
la **raíz** (*pl.* las **raíces**)	root
el **valor**	value
aprender	to learn
dejarle + *inf.*	to allow (*someone*) to (*do something*)
esconder	to hide
identificarse (con)	to identify oneself (with)
nacer (zc)	to be born
olvidar	to forget
preservar	to preserve, maintain
ser consciente de	to be conscious of
tratar de mantener las costumbres	to try to maintain one's customs
bilingüe	bilingual

OTRAS EXPRESIONES

la **parte**	part
gracias por + *noun* or *inf.*	thanks for (*noun* or *pres. part.*)
hace (mucho tiempo)	(a long time) ago
para	for, in order, toward
por	around, because of, by, for, through
por ciento	percent
por eso	for that (reason), that's why
por si acaso	just in case
se me hace	it seems to me (*Mex.*)

Repaso: por favor, por supuesto

El trabajo

Chile

Cultura

◆ The Business Environment; Job Skills

◆ Interviewing for a Job

◆ The Changing Roles of Women in the Working World

◆ **Señas culturales: La Isla de Pascua**

Lengua

◆ Professions and Occupations

◆ Looking for Work

◆ Formal Commands (12.1)

◆ Familiar Commands (12.2)

◆ Reciprocal Actions (12.3)

	Los indígenas incas y araucanos habitan en Chile		El español Pedro de Valdivia funda Santiago		Independencia de España	Guerra contra Perú extiende el territorio chileno
Chile	**hasta el siglo XVI**	**1500–1600**	**1534** **1541**	**1600–1750**	**1776–1783** **1818**	**1836–1839**
Los Estados Unidos y el Canadá	Varias tribus indígenas habitan en Norteamérica	Exploración española de Norteamérica	Jacques Cartier reclama para Francia el Canadá	Fundación de las colonias británicas en Norteamérica	Guerra de Independencia en los EE. UU.	

Instantánea

ORIGEN DEL NOMBRE

Chile: incierto; posiblemente de *tchili*, palabra indígena que significa «nieve» o de *chilli* que significa «fin de la tierra»

POBLACIÓN

15.265.600

LENGUAS

El español (oficial), el mapuche, el aimara

▲ *La bolsa de valores* (stock market/exchange) *en Santiago de Chile.*

For additional practice, check out the *Manual de práctica,* the Interactive CD-ROM, and the Online Learning Center (**www.mhhe.com/entrevistas2**)!

1846–1848	1879–1883	1898	1952	1970	1973	1982	1989	1994	1999	2000
	Guerra del Pacífico contra Perú y Bolivia		Salvador Allende Gossens gana la presidencia		Allende es asesinado; Augusto Pinochet Ugarte inicia su dictadura	Pinochet se retira del poder; se elige a Patricio Alwyn		Se detiene a Pinochet en la Gran Bretaña por crímenes contra la humanidad	Se elige a Ricardo Lagos como presidente	
Guerra Mexicano-Americana		Guerra Hispano-Americana	Puerto Rico se hace Estado Libre Asociado de los EE. UU.			El Canadá se separa legalmente de Inglaterra	Tratado de Libre Comercio entre los EE. UU., el Canadá y México			

Vocabulario

🔵 El mundo del trabajo

Profesiones y oficios[a]

la fotógrafa

el abogado

la mujer mecánico

la doctora   el enfermero

la arqueóloga

la bibliotecaria

el veterinario

la pilota

el/la arquitecto/a	architect	**el/la empleado/a**	employee
el/la artista	artist	**el/la entrenador(a)**	(personal) trainer
el/la asesor(a)	consultant	**(personal)**	
el/la asistente social	social worker	**el/la escritor(a)**	writer
el/la banquero/a	banker	**el hombre / la mujer**	businessman /
el bombero / la mujer	firefighter	**de negocios**	businesswoman
bombero		**el/la ingeniero/a**	engineer
el/la científico/a	scientist	**el político / la mujer político**	politician
el/la cirujano/a	surgeon	**el/la programador(a)**	(computer)
el/la contable	accountant		programmer
el/la director(a)	director	**el/la secretario/a**	secretary
el/la diseñador/a	designer	**el/la traductor(a)**	translator

[a]*occupations*

Las condiciones de trabajo

Prefiero un trabajo con...

un horario flexible	⟷	**una jornada**[a] tradicional
el sueldo mínimo	⟷	un sueldo **según la experiencia**
un trabajo de tiempo parcial	⟷	un trabajo **de tiempo completo**
mucha **responsabilidad**	⟷	poca responsabilidad
mucho **prestigio**	⟷	poco prestigio

la oportunidad de avanzar
buenas **prestaciones**[b]

[a]*workday* [b]*benefits*

Actividades

A. ¿Qué profesiones? Si tienes las siguientes habilidades (*skills*), ¿qué profesión o profesiones puedes ejercer?

1. Si tienes habilidades artísticas,...
2. Si eres bueno/a para las matemáticas,...
3. Si tienes mucha capacidad de concentrarte,...
4. Si eres bueno/a para los negocios,...
5. Si tienes don de gentes (*people skills*),...
6. Si te interesa la medicina,...
7. Si entiendes bien cómo funcionan las máquinas y otros aparatos,...
8. Si eres atleta,...
9. Si eres muy detallista (*detail-oriented*),...
10. Si tienes habilidad para las lenguas,...

B. Condiciones de trabajo. ¿Qué trabajos asocias con las siguientes descripciones? Da tres ejemplos de cada uno.

1. un trabajo con poca responsabilidad
2. un trabajo de poco prestigio
3. un trabajo que paga el sueldo mínimo
4. un trabajo de tiempo completo
5. un trabajo que ofrece oportunidades de avanzar
6. un trabajo peligroso (*dangerous*)

C. Categorías. ¿Qué cualidades y habilidades tienen las personas que ejercen las siguientes profesiones?

MODELO   profesor(a) →
Un buen profesor tiene habilidad para las lenguas y mucha paciencia.

1. editor(a) (de revista, de periódico, etcétera)
2. deportista profesional
3. artesano/a
4. productor(a) de cine
5. pintor(a)
6. escritor(a)
7. abogado/a

Si te interesa

Historically, there have been many professions that have excluded women. Thus, the names of some professions in the Spanish-speaking world do not have feminine variants. But as the reality of the workplace changes, more professions are adopting feminine terms.

Sometimes an **-a** is used at the end of a word to make it feminine: **el médico → la médica; el juez** (*judge*) **→ la jueza.** For other professions, the word **mujer** is added before the masculine term: **el policía → la mujer policía; el soldado** (*soldier*) **→ la mujer soldado.**

D. ¿Cuál es mi profesión?   Trabaja con dos o tres compañeros/as. Cada estudiante debe escoger una profesión, sin decirles a los otros miembros del grupo cuál es. Los otros deben hacerle preguntas para adivinar la profesión que escogió.

DATOS ÚTILES

- el lugar de trabajo
- el horario de trabajo
- las habilidades y cualidades necesarias para ejercer el trabajo
- las actividades típicas del trabajo

E. Debate.   De los siguientes pares de profesiones y oficios, explícale a un compañero / una compañera cuál tiene más prestigio en tu opinión y por qué.

MODELO   Creo que la profesión de filósofo tiene más prestigio que el oficio de taxista porque es un trabajo intelectual.

1. abogado ⟷ político
2. escritor ⟷ secretario
3. estrella de rock ⟷ entrenador personal
4. mesero ⟷ profesor de español
5. ¿ ? ⟷ ¿ ?

▲ *¿Qué cualidades y características son necesarias para ser mujer de negocios? ¿Y para ser hombre de negocios?*

Susana Cid Hazard

«*En Chile el horario laboral es bastante duro, muy pesado.*»

Nombre: Susana

Apellidos: (1) Cid (2) Hazard

Edad: 36 años

Nació en: Santiago de Chile

You can watch this interview on the *Entrevistas* Video or Interactive CD-ROM or listen to the audio on the Online Learning Center (**www.mhhe.com/entrevistas2**).

Vocabulario útil

el día laboral	workday	**actualmente**	currently
pesado	strenuous	**párvulo**	nursery school; *pl.* young
base económica	economic base		children
postular	to apply (for)	**kínder** *m.*	kindergarten
estadísticas	statistics		

Antes de ver

A. El mundo laboral. Completa las siguientes oraciones sobre la vida laboral en tu país.

1. El día laboral típico en mi país es de _____ horas al día, _____ días a la semana.

2. Típicamente los estudiantes trabajan por la _____.

3. El sueldo mínimo es de _____.

4. Para costearse (*cover the cost of*) los estudios, los estudiantes generalmente necesitan _____.

B. La mujer en el mundo laboral. ¿Qué papel desempeña (*plays*) la mujer en el mundo laboral en tu país? Indica lo que opinas de las oraciones en la siguiente página.

	ESTOY DE ACUERDO.	NO ESTOY DE ACUERDO.
1. Hay carreras que excluyen a las mujeres.	☐	☐
2. Si un hombre y una mujer postulan a un trabajo que ambos pueden hacer igualmente bien, el hombre va a ser elegido.	☐	☐
3. Es común que los hombres estudien ciertas carreras y las mujeres otras.	☐	☐
4. Las mujeres no tienen ninguna ventaja en el mundo laboral.	☐	☐

¡Veamos!

¿Acertaste? Ahora, revisa tus respuestas de las actividades de **Antes de ver** y adivina qué va a decir Susana sobre los mismos temas en Chile. Después, ve la entrevista y compara lo que adivinaste con lo que dijo Susana. ¿Acertaste bien?

Después de ver

A. El trabajo y la identidad. Contesta las siguientes preguntas y comparte tus respuestas con la clase.

1. Para un estudiante, ¿es preferible trabajar y estudiar o es mejor sólo estudiar? ¿Qué ventajas y desventajas tiene cada posibilidad?
2. En tu opinión, ¿tienen tanto los hombres como las mujeres aptitud natural para algunas carreras pero no para otras? Por ejemplo, ¿tienen los hombres aptitud natural para la ingeniería, pero no para la enseñanza de párvulos, y se inclinan por naturaleza las mujeres más hacia la enseñanza que hacia la ingeniería? Menciona otras carreras.

B. Un anuncio de trabajo. Estudia este anuncio de empleo de Santiago de Chile y comenta las preguntas con un compañero / una compañera de clase.

Compañía internacional hotelera[a] necesita

✱ VENDEDORES ✱

Residentes en distrito sur

(Valdivia-Puerto Montt-Concepción)

Buscamos: Sexo masculino, menos de 35 años de edad, experiencia en ventas y conocimientos[b] generales de hostelería. Transporte propio y flexibilidad de horarios.

Ofrecemos: Sueldo según experiencia, más comisión.

Para entrevista personal, contacte: Jesús Aguirre Backer, **744.39.32 *Puerto Montt***

[a]*hotel (adj.)*   [b]*knowledge*

1. ¿Qué tipo de trabajo se anuncia? ¿Qué responsabilidades tiene este puesto (*position*)?
2. ¿Para quién es la oferta: para hombres o para mujeres? ¿De qué edad?
3. ¿Por qué crees que esta compañía prefiere personas del sexo masculino para este puesto? ¿Qué ventajas y desventajas podría aportar (*could bring*) cada sexo a este tipo de trabajo?
4. ¿Por qué limita la compañía la edad de los solicitantes (*applicants*)?
5. ¿Existen estas limitaciones de sexo y edad en tu país? En tu opinión, ¿es una forma de discriminación? Explica.

12.1 Formal Commands

Giving commands (**mandatos**) in English is relatively simple. To get someone to do something you just need to use a verb: *Go home! Stay here! Help me, please!* To get someone *not* to do something, you just add *Don't* before the verb: *Don't go home!* In Spanish, however, special endings are attached to verbs in order to give commands. Since commands are spoken directly to someone (*you*), there must be endings to match *you* formal and familiar and *you* singular and plural (**tú/vos, usted, vosotros/as, ustedes**). In this chapter, you will learn the affirmative and negative forms of commands, as well as other, more socially acceptable or tactful ways of getting others to do what you want.

A. Many formal commands (used with people whom you would address as **usted** or **ustedes**) were presented in **Capítulo 4,** and you may have heard many of them when your teacher asks the class or individual students to do something. The stems for these command forms are taken from the present tense indicative **yo** form minus the **-o;** any irregularities in the indicative **yo** form also show up in the formal commands. The endings look as if the wrong conjugation has been applied: **-ar** verbs have **-e(n)** endings, and **-er** and **-ir** verbs have **-a(n)** endings.*

Infinitive	*yo* Form, Present Indicative	*usted* Command	*ustedes* Command
tomar	tomo	tome	tomen
beber	bebo	beba	beban
vivir	vivo	viva	vivan
tener	tengo	tenga	tengan
traer	traigo	traiga	traigan
reducir	reduzco	reduzca	reduzcan

Stem-changing verbs show the **ie, ue,** or **i** changes in formal commands, just as in the present indicative.

Infinitive	*yo* Form, Present Indicative	*usted* Command	*ustedes* Command
pensar	pienso	piense	piensen
volver	vuelvo	vuelva	vuelvan
pedir	pido	pida	pidan

---

* These endings are borrowed from the subjunctive mood, which you will study in **Capítulo 13.**

As you saw with the preterit, some vowel endings cause a change in the spelling of verb stems to ensure that the pronunciation doesn't change. Before the vowels **e** and **i,** the consonant **c** becomes **qu, g** becomes **gu,** and **z** becomes **c.**

Infinitive	*yo* Form, Present Indicative	*usted* Command	*ustedes* Command
explicar	explico	explique	expliquen
navegar	navego	navegue	naveguen
empezar	empiezo	empiece	empiecen

Before the vowels **a** and **o, g** becomes **j** in **-er** and **-ir** verbs.

Infinitive	*yo* Form, Present Indicative	*usted* Command	*ustedes* Command
escoger	escojo	escoja	escojan
elegir	elijo	elija	elijan

Five verbs have completely irregular formal command forms.

Infinitive	*usted* Command	*ustedes* Command
dar	dé*	den
estar	esté	estén
ir	vaya	vayan
saber	sepa	sepan
ser	sea	sean

B. To tell someone *not* to do something (a negative command), simply add **no** before the affirmative **usted(es)** command.

No lleve pantalones cortos a la entrevista de trabajo.

Don't wear shorts to the job interview.

No olviden su portafolio para la entrevista.

Don't forget your (pl.) portfolios for the interview.

C. When one or more object pronouns are used with an affirmative command, the pronouns are attached directly to the verb, indirect object first and then direct object. This new combination is subject to the same rules for written accents as other words, so a written accent may be needed to indicate the original stress of the verb form. When object pronouns accompany a negative command, they precede the conjugated verb and are separate from it.

---

* This form of the verb **dar** has a written accent to distinguish it from the preposition **de** (*of, from*).

Tráigame los papeles, por favor.	*Bring me the papers, please.*
No **me los** traiga ahora.	*Don't bring them to me now.*
¿Las cartas? Llé**veselas** al director.	*The letters? Take them to the director.*
No **se las** lleve hoy, por favor.	*Please don't take them to him today.*

D. In situations that require the **usted/ustedes** forms, it is often inappropriate to issue a direct command (to your boss or to an unknown person, for example). It is more common to make requests using the following politeness formulas. Make sure you know the meaning of these expressions.

¿**Me haría (usted) el favor de** escribir una carta de recomendación?	*Would you (form. s.) be so kind as to write me a letter of recommendation?*
¿**Podría usted** entregarle este portafolio al señor Logroño?	*Could you please deliver this portfolio to Mr. Logroño?*
¿**Le importaría** mandarme el fax mañana?	*Would you mind sending me the fax tomorrow?*

Actividades

A. Una jefa (*boss*) **difícil.** La jefa de Rosario es muy exigente. Le deja (*She leaves her*) la siguiente lista de tareas para la mañana. Convierte la lista de tareas en mandatos formales de los verbos subrayados.

1. <u>Ir</u> a la oficina de correos para comprar más estampillas.

2. <u>Buscar</u> el correo en la recepción.

3. <u>Mandar</u> este fax al banco.

4. <u>Escribirle</u> una carta al señor Domínguez.

5. No <u>olvidar</u> la conferencia a las 9:30.

6. <u>Hacer</u> cuatro fotocopias de los papeles en mi escritorio.

7. <u>Ofrecerles</u> un café a los clientes en la sala de espera (*waiting room*).

8. <u>Tomar</u> un descanso a las 11:00.

B. Eres el director / la directora. Eres director(a) de una agencia de empleados temporarios y tienes que indicarle a cada empleado/a las tareas de su trabajo para hoy. Inventa dos actividades o consejos apropiados para cada persona y díselos en forma de mandato.

MODELO   Rita Donado: dependienta →
          Señorita Donado, hable cortésmente con los clientes y sea puntual.

1. Raúl Domínguez: secretario
2. Renata Duero: asistente social
3. Ramón Díaz: mensajero (*messenger*)
4. Rigoberta Dalí: programadora
5. Rafael Duarte: mecánico

C. **¿Buscan trabajo?**   Algunos de tus amigos están buscando trabajo. Convierte las siguientes expresiones en mandatos plurales formales para darles consejos prácticos.

1. analizar sus habilidades
2. especificar sus metas
3. leer los anuncios en el periódico
4. hablar con amigos/as y parientes sobre las posibilidades de empleo
5. visitar compañías y tiendas
6. fijar citas con los jefes / las jefas
7. no preocuparse demasiado; no estar nervioso/a
8. no aceptar la primera oferta
9. ¿ ?

D. **¡Más cortés, por favor!**   Cambia los siguientes mandatos directos por una forma más cortés, usando las expresiones que has aprendido en este capítulo. Trata de dar dos formas para cada mandato, si es posible.

MODELO   ¡Tráigame esas cartas! →
¿Me haría el favor de traerme esas cartas?
¿Me trae esas cartas, por favor?

1. Llene esta solicitud (*application*).
2. No se sienten allí.
3. Hablen con el recepcionista.
4. Busque su cheque en la oficina de enfrente.
5. Pídale una copia a la secretaria.

▲ *¿Qué les dice este gerente* (manager) *a sus empleados?*

Análisis cultural

La siguiente cita tomada de una fuente escrita en inglés para anglohablantes va a aumentar tus conocimientos sobre algunos fenómenos culturales en Chile. ¿Es consistente esta información con la perspectiva de Susana de la **Entrevista 1?** Usa lo que has aprendido en este capítulo sobre Chile, más tu propia experiencia, para contestar las preguntas que siguen la cita.

66Although Chilean women won the vote in 1949, they are still very much underrepresented on the national political scene, even if they are prominent in politics at a local level and in many of the professions. Although women were at the forefront of the political struggles of the early 1970s, they became even more involved under the military government [of Augusto Pinochet]. With political parties and trade unions, both traditionally male-dominated, banned, a new generation of grassroots social movements, such as shanty town organizations and soup kitchens, filled the political vacuum. Many of these were headed by women. **Democracia en el país y en la casa** (*Democracy in the country and in the home*) was one of the most common rallying cries of this movement, which did have some success in changing ingrained male attitudes. However, many women's organizations have found it hard to cope with the return to democracy, during which power has largely reverted to male-run political parties.

Figures from 1987 showed that women's average earnings were only 71 percent of those of men, and little progress has been made since. It also appears that it is middle-class, educated women who have made most economic and social advances in the past generation. Poorer women still have larger families, are far more likely to be single parents, and to believe with 23-year-old Nora that: 'I want to have a baby so that I can have something of my own, because I've never had anything of my own.'**99**

Source: *Chile in Focus: A Guide to the People, Politics and Culture*

1. ¿Cuándo ganaron las mujeres el derecho al voto en tu país? ¿Cómo se compara esto con Chile?

2. ¿En qué aspectos de la sociedad de tu país tienen las mujeres igual o mayor representación o poder que los hombres? ¿Cómo se compara esto con Chile?

3. ¿Hay organizaciones de mujeres en tu país? ¿Cómo se comparan con las organizaciones en que participan las mujeres chilenas?

4. Con respecto a los sueldos y el poder económico que tienen las mujeres, ¿cómo se compara tu país con Chile?

5. Que tú sepas (*As far as you know*), ¿son iguales las oportunidades para mujeres de distintas clases sociales en tu país? ¿Tienen aspiraciones diferentes o todas quieren las mismas cosas?

● The Spanish **s**

By now you have seen many examples of the pronunciation of both **s** and **z** as [s] in Spanish. One major error to avoid in pronunciation is the use of the English [z] sound in cognate words that should have an [s] sound in Spanish.

ENGLISH [Z]	SPANISH [S]
mu<u>s</u>ic	mú<u>s</u>ica
pre<u>s</u>ident	pre<u>s</u>idente

Make sure you pronounce the letter **z** as [s], unless you are imitating Castilian Spanish, in which case **z** = English *th* as in *think*. Listen to your instructor pronounce the following words.

almuerzo	taza
cazar (*to hunt*)	zapato

In many dialects of Spanish, the **s** at the end of a syllable has a different pronunciation. Instead of [s], you hear a puff of air (or *aspiration*, symbolized by a superscripted *h*), and some speakers delete the [s] altogether.

SPELLING	ASPIRATED [S]	DELETED [S]
es-tar	[e^h-tar]	[e-tar]
los nuevos	[lo^h nue-vo^h]	[lo nue-vo]
mis-mo	[mi^h-mo]	[mi-mo]

The *Manual de práctica* has activities to practice the material explained here.

¿Tienes un trabajo de tiempo ▶
parcial como este estudiante en
Santiago de Chile?

● ¿Qué hago para buscar empleo?

consultar con **una agencia de colocaciones**	*to consult with a job placement agency*
definir los objetivos personales	*to define personal objectives*
fijar una cita para la entrevista	*to set up an appointment for the interview*
leer **los anuncios (de empleo)**	*to read (job) ads*
llenar solicitudes	*to fill out applications*
pedir (i, i) **cartas de recomendación**	*to ask for letters of recommendation*
preparar **un currículum (vitae)**	*to prepare a résumé*

Las ofertas de empleo

Importante **empresa**[a] informática **requiere**

PROGRAMADOR(A)

REQUISITOS:
- **competencia**[b] en dos lenguas de programación
- inglés técnico, **nivel** alto
- **experiencia mínima** de 3 años
- **formación**[c] en negocios **deseable**[d]
- transporte propio

OFRECEMOS:
- horario fijo de 9 a 5, lunes a viernes
- sueldo acorde a[e] la experiencia
- **futuro prometedor**[f] con satisfacción profesional

---

[a]*company* [b]*skill* [c]*background* [d]*desirable* [e]acorde... *according to; commensurate with*
[f]futuro... *promising future*

los conocimientos	knowledge
el formulario	form
la fuerza física	physical strength
el puesto	job, position
exigir (j)	to demand
ganar	to earn
amplio/a	ample, broad
arriesgado/a	risk-taking
multilingüe	multilingual

Actividades

A. Requisitos. ¿Cuáles son los requisitos que probablemente se necesitan para los siguientes trabajos? Añade otros trabajos que te interesan e indica los requisitos de éstos.

1. ingeniero eléctrico / ingeniera eléctrica
2. profesor(a)
3. decorador(a) de interiores
4. mensajero/a ciclista
5. traductor(a)
6. hombre/mujer de negocios
7. vendedor(a) de *software*
8. ¿ ?

B. Ventajas y desventajas. ¿Qué ventajas y desventajas tienen los siguientes trabajos? Puedes añadir otros trabajos que se te ocurran.

1. enfermero/a
2. bombero / mujer bombero
3. entrenador(a) personal
4. hombre/mujer de negocios
5. profesor(a)
6. escritor(a)
7. asesor(a)
8. ¿ ?

C. Entrevista: Tu trabajo. Pregúntale a un compañero / una compañera de clase sobre su trabajo actual, previo o el que le gustaría tener. Usa las siguientes categorías. Apunta las respuestas de tu compañero/a para luego compartirlas con el resto de la clase.

Nombre de mi compañero/a: _____   Trabajo: _____

- el sueldo
- las prestaciones
- el horario
- el ambiente laboral
- el jefe / la jefa

D. El trabajo ideal. Usando las mismas categorías de la **Actividad C,** describe las características de tu trabajo ideal.

Mi trabajo ideal es _____.

Me gustaría tener este trabajo porque _____.

- el sueldo
- las prestaciones
- el horario
- el ambiente laboral
- el jefe / la jefa

E. Prepárate para la entrevista. Antes de ir a una entrevista de trabajo, es importante considerar las siguientes preguntas. ¿Qué opinas tú?

1. ¿Qué tipo de horario deseas: fijo o flexible? ¿Por qué?
2. ¿Qué prestaciones buscas en un trabajo? (seguro médico/dental, vacaciones pagadas, estacionamiento [*parking*] gratis, acceso a un club deportivo, etcétera)
3. ¿Qué ropa te pones para la entrevista? (traje, vestido formal, ropa informal, etcétera) ¿Por qué?
4. ¿Cuáles son los puntos fuertes (*strong*) que quieres enfatizar en la entrevista? ¿Cuáles son los puntos débiles (*weak*) que debes evitar mencionar o explicar?
5. ¿Qué preguntas quieres hacerle al entrevistador / a la entrevistadora sobre el trabajo?

F. En la entrevista. Eres director(a) de personal y vas a entrevistar a un compañero / una compañera de clase para un trabajo.

Paso 1. Escribe un anuncio de trabajo, siguiendo los modelos que has visto en este capítulo. Incluye tu nombre como persona de contacto y entrégale una copia a tu profesor(a). (También guarda una copia para ti.)

Paso 2. Prepara una lista de preguntas apropiadas para el puesto que describiste en el anuncio.

Paso 3. El profesor / La profesora va a repartir (*distribute*) los anuncios a la clase, y tú vas a entrevistar a la persona que reciba tu anuncio. Usa las preguntas del **Paso 2.** Al terminar, tienes que anunciar a la clase si vas a darle el trabajo a la persona y explicar por qué sí o por qué no.

Lenguaje funcional
La entrevista de trabajo

The job interview is the perfect opportunity for boss and employee to begin to get to know each other. Don't forget that the applicants also interview the boss! Here are some good questions to ask. Can you think of others?

PREGUNTAS DEL JEFE / DE LA JEFA

¿Es usted capaz (*capable*) de + *inf.*?
   (¿Sabe usted + *inf.*?)
¿Tiene los conocimientos necesarios
   para... ?
¿Dónde estudió?
¿Qué carrera estudió?
¿Tiene usted experiencia en... ?
¿A qué se dedica usted fuera del
   trabajo? ¿Cuáles son sus intereses?

PREGUNTAS DEL / DE LA SOLICITANTE

¿De cuántas horas es la jornada?
¿Cuáles son las responsabilidades de este
   puesto?
¿Qué ventajas ofrece esta empresa?
¿Qué prestaciones se ofrecen?

Entrevista 2

You can watch this interview on the *Entrevistas* Video or Interactive CD-ROM or listen to the audio on the Online Learning Center (**www.mhhe.com/entrevistas2**).

Hernán Fuentes Estévez

«Bueno, el ambiente en las oficinas es bien formal en Chile.»

Nombre: Hernán

Apellidos: (1) Fuentes (2) Estévez

Edad: 68 años

Nació en: Santiago de Chile

Vocabulario útil

marcar (qu)	to emphasize	**ponte**	put on
tendencia	trend	**preocúpate de que sean**	take care that they are
se les dice	they are called		
que vaya	he should go	**calidad** *f.*	quality
zapatos lustrados	polished shoes	**la norma europea**	European style
detalles *m.*	details	**cuadra con**	matches

Antes de ver

El ambiente laboral.   Don Hernán va a hablar del ambiente laboral en Chile. Lee las siguientes oraciones e indica en la segunda columna cuáles, en tu opinión, describen la oficina típica en tu país.

	EN TU PAÍS	EN CHILE
1. En las oficinas, el ambiente es bien formal.	☐	☐
2. Los hombres llevan traje y corbata y las mujeres visten con vestido.	☐	☐
3. Se puede llevar *bluejeans*.	☐	☐
4. Los jefes marcan una distancia entre ellos y sus empleados.	☐	☐
5. Se puede tratar (*address*) al jefe / a la jefa de una manera informal, por ejemplo, por sólo su nombre.	☐	☐

¡Veamos!

A. Comparaciones. En la tercera columna de la actividad en **Antes de ver,** indica qué oraciones describen el ambiente laboral en Chile, según don Hernán.

B. Lo positivo, lo negativo. Haz dos listas: una de las cosas positivas que ayudan a conseguir un trabajo en Chile, según don Hernán, y otra de las cosas negativas que causan una mala impresión.

Cosas positivas	Cosas negativas

Después de ver

Trabajos anteriores. Contesta las siguientes preguntas sobre tus experiencias laborales.

1. ¿Has tenido una entrevista de trabajo alguna vez? ¿Qué te preguntaron?
2. ¿Qué hiciste en preparación para la entrevista? ¿Qué hiciste para causar una primera impresión positiva?
3. ¿Cómo fue la entrevista? ¿Cómo te sentías durante la entrevista?
4. ¿Conseguiste el trabajo? ¿Por qué sí o por qué no?

Piénsalo bien

En los últimos 30 años... Es obvio que don Hernán ha visto muchos cambios en el ambiente laboral en Chile. ¿Qué cambios han ocurrido en el ambiente laboral en tu propio país en los últimos 30 años? Entrevista a algunas personas de otras generaciones (tu profesor[a], tus padres, tus abuelos, etcétera) para saber más de los siguientes temas.

- el modo de vestir
- la manera de hablarse (jefes y empleados)
- los trabajos masculinos y femeninos
- ¿ ?

Luego, compara la realidad actual con lo que dicen tus entrevistados y presenta tus resultados a la clase.

MODELO   Antes, los hombres vestían traje y corbata, pero actualmente la ropa no es tan importante en las oficinas.

12.2 Familiar Commands

A. Although the politeness formulas and direct commands you learned in **Forma y función 12.1** are used in formal situations, you should use familiar commands with people you address as **tú.** In general, these commands are equivalent to the **tú** form of the present indicative, minus the final **-s.** (Any irregularities, such as stem changes, are also present.)

Infinitive	*tú* Form, Present Indicative	*tú* Command	Translation
asistir	asistes	**Asiste a esa reunión.**	Attend that meeting.
cerrar	cierras	**Cierra la puerta.**	Close the door.
escuchar	escuchas	**Escucha este anuncio.**	Listen to this announcement.
leer	lees	**Lee este reportaje.**	Read this report.
pedir	pides	**Pide ayuda.**	Ask for help.
volver	vuelves	**¡Vuelve aquí!**	Come back here!

Eight common verbs have irregular **tú** commands.

Infinitive	*tú* Command	Translation
decir	**¡Di la verdad!**	Tell the truth!
hacer	**Haz la tarea.**	Do the homework.
ir	**¡Ve a la oficina!**	Go to the office!
poner	**Pon los libros allí.**	Put the books over there.
salir	**¡Sal de aquí!**	Get out of here!
ser	**¡Sé eficiente!**	Be efficient!
tener	**¡Ten cuidado!**	Be careful!
venir	**Ven a las 2:00.**	Come at 2:00.

B. Negative **tú** commands are similar to the **tú** form of the present indicative, but, like negative **usted** commands, they use the opposite vowel in the ending: **-es** for **-ar** verbs and **-as** for **-er/-ir** verbs.

Infinitive	*tú* Form, Present Indicative	Negative *tú* Command	Translation
asistir	asistes	No asistas a esa reunión.	Don't attend that meeting.
cerrar	cierras	No cierres la puerta.	Don't close the door.
escuchar	escuchas	No escuches este anuncio.	Don't listen to this announcement.
leer	lees	No leas este reportaje.	Don't read this report.
pedir	pides	No pidas ayuda.	Don't ask for help.
volver	vuelves	¡No vuelvas aquí!	Don't come back here!

You may have noticed that these negative **tú** commands could also be described as the negative **usted** commands plus a final **-s**. This fact will help you remember the negative forms of irregular verbs.

Infinitive	Negative *usted* Command	Negative *tú* Command
decir	no diga	no digas
hacer	no haga	no hagas
ir	no vaya	no vayas
poner	no ponga	no pongas
salir	no salga	no salgas
ser	no sea	no seas
tener	no tenga	no tengas
venir	no venga	no vengas

C. Just as with formal commands, object pronouns are attached to the end of affirmative familiar commands (adding an accent mark if necessary to indicate the original stress of the verb form). They precede and are separated from negative familiar commands. **¡OJO!** Remember that reflexive pronouns fall under this rule as well.

Tráeme el informe sobre ese proyecto.	*Bring me the report on that project.*
Pídele más información.	*Ask her for more information.*
Siéntate y **ponte** cómodo.	*Have a seat and make yourself comfortable.*
Díselo a mi secretario, por favor.	*Tell (it to) my secretary, please.*
No me traigas ese informe hoy.	*Don't bring me that report today.*
No le pidas más información.	*Don't ask her for more information.*

Si te interesa

Remember that in some countries, like Argentina for example, **vos** instead of **tú** forms are used. But the way they are formed varies from region to region. In Buenos Aires, affirmative **vos** commands are formed by removing the final **-r** from the infinitive and adding an accent to the final vowel (**pensar** → **pensá; beber** → **bebé; vivir** → **viví**), whereas negative **vos** commands are the same as negative **tú** commands. (These forms will not be practiced in *Entrevistas.*)

No te sientes allí, por favor.	*Don't sit there, please.*
No te pongas nervioso.	*Don't get nervous.*
No se lo digas a mi secretario.	*Don't tell (it to) my secretary.*

Actividades

Si te interesa

Recall that in most of Spain, you would address two or more people informally as **vosotros/as.** Affirmative **vosotros/as** commands are formed by removing the final **-r** of the infinitive and replacing it with a **-d: tomar** → **tomad; beber** → **bebed; asistir** → **asistid.** Negative **vosotros/as** commands are the same as the subjunctive forms you will study in **Capítulo 13.**

In colloquial speech in today's Spain, it is common to hear the infinitive used for **vosotros/as** commands: **¡Tomar esto!, ¡Sentaros allí!,** and so on.

A. ¿Quién lo dijo? Mario Sabater, de 18 años, trabaja en una oficina y vive con su familia. Todo el día le piden que haga o no haga ciertas cosas. ¿Quién le dio los siguientes mandatos: su jefe o alguien de su familia?

	SE LO DIJO SU JEFE.	SE LO DIJO ALGUIEN DE SU FAMILIA.
1. Tráeme un vaso de agua.	☐	☐
2. Ponga los libros en mi escritorio.	☐	☐
3. Ayúdeme con esto.	☐	☐
4. Dame los papeles.	☐	☐
5. Léeme ese artículo.	☐	☐
6. Salga a tomar café.	☐	☐
7. Vete a buscar el correo.	☐	☐
8. Saca la basura.	☐	☐

B. Buscar empleo. Uno de tus amigos quiere conseguir trabajo pero no sabe qué hacer. Convierte los siguientes verbos en mandatos informales y combina los verbos con las expresiones apropiadas para hacer oraciones lógicas. **¡OJO!** Algunos mandatos deben ser negativos.

MODELOS   Pon tu mejor camisa.

              No llegues tarde a tu entrevista.

considerar consultar (con) criticar decir estar fijar leer llenar llevar olvidar pedir preparar	**+**	cartas de recomendación una agencia de colocaciones cosas negativas el currículum tonterías (*foolish things*) en la entrevista los anuncios de empleo los objetivos personales nervioso/a durante la entrevista ropa informal solicitudes una cita para la entrevista

C. El entrenamiento. Un estudiante de intercambio chileno ha conseguido trabajo como cajero (*cashier*) en la cafetería estudiantil donde trabajas. Tienes que ayudarlo a comportarse (*behave, act*) bien en el trabajo, dándole la siguiente información. Convierte los verbos entre paréntesis en mandatos informales (afirmativos o negativos, según el caso).

1. (ponerse) el uniforme antes de llegar
2. (llegar) treinta minutos antes de la hora de empezar
3. (verificar) todos los billetes (*bills* [*currency*]) grandes
4. no (dejar) la caja abierta
5. (contar) el cambio con cuidado
6. no (dudar) en (*to hesitate*) consultar con el jefe si hay algún problema
7. no (salir) de la cafetería
8. no (hablar) demasiado con los amigos
9. no (comer) ni (beber) en la caja
10. no (olvidarse) de marcar la ficha (*to punch out*) al salir

12.3 Reciprocal Actions

In **Capítulo 6,** you learned how to express *reflexive actions:* **me visto, te preocupas, nos dormimos,** and so on, in which the subject is doing something to himself or herself. It is also possible to use the *plural* reflexive pronouns **(nos, os, se)** to express *reciprocal actions*—what people do to/for each other.

Los empleados **se saludan** al llegar.	*The employees greet each other upon arriving.*
Mi jefe y yo siempre **nos escribimos** por correo electrónico.	*My boss and I always write to each other through e-mail.*
Ustedes tienen que **conocerse** bien para poder trabajar juntos.	*You have to know each other well in order to work together.*

Note that the last sentence is ambiguous: With a reciprocal reading **conocerse** means *to know each other,* but as a reflexive verb it could also mean *to know yourselves* (i.e., each person knows himself/herself well). In the first two examples, the reflexive meaning is possible but nonsensical.

Análisis estructural

Lee las siguientes oraciones y di si la interpretación más lógica es una acción reflexiva o recíproca.

1. Mis compañeros de oficina se hablan todos los días.
2. Las secretarias se llaman por teléfono.
3. Los candidatos se miran al espejo antes de empezar la entrevista.

Actividades

A. El ambiente ideal. ¿Cómo se tratan las personas en el trabajo ideal? Usa los siguientes verbos para hacer oraciones lógicas, expresando tus recomendaciones. También añade otras sugerencias que se te ocurran.

MODELO   apoyarse (*to support each other*) →
         Los empleados se apoyan en momentos difíciles.

- ayudarse
- conocerse bien
- considerarse amigos
- criticarse
- hablarse con cortesía

- gritarse
- respetarse
- verse fuera del trabajo
- ¿ ?

B. Comportamientos (*Behavior*) **apropiados.**   En muchas empresas se recomienda evitar las relaciones personales entre empleados. Trabaja con un compañero / una compañera para completar las oraciones para decir qué cosas son apropiadas y cuáles no se deben hacer. En cada caso, explica el porqué de tus respuestas. Puedes usar las frases de la siguiente lista u otras que se te ocurran.

- escribirse cartas y mensajes electrónicos personales
- llamarse por teléfono
- verse en las reuniones

- hablarse en los pasillos
- salir juntos/as fuera del trabajo
- mirarse con cariño
- ¿ ?

1. Dos empleados que son amigos pueden... / no deben...
2. Dos empleados enamorados (*in love*) pueden... / no deben...
3. Un empleado / Una empleada y el jefe / la jefa (no) deben...

Señas culturales

▲ *Algunas de las estatuas de la Isla de Pascua*

La Isla de Pascua, 45 millas cuadradas de roca volcánica, es una posesión chilena a 2.490 millas de la costa de Sudamérica. Sus cientos de estatuas de basalto son únicas en Oceanía. Su origen aún no se ha establecido con certidumbre, ya que[a] los datos de esta cultura prehistórica fueron destruidos por los europeos. Muchos investigadores creen que la Isla de Pascua fue poblada[b] por primera vez antes de 500 d.C.[c] por polinesios provenientes[d] de las Islas Marquesas. Estos pobladores permanecieron en aislamiento[e] total por 1.200 años, tiempo durante el cual desarrollaron[f] un sistema de escritura original y las famosas estatuas.

Describe las estatuas que se ven en la foto. ¿Qué emociones inspiran? ¿Sabes de otros monumentos históricos de origen desconocido?

[a]*ya... since*   [b]*fue... was inhabited*   [c]*después de Cristo* (A.D.)   [d]*originating*   [e]*isolation*   [f]*they developed*

Lectura

Sobre la lectura   El trabajo es una parte importante de la vida de todos, pero puede provocar diferentes reacciones, según las circunstancias. La lectura de este capítulo es la letra de una canción de Víctor Jara en la que se expresa la realidad de un grupo de obreros oprimidos (*oppressed workers*) de Chile.

Antes de leer

A. La vida del minero.   ¿Qué vida tiene un minero? ¿Qué actividades hace? Di cuáles de las siguientes acciones crees que hace el minero típico.

- ☐ abrir nuevos filones (*veins*) de carbón (*coal*)
- ☐ disfrutar de mucho tiempo libre
- ☐ ganar mucho dinero
- ☐ gritar a los compañeros
- ☐ sangrar (*bleed*)
- ☐ subir después de trabajar
- ☐ sudar (*sweat*)
- ☐ sufrir de dolores musculares
- ☐ tener buenas relaciones con el patrón (*jefe*)
- ☐ trabajar bajo la tierra
- ☐ vivir en la pobreza

B. Identificación.   Revisa brevemente la lectura y di qué palabras o frases expresan las siguientes ideas.

1. la desesperación del minero
2. el optimismo del minero
3. la descripción de las actividades del minero

Canción del minero

por Víctor Jara

Voy	Abro	Mira
Vengo	Saco	Oye
Subo	Sudo	Piensa
Bajo	Sangro	Grita
Todo para qué	Todo pa'l^a patrón	Nada es lo peor
Nada para mí	Nada pa'l dolor	Todo es lo mejor
Minero soy	Minero soy	Minero soy
A la mina voy	A mi casa voy	A la tierra voy
A la muerte voy	A la pena voy	A la muerte voy
Minero soy	Minero soy	Minero soy
		Humano soy

^apara el

Si te interesa

▲ *Víctor Jara*

La nueva canción es un movimiento artístico que se popularizó en Hispanoamérica durante la segunda mitad del siglo XX. Los artistas de diferentes países se conocen como «cantautores» **(cantante + autor)** y comparten las siguientes características: respetar la cultura y la música tradicional de su país, tocar instrumentos tradicionales y usar su arte para combatir la injusticia y la represión y para mejorar las condiciones de los agricultores y obreros.

   Víctor Jara (1932–1973), un cantautor chileno, nació en un pueblo cerca de Santiago de Chile, donde su madre le enseñó a cantar y tocar la guitarra. Después de estudiar teatro y la música tradicional chilena, conoció a la cantante famosa Violeta Parra, se interesó en la política chilena y empezó a apoyar en sus canciones al gobierno socialista del presidente Salvador Allende. Pero después del golpe militar del general Augusto Pinochet (el 11 de septiembre de 1973), los militares lo detuvieron, lo torturaron, le rompieron las manos para que no pudiera (*he couldn't*) tocar sus canciones de justicia social. Lo mataron pocos días después. Después de la muerte de Jara, Pinochet prohibió sus canciones, pero su música siguió inspirando a la gente oprimida de toda Hispanoamérica.

Después de leer

A. Comprensión. Indica si las siguientes oraciones son ciertas o falsas, según la lectura. Luego, di en qué línea y estrofa se encuentra la información y corrige la información falsa.

	CIERTO	FALSO
1. Los mineros tienen un trabajo difícil en el que arriesgan (*risk*) su vida.	☐	☐
2. Los mineros están contentos con las condiciones de su trabajo.	☐	☐
3. Los mineros tienen buenas relaciones con el patrón.	☐	☐
4. Los mineros son bien pagados.	☐	☐

B. Interpretación.   Comenta las siguientes preguntas con un compañero / una compañera.

1. ¿Cómo indica el poeta que la vida del minero es monótona?
2. ¿En qué se diferencia el tono de la tercera estrofa del de las primeras dos?
3. ¿A qué se refiere la expresión «A la tierra voy»? ¿Crees que el poeta hable de su trabajo o del fin de su vida?
4. ¿Qué características de la «Canción del minero» corresponden a las del género musical **La nueva canción?** (Lee de nuevo el **Si te interesa** al principio de esta sección si es necesario.)

C. Tu trabajo.   Escribe la letra de una canción en la que expresas tus sentimientos hacia un trabajo que has hecho o que te gustaría hacer.

Paso 1. Usando el siguiente formato en la primera estrofa de tu canción, escribe cuatro de las acciones que haces en el trabajo. **¡OJO!** Debes usar un verbo en forma **yo** del presente del indicativo en las primeras dos líneas.

Siempre _____
Nunca _____
_____ soy.
A _____ voy
A _____ voy
_____ soy.

Paso 2. Usando el mismo formato del **Paso 1** en la segunda estrofa, escribe cuatro reacciones personales o críticas al trabajo.

D. Información actual.   Víctor Jara compuso esta canción en 1961. Desde entonces, la política y la economía chilenas han evolucionado, y ahora Chile tiene un tratado de libre comercio con los Estados Unidos. Trabaja con dos compañeros/as para contestar las siguientes preguntas, buscando más información en el Internet si es necesario.

1. Revisa la siguiente lista de derechos actualmente garantizados a los obreros chilenos. ¿Cuáles afectan los problemas mencionados por el minero de la canción?

☐ un ambiente sano y seguro
☐ la baja (*leave*) por maternidad
☐ el derecho a la huelga
☐ la igualdad de sueldos
☐ la libertad de asociación libre (*right to assembly*)

☐ la negociación (*bargaining*) colectiva
☐ el seguro contra accidentes
☐ el sueldo mínimo
☐ el pago por horas extras
☐ las vacaciones pagadas

2. ¿Existen los mismos derechos en tu país, según la ley? Compara la lista anterior con los derechos que tienen los obreros de tu país.
3. ¿Siempre se respetan estos derechos en tu país? ¿Qué problemas de los obreros no se resuelven con una lista de este tipo? En tu opinión, ¿se necesitan más leyes que protejan a los obreros?

Redacción

El currículum. Imagina que estás solicitando un trabajo de verano en Chile. Escribe una carta de presentación (*letter of introduction*) y un currículum para informar a tu posible jefe/a de tus experiencias laborales y conocimientos. Sigue los pasos en el *Manual de práctica* para elaborar tus documentos.

Exploración

Investigación cultural. Busca más información sobre Chile en la biblioteca, en el *Entrevistas* Online Learning Center **(www.mhhe.com/entrevistas2)** o en otros sitios del Internet y preséntala a la clase. El *Manual de práctica* contiene más ideas para tu presentación.

Léxico activo

PROFESIONES Y OFICIOS

el/la **abogado/a**	lawyer
el/la **arqueólogo/a**	archaeologist
el/la **artista**	artist
el/la **asesor(a)**	consultant
el/la **asistente social**	social worker
el/la **banquero/a**	banker
el/la **bibliotecario/a**	librarian
el **bombero** / la **mujer bombero**	firefighter
el/la **científico/a**	scientist
el/la **cirujano/a**	surgeon
el/la **contable**	accountant
el/la **director(a)**	director
el/la **diseñador(a)**	designer
el/la **empleado/a**	employee
el/la **enfermero/a**	nurse
el/la **entrenador(a) (personal)**	(personal) trainer
el/la **escritor(a)**	writer
el/la **fotógrafo/a**	photographer
el **hombre** / la **mujer de negocios**	businessman/ businesswoman
el/la **ingeniero/a**	engineer
el **mecánico** / la **mujer mecánico**	mechanic
el/la **médico/a**	doctor
el/la **piloto/a**	pilot
el **político** / la **mujer político**	politician
el/la **programador(a)**	(computer) programmer
el/la **secretario/a**	secretary
el/la **traductor(a)**	translator
el/la **veterinario/a**	veterinarian

PARA PEDIR CON CORTESÍA

¿Le importaría… ?	Would you (*form.*) mind . . . ?
¿Me haría el favor de… ?	Would you (*form.*) please . . . ?
¿Podría usted… ?	Could you (*form.*) . . . ?

PARA CONSEGUIR TRABAJO

la **agencia de colocaciones**	job placement agency
el **anuncio (de empleo)**	(job) ad
la **carta de recomendación**	letter of recommendation
la **cita**	appointment
el **currículum (vitae)**	résumé
la **empresa**	company
el **formulario**	form
el **objetivo**	objective
la **oferta**	offer
el **puesto**	job, position
la **solicitud**	application

definir	to define
exigir (j)	to demand
fijar	to arrange, set up
ganar	to earn
llenar	to fill (in/out)
ofrecer (zc)	to offer
requerir (ie, i)	to require

LOS REQUISITOS

la **competencia**	skill
los **conocimientos**	knowledge
la **experiencia mínima**	minimum experience
la **formación**	background
la **fuerza física**	physical strength
el **nivel**	level
amplio/a	ample, broad
arriesgado/a	risk-taking

capaz (*pl.* **capaces**)	capable
deseable	desirable
multilingüe	multilingual

LAS CONDICIONES DE TRABAJO

el **futuro prometedor**	promising future
el **horario (flexible)**	(flexible) schedule
la **jornada tradicional**	traditional workday
la **oportunidad de avanzar**	opportunity for advancement
las **prestaciones**	benefits
el **prestigio**	prestige
la **responsabilidad**	responsibility
el **sueldo (mínimo)**	(minimum) wage, salary
de tiempo completo/parcial	full-time/part-time
según la experiencia	based on experience

El mundo actual

El Salvador, Guatemala, Honduras,
Nicaragua y Panamá

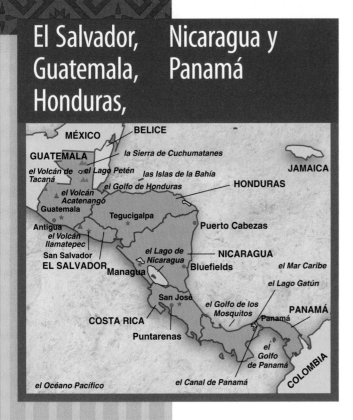

MÉXICO
BELICE
GUATEMALA
la Sierra de Cuchumatanes
el Volcán de Tacaná
el Lago Petén
las Islas de la Bahía
JAMAICA
el Volcán Acatenango
el Golfo de Honduras
HONDURAS
Guatemala
Tegucigalpa
Antigua
el Volcán Ilamatepec
Puerto Cabezas
San Salvador
EL SALVADOR
el Lago de Nicaragua
NICARAGUA
Managua
Bluefields
el Mar Caribe
el Lago Gatún
San José
el Golfo de los Mosquitos
PANAMÁ
COSTA RICA
Panamá
Puntarenas
el Golfo de Panamá
COLOMBIA
el Océano Pacífico
el Canal de Panamá

Cultura

◆ The Impact of Technology on Culture

◆ Cultural Images in the Media

◆ Conflict and Peace in Central America

◆ **Señas culturales: La ropa tradicional de los mayas**

Lengua

◆ Newspapers, Television, Movies, and the Internet

◆ The Present Subjunctive (13.1)

◆ Basic Uses of the Present Subjunctive (13.2)

◆ The Subjunctive with Expressions of Doubt (13.3)

◆ The Subjunctive with Expressions of Emotion (13.4)

El Salvador, Guatemala, Honduras, Nicaragua y Panamá	Mayas, nahuas y otras civilizaciones indígenas	Vasco Núñez de Balboa recorre Panamá y encuentra el Océano Pacífico				Independencia de España de los países de Centroamérica		El estadounidense William Walker es presidente de Nicaragua hasta su ejecución
	hasta el siglo XVI	**1500– 1600**	**1513**	**1534**	**1600– 1750**	**1776– 1783**	**1821**	**1846– 1848** **1856– 1860**
Los Estados Unidos y el Canadá	Varias tribus indígenas habitan en Norteamérica	Exploración española de Norteamérica		Jacques Cartier reclama para Francia el Canadá	Fundación de las colonias británicas en Norteamérica	Guerra de Independencia en los EE. UU.		Guerra Mexicano-Americana

Instantánea

ORIGEN DEL NOMBRE

El Salvador (*The Savior* [Jesucristo]); **Guatemala:** de *Quauhtlemallan* (nahua), que significa «Tierra de muchos árboles»; **Honduras** (*Depths*): referencia a las aguas de la costa norteña; **Nicaragua:** de *Nicarao*, nombre de un cacique indígena; **Panamá:** «Abundancia de peces (*fish*)»

POBLACIÓN

El Salvador: 6.178.700;
Guatemala: 14.223.400;
Honduras: 6.606.100;
Nicaragua: 5.777.700;
Panamá: 2.991.000

LENGUAS

El Salvador: El español (oficial), el nahua; **Guatemala:** El español (oficial), varios dialectos maya quiché; **Honduras:** El español (oficial), varias lenguas indígenas; **Nicaragua:** El español (oficial), el inglés, el misquito, varias lenguas indígenas; **Panamá:** El español (oficial), el inglés, el inglés criollo

◄ *Esta joven guatemalteca se gana la vida* (earns a living) *tejiendo* (weaving) *alfombras.*

El Salvador

Guatemala

Honduras

Nicaragua

Panamá

For additional practice, check out the *Manual de práctica*, the Interactive CD-ROM, and the Online Learning Center (**www.mhhe.com/entrevistas2**)!

				Violeta Barrios de Chamorro es elegida presidenta de Nicaragua	El huracán Mitch causa mucha destrucción y muchas muertes en Centroamérica	Se elige a Enrique Bolaños Geyer como presidente de Nicaragua
	Se abre el Canal de Panamá	Revolución sandinista en Nicaragua	Guerra civil en El Salvador			
1898	**1914**	**1952**	**1979–1988**	**1979–1991**	**1982**	**1990**	**1994**	**1998**	**2002**
Guerra Hispano-Americana		Puerto Rico se hace Estado Libre Asociado de los EE. UU.		El Canadá se separa legalmente de Inglaterra		Tratado de Libre Comercio entre los EE. UU., el Canadá y México		

🌓 El periódico en línea

El-noticiero.com.ni

Managua, viernes 14 de noviembre de 2003
actualizada 13:30

Pronóstico del tiempo[a]

Pacífico: Nublado
Temp: 31°C / 88°F
MÁS

Secciones

Portada[b]
Nacionales
Internacionales
Editoriales
Anuncios
Cultura
Deportes

Revista semanal

Inundaciones causan daños de millones

Claudio Hernández Salcedo
chernandezs@el-noticiero.com.ni

Managua. Las recientes lluvias provocaron inundaciones (Foto) en la región capitalina que desplazaron a miles de ciudadanos y causaron daños que superarán los 17 millones de córdobas, según fuentes oficiales. MÁS

Cotización dólar

Oficial:
15,2954 córdobas

Mercado negro:
compra 14,95
venta 15,55

Economía

Servicios

Ediciones anteriores
Foros de opinión
Cartas al director
Cartelera de cine

Campaña de protección del Lago de Nicaragua

María Luz Gutiérrez Soto
mlgutierrezs@el-noticiero.com.ni

Granada. Los dirigentes de la Asociación de Municipios de la Cuenca del Gran Lago (AMUGRAN) se reunieron hoy en Granada para iniciar una campaña de protección de uno de los recursos naturales más importantes del país (Foto). MÁS

Encuestas

¿Es bueno que el dólar tenga tanta importancia en la economía nacional?

☐ Sí
☐ No

Ver resultados
(930 votos)

[a]Pronóstico… *Weather forecast*
[b]*Front page*

el crucigrama	crossword puzzle
el encabezado	headline
el/la lector(a)	reader
la noticia	piece of news; *pl.* news
el obituario	obituary
la prensa	press
el reportaje	report
el/la reportero/a	reporter
la reseña	review
la tira cómica	comic strip, cartoon

abonarse	to subscribe		
estar al corriente	to be up-to-date		
estar desinformado/a	to be uninformed		
estar enterado/a de	to know about		
exponer (*irreg.*)	to report; to expose		
mantenerse informado/a	to stay informed		
publicar (qu)	to publish		
actual(mente)	current(ly)		

La comunicación electrónica

el café cibernético	Internet café	**chatear**	to chat (online)
el *chat*	chatroom	**conectarse**	to get connected
el correo electrónico	e-mail	**estar conectado/a**	to be connected
el enlace	link	**hacer clic (en)**	to click (on)
el Internet	Internet	**navegar (gu)**	to surf (*the Internet*)
el *mail*	e-mail (message)	**platicar (qu)**	to chat (*in general*)
el mensaje	message		

Actividades

A. ¿En qué sección?   ¿En qué sección del periódico puedes encontrar la siguiente información?

VOCABULARIO ÚTIL

cultura y sociedad	culture and society
deportes	sports

1. el resultado del último partido de béisbol en Managua
2. opiniones sobre una cuestión política local
3. las temperaturas altas y bajas en la región
4. las noticias más importantes del día
5. el horario de los espectáculos, películas y conciertos de la semana
6. la crítica de un restaurante nuevo
7. las últimas aventuras de Mafalda y de Carlitos Brown
8. la noticia de una muerte

B. Los periódicos que tú lees.   ¿Cómo es el periódico de tu ciudad, o el que lees con más frecuencia? Contesta las preguntas.

1. ¿Qué secciones tiene?
2. ¿Abarca (*Does it cover*) los eventos locales, nacionales e internacionales?
3. ¿Hay una sección dedicada a los deportes?
4. ¿Tiene crucigramas u otras diversiones? ¿Son difíciles o fáciles?
5. ¿Son objetivos o subjetivos los reportajes que contiene?
6. ¿Ofrece análisis de las noticias del día? ¿En qué sección?
7. ¿Hay muchos anuncios o pocos? ¿Qué venden?

C. Encuesta: ¿Estás enterado/a?

Paso 1. Pregúntales a cinco compañeros/as de clase sobre sus hábitos de lectura.

1. ¿Con qué frecuencia lees las noticias?
   - Las leo con frecuencia.
   - Las leo de vez en cuando.
   - Las leo _____ veces por semana.
   - No las leo nunca.
2. ¿Te has abonado a algún periódico o revista de noticias? ¿A cuál(es)?
3. ¿Cómo te mantienes informado/a de las actualidades (*current events*): por televisión, radio, Internet, etcétera? Explica por qué.

Paso 2. Presenta los resultados a la clase, resumiendo información cuando sea (*it is*) posible.

MODELOS   Melisa se mantiene informada, leyendo las noticias con frecuencia.

Alberto está muy desinformado porque no lee las noticias nunca.

La televisión y el cine

Encuesta televisiva[a]

1. ¿Cuál es su **canal** favorito?
2. ¿Prefiere usted **la televisión de antena parabólica** o **la televisión por cable**?
3. ¿Tiene usted **video** o **DVD**[b]?
4. ¿Cuántos **televidentes**[c] hay en su familia?
5. ¿Qué tipos de **programas** mira usted con frecuencia?

☐ **los concursos**[d]   ☐ **las películas**
☐ **los documentales**   ☐ **cómicas**
☐ **los noticieros**[e]   ☐ **de acción**
☐ **los programas educativos** ☐ **de amor**
☐ **las telenovelas**[f]   ☐ **de horror**

---

[a]*television (adj.)* [b]*video… VCR or DVD player* [c]*TV viewers* [d]*game shows* [e]*newscasts* [f]*soap operas*

Los programas

el acontecimiento	event, happening	**mentir (ie, i)**	to lie
el chisme	bit of gossip; *pl.* gossip		
el desastre (natural)	(natural) disaster	**abrumador(a)**	overwhelming
la manifestación	demonstration	**chocante**	shocking
la mentira	lie	**cómico/a**	funny, comical
el suceso	event, happening	**controvertido/a**	controversial
la verdad	truth	**dudoso/a**	doubtful
		escandaloso/a	scandalous
dudar	to doubt	**lamentable**	lamentable, regretful
lamentar	to lament, regret	**ridículo/a**	ridiculous

Si te interesa

In recent years, Hispanic TV channels have had enormous success with programming similar to that offered in the United States. Two very popular programs are *Cristina*, an interview program in which experts participate along with laypeople from the audience, and *Sábado gigante*, a variety show that features artists, singers, games, comedy skits, and so on.

▲ *Cristina Saralegui, anfitriona de* Cristina, *le solicita opiniones a un espectador de su* show.

Actividades

A. Tipos de programas. ¿Qué tipo de emisión (*broadcast*) representan los siguientes programas estadounidenses?

1. *CNN News of the World*
2. *General Hospital*
3. *National Geographic*
4. *Gone with the Wind*
5. *Evening News with Dan Rather*
6. *Friends*
7. *The Price Is Right*
8. *Scream*

B. Géneros cinematográficos. ¿Qué suele ocurrir en los distintos tipos de películas? Escoge los detalles más comunes del argumento (*plot*) de cada género cinematográfico.

GÉNERO

1. _____ la película de horror
2. _____ la película de acción
3. _____ la película de amor
4. _____ la película cómica
5. _____ la película histórica
6. _____ el documental

CARACTERÍSTICAS

a. Da miedo. (*It scares you.*)
b. Contiene escenas violentas.
c. Tiene un final feliz.
d. Relata información histórica.
e. Da risa. (*It makes you laugh.*)
f. Contiene escenas románticas.
g. Expone detalles sobre un suceso.
h. Es realista.
i. Hay monstruos y personajes supernaturales.

Lenguaje funcional

Para expresar reacciones

The following formulas are useful to comment on things and events.

¡Qué + NOUN + **más/tan** + ADJECTIVE!

¡Qué noticia más triste!	What a sad piece of news!
¡Qué programas tan interesantes!	What interesting shows!

¡Qué + ADJECTIVE!

¡Qué triste!	How sad!

OTRAS EXPRESIONES

¡Qué barbaridad!	How awful!
¡Qué bien!	Great! How wonderful!
¡Qué escándalo!	What a scandal!

C. Tus reacciones.   ¿Cómo reaccionas a las siguientes noticias?

> MODELO   Un desastre natural →
> ¡Qué tragedia! / ¡Qué cosa más triste!

1. Ciudadanos pierden millones en fracaso (*failure*) bancario
2. Presidente vomita delante de líderes mundiales
3. Futbolista famoso acusado de robos
4. Ovejas (*Sheep*) clonadas en Escocia
5. Médicos franceses compran órganos humanos en el mercado negro
6. Nuevas tarifas en los cigarrillos
7. Deportista salvadoreño vuelve con siete medallas de oro en Juegos Olímpicos

D. Entrevista.   Entrevista a un compañero / una compañera de clase para saber la siguiente información. Luego, haz un resumen de la información para la clase.

1. su película favorita
   a. título
   b. director(a) y actores principales
   c. breve resumen del argumento
   d. razón por la que le gusta tanto
2. el programa menos interesante para él/ella
   a. título
   b. razón por la que no le interesa
3. la revista que lee con mayor frecuencia
   a. título
   b. aspectos interesantes
4. su canal favorito
   a. nombre/número
   b. programas que presenta

David Guzmán Arias

«Pienso que la televisión tiene un papel más importante que el periódico... »

Nombre: David

Apellidos: (1) Guzmán (2) Arias

Edad: 29 años

Nació en: Tegucigalpa, Honduras

You can watch this interview on the *Entrevistas* Video or Interactive CD-ROM or listen to the audio on the Online Learning Center (**www.mhhe.com/entrevistas2**).

Vocabulario útil

si sucede algo	if something happens	**dejo de verla**	I stop watching it
prender la televisión	to turn on the TV	**sin embargo**	however
hasta cierto punto	up to a point	**por medio de**	by means of
la trama	plot		

Antes de ver

¿Cómo te mantienes informado/a?   ¿Qué medios de comunicación usas para mantenerte informado/a de lo que pasa en el mundo? Cambia las siguientes oraciones si es necesario para describir tus preferencias.

1. Leo todo el periódico todos los días.
2. Leo sólo los encabezados.
3. Si sucede algo importante, lo primero que hago es prender la televisión para ver qué pasó.
4. Me gustan las teleseries y telenovelas porque reflejan bien la vida moderna.
5. El Internet es una forma muy práctica de estar al corriente de las cosas.
6. Me comunico con mucha gente por correo electrónico y así sé lo que pasa en el mundo.

¡Veamos!

¿Y David?   Primero, revisa las oraciones en la siguiente página. Después, mientras ves la entrevista, indica si son ciertas o falsas.

1. David lee el periódico todos los días.   ☐   ☐
2. David no tiene sección favorita: Lee todo el periódico.   ☐   ☐
3. David piensa que más gente tiene acceso a la televisión   ☐   ☐
   que a los periódicos.
4. Las telenovelas son importantes porque unen a las   ☐   ☐
   familias: Todos las ven.
5. David se comunica por computadora desde su casa.   ☐   ☐
6. David usa el Internet para su trabajo y sus asuntos   ☐   ☐
   económicos.

Después de ver

A. ¿Entendiste?   Contesta las siguientes preguntas. Puedes ver de nuevo la entrevista si es necesario.

1. ¿Qué hace la gente cuando sucede algo importante? ¿Cómo se mantiene informada?
2. ¿Qué tipo de programa de televisión es muy popular en Honduras?
3. ¿Qué palabras usa David para indicar la importancia de ese tipo de programa en la sociedad centroamericana?
4. Según David, ¿quién tiene acceso directo —en casa o en el trabajo— a las computadoras en su país?
5. ¿Para qué usa David el Internet?

B. Comparaciones.   ¿En qué se parecen los medios de comunicación en tu país a los de la descripción de David? ¿En qué se diferencian? Contesta con **Son similares/diferentes porque…**

C. Entrevista: En tu opinión.   Hazle las siguientes preguntas a un compañero / una compañera de clase.

1. ¿Prefieres leer el periódico o mirar las noticias en la televisión? ¿Por qué?
2. En tu opinión, ¿quiénes usan más el Internet, los jóvenes o las personas mayores de 50 años? Explica tu respuesta.
3. ¿Están al corriente tus amigos de las actualidades nacionales e internacionales? ¿Cómo se enteran, en general (por televisión, radio, periódicos, revistas, oralmente, etcétera)?
4. ¿Cómo se enteran de las noticias universitarias los estudiantes de tu universidad?
5. ¿Te gustan las telenovelas? ¿Cuáles? ¿Por qué te gustan?
6. ¿Dónde crees que la gente use más el Internet, en el trabajo o en la casa? ¿Y para qué lo usa? Explica tus respuestas.

13.1 The Present Subjunctive

Introduction

So far in your study of Spanish you have learned many verb forms that allow you to distinguish time frames (tense, e.g., present vs. past) and ways of carrying out actions (aspect, e.g., progressive vs. habitual). All of these forms are known as *indicative* forms because in each case, they *indicate* facts or report actions and states that speakers believe, to the best of their knowledge, to be true, valid, and real.

There is also a parallel set of verb forms in Spanish called the *subjunctive,* which is used to reveal a speaker's doubt, uncertainty, or negation of the reality of an action or state—a more *subjective* view of things. The subjunctive is not a tense, but it is rather a verbal *mood:* There are present, past, perfect, and progressive subjunctive forms that allow you to express many of the subtleties of time frame and aspect that are possible in the indicative.

As with any aspect of language that allows for subtlety of meaning, the subjunctive is a tricky feature of Spanish that English speakers may spend many years trying to perfect. In some cases, there are specific words or expressions in a sentence that make the subjunctive absolutely necessary; at other times, a speaker can use either the indicative or the corresponding subjunctive form, depending on the exact nuance intended. This textbook concentrates on the basic uses of the subjunctive mood.

Forms

The basic rules for the formation of the present subjunctive verb forms in Spanish are the same as those for the formal commands you learned in **Capítulos 4** and **12.** The subjunctive, however, has the entire range of personal endings, not just **usted** and **ustedes** forms. Thus, regular **-ar** verbs take the endings **-e, -es, -e, -emos, -éis, -en;** and regular **-er** and regular **-ir** verbs take **-a, -as, -a, -amos, -áis, -an.**

Infinitive	Present Subjunctive Forms
lamentar	lamente, lamentes, lamente, lamentemos, lamentéis, lamenten
leer	lea, leas, lea, leamos, leáis, lean
transmitir	transmita, transmitas, transmita, transmitamos, transmitáis, transmitan

Just as with commands, the verb stem for the subjunctive is identical to the **yo** form of the indicative, minus the **-o;** that is, any irregularities in the indicative **yo** form are present throughout the subjunctive paradigm.

Infinitive	yo Form, Present Indicative	Present Subjunctive Forms
tener	tengo	tenga, tengas, tenga, tengamos, tengáis, tengan
traer	traigo	traiga, traigas, traiga, traigamos, traigáis, traigan
reducir	reduzco	reduzca, reduzcas, reduzca, reduzcamos, reduzcáis, reduzcan

Stem-changing verbs show the **-ie-** and **-ue-** in the same four forms of the subjunctive as the indicative.

Infinitive	yo Form, Present Indicative	Present Subjunctive Forms
pensar	pienso	piense, pienses, piense, pensemos, penséis, piensen
volver	vuelvo	vuelva, vuelvas, vuelva, volvamos, volváis, vuelvan

Stem-changing **-ir** verbs that have irregular third-person forms in the preterit (**e → i, o → u**) have this same stem change in the **nosotros/as** and **vosotros/as** forms of the present subjunctive. Note that such verbs maintain the present indicative stem changes found in the other conjugations (**e → ie, o → ue**).

Infinitive	yo Form, Present Indicative	Third-Person, Preterit	Present Subjunctive Forms
sentir	siento	sintió, sintieron	sienta, sientas, sienta, sintamos, sintáis, sientan
dormir	duermo	durmió, durmieron	duerma, duermas, duerma, durmamos, durmáis, duerman

As you saw with the preterit and the formal commands, some vowels in verb endings cause a change in the spelling of verb stems to ensure that the pronunciation remains the same. Before the vowels **e** and **i,** the consonant **c** becomes **qu, g** becomes **gu,** and **z** becomes **c.**

Infinitive	yo Form, Present Indicative	Present Subjunctive Forms
abarcar	abarco	abarque, abarques, abarque, abarquemos, abarquéis, abarquen
navegar	navego	navegue, navegues, navegue, naveguemos, naveguéis, naveguen
empezar	empiezo	empiece, empieces, empiece, empecemos, empecéis, empiecen

Before the vowels **a** and **o**, **g** becomes **j** in **-er** and **-ir** verbs.

Infinitive	yo Form, Present Indicative	Present Subjunctive Forms
escoger	escojo	escoja, escojas, escoja, escojamos, escojáis, escojan

A few verbs have completely irregular stems in the subjunctive, but notice the regularity of their endings.

Infinitive	Present Subjunctive Forms
dar*	dé, des, dé, demos, deis, den
estar	esté, estés, esté, estemos, estéis, estén
haber	haya, hayas, haya, hayamos, hayáis, hayan
ir	vaya, vayas, vaya, vayamos, vayáis, vayan
saber	sepa, sepas, sepa, sepamos, sepáis, sepan
ser	sea, seas, sea, seamos, seáis, sean

Análisis estructural

Di si las siguientes formas verbales están en el indicativo (**I**) o el subjuntivo (**S**). Después, di qué persona es el sujeto de cada verbo. Usa estos sujetos: **yo, tú, nosotros/as, ellos.**

		I/S	SUJETO
MODELO			
hablar:	hablemos	S	nosotros/as
1. creer:	crea	___	___
2. crear:	creas	___	___
3. saber:	sepamos	___	___
4. desempeñar:	desempeñan	___	___
5. sentir:	sienten	___	___
6. sentar:	sienten	___	___

---

* The accent on **dé** is needed to distinguish this subjunctive verb form from the preposition **de**.

Actividades

A. Expectativas del público. Completa las siguientes oraciones con el presente del subjuntivo de los verbos entre paréntesis para describir algunas expectativas del público respecto a los medios de comunicación.

1. Los ciudadanos necesitan que los medios de comunicación (ser) fuentes fiables (*reliable*) de información.
2. Algunos reporteros insisten en que sus fuentes (mantenerse) secretas.
3. Muchos lectores prefieren que los periódicos sólo (publicar) noticias sobre eventos nacionales.
4. El gobierno debe prohibir que las estaciones de cable (transmitir) programas violentos o pornográficos.
5. Es necesario que el gobierno (limitar) la difusión de algunas noticias por razones de seguridad nacional.
6. Los televidentes quieren que los noticieros (informar) sobre los sucesos más trágicos del día.

B. Películas y programas. Completa las siguientes oraciones con el subjuntivo del verbo entre paréntesis. Luego, indica si estás de acuerdo o no con cada oración.

	ESTOY DE ACUERDO.	NO ESTOY DE ACUERDO.
1. No me gusta que los actores (ganar) tanto dinero por cada película.	☐	☐
2. Es importante que los directores (hacer) películas con temas educativos.	☐	☐
3. Prefiero programas que (abarcar) temas políticos.	☐	☐
4. Este verano no hay ninguna película que (tener) un argumento interesante.	☐	☐
5. No creo que (ser) posible convertir una telenovela en película.	☐	☐
6. Quiero que la compañía de cable (instalar) líneas digitales en mi barrio.	☐	☐

● 13.2 Basic Uses of the Present Subjunctive

Criteria and Cues

As stated previously, the subjunctive mood in Spanish is used to reveal the speaker's underlying subjective interpretation of some action, state, or entity. The expression of a subjective view of reality is quite common in everyday speech, and consequently many beginning students of Spanish tend to overuse the subjunctive. However, this verbal mood actually appears only under very strict circumstances. Specifically, the subjunctive occurs primarily in sentences that meet the following three criteria.

1. The sentence has a main clause **(una cláusula principal)** and a dependent clause **(una cláusula subordinada).** A dependent clause is a secondary clause within the main sentence that is introduced by a relative pronoun (the most common one is **que).***

MAIN CLAUSE	RELATIVE PRONOUN	DEPENDENT CLAUSE
Quiero	**que**	*leas* **este artículo.**

2. The subject of the dependent clause is different from that of the main clause.

SUBJECT = **yo**		SUBJECT = **esa historia**
Dudo	**que**	**esa historia** *sea* **cierta.**

3. The main clause contains an expression that cues the subjunctive in the dependent clause (e.g., **Dudo,** above). In this and subsequent chapters you will learn which expressions can cue the use of the subjunctive in dependent clauses.

There are two broad categories of cues for the subjunctive:

- Cues that *always* require a subjunctive verb form in the dependent clause
- Cues that allow an indicative or subjunctive verb form in the dependent clause, depending on what nuance the speaker wishes to convey

When analyzing dependent clauses, you should determine right away which context you are dealing with and what changes of meaning each mood entails if both subjunctive and indicative moods are possible. In this chapter you will focus on the first category of cues; you will study the second category of cues in **Capítulo 14.**

Expressions of Volition

The subjunctive is obligatory in a dependent clause when the main clause contains a verb of *will, volition,* or *influence* over the subject of the dependent clause, and the subject of the dependent clause is different from that of the main clause.

Los jóvenes **quieren** que la televisión los **distraiga.**	*Young people want TV to distract them.*

In this example, the verb **quieren** cues the subjunctive in the dependent clause (**distraiga,** from **distraer**).

Here are some common expressions of will, volition, and influence that require the subjunctive in the dependent clause.

Quiero que lo **leas.**	*I want you to read it.*
Prefiero que lo **leas.**	*I prefer that you read it.*

---

* These secondary clauses are called "dependent" because they cannot stand alone as a sentence. For example, "that he reads the paper every day" is not a complete sentence, but it could be a dependent clause within a complex sentence such as "I didn't know that he reads the paper every day." The main clause, "I didn't know," can stand alone as a complete sentence.

Te **sugiero** que lo **leas.***	*I suggest that you read it.*
Te **recomiendo** que lo **leas.***	*I recommend that you read it.*
Es importante que lo **leas.**†	*It's important for you to read it.*
Es necesario que lo **leas.**†	*It's necessary for you to read it.*
Insisto en que lo **leas.**	*I insist that you read it.*
Prohíbo que lo **leas.**	*I prohibit you to read it.*
Permito que lo **leas.**	*I permit you to read it.*

Note that the English translation of many Spanish sentences with the subjunctive does not have an obvious two-clause structure. Instead, English often expresses this change of subject in Spanish with the construction (for) + *subject* + to + *verb.*

Quieren que la televisión los distraiga.	*They want (for) TV to distract them.*
Necesito que él lo haga.	*I need (for) him to do it.*

Análisis estructural

Analiza las siguientes oraciones, indicando estos aspectos.

[ ]	dependent clause
M-S	main-clause subject
D-S	dependent-clause subject
ind./subj.	dependent-clause verb in indicative or subjunctive
*	expression that cues the subjunctive in the dependent clause

MODELO   Nuestro profesor quiere que nosotros leamos el artículo. →

Nuestro
profesor   quiere   [que   nosotros   leamos   el artículo].
M-S   *   D-S   subj.

1. Mis padres prefieren que yo compre el periódico en ese quiosco.
2. Los reporteros insisten en que los censores no limiten la libertad de expresión.
3. La constitución estadounidense prohíbe que el gobierno establezca una religión oficial.
4. Es importante que los programas de televisión para niños sean educativos.
5. Muchos padres no permiten que sus hijos vean demasiada televisión.

---

* **Sugerir (ie, i)** and **recomendar (ie)** both require indirect object pronouns, which refer to the same person as the subject of the dependent clause: *I suggest (to you) that you read it.*
† The expressions **Es importante** and **Es necesario** are two of the many *impersonal expressions* that cue the subjunctive in a dependent clause. The subject of the dependent clause will *always* be different from the impersonal subject of the impersonal expression: **Es importante que estudies.** (*It's important for you to study.*)

Actividades

A. El papel de la televisión. Usando los siguientes elementos, forma oraciones completas sobre el papel de la televisión en la vida de las personas. Después, indica si estás de acuerdo o no con las ideas mencionadas.

	ESTOY DE ACUERDO.	NO ESTOY DE ACUERDO.
1. los expertos / recomendarle que / los niños / mirar / menos de una hora de televisión cada día	☐	☐
2. muchos padres / querer que / sus hijos / hacer la tarea / en vez de mirar la televisión	☐	☐
3. los profesores / insistir en que / sus alumnos / aprender a criticar / las noticias en la televisión	☐	☐
4. es necesario que / el gobierno / gastar más dinero / en programas educativos	☐	☐
5. yo / preferir que / los canales de televisión / limitar / los anuncios que ponen	☐	☐

B. Dos periódicos diferentes. ¿En qué se diferencian las opiniones en los periódicos conservadores y liberales? Escribe oraciones completas sobre cada actividad de la derecha, dando una versión que exprese una opinión conservadora y otra que exprese una opinión liberal.

MODELO   Es importante que el gobierno controle más la economía. (liberal)

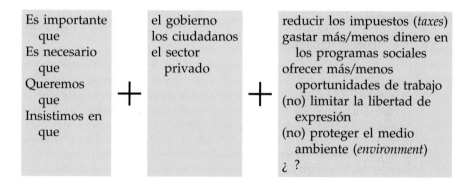

Es importante que
Es necesario que
Queremos que
Insistimos en que

+

el gobierno
los ciudadanos
el sector privado

+

reducir los impuestos (*taxes*)
gastar más/menos dinero en los programas sociales
ofrecer más/menos oportunidades de trabajo
(no) limitar la libertad de expresión
(no) proteger el medio ambiente (*environment*)
¿ ?

C. Un editorial. Completa la carta al editor de un periódico nicaragüense en la siguiente página con el indicativo o subjuntivo de los verbos entre paréntesis.

Estoy de acuerdo con todos los lectores de su periódico que (expresar)[1] disgusto por los actos inhumanos cometidos en ciertas regiones en guerra (*at war*). Pero es importante que nosotros (reconocer)[2] que aquí en Centroamérica (existir)[3] las mismas condiciones de violencia. Recomiendo que nuestras autoridades (hacer)[4] los sacrificios necesarios para poner fin a estas conductas vergonzosas (*shameful*). Todos debemos insistir en que la represión (ser)[5] una cosa del pasado. Los centroamericanos queremos que nuestros hijos (tener)[6] una vida libre de la ansiedad y del miedo que vivieron sus abuelos.

José Serrano Villa, Managua

Análisis cultural

La siguiente cita tomada de una fuente escrita en inglés para anglohablantes va a aumentar tus conocimientos sobre algunos fenómenos culturales en Nicaragua. Usa lo que has aprendido en este capítulo sobre Centroamérica, más tu propia experiencia, para contestar las preguntas que siguen la cita.

66In the other countries of Central America, newspapers are devoted largely to the reporting of international news and local traffic accidents, either because it is too dangerous to report on national issues (witness Guatemala) or because there is just not that much to say about the polity (as in Honduras). In Nicaragua, though, everything is a big deal—or at least an attempt is made to make it a big deal. Nicaraguans avidly read their newspapers, but they do not read them to find out what has happened, or what is going to happen. Naked information is gleaned from rumors, which spread unbelievably fast, perhaps because of the prevalence of large families and Nicaraguans' penchant for gab. Newspapers are read to see the puffy reactions, the official [one] and that of the opposition, to events. Revealingly, sometimes front-page news is simply a commentary on (usually a denial of) a rumor sweeping through Managua.**99**

Source: *My Car in Managua*

1. ¿Qué sabes de la situación política en los países mencionados en este texto (Guatemala, Honduras y Nicaragua)? ¿Por qué es peligroso o inútil escribir sobre la política en cada país?

2. ¿Qué papel juegan los rumores y los chismes en divulgar las noticias en Nicaragua? ¿Por qué crees que son tan importantes o frecuentes los rumores? ¿Es parecido en tu ciudad o región?

3. ¿En qué se parecen y se diferencian las ideas sobre los periódicos del autor de esta cita y lo que dice David en la **Entrevista 1?**

⬤ **p, t,** and **c/qu**

The consonants **p, t,** and **c** (the [k] sound, spelled **qu** before **i** and **e**) have similar pronunciations in English and Spanish, with one important difference. The English consonants are pronounced with a puff of air, which can be quite strong when the sound begins a stressed syllable. In Spanish, it is important to avoid this aspiration or puff of air if you want to have a native-like accent. Listen to the [p], [t], and [k] sounds as your instructor contrasts the following English and Spanish words. The vowels will be different as well, of course, but focus your attention on the consonants.

English (with Aspiration)	Spanish (with No Aspiration)
attack	**ataque**
capable	**capaz**
key	**¿quién?**
pan	**pan**
periodical	**periódico**
quad	**¿cuánto?**
too	**tú**

The *Manual de práctica* has activities to practice the material explained here.

▲ *Estos nicaragüenses se reúnen en el parque para mirar la televisión.*

● La política y la comunicación en Centroamérica

Los **ciudadanos** de Centroamérica han tenido una **historia** tumultuosa, llena de **injusticias** sociales y económicas y de **abusos** a los **derechos**[a] humanos.

En las **décadas** de los años 80 y 90 los **nicaragüenses,** los **guatemaltecos** y los **salvadoreños** en particular experimentaron **revoluciones, guerras civiles** y **guerrillas**[b] que causaron mucha destrucción y muchas **muertes.** Durante esos años, los **gobiernos** frecuentemente **suspendían** los derechos básicos —como **la libertad de palabra,**[c] **la libertad de prensa** y el derecho a reunirse— y se dificultaba la comunicación personal y pública.

▲ *En una manifestación en Centroamérica*

Buscando **estabilidad** política y protección para su familia y sí mismos, muchos centroamericanos salieron de su respectivo país en los años 80 y 90 como **refugiados** o **exiliados** políticos hacia otros lugares como México, Europa, el Canadá y los Estados Unidos. El **exilio,** para algunos, fue una oportunidad de atraer la atención de **la comunidad internacional** hacia la situación en Centroamérica. El libro *Me llamo Rigoberta Menchú,* por ejemplo, es **el testimonio** de una joven **indígena** guatemalteca sobre **las atrocidades** cometidas contra su gente. Este testimonio presentó una **imagen** de Centroamérica que tuvo gran impacto **en el extranjero.** Menchú ganó el **Premio Nobel de la Paz** en 1992, y su libro contribuyó en gran medida[d] a **difundir**[e] una idea positiva de las culturas indígenas de la región.

En los años 90, los diferentes grupos y **partidos políticos** comenzaron a dialogar para **resolver** los conflictos. Como resultado, se firmaron **pactos**[f] y se celebraron **elecciones.** Ahora los centroamericanos pueden informarse de los acontecimientos actuales por todos los medios de comunicación: radio, televisión, teléfono, periódico, Internet y otros, y es más fácil que expresen sus opiniones sin miedo.

el desinterés	indifference
el ejército	army
la manifestación	demonstration
influir (y) en	to influence

[a]*rights* [b]*guerrilla wars* [c]*libertad… freedom of speech* [d]*en… in great part* [e]*disseminate* [f]*truces*

Actividades

A. Definiciones. Di qué palabra o frase corresponde a las siguientes definiciones.

1. un acuerdo entre dos grupos que quieren terminar una guerra
2. un conflicto organizado entre dos o más grupos dentro de un país
3. un derecho que permite la expresión libre en los periódicos, la televisión u otros medios de comunicación
4. una época de diez años
5. el fin de la vida de una persona
6. un grupo de personas que tienen la misma ideología política
7. una persona que tiene que salir de su país por razones políticas
8. tener impacto

B. ¿Estás de acuerdo? Escoge la mejor palabra o expresión para completar cada oración. Luego, indica si estás de acuerdo o no con cada oración. Si no, trata de explicar por qué.

	ESTOY DE ACUERDO.	NO ESTOY DE ACUERDO.
1. Los (ciudadanos/extranjeros) en mi país han tenido estabilidad política.	☐	☐
2. Últimamente (*Recently*) los países de Centroamérica han tenido varios años de (guerra/paz).	☐	☐
3. Durante un período de inestabilidad política, es común suspender la libertad de (ejército/prensa).	☐	☐
4. Siempre se debe respetar (los derechos / la derecha) de los ciudadanos.	☐	☐
5. (La comunidad internacional / El prejuicio) siempre muestra interés por Centroamérica.	☐	☐
6. Las diferencias de opinión se (resuelven/ suspenden) si se respetan las libertades básicas.	☐	☐

C. Cultura e imagen. ¿Qué imagen de tu país se transmite en los medios de comunicación? ¿Qué pensaría (*would think*) un centroamericano que sólo ve las películas y los programas de televisión producidos en tu país? Escoge entre las siguientes posibilidades o añade otras que se te ocurran. Explica tu respuesta.

- Mi país es violento.
- Hay mucha diversidad (cultural, étnica, etcétera) en mi país.
- Mi país es muy avanzado en cuanto a la tecnología.
- Todos son iguales en mi país.
- Todo el mundo es rico.
- Los reportajes de la prensa son muy superficiales; no contienen mucha información relevante.
- El público no está al corriente de lo que pasa en el mundo.
- ¿ ?

D. Tus representantes políticos. ¿Qué esperas (*do you expect*) de los políticos que te representan? Completa las frases de la izquierda con las frases de la derecha para expresar tus opiniones. Puedes añadir otras ideas que se te ocurran. ¡OJO! Es necesario usar el subjuntivo en la cláusula subordinada.

CLÁUSULA PRINCIPAL		CLÁUSULA SUBORDINADA
1. Quiero que mis representantes…		comunicarse con nosotros
2. Prefiero que mis representantes…		conocer las leyes del país
		contestar mis cartas y llamadas
	+	decirnos la verdad
3. Insisto en que mis representantes…		pertenecer a mi partido
		respetar nuestros derechos
4. Les recomiendo a mis representantes que…		ser honestos y justos
		tener un sitio de Internet
		vivir en mi región
		¿ ?

E. Los efectos de la tecnología. Lee las siguientes oraciones y di si estás de acuerdo o no con cada una. Luego, con dos o tres compañeros/as, escribe una lista de ideas a favor o en contra de (*opposed to*) cada tema.

1. El correo electrónico es mejor que las cartas para mantenerse en contacto.
2. Va a haber menos conflictos entre los países gracias a la comunicación rápida entre todos los ciudadanos del mundo.
3. El Intenet permite que todos tengan acceso instantáneo a muchísima información.
4. La comunicación global borra (*erases*) la distinción cultural de los diferentes grupos del mundo.

Es verdad que la tecnología hace ▶ *la vida más fácil, pero al mismo tiempo la complica, ¿no crees?*

Entrevista 2

Claudia Bautista Nichola

«*Vivo en dos lugares: Los Ángeles, California, y San Salvador, El Salvador.*»

Nombre: Claudia

Apellidos: (1) Bautista (2) Nichola

Edad: 33 años

Nació en: San Salvador, El Salvador

You can watch this interview on the *Entrevistas* Video or Interactive CD-ROM or listen to the audio on the Online Learning Center (**www.mhhe.com/entrevistas2**).

Vocabulario útil

por la razón de	on account of	**después de haber**	after having left
por lo tanto	therefore	**salido**	
abiertamente	openly	**delitos**	crimes
lamento que haya	I regret that there may be		

Antes de ver

A. Una perspectiva histórica. Lee las siguientes oraciones e indica si se refieren más a la actualidad (el presente) o al pasado.

	ACTUALIDAD	PASADO
1. Muchos de los salvadoreños viajaron a los Estados Unidos durante la década de los 80.	☐	☐
2. Trato de mantenerme al corriente de lo que pasa.	☐	☐
3. No nos mandamos cartas porque se pierden las cosas; por lo tanto no usamos el correo.	☐	☐
4. Después de firmar el pacto de la paz, ya no (*no longer*) tenemos miedo.	☐	☐
5. Muchos criminales han regresado a El Salvador y han causado muchos delitos.	☐	☐

B. Predicciones. Lee las siguientes oraciones y adivina qué va a decir Claudia, escogiendo una de las palabras entre paréntesis.

1. Me mantengo en contacto por medio (de las cartas / del teléfono).
2. Hoy, muchos de los salvadoreños nos sentimos más (inseguros/ seguros) de hablar sobre la guerra.

---

3. Lamento que haya muchos problemas por razones (económicas/ filosóficas).
4. Espero que las cosas se (resuelvan/suspendan).

¡Veamos!

¿Acertaste?   Revisa tus respuestas para la **Actividad B** de **Antes de ver** para ver si adivinaste bien.

Después de ver

¿Cierto o falso?   Indica si las siguientes afirmaciones son ciertas o falsas, según Claudia.

	CIERTO	FALSO
1. Claudia mantiene contacto con la familia por correo electrónico.	☐	☐
2. Ella no está al corriente de los sucesos en El Salvador.	☐	☐
3. Claudia no mira la televisión para saber lo que pasa en su país.	☐	☐
4. Antes, los salvadoreños tenían miedo de hablar abiertamente de la política.	☐	☐
5. Claudia lamenta que haya violencia en El Salvador.	☐	☐

Piénsalo bien

Claudia habla de su vida después de salir de su país por razones políticas. Comenta este tema con dos o tres compañeros/as de clase, contestando las siguientes preguntas.

1. Claudia se refugió en los Estados Unidos a causa de la inestabilidad política en El Salvador. Imagina que tú estás en una situación parecida. ¿Te quedas en tu país o te vas? Explica el porqué de tu respuesta.
2. Claudia se mantiene en contacto con la familia en El Salvador por varios medios. Si tú estás lejos de tu familia, ¿cómo te mantienes en contacto con tus amigos y familiares?
3. Aunque ya no hay guerra en El Salvador, Claudia sigue viviendo en Los Ángeles. ¿Por qué crees que ella no ha regresado definitivamente (*for good*) a su país?
4. ¿Qué dice Claudia con respecto al futuro de su país? ¿Crees que su opinión sea justificada?
5. La comunidad salvadoreña en los Estados Unidos es muy grande, y muchas personas viven un tiempo en cada lugar. ¿Qué efectos puede tener este intercambio de personas e ideas en la cultura local de El Salvador? Menciona aspectos positivos y negativos.

Forma y función

13.3 The Subjunctive with Expressions of Doubt

In **Forma y función 13.2** you learned that the subjunctive is used in dependent clauses after verbs of will, volition, and influence in the main clause. The subjunctive is also used to indicate doubt or uncertainty about actions and states in clauses after expressions such as **es (im)probable que, es (im)posible que, dudo que, no creo que,** and so on.

Statement (Indicative)	Statement with Doubt/ Uncertainty (Subjunctive)	Translation
La gente prefiere a los artistas internacionales.	Es posible que la gente prefiera a los artistas internacionales.	It's possible that people prefer international artists.
Las telenovelas son los programas más populares.	Es probable que las telenovelas sean los programas más populares.	It's likely that soap operas are the most popular shows.
Los turistas aprecian los aspectos más finos de la cultura guatemalteca.	Dudo que los turistas aprecien los aspectos más finos de la cultura guatemalteca.	I doubt that tourists appreciate the finer details of Guatemalan culture.

Conversely, if the expression in the main clause indicates certainty (to the best of the speaker's knowledge), the dependent-clause verb must be in the indicative.

Statement (Indicative)	Statement Affirmed (Indicative)	Translation
Las películas influyen en el desarrollo de la cultura.	Es obvio (No dudo) que las películas influyen en el desarrollo de la cultura.	It's obvious (I don't doubt) that films influence the development of culture.

In affirmative sentences, the verbs **creer** and **pensar** are frequently used to report what one believes to be true and valid, and consequently must be followed by **que** + *indicative verb*. But when using these verbs in questions (**¿Crees que... ?**) or in the negative (**No creo que, No pienso que),** the speaker is expressing doubt about the action in the dependent clause; therefore, the dependent-clause verb must be in the subjunctive.*

Creo que los medios de comunicación **contribuyen** al desarollo de El Salvador.	*I think that the media contribute to the development of El Salvador.*
Pues yo **no creo que contribuyan** al desarrollo de la cultura.	*Well, I don't think they contribute to the development of the culture.*
¿**Crees que** los medios de comunicación **contribuyan** a la creación de la identidad nacional?	*Do you think that the media contribute to the creation of the national identity?*

Análisis estructural

¿Cuáles de las siguientes frases expresan duda? ¿Cuáles *no* expresan duda?

	INDICA DUDA. (SUBJUNTIVO)	NO INDICA DUDA. (INDICATIVO)
1. Creemos que…	☐	☐
2. Ella no duda que…	☐	☐
3. Es cierto que…	☐	☐
4. Es completamente obvio que…	☐	☐
5. Es imposible que…	☐	☐
6. Es probable que…	☐	☐
7. No creen que…	☐	☐
8. No es verdad que…	☐	☐

Actividades

A. La televisión en el siglo XXI. ¿Cuál va a ser el futuro de los medios de comunicación en el siglo XXI? Completa las siguientes oraciones usando la forma correcta de los verbos entre paréntesis. Luego, indica si estás de acuerdo con cada oración o no. **¡OJO!** Cuidado al escoger entre el subjuntivo y el indicativo.

	ESTOY DE ACUERDO.	NO ESTOY DE ACUERDO.
1. Creo que los estudios más importantes (ir) a mejorar la calidad de la programación.	☐	☐
2. No creo que nosotros (poder) limitar la violencia en la televisión.	☐	☐

---

* The exact usage of the indicative and subjunctive with **creer** and **pensar** in questions is a matter of great subtlety, and you may hear much variation among native speakers. For now, stick to this rule of thumb: in the affirmative, use the indicative after **creer** and **pensar;** in questions and negative sentences, use the subjunctive.

CAPÍTULO 13 • El mundo actual

	ESTOY DE ACUERDO.	NO ESTOY DE ACUERDO.

3. No es probable que (haber) más de 800 canales por cable. ☐ ☐

4. Dudo que (permitirse) la pornografía en la televisión. ☐ ☐

5. Va a ser imposible que (verse) los crímenes en el acto de ser cometida. ☐ ☐

6. Es cierto que los programas (representar) muchas ideas preconcebidas (*preconceived*). ☐ ☐

7. Es obvio que el dinero (hacer) un papel importante en la producción de las películas. ☐ ☐

8. Es probable que la televisión (tener) menos importancia que las computadoras. ☐ ☐

B. ¿Qué imagen proyectamos?   Los siguientes temas representan comentarios de diferentes centroamericanos sobre los Estados Unidos y Norteamérica en general; están basados en la imagen proyectada en los medios de comunicación. Pero, ¿es una imagen fiel (*accurate*)? Da tu opinión sobre los siguientes temas, usando las expresiones de la lista. Explica el porqué de tus respuestas.

Creo que…   No creo que…
Es cierto que…   No es cierto que…
Es obvio que…   Dudo que…

1. Los Estados Unidos es un país violento.
2. Hay mucha diversidad cultural en los Estados Unidos.
3. Los norteamericanos son muy avanzados en cuanto a la tecnología.
4. Todos los ciudadanos son iguales en los Estados Unidos.
5. Los norteamericanos tienen mucho dinero.
6. Existen muchas oportunidades de trabajo en Norteamérica.
7. Los padres norteamericanos no les enseñan a sus hijos los valores fundamentales.
8. Los jóvenes norteamericanos no respetan a los mayores.

C. Entrevista: Imágenes de nuestra sociedad.   Habla con un compañero / una compañera de clase para saber sus opiniones sobre los siguientes temas. **¡OJO!** Cuidado con el uso del indicativo y del subjuntivo en las respuestas.

1. ¿Es verdad que muchas mujeres trabajan fuera de la casa?
2. ¿Es cierto que todos los norteamericanos tienen armas de fuego (*firearms*) en casa?
3. ¿Crees que la televisión contribuya a la violencia en nuestra sociedad?
4. ¿Es importante que los niños miren programas educativos en la televisión?
5. ¿Es posible que las películas puedan cambiar los valores sociales de un país?

13.4 The Subjunctive with Expressions of Emotion

Since subjectivity is the hallmark of the subjunctive mood, it is not surprising that the subjunctive is required after expressions that indicate a speaker's subjective or emotional reactions to a statement.

Statement (Indicative)	Subjective Reaction to Statement (Subjunctive)	Translations
Ya no quieren vivir en El Salvador.	**Es triste que ya no quieran vivir en El Salvador.**	It's sad that they no longer want to live in El Salvador.
Va a seguir así.	**Siento que vaya a seguir así.**	I'm sorry that it is going to continue like that.
El exilio tiene un impacto fuerte en la cultura local.	**Lamento que el exilio tenga un impacto fuerte en la cultura local.**	I lament (the fact) that exile has a strong impact on the local culture.

There are many more expressions of emotion that require the subjunctive in a dependent clause. You cannot memorize all of them, but as you become more familiar with Spanish you will learn to recognize which expressions take the subjunctive just from the "feel of it." Here are some of the most common expressions of emotion that cue the subjunctive.

Es importante que…	*It's important that . . .*
Es mejor que…	*It's better that . . .*
Espero que…	*I hope that . . .*
Me gusta que…	*I like (the fact) that . . .*
Me sorprende que…	*It surprises me that . . .*
Siento que…	*I'm sorry that . . .*
Es lamentable que…	*It's too bad that . . .*
Es una lástima que…	*It's a shame that . . .*
Me molesta que…	*It bothers me that . . .*
Temo que…	*I'm afraid that . . . / I fear that . . .*

Note that the subjunctive is used only if the subject in the dependent clause is *not* the same as that of the main clause. If there is no **que**, the second verb in the sentence is in the infinitive. With impersonal expressions (**es triste, es necesario, es lamentable,** and so on), if the subject of the dependent clause is not specified, the infinitive is used.

Prefieren usar ropa común.	*They prefer to wear mainstream clothing.*
Prefieren que yo **use** ropa común.	*They prefer that I wear mainstream clothing.*

| Es triste perder eso. | *It's sad to lose that.* |
| Es triste que perdamos eso. | *It's sad that we are losing that.* |

Análisis estructural

Identifica el sujeto lógico de los verbos subrayados en las siguientes oraciones.

1. Espero ver muchos espectáculos folclóricos durante mi viaje a Guatemala.
2. Espero que tengamos la oportunidad de ver a unos artistas nacionales.
3. Es una lástima que los indígenas guatemaltecos no puedan mantener su cultura.
4. Me molesta que los turistas no respeten las costumbres locales.
5. El gobierno quiere controlar la imagen nacional que proyectan los medios de comunicación.

Actividades

A. ¿Cómo reaccionas?   Oyes las siguientes noticias en la radio. ¿Cuál es tu reacción?

+	⟵————————⟶	–
Me gusta que	Me sorprende que	Es lamentable que
Me alegro de		Es triste que
(*I'm happy*) que		Siento que
Espero que		Me molesta que

MODELO   El presidente renuncia a su puesto. →
¡Me sorprende que el presidente renuncie a su puesto!

1. El gobierno va a limitar la libertad de expresión en el Internet.
2. Una nueva película con mi actor favorito sale en el verano.
3. La universidad ya no ofrece clases de periodismo (*journalism*).
4. El canal de televisión en mi ciudad reduce los noticieros.
5. Los actores de la telenovela más popular se declaran en huelga.
6. El gobierno de Guatemala contribuye con millones de quetzales (*Guatemalan currency*) a un fondo (*fund*) para grupos indígenas.

B. La vida en el exilio.   Completa las siguientes oraciones con ideas lógicas, según la perspectiva de una persona que tuvo que salir de su país por razones políticas.

1. Lamento que las condiciones en mi país…
2. Espero que en el futuro…
3. Es importante que los extranjeros que visitan mi país…
4. Temo que en el futuro mis hijos…

C. Entrevista: Cambios culturales. Hazle las siguientes preguntas a un compañero / una compañera de clase para saber sus actitudes sobre la cultura actual de su país.

1. Cuando invitas a tus amigos o parientes a casa, ¿prefieres preparar platos nacionales o internacionales? ¿Son los mismos platos que preparaban tus padres o tus abuelos?
2. ¿Quieres que la televisión presente más programas educativos (documentales, deportivos, etcétera)?
3. En tu opinión, ¿es triste o es mejor que la cultura actual sea diferente a la de tus abuelos/antepasados?
4. Para ti, ¿es importante que tus hijos conozcan todas las obras más importantes de las generaciones anteriores (libros, obras de arte, películas, etcétera)? ¿Por qué sí o por qué no?

Señas culturales

▲ *Una mujer guatemalteca con su ropa típica*

Los tejidos y bordados[a] mayas, decorados con diseños geométricos, florales y de animales, han sido una expresión artística desde hace más de dos milenios. Los trajes típicos sirven para identificar tanto una región o un pueblo particular como el estatus social de una persona.

El conjunto[b] de ropa femenina incluye una blusa multicolor que se llama **huipil,** una falda de un solo color o estampado,[c] un cinturón —o **faja**— tejido o bordado y un adorno para la cabeza o el pelo llamado **listón.**

Los hombres llevan pantalones cortos o camisa y pantalones teñidos[d] de una tela llamada **jaspe,** una corta saya[e] de lana o **rodillera,** sobretodo[f] de lana negra —llamado **gabán**— y sombrero.

¿Qué significado tienen ciertos tipos o ciertas marcas de ropa en tu país? ¿Visten los miembros de tu familia ropa que refleja su país de origen?

[a]tejidos... *textiles and embroidery* [b]*combination* [c]*embossed* [d]*dyed* [e]*kilt* [f]*robe*

Lectura

Sobre la lectura   En los últimos años se han visto cambios sociales dramáticos en Centroamérica y estos cambios se reflejan en los medios de comunicación. La siguiente lectura es una adaptación de un artículo sobre una nueva serie televisiva en Nicaragua.

Antes de leer

A. El título.   El título de un artículo frecuentemente revela muchos detalles del contenido. A continuación hay cuatro oraciones **falsas**. ¿Qué pistas (*clues*) en el título te indican por qué no son verdaderas?

1. Este programa va a tratar los problemas que experimentan las personas mayores.
2. El programa tiene que ver con varios países centroamericanos.
3. Muy pocas personas van a ver *Sexto sentido* porque el Canal 2 no tiene muchos televidentes.
4. El programa va a influir en la sociedad nicaragüense.

B. Cognados falsos.   Ya has estudiado muchos ejemplos de cognados, palabras españolas que se parecen a una palabra inglesa en su forma y en su significado, por ejemplo, **construcción** = *construction*. Los cognados falsos son palabras españolas que se parecen a una palabra inglesa en su forma pero **no** en su significado. Utilizando el contexto para ayudarte, adivina el significado de los siguientes cognados falsos subrayados.

1. los conflictos en la universidad y el <u>colegio</u>
2. Este país tiene la tasa de <u>embarazos</u> de adolescentes más alta de Centroamérica.
3. La serie <u>pretende</u> que los chavalos y chavalas (chicos y chicas) decidan por sí mismos/as y tomen el control de su vida.
4. la gente joven que ha <u>experimentado</u> avances sexuales
5. La opinión pública nica (nicaragüense) muestra gran interés por esta serie <u>juvenil</u>.
6. El proyecto fue <u>impulsado</u> por *Puntos de Encuentro,* una organización feminista.

C. Definiciones.   Adivina el significado de las siguientes palabras o frases. Luego, comprueba tus definiciones con un diccionario. ¿Puedes definirlas en español?

1. los altibajos
2. el derecho al trabajo
3. la anticoncepción
4. las relaciones equitativas entre hombres y mujeres
5. la violencia intrafamiliar
6. el derecho a decidir
7. los mitos sexuales
8. los avances sexuales no deseados
9. los departamentos del país

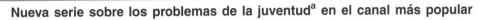

Nueva serie sobre los problemas de la juventud[a] en el canal más popular

Sociedad civil nicaragüense irrumpe en[b] la televisión con *Sexto sentido*

Esquivando[c] al conservadurismo, la sociedad civil nicaragüense inaugura un espacio masivo de comunicación con la juventud a través de *Sexto sentido: Es tu vida, ¡atrévete!,*[d] serie televisiva que se transmite por el Canal 2, el de mayor audiencia y cobertura en el país centroamericano. La opinión pública nica muestra gran interés por esta serie juvenil que tocará,[e] a lo largo de dos temporadas, los problemas para este grupo de población.

Con un equipo profesional seleccionado de entre los mejores del país, *Sexto sentido* relata los altibajos de tres hombres y tres mujeres jóvenes. Los personajes principales son de diferentes lugares de Nicaragua, pretendiendo buscar un equilibrio[f] no solamente centrado en la vida de los jóvenes capitalinos, sino también de los departamentos y de diversas condiciones económicas.

La historia se desarrolla en una casa donde se encuentran los seis personajes, enfrentados a[g] situaciones diversas, problemas entre adolescentes y jóvenes que van desde conflictos en la universidad y el colegio hasta relaciones entre los amigos y la solidaridad.

Algunos temas concretos son la violencia intrafamiliar, el derecho a decidir, el alcoholismo, la discriminación, el derecho al trabajo, la anticoncepción, las relaciones con los padres, la preparación profesional, la preferencia sexual, las relaciones equitativas entre hombres y mujeres, así como el aborto y algunos mitos sexuales.

Existe en Nicaragua una gran necesidad de abordar[h] el tema de la sexualidad de los adolescentes, ya que el país tiene la tasa de embarazo de adolescentes más alta de Centroamérica (año 2000). Además, evidencia reciente sugiere que hay un alto porcentaje de gente joven que ha experimentado avances sexuales no deseados o que han tenido relaciones sexuales sin protección.

La serie pretende que los chavalos y chavalas[i] decidan por sí mismos/as y tomen el control de su vida. Según los productores: «Ése es el lema,[j] tomar el control de tu vida, no tomar lo que las personas decidan por vos y lo que es mejor para vos, sino que vos decidás por vos lo que considerás que es mejor para tu vida, tomando en cuenta los riesgos que significan tener el control de tu vida y tomar tus propias decisiones. La idea no es que se lancen a actuar[k] sin pensar en las consecuencias de los actos.»

El proyecto fue impulsado por *Puntos de Encuentro*, organización feminista que desde hace once años se dedica a la comunicación y educación desde una perspectiva multicultural.

[Página principal]   [Noticias del día]   [Contáctenos]

---

[a]*youth* [b]*irrumpe… invades* [c]*Avoiding* [d]*take a chance! (go for it!)* [e]*will deal with* [f]*balance* [g]*enfrentados… faced with* [h]*broach*
[i]*chavalos… guys and gals (colloquial)* [j]*motto* [k]*se… they act rashly*

CAPÍTULO 13 • El mundo actual

Después de leer

A. ¿Entendiste?   Contesta las siguientes preguntas, según la lectura.

1. ¿Cómo es la sociedad nicaragüense?
2. ¿Crees que muchas personas vean *Sexto sentido*?
3. ¿Cuánto tiempo va a durar la serie?
4. ¿Dónde se desarrolla la historia?
5. ¿Cuántos personajes principales hay en la serie? ¿Cómo son los personajes?
6. ¿Qué tipos de situaciones van a enfrentar los personajes?

B. El título.   ¿Qué conexión hay entre el título y el contenido de esta serie? Explica la importancia de cada parte del título, usando detalles del artículo.

Parte del título	Importancia
Sexto sentido:	
Es tu vida,	
¡atrévete!	

C. Comparaciones.   Contesta las siguientes preguntas con un compañero / una compañera.

1. ¿Existen en tu país programas parecidos a *Sexto sentido*? De ser que sí (*If so*), ¿qué temas tratan?
2. ¿Qué tono tienen estos programas: cómico, irónico, serio, etcétera?
3. ¿Crees que la tele sea un medio eficaz para tratar problemas sociales de los jóvenes?
4. ¿Son universales los temas presentados en *Sexto sentido* o son específicos a Nicaragua?
5. En general, ¿crees que los jóvenes de tu país tomen sus propias decisiones o es que siguen las decisiones de otras personas como sus padres, profesores, curas (*priests*), etcétera?
6. ¿Qué problemas enfrentan los jóvenes de tu país que no se mencionan en este artículo?

D. Una nueva serie.   Trabaja con dos o tres compañeros/as, imaginando que ustedes son los productores de una nueva serie parecida a *Sexto sentido*. En esta nueva serie, tres jóvenes nicaragüenses y tres jóvenes norteamericanos van a convivir en una casa por unos meses. Como grupo, tienen que decidir lo siguiente:

- dónde queda la casa
- el sexo y la edad de cada persona
- la mezcla de personalidades de los seis personajes
- los problemas que probablemente el grupo va a enfrentar

¡OJO! Cuidado con el uso del subjuntivo en expresiones como **dudamos que…** , **es necesario que…** , **es posible que…** , **es probable que…** , etcétera.

PORTAFOLIO CULTURAL

Redacción

Un *mail* de Panamá. Imagina que has recibido un *mail* de un amigo / una amiga de Panamá que ve muchos de los programas de la televisión norteamericana que se difunden allí. Él/Ella te dice que no comprende algunos de los aspectos de la vida norteamericana que ha visto en la televisión. Escríbele una carta de respuesta en la que le describes lo que, en tu opinión, es un retrato más realista de tu país. Sigue los pasos en el *Manual de práctica* para elaborar tu respuesta.

Exploración

Investigación cultural. Busca más información sobre Centroamérica en la biblioteca, en el *Entrevistas* Online Learning Center **(www.mhhe.com/entrevistas2)** o en otros sitios del Internet y preséntala a la clase. El *Manual de práctica* contiene más ideas para tu presentación.

Léxico activo

EL PERIÓDICO EN LÍNEA

el **anuncio**	advertisement
el **crucigrama**	crossword puzzle
el **editorial**	opinion page
el **encabezado**	headline
el/la **lector(a)**	reader
el **obituario**	obituary
la **noticia**	piece of news; *pl.* news
la **portada**	front page
la **prensa**	press
el **pronóstico del tiempo**	weather report
el **reportaje**	report
el/la **reportero/a**	reporter
la **reseña**	review
la **tira cómica**	comic strip, cartoon
abonarse	to subscribe
estar al corriente	to be up-to-date
estar desinformado/a de	to be uninformed about
estar enterado/a de	to know about
exponer (*irreg.*)	to report, expose
mantenerse informado/a	to stay informed
publicar (qu)	to publish
actual(mente)	current(ly)

LA TELEVISIÓN Y EL CINE

el **acontecimiento**	event, happening
el **canal**	channel
el **chisme**	bit of gossip; *pl.* gossip

el **cine**	movie theater; the movies
el **concurso**	game show
el **desastre (natural)**	(natural) disaster
el **documental**	documentary
el **DVD**	DVD; DVD player
la **mentira**	lie
el **noticiero**	newscast
la **película (cómica, de acción, de amor, de horror)**	(comedy, action, romance, horror) film, movie
el **programa (educativo)**	(educational) program
el **suceso**	event, happening
la **telenovela**	soap opera
el/la **televidente**	TV viewer
la **televisión por antena parabólica**	satellite TV
la **televisión por cable**	cable TV
la **verdad**	truth
el **video**	video; VCR
dudar	to doubt
lamentar	to lament, regret
mentir (ie, i)	to lie
abrumador(a)	overwhelming
chocante	shocking
cómico/a	funny, comical
controvertido/a	controversial
dudoso/a	doubtful
escandaloso/a	scandalous

lamentable	lamentable, regretful	**la guerrilla**	guerilla war
ridículo/a	ridiculous	**la historia**	history
televisivo/a	television (*adj.*)	**la imagen** (*pl.* **imágenes**)	image
		el/la indígena	indigenous person, native

LA COMUNICACIÓN ELECTRÓNICA

el **café cibernético**	Internet café	**la injusticia**	injustice
el *chat*	chatroom	**la libertad de palabra/prensa**	freedom of speech / the press
el **correo electrónico**	e-mail	**la manifestación**	demonstration
el **enlace**	link	**la muerte**	death
el **Internet**	Internet	el **pacto**	truce, pact
el *mail*	e-mail (message)	el **partido político**	political party
el **mensaje**	message	el **Premio Nobel de la Paz**	Nobel Peace Price
		el/la **refugiado/a**	refugee
chatear	to chat (online)	**la revolución**	revolution
conectarse	to get connected	el **testimonio**	testimony
estar conectado/a	to be connected		
hacer clic (en)	to click (on)	**difundir**	to disseminate
navegar (gu)	to surf (*the Internet*)	**influir (y) en**	to influence
platicar (qu)	to chat (*in general*)	**resolver (ue)**	to resolve
		suspender	to suspend

LA POLÍTICA Y LA COMUNICACIÓN

el **abuso**	abuse	**guatemalteco/a**	Guatamalan
la **atrocidad**	atrocity	**nicaragüense**	Nicaraguan
la **comunidad internacional**	international community	**salvadoreño/a**	Salvadoran
la **década**	decade		

Repaso: el/la ciudadano/a, en el extranjero

LENGUAJE FUNCIONAL: PARA EXPRESAR REACCIONES

los **derechos**	rights	**¡Qué** + *adj.*!	What a + *adj.*!
el **desinterés**	indifference	**¡Qué** + *noun* + **más/tan** + *adj.*!	What a/an + *adj.* + *noun*!
el **ejército**	army	**¡Qué barbaridad!**	How awful!
las **elecciones**	elections	**¡Qué bien!**	Great! How wonderful!
la **estabilidad**	stability	**¡Qué escándalo!**	What a scandal!
el/la **exilado/a**	exile (*person*)		
el **exilio**	exile		
el **gobierno**	government		
la **guerra civil**	civil war		

Grupos minoritarios y mayoritarios

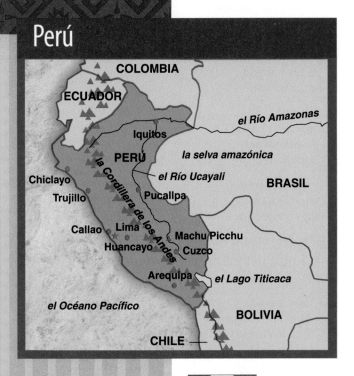

Perú

COLOMBIA

ECUADOR

el Río Amazonas

Iquitos

PERÚ

la selva amazónica

la Cordillera de los Andes

el Río Ucayali

BRASIL

Chiclayo

Pucallpa

Trujillo

Callao

Lima

Machu Picchu

Huancayo

Cuzco

Arequipa

el Lago Titicaca

el Océano Pacífico

BOLIVIA

CHILE

Cultura

◆ Ethnic Groups: Recipe for Diversity Within a Country

◆ Stereotypes: A Necessary Evil?

◆ **Señas culturales: Machu Picchu**

Lengua

◆ Peruvian Society; Ethnic Groups

◆ Societal Problems and Solutions

◆ The Subjunctive with Noun Antecedents (14.1)

◆ Comparisons (14.2)

◆ The Future Tense (14.3)

◆ The Subjunctive with Future Actions (14.4)

Perú				Conquista de los incas por Francisco Pizarro				Independencia de España		
		El Imperio inca								
hasta el siglo XVI	hasta 1531	1500–1600	1531–1533	1534		1600–1750	1776–1783	1821	1846–1848
Varias tribus indígenas habitan en Norteamérica		Exploración española de Norteamérica		Jacques Cartier reclama para Francia el Canadá		Fundación de las colonias británicas en Norteamérica	Guerra de Independencia en los EE. UU.		Guerra Mexicano-Americana

Los Estados Unidos y el Canadá

Instantánea

ORIGEN DEL NOMBRE

Perú: incierto; posiblemente de las palabras indígenas **Beru** (nombre de una tribu), **Pelu** (nombre de un río) o **Biru** (nombre de una región del país)

POBLACIÓN

27.083.400

LENGUAS

El español y el quechua (oficiales), el aimara

◀ *«El candelabro» es uno de los diseños misteriosos que se encuentran cerca de Nasca, Perú.*

For additional practice, check out the *Manual de práctica,* the Interactive CD-ROM, and the Online Learning Center (**www.mhhe.com/entrevistas2**)!

1879–1883	1898	1952	1982	1990	1992	1994	1996	2000	2001
Lucha sin éxito contra Chile en la Guerra del Pacífico				Alberto Fujimori gana las elecciones	Fujimori disuelve el Congreso, suspende la constitución e impone la censura	Rebeldes del grupo Túpac Amaru toman la residencia del embajador japonés en Lima, tomando 72 rehenes		Caída del gobierno de Fujimori después de elecciones fraudulentas	Elección de Alejandro Toledo, primer presidente de origen indígena
	Guerra Hispano-Americana	Puerto Rico se hace Estado Libre Asociado de los EE. UU.	El Canadá se separa legalmente de Inglaterra			Tratado de Libre Comercio entre los EE. UU., el Canadá y México			

● La sociedad peruana

Los grupos étnicos

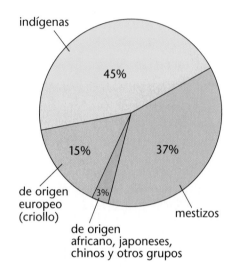

indígenas

45%

15%

3%

37%

de origen
europeo
(criollo)

de origen
africano, japoneses,
chinos y otros grupos

mestizos

La mayoría de los **peruanos** es **indígena** quechua y aimara.

Entre los indígenas, el grupo más **numeroso** es de origen **incaico.**

Los mestizos son una mezcla de origen **europeo** e indígena.

Los criollos y los mestizos son **minorías,** pero juntos controlan el país.

Los asiáticos (japoneses y chinos) forman un grupo **minoritario**
importante.

Las regiones

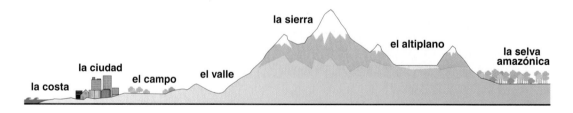

la sierra

el altiplano

la selva
amazónica

la ciudad

el campo

el valle

la costa

¿Cómo se distinguen los grupos étnicos?

el habla

el vestuario

la gastronomía

el acento	accent
la costumbre	custom, practice
la creencia (tradicional)	(traditional) belief
el nivel de educación	level of education
la religión	religion
el territorio ancestral	ancestral land
la tradición	tradition

Actividades

A. Definiciones. Di la palabra o expresión que corresponde a cada definición.

1. la región donde ha vivido un grupo durante siglos
2. la cocina típica de un grupo étnico
3. las prácticas culturales de un grupo
4. la manera de pronunciar las palabras
5. la región cerca del mar
6. los habitantes originales de una región
7. el grupo más grande dentro de una sociedad
8. una persona de origen europeo e indígena

B. La geografía peruana. Usando el mapa de Perú al principio del capítulo, di dónde están los dos lugares, según el modelo.

MODELO   Lima/Arequipa →
Lima está en la costa, pero Arequipa está en la sierra, al sureste de Lima.

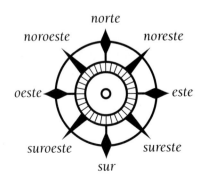

Grupos minoritarios y mayoritarios • CAPÍTULO 14

1. Lima/Cuzco
2. Iquitos / Machu Picchu
3. Chiclayo/Huancayo
4. Lima/Trujillo
5. el Lago Titicaca / el Río Amazonas

C. Diferencias regionales. Trabaja con un compañero / una compañera para contestar las siguientes preguntas sobre las diferencias regionales de tu país.

1. ¿Cuáles son las regiones culturales de tu país?
2. ¿Corresponden a regiones geográficas?
3. ¿Se diferencian los habitantes de las montañas de los de la costa? ¿En qué aspectos?
4. ¿En qué se diferencian los habitantes de las ciudades de los de las zonas rurales (del campo)?

D. Símbolos de identidad. Cada grupo cultural o social tiene sus propias símbolos de identidad. ¿Cómo se reconocen los siguientes grupos? Considera las categorías indicadas, y añade otro grupo que se te ocurra.

	El habla	El vestuario	Las costumbres	Las creencias
1. un(a) intelectual de Nueva York				
2. un(a) aristócrata de Boston				
3. un(a) tablista (*surfer*) de California				
4. un(a) canadiense de Quebec				
5. un programador / una programadora de computadoras				
6. ¿ ?				

E. Estereotipos. Para cada símbolo de identidad que identificaste en la **Actividad D,** contesta las siguientes preguntas con la ayuda de un compañero / una compañera.

1. ¿Qué función tienen las costumbres, el habla, las creencias, etcétera, dentro de cada grupo? Es decir, ¿por qué es un símbolo importante para las personas de cada grupo?
2. ¿Crees que sea algo consciente o inconsciente? ¿Por qué?
3. ¿Qué costumbres, acentos, etcétera, existen en tu propio grupo cultural que sirven la misma función?
4. ¿Crees que todos los miembros del grupo compartan esta característica o es un estereotipo? ¿Entiendes esta característica de manera superficial o conoces el contexto del uso entre los miembros del grupo?

Sandra Montiel Nemes

«Para entender esto hay que saber que el Perú es muy rico geográficamente.»

Nombre: Sandra

Apellidos: (1) Montiel (2) Nemes

Edad: 34 años

Nació en: Lima, Perú

You can watch this interview on the *Entrevistas* Video or Interactive CD-ROM or listen to the audio on the Online Learning Center **(www.mhhe.com/entrevistas2)**.

Vocabulario útil

coloridas	colorful	**aislados**	isolated
anchas	wide	**tribus** *f.*	tribes
una encima de otra	one on top of another	**cazan**	they hunt
cultivaban	(they) used to grow	**pescar (qu)**	to fish

Antes de ver

Buscar información. Usa la información al principio de este capítulo (página 404) para contestar las siguientes preguntas.

1. ¿Qué grupo étnico puede considerarse como mayoritario en Perú? ¿Qué grupos son minoritarios?
2. ¿Cuáles son las divisiones geográficas más importantes de Perú?

¡Veamos!

¿Qué dijo? Primero, lee las siguientes preguntas. Después, mientras ves la entrevista, contéstalas, según lo que dice Sandra.

1. ¿Está de acuerdo la información de Sandra con otra información sobre Perú que has leído en este capítulo?
2. ¿En qué se diferencia la ropa de los que viven en la costa de la de los que viven en la selva o en la sierra?

Después de ver

A. Diferencias regionales. Lee las siguientes oraciones e indica a qué región de Perú corresponden.

	SIERRA	SELVA	COSTA
1. Mucha gente es indígena.	☐	☐	☐
2. La gente vive en tribus cerca del río.	☐	☐	☐
3. Las mujeres llevan faldas coloridas.	☐	☐	☐
4. Está junto al desierto.	☐	☐	☐
5. Los hombres llevan chullo.	☐	☐	☐
6. Comen lo que pescan y cazan.	☐	☐	☐
7. Se come comida china y japonesa.	☐	☐	☐

B. ¿Existen todavía? ¿Hay grupos en tu país que todavía sigan costumbres tradicionales? Describe los siguientes aspectos de los grupos que conozcas.

- principios económicos (el trueque [*barter*], organizaciones agrícolas, etcétera)
- vestuario tradicional
- comidas especiales regionales o étnicas
- prácticas o creencias religiosas

▲ *Estos indígenas llevan el vestuario típico de la sierra peruana (Lima, Perú).*

• 14.1 The Subjunctive with Noun Antecedents

In **Capítulo 13,** you learned many main-clause expressions that require a subjunctive verb form in the dependent clause; in each case the main-clause phrase was a verb (e.g., **quiero**) or an impersonal expression (e.g., **es necesario**). But what if the dependent clause follows (and describes) a *noun*? Not surprisingly, if the speaker views this noun as nonexistent or indefinite, Spanish uses a subjunctive verb form in the dependent clause to convey this nuance.

	NOUN	DEPENDENT CLAUSE	
No hay	costumbres	que **se remonten** a los incas.	*There are no customs that date back to the Incas.*

In the preceding sentence, the dependent clause **que se remonten...** describes the noun antecedent **costumbres.** The dependent-clause verb is in the subjunctive (**se remonten,** from **remontarse**) because the speaker used **No hay** in the main clause, thus declaring the noun antecedent as nonexistent in his/her mind.

Contrast the preceding example with the following one.

	NOUN	DEPENDENT CLAUSE	
Hay muchas	costumbres	que **se remontan** a los incas.	*There are many customs that date back to the Incas.*

Here, by using the phrase **Hay muchas,** the speaker shows that he/she believes that the noun antecedent **costumbres** *does* exist. Thus, the dependent-clause verb is in the indicative **(se remontan)** and *not* in the subjunctive.

The use of negative indefinite expressions such as **nada, nadie,** and **ningún/ninguna** in a main clause will also trigger use of the subjunctive in a dependent clause, because these terms imply nonexistent entities.

No tengo **ningún amigo** que **sepa** hablar quechua.	*I don't have a single friend who knows how to speak Quechua.*
No veo a **nadie** aquí que **venga** de la costa.	*I don't see anyone here who comes from the coast.*

When the positive indefinite expressions **algo, alguien,** and **algún/alguna** appear in a main clause, they may or may not trigger use of the subjunctive in a dependent clause. In general, if the speaker doubts or denies the existence of the indefinite entity (as in a question), the dependent verb is in the subjunctive. Otherwise, the indicative is used.

| ¿Conoces a **alguien** que **trabaje** en la sierra? | *Do you know anyone who works in the mountains?* |
| Sí, conozco a **alguien** que **trabaja** en el Parque Nacional Manú. | *Yes, I know someone who works in Manú National Park.* |

The personal **a** is always used when **alguien** and **nadie** are objects of the verb, but it is *not* used with indefinite or nonexistent direct object nouns.

| Busco **un señor** que **sepa** hablar quechua. | *I'm looking for a man who knows how to speak Quechua. (I'm not sure if such a person exists.)* |
| Busco *al* **señor** que **sabe** hablar quechua. | *I'm looking for the man who knows how to speak Quechua. (I know he exists.)* |

Análisis estructural

Analiza las siguientes oraciones, indicando estos aspectos.

[ ]	dependent clause
ind./subj.	dependent-clause verb in indicative or subjunctive
*	noun antecedent that cues use of the subjunctive in the dependent clause

MODELO No hay ningún grupo que tenga raíces indígenas. →

        No hay <u>ningún grupo</u>   [que   <u>tenga</u>   raíces indígenas].

                      *   subj.

1. Aquí no tenemos mujeres que lleven hasta ocho faldas.
2. En la costa preparan comidas que vienen de tradiciones diferentes.
3. Pero en la sierra no hay platos que tengan influencia extranjera.
4. No conozco a ningún indígena que viva en la ciudad.
5. Tampoco hay gente de origen africano que trabaje en las minas de las sierras.
6. Mi amigo me presentó (*introduced*) a un hombre que sabe mucho de las tradiciones incaicas.

Actividades

A. La gastronomía peruana. Completa estos comentarios sobre la gastronomía peruana con la forma apropiada (indicativo o subjuntivo) de los verbos entre paréntesis.

1. Los peruanos cultivan muchas variedades de papas que no (existir) en otros países.
2. ¿Conoces algún plato que (prepararse) en Perú?
3. No hay ninguna comida indígena que te (hacer) daño (*harms*).
4. En la televisión he visto programas que te (enseñar) a cocinar platos japoneses.
5. En la costa no se venden mariscos que (ser) de mala calidad.
6. Queremos probar las diferentes especies de maíz que (cultivarse) en la sierra.

B. Oraciones incompletas.   Combina los siguientes elementos para formar oraciones completas, añadiendo las palabras necesarias. **¡OJO!** Cuidado con el uso del indicativo y del subjuntivo.

1. ¿tú **/** conocer **/** a alguien **/** que **/** hablar **/** quechua?
2. mi papá **/** tener **/** parientes **/** que **/** vivir **/** en la sierra
3. yo **/** pensar cocinar **/** un plato **/** que **/** venir **/** de la costa
4. en la ciudad **/** nosotros **/** no celebrar **/** costumbres que **/** ser **/** incaico
5. esa familia **/** buscar **/** una casa **/** que **/** estar **/** cerca del centro

C. Entrevista: Las personas que conoces.   Entrevista a un compañero / una compañera para saber la siguiente información.

¿Conoces a alguien que…

1. tenga un acento diferente? ¿Por qué tiene ese acento? ¿Es de una región específica o de otro país? ¿Te gusta su acento?
2. se vista con ropa tradicional? ¿Cómo es esa ropa?
3. prepare recetas de sus antepasados? ¿Cómo son las comidas que prepara? ¿En qué ocasiones las prepara?
4. trabaje en el mismo lugar (la misma profesión) que sus padres o abuelos? ¿Le gusta su trabajo? ¿Crees que la próxima generación también ejerza (*will practice*) esa carrera?

⬤ 14.2 Comparisons

Throughout this text you have been comparing and contrasting Hispanic and North American cultures. This section presents a summary of the language you have used to carry out these important linguistic functions.

Unequal Comparisons

To make unequal comparisons of nouns, adjectives, adverbs, and verbs, use the constructions **más… que** and **menos… que.**

NOUNS

Hay **más** indígenas **que** europeos en Perú.	*There are more indigenous people than Europeans in Peru.*
Perú tiene **menos** chinos **que** japoneses.	*Peru has fewer Chinese people than Japanese.*

ADJECTIVES

Perú es **más** grande **que** Ecuador.	*Peru is larger than Ecuador.*

ADVERBS

Gustavo habla **más** rápidamente **que** tú.	*Gustavo speaks more rapidly than you do.*

VERBS

Pero habla **menos que** tú.*	*But he talks less than you do.*

---

* Note that when comparing verbs, nothing comes between **más/menos** and **que.**

A few adjectives and adverbs have irregular comparative forms.

mayor (*older*)	Mi hermana es **mayor que** yo.	*My sister is older than I am.*
menor (*younger*)	Mi tía es **menor que** mi madre.	*My aunt is younger than my mother.*
bueno (*adj.*) → mejor	Esta receta peruana es **mejor que** la otra.	*This Peruvian recipe is better than the other one.*
bien (*adv.*) → mejor	Muchos niños indígenas hablan español **mejor que** sus padres.	*Many indigenous children speak Spanish better than their parents.*
malo (*adj.*) → peor	La discriminación es **peor** en las grandes ciudades.	*Discrimination is worse in large cities.*
mal (*adv.*) → peor	Esa quena suena **peor que** la otra.	*That Andean flute sounds worse than the other one.*

Use the expression **más/menos de** when a number follows.

Hay **más de cinco** grupos étnicos en nuestra ciudad.

There are more than five ethnic groups in our city.

Menos del cuatro por ciento de la población es de origen asiático.

Less than four percent of the population is of Asian origin.

Equal Comparisons

To make equal comparisons of nouns, use the construction **tanto/a/os/as... como.**

No tienen **tanto** dinero **como** nosotros.

They don't have as much money as we do.

No hay **tantos** problemas allí **como** aquí.

There aren't as many problems there as here.

Este libro de cocina tiene **tantas** recetas **como** el otro.

This cookbook has as many recipes as the other one.

To make equal comparisons of adjectives and adverbs, use the construction **tan... como.**

Lima es **tan** grande **como** otras capitales sudamericanas.

Lima is as big as other South American capitals.

To make equal comparisons of verbs, use the expression **tanto como.**

Los indígenas de la ciudad trabajan **tanto como** los de la sierra.

The indigenous people in the city work as much as those in the mountains.

Actividades

A. Las tres regiones de Perú. Completa las siguientes comparaciones con las palabras necesarias (+ significa **más,** − significa **menos**).

1. Hace _____ calor en la selva _____ en las montañas. (+)

2. La sierra tiene _____ habitantes _____ la capital. (−)

3. La costa tiene un clima _____ seco _____ la selva tropical. (+)

4. Tienen _____ terremotos en la costa _____ en la sierra. (=)

5. La vida en las montañas es _____ difícil _____ en la selva. (+)

6. Hay _____ desempleo (*unemployment*) en la sierra _____ en la selva. (=)

7. Hay _____ indígenas en la capital _____ en la selva. (−)

8. La sierra tiene _____ diversidad étnica _____ la selva. (−)

B. ¿Por qué se van?

Paso 1. Estudia los siguientes datos sobre la distribución de la población peruana entre 1940 y 1990. ¿Qué cambios notas? Luego, completa las oraciones que siguen la tabla con la información apropiada.

Distribución de la población peruana			
Año	Costa (%)	Sierra (%)	Selva (%)
1940	25	62	13
1961	39	52	9
1972	45	44	11
1981	51	41	8
1990	53	36	11

1. Entre 1940 y 1990, muchos peruanos se mudaron de _____ a _____.

2. En 1990, la región más poblada de Perú era _____.

3. La región que no tuvo grandes cambios de población entre 1940 y 1990 es _____.

Paso 2. ¿Por qué hubo tanta migración dentro de Perú? Explica este fenómeno comparando los datos de la costa con los de la sierra. Los siguientes aspectos pueden darte algunas ideas.

MODELO   la salud →
         Hay más hospitales en las ciudades que en la sierra.

- las actividades culturales
- el clima
- las oportunidades de trabajo
- el terrorismo
- ¿ ?

C. Grupos étnicos. Trabaja con un compañero / una compañera para describir los grupos étnicos o regionales de tu país, hablando de los siguientes aspectos y otros que se te ocurran.

1. el acceso a la educación
2. la cantidad de personas
3. el mantenimiento de la cultura y las tradiciones
4. los trabajos y las oportunidades de avanzar
5. ¿ ?

Señas culturales

▲ *Machu Picchu: La ciudad perdida de los incas*

Machu Picchu está situada en los Andes peruanos al norte de Cuzco, la antigua capital incaica. Considerada como la «ciudad perdida», Machu Picchu era desconocida por los españoles y su recuerdo se había perdido[a] aún entre los incas, hasta que fue «redescubierta»[b] en 1911.

Un punto de vista sostiene[c] que la ciudad fue construida para el emperador Pachacuti a fines del siglo XV, lo cual se confirma en el estilo imperial tardío[d] de los incas. Ya que no hay señales de ocupación después de la Conquista, Machu Picchu debió de haber sido[e] construida, ocupada y abandonada dentro de un período de cien años. El porqué del abandono sigue siendo un misterio.

Los arqueólogos especulan que Machu Picchu fue un sitio de importancia espiritual y ceremonial, además de tener destacadas[f] funciones agrícolas. Su función estratégica era probablemente secundaria.

¿Qué otras ciudades «sagradas»,[g] u otros sitios de templos abandonados, conoces? ¿Dónde están? ¿Cuál fue su importancia en el pasado? ¿Y ahora en el presente?

[a]se... *had been lost* [b]*rediscovered* [c]*maintains* [d]estilo... *late Imperial style* [e]debió... *must have been* [f]*marked* [g]*sacred*

Análisis cultural

La siguiente cita tomada de una fuente escrita en inglés para anglohablantes va a aumentar tus conocimientos sobre algunos fenómenos culturales en Perú. ¿Es consistente esta información con la perspectiva de Sandra de la **Entrevista 1?** Usa lo que has aprendido en este capítulo sobre Perú, más tu propia experiencia, para contestar las preguntas que siguen la cita.

❝Walk down the bustling central Lima pedestrian street, the Jirón de la Unión, and look into the sea of faces: the moneychangers, the street traders selling clothes, the shop assistants, the restaurant waiters, the stock market traders in ties on their lunch break, the policeman, the shoeshine boy, the beggar woman sitting with her hand held reverently outstretched. The spectrum of activities is mirrored in the variety of features. With migration from the highlands in recent years, Lima has become a more accurate reflection of all Peru's people . . . .

[Peru] is a society crisscrossed not only by its varied racial roots, but also by deep prejudices between rich and poor, and between those living in Lima and in the provinces. This prejudice survives despite the extent to which different communities have merged. Until recently, most television advertising contained almost exclusively white, European-type faces. Locally produced soap operas have generated a 'brat pack' of young actors selected because they share a similar look, with blue or green eyes and blond hair, the opposite of indigenous Peruvians' dark eyes and black hair. One study of advertising found that darker-skinned people appeared only rarely in commercials and when they did it was almost exclusively in government-paid spots.❞

Source: *Peru in Focus: A Guide to the People, Politics and Culture*

1. ¿Qué parte de tu ciudad refleja la diversidad de la sociedad en general?

2. ¿Ha experimentado tu ciudad una migración de recién llegados (*newcomers*) en los últimos años?

3. ¿Dónde vive la mayoría de la gente en tu país: en las ciudades, en las afueras o en el campo? ¿Hay una división parecida en tu país entre la capital y el resto de la nación?

4. ¿Crees que los anuncios reflejen fielmente la composición étnica de la sociedad? ¿Deben, en tu opinión, ser representativos de la diversidad? ¿Por qué sí o por qué no?

5. ¿Hay alguna apariencia física «ideal» en tu país a la que muchas personas aspiren? ¿Cómo es? ¿Cómo se establece: en los anuncios, los programas de televisión, las películas, etcétera?

Pronunciación y ortografía

● m, n, and ñ

The sounds associated with nasal consonants are made by allowing air to pass through the nose as when you hum, "mmmmmm." (Your mouth is closed and the air passes through the nasal cavity). English has the nasal sounds [m] (as in *map*), [n] (as in *note*), and [ŋ] (the *ng* sound in *sing*). Spanish has a different set of nasal sounds: [m] (as in **mapa**), [n] (as in **nota**), [ŋ] as in **húngaro** (*Hungarian*), and [ñ] (as in **señor**). The [ñ] sound does not exist in English. The closest equivalent is the *ny* combination in *canyon*; it is pronounced at more or less the same place in the mouth as the *y* in English *yes*.

The pronunciation of nasal consonants in Spanish does not always correspond to the letter used in spelling. When a nasal consonant is followed by another consonant, the nasal sound is pronounced at the same place in the mouth as the following consonant sound. For example, the word **un** (written with **n**) in **un año** is pronounced [un], but in the phrase **un beso** it is pronounced [um], because the **b** that follows is made with the lips. Observe the following patterns.

Spelling	Pronunciation	Notes
un beso	[um beso]	The sounds [m], [b], and [p] are
un mapa	[um mapa]	all made with the lips.
un peso	[um peso]	
un carro	[uŋ karro]	[ŋ] = the *ng* sound of English
un gato	[uŋ gato]	*sing*; the sounds [ŋ], [k], and [g] are all made in the back of the throat.

The *Manual de práctica* has activities to practice the material explained here.

Los problemas sociales

¿Cuáles son los problemas sociales más graves?

Enrique Soto,
43 años, Lima

Rosa Echenique,
28 años, Arequipa

Éster Losada,
32 años, Cuzco

Alejandro Yamada,
18 años, Callao

«En mi opinión, es **el crimen. Los delincuentes roban** y **engañan**[a] a la gente a toda hora.»

«En este país es **la desigualdad** entre las clases. **Los ricos** y **la clase media explotan**[b] a **los pobres,** quienes son **impotentes**[c] de cambiar su situación. Se sienten **rechazados**[d] y **marginados.**»

«Creo que hay mucha **discriminación.** Los pobres en las ciudades y los indígenas **son discriminados** de manera brutal.»

«La pobreza y la economía **subdesarrollada**[e] causan muchos problemas: **drogas,** crimen y **resentimiento** entre los pobres.»

[a]*trick, swindle* [b]*exploit* [c]*powerless* [d]*rejected* [e]*underdeveloped*

Cómo resolver los problemas

evitar el lenguaje peyorativo	to avoid pejorative language
mantener los valores tradicionales	to maintain traditional values
mejorar las condiciones de vida	to improve living conditions
proteger (j) a los obreros	to protect (the rights of) workers
romper los obstáculos sociales	to break down social barriers
superar las barreras económicas	to overcome economic barriers
tener más acceso a la enseñanza	to have more access to education

Actividades

A. Sinónimos y antónimos. Junta las palabras de la izquierda con sus sinónimos o antónimos de la derecha.

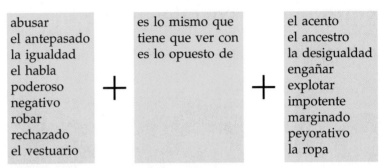

abusar		es lo mismo que		el acento
el antepasado		tiene que ver con		el ancestro
la igualdad		es lo opuesto de		la desigualdad
el habla				engañar
poderoso	**+**		**+**	explotar
negativo				impotente
robar				marginado
rechazado				peyorativo
el vestuario				la ropa

B. Definiciones. Completa las siguientes oraciones con una expresión apropiada del vocabulario.

1. Un país _____ no tiene mucha industria.

2. Las personas _____ están excluidas de la sociedad.

3. Los habitantes originales de una región son _____.

4. Las personas que trabajan en las fábricas, por ejemplo, son _____.

5. No tratar bien a una persona por su raza, clase, situación económica, etcétera, es _____.

6. Los _____ no tienen mucho dinero.

7. Una persona sin control de una situación se siente _____.

8. Las personas que cometen crímenes se llaman _____.

C. Grupos minoritarios. ¿Cuáles son los grupos minoritarios más importantes de tu país? ¿Cómo contribuyen al país, qué discriminaciones experimentan y qué aspiraciones tienen? Apunta tus ideas, según las siguientes categorías. Luego, presenta tus ideas a la clase.

MODELOS   Un grupo importante son los…

Contribuyen mucho al país porque…

Experimentan discriminación cuando…

Quieren ser (hacer, llegar a ser [*to become*], etcétera)…

Grupo	Contribuciones	Discriminaciones que experimentan	Aspiraciones

Héctor Cabral Domínguez

«*Básicamente, en el Perú, como te ven, te tratan.*»

Nombre: Héctor

Apellidos: (1) Cabral (2) Domínguez

Edad: 29 años

Nació en: Lima, Perú

You can watch this interview on the *Entrevistas* Video or Interactive CD-ROM or listen to the audio on the Online Learning Center (**www.mhhe.com/entrevistas2**).

Vocabulario útil

despreció	scorned	**marcada**	marked, distinct
el aporte	contribution	**recae**	falls upon
a nivel mundial	worldwide	**desenvolverse**	to evolve
sacar... adelante	to improve	**no se le menosprecia**	(he/she) isn't underrated
lamentablemente	unfortunately	**no se le chulea**	(he/she) isn't exploited
alcanzar	to attain	**tienden a perder**	tend to loose
conforman	comprise	**se deprimen**	get depressed

Antes de ver

¿Aceptación o discriminación?   Revisa las siguientes oraciones e indica si sugieren la **aceptación** o la **discriminación,** con respecto a un grupo minoritario.

	ACEPTACIÓN	DISCRIMINACIÓN
1. La gente de la ciudad explotó al indígena.	☐	☐
2. Lo que viene de Europa se ve mejor.	☐	☐
3. Hay muchas cosas nativas que son buenas.	☐	☐
4. El aporte indígena al país es grande.	☐	☐
5. En Perú se fijan mucho en la apariencia, el nombre y la posición económica.	☐	☐
6. Los que no encuentran lo que buscaban tienden a perder sus costumbres.	☐	☐
7. Algunas personas marginadas buscan salida (*a way out*) a través de grupos terroristas.	☐	☐

¡Veamos!

¿Cierto o falso?   Revisa las siguientes oraciones. Luego, ve la entrevista e indica si son ciertas o falsas, según Héctor.

	CIERTO	FALSO
1. Históricamente, la gente despreció a los indígenas.	☐	☐
2. Hay gran interés internacional por la cultura indígena.	☐	☐
3. Las aspiraciones de los indígenas son diferentes a las de los otros grupos étnicos.	☐	☐
4. Los indígenas tienen las mismas oportunidades que todos los demás peruanos.	☐	☐
5. Si los indígenas estudian y alcanzan una profesión, no encuentran discriminación.	☐	☐
6. Algunos indígenas se integran fácilmente a la sociedad.	☐	☐

Después de ver

A. Resumen. Vuelve a ver la entrevista y resume con tus propias palabras la explicación que da Héctor de los siguientes aspectos de la sociedad peruana.

1. la historia de las relaciones entre los europeos y los indígenas
2. las aspiraciones de los peruanos de diferentes grupos étnicos
3. la discriminación en Perú
4. lo que les puede pasar a los indígenas cuando van a las ciudades

B. Discusión. En grupos de tres o cuatro estudiantes, contesten las siguientes preguntas. Luego, un miembro del grupo va a presentar un resumen a la clase.

1. ¿Son importantes las clases sociales en Norteamérica? ¿En qué sentido?
2. ¿Qué criterios determinan las diferentes clases en tu país: la educación, el dinero, el origen étnico, la lengua, la familia o geneología, el enchufe (*connections*), etcétera?
3. ¿Cómo se reconocen los diferentes grupos sociales: por el habla, la ropa, el coche, las costumbres, el barrio donde viven, etcétera?

Piénsalo bien

Héctor habla de las aspiraciones de los indígenas peruanos. ¿Son las mismas aspiraciones que tienen otros grupos que conoces? Considera los siguientes grupos para contestar esta pregunta:

- los mexicoamericanos **(Capítulo 11)**
- las personas de la generación de tus padres
- las personas de tu generación
- un grupo étnico de tu país

● 14.3 The Future Tense

Forms

From early on in your study of Spanish, you have been able to talk about future actions using either the *present tense* or the expression **ir** + **a** + *infinitive*. Spanish also has a *future tense*, which is formed by adding a special set of endings to the future stem, which is normally the infinitive of the verb. Unlike other tenses, the future tense has only one set of endings for verbs of all three conjugations (**-ar, -er,** and **-ir**).

Future Tense of Regular Verbs		
-ar	**-er**	**-ir**
mejoraré	romperé	seguiré
mejorarás	romperás	seguirás
mejorará	romperá	seguirá
mejoraremos	romperemos	seguiremos
mejoraréis	romperéis	seguiréis
mejorarán	romperán	seguirán

La situación **mejorará**.

The situation will get better.

Los jóvenes **romperán** los obstáculos sociales.

Young people will break down social barriers.

Seguiremos luchando por los derechos de los grupos minoritarios.

We will continue fighting for the rights of minority groups.

A few verbs have irregular future stems, but they take the same endings used for regular verbs. Note the similarities among the irregular stems.

Future Tense of Irregular Verbs					
INFINITIVE	STEM	FUTURE TENSE	INFINITIVE	STEM	FUTURE TENSE
caber[a]	cabr-	cabré, cabrás, cabrá,...	poner	pondr-	pondré, pondrás, pondrá,...
poder	podr-	podré, podrás, podrá,...	salir	saldr-	saldré, saldrás, saldrá,...
querer	querr-	querré, querrás, querrá,...	tener	tendr-	tendré, tendrás, tendrá,...
saber	sabr-	sabré, sabrás, sabrá,...	valer[b]	valdr-	valdré, valdrás, valdrá,...
			venir	vendr-	vendré, vendrás, vendrá,...
decir	dir-	diré, dirás, dirá,...			
hacer	har-	haré, harás, hará,...			

[a]*to fit*   [b]*to be worth*

NOTES:

- Most of the verbs similar to the preceding irregular verbs have corresponding irregular stems in the future tense: **mantener** → **mantendr-** → **mantendré, mantendrás, mantendrá,...** , *but* **predecir** (*to predict*) → **predecir-** → **prediciré, predecirás, predecirá,...** .
- The future of **hay** is **habrá** (*there will be*).

Uses

The future tense in Spanish corresponds closely to the English future: *will/shall* + *verb.* Just as in English, the Spanish future often implies more force of will than the **ir** + **a** + *infinitive* construction.

Van a superar las barreras económicas.	*They are going to overcome the economic obstacles.* (simple report of future action)
Superarán las barreras económicas.	*They will overcome the economic obstacles.* (implies determination)

In requests, English *will* often indicates willingness to do something, not future time. In these cases, Spanish uses other expressions, not the future.

Will you help me?	**¿Puedes** ayudarme?
Will you please close the window?	**¿Te importa** cerrar la ventana?

Actividades

A. ¿Cambiará el país?   Imagina que eres Héctor. Contesta las siguientes preguntas, usando las formas apropiadas del futuro.

> MODELO   ¿Van a luchar por cambiar el país? →
> Sí, lucharán por cambiarlo.

1. ¿Van a mejorar la economía?
2. Los grupos como Sendero Luminoso, ¿van a atraer a más jóvenes?
3. Los jóvenes, ¿van a encontrar medios para triunfar?
4. ¿Va a afirmar el gobierno los derechos de todos los grupos minoritarios?
5. ¿Van a perderse las tradiciones indígenas?

B. ¿Cómo mejorar la vida?   Escribe una lista de cinco cosas que harás para mejorar tu vida, usando verbos en el futuro.

> MODELO   Terminaré mis estudios.

C. Mi vida en 2020.   ¿Cómo será tu vida en el año 2020? Descríbele a un compañero / una compañera tus predicciones sobre los siguientes aspectos de tu vida, usando verbos en el futuro.

1. la carrera	**4.** el país
2. la familia	**5.** los pasatiempos
3. el mundo	**6.** ¿ ?

D. La utopía. Trabaja con un compañero / una compañera para describir una sociedad utópica o ideal del futuro. Comenten las siguientes ideas, usando verbos en el futuro.

MODELO   el crimen →
          No habrá delincuentes en la sociedad ideal.

1. la comida
2. los medios de comunicación
3. la política
4. la tecnología

5. el trabajo
6. los viajes
7. ¿ ?

● 14.4 The Subjunctive with Future Actions

So far in your study of the subjunctive you have seen that certain verbs and impersonal expressions in the main clause (for example, **Quiero, Es necesario**) trigger the subjunctive in dependent clauses. These expressions imply that the action in the dependent clause has not happened yet or is not yet true. (If it were true already, the speaker would not try to influence it or have doubts about it!) Not surprisingly, Spanish requires the use of the subjunctive in *any* dependent clause that expresses an action that has not yet been carried out or is not yet true—that is, any future action.

Some expressions introduce dependent clauses that always imply future or as-yet-untrue actions and, therefore, *always* require the subjunctive. You should memorize them.

Expressions That *Always* Trigger Subjunctive in a Dependent Clause			
a menos que	unless	en caso de que	in case
a no ser que	unless	para que	so that, in
antes (de) que	before		order that
con tal (de) que	provided that	sin que	without

Muchos indígenas van a la ciudad **para que** sus hijos **puedan** tener acceso a una buena educación.

Many indigenous people go to the city so that their children can have access to a good education.

Habrá muchos policías **en caso de que** la manifestación se **ponga** violenta.

There will be many police officers in case the demonstration turns violent.

Other expressions introduce dependent clauses that may or may not imply future actions. If the actions are habitual or completed, the indicative is used; if future actions are implied, these dependent clauses take the subjunctive.

Expressions That *Sometimes* Trigger Subjunctive in a Dependent Clause
(*Implied Future* = Subjunctive; *Habitual* or *Completed* = Indicative)

cuando	when(ever)	**hasta que**	until
después (de) que	after	**tan pronto como**	as soon as
en cuanto	as soon as		

Cuando **llego** a Lima, siempre me recoge mi tío Alberto.	*When(ever) I arrive in Lima* (habitual action: present indicative), *my uncle Alberto always picks me up.*
Cuando **llegué** a Machu Picchu, me impresionaron mucho las ruinas.	*When I arrived in Machu Picchu* (completed action: preterit), *I was surprised by the ruins.*
Cuando **llegue** a casa, estaré muy cansado del viaje.	*When I get home* (in the future), *I will be very tired from the trip.*

Análisis estructural

Estudia las siguientes oraciones y di si los verbos en la cláusula subordinada se refieren a acciones futuras, acciones habituales en el presente o acciones completas.

1. Los incas tenían un imperio grande cuando llegaron los españoles a Perú.
2. Los indígenas de la sierra mantienen algunas costumbres después de que llegan a las ciudades de la costa.
3. La gente del campo tendrá mejores oportunidades en cuanto aprendan a hablar español.
4. Seguiremos luchando contra la discriminación hasta que ya no exista.
5. Los pobres de las ciudades tendrán una vida mejor tan pronto como superen las barreras económicas que existen.

Actividades

A. **Una carta desde Perú.** Completa la siguiente carta con la forma apropiada del subjuntivo de los verbos **dar, empezar, irse, poder, regresar** y **tener.**

Queridos papis:

¡Saludos desde Cuzco! Estoy pasándola bien aquí en Perú, y quería contarles mis planes para el resto de las vacaciones.

No me queda mucho tiempo aquí, pues pensaba viajar por esta zona hasta que mis amigos _____[1] las clases. Son muy amables: me invitan a su casa y hemos hecho muchas excursiones juntos. Voy a invitarlos a visitarme en México para que ustedes _____[2] conocerlos también. Les van a caer muy bien.

Un problemita: Resulta que no me queda mucho dinero, entonces no podré comprar el boleto de avión de vuelta a menos que ustedes me _____³ el dinero. ¿Podrían mandármelo antes de que yo _____⁴ de Cuzco? No se preocupen; cuando yo _____⁵ a casa, ¡les devolveré todo el dinero que me prestaron[a]!

Les diré la fecha del vuelo de vuelta tan pronto como _____⁶ el boleto comprado. Hasta muy pronto.

Un fuerte abrazo cariñoso de su hijo,
Antonio

[a]me… *you loaned me*

B. Un viaje a Perú. Ramón y su familia están planeando un viaje a Perú. Lee los siguientes comentarios de Ramón y complétalos con la forma apropiada (indicativo o subjuntivo) de los verbos subrayados.

1. Siempre llevo demasiadas cosas cuando <u>ir</u> de viaje. Pero cuando <u>ir</u> a Perú, sólo llevaré lo necesario.
2. Frecuentemente, cuando <u>salir</u> de viaje, no llevo mi pasaporte. Pero esta vez llevaré mis documentos en caso de que los agentes me los <u>pedir</u> en la frontera.
3. En general, no me gusta pleanear demasiado. Pero esta vez nuestro agente de viajes nos hará un itinerario antes de que nosotros <u>viajar</u>.
4. Según la página Web de nuestro hotel, será imposible conseguir una habitación a menos que yo <u>tener</u> una reserva.
5. ¡No estaré contento hasta que <u>ver</u> las ruinas de Machu Picchu!
6. Cuando <u>estar</u> en Lima, quiero ver todas las atracciones de la ciudad.
7. Pero no quiero visitar los monumentos sin que nuestro guía nos <u>explicar</u> su historia.
8. Normalmente, cuando yo <u>cenar</u> en restaurantes elegantes, pago con tarjeta de crédito. Pero cuando nosotros <u>pagar</u> en Perú, usaremos cheques de viajero.

C. ¿Un futuro prometedor? Trabaja con un compañero / una compañera para completar las siguientes oraciones con ideas originales sobre el futuro.

1. Siempre habrá problemas sociales a menos que…
2. El gobierno debe presentar un nuevo programa de educación para que…
3. Los indígenas se quedarán en la sierra cuando…
4. Nadie en Perú hablará quechua a no ser que…
5. Los grupos como Sendero Luminoso desaparecerán tan pronto como…

Sobre la lectura   En esta lectura, vas a leer algunos párrafos de un testimonio etnográfico de Ranin Ama,* una mujer shipiba, grabado (*recorded*) por la lingüista Pilar Valenzuela en 1998. En los párrafos que se presentan a continuación, Ranin Ama habla de los cambios en la cultura shipiba que, en su opinión, se deben al contacto de los shipibos con los «mestizos»† y europeos.

Si te interesa

The Shipibo are the third largest group of indigenous peoples of the Amazon region. They number about 130,000, distributed in about 130 settlements (**comunidades nativas**) of around 1,000 inhabitants each. They are unique in that they have maintained their language and customs to a greater extent than any other indigenous group in contact with Westerners. The Shipibo have had radio broadcasts in their language for many years, but only after the introduction of television in 1997 have young people begun to prefer Spanish over Shipibo. The Shipibo traditionally live off the river and the jungle, with a diet consisting of fish and bananas.

Antes de leer

A. Lluvia de ideas.   En su testimonio, Ranin Ama lamenta que muchas cosas hayan cambiado (*have changed*). ¿Qué sabes de los indígenas amazónicos y sus tradiciones? ¿Qué cosas han cambiado probablemente? Trabaja con dos compañeros/as para hacer una lista de todos los temas que se te ocurran en las siguientes categorías:

- el alojamiento
- la comida
- las costumbres
- las creencias religiosas
- la lengua
- las relaciones familiares
- el vestuario

B. ¿Antes o después?   Revisa las siguientes acciones e indica cuáles probablemente son parte de la cultura tradicional shipiba y cuáles son parte de la vida moderna «mestiza».

	LA VIDA TRADICIONAL SHIPIBA	LA VIDA MODERNA «MESTIZA»
1. llevar pantalones	☐	☐
2. hilar (*to spin thread*)	☐	☐
3. hablar en shipibo	☐	☐
4. comprar las cosas con dinero	☐	☐
5. ponerse la pampanilla‡	☐	☐

---

* Most Shipibos have a Shipibo name (their real name) and a Spanish name. Ranin Ama's Spanish name is Agustina Valera Rojas.
† For the Shipibo, the term **mestizo/a** means *anyone who speaks Spanish,* even a native Shipibo.
‡ See the photo that accompanies the reading in this section.

	LA VIDA TRADICIONAL SHIPIBA	LA VIDA MODERNA «MESTIZA»
6. aprender a hablar el castellano (español)	☐	☐
7. preparar *masato*	☐	☐
8. sacar yuca	☐	☐

Si te interesa

Masato is a beverage made by chewing manioc root and fermenting the saliva. The practice is gender-specific: Only women are allowed to prepare it.

C. Identifica el sujeto. Recuerda que en español el sujeto de la oración muchas veces puede encontrarse **después** del verbo. Esta construcción es muy común con verbos como **gustar (Me gusta *la selva*)** y en las cláusulas subordinadas (Me dijeron **que venía *Juan***). Revisa las siguientes oraciones de la lectura e identifica el sujeto de los verbos subrayados.

1. «Ahora <u>veo</u> que se cumplió lo que <u>decían</u> mis abuelas y abuelos.»
2. «<u>Poseo</u> consejos porque <u>hice</u> caso a lo que me <u>decía</u> mi madre.» (**poseer** = *to possess*, **hacer caso a** = *to take heed of*)
3. «Ésas <u>son</u> cosas que se <u>ponían</u> las abuelas antiguamente.»
4. «…esas cositas nos <u>enseñó</u> nuestra madre.»
5. «Si <u>sabemos</u> hacer estas cosas, nunca nos <u>falta</u> la ropa.» (**faltar** = *to be lacking*)
6. «Mamá, te <u>llama</u> la tía.»

Testimonio de una mujer shipiba

Me siento muy triste cuando recuerdo las palabras de mis abuelos: «Algún día ustedes los jóvenes serán como los mestizos, sin ser mestizos van a vivir usando la vestimenta[a] de ellos.» Ahora veo que se cumplió[b] lo que decían mis abuelas y abuelos. En esa etapa estamos. Mi hija señorita no quiere ponerse la pampanilla, a pesar de que yo le quiero hacer usarla; ya se acostumbró a usar pantalones. Con respecto a nuestra vestimenta propia, mi hija dice: «Ésas son cosas que se ponían las abuelas antiguamente.»

▲ *Ranin Ama y su y su hija demuestran la vestimenta tradicional de las mujeres shipibas la* **pampanilla,** *una falda bordada con diseños impresionantes.*

Mi madre me crió,[c] dándome consejos. Poseo consejos porque hice caso a lo que me decía mi madre. Como mi madre sabía hacer de todo, ella me enseñó. Nosotras las mujeres shipibas no somos como las mestizas que solamente hacen las cosas con dinero. Nosotras no hacemos las cosas con dinero. Mi madre nos enseñó a ir al monte, a cortar leña,[d] traer plátano, sacar yuca, preparar *masato*, preparar *chapo*[e] especial; esas cositas nos enseñó nuestra madre.

[a]vestuario [b]*se… came true* [c]*me… raised me* [d]*(fire)wood* [e]*Shipibo word for banana paste used to make a drink*

Pero las cosas de antes se están perdiendo. Mi hija no sabe hacer nada, ni hilar puede. A veces me pregunta: «Mamá, ¿cómo se teje el hilo[f] de algodón?» Entonces, yo le respondo: «Hija, antes era así, ahora ya no.» Si sabemos hacer estas cosas, nunca nos falta la ropa; aunque nos falten otras cosas, la ropa la hacemos nosotras mismas, dura más que la ropa de los mestizos, no se envejece[g] tan rápido como la ropa de la tienda.

Algunos jóvenes shipibos hablan en nuestro idioma, pero hay otros que ni lo hablan ni lo entienden. Los niños de la nueva generación desconocen[h] muchas cosas. Así es ahorita, nuestros hijos pequeños nos preguntan: «Mamá, ¿cuánto es *pichika*[i]?» Entonces yo les digo: «*Pichika* es esta cantidad», mostrándoles los cinco dedos de la mano. Ésta es la razón por la que se está perdiendo nuestra lengua;

por eso los profesores bilingües tienen que enseñar en nuestra propia lengua a los niños. Si no se practican, es probable que desaparezcan nuestra cultura y nuestra lengua.

Yo opino que debemos hablarles en shipibo a nuestros hijos. Hay algunos niños que no quieren hablar en shipibo. Mi hijo menor, el pelachito,[j] no quiere hablar en shipibo. Cuando tiene sed, me pide en castellano: «Mamá, dame agua.» Ya no quiere conversar en nuestro idioma. Cuando su hermana me llama, siempre me dice en castellano: «Mamá, te llama la tía.» Pero el mayorcito[k] siempre le reclama [al pelachito]: «¿Por qué hablas en castellano? ¿Acaso eres mestizo?[l]» El pelachito le contesta: «Quiero aprender bien el castellano.» El mayorcito no habla castellano, ni entiende. ■

[f]*thread* [g]*no… it doesn't get old, worn out* [h]*are unfamiliar with* [i]*cinco (en shipibo)* [j]*peladito (de poco pelo)* [k]*oldest (child)*
[l]*¿Acaso… Are you "mestizo" or what?*

Después de leer

A. Las generaciones. ¿Cuántas generaciones se mencionan en el testimonio? Identifica cuáles son. Luego, lee las siguientes oraciones y di qué generación las dijo.

1. «Algún día ustedes los jóvenes serán como los mestizos, sin ser mestizos van a vivir usando la vestimenta de ellos.»
2. «Ésas son cosas que se ponían las abuelas antiguamente.»
3. « …antes era así, ahora ya no.»
4. «Mamá, dame agua.»
5. «¿Por qué hablas en castellano? ¿Acaso eres mestizo?»

B. El español regional. Ranin Ama y sus hijos, como muchos shipibos, no hablan español como primer idioma. Es decir, su español regional contiene ciertas características que no son parte del español estándar. ¿En qué se diferencia el español regional de los shipibos del español estándar? Empareja las citas de la lectura con las características del español regional.

CARACTERÍSTICAS DEL ESPAÑOL REGIONAL

1. _____ palabras propias de (*specific to*) la región
2. _____ préstamos (*borrowed words*) de otras lenguas
3. _____ omisión de pronombres de complemento directo
4. _____ uso redundante de los pronombres de sujeto

CITAS DE LA LECTURA

a. «Entonces, **yo** le respondo:… »
b. « …preparar **masato**, preparar **chapo**… »
c. «El mayorcito no habla castellano, ni [lo] entiende.»
d. «El **pelachito** le contesta:… »

C. Tu interpretación. Trabaja con un compañero / una compañera para contestar las siguientes preguntas.

1. ¿Cómo ven Ranin Ama y sus hijos a los «mestizos»? ¿Se sienten inferiores o superiores a ellos? ¿Cómo lo sabes?
2. ¿Cuál es la actitud de Ranin Ama hacia los «mestizos»? ¿Parece que está agradecida, curiosa, enojada, resentida (*resentful*), sorprendida, triste, etcétera?
3. ¿Qué opina Ranin Ama de las pérdidas culturales del pueblo shipibo? ¿Cree que sea posible detener los cambios o volver al pasado?

D. Predicciones. Si los cambios culturales siguen de acuerdo con la información de la lectura, ¿cómo será la vida de los shipibos en veinte años? Combina los siguientes elementos para formar ideas lógicas, usando el futuro, y añade otras ideas que se te ocurran.

VOCABULARIO ÚTIL

todavía   still
ya no   no longer

MODELO   Las mujeres shipibas ya no llevarán la pampanilla.

1. Las mujeres shipibas…	aprender shipibo
2. Los hombres shipibos…	hablar español
3. Las niñas shipibas…	llevar la vestimenta tradicional
4. Los niños shipibos…	mantener las costumbres
	mudarse a las ciudades
	vivir de la selva
	¿ ?

E. Recomendaciones. Es triste perder la cultura y las costumbres propias. ¿Qué se puede hacer para que no ocurra esto? Trabaja con un compañero / una compañera para inventar consejos para un grupo étnico norteamericano (o de otro lugar) para prevenir la pérdida cultural. **¡OJO!** Cuidado con el uso del subjuntivo.

MODELO   Es importante que los niños aprendan la lengua de la familia.

1. Es importante que…

2. Les recomendamos a _____ que…

3. Les aconsejamos a _____ que _____ para que…

4. ¿ ?

F. Tus tradiciones. Contesta las siguientes preguntas con un compañero / una compañera.

1. ¿Hay artesanías, celebraciones, costumbres, leyendas, símbolos, tradiciones, vestuario, etcétera, en tu cultura o familia que se estén perdiendo? ¿Por qué?
2. ¿Hay artesanías, celebraciones, costumbres, etcétera, familiares o culturales que hayas (*you have*) redescubierto? ¿Cómo lo hiciste?

3. ¿Por qué motivos crees que prefiere hablar en español el hijo menor de Ranin Ama? ¿Hay personas en tu familia que no tengan interés en mantener las tradiciones de la familia?
4. Los consejos obviamente son muy importantes en la transmisión de la cultura shipiba. (Ranin Ama dice: «Mi madre me crió, dándome consejos.*») ¿Cómo se transmiten de generación en generación la cultura y los conocimientos en tu familia? ¿y en la cultura norteamericana en general?

PORTAFOLIO CULTURAL

Redacción

Encuesta. En esta actividad vas a entrevistar a otros estudiantes de tu universidad para saber qué problemas sociales les preocupan más. Sigue los pasos en el *Manual de práctica* para elaborar tu encuesta.

Exploración

Investigación cultural. Busca más información sobre Perú en la biblioteca, en el *Entrevistas* Online Learning Center (**www.mhhe.com/entrevistas2**) o en otros sitios del Internet y preséntala a la clase. El *Manual de práctica* contiene más ideas para tu presentación.

Léxico activo

PARA HABLAR DE LA POBLACIÓN DE UN PAÍS

el/la **asiático/a**	Asian (person)
el/la **criollo/a**	American-born children of European parents and their descendants
el/la **europeo/a**	European
la **mayoría**	majority
el/la **mestizo/a**	mixed-race (person)
la **minoría**	minority
étnico/a	ethnic
incaico/a	Incan
minoritario/a	minority (*adj.*)
numeroso/a	numerous
peruano/a	Peruvian

Repaso: el/la indígena

LOS RASGOS DISTINTIVOS DE UNA CULTURA

el **acento**	accent
la **creencia (tradicional)**	(traditional) belief
la **gastronomía**	(style of) cooking, gastronomy
el **habla** (*pl.* las **hablas**)	speech
el **nivel de educación**	level of education
la **religión**	religion
el **territorio ancestral**	ancestral territory
la **tradición**	tradition
el **vestuario**	clothing, style of dress
distinguir (distingo)	to distinguish

Repaso: la costumbre

LAS REGIONES

el **altiplano**	plateau, high plain
la **costa**	coast
el **valle**	valley
amazónico/a	Amazon (*adj.*)

Repaso: el campo, la ciudad, la selva, la sierra

---

* Ranin Ama also says, **Poseo consejos,… .** In Shipibo culture, a person with **consejos** is highly respected.

LOS PROBLEMAS SOCIALES

la **clase media**	middle class
el **crimen**	crime
el/la **delincuente**	delinquent (person)
la **desigualdad**	inequality
la **discriminación**	discrimination
la **droga**	drug
el **resentimiento**	resentment
engañar	to trick, swindle
explotar	to exploit
robar	to rob, steal
ser discriminado/a	to be discriminated against
impotente	powerless
marginado/a	marginalized
pobre	poor
rechazado/a	rejected
rico/a	rich, wealthy
subdesarrollado/a	underdeveloped

CÓMO RESOLVER LOS PROBLEMAS

evitar el lenguaje peyorativo	to avoid pejorative language
mantener los valores tradicionales	to maintain traditional values
mejorar las condiciones de vida	to improve living conditions
proteger (j) a los obreros	to protect (the rights of) workers
romper los obstáculos sociales	to break down social barriers
superar las barreras económicas	to overcome economic barriers
tener más acceso a la enseñanza	to have more access to education

REPASO DE LAS COMPARACIONES

más/menos _____ **que**	more/less _____ than
más/menos de + *number*	more/less than + *number*
mayor/menor	older/younger
mejor/peor	better/worse
tan + *adj./adv.* + **como**	as + *adj./adv.* + as
tanto/a/os/as + *noun* + **como**	as much/many + *noun* + as
verb + **tanto como**	*verb* + as much as

LAS CONJUNCIONES + *SUBJUNTIVO*

a menos que	unless
a no ser que	unless
antes (de) que	before
con tal (de) que	provided that
en caso de que	in case
para que	so that, in order that
sin que	without

LAS CONJUNCIONES + *SUBJUNTIVO/INDICATIVO*

cuando	when(ever)
después (de) que	after
en cuanto	as soon as
hasta que	until
tan pronto como	as soon as

Conexiones y comunidad

Paraguay y Uruguay

BOLIVIA

el Río Paraguay   BRASIL

PARAGUAY

el Río Paraná

la Cordillera de
Amambay

el Gran
Chaco   Asunción ★   las Cataratas
del Iguazú

CHILE

el Río Uruguay

la Cuchilla de Haedo

URUGUAY

la Cuchilla Grande   el Río Negro

Durazno
Montevideo

Buenos Aires ★   Punta del Este

ARGENTINA

el Río de la Plata

el Océano Pacífico

la Cordillera de los Andes

el Océano Atlántico

Paraguay

Uruguay

Cultura

◆ Connecting with Fellow Beings: A
  Universal Necessity

◆ Friends and Loves Across Cultures

◆ **Señas culturales: El mate**

Lengua

◆ Friendships

◆ Dating and Relationships

◆ The Conditional (15.1)

◆ Results and Consequences (15.2)

◆ The Subjunctive (Summary) (15.3)

Paraguay y Uruguay

Los Estados Unidos
y el Canadá

	Paraguay habitado por indígenas guaraníes y otras tribus		Llegada de los españoles a Paraguay			Independencia de España en Paraguay y Uruguay	
hasta el siglo XVI	**hasta 1534**	**1500–1600**	**1534**	**1534**	**1600–1750**	**1776–1783**	**1811**	**1846–1848**
Varias tribus indígenas habitan en Norteamérica		Exploración española de Norteamérica	Jacques Cartier reclama para Francia el Canadá		Fundación de las colonias británicas en Norteamérica	Guerra de Independencia en los EE. UU.		Guerra Mexicano-Americana

Instantánea

ORIGEN DEL NOMBRE

Paraguay: del Río Paraguay, de la palabra indígena que significa **agua.**

Uruguay: posiblemente de las palabras indígenas **guay** (*tail*) y **uru** (*bird*), refiriéndose a una especie de pájaro nativo del área que tiene una cola (*tail*) larga y magnífica

POBLACIÓN

Paraguay: 6.028.900
Uruguay: 3.452.600

LENGUAS

Paraguay: el español, el guaraní (oficiales)
Uruguay: el español (oficial)

For additional practice, check out the *Manual de práctica*, the Interactive CD-ROM, and the Online Learning Center (**www.mhhe.com/entrevistas2**)!

▲ *Éstas son ruinas de la misión jesuita Jesús y Trinidad en Paraguay. Los misioneros jesuitas establecieron misiones en Paraguay, Uruguay y Brasil durante el siglo XVII.*

Guerra de la Triple Alianza (Argentina, Uruguay y Brasil) contra Paraguay		Guerra del Chaco entre Paraguay y Bolivia		El General Alfredo Stroessner toma el poder en Paraguay	El General Andrés Rodríguez gana las primeras elecciones libres paraguayas en décadas		Nueva Constitución paraguaya	Jorge Batlle, hijo de una familia de políticos, es elegido presidente de Uruguay
1865–1870	1898	1932–1935	1952	1954	1982	1989	1992	1994	1999
	Guerra Hispano-Americana		Puerto Rico se hace Estado Libre Asociado de los EE. UU.		El Canadá se separa legalmente de Inglaterra			Tratado de Libre Comercio entre los EE. UU., el Canadá y México	

● Las amistades[a]

> ### ¿Qué significa ser buen amigo? Indica las afirmaciones que son verdaderas para ti.
>
> El amigo ideal...
>
> ❏ sabe **expresar sus sentimientos.**[b]
> ❏ me **engaña** de vez en cuando.
> ❏ me hace favores **sin dudar.**[c]
> ❏ es paciente en **llegar a conocerme.**[d]
> ❏ **mantiene la distancia entre los dos.**
> ❏ **muestra cariño en público.**
> ❏ me hace reír.
> ❏ necesita mucha atención.
> ❏ nunca me **hace daño.**
> ❏ no me **avergüenza**[e] delante de **los demás.**[f]
> ❏ no me dice la verdad en ciertas situaciones.
> ❏ **revela mis secretos.**
> ❏ **se pelea**[g] conmigo.
> ❏ me **presta** dinero.
> ❏ siempre es **honesto/a** conmigo.
> ❏ **trata de** cambiarme.
> ❏ no deja que **me sienta** solo/a **(aislado/a).**
> ❏ no **duda en** demostrar su **amor.**[h]

La historia de un amor

Rafael y Julieta **se enamoraron**[i] a los 16 años. Esta **pareja** moderna vivió junta antes de **casarse.**[j] Decidieron casarse a los 23 años. **La boda**[k] se celebró en la catedral de Montevideo. **Se quieren** mucho **a pesar de** los problemas con sus padres.

---

[a]*friendships* [b]*feelings* [c]*sin... without hesitation* [d]*llegar... getting to know me*
[e]*embarrass* [f]*los... others* [g]*se... fights* [h]*love* [i]*se... fell in love* [j]*getting married* [k]*wedding*

¿Qué problemas enfrentan[a] las parejas de hoy?

divorciarse	to divorce, get divorced
comunicarse (qu) bien/mal	to communicate well/poorly
llevarse bien/mal	to get along well/poorly
quejarse	to complain (about)
separarse	to separate, get separated
tener celos	to be jealous

**tener personalidades/
    valores incompatibles**
	to have incompatible
	    personalities/values

Actividades

A. Asociaciones.   ¿Qué acciones asocias con los diferentes tipos de personas? Completa las oraciones con expresiones del vocabulario. ¿Qué tipos de personas pueden ser buenos amigos, en tu opinión?

MODELO   una persona indiscreta →
Una persona indiscreta revela mis secretos, así que no es un buen amigo.

1. una persona generosa
2. una persona ofensiva
3. una persona que cuenta muchos chistes
4. una persona que roba mi dinero
5. una persona que tiene muchos problemas

B. Definiciones.   ¿Qué palabra o expresión del vocabulario corresponde a las siguientes definiciones?

1. la ceremonia en que dos personas se casan
2. dejar de vivir juntos
3. una persona simpática, amable
4. sentirse lejos de los amigos y parientes
5. ser compatibles

▲ *Esta pareja uruguaya celebra su boda en Montevideo.*

C. Comparaciones.   Mira los siguientes dibujos y describe la relación que probablemente tiene cada pareja. ¿Qué hay de positivo o de negativo en cada caso?

los Martínez

los Guzmán

[a]*face*

D. Entrevista: Una persona importante. Hazle las siguientes preguntas a un compañero / una compañera para saber más de una persona importante (amigo/a o pariente) en su vida.

1. ¿Con quién te llevas lo mejor?
2. ¿En qué te pareces a esa persona? ¿En qué te diferencias de él/ella?
3. ¿Cuánto tiempo pasas con él/ella, normalmente? ¿Qué hacen juntos/as?
4. Cuando él/ella no está, ¿te sientes aislado/a o solo/a? ¿Por qué sí o por qué no?
5. ¿Qué característica valoras más en esta persona? ¿Por qué?

E. Anuncios personales

Paso 1. Busca algunos anuncios personales en un periódico hispano en línea de Paraguay o Uruguay, imprímelos y llévalos a clase para poder hacer el **Paso 2.**

Paso 2. Revisa tus anuncios y los de un compañero / una compañera, para hacer de trotaconventos (*matchmaker*) y tratar de unir a las parejas compatibles. Explica el porqué de tus ideas y compártelas con la clase.

MODELO   Creo que [nombre] es bueno/a para [nombre] porque a los dos les gusta [actividad o cosa] y los dos buscan [características].

Señas culturales

▲ *Una jícara*

El mate, también conocido como el té paraguayo, es una bebida preparada con las hojas de la yerba[a] mate. Es una bebida no alcohólica pero cafeinada que toman uruguayos y paraguayos (y argentinos también) de todas las clases sociales y económicas.

Típicamente, el mate se consume en grupos, pero se usa sólo una vasija[b] —llamada **jícara**— que todos comparten. La persona que lo sirve, llamada «cebador», llena la jícara con hojas picadas[c] de yerba mate y les añade agua casi hervida, lo cual produce una espuma.[d] Entonces, le pasa la vasija al primero del grupo, quien utiliza una pajita[e] de plata para tomar la infusión. Después de escurrir[f] la vasija, el que bebe se la devuelve al cebador, quien la llena de nuevo con agua caliente para pasársela a la persona que sigue.

¿Conoces otros ritos nacionales en torno a[g] una bebida? ¿Cuáles son?

[a]*herb* [b]*receptacle, often a hollowed-out gourd* [c]*crushed* [d]*foam* [e]*straw* [f]*emptying* [g]*en... surrounding*

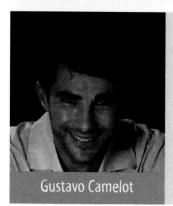

Gustavo Camelot

«*Tu pareja es tu mejor amigo o tu mejor amiga,...* »

Nombre: Gustavo

Apellido: Camelot

Edad: 36 años

Nació en: Montevideo, Uruguay

You can watch this interview on the *Entrevistas* Video or Interactive CD-ROM or listen to the audio on the Online Learning Center (**www.mhhe.com/entrevistas2**).

Vocabulario útil

ternura	affection, tenderness	**entrás* a desconfiar**	you begin to mistrust
transparente	open, sincere	**dañarse**	to fall apart, get hurt
transparencia	openness, sincerity	**ateo**	atheist
enteramente	entirely	**que te frene**	that stops you
confianza	trust	**enfrentaron**	they confronted, faced

Antes de ver

A. Las amistades y las parejas.   Lee las siguientes oraciones e indica qué rasgos, en tu opinión, caracterizan mejor a un amigo / una amiga o a una pareja. Es posible que una descripción se aplique a ambos tipos de relaciones.

	AMIGO/A	PAREJA
1. Es como un hermano / una hermana.	☐	☐
2. Es totalmente honesto/a contigo.	☐	☐
3. Te respeta.	☐	☐
4. Tiene celos de ti.	☐	☐
5. Desconfía de ti.	☐	☐
6. Siempre está allí cuando lo/la necesitas.	☐	☐
7. Es como otro miembro de un equipo contigo para toda la vida.	☐	☐

B. En una pareja.   Escoge la mejor opción para completar las siguientes oraciones, según tu opinión. Después, explica el porqué de tu opinión.

---

* As in Argentina, many people in Paraguay and Uruguay use **vos** instead of **tú** forms. Some of the other **vos** forms you will hear Gustavo say are **te llevás, te quedás,** and **querés (quieres).**

1. El respeto es una cualidad (esencial/opcional) entre amigos y entre una pareja.
2. Los celos son (necesarios en / el comienzo del fin de) una relación.
3. Una buena pareja (puede separarse / trata de mantenerse unida).
4. Hoy en día es frecuente el divorcio a causa de la (situación económica / sociedad mayormente atea).
5. Vivir juntos antes de casarse (ayuda a la pareja a enfrentar los problemas juntos / contribuye al alto número de divorcios).

¡Veamos!

¿A quiénes se refiere? Indica a cuál de los tres tipos de relaciones se refiere Gustavo al decir las siguientes frases: a una buena amistad, a una amistad en peligro o a una pareja.

	BUENA AMISTAD	AMISTAD EN PELIGRO	PAREJA
1. …«ternura»…	☐	☐	☐
2. …brindarse (*give of oneself*) enteramente…	☐	☐	☐
3. …problemas de falta de confianza…	☐	☐	☐
4. …dicen cosas que no son lo que realmente quieren decir…	☐	☐	☐
5. …lo elegiste, la elegiste (*you chose him/her*)…	☐	☐	☐
6. …te llevás fantástico con esa persona…	☐	☐	☐
7. …querés convertirte en un equipo…	☐	☐	☐

Después de ver

A. Comparaciones. Ve de nuevo la entrevista y apunta las características de la amistad, según la opinión de Gustavo. Después, comenta si compartes esta opinión o no.

La amistad para Gustavo	La amistad para mí

B. Discusión. Trabaja con dos o tres compañeros/as para comentar las siguientes preguntas. Luego, compartan sus opiniones con el resto de la clase.

1. ¿Cuál de las características que apuntaste en la **Actividad A** crees que sea la más esencial en una buena amistad?
2. En tu opinión, ¿cuáles son los factores que contribuyen a que una amistad se dañe?
3. ¿Es tu pareja necesariamente tu mejor amigo/a?
4. Gustavo dice que muchas parejas en Uruguay nunca enfrentan los problemas de la rutina diaria y que esto trae los problemas que producen el divorcio. ¿Estás de acuerdo con esta afirmación? ¿Hay otros factores más importantes que contribuyan a la alta incidencia de divorcios?

15.1 The Conditional

Forms

The conditional is frequently used to express what someone *would* do *if* a given set of circumstances were true. It is formed in Spanish by adding a set of personal endings to the conditional verb stem. As with the future tense, the conditional stem is generally the infinitive; there is only one set of endings for **-ar, -er,** and **-ir** verbs.

Conditional of Regular Verbs		
-ar	**-er**	**-ir**
prestaría	recogería	mentiría
prestarías	recogerías	mentirías
prestaría	recogería	mentiría
prestaríamos	recogeríamos	mentiríamos
prestaríais	recogeríais	mentiríais
prestarían	recogerían	mentirían

The verbs that have irregular stems in the future tense have those same stems in the conditional.

INFINITIVE	STEM	CONDITIONAL	INFINITIVE	STEM	CONDITIONAL
		Conditional of Irregular Verbs			
caber	cabr-	cabría, cabrías, cabría,...	poner	pondr-	pondría, pondrías, pondría,...
poder	podr-	podría, podrías, podría,...	tener	tendr-	tendría, tendrías, tendría,...
querer	querr-	querría, querrías, querría,...	salir	saldr-	saldría, saldrías, saldría,...
saber	sabr-	sabría, sabrías, sabría,...	valer	valdr-	valdría, valdrías, valdría,...
			venir	vendr-	vendría, vendrías, vendría,...
decir	dir-	diría, dirías, diría,...			
hacer	har-	haría, harías, haría,...			

NOTES:

- The endings for the **yo** and **usted/él/ella** forms are identical; you will know which person is meant by the context.
- The conditional form of **hay** is **habría** (*there would be*).

Uses

You have already learned some forms of the conditional to make polite requests.

| ¿Te **gustaría** ir al cine conmigo? | Would you like to go to the movies with me? |
| ¿Me **haría** el favor de mandar estas cartas? | Would you please send these letters for me? |

The conditional forms of **querer, poder,** and **deber** are also useful for softening requests and expressing obligations.

¿**Querrías** tomar algo, Rafael?	Would you like something to drink, Rafael?
¿**Podría** usted venir a las 8:00?	Could you (Would you please) come at 8:00?
Deberíamos invitar a Alicia.	We should invite Alicia.

The conditional has other uses, but the most important one you should be aware of for now is the expression of reactions (what you *would* do) in a hypothetical circumstance (if certain conditions were true).

Yo, en tu lugar, no **iría** a Montevideo.	If I were you, I wouldn't go to Montevideo.
Ramón es un amigo muy discreto; nunca le **revelaría** mis secretos a nadie.	Ramón is a very discreet friend; he would never reveal my secrets to anyone.
Yo no **saldría** con él, Marisa. No es muy simpático.	I wouldn't go out with him, Marisa. He's not very nice.

NOTES:

- In some cases, English *would* is *not* a signal of the conditional tense. When *would* + *verb* describes a habitual action in the past, Spanish uses the imperfect, as you learned in **Capítulo 9.**

| My dad *would* always *give* us some money on the weekends. | Mi padre siempre nos **daba** dinero los fines de semana. |

- When *wouldn't* + *verb* indicates *refusal* in the past, Spanish uses the preterit of **querer.**

| Antonio *wouldn't help* us. | Antonio **no quiso ayudar**nos. |

Actividades

A. Amigos diversos. ¿Por qué sería interesante tener amigos de orígenes diferentes? Completa las siguientes oraciones con ideas originales.

1. Yo tendría la oportunidad de…
2. Podría aprender (a)…
3. Sería interesante…
4. Me ayudaría a…

B. El amigo / La amiga ideal. Primero, conjuga los verbos entre paréntesis en el condicional para describir las características del amigo / de la amiga ideal. Después, indica si estás de acuerdo o no con cada idea.

El amigo / La amiga ideal…

1. siempre (ayudarme) en una situación difícil.
2. (mentir) para protegerme.
3. (revelar) mis secretos.
4. (hacerme) favores sin explicación.
5. nunca (pelearse) conmigo.
6. (ser) honesto/a conmigo.
7. (acompañarme) a todas partes.
8. siempre (decirme) la verdad.

C. **Situaciones difíciles.** Las siguientes personas se encuentran en situaciones difíciles. ¿Qué harías por ellas? **¡OJO!** Contesta con el condicional; puedes usar los verbos entre paréntesis o ideas originales que se te ocurran.

1. A tu amigo Raúl le robaron la cartera y se quedó sin dinero. (prestarle dinero)
2. Un estudiante de intercambio está solo en su residencia todo el fin de semana. (invitarlo a mi casa)
3. Tu prima Cristina se encuentra sin trabajo después de terminar la escuela secundaria. (ayudarla a buscar trabajo)
4. Tu profesor(a) de español deja caer (*drops*) todos los papeles de la clase. (recogerlos)
5. Algunos amigos de tu residencia estudian hasta muy tarde en la biblioteca y tienen miedo de caminar a casa. (llamar un taxi)

D. **Motivos para casarse**

Paso 1. Lee los resultados de esta encuesta sobre los motivos para casarse. ¿En qué se diferencian los motivos de los chicos y los de las chicas?

MODELOS   Los chicos se casarían _____, pero las chicas, no.

Las chicas _____, pero los chicos, no.

_____ sería más importante para los/las chicos/as.

Paso 2. Explícale a un grupo de compañeros/as el motivo más importante para ti y el motivo menos probable.

Yo me casaría _____.
No me casaría _____.

¿Por qué se casarían los chicos?

1. Por amor.
2. Para formar una familia.
3. Para compartir su vida con la chica a la que aman.
4. Para no quedarse solos de viejos.
5. Para entregarse totalmente a ella.
6. Para legalizar su situación.
7. Porque no encuentran otra solución.
8. Por educación.[a]
9. Por imposiciones familiares.
10. Por dinero o algo similar.

¿Por qué se casarían las chicas?

1. Por amor.
2. Para compartir su vida con el chico al que aman.
3. Porque es una forma de demostrar su amor.
4. Para legalizar la relación.
5. Para tener a alguien en quien depositar toda su confianza.
6. Para formar una familia.
7. Por tradición.
8. Por causas morales, éticas o religiosas.
9. Por imposición de los padres.
10. Por dinero o algo similar.

[a]Por… *As a matter of courtesy.*

● 15.2 Results and Consequences

Si Clauses

In English, the results and consequences of different situations are expressed in complex sentences with an *if . . . then . . .* pattern: *If you break it, (then) you'll have to pay for it.* Spanish has a similar construction using the word **si** (*if*). Note that the **si** clause can go before or after the main clause.

1. Habitual situations, habitual results: **si** clause → *present indicative,* main clause → *present indicative.*

Si mis amigos me **engañan,** ya no los **considero** amigos.	*If my friends deceive me, I no longer consider them friends.*
Ramón siempre me **ayuda si** se lo **pido.**	*Ramón always helps me if I ask him to.*

2. Possible (present) situations, future results: **si** clause → *present indicative,* main clause → *future tense.*

Si tratas de cambiarme, no **seré** tu amigo.	*If you try to change me, I won't be your friend.*
Podrás ir con nosotros **si** tu amigo te **presta** el dinero.	*You can (will be able to) go with us if your friend lends you the money.*

3. Hypothetical or contrary-to-fact situations, conditional results: **si** clause → *imperfect subjunctive,* main clause → *conditional.* As shown in the preceding formula, you can use the *conditional* verb forms that you learned in **Forma y función 15.1** to express the results of a hypothetical situation. However, to express the hypothetical or contrary-to-fact situation (the **si** clause), Spanish uses the *imperfect* (also called *"past"*) *subjunctive.*

Si me **prestaras** el dinero, **iría** contigo.	*If you loaned me the money, I'd go with you. (But you haven't loaned it to me.)*
Si mis amigos **estuvieran** aquí, nos **divertiríamos** mucho.	*If my friends were here, we'd have a lot of fun. (But they aren't here.)*

Forms of the Imperfect Subjunctive

The imperfect subjunctive of *all* verbs is formed by deleting the **-ron** ending from the **ustedes/ellos/ellas** form of the preterit and adding the endings **-ra, -ras, -ra, -ramos, -rais, -ran.** Technically, there are *no* irregular verbs in the imperfect subjunctive; any apparent irregularities come from the preterit stem. As such, you should review the irregular preterit forms you learned in **Capítulo 8.**

Imperfect Subjunctive

INFINTIVE	ustedes/ellos/ellas PRETERIT	STEM	IMPERFECT SUBJUNCTIVE FORMS	
prestar	prestaron	presta-	prestara prestaras prestara	prestáramos prestarais prestaran
aprender	aprendieron	aprendie-	aprendiera aprendieras aprendiera	aprendiéramos aprendierais aprendieran
salir	salieron	salie-	saliera salieras saliera	saliéramos salierais salieran
estar	estuvieron	estuvie-	estuviera estuvieras estuviera	estuviéramos estuvierais estuvieran
decir	dijeron	dije-	dijera dijeras dijera	dijéramos dijerais dijeran
ir/ser	fueron	fue-	fuera fueras fuera	fuéramos fuerais fueran
oír	oyeron	oye-	oyera oyeras oyera	oyéramos oyerais oyeran
sentir	sintieron	sintie-	sintiera sintieras sintiera	sintiéramos sintierais sintieran

NOTES:

- The vowel immediately preceding the **-r-** in the **nosotros** ending requires an accent: **anduviéramos, habláramos, leyéramos,** and so on.
- The imperfect subjunctive of **hay** is **hubiera** (**si hubiera...** = *if there were . . .*).

Actividades

A. Tus reacciones. ¿Cómo reaccionarías en las siguientes situaciones? Escoge una de las posibilidades, o inventa una respuesta original.

1. Si mi mejor amigo/a no supiera expresar sus sentimientos,…
   a. le recomendaría un buen psicólogo.
   b. yo tomaría la iniciativa para empezar la conversación.
2. Si no me dijera la verdad,…
   a. ya no sería mi mejor amigo/a.   b. le pediría una explicación.
3. Si revelara un secreto importante mío (*of mine*)…
   a. lo/la confrontaría.   b. yo revelaría un secreto suyo (*of his/hers*).

4. Si me pidiera una gran cantidad de dinero,...
   a. se la daría sin preguntas.   **b.** le preguntaría para qué la necesita.
5. Si no me dejara en paz (*leave me alone*),...
   a. le gritaría (*I would shout*).   **b.** iría a otro lugar para estar solo/a.

B. Vivir lejos de la comunidad.   Muchas personas prefieren vivir cerca de la comunidad o barrio donde crecieron, pero no siempre es posible. ¿En qué circunstancias vivirías tú lejos de tus raíces? Considera las siguientes posibilidades y añade otras que se te ocurran. Usa el imperfecto de subjuntivo.

Yo viviría lejos de mi comunidad si...

1. (conseguir) una oferta de trabajo muy buena en otra ciudad / otro país.
2. (tener) problemas o peleas (*fights*) con un(a) pariente.
3. ya no (tener) amistades en la comunidad.
4. (cometer) un crimen.
5. (enamorarse) de alguien de otra ciudad / otro país.
6. no (estar) de acuerdo con la política local.
7. ¿ ?

C. ¿En qué circunstancias?   ¿En qué circunstancias harías las siguientes cosas? Completa las oraciones de manera lógica con el imperfecto de subjuntivo.

1. Me casaría con un extranjero / una extranjera si...
2. Contradiría (*I would contradict*) los deseos de mi familia si...
3. Tendría celos de mi novio/a (esposo/a) si...
4. Dejaría la universidad si...
5. Cambiaría de casa si...
6. Estaría enojado/a con un amigo / una amiga si...

D. Una comunidad mejor.   ¿Qué cosas cambiarías para mejorar tu comunidad o la sociedad en general? Trabaja con un compañero / una compañera de clase para apuntar algunos problemas sociales que te gustaría cambiar. Después, di cómo se podrían mejorar esas cosas (un cambio posible) y cuáles serían las consecuencias o los resultados probables de ese cambio.

MODELO   Si tuviéramos leyes menos permisivas tendríamos menos divorcios.

Problema social	Cambio posible	Consecuencia(s) o resultado(s)

▲ *¿Qué estarías haciendo con tus amigos si no estuvieras en la clase de español en este momento?*

Análisis cultural

La siguiente cita tomada de una fuente escrita en inglés para anglohablantes va a aumentar tus conocimientos sobre algunos fenómenos culturales en Paraguay y Uruguay. ¿Es consistente esta información con la perspectiva de Gustavo de la **Entrevista 1?** Usa lo que has aprendido en este capítulo sobre Paraguay y Uruguay, más tu propia experiencia, para contestar las preguntas que siguen la cita.

❝Those untutored in Latin American affairs frequently confuse Uruguay and Paraguay because the names have a similar sound and because of the two countries' geographic proximity. Two more dissimilar nations, however, could not be found. Landlocked Paraguay is still Indian country; half the population is bilingual and speaks Guaraní as well as Spanish; there is even a literature in the language, and newspapers print a portion of their news in it. The people of Paraguay are poor in a land of potential wealth; the women still far outnumber the men; about 500,000 Paraguayans live in exile because of the unpleasant political and economic conditions in the country, for General Alfredo Stroessner, who was in power from 1954 to 1989, maintained the ancient tradition of Francia and López, and ruled the nation with a stern hand. Asunción, the capital, is a picturesque city of about 500,000, but it is a far cry from Uruguay's bustling Montevideo. There are no other cities of consequence in Paraguay.

(sigue)

Uruguay, in contrast, is one of the most literate, intelligent, and homogeneous countries in Latin America. Its population is almost entirely Spanish and Italian, the Indian influence is practically nil, and it has the one large capital in Latin America with no sprawling slums. The extremes of rich and poor are not obvious in Uruguay; the middle class predominates in the national life.**99**

Source: *The Epic of Latin America, Fourth Edition*

1. ¿A qué se debe la confusión que tienen muchas personas respecto a Paraguay y Uruguay? ¿Conoces otros casos de nombres geográficos que causen confusión?

2. ¿En qué se parecen Paraguay y Uruguay? ¿En qué son diferentes? Piensa en los siguientes temas: la etnicidad de la población, las lenguas que se hablan en cada país, el nivel socioeconómico de la población.

3. ¿Cuáles son los factores que, en tu opinión, contribuyen al alto nivel de pobreza en Paraguay? ¿Y qué factores ayudan a Uruguay a estar en una mejor situación socioeconómica?

4. Basándote en la cita y en lo que has aprendido en éste y otros capítulos, ¿cómo crees que se manifieste el espíritu de comunidad en estos dos países?

● Written Accents (Summary and Review)

In previous chapters you have learned to use written accent marks in the following situations:

- to mark question words (**¿Cómo?**).
- to distinguish homophones in spelling (**tú** = *you* vs. **tu** = *your*).
- to help locate the stressed syllable in unfamiliar words.

The rules you studied in **Capítulo 3** are for *reading* words already printed. The rules for *writing* accent marks in your original compositions are just the opposite: They assume that you already know both how to pronounce the word (i.e., which syllable is stressed) and the word ending. When native speakers of Spanish learn how to spell, they phrase the rules in the following way.

1. Words stressed on the next-to-last syllable (called **palabras llanas** in Spanish) that end in a vowel, **n,** or **s** *do not* need an accent.
2. Words stressed on the last syllable **(palabras agudas)** that end in a consonant other than **n** or **s** *do not* need an accent.
3. Any deviation from the two previous patterns requires a written accent. Note the following cases.

- Words stressed three syllables from the end (**úl-ti-mo, có-mi-co,** and so on) have the special name **palabras esdrújulas;** since they always break rules 1 and 2, **esdrújulas** always bear a written accent mark.
- Use a written accent to show that the vowels **i** or **u** are pronounced in a separate syllable from an adjacent **a, e,** or **o** (i.e., to break up a diphthong: **Ma-rí-a, frí-o, con-ti-nú-a, re-ú-no,** and so on).

For example, suppose you want to write the word pronounced **[a-mo-ro-so].** You hear the stress on the next-to-last syllable; the word ends in a vowel, so rule 1 says that no accent is necessary **(amoroso).** To write **[u-til],** you also hear the stress on the next-to-last syllable, but the word ends in a consonant other than **n** or **s,** so you must write an accent on the **u** to indicate this exception to rule 1 **(útil).**

The *Manual de práctica* has activities to practice the material explained in this section.

🔵 Para formar pareja

Cuando se trata de **formar pareja,** las costumbres en Uruguay se parecen mucho a las de otras partes del mundo, pero quizá **el romanticismo** juegue un papel más importante que en otros lugares.

Los jóvenes típicamente **se conocen** en el colegio o en la universidad, en el trabajo, **de paseo**[a] por los parques, en las playas, en las discotecas, en los cines y en otros lugares que **frecuentan,** y vuelven a los mismos lugares cuando tienen una **cita.**

Debido[b] al estado de la economía, no se suele gastar mucho dinero cuando dos personas salen juntas. Por eso, la forma más popular de conocerse es pasar el tiempo **charlando.**

Por lo general,[c] los jóvenes empiezan a **salir en pareja** antes de los 20 años y a veces tardan en **comprometerse.**[d] Según muchos expertos, es muy **sano** desarrollar una **relación íntima** de esta manera, ya que la pareja llega a conocerse mejor.

Ya se sabe que la amistad es la base de una buena relación. Pero también es lindo pasar de la amistad a gestos[e] más románticos: regalarse flores, tomarse de la mano, comunicarse sin palabras y **mirarse profundamente a los ojos.** Así se fortalecen[f] los **lazos afectivos.**[g]

▲ *Dicen que los hispanos son más cariñosos en público que la gente de otras culturas. ¿Estás de acuerdo? ¿Por qué sí o por qué no?*

Sin duda, conseguir una buena pareja es una de las bases del **bienestar**[h] **emocional para toda la vida.**

[a]de… *on a walk* [b]*Due* [c]Por… *In general* [d]*getting engaged* [e]*gestures* [f]se… *are strengthened* [g]lazos… *emotional bonds* [h]*well-being*

Actividades

A. Definiciones.   ¿A cuáles de las palabras o expresiones en negrita (*boldface*) del vocabulario anterior se refieren las siguientes definiciones?

1. para siempre
2. hacer la promesa de casarse con alguien
3. el opuesto de **dañino** (*harmful*)
4. establecer una relación íntima
5. ir a un mismo lugar varias veces
6. conversar informalmente
7. conexiones sentimentales
8. un acuerdo entre dos personas para ir al cine, por ejemplo

B. Relaciones lógicas. Explica la relación entre los tres elementos de las siguientes series. Puedes cambiar el orden de los elementos si te ayuda a explicar la relación lógica.

MODELO   conocer **/** compatible **/** frecuentar →
                  Las personas que frecuentan los mismos lugares pueden conocer a personas compatibles con los mismos intereses.

1. salir **/** comprometerse **/** formar pareja
2. salir **/** de paseo **/** frecuentar
3. la cita **/** conocerse **/** formar pareja
4. la relación íntima **/** sano/a **/** el bienestar emocional
5. el romanticismo **/** enamorarse **/** los lazos afectivos

C. Citas. Trabaja con dos o tres compañeros/as para comentar las siguientes preguntas. Después, compara las respuestas de tu grupo con las de otros grupos.

1. En tu opinión, ¿es difícil o fácil encontrar pareja?
2. ¿Dónde se conocen las personas de tu generación?
3. ¿Qué acciones o actividades consideras románticas? ¿Por qué?
4. ¿Te gusta salir con una persona romántica? ¿Por qué sí o por qué no?
5. Entre las parejas que conoces, ¿típicamente sale sola una pareja o con otras parejas?
6. En tu región/país, ¿quién paga generalmente en las citas: el hombre, la mujer, el/la que invita, etcétera?
7. ¿Cómo sería la cita perfecta para ti?

D. El bienestar emocional. Trabaja con un compañero / una compañera para comentar las siguientes preguntas.

1. ¿Qué cualidades (físicas, emocionales, intelectuales, de personalidad, etcétera) buscas en una pareja? ¿Son estas cualidades diferentes de las que buscas en un amigo / una amiga?
2. ¿Tardas mucho en establecer una relación íntima con alguien?
3. ¿Es la pareja ideal para ti como un amigo / una amiga, o es algo diferente?
4. ¿Crees que sea posible conocer a tu pareja ideal? ¿Por qué sí o por qué no?
5. ¿Puedes sentirte emocionalmente bien sin pareja, o necesitas tener a alguien a tu lado para sentirte feliz?

You can watch this interview on the *Entrevistas* Video or Interactive CD-ROM or listen to the audio on the Online Learning Center (**www.mhhe.com/entrevistas2**).

Wanda Solla

«*Hay muchos lugares para conocerse.*»

Nombre: Wanda

Apellido: Solla

Edad: 26 años

Nació en: Montevideo, Uruguay

Vocabulario útil

cuán rígidos	how strict	**una moda**	a fad
cálido	warm	**se paga a medias**	the bill is split

Antes de ver

¿Cómo formar pareja?   Wanda va a hablar de cómo se forman las parejas en Uruguay. Lee las siguientes oraciones e indica cuáles en tu opinión describen las costumbres de tu región/país.

1. ☐ Los jóvenes comienzan a salir entre los 12 y 15 años.
2. ☐ Los padres son más rígidos con las chicas que con los chicos.
3. ☐ Los jóvenes se conocen en discotecas y en el colegio.
4. ☐ La costa/playa es un lugar común para las citas.
5. ☐ Es común salir a tomar café u otras bebidas.
6. ☐ En general la cuenta se paga a medias en una cita.
7. ☐ La gente se busca y se conoce por el Internet.
8. ☐ Las personas que se conocen en el Internet forman pareja y se casan.
9. ☐ Aún (*Still*) existe el romanticismo.

¡Veamos!

Las relaciones en Uruguay.   Primero, lee las siguientes oraciones que Wanda dice en su entrevista. Luego, mientras ves la entrevista, apunta la información que falta.

1. « ...a veces los jóvenes _____ _____ en la costa, _____ _____, que es la bebida típica de Uruguay como en Argentina también, y bueno ahí _____ muchos jóvenes.»

2. «[El] Internet es algo ____ ____ en Uruguay. Se empezó a usar como una moda en el año ____. Sí, se buscan parejas y sí, ____ ____ ____. Y se conoce a mucha gente también de otros países… y algunos hasta ____ ____ ____.»

3. «A veces surge la circunstancia de que uno de los dos no ____ _____, a veces es ____ _____,… Y bueno, a veces uno ____ ____ los dos;… »

4. «Mi país es un país muy chiquito. Muy pocos ____ _____. A ésos, nos escuchan hablar y, parecemos _____ porque somos nada más que ____ _____ de habitantes en el país entero, un millón y medio en la _____.»

Después de ver

¿Qué dijo? Revisa las oraciones de la actividad en **Antes de ver,** ve de nuevo la entrevista y di qué oraciones se aplican a Uruguay, según Wanda.

Piénsalo bien

Trabaja con dos o tres compañeros/as para comentar las siguientes preguntas. Después, compara las respuestas de tu grupo con las de otros grupos.

1. ¿A qué edad crees que sea apropiado que los jóvenes salgan en pareja? ¿Crees que haya una edad mínima? En tu opinión, ¿es la misma edad tanto para los chicos como para las chicas?
2. ¿Deben los padres darles libertad absoluta a los jóvenes cuando salen en pareja, o deben controlar la situación y poner límites? Justifica tu respuesta.
3. La costumbre de tomar mate en grupo sirve para unir a las personas en Uruguay. ¿Hay en tu región/país alguna costumbre que sirva para unir a las parejas y a la comunidad en general?
4. En épocas anteriores, siempre pagaba el hombre en una cita. ¿Cuáles eran las ventajas y las desventajas de esa costumbre? ¿Crees que sea más romántico pagar a medias?
5. ¿Crees que sea posible desarrollar una relación íntima por el Internet? ¿Conoces a alguien que se haya (*has gotten*) casado gracias al Internet?

15.3 The Subjunctive (Summary)

Fully understanding and mastering the subjunctive can take many years for English speakers. Throughout *Entrevistas*, we have strived to make your introduction to the subjunctive as simple and straightforward as possible, exposing you to only its most basic and most frequent uses. There are other uses and even other tenses of the subjunctive, but for now you need only concern yourself with the following summary table of what you learned in **Capítulos 13** and **14**. Note that most of the cue verbs (e.g., **quiero**) in the following tables are given in **yo** forms for ease of illustration.

Cases That Require the Subjunctive

FUNCTION	CUES
possibility, probability	**Es posible que... , Es probable que...**
volition, hope	**Quiero que... , Necesito que... , Espero que...**
influence	**Insisto en que... , Permito que... , Prohíbo que...**
doubt; questioning beliefs	**Dudo que... , No creo que... , No pienso que... , ¿Crees que... ?**
emotion	**Es increíble que... , Me alegro de que... , Me sorprende que...**
judgments	**Es importante que... , Es mejor que... , Me gusta que...**
contingent actions	**a menos que... , antes de que... , con tal (de) que... , para que...**
implied future actions	**cuando... , después de que... , hasta que... , tan pronto como...**

Cases That Do *Not* Require the Subjunctive

FUNCTION	CUES
certainty	**Creo que... , Pienso que... , No dudo que... , Es obvio que...**
completed or habitual actions	**cuando... , después de que... , hasta que... , tan pronto como...**

NOTES:

- In general, the subjunctive is used in dependent clauses only if the subject is different from that of the main clause. If the subject of the dependent clause is the same as that of the main clause, the infinitive is normally used instead of a dependent clause.

Julia **quiere** que sus amigos **se casen.**	*Julia wants her friends to get married.*
Julia quiere **casarse.**	*Julia wants to get married.*

- After expressions like **cuando, después de que, hasta que,** and **tan pronto como,** the subjunctive is used if the action has not yet occurred (implied future); the indicative is used if the action is habitual or has already been completed.

Mi madre va a estar contenta **cuando me case.**	*My mother is going to be happy when I get married.* (implied future action)
Mi madre estaba muy contenta **cuando me casé.**	*My mother was very happy when I got married.* (completed action)
Normalmente, las madres están contentas **cuando** sus hijos **se casan.**	*Normally, mothers are happy when(ever) their children get married.* (habitual action)

- In a dependent clause that follows a noun, the choice of indicative or subjunctive depends on the speaker's certainty of the existence of the noun.

Rafael conoce a muchos paraguayos que **viven** en este país.	*Rafael knows many Paraguayans that live in this country.* (He knows them; they exist.)
No hay ningún paraguayo que **viva** en esta ciudad.	*There aren't any Paraguayans who live in this city.* (None exist.)
¿Hay alguien aquí que **hable** guaraní?	*Is there someone here who speaks Guaraní?* (The speaker is unsure of the existence of any Guaraní speakers.)

Actividades

A. La primera cita. Completa las siguientes oraciones sobre las citas con el indicativo o el subjuntivo de los verbos entre paréntesis, según el contexto. Luego, di si estás de acuerdo o no con las afirmaciones.

1. La mujer debe esperar hasta que el hombre le (abrir) la puerta.
2. En una cita, es mejor que el hombre (pagar) la cuenta.
3. Es bueno que la mujer (escoger) las actividades de la cita.
4. El hombre siempre prefiere hacer actividades que no (costar) mucho.
5. A la mujer le gusta que el hombre la (recoger) en coche para que ella no (tener) que llegar al lugar de la cita en transporte público.
6. Cuando la cita (terminarse), la pareja debe besarse.

B. Actitudes diferentes. Completa lo que dicen las siguientes personas con el indicativo, el subjuntivo o el infinitivo de los verbos entre paréntesis, según el contexto. Luego, di si estás de acuerdo con sus opiniones o no.

1. «Muchas personas creen que los adolescentes no (ser) muy responsables hoy en día.»
2. «Muchos adolescentes necesitan que sus padres les (dar) dinero para poder salir.»
3. «Muchos padres esperan que sus hijos (conocer) a personas de la misma clase social.»

4. «Por lo general, los padres insisten en que sus hijas (seguir) reglas diferentes de las de sus hijos.»

5. «Las chicas prefieren que la pareja (salir) en grupo, en cambio, los chicos prefieren (salir) solos con ellas.»

6. «Es importante (hablar) con los adolescentes sobre las relaciones sexuales antes de que (tener) su primera cita.»

7. «Los padres prohíben que sus hijos (tener) relaciones sexuales antes de (casarse).»

8. «En Uruguay muchos jóvenes (vivir) en casa de sus padres hasta que (casarse).»

C. Consejos para Pascual. Pascual es estudiante de intercambio y ya lleva varios meses en tu ciudad sin conocer a muchas personas. ¿Qué le recomiendas? Completa las siguientes sugerencias con el indicativo, el subjuntivo o el infinitivo, según el contexto.

1. Es importante que tú…
2. Debes…
3. Te recomiendo que…
4. Es obvio que…
5. Tienes que…
6. No vas a estar contento a menos que…

D. La boda. La boda es originalmente una institución religiosa, pero hoy en día hay muchas bodas seculares. ¿Qué opinas tú sobre esta institución? Comenta las siguientes preguntas con dos compañeros/as. Luego, compara las respuestas de tu grupo con las de otros grupos.

Expresiones útiles: Es posible que… , Es importante que la pareja… , Dudo que la boda… , Es verdad que… , Cuando yo me case (mi hermano/a se case)… , Me gusta que… , Yo no me caso (Mi hermano/a no se casa) a menos que… , Creo que…

1. ¿Quieres casarte algún día? (Si ya estás casado/a, da tu opinión sobre los deseos de un hermano soltero / una hermana soltera u otro/a pariente que no esté casado/a.)

2. ¿Cómo quieres (quiere tu hermano/a) que sea la ceremonia?

3. ¿Crees que la boda sea una ceremonia anticuada e innecesaria?

4. ¿En qué circunstancias debe casarse una pareja?

5. ¿Es bueno que dos personas vivan juntas antes de casarse?

6. ¿Qué aspectos de las bodas te gustan en general?

7. ¿Qué ventajas e inconvenientes tiene el casarse? ¿Y el *no* casarse?

Sobre la lectura ¿Ya has buscado pareja en el Internet? En esta lectura vas a leer sobre algunos consejos a los internautas (*Internet surfers*) que piensan probar este modo de buscar pareja.

Antes de leer

A. Para comenzar. Basándote en tus experiencias y opiniones personales, explica cuáles son las ventajas y las desventajas de buscar pareja en el ciberespacio.

VOCABULARIO ÚTIL

la distancia	**eficaz**	**peligroso/a**
anónimo/a	**fácil**	

B. Consejos

Paso 1. ¿Qué le recomiendas a un amigo / una amiga que quiere buscar pareja en el Internet? Forma oraciones completas con las siguientes frases para dar consejos sobre cómo escribir un buen anuncio personal y realizar la primera cita. Usa mandatos afirmativos o negativos.

MODELOS   poner tu foto en tu perfil →
          Pon tu foto en tu perfil.
          No pongas tu foto en tu perfil.

1. compartir tus esperanzas y tus sueños para el futuro
2. contar cuáles son tus pasatiempos e intereses
3. dar tu número de teléfono
4. incluir una descripción de lo que te gustaría hacer en tu primera cita
5. citarse (*set up a date*) con la persona en un lugar solitario
6. usar mucha creatividad al escribir tu perfil

Paso 2. Escribe dos consejos originales para añadir a la lista del **Paso 1.**

C. El contexto. Usa el contexto para adivinar el significado de las palabras subrayadas y escoge la mejor traducción entre paréntesis.

1. Cuéntale al mundo qué es lo que hace de ti una persona especial y qué esperas poder <u>aportar</u> (*to contribute / to enjoy / to meet*) a una relación.
2. Simplemente intenta no exagerar en tu lista de <u>requisitos</u> (*desires / requirements / restrictions*) y preferencias.
3. Recuerda que la primera impresión es la que más <u>perdura</u> (*deceives / goes away / lasts*).
4. Antes de ir a tu cita, informa a tus amigos, familiares o a alguien en quien de verdad puedas <u>confiar</u> (*keep a secret / keep calm / trust*).
5. Si la otra persona insiste en llevarte a otro lugar más <u>apartado</u> (*apparent / private / remote*), ¡dile que no!

¡Busca y encuentra tu media naranja[a]!

Citas en el ciberespacio

¡Donde los paraguayos encuentran el amor!

Búsqueda rápida		Ingreso a miembros	
Yo soy: hombre	Edad desde: 21 hasta: 35	Nombre de usuario	
Busco: mujer	Ciudad: Asunción	Clave	

Recomendaciones para tu perfil

Está demostrado que tu perfil será el primer contacto que tendrás con los demás. A continuación, te damos algunos consejos para que tu perfil sea más atractivo cuando otros lo lean.

La foto: Pon tu foto en tu perfil. Recuerda que el amor a primera vista siempre funciona.

Pasatiempos e intereses: No temas contar cuáles son tus pasatiempos y tus intereses en tu perfil personal. Lo que tú haces en tu tiempo libre refleja muy bien qué clase de persona eres.

Virtudes y atributos: No dudes en hablar sobre tus virtudes y atributos como persona. Éste no es el momento de ser modesto ni tímido. Cuéntale al mundo qué es lo que hace de ti una persona especial y qué esperas poder aportar a una relación, ya sea un muy buen sentido del humor o una actitud positiva o despreocupada[b] frente a la vida.

Sé creativo/a: Usa la creatividad al escribir tu perfil. ¿Qué te parece incluir un poema o una descripción de lo que considerarías una primera cita maravillosa? ¡Crea un perfil que se distinga de los demás!

Esperanzas y sueños: El hecho de compartir tus esperanzas y tus sueños para el futuro es una excelente forma de darte a conocer.[c] ¿Quién sabe?, Quizás encuentres a alguien que siempre haya soñado con[d] dar la vuelta al mundo navegando[e] o con jubilarse[f] a los 45 años igual que tú.

Sé realista: Intenta ser realista al describir las características que estás buscando en la otra persona. Incluir una lista con unas pocas características importantes está bien, simplemente intenta no exagerar en tu lista de requisitos y preferencias.

La primera impresión: Diviértete mientras escribes tu perfil y no dudes en transmitir tu personalidad. Elige las palabras que mejor transmitan tu actitud y tu manera de ver la vida y cuida las faltas de ortografía.[g] Recuerda que la primera impresión es la que más perdura.

Consejos para el primer encuentro

Una vez hayas conocido[h] a alguien que te interese, el siguiente paso será pedirle una cita. A continuación, te damos algunos consejos que esperamos que te sirvan de ayuda.

- Sé tu mismo/a, tanto antes como después de tu cita. No sientas vergüenza, debes estar seguro/a de que eres maravilloso/a tal y como tú eres.[i]
- Antes de ir a tu cita, informa a tus amigos, familiares o a alguien en que de verdad puedas confiar. Diles adónde vas y con quién. Asegúrate de que tomen nota de ello, e indica más o menos cuándo piensas regresar.
- Siempre cítate en un lugar público. Si la otra persona insiste en llevarte a otro lugar más apartado, o solitario, ¡dile que no y deshazte[j] de él/ella!
- Lleva contigo tu teléfono móvil o celular, si es posible.
- Nunca dejes tus objetos personales desatendidos. Recuerda en todo momento dónde pusiste tu bolso, cartera o chaqueta. Sobre todo, ten cuidado con las llaves de tu casa.
- No bebas mucho alcohol, ya que a veces te puede hacer perder la cabeza. Y tampoco le quites el ojo a tu copa.

---

[a]media... *soul mate*   [b]*worry-free*   [c]darte... *letting yourself be known*   [d]haya... *has dreamed of*   [e]*sailing*   [f]*retiring*   [g]cuida... *be mindful of spelling errors*   [h]Una... *Once you have met*   [i]tal... *just as you are*   [j]*rid yourself*

Después de leer

A. ¿Entendiste? Compara tus consejos de la **Actividad B** de **Antes de leer** para ver si corresponden a los consejos de la lectura. Si son diferentes, ¿cuáles prefieres? ¿Crees que los consejos de la lectura sean apropiados? ¿poco realistas? ¿demasiado cautelosos (*cautious*)?

B. Encuentros. Lee los siguientes anuncios personales dejados en *Citas en el ciberespacio* y contesta las preguntas que siguen en la página 458.

Rosa120
Ubicación: Asunción, Paraguay
24 años, buscando solamente amistad, cabello rubio, ojos marrones, 188cm, delgada
Me considero una persona apasionada por la vida y muy agradecida por todo lo bueno que he conquistado hasta hoy. Trato de vivir la vida y aprender de ella, que es lo que nos hace cada vez más humanos. Soy sociable, romántica, me encanta el deporte, me gusta salir a cenar, bailar con amigos y conocer a nuevas personas con quienes pueda entablar una amistad, ¿y por qué no?... una relación.

Arnaldito
Ubicación: Villarrica, Paraguay
24 años, cabello negro, ojos marrones, atlético, músculos definidos, atractivo, fumador ocasional
Hasta hoy día he tenido mala suerte en el amor. Sin embargo la esperanza es lo único que no se pierde. Sólo hay que perseverar y no dejar pasar las oportunidades que se presentan. Sé que algún día aparecerá esa mujer que haga de mi mundo un paraíso, y estoy preparado para darme por completo en nombre del amor.

Daniel90
Ubicación: San Lorenzo, Paraguay
26 años, delgado, atractivo, 180cm, ojos verdes, cabello castaño oscuro, ¡adrenalina a full!
Me gusta todo aquello que haga latir fuerte el corazón. Me gusta vivir el momento. Ya sea a alto o bajo voltaje. No tengo tabúes: cuánto más arriesgado, mejor.

PedroCanovas
Ubicación: Asunción, Paraguay
22 años, cabello negro, ojos cafés, 190cm
Soy una persona muy aventurera: Me gusta descubrir cosas, viajar, charlar, conocer a gente. Mi profesión hace que esté en contacto con mucha gente, pero quizá por eso se me ha pasado por alto estar con alguien en especial. En mi país estoy preparando las maletas para emprender algún tipo de viaje. ¿Adónde? No sé, pero quizá donde estés tú. ¿Qué te parece? Lo cierto es que saldré a buscar nuevos horizontes, ya que estoy soltero y sin hijos todavía.

Crystell
Ubicación: Asunción, Paraguay
18 años, buscando un hombre con quien compartir actividades, solamente amistad, esbelta, atractiva, 165cm, cabello castaño oscuro, ojos marrones
A ver... soy una joven a quien le gusta conocer a gente de diferentes nacionalidades con buena onda. Me gusta conocer o hacer amigos para conocer sus ideas, pensamientos, etcétera. Estoy en el sexto curso, y este año termino el colegio y comienzo la facultad. Me gustan los deportes extremistas, soy bastante aventurera y me encanta viajar.

---

1. ¿Han seguido estas personas los consejos dados en la lectura? Identifica ejemplos específicos en tu respuesta.
2. ¿Cómo describirías la personalidad de cada persona, según su descripción física y lo que dice sobre sus pasatiempos e intereses?
3. De todas las personas que se anuncian, ¿cuáles se llevarían mejor? Forma todas las parejas compatibles, según las descripciones. Luego, justifica tus opiniones frente a la clase.

C. **Tu anuncio.** Escribe un anuncio personal en el que describas tu apariencia física, tu personalidad, tus pasatiempos e intereses. Sigue los consejos de la lectura. Puedes usar los anuncios de la **Actividad B** como modelo.

D. **La primera conversación.** Imagina la primera correspondencia o conversación entre dos personas que acaban de encontrarse en el ciberespacio. ¿Cómo se saludarían? ¿Qué preguntas se harían? ¿Cómo se terminaría el encuentro? Escribe el diálogo entero.

PORTAFOLIO CULTURAL

Redacción

Manual de vida. Vas a desarrollar un manual en el que explicas tus recomendaciones para mantener el bienestar en la vida. Vas a resumir tus opiniones y consejos sobre muchos de los temas estudiados en *Entrevistas* y así revelar mucho sobre tu personalidad. Sigue los pasos en el *Manual de práctica* para elaborar tu manual.

Exploración

Investigación cultural. Busca más información sobre Paraguay o Uruguay en la biblioteca, en el *Entrevistas* Online Learning Center (**www.mhhe.com/entrevistas2**) o en otros sitios del Internet y preséntala a la clase. El *Manual de práctica* contiene más ideas para tu presentación.

Léxico activo

LA AMISTAD, EL AMOR Y LAS BODAS

el **amor**	love
la **pareja**	couple; partner; mate
casarse	to marry, get married
enamorarse (de)	to fall in love (with)
expresar los sentimientos	to express one's feelings
llegar (gu) a conocer	to get to know
mostrar (ue) cariño en público	to show affection in public
prestar	to loan
quererse (ie)	to love each other
honesto/a	honest

a pesar de	in spite of, despite
los demás	others
sin dudar	without hesitation

Repaso: engañar, tratar de + *inf.*

PROBLEMAS ENTRE AMIGOS/PAREJAS

avergonzar (üe) (c)	to embarrass
comunicarse (qu) bien/mal	to communicate well/poorly
divorciarse	to divorce, get divorced
dudar en + *inf.*	to hesitate to (*do something*)
hacer daño	to hurt, harm
llevarse bien/mal	to get along well/poorly

mantener la distancia entre los dos	to maintain distance between the two	los **lazos afectivos**	emotional bonds
pelearse	to fight	la **relación íntima**	intimate relationship
quejarse	to complain	el **romanticismo**	romanticism
revelar los secretos	to reveal one's secrets	**comprometerse**	to get engaged
separarse	to separate, get separated	**frecuentar**	to frequent
tener celos	to be jealous	**mirarse (profundamente) a los ojos**	to stare (deeply) into each other's eyes
tener personalidades/ valores incompatibles	to have incompatible personalities/values	**salir en pareja**	to go out as a couple
aislado/a	isolated	**sano/a**	healthy
		de paseo	on a walk
		para toda la vida	for life

PARA SUGERIR/PEDIR CON CORTESÍA

Deberíamos…	We should . . .
¿Querría usted… ?	Would you (*form.*) . . . ?

Repaso: **charlar, conocerse**

PARA FORMAR PAREJA

el **bienestar emocional**	emotional well-being
la **cita**	date

Appendix A: Basic Pronunciation Guide

LETTER(S)	PRONUNCIATION (OR CLOSEST ENGLISH SOUND)	EXAMPLES
a	like *a* in *father*	ca**sa**, **ga**to
b	hard **b**: like *b* in *boy* at the beginning of an utterance or after **m, n**	**b**ien, en **B**ogotá
(same as **v**)	soft **b**: upper and lower lips do not close completely; used everywhere else	muy **b**ien, La Ha**b**ana
c	hard **c**: like *c* in *car*; used before **a, o, u**, but with no puff of air (aspiration)	a**c**á, **c**ostar, **c**una
	soft **c**: before **e, i**; like *th* in *think* (Spain only); like *s* in *see* (other countries)	**c**ena, **c**in**c**o
ch	like *ch* in *church*	**ch**icle, mu**ch**acho
d	like *d* in *dog* at the beginning of an utterance or after **n, l**	**d**oy, un **d**ía, el **d**ía
	like *th* in *this* everywhere else	na**d**a, hay **d**os
e	like *e* in *café*	caf**é**, **e**char
f	like *f* in *fun*	**f**olclórico, **f**ijar
g	hard **g** (before **a, o, u**): like *g* in *go*	**g**ota, ten**g**o
	soft **g** (before **e, i**): like *h* in *hotel*; stronger in some dialects	**g**eneral, **g**itano
h	always silent	**h**ora, **h**uerto
i	like *i* in *machine*	c**i**ta, rub**í**
j	like *h* in *hotel*; stronger in some dialects	**j**ugar, fi**j**ar
k	like *k* in *kite*; used only in foreign words	**k**ilómetro
l	like *l* in *light*	**l**eche, a**l**a
ll	like *y* in *yes* in most dialects	**ll**ámame, ca**ll**e
m	like *m* in *mother*	**m**amá, **m**udarse
n	like *n* in *nest*	**n**o, **n**egar
	like *m* in *mother* before **b, m, p**	u**n** beso, e**n** peso
ñ	like *ny* in *canyon*	a**ñ**o, paname**ñ**o
o	like *o* in *joke*	b**o**b**o**, ch**o**que

LETTER(S)	PRONUNCIATION (OR CLOSEST ENGLISH SOUND)	EXAMPLES
p	like *p* in *pat*, but with no puff of air (aspiration)	**p**adre, a**p**io
qu	like hard **c**: used only before **e, i**	**qu**ien, **qu**e
r	single flap **r**: single tap of tongue against roof of mouth between vowels, at end of word, or after a consonant except **l, n**	ca**r**o, habla**r**
	trilled **r**: trilled like **rr** at beginning of word or after **l, n**	**r**ojo, En**r**ique, al**r**ededor
rr	trilled **r**: multiple flaps of tongue against roof of the mouth	ca**rr**o, puerto**rr**iqueño
s	like *s* in *sing*	**s**andía, mú**s**ica
t	like *t* in *touch* but with no puff of air (aspiration)	**t**odo, a**t**ún
u	like *oo* in *pool* but never like *u* in *music*	t**ú**, ab**u**so
v (same as **b**)	hard **b/v**: like *b* in *boy* at the beginning of an utterance or after **m, n**	¡**V**amos!, en **V**enezuela
	soft **b/v**: upper and lower lips do not close completely; used everywhere else	Las **V**egas, una **v**entana
w	like *w* in *will*; used only in foreign words	**W**ashington
x	like *x* in *extra*	e**x**amen
	like *h* in *hotel*	Mé**x**ico
y	like *y* in *yes* at beginning of syllable	**y**o, ma**y**a
	like *i* in *machine* at end of a syllable	ho**y**, esto**y**
z	like *th* in *think* (Spain only); like *s* in *sing* (other countries)	**z**apato, ca**z**ar

Appendix B: Verb Charts

A. Regular Verbs: Simple Tenses

INFINITIVE / PRESENT PARTICIPLE / PAST PARTICIPLE	INDICATIVE PRESENT	IMPERFECT	PRETERIT	FUTURE	CONDITIONAL	SUBJUNCTIVE PRESENT	IMPERFECT	IMPERATIVE
hablar / hablando / hablado	hablo	hablaba	hablé	hablaré	hablaría	hable	hablara	habla / no hables
	hablas	hablabas	hablaste	hablarás	hablarías	hables	hablaras	hable
	habla	hablaba	habló	hablará	hablaría	hable	hablara	hablemos
	hablamos	hablábamos	hablamos	hablaremos	hablaríamos	hablemos	habláramos	hablad / no habléis
	habláis	hablabais	hablasteis	hablaréis	hablaríais	habléis	hablarais	hablen
	hablan	hablaban	hablaron	hablarán	hablarían	hablen	hablaran	
comer / comiendo / comido	como	comía	comí	comeré	comería	coma	comiera	come / no comas
	comes	comías	comiste	comerás	comerías	comas	comieras	coma
	come	comía	comió	comerá	comería	coma	comiera	comamos
	comemos	comíamos	comimos	comeremos	comeríamos	comamos	comiéramos	comed / no comáis
	coméis	comíais	comisteis	comeréis	comeríais	comáis	comierais	coman
	comen	comían	comieron	comerán	comerían	coman	comieran	
vivir / viviendo / vivido	vivo	vivía	viví	viviré	viviría	viva	viviera	vive / no vivas
	vives	vivías	viviste	vivirás	vivirías	vivas	vivieras	viva
	vive	vivía	vivió	vivirá	viviría	viva	viviera	vivamos
	vivimos	vivíamos	vivimos	viviremos	viviríamos	vivamos	viviéramos	vivid / no viváis
	vivís	vivíais	vivisteis	viviréis	viviríais	viváis	vivierais	vivan
	viven	vivían	vivieron	vivirán	vivirían	vivan	vivieran	

B. Regular Verbs: Perfect Tenses

INDICATIVE PRESENT PERFECT		PAST PERFECT		PRETERIT PERFECT		FUTURE PERFECT		CONDITIONAL PERFECT		SUBJUNCTIVE PRESENT PERFECT		PAST PERFECT	
he	hablado	había	hablado	hube	hablado	habré	hablado	habría	hablado	haya	hablado	hubiera	hablado
has	comido	habías	comido	hubiste	comido	habrás	comido	habrías	comido	hayas	comido	hubieras	comido
ha	vivido	había	vivido	hubo	vivido	habrá	vivido	habría	vivido	haya	vivido	hubiera	vivido
hemos		habíamos		hubimos		habremos		habríamos		hayamos		hubiéramos	
habéis		habíais		hubisteis		habréis		habríais		hayáis		hubierais	
han		habían		hubieron		habrán		habrían		hayan		hubieran	

C. Irregular Verbs

INFINITIVE / PRESENT PARTICIPLE / PAST PARTICIPLE	INDICATIVE					SUBJUNCTIVE		IMPERATIVE
	PRESENT	IMPERFECT	PRETERIT	FUTURE	CONDITIONAL	PRESENT	IMPERFECT	
andar / andando / andado	ando	andaba	anduve	andaré	andaría	ande	anduviera	anda /
	andas	andabas	anduviste	andarás	andarías	andes	anduvieras	no andes
	anda	andaba	anduvo	andará	andaría	ande	anduviera	ande
	andamos	andábamos	anduvimos	andaremos	andaríamos	andemos	anduviéramos	andemos
	andáis	andabais	anduvisteis	andaréis	andaríais	andéis	anduvierais	andad / no andéis
	andan	andaban	anduvieron	andarán	andarían	anden	anduvieran	anden
caer / cayendo / caído	caigo	caía	caí	caeré	caería	caiga	cayera	cae /
	caes	caías	caíste	caerás	caerías	caigas	cayeras	no caigas
	cae	caía	cayó	caerá	caería	caiga	cayera	caiga
	caemos	caíamos	caímos	caeremos	caeríamos	caigamos	cayéramos	caigamos
	caéis	caíais	caísteis	caeréis	caeríais	caigáis	cayerais	caed / no caigáis
	caen	caían	cayeron	caerán	caerían	caigan	cayeran	caigan
dar / dando / dado	doy	daba	di	daré	daría	dé	diera	da /
	das	dabas	diste	darás	darías	des	dieras	no des
	da	daba	dio	dará	daría	dé	diera	dé
	damos	dábamos	dimos	daremos	daríamos	demos	diéramos	demos
	dais	dabais	disteis	daréis	daríais	deis	dierais	dad / no deis
	dan	daban	dieron	darán	darían	den	dieran	den
decir / diciendo / dicho	digo	decía	dije	diré	diría	diga	dijera	di /
	dices	decías	dijiste	dirás	dirías	digas	dijeras	no digas
	dice	decía	dijo	dirá	diría	diga	dijera	diga
	decimos	decíamos	dijimos	diremos	diríamos	digamos	dijéramos	digamos
	decís	decíais	dijisteis	diréis	diríais	digáis	dijerais	decid / no digáis
	dicen	decían	dijeron	dirán	dirían	digan	dijeran	digan
estar / estando / estado	estoy	estaba	estuve	estaré	estaría	esté	estuviera	está /
	estás	estabas	estuviste	estarás	estarías	estés	estuvieras	no estés
	está	estaba	estuvo	estará	estaría	esté	estuviera	esté
	estamos	estábamos	estuvimos	estaremos	estaríamos	estemos	estuviéramos	estemos
	estáis	estabais	estuvisteis	estaréis	estaríais	estéis	estuvierais	estad / no estéis
	están	estaban	estuvieron	estarán	estarían	estén	estuviera	estén
haber / habiendo / habido	he	había	hube	habré	habría	haya	hubiera	
	has	habías	hubiste	habrás	habrías	hayas	hubieras	
	ha	había	hubo	habrá	habría	haya	hubiera	
	hemos	habíamos	hubimos	habremos	habríamos	hayamos	hubiéramos	
	habéis	habíais	hubisteis	habréis	habríais	hayáis	hubierais	
	han	habían	hubieron	habrán	habrían	hayan	hubieran	
hacer / haciendo / hecho	hago	hacía	hice	haré	haría	haga	hiciera	haz /
	haces	hacías	hiciste	harás	harías	hagas	hacieras	no hagas
	hace	hacía	hizo	hará	haría	haga	hiciera	haga
	hacemos	hacíamos	hicimos	haremos	haríamos	hagamos	hiciéramos	hagamos
	hacéis	hacíais	hicisteis	haréis	haríais	hagáis	hicierais	haced / no hagáis
	hacen	hacían	hicieron	harán	harían	hagan	hicieran	hagan

C. Irregular Verbs (*continued*)

Infinitive / Present Participle / Past Participle	INDICATIVE					SUBJUNCTIVE		IMPERATIVE
	Present	Imperfect	Preterit	Future	Conditional	Present	Imperfect	
ir yendo ido	voy vas va vamos vais van	iba ibas iba íbamos ibais iban	fui fuiste fue fuimos fuisteis fueron	iré irás irá iremos iréis irán	iría irías iría iríamos iríais irían	vaya vayas vaya vayamos vayáis vayan	fuera fueras fuera fuéramos fuerais fueran	ve / no vayas vaya vamos / no vayamos id / no vayáis vayan
oír oyendo oído	oigo oyes oye oímos oís oyen	oía oías oía oíamos oíais oían	oí oíste oyó oímos oísteis oyeron	oiré oirás oirá oiremos oiréis oirán	oiría oirías oiría oiríamos oiríais oirían	oiga oigas oiga oigamos oigáis oigan	oyera oyeras oyera oyéramos oyerais oyeran	oye / no oigas oiga oigamos oíd / no oigáis oigan
poder pudiendo podido	puedo puedes puede podemos podéis pueden	podía podías podía podíamos podíais podían	pude pudiste pudo pudimos pudisteis pudieron	podré podrás podrá podremos podréis podrán	podría podrías podría podríamos podríais podrían	pueda puedas pueda podamos podáis puedan	pudiera pudieras pudiera pudiéramos pudierais pudieran	
poner poniendo puesto	pongo pones pone ponemos ponéis ponen	ponía ponías ponía poníamos poníais ponían	puse pusiste puso pusimos pusisteis pusieron	pondré pondrás pondrá pondremos pondréis pondrán	pondría pondrías pondría pondríamos pondríais pondrían	ponga pongas ponga pongamos pongáis pongan	pusiera pusieras pusiera pusiéramos pusierais pusieran	pon / no pongas ponga pongamos poned / no pongáis pongan
querer queriendo querido	quiero quieres quiere queremos queréis quieren	quería querías quería queríamos queríais querían	quise quisiste quiso quisimos quisisteis quisieron	querré querrás querrá querremos querréis querrán	querría querrías querría querríamos querríais querrían	quiera quieras quiera queramos queráis quieran	quisiera quisieras quisiera quisiéramos quisierais quisieran	quiere / no quieras quiera queramos quered / no queráis quieran
saber sabiendo sabido	sé sabes sabe sabemos sabéis saben	sabía sabías sabía sabíamos sabíais sabían	supe supiste supo supimos supisteis supieron	sabré sabrás sabrá sabremos sabréis sabrán	sabría sabrías sabría sabríamos sabríais sabrían	sepa sepas sepa sepamos sepáis sepan	supiera supieras supiera supiéramos supierais supieran	sabe / no sepas sepa sepamos sabed / no sepáis sepan
salir saliendo salido	salgo sales sale salimos salís salen	salía salías salía salíamos salíais salían	salí saliste salió salimos salisteis salieron	saldré saldrás saldrá saldremos saldréis saldrán	saldría saldrías saldría saldríamos saldríais saldrían	salga salgas salga salgamos salgáis salgan	saliera salieras saliera saliéramos salierais salieran	sal / no salgas salga salgamos salid / no salgáis salgan

C. Irregular Verbs (continued)

INFINITIVE / PRESENT PARTICIPLE / PAST PARTICIPLE	INDICATIVE PRESENT	IMPERFECT	PRETERIT	FUTURE	CONDITIONAL	SUBJUNCTIVE PRESENT	IMPERFECT	IMPERATIVE
ser / siendo / sido	soy	era	fui	seré	sería	sea	fuera	sé /
	eres	eras	fuiste	serás	serías	seas	fueras	no seas
	es	era	fue	será	sería	sea	fuera	sea
	somos	éramos	fuimos	seremos	seríamos	seamos	fuéramos	seamos
	sois	erais	fuisteis	seréis	seríais	seáis	fuerais	sed / no seáis
	son	eran	fueron	serán	serían	sean	fueran	sean
tener / teniendo / tenido	tengo	tenía	tuve	tendré	tendría	tenga	tuviera	ten /
	tienes	tenías	tuviste	tendrás	tendrías	tengas	tuvieras	no tengas
	tiene	tenía	tuvo	tendrá	tendría	tenga	tuviera	tenga
	tenemos	teníamos	tuvimos	tendremos	tendríamos	tengamos	tuviéramos	tengamos
	tenéis	teníais	tuvisteis	tendréis	tendríais	tengáis	tuvierais	tened / no tengáis
	tienen	tenían	tuvieron	tendrán	tendrían	tengan	tuvieran	tengan
traer / trayendo / traído	traigo	traía	traje	traeré	traería	traiga	trajera	trae /
	traes	traías	trajiste	traerás	traerías	traigas	trajeras	no traigas
	trae	traía	trajo	traerá	traería	traiga	trajera	traiga
	traemos	traíamos	trajimos	traeremos	traeríamos	traigamos	trajéramos	traigamos
	traéis	traíais	trajisteis	traeréis	traeríais	traigáis	trajerais	traed / no traigáis
	traen	traían	trajeron	traerán	traerían	traigan	trajeran	traigan
venir / viniendo / venido	vengo	venía	vine	vendré	vendría	venga	viniera	ven /
	vienes	venías	viniste	vendrás	vendrías	vengas	vinieras	no vengas
	viene	venía	vino	vendrá	vendría	venga	viniera	venga
	venimos	veníamos	vinimos	vendremos	vendríamos	vengamos	viniéramos	vengamos
	venís	veníais	vinisteis	vendréis	vendríais	vengáis	vinierais	venid / no vengáis
	vienen	venían	vinieron	vendrán	vendrían	vengan	vinieran	vengan
ver / viendo / visto	veo	veía	vi	veré	vería	vea	viera	ve /
	ves	veías	viste	verás	verías	veas	vieras	no veas
	ve	veía	vio	verá	vería	vea	viera	vea
	vemos	veíamos	vimos	veremos	veríamos	veamos	viéramos	veamos
	veis	veíais	visteis	veréis	veríais	veáis	vierais	ved / no veáis
	ven	veían	vieron	verán	verían	vean	vieran	vean

D. Stem-Changing and Spelling Change Verbs

INFINITIVE / PRESENT PARTICIPLE / PAST PARTICIPLE	INDICATIVE PRESENT	IMPERFECT	PRETERIT	FUTURE	CONDITIONAL	SUBJUNCTIVE PRESENT	IMPERFECT	IMPERATIVE
construir (y) / construyendo / construido	construyo	construía	construí	construiré	construiría	construya	construyera	construye /
	construyes	construías	construiste	construirás	construirías	construyas	construyeras	no construyas
	construye	construía	construyó	construirá	construiría	construya	construyera	construya
	construimos	construíamos	construimos	construiremos	construiríamos	construyamos	construyéramos	construyamos
	construís	construíais	construisteis	construiréis	construiríais	construyáis	construyerais	construid / no construyáis
	construyen	construían	construyeron	construirán	construirían	construyan	construyeran	construyan
dormir (ue, u) / durmiendo / dormido	duermo	dormía	dormí	dormiré	dormiría	duerma	durmiera	duerme /
	duermes	dormías	dormiste	dormirás	dormirías	duermas	durmieras	no duermas
	duerme	dormía	durmió	dormirá	dormiría	duerma	durmiera	duerma
	dormimos	dormíamos	dormimos	dormiremos	dormiríamos	durmamos	durmiéramos	durmamos
	dormís	dormíais	dormisteis	dormiréis	dormiríais	durmáis	durmierais	dormid / no durmáis
	duermen	dormían	durmieron	dormirán	dormirían	duerman	durmieran	duerman

D. Stem-Changing and Spelling Change Verbs (*continued*)

INFINITIVE PRESENT PARTICIPLE PAST PARTICIPLE	INDICATIVE					SUBJUNCTIVE		IMPERATIVE
	PRESENT	IMPERFECT	PRETERIT	FUTURE	CONDITIONAL	PRESENT	IMPERFECT	
pedir (i, i) pidiendo pedido	pido pides pide pedimos pedís piden	pedía pedías pedía pedíamos pedíais pedían	pedí pediste pidió pedimos pedisteis pidieron	pediré pedirás pedirá pediremos pediréis pedirán	pediría pedirías pediría pediríamos pediríais pedirían	pida pidas pida pidamos pidáis pidan	pidiera pidieras pidiera pidiéramos pidierais pidieran	pide / no pidas pida pidamos pedid / no pidáis pidan
pensar (ie) pensando pensado	pienso piensas piensa pensamos pensáis piensan	pensaba pensabas pensaba pensábamos pensabais pensaban	pensé pensaste pensó pensamos pensasteis pensaron	pensaré pensarás pensará pensaremos pensaréis pensarán	pensaría pensarías pensaría pensaríamos pensaríais pensarían	piense pienses piense pensemos penséis piensen	pensara pensaras pensara pensáramos pensarais pensaran	piensa / no pienses piense pensemos pensad / no penséis piensen
producir (zc) produciendo producido	produzco produces produce producimos producís producen	producía producías producía producíamos producíais producían	produje produjiste produjo produjimos produjisteis produjeron	produciré producirás producirá produciremos produciréis producirán	produciría producirías produciría produciríamos produciríais producirían	produzca produzcas produzca produzcamos produzcáis produzcan	produjera produjeras produjera produjéramos produjerais produjeran	produce / no produzcas produzca produzcamos producid / no produzcáis produzcan
reír (i, i) riendo reído	río ríes ríe reímos reís ríen	reía reías reía reíamos reíais reían	reí reíste rió reímos reísteis rieron	reiré reirás reirá reiremos reiréis reirán	reiría reirías reiría reiríamos reiríais reirían	ría rías ría riamos riáis rían	riera rieras riera riéramos rierais rieran	ríe / no rías ría riamos reíd / no riáis rían
seguir (i, i) (g) siguiendo seguido	sigo sigues sigue seguimos seguís siguen	seguía seguías seguía seguíamos seguíais seguían	seguí seguiste siguió seguimos seguisteis siguieron	seguiré seguirás seguirá seguiremos seguiréis seguirán	seguiría seguirías seguiría seguiríamos seguiríais seguirían	siga sigas siga sigamos sigáis sigan	siguiera siguieras siguiera siguiéramos siguierais siguieran	sigue / no sigas siga sigamos seguid / no sigáis sigan
sentir (ie, i) sintiendo sentido	siento sientes siente sentimos sentís sienten	sentía sentías sentía sentíamos sentíais sentían	sentí sentiste sintió sentimos sentisteis sintieron	sentiré sentirás sentirá sentiremos sentiréis sentirán	sentiría sentirías sentiría sentiríamos sentiríais sentirían	sienta sientas sienta sintamos sintáis sientan	sintiera sintieras sintiera sintiéramos sintierais sintieran	siente / no sientas sienta sintamos sentid / no sintáis sientan
volver (ue) volviendo vuelto	vuelvo vuelves vuelve volvemos volvéis vuelven	volvía volvías volvía volvíamos volvíais volvían	volví volviste volvió volvimos volvisteis volvieron	volveré volverás volverá volveremos volveréis volverán	volvería volverías volvería volveríamos volveríais volverían	vuelva vuelvas vuelva volvamos volváis vuelvan	volviera volvieras volviera volviéramos volvierais volvieran	vuelve / no vuelvas vuelva volvamos volved / no volváis vuelvan

Vocabularies

This Spanish-English vocabulary contains all of the words that appear in the text, with the following exceptions: (1) most identical cognates that do not appear in the chapter vocabulary lists; (2) conjugated verb forms, with the exception of certain forms of **haber** and expressions found in the chapter vocabulary lists; (3) diminutives in **-ito/a;** (4) absolute superlatives in **ísimo/a;** and (5) some adverbs in **-mente.** Active vocabulary is indicated by the number of the chapter in which a word or given meaning is first listed; vocabulary that is glossed in the text is not considered to be active vocabulary and is not numbered. Only meanings that are used in this text are given.

The gender of nouns is indicated, except for masculine nouns ending in **-o** and feminine nouns ending in **-a.** Stem changes and spelling changes are indicated for verbs: **dormir (ue, u); llegar (gu).**

The English-Spanish vocabulary contains only the active vocabulary items that appear in the end-of-chapter lists. A number in parentheses identifies the first chapter in which an active item is presented.

The following abbreviations are used:

adj.	adjective		*m.*	masculine
adv.	adverb		*Mex.*	Mexico
Carib.	Caribbean		*neut. pron.*	neuter pronoun
conj.	conjunction		*n.*	noun
def. art.	definite article		*obj. of prep.*	object of preposition
d.o.	direct object		*pl.*	plural
f.	feminine		*poss.*	possessive
fam.	familiar		*p.p.*	past participle
form.	formal		*P. R.*	Puerto Rico
gram.	grammatical		*prep.*	preposition
indef. art.	indefinite article		*pron.*	pronoun
inf.	infinitive		*refl. pron.*	reflexive pronoun
inv.	invariable		*s.*	singular
i.o.	indirect object		*Sp.*	Spain
irreg.	irregular		*sub. pron.*	subject pronoun
Lat. Am.	Latin America			

Spanish-English Vocabulary

A

a to (2); at
abajo below, underneath
abandonado abandoned
abandono abandonment
abarcar (qu) to take in; to comprise
abierto/a (*p.p. of* **abrir**) open
abogado/a lawyer (12)
abonarse to subscribe (13)
abordar to board (10)

aborto abortion
abrazo hug
abrigo overcoat (7)
abril *m.* April (6)
abrir (*p.p.* **abierto/a**) to open; **abra la boca** open your (*form. s.*) mouth (6)
abrumador(a) overwhelming (13)
absoluto/a absolute; complete
abstracto/a abstract

abuelo/a grandfather/ grandmother (3); *pl.* grandparents (3)
abundancia abundance
aburrido/a boring (2); **estar** (*irreg.*) **aburrido/a** to be bored (6)
aburrir(le) to bore (*someone*) (9)
abusar de to abuse
abuso abuse (13)
acá here (4)

acabar to finish; **acabarse** to run out of
academia academy
académico/a academic
acampar to camp (8)
acaso: por si acaso just in case (11)
accesible accessible
acceso access; **tener** (*irreg.*) **más acceso a la enseñanza** to have more access to education (14)
accesorio prop
accidente *m.* accident
acción *f.* action; **Día** (*m.*) **de Acción de Gracias** Thanksgiving (9); **película de acción** action film, movie (13)
aceite *m.* oil (5); **aceite de oliva** olive oil (5)
acento accent (14)
aceptable acceptable
aceptación *f.* acceptance
aceptar to accept; **¿aceptan tarjetas de crédito?** do you accept credit cards? (7)
acerca de about
acertar (ie) to guess right
ácido/a sour, tart
acogedor(a) welcoming (4)
acompañar to accompany, go with
acondicionado: aire acondicionado air conditioning
aconsejar to advise
acontecimiento event, happening (13)
acorde a according to (12); depending on (12)
acordeón *m.* accordion
acostarse (ue) to go to bed (6)
acostumbrarse a to get used to, become accustomed to (10)
acreditación *f.* accreditation
acreditado/a accredited
actitud *f.* attitude
actividad *f.* activity
activista *m., f.* activist
activo/a active
acto act; **en el acto** on the spot

actor *m.* actor
actriz *f.* (*pl.* **actrices**) actress
actual current; contemporary (13)
actualidad *f.* present time; *pl.* current events
actualizado/a modern, up-to-date
actualmente currently (13)
actuar (actúo) to act
acuático: esquí acuático water skiing
acuerdo agreement; **estar** (*irreg.*) **de acuerdo** to agree; **ponerse** (*irreg.*) **de acuerdo** to agree
acusado/a accused
adaptación *f.* adaptation
adaptado/a adapted; adjusted
adaptarse to adapt
adecuado/a appropriate
adelante: sacar (qu) adelante to improve
además moreover; **además de** besides
adicional additional (2)
adiós good-bye (1)
adivinar to guess
adjetival adjectival
adjetivo adjective (2)
administración *f.* administration; **administración de empresas** business administration; **edificio de administración** administration building (2)
admiración *f.* admiration; amazement
admirador(a) fan
admirar to admire
admitir to admit
adolescencia adolescence (9)
adolescente *m., f.* adolescent, teenager (9)
¿adónde? (to) where? (2)
adoptar to adopt
adoptivo/a adoptive
adorno adornment, decoration
adrenalina adrenaline
aduana *s.* customs (10)
adulto/a adult (9); **edad** (*f.*) **adulta** adulthood (9)

adverbio adverb (11)
aeróbico aerobic; **hacer** (*irreg.*) **ejercicio aeróbico** to do aerobic exercise (6)
aeropuerto airport (10)
afectar to affect
afectivo/a emotional; **lazos afectivos** emotional bonds (15)
afeitarse to shave (6)
afición *f.* liking, taste, fondness
aficionado/a fan (8)
afín similar
afirmación *f.* statement
afirmar to affirm
afirmativo/a *adj.* affirmative
africano/a *n., adj.* African
afuera outside; *pl.* suburbs, outskirts (4)
agarrado/a cheek-to-cheek
agarrar to grab, seize
agencia agency; **agencia de colocaciones** job placement agency (12); **agencia de empleados temporarios** temporary employment agency; **agencia de viajes** travel agency (10)
agente *m., f.* agent; **agente de inmigración** immigration agent (11); **agente de viajes** travel agent (10)
agitado/a agitated, shaken
agonía agony, torment
agosto August (6)
agradable pleasant, nice
agradecido/a thankful
agregar (gu) to add
agresivo/a aggressive
agrícola *adj. m., f.* agricultural
agricultor(a) farmer
agricultura agriculture
agrio/a sour (5)
agua *f.* (*but* **el agua**) water (5); **agua corriente** running water; **agua embotellada** bottled water; **agua mineral** mineral water (5); **cortar el agua** to shut off the water; **esquiar (esquío) en el agua** to water ski (8)

aguacate *m.* avocado (5)
aguantar to endure
agudo/a sharp; acute
águila *f. (but* **el águila***)* eagle
ahí there (4)
ahora now; **ahora mismo** at once; **hasta ahora** until now
ahorrar to save (11)
aimara *m.* Aymara (*indigenous language of the Andes*)
aire *m.* air; **aire acondicionado** air conditioning; **al aire libre** outdoors
aislado/a isolated (15)
ajedrez *m.* chess; **jugar (ue) (gu) al ajedrez** to play chess (8)
ajo garlic (5); **diente de ajo** clove of garlic
al (*contraction of* **a** + **el**) to the (2); **al igual que** just like (3); **al lado (de** + *noun*) beside (+ *noun*) (2)
albañil *m., f.* bricklayer
álbum *m.* album
alcanzar (c) to reach
alcohol *m.* alcohol (8)
alcohólico/a alcoholic; **bebida alcohólica** alcoholic drink (8)
alcoholismo alcoholism
aldea village
alegre happy (1)
alegría happiness
alemán, alemana *n., adj.* German (1)
Alemania Germany
alergia allergy
alérgico/a allergic
alfabeto alphabet
alfiler *m.* pin
alfombra rug, carpet (4)
alga *f. (but* **el alga***)* algae
álgebra *m.* algebra
algo something, some (5); **algo de** some (5)
algodón *m.* cotton (7)
algoritmo algorithm
alguien someone
algún, alguno/a some (5); any
alianza alliance
alimenticio/a nutritional

alimento food
allá over there (4)
allí there (4)
alma *f. (but* **el alma***)* soul
almacén *m.* department store
almorzar (ue) (c) to eat lunch (4)
almuerzo lunch (5)
alojamiento lodging
alojarse to lodge, stay
alquilar to rent
alrededor de *prep.* around
alternativa *n.* alternative, choice
altibajos *pl.* ups and downs
altiplano high plain (14)
alto/a tall (1); high; **en voz alta** aloud; **hasta altas horas de la noche** until late at night
altura height
alumno/a student
amable friendly (1)
amar to love
amargo/a bitter (5)
amarillo/a yellow (7)
Amazonas: Río Amazonas Amazon River
amazónico/a *adj.* Amazon (14)
ambicioso/a ambitious
ambiente *m.* atmosphere (4); **encontrarse (ue) en ambiente** to be in the mood (8); **medio ambiente** environment
ambiguo/a ambiguous
ambos/as *pl.* both
ambulante wandering; **vendedor(a) ambulante** street vendor
americano/a: fútbol (*m.*) **americano** football (8)
amigo/a friend (2); **charlar con amigos** to chat with friends (8); **encontrarse (ue) con amigos** to get together (meet) with friends (8)
amistad *f.* friendship (15)
amor *m.* love (15); **película de amor** romance film, movie (13)
amoroso/a affectionate, loving
amplio/a ample, broad (12)
amueblado/a furnished
análisis *m. s., pl.* analysis

analítico/a analytical
analizar (c) to analyze
anaranjado/a orange (*color*) (7)
ancestral: territorio ancestral ancestral territory (14)
ancho/a wide
anciano/a *n.* elderly person (9); *adj.* old
andaluz(a) *adj. (m. pl.* **andaluces***)* Andalusian
andar *irreg.* to walk; **andar en bicicleta/motocicleta** to ride a bicycle/motorcycle (8)
anécdota anecdote
anfitrión, anfitriona host, hostess (8)
anglohablante *m., f.* English speaker; *adj.* English-speaking
anillo ring (7); **anillo de diamantes** diamond ring (7)
animal *m.* animal; **animal doméstico** pet
aniversario anniversary
anoche *adv.* last night
anónimo/a anonymous
ansiedad *f.* anxiety; **sufrir de ansiedad** to suffer from anxiety (6)
ansioso/a: estar (*irreg.*) **ansioso/a (por)** to be worried (about) (11)
ante *prep.* before; faced with; in the presence of
antecedente *m.* antecedent
antelación *f.:* **con antelación** in advance
antena: televisión (*f.*) **de antena parabólica** satellite TV (13)
antepasado/a ancestor (13)
anterior previous
antes *adv.* before; **antes de** (*prep.*) + *inf.* before (*doing something*) (11); **antes (de) que** (*conj.*) before (14)
antibiótico antibiotic
anticoncepción *f.* contraception
anticonceptivo/a contraceptive
anticuado/a antiquated, old-fashioned
antipático/a unfriendly (1)

antónimo antonym

antropología anthropology (2)

antropológico/a anthropological

anunciar to announce

anuncio advertisement; announcement; **anuncio de empleo** job ad (12)

añadir to add

año year; **el año pasado** last year; **cada año** each year (9); **¿cuántos años (tiene)?** How old (are you [*form. s.*]/is he/she)? (3); **tener** (*irreg.*) _____ **años (y medio)** to be _____ (and a half) years old (3)

apagar (gu) to turn off (*light*)

aparato appliance

aparecer (zc) to appear

apariencia appearance

apartamento apartment

aparte *adv.* apart; besides; **hoja de papel aparte** separate piece of paper

apasionado/a por la vida passionate for life

apellido last name

apestar a to reek of

aplastar to crush

aplicar (qu) to apply

aportar to contribute

apoyar to support

apoyo support

apreciar to appreciate

aprender to learn (11)

aprobar (ue) to approve, pass

apropiado/a appropriate

aproximado/a approximate (6)

aptitud *f.* aptitude; ability

apuntar to note, jot down

apunte *m.* note

aquel, aquella *adj.* that (over there) (4)

aquél, aquélla *pron.* that one (over there) (4)

aquello that; that thing (4)

aquí here (4); **aquí lo/la/los/las tiene** here you go (7)

árbol *m.* tree

archivo archive, file

área *f.* (*but* **el área**) area

arepa cornmeal griddlecake

arete *m.* earring (7)

argentino/a *n., adj.* Argentine

argumento argument; plot (*of a play, film*)

aristócrata *m., f.* aristocrat

arma *f.* (*but* **el arma**) **de fuego** firearm

armar to assemble, prepare

armario wardrobe (*furniture*) (4)

armonía harmony, agreement

arqueológico/a archaeological

arqueólogo/a archaeologist (12)

arquitecto/a architect (12)

arquitectura architecture (2); **arquitectura paisajista** landscape architecture

arrabales *pl.* slums

arrancar (qu) to pull up, uproot; **arrancar a** to steal away

arriesgado/a risk-taking (12)

arrogante arrogant; brave

arroz *m.* rice (5)

arte *m.* (*but* **las artes**) art (2); **hacer** (*irreg.*) **artes marciales** to practice martial arts (8); **obra de arte** work of art

artefacto artefact

artesanía *s.* crafts; **mercado de artesanías** handicrafts market (7)

artesano/a artisan

artículo article (1)

artista *m., f.* artist (12)

artístico/a artistic

arveja green pea

asado/a roasted

asar to roast

asegurarse to make sure

asesinado/a assassinated

asesor(a) consultant (12)

así thus, so; **así así** so-so, fair; **así que** so (that), therefore

asiático/a *n., adj.* Asian (14)

asignatura course, subject (*school*)

asistente (*m., f.*) **social** social worker (12)

asistir (a) to attend

asociación *f.* association

asociar to associate; to combine

aspecto aspect; appearance

aspiración *f.* aspiration, hope

aspirar (a) to aspire (to)

aspirina aspirin

asunto subject, topic, issue

atacar (qu) to attack

atardecer *m.* dusk

atención *f.* attention

atentado *n.* attack

ateo/a atheist (15)

ático attic

atípico/a atypical

atlántico: Océano Atlántico Atlantic Ocean

atleta *m., f.* athlete

atlético/a athletic

atormentar to torment, torture

atracción *f.* attraction; *pl.* amusements

atractivo/a attractive

atraer (*like* **traer**) to attract

atrapar to trap

atravesar (ie) to cross

atreverse to dare

atributo *n.* attribute

atrocidad *f.* atrocity (13)

atún *m.* tuna

auditorio/a auditory

aula *f.* (*but* **el aula**) classroom (2)

aumentar to augment, increase

aun *adv.* even

aún *adv.* still, yet

aunque although

aurora dawn

ausencia absence

auto car (10)

autobús *m.* bus (10); **estación** (*f.*) **de autobuses** bus station; **ir** (*irreg.*) **en autobús** to go by bus (10); **parada de autobuses** bus stop (10); **perder (ie) un autobús** to miss a bus; **subir a un autobús** to get in a bus (10)

autóctono/a aboriginal, native

autodescubrimiento self-discovery

automóvil *m.* automobile

autonomía autonomy

autónomo/a autonomous

autopista superhighway (10)
autor(a) author
autoridad *f.* authority
autoritario/a authoritarian; imperious
avance *m.* advance; **avances sexuales** sexual advances
avanzar (c) to advance; **oportunidad** (*f.*) **de avanzar** opportunity for advancement (12)
avenida avenue
avergonzar (üe) (c) to embarrass (15)
avión *m.* airplane (10); **ir** (*irreg.*) **en avión** to go by airplane (10)
ayer yesterday
ayuda help; **pedir (i, i) ayuda** to ask for help
ayudar to help (11)
ayuntamiento city/town hall (10)
azteca *adj. m., f.* Aztec
azúcar *m.* sugar (5)
azul blue; **ojos azules** blue eyes (1)

B
bachillerato bachelor's degree
bailar (pegados, separados) to dance (close, apart) (8); **sacar (qu) a alguien a bailar** to ask someone to dance (8); **salir** (*irreg.*) **a bailar** to go out dancing (3)
baile *m.* dance (8)
bajar de to get off, get down from (10)
bajo *prep.* under
bajo/a *adj.* short (*height*) (1); low; **clase** (*f.*) **baja** lower class
bala bullet
balance *m.* balance, equilibrium
balón *m.* large ball
baloncesto basketball (*Sp.*) (8); **jugar (ue) (gu) al baloncesto** to play basketball (4)
balonmano handball; **jugar (ue) (gu) al balonmano** to play handball

banana banana (5)
bancario/a *adj.* banking, financial
banco bank (10)
banda gang
bandera flag
bandoneón *m.* large concertina
banquero/a banker (12)
bañarse to bathe, take a bath (6)
bañera bathtub (4)
baño: cuarto de baño bathroom (4); **traje de baño** bathing suit (7)
barato/a inexpensive, cheap
barbaridad: ¡qué barbaridad! how awful!
barco ship, boat (10); **perder (ie) un barco** to miss a boat
barmitzvah *m.* bar mitzvah (9)
barra bar
barrer to sweep
barrera barrier; **superar las barreras económicas** to overcome economic barriers (14)
barriga stomach
barrio neighborhood (4); **mercado del barrio** neighborhood market (5)
barro mud; clay
basalto basalt
basar to base, support
base *f.* base, foundation
básico/a basic
básquetbol *m.* basketball (8); **jugar (ue) (gu) al básquetbol** to play basketball
bastante *adv.* somewhat, rather (11)
bastar to be enough, sufficient
bastón *m.* walking stick, cane
basura garbage
bata bathrobe
batalla battle
batata sweet potato
batir to beat
batmitzvah *f.* bat mitzvah (9)
bebé *m., f.* baby (9)
beber to drink (3); **beber un refresco** to drink a soft drink (3); **beber una cerveza** to

drink a beer (3); **beber vino** to drink wine (3)
bebida drink (5); **bebida alcohólica** alcoholic drink (8)
beca scholarship
béisbol *m.* baseball (8); **jugar (ue) (gu) al béisbol** to play baseball (4)
beisbolista *m., f.* baseball player
bello/a beautiful
beneficios *pl.* benefits (12)
benigno/a benign
beso kiss
bestia animal, beast
biblioteca library (2)
bibliotecario/a librarian (12)
bicicleta bicycle; **andar** (*irreg.*) **en bicicleta** to ride a bicycle (8)
bicultural bicultural (11)
bien *adv.* well; **caerle** (*irreg.*) **bien** to make a good impression (*on someone*) (9); **(no) comunicarse (qu) bien** to (not) communicate well (15); **estoy (muy) bien, gracias** I'm (very) fine, thanks (1); **irle** (*irreg.*) **bien** to go well (*for someone*) (11); **(no) llevarse bien** to (not) get along well (15); **pasarlo bien** to have a good time; **¡qué bien!** great! how wonderful! (13); **quedarle bien** to fit well (7); **sentirse (ie, i) bien** to feel good (6)
bienestar *m.* **(emocional)** (emotional) well-being (15)
bilingüe bilingual (11)
billar *m. s.* billiards, pool; **jugar (ue) (gu) al billar** to play billiards (pool) (8)
billete *m.* ticket (10)
biográfico/a biographical
biología biology (2)
bistec *m.* roast beef (5)
blanco/a white (7)
blando/a soft
bloque *m.* block; **bloque de pisos** apartment building (4)
bloqueado/a blocked

bloqueo blockade
blusa blouse (7)
boca mouth; **abra la boca** open your (*form. s.*) mouth (6)
bocadillo sandwich
boda wedding (15)
boleto ticket (10)
bolígrafo ballpoint pen (2)
boliviano/a *n., adj.* Bolivian
bolsa purse (7)
bolsillo pocket
bolso pocketbook; handbag
bombardeo bombing
bombero, mujer (*f.*) **bombero** firefighter (12)
bombilla electric lightbulb
bonito/a pretty (1)
bordado/a embroidered
borracho/a: estar (*irreg.*) **borracho/a** to be drunk (8)
borrar to erase
bosque *m.* forest (10)
botas *pl.* boots (7)
botella bottle
boxeador(a) boxer
boxeo boxing
brazo arm
brecha (generacional) (generation) gap
breve *adj.* brief
brindar to offer, give; **brindarse** to give of oneself
británico/a *adj.* British
bucear to snorkle (8)
buen, bueno/a good (1); **buenas noches** good night (1); **buenas tardes** good afternoon/ evening (1); **bueno, me lo/la/los/las llevo** OK, I'll take it/them (7); **buenos días** good morning (1); **en buena forma** in good shape; **hace buen tiempo** it's good weather (6); **¡qué buena idea!** what a good idea! (8)
busca: en busca de in search of
buscar (qu) to look for (11); **busco _____** I'm looking for _____ (7)
búsqueda search

C

caballo horse; **montar a caballo** to go horseback riding (8)
cabello hair
caber *irreg.* to fit
cabeza head; **dolor** (*m.*) **de cabeza** headache (6)
cable *m.*: **televisión** (*f.*) **por cable** cable TV (13)
cabo: al fin y al cabo in the end
cacique *m.* chief
cada *inv.* each; **cada año/mes** each year/month (9); **cada uno** each one; **cada vez** each time
caerse *irreg.* to fall; **caerle bien/mal** to make a good/bad impression (*on someone*) (9)
café *m.* coffee (5); **café** (*m.*) **cibernético** Internet café (13); **café con leche** coffee with milk; **tomar un café** to have coffee (6)
cafeinado/a caffeinated
cafetería cafeteria (2)
caída *n.* drop; **caída del sol** sunset
caja box; cash register, check-out (7)
cajero/a cashier
cajón *m.* large box
calcetín *m.* sock (7)
calculadora calculator
calcular to calculate
cálculo calculus
calefacción *f.* heating (*system*)
calendario calendar
calentar (ie) to warm up
calidad *f.* quality (7)
cálido/a warm
calificación *f.* rating; grade
calle *f.* street (4); **calle (transitada, residencial)** (busy, residential) street (4)
calmar to calm; **calmar el hambre** (*f.*) to curb one's hunger
calor *m.* heat; **hace calor** it's hot (6)
cama bed (4); **quedarse en cama** to stay, remain in bed (6)
camarero/a waiter/waitress

camarón *m.* shrimp, prawn (5)
cambiante changing
cambiar (por) to change, exchange (for) (7)
cambio change; **casa de cambio** money-changer; **en cambio** on the other hand (10); **tasa de cambio** exchange rate
cambur *m.* plantain
camello camel
caminar to walk (10)
camino road; **en camino** en route
camión *m.* truck
camisa shirt (7)
camiseta T-shirt (7)
campamento camp
campaña campaign
camping *m.*: **hacer** (*irreg.*) **camping** to go camping
campo country(side) (10)
canadiense *n., adj.* Canadian (1)
canal *m.* canal; **canal** (*televisión*) (*television*) channel (13)
cancelar to cancel; **cancelar una reserva** to cancel a reservation (10)
cancha field (*football, baseball*); court (*tennis*)
canción *f.* song
candelabro candelabra
candidato/a candidate
cangrejo crab (5)
canoa canoe
cansado/a tired; **estar** (*irreg.*) **cansado/a** to be tired (6)
cantante *m., f.* singer
cantar to sing (8)
cántaro pitcher
cantautor(a) singer-songwriter
cantidad *f.* quantity (5)
cantina bar
capacidad *f.* capacity
capaz (*pl.* **capaces**) capable (12)
capitalino/a *person from the capital*
capítulo chapter
cara face
carácter *m.* (*pl.* **caracteres**) character, personality

característica characteristic
caracterizar (c) to characterize
caramelo candy
caraota bean
carbón *m.* coal
cárcel *f.* jail
carga load; cargo
cargador(a) carrier
cargar (gu) to carry
Caribe *n. m.* Caribbean (Sea)
caribeño/a *adj.* Caribbean; *n. person of the Caribbean*
caries *f. s., pl.* (tooth) decay
cariño: mostrar (ue) cariño en público to show affection in public (15)
cariñoso/a affectionate (3)
carne *f.* **(de res/vaca, de cerdo)** meat (beef, pork) (5)
carnicería butcher's shop (5)
caro/a expensive (5)
carpintero/a carpenter
carrera major (*university*) (2); career (2)
carretera highway
carro *m.* car (10)
carroza float (*parade*)
carta letter (3); **carta de presentación** letter of introduction; **carta de recomendación** letter of recommendation (12); **escribir cartas** to write letters (3)
cartel *m.* poster (4)
cartelera billboard
cartera wallet (7)
casa house (4); **casa de cambio** money-changer; **casa particular** private / single-family house (4); **quedarse en casa** to stay, remain at home (6)
casado/a married (3); **estar** (*irreg.*) **casado/a** to be married (3)
casarse to marry, get married (15)
casi almost; **casi nunca** almost never (9); **casi siempre** almost always (9)
caso case; **en caso de que** (*conj.*) in case

castaño/a brown; **ojos castaños** brown eyes (1); **pelo castaño** brown hair (1)
castellano/a Castilian
castigo punishment
castillo castle
casualidad *f.* chance; coincidence; **por casualidad** by chance
catalán, catalana *n., adj.* Catalonian
catarata waterfall (10)
catedral *f.* cathedral (10)
categoría category; class
católico/a *n., adj.* Catholic (15)
catorce fourteen (1)
causa: a causa de because of
causar to cause
cauteloso/a cautious, wary
cazar (c) to hunt
cebolla onion (5)
ceder to give up, transfer
ceiba silkwood tree
ceja eyebrow
celebración *f.* celebration
celebrar to celebrate (9)
celeste *m., f.* celestial
celos *pl.* jealousy; **tener** (*irreg.*) **celos** to be jealous (15)
celular: teléfono celular cell phone
cementerio cemetery
cena dinner (5)
cenar to eat dinner (2)
censura censure
centígrado/a centigrade
centrado/a centered
céntrico/a central
centro downtown (10); **centro comercial** shopping center, mall (7)
Centroamérica Central America
centroamericano/a *n., adj.* Central American
cepillarse los dientes to brush one's teeth (6)
cerámica *n. s.* ceramics, pottery
cerca de *prep.* close to
cercano/a *adj.* near, close

cerdo pork; **carne** (*f.*) **de cerdo** pork (5)
ceremonia ceremony
cereza cherry
cero zero (1)
cerrar (ie) to close (4)
cerro mount(ain) (10)
certidumbre *f.* certainty
cerveza beer (3); **beber una cerveza** to drink a beer (3); **tomar una cerveza** to have a beer (6)
cesto basket
chambelán young gentleman
champiñón *m.* mushroom (5)
chaqueta jacket (7)
charlar to chat (4); **charlar con amigos** to chat with friends (8)
chat *m.* online chat (13)
chatear to chat online (13)
chaval(a) guy (gal)
cheque *m.* check
¡chévere! cool! great! (*Carib.*) (8); **¡qué chévere!** how cool/great! (*Carib.*) (8)
chícharo green pea
chico/a *n. m., f.* young man / young woman; *adj.* small
chileno/a *n., adj.* Chilean
chimenea fireplace (4)
chino/a *n., adj.* Chinese (1)
chinola passion fruit
chisme *m.* gossip (13)
chismear to gossip
chiste *m.* joke; **contar (ue) chistes** to tell jokes (8)
chocante shocking (13)
choque *m.* collision, crash
ciberespacio cyberspace
cibernético *adj.* Internet; **café** (*m.*) **cibernético** Internet café (13)
ciclismo *n.* cycling (8)
ciclista *m., f.* cyclist
cielo sky; heaven
cien, ciento one hundred (3); **por ciento** percent (11)
ciencia science (2); **ciencias sociales** social sciences (2); **Facultad** (*f.*) **de Ciencias** School of Sciences (2)

científico/a scientist (12); *adj.* scientific

cierto/a certain; true; **hasta cierto/a…** until a certain . . .

cigarillo cigarette

cigarro cigar

cinco five (1)

cincuenta fifty (3)

cine *m.* movie theater (13); the movies (13); **ir** (*irreg.*) **al cine** to go to the movies (8)

cinematográfico/a cinematic

cinturón *m.* belt (7)

circunstancia circumstance

cirujano/a surgeon (12)

cita appointment, date (12); **fijar citas** to set appointments

citarse to set up a date

ciudad *f.* city (4); **ciudad universitaria** campus (2)

ciudadanía citizenship; **tener** (*irreg.*) **la ciudadanía** to have citizenship (11)

ciudadano/a citizen (11)

civilización *f.* civilization

claro/a clear; light; **piel** (*f.*) **clara** light(-colored) skin (1)

clase *f.* class (2); **clase baja** lower class; **clase media** middle class (14); **compañero/a de clase** classmate

clásico/a classical

clasificación *f.* classification

clasificar (qu) to classify

cláusula clause

clave *f.* key; password

clic: hacer (*irreg.*) **clic (en)** to click (on) (13)

cliente *m., f.* customer (7)

clima *m.* climate

clínica *n.* clinic

cobertura coverage

cocción *f.* boiling; preparation

coche *m.* car (10); **coche-bomba** car bomb; **subir a un coche** to get in a car (10)

cocina kitchen (4); cooking; **cocina de gas** gas stove (4); **cocina eléctrica** electric stove (4)

cocinar to cook (5)

cocinero/a cook

coco coconut

cocodrilo crocodile

codificar (qu) to codify

codo elbow

cognado cognate

coincidir to coincide

cola tail (*of an animal*); line (*of people*)

colección *f.* collection

coleccionar (estampillas/ monedas) to collect (stamps/coins) (8)

colectivo bus (*Bolivia*) (10)

colegio high school

colesterol *m.* cholesterol

colina hill

collar *m.* **(de plata)** (silver) necklace (7)

colocaciones *f. pl.*: **agencia de colocaciones** job placement agency (12)

colocar (qu) to place

colombiano/a *n., adj.* Colombian (1)

colonia colony

color *m.* color (7)

colorido/a colorful

columna column

combatir to fight

combinación *f.* combination

combinar to combine

comedor *m.* dining room (4)

comentar to comment, make comments on

comentario comment; remark; *pl.* commentaries

comenzar (ie) (c) to begin

comer to eat (3); **¿qué desea(n) de comer?** what would you like to eat? (5)

comercial: centro comercial shopping center, mall (7)

comerciante *m., f.* businessperson

comercio business

cometer to commit

cómico/a funny, comical (13); **película cómica** comedy film, movie (13); **tira cómica** comic strip, cartoon (13)

comida food (5); meal (5); **comida rápida** fast food; **preparar la comida** to prepare the meal/food (4)

comienzo *n.* beginning

comino cumin (*spice*)

comisión *f.* commission

como as, like (1); **tan pronto como** as soon as

¿cómo? how (2); **¿cómo es/son _____?** what is/are _____ like? (1); **¿cómo está(s)** how are you? (1); **¿cómo se dice _____ en español?** how do you say _____ in Spanish? (1); **¿cómo se escribe?** how do you write/spell it? (1); **¿cómo te llamas? / ¿cómo se llama usted?** what's your name? (1)

cómoda dresser, chest of drawers (4)

cómodo/a comfortable

compacto/a: disco compacto compact disc

compañero/a companion; **compañero/a de clase** classmate; **compañero/a de cuarto** roommate

compañía company

comparación comparison (5)

comparar to compare

compartir to share (4)

competencia skill (12)

complementar to complement

complemento *gram.* pronoun; **pronombre** (*m.*) **de complemento directo** direct object pronoun (5)

completar to complete

completo/a complete; **de tiempo completo** full-time (12); **por completo** completely; **trabajo de tiempo completo** full-time job

complicar (qu) to complicate

comportamiento behavior

comportarse to behave, act

composición *f.* composition

compra: hacer (*irreg.*) **la compra** to do the shopping (5); **ir** (*irreg.*) **de compras** to go shopping (3)

comprar to buy (5)

comprender to understand

comprobar (ue) to verify

comprometerse to get engaged (15)

compromiso commitment; engagement

computación *f.* computer science (2)

computadora computer

común *adj.* common

comunicación *f.* communication

comunicar (qu) to communicate; **(no) comunicarse bien** to (not) communicate well (15); **comunicarse mal** to communicate poorly (15)

comunidad *f.* community; **comunidad internacional** international community (13)

comunión *f.*: **primera comunión** first communion (9)

con with (2); **con frecuencia** frequently (9)

conceder to grant, concede

concentración *f.* concentration

concentrar to concentrate; to focus; **concentrarse en** to concentrate in, be concentrated in (10)

concepto concept, idea

concierto concert

concluir (y) to conclude

conclusión *f.* conclusion

concreto/a concrete, specific

concurso contest; game show (13)

condición *f.* condition (12); **condiciones de trabajo** working conditions (12); **mejorar las condiciones de vida** to improve living conditions (14)

condimentos condiments

condominio condominium (4)

conducir *irreg.* to drive (10)

conducta conduct, behavior

conectarse to connect (*to the Internet*) (13)

conexión *f.* connection

confiable trustworthy

confiado/a trusting (9)

confianza trust

confiar (confío) to trust

confirmación *f.* confirmation (9)

confirmar to confirm; **confirmar una reserva** to confirm a reservation (10)

conflicto conflict; **conflicto cultural** cultural conflict (11); **conflicto generacional** generational conflict (11)

conformar to conform

conformista *adj. m., f.* conformist

confrontación *f.* confrontation

confrontar to confront

confusión *f.* confusion

congelado/a frozen

congestionado/a: estar (*irreg.*) **congestionado/a** to be congested

congreso congress

conjugar (gu) to conjugate

conjunción *f.* conjunction

conjunto collection; band (*of musicians*); combination

conmigo with me

conocer (zc) to know, be familiar with (*someone, something*); to meet; **conocer a otras personas** to meet new/other people (8); **llegar (gu) a conocer** to get to know (15)

conocido/a known; famous

conocimiento awareness; *pl.* knowledge (12)

conquista conquest

consciente conscious; aware; **ser** (*irreg.*) **consciente de** to be conscious of (11)

consecuencia consequence

conseguir (i, i) (g) to get, obtain (5)

consejo advice

conservador(a) conservative

conservadurismo conservatism

conservar to preserve, conserve

consideración *f.* consideration

considerar to consider

consistente consistent

consistir en to consist of

constante constant

constitución *f.* constitution

construcción *f.* construction

construir (y) to build

consuelo consolation, comfort

consulado *n.* consulate

consultar to consult

consultorio doctor's office (6)

consumir to eat; to use up

contabilidad *f.* accounting

contable accountant (12)

contacto contact

contaminar to contaminate

contar (ue) to count; to tell; **contar chistes** to tell jokes (8); **contar con** to count on

contener (*like* **tener**) to contain

contenido *s.* contents

contento/a: estar (*irreg.*) **contento/a** to be happy (6)

contestar to answer

contexto context

contigo *fam. s.* with you

continuación *f.* continuation

continuo/a continuous

contra: en contra opposed

contrabajo double bass

contracción contraction

contradecir (*like* **decir**) to contradict

contrastar to contrast

contraste *m.* contrast (10)

contratar to hire

contribuir (y) to contribute

controlar to inspect; to control

controvertido/a controversial (13)

conveniencia convenience

convento convent

conversación *f.* conversation

conversar to converse, talk (3)

convertir (ie, i) to change; **convertirse en** to turn into

convivir to live together

copa (wine) glass; **tomar una copa** to have a drink (6)

copia copy
copiar to copy
corazón *m.* heart
corbata (7)
cordillera mountain range (10)
Corea Korea
correcto/a correct
corregir (i, i) (j) to correct
correo mail; post office; **correo electrónico** e-mail (13); **oficina de correos** post office (10)
correr to run (8); **correr el riesgo** to run the risk (11)
correspondencia correspondence
corresponder to correspond
correspondiente corresponding
corriente *n. f.* current; **agua** (*f.* [*but* **el agua**]) **corriente** running water; *adj.* current, present; **estar** (*irreg.*) **al corriente** to be up-to-date (13)
corrupción *f.* corruption
cortar to cut; **cortar el agua** to shut off the water
cortés courteous, polite
corto/a short (*in length*); **pantalones** (*m. pl.*) **cortos** shorts (7); **pelo corto** short hair (1)
cosa thing
cosecha harvest (11)
coser to sew (8)
cosmopolita *adj. m., f.* cosmopolitan (10)
costa coast (14)
costar (ue) to cost (7); **¿cuánto cuesta(n)?** how much does it / do they cost? (7); **cuesta(n)** _____ it costs / they cost _____ (7)
costarricense *n., adj.* Costa Rican
costearse to cover the cost of
costumbre *f.* custom (11); **tratar de mantener las costumbres** to try to maintain one's customs (11)
cotidiano/a *adj.* daily
cotización *f.* price
coyote *m. smuggler of illegal immigrants* (11)

creación *f.* creation
crear to create
creatividad *f.* creativity
creativo/a creative
crecer (zc) to grow
crédito credit; **¿aceptan tarjetas de crédito?** do you accept credit cards? (7); **tarjeta de crédito** credit card
creencia (tradicional) (traditional) belief (14)
creer (y) to believe
creíble believable
crema cream
cremoso/a creamy
crepúsculo sunset
crianza upbringing
criar(se) ([me] crío) to bring up (be brought up)
crimen *m.* crime (14)
criminalidad *f.* crime (rate)
criollo/a Creole; *American-born person of European parents and their descendants* (14)
criterio criterion
crítica criticism
criticar (qu) to criticize
crítico/a critic
crónico/a chronic
cronológico/a chronological
crucigrama *m.* crossword puzzle (13); **hacer** (*irreg.*) **crucigramas** to do crossword puzzles (3)
crudo/a raw (5)
cruz *f.* cross
cruzar (c) to cross (10); **para cruzar la frontera** getting across the border (11)
cuaderno notebook (2)
cuadra (city) block (10)
cuadrado/a squared
cuadro picture, painting (4); statistical chart
cual: tal cual just as
¿cuál(es)? what? which? (2)
cualidad *f.* quality; **cualidades gerenciales** managing abilities
cualquier(a) any
cuando when(ever) (14); **de vez en cuando** sometimes

¿cuándo? when? (2)
cuanto: en cuanto as soon as; **en cuanto a** with regard to
¿cuánto/a? how much? (2)
¿cuántos/as? how many? (2); **¿cuántos años (tiene)?** how old (are you [*form. s.*]) / is he/she? (3)
cuarenta forty (3)
cuarenta y uno forty-one (3)
cuarto *n.* quarter (*of an hour*); room; **compañero/a de cuarto** roommate; **cuarto de baño** bathroom (4); **menos cuarto** a quarter to (*hour*) (6); **y cuarto** a quarter past (*hour*) (6)
cuatro four (1)
cuatrocientos/as four hundred (7)
cubano/a *n., adj.* Cuban
cubierta cover
cubierto/a (*p.p. of* **cubrir**) covered
cubo cube
cubrir (*p.p.* **cubierto/a**) to cover
cucharada tablespoon
cucharadita teaspoon
cuenta bill (*restaurant*), check (5); reckoning; **darse** (*irreg.*) **cuenta de** to realize; **tener** (*irreg.*) **en cuenta** to keep in mind
cuento story; **escribir cuentos** to write stories (8)
cuerda string
cuero leather (7)
cuerpo body
cuestión *f.* question
cuidado care; **cuidado de párvulos** childcare; **tener** (*irreg.*) **cuidado** to be careful
cuidar (de) to take care (of)
cultivar to cultivate
cultura culture
cultural: conflicto cultural cultural conflict (11)
cumbre *f.* summit, top; pinnacle
cumpleaños *m. s., pl.* birthday (9)
cumplir (con) to fulfill, carry out
cuñado/a brother-in-law / sister-in-law (3); *pl.* siblings-in-law (3)

curandero/a healer
curarse de to cure oneself of, be cured of
curiosidad *f.* curiosity
curioso/a curious
currículum *m.* **(vitae)** résumé (12)
cursar to take classes
curso course
cuyo/a/os/as whose

D

dama lady; **primera dama** First Lady
danza dance
dañar to hurt, harm (15)
dañino/a harmful
daño damage, hurt; **hacer** (*irreg.*) **daño** to hurt, harm (15)
dar *irreg.* to give; **dar un paseo** to take a walk (3); **dar vueltas** to go around; **darse cuenta de** to realize
datos *pl.* data, facts
de *prep.* of; from
debajo de under, below
debate *m.* debate; dispute
deber + *inf.* ought to, should (*do something*) (6); **debe descansar más** you (*form. s.*) must get more rest (6); **deberíamos...** we should . . . (15)
debido a due to
débil weak
década decade (13)
decidir to decide
decir *irreg.* (*p.p.* **dicho/a**) to say; to tell (5); **diga «aaaa»** say (*form. s.*) "ahhh" (6); **se dice** _____ you say _____ (1)
decisión *f.* decision
declarar to declare
decoración *f.* decoration; decor
decorador(a) decorator; **decorador(a) de interiores** interior decorator
decorar to decorate
dedicarse (qu) a to dedicate oneself to (12)
dedo finger; **dedo del pie** toe

deducir (*like* **conducir**) to deduct; to infer
defectuoso/a defective
defender (ie) to defend
definición *f.* definition
definido defined; *gram.* definite
definir to define (12)
definitivamente once and for all
degradante degrading
dejar to leave; **dejar en paz** to leave alone; **dejarle** + *inf.* to let, allow (*someone*) to (*do something*) (11); **dejarle pasar** to allow (*someone*) to pass (11)
del (*contraction of* **de** + **el**) of/from the (2)
delante de in front of
delfín dolphin
delgado/a thin (1)
delicioso/a delicious; rich (5)
delincuencia delinquency
delincuente *n. m., f.* delinquent (14)
delito crime, offense
demandar to demand
demás: los/lás demás others (15)
demasiado *adv.* too, too much (11)
demasiado/a *adj.* too much; *pl.* too many
democracia democracy
demostrar (ue) to demonstrate
demostrativo/a demonstrative
dentista *m., f.* dentist
dentro (de) in, within, inside (2); **por dentro** on the inside (4)
departamento department; apartment (*Lat. Am.*)
depender de to depend on
dependiente/a salesperson (7)
deportación *f.* deportation
deportar to deport (11)
deporte *m.* sport (8); **practicar (qu) un deporte** to practice a sport (8)
deportista *m., f.* sports player (8)
deportivo/a *adj.* sporting
deprimido/a depressed (9)
deprimir to depress

derecha *n.* right-hand side; **a la derecha (de)** to the right (of) (2); **doblar a la derecha** to turn right (10)
derecho *n.* right (*legal*) (13); straight ahead; **seguir (i, i) (g) derecho** to continue straight ahead (10)
derrotar to defeat
desagradable unpleasant
desalentarse (ie) to get discouraged
desaparecer (zc) to disappear
desarrollar to develop
desarrollo development
desastre *m.* **(natural)** (natural) disaster (13)
desastroso/a disastrous
desatender (ie) to neglect
desayunar to eat breakfast (2)
desayuno breakfast
desbordar (un avión) to get off (an airplane) (10)
descansar to rest (3); **debe / tiene que descansar más** you (*form. s.*) must / have to get more rest (6)
descanso rest; break
descomponer (*like* **poner**) to break
desconfiar (desconfío) to distrust
desconocer (*like* **conocer**) to be unfamiliar with
desconocido/a unknown
descortés impolite
describir (*p.p.* **descrito/a**) to describe
descriminación *f.* discrimination
descripción *f.* description
descubierto/a (*p.p. of* **descubrir**) discovered
descubrimiento discovery
descuento discount (7)
desde *prep.* from; **desde la(s)** _____ **hasta la(s)** _____ from _____ until _____ (time) (6)
deseable desirable (12)
desear to want, desire (5); **¿qué desea(n) (de comer)?** what would you like (to eat)? (5)

desempeñar to carry out
desempleo unemployment
desenvolverse (ue) to evolve
deseo wish, desire
desesperación *f.* desperation
desesperado/a desperate
deshacerse (*like* **hacer**) **de** to rid oneself of
deshidratación *f.* dehydration
desierto desert (10)
desigualdad *f.* inequality (14)
desilusionado/a disillusioned (9)
desinformado/a: estar (*irreg.*) **desinformado/a de** to be uninformed about (13)
desinterés *m.* lack of interest, indifference; apathy (13)
despedida farewell
despedirse (i, i) to say good-bye
despegue *m.* takeoff (*plane*)
despertador *m.* alarm clock
despertarse (ie) to wake up (6)
desplazar (c) to displace
despreciar to despise
despreocupado/a worry-free
después *adv.* after; **después de** (*prep.*) after (11); **después (de) que** (*conj.*) after
destacado/a outstanding
destacar (qu) to emphasize
destinado/a destined (for)
destino destination (10); destiny, fate
destrucción *f.* destruction
destruir (y) to destroy
desván *m.* attic
desventaja disadvantage
desvivirse (por) to be eager (to)
detalle *m.* detail
detallista *m., f.* detail-oriented
detener (*like* **tener**) to stop, detain (11)
detenido/a thorough, slow
determinar to determine
detrás (**de** + *noun*) behind (*something*) (2)
devastado/a devasted
devolver (ue) (*p.p.* **devuelto/a**) to return (*something*) (7)

devoto/a devout (15)
devuelto/a (*p.p. of* **devolver**) returned
día *m.* day (1); **buenos días** good morning (1); **Día de (Acción de) Gracias** Thanksgiving (9); **Día de la Hispanidad** Hispanic Awareness Day; **Día de la Independencia** Independence Day; **Día de la Madre (del Padre)** Mother's (Father's) Day; **Día de la Raza** Hispanic Awareness Day; **Día de los Enamorados (de San Valentín)** St. Valentine's Day; **Día de los Muertos** All Souls' Day (9); **Día de los Reyes Magos** Epiphany (January 6) (9); **Día de los Santos** All Saints' Day (9); **Día de Santa Bárbara** Saint Barbara's feast day (9); **día del santo** saint's day (9); **Día del Trabajador** Labor Day (9); **día feriado** holiday; **días de entresemana** weekdays; **hoy en día** nowadays; **todos los días** every day (9)
diabético/a diabetic
diagnosticar (qu) to diagnose
dialecto dialect
dialogar (gu) to dialogue
diálogo dialogue
diamante *m.* diamond; **anillo de diamantes** diamond ring (7)
diario/a *adj.* daily (6); **diario** *n. m.* newspaper
dibujar to draw (8)
dibujo drawing
diccionario dictionary
dicho/a (*p.p. of* **decir**) said
diciembre *m.* December (6)
dictado dictation
dictadura dictatorship
diecinueve nineteen (1)
dieciocho eighteen (1)
dieciséis sixteen (1)
diecisiete seventeen (1)

diente *m.* tooth; **cepillarse los dientes** to brush one's teeth (6); **diente de ajo** clove of garlic
dieta diet
diez ten (1)
diferencia difference; **a diferencia de** unlike (3)
diferenciarse to be different, distinguish oneself (10)
diferente (de) different (from/than) (1)
difícil difficult (2)
dificultad *f.* difficulty
dificultar to make difficult
difundirse to diffuse, spread (13)
difusión *f.* diffusion
dimitir to resign
Dinamarca Denmark
dinero money
dios *m.* god
diplomático/a diplomat
diptongo diphthong
directo/a direct; straight
director(a) director (12)
dirigente director
dirigir (j) to direct
disciplina discipline
disciplinar to discipline, control
disco compacto compact disc
discoteca discotheque (8)
discriminación *f.* discrimination (14)
discriminado/a: ser (*irreg.*) **discriminado/a** to be discriminated against (14)
discriminar to discriminate (11)
disculpar to excuse; **disculpe** excuse me
discusión *f.* discussion
discutir to discuss (3); to argue (3)
diseñador(a) designer (12)
diseñar to draw; to design
diseño design (2)
disfrutar to enjoy
disgustar not to like (9)
disgusto annoyance; irritation; dislike

disponible available
disputa dispute
distancia distance
distinción *f.* distinction
distinguir (distingo) to distinguish (14)
distinto/a different, distinct (from) (3)
divertirse (ie, i) to enjoy oneself (6)
dividir to divide
divino/a divine
divisa currency
división *f.* division
divorciado/a divorced (3); **estar** (*irreg.*) **divorciado/a** to be divorced (3)
divorciarse to divorce, get divorced (15)
divorcio divorce
divulgar (gu) to divulge
doblar to turn; **doblar a la derecha/izquierda** to turn right/left (10)
doble double
doce twelve (1)
doctor(a) doctor
documental *m.* documentary (13)
documento document (11)
dólar *m.* dollar
doler (ue) to hurt, ache; **me/te duele(n)** _____ my/your _____ hurt(s) (6)
dolor *m.* pain; **dolor de cabeza** headache (6)
doméstico/a domestic; **animal** (*m.*) **doméstico** pet
dominante dominant
domingo Sunday (1)
dominicano/a *n., adj. of or from the Dominican Republic*
don *m.* gift, skill; *title of respect used with a man's first name*
¿dónde? where?; **¿de dónde eres?** where are you (*fam. s.*) from? (1); **¿de dónde es?** where are you (*form. s.*) / he/she from? (1)
doña *title of respect used with a woman's first name*

dormir (ue, u) to sleep (4); **dormir la siesta** to take a siesta (nap) (4); **dormirse** to fall asleep (6)
dormitorio bedroom (4)
dos two (1)
dos mil two thousand (7)
doscientos/as two hundred (7)
dramático/a dramatic
droga drug (14)
ducha shower (4)
ducharse to shower, take a shower (6)
duda doubt; **sin duda** without a doubt
dudar to doubt (13); **dudar en** + *inf.* to hesitate to (*do something*) (13); **sin dudar** without hesitation (15)
dudoso/a doubtful (13)
dueño/a owner
dulce *adj.* sweet (5)
dulzón (dulzona) sweet
duna dune
duración *f.* duration
duradero/a lasting
durante during
durar to last
durazno peach
duro/a hard; firm
DVD DVD player (13)

E

echar to throw out; **echar una siesta** to take a siesta (nap) (3)
economía economy
económico/a economic; **superar las barreras económicas** to overcome economic barriers (14)
ecuador *m.* equator
ecuatoriano/a *n., adj.* Ecuadorian
edad *f.* age; **edad adulta** adulthood (9); **¿qué edad (tiene)?** how old (are you [*form. s.*] / is he/she)? (3)
edición *f.* edition
edificio building; **edificio de administración** administration building (2)

editor(a) editor
editorial *m.* editorial
educación *f.* education (2); **Facultad** (*f.*) **de Educación** School of Education (2); **nivel** (*m.*) **de educación** level of education (14)
educar (qu) to educate
educativo/a educational; **programa** (*m.*) **educativo** educational program (13)
efectivo: en efectivo cash (*money*)
efecto effect
eficaz (*pl.* **eficaces**) effective
eficiente efficient
egoísta *adj. m., f.* selfish, egotistical
ejecución *f.* execution
ejemplo example; **por ejemplo** for example
ejercer (z) to engage in
ejercicio exercise; **hacer** (*irreg.*) **ejercicio (aeróbico)** to do (aerobic) exercise (6)
ejército army (13)
el *def. art. m.* the (1); **el más/menos** + *adj.* the most/least + *adj.* (5); **el mejor/peor** + *noun* the best/worst + *noun* (5)
él *sub. pron.* he (1); *obj. of prep.* him
elaborar to manufacture, produce
elección *f.* election (13)
electo/a: presidente electo president elect
electricidad *f.* electricity
eléctrico/a electric; **cocina eléctrica** electric stove (14)
electrodoméstico electric appliance
electrónico/a electronic; **correo electrónico** e-mail (13)
elefante *m.* elephant
elegancia elegance
elegante elegant (4)
elegir (i, i) (j) to choose; to elect
elemento element

ella *sub. pron.* she (1); *obj. of prep.* her

ellos/as *sub. pron.* they (1); *obj. of prep.* them

embajador(a) ambassador

embarazo pregnancy

embargo: sin embargo *conj.* however

embotellado/a bottled; **agua** (*f.* [*but* **el agua**]) **embotellada** bottled water

embotellamiento traffic jam

embutido sausage

emigrante emigrant

emigrar to emigrate

emisión *f.* broadcast

emocionado/a emotional; moved (9)

emocional emotional

emocionante moving, touching

empanada *turnover pie or pastry*

emparejar to match

empate *m.* tie (*sports*)

emperador(a) emperor/empress

empezar (ie) (c) to begin

empleado/a employee (12); **agencía de empleados temporarios** temporary employment agency

empleo job; **anuncio de empleo** job ad (12)

emprender un viaje to take a trip

empresa company (12); **administración** (*f.*) **de empresas** business administration

en in (2)

enamorado/a (de) in love (with); **Día** (*m.*) **de los Enamorados** St. Valentine's Day

enamorarse (de) to fall in love (with) (15)

encabezado *n.* headline (13)

encantado/a nice to meet you (1)

encantador(a) delightful, charming (1)

encantar to charm, delight (7); **encantarle** to charm, delight (*someone*); to love (*thing*) (7)

encender (ie) to turn on

enchufe *m.* connection

encima de on top of

encontrar (ue) to find; **encontrarse con amigos** to get together (meet) with friends (8); **encontrarse en ambiente** to be in the mood (8)

encuentro *n.* get-together; (chance) meeting

encuesta survey

enero January (6)

enfatizar (c) to emphasize

enfermarse to get sick

enfermedad *f.* sickness (6)

enfermería infirmary, hospital

enfermero/a *n.* nurse (12)

enfermo/a *n.* sick person; *adj.* sick; **estar** (*irreg.*) **enfermo/a** to be sick (6)

enfrentarse con to face, confront

enfrente (de) in front (of) (2)

engañar to deceive; to trick, swindle (14)

enlace link (13)

enlatado/a canned

enojado/a angry; **estar** (*irreg.*) **enojado/a** to be angry (6)

enorme enormous

enriquecer (zc) to enrich (13)

ensalada salad (5)

enseñanza teaching; **tener** (*irreg.*) **más acceso a la enseñanza** to have more access to education (14)

enseñar to teach (2)

entablar to begin, start

entender (ie) to understand (4)

enterado/a: estar (*irreg.*) **enterado/a de** to know about (13)

enterarse de to find out about

entero/a entire, whole

entonces then

entrada entrance; ticket; **(de) entrada** (as) an appetizer (5)

entrar (en + *place*) to enter (*a place*) (2)

entre between (2); **estar** (*irreg.*) **entre dos culturas** to be (caught) between two cultures (11); **estar** (*irreg.*) **entre medio** to be in the middle; **mantener** (*like* **tener**) **un espacio entre los dos** to maintain a distance between the two

entregar (gu) to hand in

entrenador(a) (personal) (personal) trainer (12)

entrenamiento training

entrenar to train

entresemana: días (*m. pl.*) **de entresemana** weekdays

entretenido/a amused, entertained

entrevista interview

envasado/a canned, packed

envase *m.* container

enviar (envío) to send

envolver (ue) to wrap

época era, age

equilibrado/a well-balanced

equilibrio balance

equipado/a equipped

equipaje *m.* baggage; **facturar el equipaje** to check luggage (10)

equipo team (8)

equitación *f.* horseback riding (8)

equitativo/a equitable, fair

equivocado/a mistaken

equivocarse (qu) to be mistaken

error *m.* error, mistake

eructar to burp

esbelto/a graceful, slender

escala scale; ladder

escalar montañas to go mountain climbing (8)

escándalo scandal; **¡qué escándalo!** what a scandal! (13)

escandaloso/a scandalous (13)

escapar (de) to escape (from) (11)

escaso/a scarce

escena scene

escenificación *f. adaptation for the stage*

esclavo/a slave

Escocia Scotland

escoger (j) to choose

esconder to hide (11)

escribir (*p.p.* **escrito/a**) to write (3); **escribir cartas** to write letters (3); **escribir cuentos/poesía** to write stories/poetry (8); **se escribe** _____ it's spelled _____ (1)

escrito/a (*p.p. of* **escribir**) written

escritor(a) writer (12)

escritorio desk (4)

escritura writing

escuchar to listen (to) (2)

escuela school; **escuela secundaria** high school

escultor(a) sculptor

escultura sculpture

escurrir to drain

ese/a *adj.* that (4)

ése/a *pron.* that (one) (4)

esencial essential

esfuerzo effort

eso *neut. pron.* that (stuff) (4); **a eso de la(s)** _____ around _____; **por eso** for that (reason), that's why

espacio space; **mantener** (*like* **tener**) **un espacio entre los dos** to maintain distance between the two (15)

espaguetis *m. pl.* spaghetti

espalda back (*of a person*)

España Spain

español *n. m.* Spanish (*language*) (2)

español(a) *n.* Spaniard; *adj.* Spanish (1); **tortilla española** *omelette made of eggs, potatoes, and onions (Sp.)*

especia spice

especial special

especialización *f.* specialization, major

especializado/a: tienda especializada speciality shop/store (7)

especializarse (c) to specialize, major in

especie *f. s.* species

especificar (qu) to specify

específico/a specific

espectáculo spectacle, sight

espectador(a) spectator

especular to speculate

espejo mirror

espera: sala de espera waiting room

esperanza hope; **tener** (*irreg.*) **esperanza** to have hope, be hopeful (11)

esperar to hope; to wait for

espinacas *pl.* spinach

espíritu *m.* spirit

espiritual spiritual

espontáneo/a spontaneous

esposo/a husband/wife (3)

espuma foam

esquela obituary

esquí *m.* skiing (8); *pl.* skis; **esquí acuático** water skiing

esquiar (esquío) (en el agua) to (water) ski (8)

estabilidad *f.* stability (13)

estable *adj.* stable

establecer (zc) to establish

estación *f.* season (*of the year*) (6); station; **estación de trenes / del metro** train/subway station (10)

estacionamiento parking lot

estadio stadium (2)

estadística statistic

estado *n.* state

Estados Unidos United States

estadounidense *n., adj.* American (*from the United States*) (1)

estampado/a embossed

estampilla stamp; **coleccionar estampillas** to collect stamps (8)

estancado/a stuck

estantería *s.* shelving, bookcase (4)

estar *irreg.* to be (2); **está nublado** it's cloudy (6); **estar aburrido/a** to be bored (6); **estar al corriente** to be up-to-date (13); **estar ansioso/a (por)** to be anxious (about) (11); **estar borracho/a** to be drunk (8); **estar cansado/a**

to be tired (6); **estar casado/a** to be married (3); **estar conectado/a** to be connected (*to the Internet*) (13); **estar congestionado/a** to be congested; **estar contento/a** to be happy (6); **estar de acuerdo** to agree; **estar de moda** to be in fashion; **estar de vacaciones** to be on vacation (10); **estar de viaje** to be on a trip (10); **estar desinformado/a de** to be uninformed about (13); **estar divorciado/a** to be divorced (3); **estar en peligro** (**de** + *inf.*) to be in danger (*of doing something*); **estar en su punto** to be at one's best (8); **estar enfermo/a** to be sick (6); **estar enojado/a** to be angry (6); **estar enterado/a de** to know about (13); **estar entre dos culturas** to be (caught) between two cultures (11); **estar entre medio** to be in the middle; **estar fatal** to feel awful; **estar hecho/a a mano** to be made by hand (7); **estar hecho/a bien/mal** to be well/poorly made (7); **estar hecho/a de** to be made of; **estar jubilado/a** to be retired (3); **estar listo/a** to be ready; **estar muerto/a de** to be dying of; **estar orgulloso/a** to feel proud, be proud; **estar relajado/a** to be relaxed (8); **estar resfriado/a** to have a cold; **estar tranquilo/a** to be calm (8); **estar triste** to be sad (6); **estoy (muy) bien, gracias** I'm (very) fine, thanks (1)

estatua statue

estatus *m.* status

este *m.* east

este/a *adj.* this (4)

éste/a *pron.* this (one) (4)

este... uh . . . (*pause sound*) (8)

estéreo stereo

estereotipado/a stereotyped
estereotipo stereotype
estilo style
estímulo stimulus
esto *neut. pron.* this (stuff) (4)
estómago stomach
estratégico/a strategic
estrecho/a close (3); **Estrecho de Magallanes** Strait of Magellan
estrella star
estrés *m.* stress; **sufrir de estrés** to suffer from stress (6)
estresado/a stressed
estricto/a strict
estrofa verse
estructura structure
estructural structural
estudiante *m., f.* student (2); **estudiante posgraduado** graduate student
estudiantil *adj.* student; **hostal/residencia estudiantil** student hostel/residence
estudiar to study (2)
estudio study; *pl.* studies, schooling (2)
estupendo/a stupendous
etapa step, stage (9)
ética *s.* ethics
etnicidad ethnicity
étnico/a ethnic (14)
etnografía ethnography
Europa Europe
europeo/a *adj.* European (14)
evaluación *f.* evaluation
evaluar (evalúo) to evaluate
evento event
evidencia evidence
evidente evident
evitar to avoid; **evitar el lenguaje peyorativo** to avoid pejorative language (14)
evolucionar to evolve
exacto/a exact (6)
exageración *f.* exaggeration
exagerar to exaggerate
examen *m.* test
examinar to examine
excelencia excellence
excelente excellent

excepcional exceptional
excepto *adv.* except
excesivo/a excessive
excluir (y) to exclude
exclusivo/a exclusive
excursión *f.* excursion; **hacer** (*irreg.*) **una excursión** to go on an outing (excursion) (10)
excusa excuse
exhibir to exhibit
exigente demanding
exigir (j) to demand (12)
exilado/a exiled (13)
exilio exile (13)
existir to exist
éxito success; **tener** (*irreg.*) **éxito** to be successful (11)
exitoso/a successful
exótico/a exotic; strange
expandir to expand
expansión *f.* expansion
expectativa: tener (*irreg.*) **expectativas** to have expectations (11)
expedir (i, i) to expedite; to issue
experiencia experience; **experiencia (mínima)** (minimum) experience (12); **según la experiencia** based on experience (12)
experimentar to test, try out
experimento experiment
experto/a *n., adj.* expert
explicación *f.* explanation
explicar (qu) to explain
exploración *f.* exploration
explorar to explore
explosión *f.* explosion
explotar to exploit (14)
exponer (*like* **poner**) to expose, report (13)
exportación *f.* exportation
expresar (los sentimientos) to express (one's feelings) (15)
expresión *f.* expression
expulsado/a expelled; thrown out
exquisito/a exquisite
extender (ie) to extend
extensión *f.* extension

exterior *m.* exterior (4)
extinción *f.* extinction
extranjero abroad (11)
extranjero/a *n.* foreigner; *adj.* foreign (13)
extraño/a strange
extraordinario/a extraordinary
extraviar to lose
extremista *n., adj. m., f.* extremist
extremo *n.* extreme
extrovertido/a extroverted

F
fábrica factory
fabricar (qu) to make
fácil easy (2)
facilitar to facilitate, make easy
factor *m.* factor, cause
facturar el equipaje to check luggage (10)
facultad *f.* school, college (2); **Facultad de Ciencias** School of Sciences (2); **Facultad de Educación** School of Education (2); **Facultad de Letras** School of Liberal Arts (Humanities) (2)
falda skirt (7)
falsificación *f.* falsification
falso/a false
falta lack
faltar to be missing/lacking; **falta(n) _____ minuto(s) para la(s) _____** it is _____ minute(s) to _____ (6)
familia family (3)
familiar *adj. pertaining to a family*
famoso/a famous
fanático/a fan (*sports*)
fantasía fantasy
fantástico/a fantastic (9)
farmacéutico/a *n.* pharmacist; *adj.* pharmaceutical
farmacia pharmacy
fascinar(le) to fascinate (*someone*) (9)
fatal awful (9); **estar** (*irreg.*) **fatal** to feel awful
fatiga fatigue
favor *m.* favor; **por favor** please

favorito/a favorite
febrero February (6)
fecha date (*calendar*)
feliz (*pl.* **felices**) happy (9); **ser** (*irreg.*) **feliz** to be happy
femenino/a feminine
feminista *m., f.* feminist
fenómeno phenomenon
feo/a ugly (1)
feriado: día (*m.*) **feriado** holiday
feroz (*pl.* **feroces**) ferocious
festivo/a festive
fiable reliable
ficha index card; filing card; **marcar (qu) la ficha** to punch out (*time clock*)
fidelidad *f.* faithfulness
fiebre *f.* fever; **tener** (*irreg.*) **fiebre** to have a fever (6)
fiel accurate, faithful
fiesta party (8)
figura figure
fijar to arrange, set up (12); **fijar citas** to set appointments; **fijarse en** to take note of
fijo/a: seguir (i, i) (g) / mantener (*like* **tener**) **una rutina fija** to follow/maintain a fixed (regular) routine (6)
filón vein (*mine*)
filosofía philosophy (2)
filósofo/a philosopher
fin *m.* end; **al fin y al cabo** in the end; **fin de semana** weekend; **por fin** finally
final *n. m.* end; *adj.* final
fino/a *adj.* fine
firmar to sign
física *s.* physics
físico/a physical (6); **fuerza física** physical strength (12); **salud** (*f.*) **física** physical health (6)
flan *m. type of custard topped with caramel*
flexibilidad *f.* flexibility
flexible: horario flexible flexible schedule (12)
flor *f.* flower
florería flower shop

floristería flower shop
folclor *m.* folklore (14)
folclórico/a folkloric
folleto brochure
fondo fund
forma form, shape; **en buena forma** in good shape
formación *f.* background (12)
formal formal (4)
formar to form; **formar pareja** to form a romantic relationship, find a mate (15)
formato format
fórmula formula; prescription
formulario form, application (12)
foro forum
fortalecer (zc) to strengthen
foto picture
foto(grafía) photo(graph); photography
fotocopia photocopy
fotógrafo/a photographer (12)
fracaso failure
fradulento/a fradulent
fragmentación *f.* fragmentation
fragmento excerpt
francés *n. m.* French (*language*) (2)
francés, francesa *n., adj.* French (1)
Francia France
frase *f.* sentence; phrase
fraude *m.* fraud
frecuencia frecuency (9); **con frecuencia** frequently (9)
frecuentar to visit often, frequent (15)
frecuente frequent
fregadero sink (*kitchen*) (4)
freír (i, i) (*p.p.* **frito/a**) to fry (5)
frenar to brake; to stop
frenético/a frenzied, frantic
frente a *prep.* in the face of; versus; facing
fresco/a fresh (5); cool; **hace fresco** it's cool (*weather*) (6)
frigorífico refrigerator
frijol *m.* bean (5)
frío *n.:* **hace frío** it's cold (6)
frío/a *adj.* cold

frito (*p.p. of* **freír**) fried (5)
frontera border (11); **para cruzar (c) la frontera** getting across the border (11)
fronterizo/a *adj.* frontier, border
fruncir (z) to knit (*eyebrows*)
frustrado/a frustrated (9)
fruta fruit (5)
frutería fruit store (5)
fuego fire; **arma** (*f.* [*but* **el arma**]) **de fuego** firearm
fuente *f.* source; fountain
fuera de outside (of); **por fuera** on the outside (4)
fuerte strong
fuerza strength; **fuerza física** physical strength (12)
fumar to smoke (8)
función *f.* function
funcional functional; **lenguaje funcional** functional language (1)
funcionamiento: en funcionamiento functioning
funcionar to function, work
fundación *f.* foundation, founding
fundamental basic
fundar to found, be founded
fútbol *m.* soccer; **fútbol americano** football (8); **jugar (ue) (gu) al fútbol** to play soccer (4)
futbolista *m., f.* soccer player
futuro *n.* future; **futuro prometedor** promising future (12)
futuro/a *adj.* future

G

gamba shrimp, prawn (5)
ganado livestock
ganar to win (8); to earn (12)
ganas *pl.:* **tener** (*irreg.*) **ganas de** + *inf.* to feel like (*doing something*) (8)
gandules *pl.* green peas
ganga bargain (7)
garaje *m.* garage (4)
garantizar (c) to guarantee

garganta throat (6); **tiene la garganta inflamada** your (*form. s.*) throat is inflamed (6)

gas *m.*: **cocina de gas** gas stove (4); **horno de gas** gas stove

gastar to spend (*money*)

gasto expense

gastronomía (style of) cooking, gastronomy (14)

gastronómico/a gastronomic

gato/a cat (3)

gauchesco/a *adj. pertaining to gauchos*

gaucho/a Argentine rancher

gaviota seagull

gélido/a icy cold

gemelo/a twin (3)

genealogía geneology

genealógico/a genealogical

generación *f.* generation

generacional: conflicto generacional generational conflict (11)

general: en general in general

género gender; genre

gente *f. s.* people

geografía geography

geográfico/a geographical

geología geology

geométrico/a geometric

gerencial: cualidades (*f.*) **gerenciales** managing abilities

gerente *m., f.* manager

gesto gesture

gigante *adj.* giant, huge

gimnasio gymnasium (2)

girar to turn

gobernante governing

gobierno government (13)

gol goal

golf *m.* golf (8); **jugar (ue) (gu) al golf** to play golf

golfo gulf

golpe *m.* **militar** military coup

gordo/a fat (1)

gorra cap

gozar (c) de to enjoy

gracias thank you; **Día** (*m.*) **de (Acción de) Gracias** Thanksgiving (9); **gracias por** thanks for (11)

gracioso/a funny

grado degree

graduación *f.* graduation

gráfico/a *adj.* graphic

gramática grammar

gran, grande big, large (1); **quedarle grande** to fit large (*clothing*) (7)

granizado small snow cone

granjero/a farmer

grano grain

grasa *n.* fat

gratis *adv. inv.* free (*of charge*)

grave serious

gregario/a gregarious (3)

griego/a *n., adj.* Greek

gripe *f.* flu; **tener** (*irreg.*) **gripe** to have the flu (6)

gris gray (7)

gritar to yell, shout

grúa crane (*construction*)

grupo group

guante *m.* glove

guapo/a handsome, good-looking, pretty (1)

guaraní *m.* Guarani (*indigenous language of Paraguay*)

guardar to keep; to save

guardería day care center

guatemalteco/a *n., adj.* Guatemalan (13)

guayabera *embroidered shirt of light material worn in tropical climates*

gubermental governmental

güero/a blond; light-complected

guerra war; **guerra civil** civil war (13)

guerrilla guerilla war (13)

guía *m., f.* guide; *f.* guidebook

guiar (guío) to guide

guineo banana

güiro *musical instrument made from a gourd*

guisante *m.* green pea

guitarra guitar

gustar(le) to be pleasing (*to someone*) (9); **(no) me gusta(n)** _____ I (don't) like _____ (2); **(no) te gusta(n)** _____ you (*fam. s.*) (don't) like _____ (2); **me gustaría** + *inf.* I would like to (*do something*) (8); **me/te gustaría** _____ I/you (*fam. s.*) would like _____ (5); **¿te gustaría** + *inf.?* would you (*fam. s.*) like to (*do something*)? (8)

gusto taste; pleasure (7); **mucho gusto** nice (pleasure) to meet you (1)

H

haber *irreg.* to have (*auxiliary*)

habichuela bean

habilidad *f.* ability; skill

habitación *f.* (bed)room (4)

habitante *m., f.* inhabitant

habitar to live

hábito habit

habla *f.* (but **el habla**) speech (14)

hablador(a) talkative

hablar to speak (2)

hacer *irreg.* (*p.p.* **hecho/a**) to make (3); to do (3); **hace (mucho tiempo)** (a long time) ago (11); **hace buen/mal tiempo** it's good/bad weather (6); **hace fresco** it's cool (*weather*) (6); **hace frío/calor** it's cold/hot (6); **hace sol** it's sunny (6); **hace viento** it's windy (6); **hacer artes marciales** to practice martial arts (8); **hacer camping** to go camping; **hacer clic (en)** to click (on) (13); **hacer crucigramas** to do crossword puzzles (3); **hacer daño** to hurt, harm (15); **hacer ejercicio (aeróbico)** to do (aerobic) exercise (6); **hacer la compra** to do the shopping (5); **hacer la rabona** to play hookey; **hacer un viaje** to take a trip (10); **hacer una excursión** to go on an excursion/outing (10);

¿me haría el favor de... ? would you (*form. s.*) please . . . ? (12); **¿qué tiempo hace?** what's the weather like? (6); **se me hace** it seems to me (*Mex.*) (11)

hacia toward; **hacia el norte (sur, este, oeste)** to the north (south, east, west) (10)

hallar to find

hambre *f.* (*but* **el hambre**) hunger; **calmar el hambre** to curb one's hunger; **tener** (*irreg.*) **hambre** to be hungry (5)

hamburguesa hamburger

harina flour

hasta *prep.* until; **desde la(s) _____ hasta la(s) _____** from _____ until _____ (*time*) (6); **hasta ahora** until now; **hasta altas horas de la noche** until late at night; **hasta cierto/a...** until a certain . . . ; **hasta pronto/mañana/luego** until (see you) soon/tomorrow/later (1); **hasta que** (*conj.*) until

hay (*from* **haber**); **(no) hay** there is/are (not); **hay hielo** it's icy; **hay niebla** it's foggy; **hay que** + *inf.* you (one) must (*do something*) (6)

hecho *n.* fact; **de hecho** in fact

hecho/a (*p.p. of* **hacer**) made; **estar** (*irreg.*) **hecho/a a mano** to be made by hand (7); **estar** (*irreg.*) **hecho/a bien/mal** to be well/poorly made (7); **estar** (*irreg.*) **hecho/a de** to be made of

helado *n.* ice cream

hemisferio hemisphere

heredar to inherit

herencia *f.* heritage; inheritance

hermanastro/a stepbrother/ stepsister (3)

hermano/a brother/sister (3); *m. pl.* siblings (3)

herramienta tool

hervir (ie, i) to boil

hielo ice; **hay hielo** it's icy; **patinar (sobre hielo)** to (ice) skate (8)

higiene *f.* hygiene

higiénico/a hygienic

hijo/a son/daughter (3); *m. pl.* children (3); **hijo/a único/a** only child (3)

hilar to spin, weave

hilo thread

hispánico/a *adj.* Hispanic

hispanidad *f.*: **Día** (*m.*) **de la Hispanidad** Hispanic Awareness Day

hispano/a *n., adj.* Hispanic

hispanohablante *m., f.* Spanish speaker

historia story; history (13)

histórico/a historical

hogar *m.* home

hogareño/a family oriented

hoja leaf; sheet of paper; **hoja de papel aparte** separate piece of paper

hola hello (1)

hombre *m.* man; **hombre de negocios** businessman (12)

homenaje *m.* homage

honesto/a honest, sincere (15)

hora hour (6); time; **hasta altas horas de la noche** until late at night; **¿qué hora es?** what time is it? (6); **¿tiene(s) la hora?** do you have the time? (6)

horario (fijo/flexible) (fixed/ flexible) schedule (12)

horizonte *m.* horizon

hornear to bake

horno eléctrico / de gas electric/gas stove (4)

horóscopo horoscope

horrible terrible, horrible (9)

horroroso/a horrific

hospital *m.* hospital

hospitalario/a hospitable

hostal *m.* inexpensive hotel; **hostal estudiantil** student hostel

hostelería hotel management

hotelero/a *adj.* hotel

hoy today; **hoy en día** nowadays

huaraches *pl.* traditional Mexican sandals

huelga strike

huella footprint; trace

huevo egg (5)

humanidad *f.* humanity

humanitario/a humanitarian

humano *n.* human; **ser** (*n. m.*) **humano** human being

humano/a *adj.* human

humedad *f.* humidity

húmedo/a humid

humilde humble (4)

humo smoke

humor *m.* humor; mood; **sentido del humor** sense of humor

húngaro/a *n., adj.* Hungarian

huracán *m.* hurrricane

I

ida: de ida *adj.* one-way (10); **de ida y vuelta** *adj.* round-trip (10)

identidad *f.* identity (11)

identificación *f.* identification

identificar (qu) to identify; **identificarse con** to identify with (11)

ideología ideology

idiom *m.* language

ídolo idol

iglesia church (15)

igual equal; **al igual que** just like (3)

igualdad *f.* equality

igualmente likewise / same here (1)

ilegal illegal (11)

ilógico/a illogical

iluminar to illuminate, light up

ilustrar to illustrate

imagen *f.* (*pl.* **imágenes**) image (13)

imaginar to imagine

impacto impact

impartir to impart, grant

imperfecto *gram.* imperfect (*tense*)
imperio empire
impermeable *m.* raincoat (7)
implicar (qu) to implicate
implícito/a implicit
imponer (*like* **poner**) to impose
importado/a imported
importancia importance
importante important (2); **es importante** + *inf.* it's important to (*do something*) (6)
importar to matter, be important; **(no) importar(le)** to (not) matter (*to someone*) (9); **¿le importaría... ?** would you (*form. s.*) mind . . . ? (12)
imposible impossible
imposición *f.* imposition
impotente impotent, powerless (14)
imprescindible indispensable
impresión *f.* impression
impresionable impressionable; emotional
impresionante impressive
impresionar to impress
imprimir to print
impuesto *n.* tax
impulsar to give impulse to; to promote
impulsivo/a impulsive
inaugurar to inaugurate, open
inca *n. m., f.* Inca; *adj. m., f.* Incan
incaico/a Incan (14)
incentivo incentive
incertidumbre *f.* uncertainty; **vivir con la incertidumbre** to live with uncertainty (11)
incidencia incidence
incidente *m.* incident
incierto/a uncertain
inclinación *f.* inclination
inclinado/a inclined
incluir (y) to include
incompatible: tener (*irreg.*) **valores/personalidades incompatibles** to have incompatible values/ personalities (15)

incompleto/a incomplete
inconsciente unconscious
inconveniente inconvenient
incorporar to incorporate
increíble incredible, unbelievable
independencia independence; **Día** (*m.*) **de la Independencia** Independence Day
independiente independent
indicar (qu) to indicate
indicativo *gram.* indicative (*mood*)
indígena *n. m., f.* indigenous person, native (13); *adj. m., f.* indigenous, native
indio/a *n.* Indian
indirecto indirect
indiscreto/a indiscreet
indispensable essential
individual *adj.* individual
individuo *n.* person; individual
indocumentado/a undocumented person (11)
industria industry
ineficaz (*pl.* **ineficaces**) ineffective
inestabilidad *f.* instability
inestable unstable
infancia infancy (9)
infección *f.* infection
infeliz (*pl.* **infelices**) unhappy (9)
inferencia inference
inferir (ie, i) to infer
infinitivo infinitive
inflamado/a inflamed; **tiene la garganta inflamada** your (*form. s.*) throat is inflamed (6)
influencia influence (11)
influenciar to influence
influir (y) en to influence (13)
información *f.* information
informado/a: mantenerse (*like* **tener**) **informado/a** to stay informed (13)
informal informal (2)
informar to inform
informática computer science (2)
informe *m.* report
infusión *f.* infusion

ingeniería engineering
ingeniero/a engineer (12)
Inglaterra England
inglés *n. m.* English (*language*) (2)
inglés, inglesa *n., adj.* English (1)
ingrediente *m.* ingredient
ingreso entry
iniciar to initiate
iniciativa initiative
injusticia injustice (13)
inmaculado/a immaculate
inmediato/a immediate
inmejorable unsurpassable
inmigración *f.* immigration; **agente** (*m., f.*) **de inmigración** immigration agent (11)
inmigrante *n. m., f.* immigrant
innato/a innate
innecesario/a unnecessary
innovación *f.* innovation
innovador(a) innovative
inocente naive, inexperienced (9)
inolvidable unforgettable
inquilino/a *n.* tenant
inseguridad *f.* insecurity
inseguro/a insecure
insistencia insistence
insistir to insist
insomnio insomnia; **sufrir de insomnio** to suffer from insomnia (6)
insoportable insufferable
inspirar to inspire
instalación *f.* installation
instalar to install
instantánea *n.* snapshot
instantáneo/a *adj.* instantaneous
institución *f.* institution
instrumento instrument
integrarse to integrate oneself
integridad *f.* integrity
intelectual *n., adj. m., f.* intellectual
inteligente intelligent
intención *f.* intention; **tener** (*irreg.*) **la intención de** + *inf.* to intend to (*do something*) (11)
intentar to try
intercambio *n.* exchange

interés *m.* interest

interesado/a interested (9)

interesante interesting (2)

interesar(le) to interest (*someone*) (9); **(no) me interesa(n)** it/that does (not) interest me (8)

intergeneracional intergenerational

interior *m.* (4); **decorador(a) de interiores** interior decorator; **ropa interior** underwear (7)

internacional international

internauta Internet surfer

Internet *m.* Internet (13)

interpretación *f.* interpretation

interpretar to interpret, explain

interrogativo/a interrogative (2)

interrumpir to interrupt

intimidad *f.* intimacy

intimidado/a intimidated, threatened (9)

íntimo/a intimate, private; close (*relationship*); **relación** (*f.*) **íntima** intimate relationship (15)

intocable untouchable

intrafamiliar within a family

introvertido/a introverted

intuir (y) to intuit, sense

inundación *f.* flood

inútil useless

inventar to invent, discover

investigación *f.* research

investigador(a) researcher

investigar (gu) to research

invierno winter (6)

invitación *f.* invitation

invitado/a guest (8)

invitar to invite

ir *irreg.* to go (2); **ir a pie** to go on foot (walk) (10); **ir al teatro/cine** to go to the theater/movies (8); **ir de compras** to go shopping (3); **ir de vacaciones** to go on vacation (10); **ir de viaje** to go on a trip (10); **ir en (tren/avión/autobús)** to go by (train/airplane/bus) (10); **irle bien/mal** to go well/poorly

(*for someone*) (11); **irse** to go away, leave; **¡vamos!** let's go! (8)

Irlanda Ireland

irlandés, irlandesa *n., adj.* Irish

irónico/a ironic

irritado/a irritated (9)

irritante irritating, annoying

irritar(le) to irritate (*someone*) (9)

irrumpir to burst into, erupt

isla island; **Islas Malvinas** Falkland Islands

Italia Italy

italiano *n. m.* Italian (*language*)

italiano/a *n., adj.* Italian (1)

itinerario itinerary (10)

izquierda *n.* left-hand side; **a la izquierda (de + *noun*)** to the left (of + *noun*) (2); **de la izquierda** on the left; **doblar a la izquierda** to turn left (10)

J

jabón *m.* soap

jamás never, not ever (8); **nunca jamás** never ever (8)

jamón *m.* ham (5)

Januká *m.* Hanukkah (9)

japonés, japonesa *n., adj.* Japanese (1)

jaqueca migraine

jarabe *m.* **(para la tos)** (cough) syrup

jardín *m.* garden (4)

jardinero/a gardener

jefe/a boss, chief

jerez *m.* (*pl.* **jereces**) sherry

jerga slang, jargon

jesuita *n., adj. m., f.* Jesuit

jícara cup, small bowl

jitomate *m.* tomato (*Mex.*)

jornada tradicional traditional workday (12)

joven *n. m., f.* (*pl.* **jóvenes**) young person (9); *adj.* young

joyería jewelry store (7)

jubilado/a: estar (*irreg.*) **jubilado/a** to be retired (3)

jubilarse to retire

juego game; **Juegos Olímpicos** Olympics

jueves *m. s., pl.* Thursday (1)

juez(a) (*m. pl.* **jueces**) judge

jugador(a) player (8)

jugar (ue) (gu) to play (4); **jugar a los naipes** to play cards (8); **jugar a los videojuegos** to play video games (8); **jugar al ajedrez** to play chess (8); **jugar al baloncesto** to play basketball (*Sp.*) (4); **jugar al balonmano** to play handball; **jugar al básquetbol** to play basketball; **jugar al béisbol** to play baseball (4); **jugar al billar** to play billiards (pool) (8); **jugar al fútbol** to play soccer (4); **jugar al golf** to play golf

jugo juice

juguete *m.* toy

julio July (6)

jungla jungle

junio June (6)

juntar to join, gather, collect

junto/a together (3)

jurar to swear (*an oath*)

justicia justice

justificado/a justified

justificar (qu) to justify

justo/a fair

juvenil *adj.* youth

juventud *f.* youth

K

kilograma *m.* kilogram

kilómetro kilometer

kínder *m.* kindergarten

Kwanzaa *m.* Kwanzaa (9)

L

la *def. art. f.* the (1); *d.o. f.* her, it, you (*form. s.*); **la más/menos + *adj.*** the most/least + *adj.* (5); **la mejor/peor + *noun*** the best/worst + *noun* (5)

labio lip

laboral *adj. pertaining to work or labor*

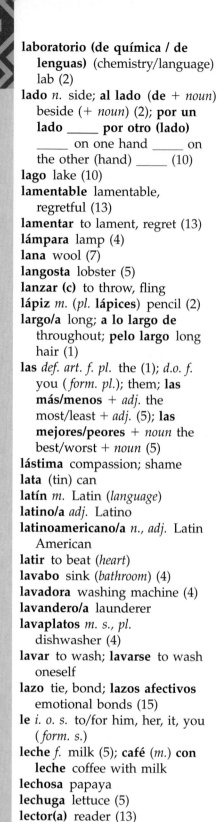

laboratorio (de química / de lenguas) (chemistry/language) lab (2)

lado *n.* side; **al lado (de** + *noun*) beside (+ *noun*) (2); **por un lado** _____ **por otro (lado)** _____ on one hand _____ on the other (hand) _____ (10)

lago lake (10)

lamentable lamentable, regretful (13)

lamentar to lament, regret (13)

lámpara lamp (4)

lana wool (7)

langosta lobster (5)

lanzar (c) to throw, fling

lápiz *m.* (*pl.* **lápices**) pencil (2)

largo/a long; **a lo largo de** throughout; **pelo largo** long hair (1)

las *def. art. f. pl.* the (1); *d.o. f.* you (*form. pl.*); them; **las más/menos** + *adj.* the most/least + *adj.* (5); **las mejores/peores** + *noun* the best/worst + *noun* (5)

lástima compassion; shame

lata (tin) can

latín *m.* Latin (*language*)

latino/a *adj.* Latino

latinoamericano/a *n., adj.* Latin American

latir to beat (*heart*)

lavabo sink (*bathroom*) (4)

lavadora washing machine (4)

lavandero/a launderer

lavaplatos *m. s., pl.* dishwasher (4)

lavar to wash; **lavarse** to wash oneself

lazo tie, bond; **lazos afectivos** emotional bonds (15)

le *i. o. s.* to/for him, her, it, you (*form. s.*)

leche *f.* milk (5); **café** (*m.*) **con leche** coffee with milk

lechosa papaya

lechuga lettuce (5)

lector(a) reader (13)

lectura *n.* reading

leer (y) to read (3); **leer el periódico** to read the newspaper (3); **leer novelas** to read novels (3); **leer revistas** to read magazines (3)

legal legal (11)

legalizar (c) to legalize

lejano/a distant, far

lejos *adv.* far away

lema *m.* slogan, motto

lengua tongue; language; **laboratorio de lenguas** language lab (2); **lengua nativa** native language (11); **saque la lengua** stick out your (*form. s.*) tongue (6)

lenguaje *m.* language (1); **evitar el lenguaje peyorativo** to avoid pejorative language (14); **lenguaje funcional** functional language (1)

lento/a slow

leña firewood

les *i. o. pl.* to/for you (*form. pl.*), them

letra letter (*of the alphabet*); lyrics; *pl.* humanities (2); **Facultad** (*f.*) **de Letras** School of Liberal Arts (Humanities) (2)

levantar to lift, raise up; **levantar pesas** to lift weights (8); **levantarse** to get up (6)

léxico vocabulary

ley *f.* law (11)

leyenda legend

libertad *f.* liberty, freedom; **libertad de palabra** freedom of speech (13); **libertad de prensa** freedom of the press (13)

libertador(a) liberator

libra pound

libre free (unfettered); **al aire libre** outdoors; **mercado libre** farmers' market (5)

librería bookstore (2)

libro book (2); **libro de texto** textbook (2)

licenciatura university degree

licor *m.* liquor

líder *m.* leader

liga league

ligero/a light (*not heavy*)

limitación *f.* limitation

limitar to limit

límite *m.* limit; frontier

limítrofe bordering

limón *m.* lemon (5)

limpiar to clean

limpieza cleaning; cleanliness

lindo/a pretty

línea line

lingüista *n. m., f.* linguist

líquido liquid

lista list

listo/a ready, prepared; **estar** (*irreg.*) **listo/a** to be ready; **ser** (*irreg.*) **listo/a** to be clever

literario/a literary

literatura literature (2)

litro liter

llamada (telephone) call

llamar to call; **llamarse** to be called; **me llamo** _____ my name is _____ (1)

llanura flatland, prairie (10)

llave *n. f.* key

llavero key chain, key ring

llegada arrival

llegar (gu) to arrive (2); **llegar a conocer** to get to know (15); **llegar a ser** to become

llenar to fill (out, in) (12)

lleno/a full

llevar to take (*a class*) (2); to carry (2); to wear (*clothing*) (7); **bueno, me lo/la/los/las llevo** OK, I'll take it/them (7); **(no) llevarse bien** to (not) get along well (15); **¿qué número/talla lleva?** what size (*shoes/clothing*) do you (*form. s.*) wear? (7)

llorar to cry (9)

llover (ue) to rain; **llueve** it's raining (6)

lo *d.o. m.* him, it, you (*form. s.*)

local *adj.* local

localización *f.* location

loco/a mad, crazy

locura madness, craziness
lógico/a logical
lograr to achieve, attain
lonche *m.* lunch
los *def. art. m. pl.* the (1);
  d.o. them, you (*form. pl.*);
  los/lás demás others (15);
  los más/menos + *adj.* the
  most/least + *adj.* (5); **los**
  mejores/peores + *noun*
  the best/worst + *noun* (5)
lucha *n.* fight
luchar to fight
luego then; **hasta luego** until
  (see you) later (1)
lugar *m.* place
lujo luxury (4)
lujoso/a luxurious (4)
luminoso/a luminous, bright
lunes *m. s., pl.* Monday (1)
lustrar to polish
luz *f.* (*pl.* **luces**) light(ing) (4);
  (overhead) light (4);
  electricity (4)

M
maceta flowerpot
madera wood
madrastra stepmother (3)
madre *f.* mother (3); **Día** (*m.*)
  de la Madre Mother's Day
madrina godmother (3)
madrugada dawn, early
  morning hours
madurar to mature; to ripen
maduro/a ripe (5)
maestría mastery, skill
maestro/a teacher
Magallanes: Estrecho de
  Magallanes Strait of Magellan
magnífico/a magnificent; great
magos *pl.*: **los Reyes** (*m.*) **Magos**
  the Magi; **Día** (*m.*) **de los Reyes**
  Magos Epiphany (January 6),
  Day of the Magi (9)
mail *m.* e-mail (*message*) (13)
maíz *m.* corn (5)
majestad *f.* majesty
mal, malo/a *adj.* bad (1); **caerle**
  (*irreg.*) **mal** to make a bad

impression (*on someone*) (9);
  comunicarse (qu) mal to
  communicate poorly (15); **hace**
  mal tiempo it's bad weather
  (6); **irle** (*irreg.*) **mal** to go
  poorly (*for someone*) (11);
  pasarlo mal to have a bad
  time; **quedarle mal** to fit
  poorly (7); **sentirse (ie, i) mal**
  to feel bad (6)
maldad *f.* evil
maldito/a cursed, damned
malestar *n. m.* discomfort,
  malaise
maleta suitcase (10)
maltratar to mistreat
Malvinas: Islas Malvinas
  Falkland Islands
mamá *f.* mother
mamón *m.* papaya
mandar to send; to order;
  mandar de regreso to
  deport (11)
mandato command
manejar to drive (10)
manera manner, way
manía mania, fad, obsession
manicero/a peanut vendor
manifestación *f.*
  demonstration (13)
mano *f.* hand; **estar** (*irreg.*)
  hecho/a a mano to be made
  by hand (7)
mantener (*like* **tener**) to maintain
  (6); **mantener los valores**
  tradicionales to maintain
  traditional values (14);
  mantener un espacio entre
  los dos to maintain distance
  between the two (15);
  mantener una rutina fija to
  maintain a fixed (regular)
  routine (6); **mantenerse a**
  raya to keep away; **mantenerse**
  informado/a to stay informed
  (13); **tratar de mantener las**
  costumbres to try to maintain
  one's customs (11)
mantenimiento maintenance
mantequilla butter (5)

manual *m.*: **manual de práctica**
  workbook
manzana apple (5)
mañana *n.* morning; *adv.*
  tomorrow; **de la mañana**
  in the morning (2); **hasta**
  mañana until (see you)
  tomorrow (1); **por la mañana**
  during the morning (2)
mapa *m.* map
maqueta scale model
maquillarse to put on makeup
máquina machine
mar *m., f.* sea, ocean
maravilla marvel
maravilloso/a marvelous (9)
marca brand
marcar (qu) to mark; **marcar la**
  ficha to punch out (*time clock*)
marcha: sobre la marcha off the
  cuff
marcial: hacer (*irreg.*) **artes**
  marciales to practice martial
  arts (8)
marginado/a marginalized (14)
marisco shellfish (5)
marrón brown
martes *m. s., pl.* Tuesday (1)
marzo March (6)
más *adv.* more; more or less;
  más + *adj.* + **que** more +
  adj. + than (5); **más o menos**
  so-so (1)
masa dough, mix
máscara mask
mascota *n.* pet
masculino/a masculine
masivo/a massive
master *m.* master's degree
matar to kill
mate *m.* tea
matemáticas mathematics (2)
materia subject (*school*)
maternidad *f.* maternity
materno/a maternal (3)
matrícula registration
matrimonio matrimony,
  marriage
maya *n., adj. m., f.* Maya(n)
mayo May (6)

mayor (que) older (than) (3); **persona mayor** older person (9)

mayoría majority (14)

mayoritario/a *adj.* majority

me *d.o.* me; *i.o.* to/for me; *refl. pron.* myself

mecánico/a mechanic (12)

medalla medal

media *n.* average; half (*an hour*) **a la(s) _____ y media** at _____:30 (at half past) (2); **clase** (*f.*) **media** middle class (14)

mediano/a *adj.* medium; average

medianoche *f.* midnight; **a medianoche** at midnight (6)

medias *pl.* stockings

medicamento medicine

medicina medicine; **tomar medicina** to take medicine

médico/a doctor (12)

medio *n. s.* means, middle; **estar** (*irreg.*) **entre medio** to be in the middle; **medio ambiente** environment; **tener** (*irreg.*) **_____ años y medio** to be **_____** and a half years old (3)

mediodía *m.* noon, midday; **a mediodía** at noon (6)

medir (i, i) to measure (5)

mediterráneo/a *adj.* Mediterranean

mejor better (5); **mejor que** better than (5)

mejorar to improve; **mejorar las condiciones de vida** to improve living conditions (14)

melancólico/a melancholic

memoria memory

mencionar to mention

menor (que) younger (than) (3)

menos less; least; **a menos que** (*conj.*) unless; **más o menos** so-so (1); **menos** + *adj.* + **que** less + *adj.* + than (5); **menos cuarto** a quarter to (*hour*) (6); **menos quince** fifteen minutes to (*hour*) (6); **por lo menos** at least

menospreciar to despise, scorn (13)

mensaje *m.* message (13)

mensajero/a messenger

mensual monthly

mental: salud mental mental health (6)

mente *f.* mind

mentir (ie, i) to lie (13)

mentira lie (13)

menú *m.* menu

menudo: a menudo frequently

mercado market; **mercado de artesanías** handicrafts market (7); **mercado libre / del barrio** farmers'/neighborhood market (5)

merendar (ie) to snack (5)

merengada milkshake

merengue *m.* merengue (*dance*)

merienda (afternoon) snack (5)

mermelada marmalade

mes *m.* month (6); **cada mes** each month (9)

mesa table (4); **poner** (*irreg.*) **la mesa** to set the table

mesero/a waiter/waitress (5)

mesilla de noche night table (4)

mestizo/a *n.* mixed-race (person) (14)

meta goal

metáfora metaphor

meteorológico/a meteorological

meteorólogo/a meteorologist

metro meter; subway (10); **estación** (*f.*) **del metro** subway station (10)

mexicano/a *n., adj.* Mexican (1)

mexicanoamericano/a *n., adj.* Mexican-American

mezcla mixture (11)

mezclar to mix; to blend

mezclilla denim

mezquita mosque

mi(s) *poss.* my

micro city bus (*Chile*)

miedo fear; **tener** (*irreg.*) **miedo** to be afraid (11)

miembro/a member (3)

mientras *adv.* meanwhile; **mientras que** (*conj.*) while (10)

miércoles *m. s., pl.* Wednesday (1)

migración *f.* migration

mil thousand, one thousand (7)

milenario/a millenary, *pertaining to the millennium*

milenio millennium

militar *adj.* military

milla mile

millón *m.* million

mimar to spoil (*child*)

mina mine

mineral: agua (*f.* [*but* **el agua**]) **mineral** mineral water (5)

minero/a miner

miniatura miniature

minidiálogo minidialogue

minifalda miniskirt

mínimo/a *adj.* minimum; **experiencia mínima** minimun experience (12)

minoría minority (14)

minoritario/a *adj.* minority (14)

minuto minute: **falta(n) _____ minuto(s) para la(s) _____** it is _____ minute(s) to _____ (6)

mío/a/os/as *poss.* my, (of) mine

mirar to look (at), watch; **mirar la televisión** watch TV (3); **mirarse (profundamente) a los ojos** to stare (deeply) into each other's eyes (15)

misión *f.* mission

misionero/a missionary

misisipí Mississippi

mismo/a same; self; **ahora mismo** at once

misterio mystery

misterioso/a mysterious

mitad *f.* half

mito myth

mixto/a mixed

mochila backpack (2)

moda fashion; **de moda** fashionable; **de última moda** the latest fashion; **estar** (*irreg.*) **de moda** to be in fashion

modales *m. pl.* manners, behavior

modelo model; *m., f.* model (*fashion*)

moderno/a modern (4)

modestia modesty

modesto/a modest

modificar (qu) to modify

modo way, manner

molestar to bother (8)

molesto/a annoying (9)

molido/a ground, grated

molondrones *m. pl.* okra

momento moment, instant

moneda currency; coin; **coleccionar monedas** to collect coins (8)

monótono/a monotonous

monstruo monster

montaña mountain; **escalar montañas** to go mountain climbing (8); **las Montañas Rocosas** the Rocky Mountains

montar a caballo to go horseback riding (8)

monte *m.* mount(ain)

monumento monument (10)

moqueta rug

morado/a purple (7)

moreno/a dark-skinned (1); **piel** (*f.*) **morena** dark skin (1)

morir(se) (ue, u) (*p.p.* **muerto/a**) to die

mostrador *m.* display counter (7)

mostrar (ue) to show (*something to someone*) (7); **mostrar cariño en público** to show affection in public (15)

motivar to motivate

motivo motive, reason

motocicleta motorcycle; **andar** (*irreg.*) **en motocicleta** to ride a motorcycle (8)

moverse (ue) to move (around)

móvil: teléfono móvil cell phone

movimiento movement

muchacho/a boy/girl

muchedumbre *f.* crowd

mucho *adv.* a lot, much (2)

mucho/a *adj.* much, a lot (of) (2); *pl.* many; **hace mucho tiempo** a long time ago (11); **mucho gusto** nice (pleasure) to meet you (1)

mudarse to move (*to another house*)

mueble *m.* piece of furniture

muerte *f.* death (13)

muerto/a (*p.p. of* **morir**) dead; **Día** (*m.*) **de los Muertos** All Souls' Day (9); **estar** (*irreg.*) **muerto/a de** to be dying of

mujer *f.* woman; **mujer bombero** (female) firefighter (12); **mujer de negocios** businesswoman (12)

multilingüe multilingual (12)

mundial *adj.* world

mundo world

municipio municipality

muñeca wrist; doll

músculo muscle

museo museum (10)

música music (2); **tocar (qu) música** to play music (8)

músico/a musician

muy very

N

nacer (zc) to be born (11)

nacimiento birth

nación *f.* nation

nacional national

nacionalidad *f.* nationality (1)

nada nothing (5); none; **nada de** no, not any (5); **para nada** (not) at all

nadar to swim (8)

nadie nobody, not anybody (8)

nahua *m.* Nahuatl (*indigenous language of the Aztecs*)

náhuatl *m.* Nahuatl (*indigenous language of the Aztecs*)

nailón *m.* nylon

naipes *m. pl.*: **jugar (ue) (gu) a los naipes** to play cards (8)

naranja orange (*fruit*) (5)

narcotraficante drug dealer

nariz *f.* (*pl.* **narices**) nose

narración *f.* narration

narrador(a) narrator

narrar to narrate

natación *f.* swimming (8)

nativo/a *adj.* native, indigenous; **lengua nativa** native language (11)

natural: desastre (*m.*) **natural** natural disaster (13); **recursos naturales** natural resources

naturaleza nature

naturalización *f.* naturalization

navegar (gu) to navigate; to surf (*the Internet*) (13)

Navidad *f.* Christmas (9)

navideño/a *adj.* Christmas

necesario/a necessary (2); **es necesario** + *inf.* it is necessary to (*do something*) (6)

necesidad *f.* necessity (4)

necesitar + *inf.* to need to (*do something*) (6)

negar(se) (ie) (gu) to deny

negativo/a negative

negociación *f.* negotiation

negociar to negotiate

negocio business; **hombre** (*m.*) **de negocios** businessman (12); **mujer** (*f.*) **de negocios** businesswoman (12)

negrita: en negrita boldface

negro/a *adj.* black (10); **ojos negros** black eyes (1); **pelo negro** black hair (1)

neologismo newly coined word

nervioso/a nervous (9)

nevar (ie) to snow; **nieva** it's snowing (6)

nevera freezer (4)

ni _____ ni _____ neither _____ nor _____ (8)

nicaragüense *n., adj. m., f.* Nicaraguan (13)

niebla fog, mist; **hay niebla** it's foggy

nieto/a grandson/granddaughter (3); *pl.* grandchildren (3)

nieve *f.* snow

ningún, ninguno/a *adj.* no, not any (5)

ninguno/a *pron.* none, not any (8)

niñez *f.* (*pl.* **niñeces**) childhood (9)

niño/a child (3); boy/girl

nivel *m.* level (12); **nivel de educación** level of education (14); **nivel de vida** standard of living

no no; not (2)

Nobel: Premio Nobel de la Paz Nobel Peace Prize (13)

noche *f.* night; **buenas noches** good night (1); **de la noche** at night (*specific time*) (2); **hasta altas horas de la noche** until late at night; **mesilla de noche** night table (4); **por la noche** during the night (2); **todas las noches** every night (9)

Nochebuena Christmas Eve

noción *f.* notion

nocivo/a unhealthy, noxious

nocturno/a *adj.* nighttime

nombre *m.* name

noreste *m.* northeast

norma norm

normalidad *f.* normality

noroeste *m.* northwest

norte *m.* north

norteamericano/a *n., adj.* North American (*from the United States and/or Canada*)

norteño/a northern

noruego/a *n., adj.* Norwegian

nos *d.o.* us; *i.o.* to/for us; *refl. pron* ourselves; **nos vemos** see you around (1)

nosotros/as *sub. pron.* we (1); *obj. of prep.* us

nostálgico/a nostalgic

nota note

notar to note, notice

noticia(s) piece of news, news (13)

noticiero newscast, news show (13)

novecientos/as nine hundred (7)

novedad *f.* novelty, innovation

novela *n.* novel; **leer (y) novelas** to read novels (3)

noventa ninety (3)

noviembre November (6)

novio/a boyfriend/girlfriend

nublado cloudy; **está nublado** it's cloudy (6)

nuestro/a/os/as *poss.* our

nueve nine (1)

nuevo/a new

numérico/a numerical

número number (1); **¿qué número lleva?** what size (*shoes*) do you (*form. s.*) wear? (7)

numeroso/a numerous (14)

nunca never, not ever (8); **casi nunca** almost never (9); **nunca jamás** never ever (8)

Ñ

ñame sweet potato

O

o or

obedecer (zc) to obey

obituario obituary (13)

objetivo objective (12)

objeto object

obligación *f.* obligation

obligado/a obliged, compelled

obligatorio/a required (2)

obra work; **obra de arte** work of art

obrero/a *n.* worker; **proteger (j) a los obreros** to protect (the rights of) the workers (14)

obstáculo obstacle; **romper (*p.p.* roto/a) los obstáculos sociales** to break down social barriers (14)

obtener (*like* **tener**) to obtain, get

obvio/a obvious

ocasión *f.* occasion

occidental western

océano ocean (10); **Océano Atlántico** Atlantic Ocean; **Océano Pacífico** Pacific Ocean

ochenta eighty (3)

ocho eight (1)

ochocientos/as eight hundred (7)

octavo/a eighth

octubre October (6)

ocupación *f.* occupation

ocupado/a busy

ocupar to occupy

ocurrir to occur

oeste *m.* west

ofensivo/a offensive

oferta offer (12)

oficina office; **oficina de correos** post office (10)

oficio job, profession; trade (12)

ofrecer (zc) to offer (12)

oído (inner) ear

oír *irreg.* to hear

ojo eye (1); **mirarse (profundamente) a los ojos** to stare (deeply) into each other's eyes (15); **ojos (azules, castaños, negros, verdes)** (blue, brown, black, green) eyes (1)

olímpico: Juegos Olímpicos Olympics

oliva: aceite (*m.*) **de oliva** olive oil (5)

olvidar to forget (11)

ombligo navel

omisión *f.* omission

once eleven (1)

onda wave

onza ounce

opción *f.* option

operación *f.* operation

opinar to think, believe

opinión *f.* opinion

oportunidad (*f.*) opportunity; **oportunidad de avanzar** opportunity for advancement (12)

oprimido/a oppressed

optativo/a elective, optional (2)

optimismo optimism

optimista *n. m., f.* optimist; *adj.* optimistic (9)

opuesto/a opposite

oración *f.* sentence

orden *m.* order (*chronological*)

ordenador computer (*Sp.*) (4)
oreja (outer) ear
organizar (c) to organize
órgano organ
orgullo pride
orgulloso/a proud (9); **estar** (*irreg.*) **orgulloso/a** to feel proud, be proud
orientación *f.* orientation, direction
orientarse: para orientarse en la ciudad getting around (*lit.* orienting oneself in) the city
origen *m.* (*pl.* **orígenes**) origin (1); **¿de qué origen es/son _____?** what is/are _____'s/s' (national) origin(s)? (1); **país de origen** country of origin (11)
originalidad *f.* originality
originarse (en) to have one's/something's beginning (in)
oro gold; **pulsera de oro** gold bracelet (7)
ortografía *n.* spelling
os *d.o.* you (*fam. pl. Sp.*); *i.o.* to/for you (*fam. pl. Sp.*); *refl. pron.* yourselves (*fam. pl. Sp.*)
oscuro/a dark; **piel** (*f.*) **oscura** dark skin (1)
otoño fall (6)
otro/a other; another (3); **conocer (zc) a otras personas** to meet new/other people (8); **por un lado _____ por otro (lado) _____** on one hand _____ on the other (hand) _____ (10)
oveja sheep

P
pabellón *m.* pavilion
paciente *n., adj. m., f.* patient
pacífico/a peaceful; **Océano Pacífico** Pacific Ocean
pacifista *m., f.* pacifist
pacto pact, truce (13)
padrastro stepfather (3)

padre *m.* father (3); *pl.* parents (3); **Día** (*m.*) **del Padre** Father's Day
padrino godfather (3)
paella *rice dish with meat, fish, or seafood and vegetables* (*Sp.*)
pagar (gu) to pay (7)
página page
pago payment
país *m.* country; **país de origen** country of origin (11)
paisaje *m.* countryside
paisajista landscape; **arquitectura paisajista** landscape architecture
paja straw
palabra word; **libertad** (*f.*) **de palabra** freedom of speech (13)
pampa pampa, prairie
pan *m.* bread (5)
panadería bakery (5)
panadero/a baker
pantalón, pantalones *m.* pants (7); **pantalones cortos** shorts (7); **pantalones vaqueros** jeans (7)
panteón *m.* pantheon
papa *m.* potato (5)
papá *m.* dad, father; daddy (*Sp.*)
papel *m.* role, part; paper; **hoja de papel aparte** separate piece of paper
paquete *m.* package
par *m.* pair
para for; in order to; **para + *inf.*** in order to (*do something*) (2); **para cruzar (c) la frontera** getting across the border (11); **para nada** (not) at all; **para orientarse en la ciudad** getting around (*lit.* orienting oneself in) the city (10); **para toda la vida** for life (15)
parabólico/a: televisión (*f.*) **de antena parabólica** satellite TV (13)
parada de autobuses/taxis bus stop / taxi stand (10)
paraguayo/a *n., adj.* Paraguayan

paraíso paradise
paralelo/a *adj.* parallel
parar to stop; **parar en** to stop (over) in (10)
parcial partial; **de tiempo parcial** part-time (12)
pardo/a brown (7)
parecer (zc) to look; to seem; **este... (no) me parece muy interesante** uh . . . that seems (doesn't seem) very interesting (8); **parecerse a** to resemble, be alike, be similar (10)
parecido/a (a) similar (to) (1)
pareja couple (15); mate (15); partner (15); **formar pareja** to form a romantic relationship, find a mate (15); **salir** (*irreg.*) **en pareja** to go out as a couple (15)
paréntesis *m. s., pl.* parenthesis
pariente *m., f.* relative; **ver** (*irreg.*)**/visitar a los parientes** to see/visit the (one's) relatives (3)
parilla: a la parilla grilled
parillado/a grilled
parlamento parliament
paro: en paro unemployed
parque *m.* park
párrafo paragraph
parte *f.* part (11)
participación *f.* participation
participar to participate (2)
particular particular; private; **casa particular** private / single-family house (4)
partido game (8); **partido político** political party (13)
partir: a partir de starting on (*day, date*)
párvulos *pl.*: **cuidado de párvulos** childcare
pasado/a *adj.* past; **el año pasado** last year; **el verano pasado** last summer; **la semana pasada** last week
pasajero/a *n.* passenger
pasaporte *m.* passport

pasar to pass; to spend (*time*); **dejarle pasar** to allow (*someone*) to pass (11); **¿me pase(s) ____, por favor?** could you pass (me) ____, please? (5); **pasar el tiempo libre** to spend free time (3); **pasar tiempo con los hijos** to spend time with the (one's) children (3); **pasarlo bien/mal** to have a good/bad time; **¿qué le pasa?** what's wrong? (6)

pasatiempo pastime (8)

Pascua Easter (9)

pasear to walk, stroll (3)

paseo *n.* walk, stroll; **dar** (*irreg.*) **un paseo** to take a walk (3)

pasillo corridor, hallway (4)

pasión *f.* passion

pasivo/a passive

paso step

pastel *m.* pastry (5); cake (5); pie (5)

pastilla lozenge

patata (*Sp.*) potato

paterno/a paternal (3)

patinar (sobre hielo) to (ice) skate (8)

patio courtyard, patio (4)

patrio/a patriotic

patriota *m., f.* patriot

patrón *m.* boss; pattern

pavo turkey

paz *f.* (*pl.* **paces**) peace; **dejar en paz** to leave alone; **Premio Nobel de la Paz** Nobel Peace Prize (13)

peculiaridad *f.* peculiarity

pedagogía pedagogy; education

pedir (i, i) to ask for, request (5); order (*restaurant*); **pedir ayuda** to ask for help

pegado/a close together; **bailar pegados** to dance close together (8)

pegar (gu) to attach; to stick together

pelado/a with little hair

pelar to peel

pelearse to fight (15)

película (cómica / de acción / de amor / de terror) (comedy/action/romance/horror) film, movie (13); **ver** (*irreg.*) **una película** to watch a film (8)

peligro danger; **estar** (*irreg.*) **en peligro (de +** *inf.*) to be in danger (*of doing something*); **poner** (*irreg.*) **en peligro** to endanger

peligroso/a dangerous

pelo (castaño/negro/rubio/largo/corto) (brown/black/blond/long/short) hair (1)

pelota ball; baseball (*P. R.*)

pelotero/a baseball player (*P. R.*)

pena penalty; sorrow

pendiente *m.* earring (7); pendant (7)

pensar (ie) (de/en) to think (of, about) (4)

peor(es) (que) worse (than) (5)

peperoni pepperoni

pequeño/a little, small (1); **quedarle pequeño** to fit small (*clothing*) (7)

perder (ie) to lose (8); **perder un autobús (barco/tren/vuelo)** to miss a bus (boat/train/flight); **perderse** to get lost (10)

pérdida loss

perdonar to pardon, forgive, excuse

perdurar to last

peregrino pilgrim

perezoso/a lazy (1)

perfecto/a perfect

perfil *m.* profile

perforación *f.* piercing

perforarse to pierce

perfume *m.* perfume

perfumería perfumery

periódico (en línea) (online) newspaper (13); **leer (y) el periódico** to read the newspaper (3)

período period

perjudicar (qu) to harm

permanecer (zc) to remain

permisivo/a permissive

permitir to allow

pero but (1)

perpétuo/a perpetual

perro dog (3)

persecución *f.* persecution

perseguir (i, i) (g) to pursue, chase

perseverar to persevere

persona person; **conocer (zc) a otras personas** to meet new/other people (8); **persona mayor** older person (9)

personaje *m.* character (*fictional*)

personalidad *f.* personality; **tener** (*irreg.*) **personalidades incompatibles** to have incompatible personalities (15)

personificación *f.* personification

perspectiva perspective

pertenecer (zc) to belong

peruano/a Peruvian (14)

pesa: levantar pesas to lift weights (8)

pesado/a heavy

Pesaj *m.* Passover (9)

pesar to weigh; **a pesar de** (*prep.*) in spite of, despite (15)

pescadería fish market (5)

pescado fish (*caught*) (5)

pescar (qu) to fish

pesebre *m.* manger; Nativity scene

pesimista *n. m., f.* pessimist; *adj.* pessimistic (9)

peso weight

peyorativo/a pejorative, derogatory; **evitar el lenguaje peyorativo** to avoid pejorative language (14)

picado/a diced

picante hot, spicy (5)

pico mountain peak (10); **a las ____ y pico** at a little past ____ (*time*)

pie *m.* foot; **ir** (*irreg.*) **a pie** to go on foot (walk) (10)

piel *f.* **(clara/morena/oscura)** (light/brown/dark) skin (1)

pierna leg

pijama *m. s.* pajamas
piloto/a pilot (12)
pimienta pepper (5)
pimiento (rojo/verde) (red/green) bell pepper (5)
pingüino penguin
pintar to paint (8)
pintoresco/a picturesque
piña pineapple (5)
Pirineos Pyrenees
piscina swimming pool (4)
piso floor; flat, apartment (4); **bloque** (*m.*) **de pisos** apartment building (4)
pista clue; court (*tennis*) (*Sp.*)
pizarra chalkboard (2)
pizarrón chalkboard
pizca pinch, small amount
placer *m.*: **el placer es mío** it's my pleasure
planear to plan
planificar (qu) to plan
plano map
plano/a *adj.* flat
planta plant
plantación *f.* plantation
plantar to plant
plástico plastic
plata silver; **collar** (*m.*) **de plata** silver necklace (7)
plátano banana (5)
platicar (qu) to chat
plato plate; prepared dish (5); **(de) plato principal** (as a) main course (5); **(de) primer plato** (as a) first course (5)
playa beach (10)
plaza square, plaza (10)
población *f.* population
poblado/a populated
poblador(a) inhabitant
pobre *adj.* poor (14)
pobreza poverty (11)
poco/a little (3); *pl.* few (3); **un poco de** a little of (5)
poder *irreg.* to be able to, can (4); **¿en qué puedo servirle?** how may I help you? (7); **podría usted... ?** could you (*form. s.*) . . . ?

poder *n. m.* power
poderoso/a powerful
poema *m.* poem
poesía poetry; **escribir poesía** to write poetry (8)
poeta *m., f.* poet
poético/a poetical
pólen *m.* pollen
policía *m., mujer* (*f.*) **policía** police officer; *f.* police force
poliéster *m.* polyester
polinesio/a *n., adj.* Polynesian
política *s.* politics
político/a *n.* politician (12)
pollo chicken (5)
polo pole
poner *irreg.* to put; **poner en peligro** to endanger; **poner la mesa** to set the table; **ponerle** + *adj.* **a alguien** to make someone feel + *adj.* (9); **ponerse** to put on, wear (*clothing*) (7); **ponerse de acuerdo** to agree
popularidad *f.* popularity
popularizarse to become popular
por around, because of, by, for, through (11); **gracias por** thanks for (11); **por casualidad** by chance; **por ciento** percent (11); **por completo** completely; **por dentro** on the inside (4); **por eso** for that (reason), that's why (11); **por favor** please; **por fin** finally; **por fuera** on the outside (4); **por la mañana (tarde/noche)** in the morning (in the afternoon/evening, at night) (*in general*) (2); **por lo menos** at least; **por lo tanto** therefore; **¿por qué no (nosotros/as) ____?** why don't (*we do something*)? (8); **por si acaso** just in case (11); **por un lado ____ por otro (lado) ____** on one hand ____ on the other (hand) ____ (10); **por supuesto** of course
porcentaje *m.* percentage
porción *f.* portion

pordiosero/a beggar
pornografía pornography
pornográfico/a pornographic
poroto pigeon pea
porque because (1)
¿por qué? why?
portada front page, cover
portafolio portfolio
posada navideña *traditional Mexican Christmas celebration*
poseer (y) to possess
posesión *f.* possession (3)
posesivo/a possessive
posgrado/a graduate
posgraduado/a: estudiante posgraduado/a graduate student
posibilidad *f.* possibility
posible possible
posición *f.* position
positivo/a positive
posponer (*like* **poner**) to postpone
postal: tarjeta postal postcard
postre *m.* dessert; **de postre** for dessert (5)
postular to request; to demand
práctica practice; **manual** (*m.*) **de práctica** workbook
practicar (qu) to practice (2); **practicar un deporte** to practice a sport (8)
pradera meadow
precio price (7)
precioso/a precious; valuable
precocido/a precooked
preconcebido/a preconceived
predecir (*like* **decir**) to predict
predicción *f.* prediction
predominar to dominate
preferencia preference
preferir (ie, i) to prefer (4)
pregón *m.* street vendor's call (*Cuba*)
pregunta *n.* question
preguntar to ask (*questions*)
prehistórico/a prehistoric
prejuicio prejudice
Premio Nobel de la Paz Nobel Peace Prize (13)

prender (la televisión) to turn on (the television)
prensa press (13); **libertad** (*f.*) **de prensa** freedom of the press (13)
preocupado/a worried
preocuparse (por) to worry (about)
preparación *f.* preparation
preparar (la comida) to prepare (the meal/food) (4)
preposicional prepositional
presentación *f.* presentation; **carta de presentación** letter of introduction
presentar to present; to introduce
presente *n., adj. m.* present
preservar to preserve, maintain (11)
presidencia presidency
presidente/a (electo) president (elect)
prestaciones *f. pl.* benefits (*work*) (12)
préstamo loan
prestar to loan, lend (15)
prestigio prestige (12)
pretender to pretend; to claim
pretérito preterit
pretexto pretext, excuse
prevenir (*like* **venir**) to prevent
previo/a previous
priista *member of the PRI* **(Partido Revolucionario Institucional)** *political party in Mexico*
primavera spring (6)
primer, primero/a first; **(de) primer plato** (as a) first course (5); **primera comunión** first communion (9)
primo/a cousin (3); *pl.* cousins (3)
principal *adj.* main, principal; **(de) plato principal** (as a) main course (5)
príncipe *m.* prince
principio beginning

prisa: (no) tener (*irreg.*) **prisa** to (not) be in a hurry (8)
privado/a private
privatización *f.* privatization
privilegio privilege
probabilidad *f.* probability
probador *m.* dressing room (7)
probar (ue) to try on (7)
problema *m.* **(social)** (social) problem (14)
procedente *adj.* originating
procesión *f.* procession, parade
proceso process
producción *f.* production
producir *irreg.* to produce
producto product
productor(a) producer
profesión *f.* profession (12)
profesional professional
profesor(a) professor, teacher (2)
profundamente deeply; **mirarse profundamente a los ojos** to stare deeply into each other's eyes (15)
programa *m.* **(educativo)** (educational) program (13)
programación *f.* programming
programador(a) (computer) programmer (12)
progreso progress
prohibir (prohíbo) to prohibit
promesa promise
prometedor(a) promising; **futuro prometedor** promising future (12)
promoción *f.* promotion
pronombre *m.* pronoun (1); **pronombre** (*m.*) **de complemento directo** direct object pronoun (5)
pronóstico del tiempo weather report
pronto soon; **hasta pronto** until (see you) soon (1); **tan pronto como** as soon as
pronunciación *f.* pronunciation
pronunciar to pronounce
propio/a own

prosperidad *f.* prosperity
próspero/a: ser (*irreg.*) **próspero/a** to be prosperous (11)
protección *f.* protection
proteger (j) to protect; **proteger a los obreros** to protect (the rights of) the workers (14)
protesta *n.* protest
protestar to protest
proveniente proceeding, originating
provincia province, region
provocar (qu) to provoke
próximo/a next
proyectar to project
proyecto project
prueba quiz, test
psicología psychology (2)
psicólogo/a psychologist
psicoterapeuta *m., f.* psychotherapist
publicar (qu) to publish (13)
público *n.* public; **mostrar (ue) cariño en público** to show affection in public (15)
público/a *adj.* public
pueblo small town (4)
puerta door (4)
puerto (sea)port (10)
puertorriqueño/a *n., adj.* Puerto Rican (1)
pues _____ well _____; **pues, la verdad es que** _____ well, actually _____ (8)
puesta del sol sunset
puesto position, job (12)
pulmón *m.* lung
pulsera (de oro) (gold) bracelet (7)
puntaje *m.* points earned
punto point; period; **en punto** on the dot (6); **estar** (*irreg.*) **en su punto** to be at one's best (8); **punto de vista** point of view
puntual punctual
pupitre (student's) desk (2)
pureza purity
puro cigar
puro/a pure

Q

que that, which; than; **a menos que** (*conj.*) unless; **a no ser que** (*conj.*) unless; **al igual que** just like (3); **antes (de) que** (*conj.*) before (14); **así que** so (that), therefore; **con tal de que** (*conj.*) provided that; **después (de) que** (*conj.*) after; **en caso de que** (*conj.*) in case; **hasta que** (*conj.*) until; **hay que** + *inf.* you (one) must (*do something*) (6); **más** + *adj.* + **que** more + *adj.* + than (5); **mejor que** better than (5); **menor que** younger than (3); **menos** + *adj.* + **que** less + *adj.* + than (5); **mientras que** (*conj.*) while (10); **tener** (*irreg.*) **que** + *inf.* to have to (*do something*) (6)

¿qué? what (2); **¡qué** + *adj.*! what a + *adj!* (13); **¡qué** + *noun* + **más/tan** + *adj.*! what a/an + *adj.* + *noun!* (13); **¡qué barbaridad!** how awful! (13); **¡qué bien!** great! how wonderful! (13); **¡qué buena idea!** what a good idea! (8); **¡qué chévere!** how cool/great! (*Carib.*) (8); **¿qué desea(n) (de comer)?** what would you like (to eat)? (5); **¿qué edad tiene?** how old is he (she, you [*form. s.*])? (3); **¡qué escándalo!** what a scandal! (13); **¿qué hora es?** what time is it? (6); **¿qué le pasa?** what's wrong? (6); **¿qué le(s) traigo?** what can I bring you? (5); **¿qué número lleva?** what size (*shoes*) do you (*form. s.*) wear? (7); **¿qué recomienda (usted)?** what do you (*form. s.*) recommend? (5); **¿qué tal?** how's it going? what's up? (1); **¿qué tal éste/a/os/as aquí?** what about this (one) / these (ones) here? (7); **¿qué tal si (nosotros/as) _____?** how about if (*we do something*)? (8);

¿qué talla lleva? what size (*clothing*) do you (*form. s.*) wear? (7); **¿qué tiempo hace?** what's the weather like? (6); **¿qué tiene hoy?** what's wrong today? (6)

quechua Quechua (*language*)

quedar to be located; **quedarle (bien/mal/grande/pequeño)** to fit (well/poorly/large/small) (7); **quedarse (en cama / en casa)** to stay, remain (in bed / at home) (6)

quehacer *m.* chore

quejarse (de) to complain (about) (15)

querer *irreg.* to want (4); to love (7); **quererse** to love each other (15)

querido/a *n., adj.* dear

queso cheese (5)

quetzal *m. monetary unit of Guatemala*

quiché *m.* Quiche (*language*)

quien(es) who, whom

¿quién(es)? who? whom? (2)

quietud *f.* quietness, peacefulness

química chemistry (2); **laboratorio de química** chemistry lab (2)

quince fifteen (1); **menos quince** fifteen minutes to (*hour*) (6); **y quince** fifteen minutes past (*hour*) (6)

quinceañera girl's fifteenth birthday party (9)

quinientos/as five hundred (7)

quiosco kiosk (10)

quitarse to take off (7)

quizá(s) perhaps (11)

R

rabona: hacer (*irreg.*) **la rabona** to play hookey

radio *m.* radio (*receiver*); *f.* radio (*medium*)

raíz *f.* (*pl.* **raíces**) root (11)

ranchero/a *n.* farmhand

rancho ranch

rápido/a *adj.* fast, quick; **comida rápida** fast food

raptar to kidnap

raro/a strange; rare; **raras veces** infrequently, rarely (9)

rasgar (gu) to tear, rip

rasgo feature, trait

rato *n.* while, short time

raya stripe; **mantenerse** (*like* **tener**) **a raya** to keep away

raza race; **Día** (*m.*) **de la Raza** Hispanic Awareness Day

razón *f.* reason (11)

razonable reasonable

reacción *f.* reaction

reaccionar to react

real royal

realidad *f.* reality

realista *adj. m., f.* realistic

realizar (c) to attain, achieve

realizar to resume

reanudar to resume

rebaja reduction (7)

rebajar to reduce (*a price*)

rebanar to slice up

rebasar to exceed, overflow; to surpass

rebelde rebellious (9)

rebeldía rebellion

rebelión *f.* rebellion

rebuscado/a affected, unnatural

recaer (*like* **caer**) to fall upon

recepción *f.* reception

recepcionista *m., f.* receptionist

receta recipe; medical prescription

recetar to prescribe

rechazado/a rejected (14)

rechazar (c) to reject

recibidor *m.* entryway

recibir to receive

recibo receipt

recién recently

reciente recent

recipiente *m.* container

recíproco/a reciprocal

reclamar to claim; to demand

recoger (j) to pick up

recomendable recommendable

recomendación *f.* recommendation; **carta de recomendación** letter of recommendation (12)

recomendar (ie) to recommend (5); **¿qué recomienda (usted)?** what do you (*form. s.*) recommend? (5)

reconfirmar to reconfirm (10)

reconocer (zc) to recognize

recordar (ue) to remember (9)

recorrer to tour, travel across

recurso resource; **recursos naturales** natural resources

redacción *f.* composition

redescubierto/a (*p.p. of* **redescubrir**) rediscovered

redescubrir (*p.p.* **redescubierto/a**) to rediscover

redondo/a round

reducción *f.* reduction

reducir *irreg.* to reduce

reelecto (*p.p. of* **reelegir**) reelected

reelegir (i, i) (j) (*p.p.* **reelecto/a**) to reelect

referencia reference

referir (ie, i) to refer

reflejar to reflect

reflexión *f.* reflection

reflexivo/a reflexive

refresco soft drink (3); **beber un refresco** to drink a soft drink (3)

refrigerador *m.* refrigerator (4)

refugiado/a refugee (13)

refugio refuge, shelter

regalar to give (*as a gift*); **regalarle** to give (*something to someone*) as a gift (7)

regalo gift

regatear to bargain (7)

regeneración *f.* regeneration

región *f.* region (14)

regir (i, i) (j) to govern; to rule

regla rule

regresar to return (*to a place*) (2)

regreso: mandar de regreso to deport (11)

regular OK (1)

rehén *m.* hostage

reina queen

reinstitución *f.* reinstitution

reírse (i, i) to laugh (9)

relación *f.* relationship; **relación íntima** intimate relationship (15)

relacionado/a related

relajación *f.* relaxation (6)

relajado/a: estar (*irreg.*) **relajado/a** to be relaxed (8)

relajarse to relax

relatar to relate, tell

relativo/a relative

religión *f.* religion (14)

religioso/a religious

reliquia heirloom

rellenar to fill

relleno (de) stuffed (with)

reloj *m.* watch (7)

remedio remedy (6)

remontarse a to date back to

remoto/a remote

rencoroso/a bitter (*person*)

renovar (ue) to renew (11)

renunciar to renounce

reparar to repair

repartir to distribute

repaso review

repetición *f.* repetition

repetir (i, i) to repeat

reportaje *m.* report (13)

reportar to report

reportero/a reporter (13)

reposar to rest

reposo *n.* rest

representación *f.* representation

representante *n. m., f.* representative

representar to represent

representativo/a representative

represión *f.* repression

república republic; **República Dominicana** Dominican Republic

reputación *f.* reputation

requerir (ie, i) to require (12)

requisito requirement (12)

res *f.* head of cattle; **carne** (*f.*) **de res** beef (5)

resentido/a resentful

resentimiento resentment (14)

reseña review (13)

reserva reserve; reservation (*hotel*); **cancelar una reserva** to cancel a reservation (10); **confirmar una reserva** to confirm a reservation (10)

reservación *f.* reservation

reservado/a reserved

resfriado: tener (*irreg.*) **un resfriado** to have a cold (6)

resfriado/a: estar (*irreg.*) **resfriado/a** to have a cold

resfriarse (me resfrío) to catch a cold

resfrío *n.* cold (*illness*); **tener** (*irreg.*) **resfrío** to have a cold (6)

residencia estudiantil/ universitaria dormitory/ residence hall

residencial: calle/zona residencial residential street/zone (4)

resolución *f.* resolution

resolver (ue) (*p.p.* **resuelto/a**) to resolve (13)

respectivo/a respective

respecto respect, relation; **al respecto** about the matter; **con respecto a** with regard to

respetar to respect

respeto respect, deference

respetuoso/a respectful (9)

respirar to breathe

responder to respond, answer

responsabilidad *f.* responsibility

responsable responsible

respuesta response, answer

restaurante *n.* restaurant

resto rest, remainder; *pl.* remains

restrasado/a behind schedule

resultado result

resultar to turn out, result

resumir to sum up

retirarse to withdraw

retrato portrait

retrete *m.* toilet (4)

reunión *f.* meeting

reunir (reúno) to join, gather; **reunirse con amigos** to get together with friends (6)

revelar los secretos to reveal one's secrets (15)

revisar to check, inspect (11)

revista magazine; **leer (y) revistas** to read magazines (3)

revolución *f.* revolution (13)

revolver (ue) to mix

rey *m.* king; **Día** (*m.*) **de los Reyes Magos** Epiphany (January 6) (9); **los Reyes Magos** the Magi

rico/a rich, delicious (5); rich, wealthy (14)

ridículo/a ridiculous (13)

riesgo risk; **correr el riesgo** to run the risk (11)

rima rhyme

río river (10)

riqueza *s.* riches, wealth

risa laugh, laughter

ritmo rhythm

rito rite; ceremony

rivalidad *f.* rivalry

robar to rob, steal (14)

roca rock

rocoso/a rocky; **las Montañas Rocosas** the Rocky Mountains

rodeado/a surrounded

rojo/a red; **pimiento rojo** red (bell) pepper (5)

romanticismo romanticism (15)

romántico/a romantic

romper (*p.p.* **roto/a**) to break; **romper los obstáculos sociales** to break down social barriers (14)

ropa clothing (7); **ropa interior** underwear (7)

rosado/a pink (7)

roto/a (*p.p. of* **romper**) broken

rubio/a blond(e); **pelo rubio** blond hair (1)

rueda wheel

ruido noise (8)

ruina ruin

rumbo a on the way to

rumor *m.* rumor

Rusia Russia

rústico/a rustic

ruta route

rutina *n.* **diaria** daily routine (6); **mantener** (*like* **tener**) **una rutina fija** to maintain a fixed (regular) routine (6)

S

sábado Saturday (1)

saber *irreg.* to know (*facts, information*) (6); to find out (*about something*) (6); **saber + inf.** to know how to (*do something*) (6)

sabio/a wise (9)

sabor *m.* taste, flavor

sabroso/a savory (5)

sacar (qu) to take out; **sacar a alguien a bailar** to ask someone to dance (8); **sacar adelante** to improve; **saque la lengua** stick out your (*form. s.*) tongue (6)

sacrificio sacrifice

sagrado/a sacred, holy

sal *f.* salt (5)

sala family room; **sala de espera** waiting room

salado/a salty (5)

salario salary

salchicha sausage

salida exit; way out

salir *irreg.* to leave; to go out (3); **salir a bailar** to go out dancing (3); **salir en pareja** to go out as a couple (15)

salmón *m.* salmon

salón *m.* living room (4)

salsa de tomate ketchup

saltarín, saltarina lively

saltear to hold up, rob, waylay

salto waterfall (10)

salud *f.* health; **salud física** physical health (6); **salud mental** mental health (6)

saludable healthy

saludar to greet, say hello

saludo greeting (1)

salvadoreño/a *n., adj.* Salvadoran (13)

san *apocopated form of* **Santo**; **Día** (*m.*) **de San Valentín** St. Valentine's Day

sancochado/a parboiled

sancocho *stew made with meat, yucca, and plantains*

sándwich *m.* sandwich (5)

sangrar to bleed

sangre *f.* blood

sano/a healthy (15)

santería *religion consisting of Catholic and Western African Yoruba beliefs*

santo/a *n., adj.* saint; **Día** (*m.*) **de los Santos** All Saints' Day (9); **Día** (*m.*) **de Santa Bárbara** Saint Barbara's feast day (9); **día** (*m.*) **del santo** saint's day (9); **Semana Santa** Holy Week (9); **Viernes** (*m.*) **Santo** Good Friday (9)

sartén *f.* (frying) pan

satisfacer (*like* **hacer**) to satisfy

satisfecho/a satisfied

saxofón *m.* saxophone

saya kilt

se *refl. pron.* herself, himself, itself, yourself (*form. s.*), themselves, yourselves (*form. pl.*)

secadora dryer (4)

seco/a dry (5)

secretario/a secretary (12)

secreto *n.* secret; **revelar los secretos** to reveal one's secrets (15)

secreto/a *adj.* secret

secuencia sequence

secundario/a secondary; **escuela secundaria** high school

sed *f.* thirst; **tener** (*irreg.*) **sed** to be thirsty

seda silk (7)

seguida: en seguida right away

seguir (i, i) (g) to follow; **seguir derecho** to continue straight ahead (10); **seguir una rutina fija** to follow a fixed (regular) routine (6)

según according to; **según la experiencia** based on experience (12)
segundo/a *adj.* second
seguridad *f.* safety
seguro/a *adj.* sure; safe
seis six (1)
seiscientos/as six hundred (7)
selección *f.* selection
seleccionar to select, choose
selva jungle (10)
semáforo signal; traffic light
semana week; **fin** (*m.*) **de semana** weekend; **la semana pasada** last week; **Semana Santa** Holy Week (9)
semanal weekly
semejanza similarity
semestre *m.* semester
seminario seminary
sencillo/a simple (4)
sendero path
sensato sensible (9)
sensible sensitive (9)
sentarse (ie) to sit down
sentido *n.* sense; **sentido del humor** sense of humor
sentimiento feeling, emotion; **expresar los sentimientos** to express one's feelings (15)
sentir(se) (ie, i) to feel; **sentirse** + *adj., adv.* to feel + *adj., adv.* (9); **sentirse bien/mal** to feel good/bad (6)
seña sign, signal, gesture
señal *f.* sign; signal
señalar to indicate
señor man; Mr. (1)
señora married woman; Mrs. (1)
señorita unmarried woman; Miss, Ms. (1)
separación *f.* separation
separado/a separated; **bailar separados** to dance apart (8)
separarse to separate, get separated (15)
septiembre September (6)
ser *irreg.* to be (1); **a no ser que** (*conj.*) unless; **es** _____ he (she, it) is _____ (1); **es/son de**

it is / they are (made of) (7); **es importante** + *inf.* it's important to (*do something*) (6); **es la / son las** _____ it's _____ o'clock (6); **es necesario** + *inf.* it's necessary to (*do something*) (6); **llegar (gu) a ser** to become; **ser consciente de** to be conscious of (11); **ser (de)** to be (from) (1); **ser discriminado/a** to be discriminated against (14); **ser feliz** to be happy; **ser listo/a** to be clever; **ser próspero/a** to be prosperous (11); **ser trabajador(a)** to be hardworking; **Soy/Es** _____ I am / He (She, It) is _____ (1); **Soy/Son de** _____ I'm / They are from _____ (1)
ser (*n. m.*) **humano** human being
serie *f.* series
serio/a serious
servicio service
servir (i, i) to serve (5); **¿en qué puedo servirle?** how may I help you? (7)
sesenta sixty (3)
setecientos/as seven hundred (7)
setenta seventy (3)
sexo sex
sexto/a sixth
sexual: avances sexuales sexual advances
sexualidad *f.* sexuality
si if
sí yes (1); **sí, por supuesto** yes, of course (7)
sicología psychology
sicológico/a psychological
sicólogo/a psychologist
siempre always (9); **casi siempre** almost always (9)
sierra mountain range (10)
siesta nap; **dormir (ue, u) la siesta** to take a siesta (nap) (4); **echar una siesta** to take a siesta (nap) (3); **tomar una siesta** to take a siesta (nap) (6)

siete seven (1)
siglo century
significado meaning
significar (qu) to mean
siguiente following, next
silencioso/a silent, quiet
silla chair (2)
sillón *m.* armchair (4)
simbólico/a symbolic
simbolizar (c) to symbolize
símbolo symbol
similar (a) similar (to) (1)
simpático/a friendly, nice
sin without; **sin duda** without a doubt; **sin dudar** without hesitation (15); **sin embargo** (*conj.*) however; **sin que** without
sinagoga synagogue
sincero/a sincere
sino but (rather)
sinónimo synonym
sintaxis *f.* syntax
síntesis *f.* synthesis
síntoma *m.* symptom
sistema *m.* system
sitio place, location; **sitio de subastas** auction site
situación *f.* situation
situado/a located
soberano/a sovereign
sobras *pl.* leftovers
sobre about; on, on top of; **sobre todo** above all, especially
sobretodo robe
sobrevivir to survive
sobrino/a nephew/niece (3)
social: asistente social social worker (12); **ciencias sociales** social sciences (2); **romper** (*p.p.* **roto/a**) **los obstáculos sociales** to break down social barriers (14)
socialista *n., adj. m., f.* socialist
socializar (c) to socialize
sociedad *f.* society
socioeconómico/a socioeconomic
sociología sociology (2)
sociólogo/a sociologist
sofá *m.* sofa (4)

sol *m.* sun; **caída/puesta del sol** sunset; **hace sol** it's sunny (6)
solamente only (11)
solas: a solas alone, in private
soler (ue) + *inf.* to be in the habit of / be accustomed to (*doing something*) (4)
solicitante *m., f.* applicant
solicitar to request; to apply for
solicitud *f.* application (12)
solidaridad *f.* solidarity
solitario/a solitary
solo/a alone (3)
sólo (solamente) *adv.* only (11)
soltar (ue) (*p.p.* **suelto/a**) to let out; to let free
soltero/a unmarried (3)
solución *f.* solution
solucionar to solve
solvente debt-free
sombrero hat (7)
soneto sonnet
sonreír (i, i) to smile (9)
sonrisa smile
soñador(a) dreamy; given to dreaming
soñar (ue) (con) to dream (about) (4)
sopa soup (5)
sorprender to surprise
sorpresa surprise
soso/a tasteless, bland
sospecha suspicion
sostener (*like* **tener**) to hold up, support
sótano basement
su(s) *poss.* his, her, its, their, your (*form. s., pl.*)
suavemente softly
subasta: sitio de subastas auction site
subdesarrollado/a underdeveloped
subida *n.* climb
subir to rise, go up; **subir a un autobús (coche, taxi)** to get in a bus (car, taxi) (10)
subjetivo subjective
subjuntivo *gram.* subjunctive mood

subordinado/a subordinate
subrayar to underline
subterráneo/a underground
suburbio suburb
suceder to happen
suceso event, happening (13)
sucio/a dirty
sudamericano/a *n., adj.* South American
sudar to sweat
Suecia Sweden
sueco/a *n.* Swede; *adj.* Swedish
suegro/a father-in-law, mother-in-law
sueldo (mínimo) (minimum) wage, salary (12)
suelto/a (*p.p. of* **soltar**) free
sueño dream; **tener** (*irreg.*) **sueño** to be tired
suerte *f.* luck; **tener** (*irreg.*) **suerte** to be lucky (11)
suéter *m.* sweater (7)
suficiente sufficient, enough (11)
sufrir (de ansiedad, estrés, insomnio) to suffer (from anxiety, stress, insomnia) (6)
Suiza Switzerland
suizo/a *n., adj.* Swiss
sujeto *n.* subject
súper *adv.* super (11)
superar las barreras económicas to overcome economic barriers (14)
supermercado supermarket (5)
superstición *f.* superstition
supersticioso/a supersticious
supuesto/a (*p.p. of* **suponer**) supposed; **por supuesto** of course
sur *m.* south
sureste *m.* southeast
surfear to surf (8)
surgir (j) to arise
suroeste *m.* southwest
suspender to suspend (13)
suspirar to sigh; to yearn
sustituir (y) to substitute
suyo/a/os/as *poss.* your, of yours (*form. s., pl.*); his, of his; her, of hers

T
tabla table, chart
tablista *m., f.* surfer
tabú *m.* taboo
tacón *m.* heel (*shoe*); **zapatos de tacón alto** high-heeled shoes
taíno/a *n., adj.* Taíno (*indigenous people inhabiting islands in the Caribbean*)
tal such, such a; **con tal de que** (*conj.*) provided that; **¿qué tal?** how's it going? what's up? (1); **¿qué tal éste/a/os/as aquí?** what about this (one) / these (ones) here?; **¿qué tal si (nosotros/as) _____?** how about if (*we do something*)? (8); **tal vez** perhaps
talento talent
talla size (*clothes*); **¿qué talla lleva?** what size (*clothing*) do you (*form. s.*) wear? (7)
taller *m.* workshop
tamaño size
también also, too (1)
tampoco neither, not either (8)
tan so; **tan** + *adj./adv.* **como** as + *adj./adv.* as (5); **tan pronto como** as soon as
tanto *adv.* so much
tanto/a *adj.* so much; such; *pl.* so many; **por lo tanto** therefore; **tanto/a/os/as** + *noun* + **como** as much/many + *noun* + as (5)
tapera shack
tardar to take time (*to do something*)
tarde *n. f.* afternoon, evening; *adv.* late (6); **buenas tardes** good afternoon/evening (1); **de la tarde** in the afternoon, evening (2); **por la tarde** during the afternoon/evening (*general*) (2)
tardío/a late
tarea homework; task
tarifa rate, price, fare
tarjeta card; **tarjeta de crédito** credit card; **tarjeta postal** postcard

tarro jar
tarta pastry
tasa rate, level; **tasa de cambio** exchange rate
tatuaje *m.* tatoo
taxi *m.* taxi (10); **parada de taxis** taxi stand (10); **subir a un taxi** to get in a taxi (10)
taza cup (*coffee*); **una taza de** a cup of
te *d.o.* you (*fam. s.*); *i.o.* to/for you (*fam. s.*); *refl. pron.* yourself (*fam. s.*)
té *m.* tea (5)
teatral theatrical
teatro theater (10); **ir** (*irreg.*) **al teatro** to go to the theater (8)
techo roof
técnico/a *n.* technician; *adj.* technical
tecnología technology
tecnológico/a technological
teja roof tile
tejano/a Texan
tejer to knit (8)
tejido *n.* textile
tejido/a woven
tela fabric
telefónica telephone company office (10)
teléfono telephone (4); **teléfono celular** cell phone
telenovela soap opera (13)
teleserie *f.* television series
televidente *m., f.* television viewer (13)
televisión *f.* television (*medium*) (13); **mirar la televisión** to watch TV (3); **televisión de antena parabólica** satellite TV (13); **televisión por cable** cable TV (13)
televisivo/a *adj.* television (13)
tema *m.* theme, topic
temer to fear
temperatura temperature
temporada season
temporario/a temporary; **agencia de empleados temporarios** temporary employment agency

temprano early (6)
tendencia tendency
tender (ie) to spread out
tener *irreg.* to have; **tener celos** to be jealous (15); **tener cuidado** to be careful; **tener en cuenta** to keep in mind; **tener esperanza** to have hope, be hopeful (11); **tener éxito** to be successful (11); **tener expectativas** to have expectations (11); **tener fiebre** to have a fever (6); **tener ganas de** + *inf.* to feel like (*doing something*) (8); **tener gripe** (*f.*) to have the flu (6); **tener hambre** (*f.*) to be hungry (5); **tener la ciudadanía** to have citizenship (11); **tener la intención de** + *inf.* to intend to (*do something*) (11); **tener más acceso a la enseñanza** to have more access to education (14); **tener miedo** to be afraid (11); **tener personalidades incompatibles** to have incompatible personalities (15); **tener prisa** to be in a hurry (8); **tener que** + *inf.* to have to (*do something*) (6); **tener resfrío** to have a cold (6); **tener sueño** to be tired; **tener suerte** to be lucky (11); **tener un resfriado** to have a cold (6); **tener valores incompatibles** to have incompatible values (15); **tener _____ años (y medio)** to be _____ (and a half) years old (3); **tengo** I have (1); **tiene la garganta inflamada** your (*form. s.*) throat is inflamed (6); **tiene que descansar más** you (*form. s.*) have to get more rest (6); **¿tiene(s) la hora?** do you have the time? (6)
tenis *m.* tennis (8); **zapatos de tenis** tennis shoes (7)
tensión *f.* tension

tenso/a tense; stressed (9)
teoría theory
terapia therapy
tercer, tercero/a third
terminar to finish
término term
ternura tenderness
terraza terrace (4)
terremoto earthquake
territorio territory; **territorio ancestral** ancestral territory (14)
terror horror; **película de terror** horror film, movie (13)
terrorismo terrorism
terrorista *n. m., f.* terrorist
testimonio testimony (13)
tetera teapot
texto text; **libro de texto** textbook (2)
ti *obj. of prep.* you (*fam. s.*)
tiempo weather, time; **a tiempo** on time (6); **de tiempo completo/parcial** full-time/part-time (12); **hace buen/mal tiempo** it's good/bad weather (6); **hace mucho tiempo** a long time ago; **pasar el tiempo libre** to spend free time (3); **pasar tiempo con los hijos** to spend time with the (one's) children (3); **pronóstico del tiempo** weather report; **¿que tiempo hace?** what's the weather like? (6)
tienda store, shop (7); **tienda especializada** speciality shop/store (7)
tierno/a tender (5)
tierra earth, land
tigre *m.* tiger
tímido/a timid
tío/a uncle/aunt (3)
típico/a typical
tipo type
tira cómica comic strip, cartoon (13)
titular *m.* headline
título title
tiza chalk (2)

tocar (qu) to touch; to play; **tocar música** to play music (8)

tocino bacon

todavía still, yet

todo/a all; every; **a todo volumen** on high (*radio, television*); **para toda la vida** for life (15); **sobre todo** above all, especially; **todas las noches** every night (9); **todos los días** every day (9)

tolerante tolerant

tomar to take; to drink; **tomar medicina** to take medicine; **tomar un café (una cerveza, una copa)** to drink/have coffee (a beer, a drink) (6); **tomar una siesta** to take a siesta (nap) (6)

tomate *m.* tomato (5)

tono tone

tontería foolish thing

tonto/a silly, foolish

tormenta storm

torno: en torno surrounding

torta cake

tortilla *thin cake made of cornmeal or flour (Mex.);* **tortilla española** *omelette made of eggs, potatoes, and onions (Sp.)*

torturar to torture

tos *f.* cough; **jarabe para la tos** cough syrup

tostada toast (5)

trabajador(a) *n.* worker; *adj.* hardworking (1); **Día** (*m.*) **del Trabajador** Labor Day (9); **ser** (*irreg.*) **trabajador(a)** to be hardworking

trabajar to work (2)

trabajo job; **condiciones de trabajo** working conditions (12); **trabajo de tiempo completo/parcial** full-time/part-time job (12)

tradición *f.* tradition (14)

tradicional traditional (4); **jornado tradicional** traditional workday (12); **mantener** (*like* **tener**) **los**

valores tradicionales to maintain traditional values (14)

traducción *f.* translation

traducir *irreg.* to translate

traductor(a) translator (12)

traer *irreg.* to bring (5); **¿me trae _____, por favor?** could you bring me _____, please? (5); **¿qué le(s) traigo?** what can I bring you? (5)

tráfico traffic

tragedia tragedy

trágico/a tragic

trago drink

traje *m.* suit (7); **traje de baño** bathing suit (7)

trama plot

tranquilidad *f.* tranquility

tranquilo/a calm, peaceful; **estar** (*irreg.*) **tranquilo/a** to be calm (8)

transformación *f.* transformation

transformar to transform

transición *f.* transition

transitado/a: calle/zona transitada busy street/zone (4)

tránsito traffic

transmitir to transmit

transparente transparent

transporte transportation

tranvía *m.* cable car

trapo rag

trasladarse to move (*house*)

tratado treaty; **Tratado de Libre Comercio** NAFTA

tratar to treat; to deal with; **tratar de mantener las costumbres** to try to maintain one's customs (11)

través: a través de through, by means of

trece thirteen (1)

treinta thirty (1)

treinta y cinco thirty-five (3)

treinta y cuatro thirty-four (3)

treinta y dos thirty-two (3)

treinta y nueve thirty-nine (3)

treinta y ocho thirty-eight (3)

treinta y seis thirty-six (3)

treinta y siete thirty-seven (3)

treinta y tres thirty-three (3)

treinta y uno thirty-one (1)

tren *m.* train (1); **estación** (*f.*) **de trenes** train station (10); **ir** (*irreg.*) **en tren** to go by train (10); **perder (ie) un tren** to miss a train

tres three (1)

trescientos/as three hundred (7)

tribu *f.* (*pl.* **tribus**) tribe

trimestre *m.* trimester

triste sad; **estar** (*irreg.*) **triste** to be sad (6)

tristeza unhappiness

triunfal triumphant

triunfar to triumph

trotaconventos matchmaker

trozo piece, chunk

trucha trout

tú *sub. pron.* you (*fam. s.*) (1)

tu(s) *poss.* your (*fam. s.*)

tumultuoso/a tumultuous

turismo tourism

turista *n. m., f.* tourist

turístico/a *adj.* tourist

tuyo/a/os/as *poss.* your, of yours (*fam. s.*)

U

u or (*used instead of* **o** *before words beginning with* **o** *or* **ho**)

ubicación *f.* location

Ud.: usted *sub. pron.* you (*form. s.*) (1); *obj. of prep.* you (*form. s.*)

Uds.: ustedes *sub. pron.* you (*form. pl.*) (1); *obj. of prep.* you (*form. pl.*)

últimamente recently

último/a last; **de última moda** the latest fashion

un, uno/a *indef. art.* a, an (1); one (1); *pl.* some, any (1); **cada uno** each one; **un poco de** a little (of) (5)

único/a: hijo/a único/a only child (3)

unido/a close-knit (3); **Estados Unidos** United States

uniforme *m.* uniform
unión *f.* union
unir to unite, join
universidad *f.* university (2)
universitario/a *of or pertaining to the university;* **ciudad universitaria** campus (2); **residencia universitaria** dormitory, residence hall (2)
urbanización *f.* modern; neighborhood housing development (*Sp.*)
urbano/a urban
uruguayo/a *n., adj.* Uruguayan
usar to use (2); to wear (*clothing*)
uso *n.* use
usted (Ud., Vd.) *sub. pron.* you (*form. s.*) (1); *obj. of prep.* you (*form. s.*)
ustedes (Uds., Vds.) *sub. pron.* you (*form. pl.*) (1); *obj. of prep.* you (*form. pl.*)
usuario/a user
utensilio utensil
útil useful
utilidad *f.* utility
utilitario/a utilitarian
utilizar (c) to utilize, use
utopia Utopia
utópico/a Utopic
uva grape

V

vaca cow; **carne** (*f.*) **de vaca** beef (5)
vacación *f.* vacation; **de vacaciones** on vacation; **estar** (*irreg.*) **de vacaciones** to be on vacation (10); **ir** (*irreg.*) **de vacaciones** to go on vacation (10)
vaciar (vacío) to empty
vajilla dishes, crockery
valentín: Día (*m.*) **de San Valentín** St. Valentine's Day
valer *irreg.* to be worth
válido/a valid
valiente brave
valle *m.* valley (14)

valor *m.* value (11); **mantener** (*like* **tener**) **los valores tradicionales** to maintain traditional values (14); **tener** (*irreg.*) **valores incompatibles** to have incompatible values (15)
valorar to value
vapor steam; **al vapor** steamed
vaquero/a cowboy/cowgirl; **(pantalones)** (*m. pl.*) **vaqueros** jeans (7)
variación *f.* variation
variado/a varied
variar (varío) to vary
variedad *f.* variety
varios/as *pl.* various
varón *m.* male
vascuence *m.* Basque (*language*)
vasija receptacle
vaso (drinking) glass; **un vaso de** a glass of
Vd.: usted *sub. pron.* you (*form. s.*) (1); *obj. of prep.* you (*form. s.*)
Vds.: ustedes *sub. pron.* you (*form. pl.*) (1); *obj. of prep.* you (*form. pl.*)
vecino/a neighbor (4)
vegetal *m.* vegetable (5)
vegetariano/a vegetarian
veinte twenty (1)
veinticinco twenty-five (1)
veinticuatro twenty-four (1)
veintidós twenty-two (1)
veintinueve twenty-nine (1)
veintiocho twenty-eight (1)
veintiséis twenty-six (1)
veintitrés twenty-three (1)
veintiuno twenty-one (1)
vejez *f.* old age (9)
vendedor(a) salesperson; vendor; **vendedor(a) ambulante** street vendor
vender to sell (7)
venezolano/a Venezuelan
vengativo/a vengeful
venta sale
ventaja advantage
ventana window (4)

ver *irreg.* (*p.p.* **visto/a**) to see (3); **nos vemos** see you around (1); **ver a los parientes** to see the (one's) relatives (3); **ver la televisión** to watch TV (3); **ver una película** to watch a movie (8)
verano summer (6); **el verano pasado** last summer
veras: ¿de veras? really?
verbo verb
verdad *f.* truth (13); **pues, la verdad es que** _____ well, actually _____ (8)
verdadero/a true
verde green (5); unripe (5); **ojos verdes** green eyes (1); **pimiento** green (bell) pepper (5)
verdulería vegetable store (5)
verdura vegetable (5)
vergonzoso/a shameful
vergüenza shame
verificar (qu) to check, verify
vestido *n.* dress (7)
vestimenta clothing, style of dress
vestirse (i, i) to get dressed (6)
vestuario clothing, style of dress (14)
veterinario/a veterinarian (12)
vez *f.* (*pl.* **veces**) times; **a veces** sometimes (9); **cada vez** each time; **de vez en cuando** sometimes; **raras veces** infrequently, rarely (9); **tal vez** perhaps; **una vez** once
viajar to travel, take a trip (10)
viaje *m.* trip; **agencia de viajes** travel agency (10); **agente** (*m., f.*) **de viajes** travel agent (10); **emprender un viaje** to take a trip; **estar** (*irreg.*) **de viaje** to be on a trip (10); **hacer** (*irreg.*) **un viaje** to take a trip (10); **ir** (*irreg.*) **de viaje** to go on a trip (10)
viajero/a traveler
vianda cut of meat
viandero/a meat and grocery vendor

vicepresidente/a vice president

vida life; **apasionado/a por la vida** passionate for life; **mejorar las condiciones de vida** to improve living conditions (14); **nivel** (*m.*) **de vida** standard of living; **para toda la vida** for life (15)

video video (14)

videojuego video game; **jugar (ue) (gu) a los videojuegos** to play video games (8)

viejo/a *n.* elderly person (9); *adj.* old, stale (5)

viento: hace viento it's windy (6)

viernes *m. s., pl.* Friday (1); **Viernes Santo** Good Friday (9)

vigoroso/a vigorous

villancico Christmas carol

vino wine (3); **beber vino** to drink wine (3)

violencia violence

violento/a violent

virtud *f.* virtue

visibilidad *f.* visibility

visitar to visit; **visitar a los parientes** to visit the (one's) relatives (3)

vista view; **punto de vista** point of view

vitae: curriculum (*m.*) **vitae** résumé

viudo/a widower, widow

víveres supplies, provisions

vivir to live (3); **vivir con la incertidumbre** to live with uncertainty (11)

vivo/a alive

vocabulario vocabulary

vocación *f.* vocation

volcán *m.* volcano (10)

volcánico/a volcanic

voleibol *m.* volleyball (8); **jugar (ue) (gu) al voleibol** to play volleyball

volumen *m.* volume; **a todo volumen** on high (*radio, television*)

volver (ue) (*p.p.* **vuelto/a**) to return (*to a place*) (4)

vomitar to vomit

vosotros/as *sub. pron.* you (*fam. pl. Sp.*) (1); *obj. of prep.* you (*fam. pl. Sp.*)

votar to vote

voto: derecho al voto right to vote

voz (*pl.* **voces**)**: en voz alta** aloud

vuelo flight; **perder (ie) un vuelo** to miss a flight

vuelta *n.* turn; **dar** (*irreg.*) **vueltas** to go around; **de ida y vuelta** *adj.* round-trip (10)

vuelto (*p.p. of* **volver**) returned

vuestro/a/os/as *poss.* your (*fam. pl. Sp.*), of yours (*fam. pl. Sp.*)

Y

y and (1)

ya already; **ya no** no longer

yerba (mate) *herb used to make tea*

yo *sub. pron.* I (1)

yogur *m.* yogurt

yuca yucca

Z

zanahoria carrot (7)

zapatería shoe store

zapatero/a cobbler

zapatista *n., adj. m., f. member of the 1994 Zapatista Rebellion in Mexico*

zapato shoe (7); **zapatos de tacón alto** high-heeled shoes; **zapatos de tenis** tennis shoes (7)

zona (transitada/residencial) (busy/residential) zone (4)

zoología zoology

English-Spanish Vocabulary

A

a, an **un(a)** (1)
a lot **mucho** *adv.* (2); a lot (of) *adj.* **mucho/a** (2)
able: to be able **poder** *irreg.*
abroad *n.* **extranjero** (11)
abuse *n.* **abuso** (13)
accent *n.* **acento** (14)
accountant **contable** (12)
accustomed to (*doing something*) **soler (ue)** + *inf.* (4)
action film **película de acción** (13)
ad **anuncio;** job ad **anuncio de empleo** (12)
adjective **adjetivo** (2)
administration building **edificio de administración** (2)
adolescence **adolescencia** (9)
adolescent **adolescente** *m., f.* (9)
adult **adulto/a** (9)
adulthood **edad** (*f.*) **adulta** (9)
affectionate **cariñoso/a** (3)
afraid: to be afraid **tener** (*irreg.*) **miedo** (11)
after (*doing something*) **después de** + *inf.* (11)
airplane **avión** *m.* (10)
airport **aeropuerto** (10)
alcoholic drink **bebida alcohólica** (8)
All Saints' Day (November 1) **Día** (*m.*) **de los Santos** (9)
All Souls' Day (November 2) **Día** (*m.*) **de los Muertos** (9)
allow (*someone*) to (*do something*) **dejarle** + *inf.* (11); allow (*someone*) to pass **dejarle pasar** (11)
almost **casi;** almost always **casi siempre** (9)
alone **solo/a** (3)
also **también** (1)
always **siempre** (9); almost always **casi siempre** (9)
Amazon *adj.* **amazónico/a** (14)
ambience **ambiente** *m.* (4)
American (*from the United States*) *adj.* **estadounidense** (1)

among **entre** (2)
ample **amplio/a** (12)
ancestral land **territorio ancestral** (14)
and **y** (1)
angry: to be angry **estar** (*irreg.*) **enojado/a** (6)
annoy (*someone*) **molestarle** (9)
annoyed **molesto/a** (9)
annoying **molesto/a** (9)
anthropology **antropología** (2)
anxious: to be anxious (about) **estar** (*irreg.*) **ansioso/a** (**por**) (11)
apartment **piso** (4)
appetizer **entrada** (5); as an appetizer **de entrada** (5)
apple **manzana** (5)
application **solicitud** *f.* (12)
appointment **cita** (12)
approximate *adj.* **aproximado/a** (6)
April **abril** (6)
archaeologist **arqueólogo/a** (12)
architect **arquitecto/a** (12)
architecture **arquitectura** (2)
argue **discutir** (3)
armchair **sillón** *m.* (4)
army **ejército** (13)
around **por** (11); around ____ (*time*) **a eso de la(s)** ____ (6)
arrange **fijar** (12)
arrive (at) **llegar (gu) (a)** (2)
art(s) **arte** *m.* (*pl.* **las artes**) (2)
artist **artista** (12)
as **como** (1); as + *adj./adv.* + as **tan** + *adj./adv.* + **como** (5); as much/many + *noun* + as **tanto/a/os/as** + *noun* + **como** (5)
Asian (*person*) *n.* **asiático/a** (14)
ask for **pedir (i, i)** (5); to ask someone to dance **sacar (qu) a alguien a bailar** (8)
at **a;** at ____ (o'clock) **a la(s)** ____ (2); at ____:30, at half past ____ **a la(s)** ____ **y**

media (2); at midnight **a medianoche** (6); at noon **a mediodía** (6)
atmosphere **ambiente** (4)
atrocity **atrocidad** *f.* (13)
August **agosto** (6)
aunt **tía** (3)
avocado **aguacate** *m.* (5)
avoid pejorative language **evitar el lenguaje peyorativo** (14)
awful **fatal** (9)

B

baby **bebé** *m., f.* (9)
background **formación** *f.* (12)
backpack **mochila** (2)
bad **mal, malo/a** (1)
bakery **panadería** (5)
ballpoint pen **bolígrafo** (2)
banana **plátano** (5)
bank *n.* **banco** (10)
banker **banquero/a** (12)
bar mitzvah **barmitzvah** *m.* (9)
bargain *n.* **ganga** (7); *v.* **regatear** (7)
based on experience **según la experiencia** (12)
basketball **básquetbol** *m.* (8); **baloncesto** (*Sp.*)
bat mitzvah **batmitzvah** *f.* (9)
bathing suit **traje** (*m.*) **de baño** (7)
bathroom **cuarto de baño** (4)
bathtub **bañera** (4)
be **ser** *irreg.* (1); **estar** *irreg.* (2); to be able to **poder** (*irreg.*) (4); to be accustomed to (*doing something*) **soler (ue)** + *inf.* (4); to be afraid **tener** (*irreg.*) **miedo** (11); to be angry **estar** (*irreg.*) **enojado/a** (6); to be anxious (about) **estar** (*irreg.*) **ansioso/a** (**por**) (11); to be at one's best **estar** (*irreg.*) **en su punto** (8); to be bored **estar** (*irreg.*) **aburrido/a** (6); to be born **nacer (zc)** (11); to be

calm **estar** (*irreg.*) **tranquilo/a** (8); to be (caught) between two cultures **estar** (*irreg.*) **entre dos culturas** (11); to be connected (*to the Internet*) **estar** (*irreg.*) **conectado/a** (13); to be conscious of **ser** (*irreg.*) **consciente de** (11); to be different **diferenciarse** (10); to be divorced **estar** (*irreg.*) **divorciado/a** (3); to be drunk **estar** (*irreg.*) **borracho/a** (8); to be familiar with (*someone, some place, something*) **conocer (zc)** (6); to be (from) **ser** (*irreg.*) **(de)** (1); to be happy **estar** (*irreg.*) **contento/a** (6); to be hopeful **tener** (*irreg.*) **esperanza** (11); to be hungry **tener** (*irreg.*) **hambre** (5); to be in a hurry **tener** (*irreg.*) **prisa** (8); to be in the habit of (*doing something*) **soler (ue)** + *inf.* (4); to be in the mood **encontrarse (ue) en ambiente** (8); to be jealous **tener** (*irreg.*) **celos** (15); to be lucky **tener** (*irreg.*) **suerte** (11); to be made by hand **estar** (*irreg.*) **hecho/a a mano** (7); to be married **estar** (*irreg.*) **casado/a** (3); to be on a trip **estar** (*irreg.*) **de viaje** (10); to be on vacation **estar** (*irreg.*) **de vacaciones** (10); to be pleasing to (*someone*) **gustarle** (9); to be prosperous **ser** (*irreg.*) **próspero/a** (11); to be relaxed **estar** (*irreg.*) **relajado/a** (8); to be retired **estar** (*irreg.*) **jubilado/a** (3); to be sad **estar** (*irreg.*) **triste** (6); to be sick **estar** (*irreg.*) **enfermo/a** (6); to be successful **tener** (*irreg.*) **éxito** (11); to be tired **estar** (*irreg.*) **cansado/a** (6); to be too large/small **quedarle grande / pequeño/a** (7); to be trusting **confiado/a** (9); to be uninformed **estar** (*irreg.*) **desinformado/a** (13); to be

up-to-date **estar** (*irreg.*) **al corriente** (13); to be well/ poorly made **estar** (*irreg.*) **hecho/a bien/mal** (7); to be _____ (and a half) years old **tener _____ años (y medio)** (3); he (she, it) is _____ **es _____** (1); he (she, it) is from _____ **es de _____** (1); I am _____ **soy _____** (1); I'm from _____ **soy de _____** (1); I'm (very) fine, thanks **estoy (muy) bien, gracias** (1); it is / they are (made of) **es/son de** (7); they are from _____ **son de _____** (1)
beach *n.* **playa** (10)
bean **frijol** *m.* (5)
because **porque** (1); because of **por** (11)
bed **cama** (4)
bedroom **dormitorio** (4); **cuarto** (4); **habitación** *f.* (4)
beef **carne** (*f.*) **de res (vaca)** (5)
beer **cerveza** (3)
before (*doing something*) **antes de** + *inf.* (11)
behind (+ *noun*) **detrás (de +** *noun*) (2)
bell pepper (red/green) **pimiento (rojo/verde)** (5)
belt **cinturón** (7)
benefits **prestaciones** (12)
beside (+ *noun*) **al lado (de +** *noun*) (2)
best: to be at one's best **estar** (*irreg.*) **en su punto** (8)
better than **mejor(es) que** (5)
between **entre** (2)
bicultural **bicultural** (11)
big **grande** (1)
bilingual **bilingüe** (11)
bill *n.* (*restaurant*) **cuenta** (5)
biology **biología** (2)
birthday **cumpleaños** *m. s., pl.* (9)
bit of gossip, *pl.* gossip **chisme** *m.* (13)
bitter **amargo/a** (5)
black eyes **ojos negros** (1); black hair **pelo negro** (1)

block (city) **cuadra** (10)
blond hair **pelo rubio** (1)
blouse **blusa** (7)
blue eyes **ojos azules** (1)
board a plane (ship, train) **abordar un avión** (barco, tren) (10)
boat **barco** (10)
book **libro** (2)
bookcase **estantería** (4)
bookstore **librería** (2)
boots **botas** *pl.* (7)
border *n.* **frontera** (11)
bore (*someone*) **aburrirle** (9)
bored: to be bored **estar** (*irreg.*) **aburrido/a** (6)
boring **aburrido/a** (2)
born **nacer (zc)** (11)
bother **molestar** (8); to bother (*someone*) **molestarle** (9)
bracelet **pulsera** (7)
bread **pan** *m.* (5)
break down social barriers **romper** (*p.p.* **roto/a**) **los obstáculos sociales** (14)
bring **traer** (*irreg.*) (5)
broad **amplio/a** (12)
brother **hermano** (3)
brother-in-law **cuñado** (3)
brown **pardo/a** (7); brown eyes **ojos castaños** (1); brown hair **pelo castaño** (1); brown skin **piel** (*f.*) **morena** (1)
brush one's teeth **cepillarse los dientes** (6)
building **edificio;** administration building **edificio de administración** (2); apartment building **bloque** (*m.*) **de pisos** (4)
bus **autobús** *m.* (10), **colectivo** *m.* (10); bus stop **parada de autobuses** (10); to get off a bus **bajar de un autobús** (10); to get on a bus **subir a un autobús** (10)
businessman **hombre** (*m.*) **de negocios** (12)
businesswoman **mujer** (*f.*) **de negocios** (12)

busy **ocupado/a;** busy street **calle** (*f.*) **transitada** (4); to be busy **estar** (*irreg.*) **ocupado/a**

but **pero** (1)

butcher's shop **carnicería** (5)

butter *n.* **mantequilla** (5)

buy **comprar** (5)

by **por** (11)

C

cable TV **televisión** (*f.*) **por cable** (13)

cafeteria **cafetería** (2)

cake **pastel** *m.* (5)

calm: to be calm **estar** (*irreg.*) **tranquilo/a** (8)

camp *v.* **acampar** (8)

campus **ciudad** (*f.*) **universitaria** (2)

can *v.* **poder** *irreg.* (4)

Canadian *adj.* **canadiense** *m., f.* (1)

cancel a reservation **cancelar una reserva** (10)

capable **capaz** (*pl.* **capaces**) (12)

car **coche** *m.* (10)

career **carrera** (2)

caring **sensible** (9)

carpet **alfombra** (4)

carrot **zanahoria** (5)

carry **llevar** (2)

cartoon **tira cómica** (13)

cash register **caja** (7)

cat **gato** (3)

cathedral **catedral** *f.* (10)

celebrate **celebrar** (9)

chair **silla** (2)

chalk **tiza** (2)

chalkboard **pizarra** (2)

channel **canal** *m.* (13)

charming **encantador(a)** (1)

chat *v.* (*in general*) **charlar** (4), **conversar** (3); **platicar (qu)** (13); (*online*) **chatear** (13); to chat with friends **charlar con amigos** (8)

chatroom **chat** *m.* (13)

cheap **barato/a** (5)

check *n.* (*restaurant*) **cuenta** (5); *v.* **revisar** (11); to check luggage **facturar el equipaje** (10)

check-out **caja** (7)

cheese **queso** (5)

chemistry **química** (2); chemistry laboratory **laboratorio de química** (2)

chest of drawers **cómoda** (4)

chicken **pollo** (5)

child **niño/a** (3)

childhood **niñez** *f.* (9)

children **hijos** (3); **niños** (3)

Chinese *adj.* **chino/a** (1)

Christmas **Navidad** *f.* (9)

citizen **ciudadano/a** *n.* (11)

city **ciudad** *f.* (4); city hall **ayuntamiento** (10)

civil war **guerra civil** (13)

class **clase** *f.* (2)

classroom **aula** (2)

click (on) **hacer** (*irreg.*) **clic (en)** (13)

client **cliente** *m., f.* (7)

close *v.* **cerrar (ie)** (4); close *adj.* (*relationship*) **estrecho/a** (3); **íntimo/a**

close-knit **unido/a** (3)

closet **armario** (4)

clothing **ropa** (7); (*style of dress*) **vestuario** (14)

cloudy: it's cloudy (*weather*) **está nublado** (6)

coast *n.* **costa** (14)

coffee **café** *m.* (5)

cold: it's cold (*weather*) **hace frío** (6)

collect (stamps/coins) **coleccionar (estampillas/monedas)** (8)

college **facultad** (2)

come back **volver (ue)** (4)

comedy (*film*) **película cómica** (13)

comic strip **tira cómica** (13)

comical **cómico/a** (13)

communicate well/poorly **comunicarse (qu) bien/mal** (15)

company (*business*) **empresa** (12)

comparison **comparación** *f.* (5)

complain **quejarse** (15)

computer **ordenador** *m.* (*Sp.*) (4); computer programmer

programador(a) (12); computer science **computación** (2), **informática** (2)

condominium **condominio** (4)

confirm a reservation **confirmar una reserva** (10)

confirmation **confirmación** *f.* (9)

connected: to be connected (*to the Internet*) **estar** (*irreg.*) **conectado/a** (13)

conscious: to be conscious of **ser** (*irreg.*) **consciente de** (11)

consultant **asesor(a)** (12)

continue straight ahead **seguir (i, i) (g) derecho** (10)

contrast: in contrast **en cambio** (10)

controversial **controvertido/a** (13)

cook *v.* **cocinar** (5)

cooking (style of) **gastronomía** (14)

cool: it's cool (*weather*) **hace fresco** (6)

corn **maíz** *m.* (5)

cost *v.* **costar (ue)** (7); how much does it / do they cost? **¿cuánto cuesta(n)?** (7); it costs / they cost _____ **cuesta(n)** _____ (7)

cotton **algodón** *m.* (7)

could you bring me _____, please? **¿me trae _____, por favor?** (5); could you pass (me) _____, please? **¿me pasa(s) _____ por favor?** (5)

country of origin **país** (*m.*) **de origen** (11)

country(side) **campo** (10)

couple **pareja** (15)

courtyard **patio** (4)

cousin **primo/a** (3); *pl.* **primos** (3)

crab **cangrejo** (5)

Creole (*American-born children of European parents and their descendants*) **criollo/a** *n.* (14)

crime **crimen** *m.* (*pl.* **crímenes**) (14)

cross *v.* **cruzar (c)** (10)

crossword puzzle **crucigrama** *m.* (13)

cry *v.* **llorar** (9)
cultural conflict **conflicto cultural** (11)
cup **taza;** a cup of **una taza de** (5)
current **actual** (13)
currently **actualmente** (13)
custom **costumbre** *f.* (11)
customs **aduana** *s.* (10)
cycling **ciclismo** (8)

D

daily routine **rutina diaria** (6)
dance *n.* **baile** *m.* (8); *v.* (close/apart) **bailar (pegados/separados)** (8)
dark skin **piel** (*f.*) **oscura** (1)
date *n.* **cita** (15)
daughter **hija** (3)
day **día** *m.* (1); All Saints' Day (November 1) **Día de los Santos** (9); All Souls' Day (November 2) **Día de los Muertos** (9); Epiphany (January 6) **Día de los Reyes Magos** (9); Labor Day **Día del Trabajador** (9)
death **muerte** *f.* (13)
decade **década** (13)
December **diciembre** (6)
deceived **desilusionado/a** (9)
define **definir** (12)
delicious **delicioso/a** (5); **rico/a** (5)
delightful **encantador(a)** (1)
delinquent (*person*) **delincuente** (14)
demand **exigir (j)** (12)
demonstration **manifestación** *f.* (13)
deport **deportar** (11)
depressed **deprimido/a** (9)
desert *n.* **desierto** (10)
design *n.* **diseño** (2)
designer **diseñador(a)** (12)
desirable **deseable** (12)
desire *v.* **desear** (5)
desk **escritorio** (4); student's desk **pupitre** *m.* (2)
dessert **postre** *m.* (5); for dessert **(de) postre** (5)

detain **detener** *irreg.* (11)
diamond ring **anillo de diamantes** (7)
different (from/than) **diferente (de)** (1); **distinto/a (de)** (3); *v.* to be different **diferenciarse** (10)
difficult **difícil** (2)
dining room **comedor** *m.* (4)
direct object pronoun **pronombre** (*m.*) **de complemento directo** (5)
director **director(a)** (12)
disaster **desastre** *m.* (13)
discotheque **discoteca** (8)
discount *n.* **descuento** (7)
discriminate **discriminar** (11)
discriminated against **ser** (*irreg.*) **discriminado/a** (14)
discrimination **discriminación** *f.* (14)
discuss **discutir** (3)
dish (*prepared*) **plato** (5)
dishwasher **lavaplatos** *m. s., pl.* (4)
disillusioned **desilusionado/a** (9)
dislike (*someone*) **caerle** (*irreg.*) **mal** (9)
display counter **mostrador** (7)
displease (*someone*) **disgustarle** (9)
disseminate **difundir** (13)
distinct (from) **distinto/a (de)** (3)
distinguish **distinguir (distingo)** (14); to distinguish oneself **diferenciarse** (10)
divorce **divorciarse** (15)
divorced **estar** (*irreg.*) **divorciado/a** (3)
do **hacer** (*irreg.*) (3); do you have the time? **¿tiene(s) la hora?** (6); do you take credit cards? **¿aceptan tarjetas de crédito?** (7); to do aerobic exercise **hacer** (*irreg.*) **ejercicio aeróbico** (6); to do crossword puzzles **hacer** (*irreg.*) **crucigramas** (3); to do the shopping **hacer** (*irreg.*) **la compra** (5)
doctor **médico/a** (12)
document *n.* **documento** (11)
documentary **documental** (13)

dog **perro** (3)
door **puerta** (4)
dormitory **residencia estudiantil** (2), **residencia universitaria** (2)
doubt *v.* **dudar** (13)
doubtful **dudoso/a** (13)
downtown **centro** (10)
draw **dibujar** (8)
dream (about) **soñar (ue) (con)** (4)
dress *n.* **vestido** (7); *v.* **vestirse (i, i)** (6)
dresser (*furniture*) **cómoda** (4)
dressing room **probador** (7)
drink *n.* **bebida** (5); *v.* **beber** (3); **tomar** (8); and to drink? **¿y de beber?** (5); to drink a beer **beber una cerveza** (3); to drink a soft drink **beber un refresco** (3); to drink wine **beber vino** (3)
drive **conducir** *irreg.* (10), **manejar** (10)
drug *n.* **droga** (14)
drunk: to be drunk **estar** (*irreg.*) **borracho/a** (8)
dry **seco/a** (5)
dryer **secadora** (4)
DVD player **DVD** (13)

E

each **cada;** each month **cada mes** (9); each year **cada año** (9)
early **temprano** (6)
earn **ganar** (12)
earring **arete** *m.* (7), **pendiente** *m.* (7)
Easter **Pascua** (9)
easy **fácil** (2)
eat **comer** (3); to eat breakfast **desayunar** (2); to eat dinner **cenar** (2); to eat lunch **almorzar (ue) (c)** (4)
education **educación** *f.* (2)
educational program **programa educativo** (13)
egg **huevo** (5)
eight **ocho** (1)
eight hundred **ochocientos/as** (7)
eighteen **dieciocho** (1)

eighty **ochenta** (3)
elderly person **anciano/a** (9); **viejo/a** (9)
elections **elecciones** *f., pl.* (13)
elective **optativo/a** (2)
electricity **luz** *f.* (4)
elegant **elegante** (4)
eleven **once** (1)
e-mail **correo electrónico** (13); e-mail (*message*) **mail** *m.* (13)
embarrass **avergonzar (üe) (c)** (15)
emotional **emocionado/a** (9); emotional bonds **lazos afectivos** (15); emotional well-being **bienestar** (*m.*) **emocional** (15)
employee **empleado/a** (12)
engineer *n.* **ingeniero/a** (12)
English (*language*) **inglés** *m.* (2); English *adj.* **inglés, inglesa** (1)
enjoy oneself **divertirse (ie)** (6)
enough **suficiente** (11)
enter (*a place*) **entrar (en + *place*)** (2)
Epiphany (January 6) **Día de los Reyes Magos** (9)
escape (from) **escapar (de)** (11)
ethnic **étnico/a** (14)
European **europeo/a** (14)
event **acontecimiento** (13); **suceso** (13)
every **todo/a/os/as;** every day **todos los días** (9); every night **todas las noches** (9)
exact **exacto/a** (6)
exchange (for) **cambiar (por)** (7)
exercise *v.* **hacer** (*irreg.*) **ejercicio** (6)
exile *n.* **exilio** (13); exile (*person*) **exilado/a** *n.* (13)
expensive **caro/a** (5)
exploit **explotar** (14)
expose **exponer** *irreg.* (13)
express one's feelings **expresar los sentimientos** (15)
exterior **exterior** *m.* (4)
eye *n.* **ojo** (1); black eyes **ojos negros** (1); blue eyes **ojos azules** (1); brown eyes **ojos castaños** (1); green eyes **ojos verdes** (1)

F
facing (+ *noun*) **enfrente (de + *noun*)** (2)
fall *v.* **caer** *irreg.;* fall asleep **dormirse (ue) (u)** (6); fall in love (with) **enamorarse (de)** (15)
fall (*season*) *n.* **otoño** (6)
familiar with: to be familiar with (*someone, some place, something*) **conocer (zc)** (6)
family **familia** (3)
fan *adj.* **aficionado/a** (8)
fantastic **fantástico** *adv.* (9)
farmers' market **mercado libre** (5)
fascinate (*someone*) **fascinarle** (9)
fat **gordo/a** (1)
father **padre** *m.* (3)
feast of Saint Barbara's **Día de Santa Bárbara** (9)
February **febrero** (6)
feel + *adj., adv.* **sentirse (ie, i) +** *adj., adv.* (9); to feel good/bad **sentirse (ie, i) bien/mal** (6); to feel like (*doing something*) **tener** (*irreg.*) **ganas de + *inf.*** (8)
few **poco/a** (3)
fifteen **quince** (1); fifteen minutes past (*hour*) **y quince** (6); fifteen minutes to (*hour*) **menos quince** (6)
fifty **cincuenta** (3)
fight *v.* **pelearse** (15)
fill (in/out) **llenar** (12)
find a mate **formar pareja** (15); to find out (*about something*) **saber** *irreg.* (6)
fine: I'm (very) fine, thanks **estoy (muy) bien, gracias** (1)
firefighter **bombero, mujer** (*f.*) **bombero** (12)
fireplace **chimenea** (4)
first communion **primera comunión** (9)
first course **primer plato** (5); as a first course **de primer plato** (5)
fish (*caught*) **pescado** (5); fish market **pescadería** (5)

fit (well/poorly) **quedarle (bien/mal)** (7)
five **cinco** (1)
five hundred **quinientos/as** (7)
flat (*apartment*) **piso** (4)
flatland **llanura** (10)
flexible schedule **horario flexible** (12)
follow a fixed (regular) routine **seguir (i, i) (g) una rutina fija** (6)
food: to prepare the food **preparar la comida** (4)
football **fútbol** (*m.*) **americano** (8)
for **por** (11); **para** (11); for life **para toda la vida** (15); for that (*reason*) **por eso** (11)
forest **bosque** *m.* (10)
forget **olvidar** (11)
form *n.* **formulario** (12); to form a romantic relationship **formar pareja** (15)
formal **formal** (4)
forty **cuarenta** (3)
forty-one **cuarenta y uno** (3)
four **cuatro** (1)
four hundred **cuatrocientos/as** (7)
fourteen **catorce** (1)
freedom of speech **libertad** (*f.*) **de palabra** (13); freedom of the press **libertad** (*f.*) **de prensa** (13)
freezer **nevera** (4)
French (*language*) **francés** *m.* (2); *adj.* **francés, francesa** (1)
frequent *v.* **frecuentar** (15)
frequently **a menudo** (9), **con frecuencia** (9)
fresh **fresco/a** (5)
Friday **viernes** (1)
fried **frito/a** (5)
friend **amigo/a** (2)
friendly **amable** (1)
friendship **amistad** *f.* (15)
from ____ until ____ **desde la(s) ____ hasta la(s) ____** (6); to be (from) **ser** (*irreg.*) **(de)** (1)

fruit **fruta** (5); fruit store **frutería** (5)

frustrated **frustrado/a** (9)

fry **freír (i, i)** (5)

full-time job **trabajo de tiempo completo** (12)

functional language **lenguaje funcional** (1)

funny **cómico/a** (13)

G

game **partido** (8); game show **concurso** (13)

garage **garaje** *m.* (4)

garden **jardín** *m.* (4)

garlic **ajo** (5)

gas stove **cocina de gas** (4)

gastronomy **gastronomía** (14)

generational conflict **conflicto generacional** (11)

German *adj.* **alemán, alemana** (1)

get **conseguir (i, i) (g)** (5); getting across the border **para cruzar (c) la frontera** (11); getting around (*lit.* orienting oneself in) the city **para orientarse en la ciudad** (10); to get along well/poorly **llevarse bien/mal** (15); to get connected (*to the Internet*) **conectarse** (13); to get divorced **divorciarse** (15); to get dressed **vestirse (i, i)** (6); to get engaged **comprometerse** (15); to get lost **perderse (ie)** (10); to get married **casarse** (15); to get off a bus (car/taxi) **bajar de un autobús (coche, taxi)** (10); to get off a plane (ship, train) **desbordar un avión (barco, train)** (10); to get on a bus (in a car/taxi) **subir a un autobús (coche, taxi)** (10); to get separated **separarse** (15); to get to know **llegar (gu) a conocer** (15); to get together with friends **reunirse (me reúno) con amigos** (6), **encontrarse (ue) con amigos** (8); to get up **levantarse** (6)

girl's fifteenth birthday party **quinceañera** (9)

give **dar** *irreg.* (3); to give (*something to someone*) as a gift **regalarle** (7)

glass (of wine) **una copa (de vino)** (5)

go **ir** *irreg.* (2); to go back **regresar** (2); to go by bus **ir** (*irreg.*) **en autobús** (10); to go by plane **ir** (*irreg.*) **en avión** (10); to go by train **ir** (*irreg.*) **en tren** (10); to go horseback riding **montar a caballo** (8); to go mountain climbing **escalar montañas** (8); to go on a trip **ir** (*irreg.*) **de viaje** (10); to go on an excursion/outing **hacer** (*irreg.*) **una excursión** (10); to go on foot (walk) **ir** (*irreg.*) **a pie** (10); to go on vacation **ir** (*irreg.*) **de vacaciones** (10); to go out as a couple **salir** (*irreg.*) **en pareja** (15); to go out (dancing) **salir** (*irreg.*) **(a bailar)** (3); to go shopping **ir** (*irreg.*) **de compras** (3); to go to bed **acostarse (ue)** (6); to go to the movies **ir** (*irreg.*) **al cine** (8); to go to the theater **ir** (*irreg.*) **al teatro** (8); to go well/poorly for (*someone*) **irle** (*irreg.*) **bien/mal** (11); let's go! **¡vamos!** (8)

godfather **padrino** (3)

godmother **madrina** (3)

gold bracelet **pulsera de oro** (7)

golf **golf** *m.* (8)

good **buen, bueno/a** (1); good afternoon/evening **buenas tardes** (1); Good Friday **Viernes Santo** (9); good morning **buenos días** (1); good night **buenas noches** (1); good-bye **adiós** (1); good-looking **guapo/a** (1)

gossip *n.* **chisme** (13)

government **gobierno** (13)

grandchildren **nietos** (3)

granddaughter **nieta** (3)

grandfather **abuelo** (3)

grandmother **abuela** (3)

grandparents **abuelos** (3)

grandson **nieto** (3)

grape **uva** (5)

gray **gris** (7)

great! **¡qué bien!** (13)

green **verde** (5); green (bell) pepper **pimiento verde** (5); green eyes **ojos verdes** (1)

greetings **saludos** (1)

gregarious **gregario/a** (3)

Guatamalan **guatemalteco/a** *n., adj.* (13)

guerilla war **guerrilla** (13)

guest **invitado/a** (8)

gym(nasium) **gimnasio** (2)

H

habit **costumbre** *f.* (11); to be in the habit of (*doing something*) **soler (ue)** + *inf.* (4)

hair **pelo** (1); black hair **pelo negro** (1); blond hair **pelo rubio** (1); brown hair **pelo castaño** (1); long hair **pelo largo** (1); short hair **pelo corto** (1)

half past **y media** (6)

hallway **pasillo** (4)

ham **jamón** (5)

hand: on one hand _____ on the other (hand) _____ **por un lado** _____ **por otro (lado)** _____ **/ en cambio** (10)

handicrafts market **mercado de artesanías** (7)

handsome **guapo/a** (1)

Hanukkah **Januká** *m.* (9)

happening **acontecimiento** (13); **suceso** (13)

happy **alegre** (1), **feliz** (*pl.* **felices**) (9); to be happy **estar** (*irreg.*) **contento/a** (6)

hardworking **trabajador(a)** (1)

harm *v.* **hacer** (*irreg.*) **daño** (15)

hat **sombrero** (7)

have **tener** *irreg.*; to have a cold **tener** (*irreg.*) **resfrío** (6), **tener** (*irreg.*) **un resfriado** (6); to

have a fever **tener** (*irreg.*) **fiebre** (6); to have citizenship **tener** (*irreg.*) **la ciudadanía** (11); to have coffee (a beer, a drink) **tomar un café (una cerveza, una copa)** (6); to have expectations **tener** (*irreg.*) **expectativas** (11); to have fun **divertirse (ie)** (6); to have hope **tener** (*irreg.*) **esperanza** (11); to have incompatible personalities **tener** (*irreg.*) **personalidades incompatibles** (15); to have incompatible values **tener** (*irreg.*) **valores incompatibles** (15); to have more access to education **tener** (*irreg.*) **más acceso a la enseñanza** (14); to have the flu **tener** (*irreg.*) **gripe** (6); to have to (*do something*) **tener** (*irreg.*) **que** + *inf.* (6); I have _____ **tengo** _____ (1); to intend to (*do something*) **tener** (*irreg.*) **la intención de** + *inf.* (11)

he **él** (1)

headache **dolor** (*m.*) **de cabeza** (6)

headline **encabezado** (13)

healthy **sano/a** (15)

hello **hola** (1)

help *v.* **ayudar** (11)

here **acá** (4); here you (*form. s.*) go **aquí lo/la/los/las tiene** (7)

hesitate to (*do something*) **dudar en** + *inf.* (15)

hide *v.* **esconder** (11)

history **historia** (13)

Holy Week **Semana Santa** (9)

honest **honesto/a** (15)

hope: to have hope **tener** (*irreg.*) **esperanza** (11)

hopeful: to be hopeful **tener** (*irreg.*) **esperanza** (11)

horrible *adv.* **horrible** (9)

horror film **película de horror** (13)

horseback riding **equitación** *f.* (8)

host/hostess **anfitrión, anfitriona** (8)

hot (*spicy*) **picante** (5); it's hot (*weather*) **hace calor** (6)

house (private, single-family) **casa (particular)** (4)

how? **¿cómo?** (2); how about if (*we do something*)? **¿qué tal si (nosotros/as) _____?** (8); how are you (*form. s.*)? **¿cómo está usted?** (1); how are you (*fam. s.*)? **¿cómo estás?** (1); how awful! **¡qué barbaridad!** (13); how cool/great! (*Carib.*) **¡qué chévere!** (8); how do you say _____ in Spanish? **¿cómo se dice _____ en español?** (1); how do you spell _____? **¿cómo se escribe _____?** (1); how many? **¿cuántos/as?** (2); how may I help you (*form. s.*)? **¿en qué puedo servirle?** (7); how much? **¿cuánto/a?** (2); how much does it / do they cost? **¿cuánto cuesta(n)?** (7); how old is he (she, you [*form. s.*])? **¿cuántos años tiene?** (3), **¿qué edad tiene?** (3); how wonderful! **¡qué bien!** (13); how's it going? **¿qué tal?** (1)

humanities **letras** (2)

humble **humilde** (4)

hungry: to be hungry **tener** (*irreg.*) **hambre** (5)

hurry: to be in a hurry **tener** (*irreg.*) **prisa** (8)

hurt **hacer** (*irreg.*) **daño** (15)

hurt: my _____ hurt(s) **me duele(n)** _____ (6)

husband **esposo** (3)

I

I **yo** (1)

ice skate **patinar sobre hielo** (8)

identify oneself (with) **identificarse (qu) (con)** (11)

identity **identidad** *f.* (11)

illegal **ilegal** (11)

illness **enfermedad** *f.* (6)

image **imagen** *f.* (*pl.* **imágenes**) (13)

immigration agent **agente de inmigración** (11)

important **importante** (2); it's important to (*do something*) **es importante** + *inf.* (6)

improve living conditions **mejorar las condiciones de vida** (14)

in **en** (2); in (+ *noun*) **dentro (de** + *noun*) (2); in contrast **en cambio** (10); in front of (+ *noun*) **enfrente (de** + *noun*) (2); in order that **para que** (14); in order to (*do something*) **para** + *inf.* (2); in spite of **a pesar de** (15); in the morning (in the afternoon/evening, at night) (*in general*) **por la mañana (tarde, noche)** (2); in the morning (in the afternoon/evening, at night) (*specific time*) **de la mañana (tarde, noche)** (2)

Incan **incaico/a** (14)

indifference **desinterés** (13)

indigenous person, native *n.* **indígena** *m., f.* (13)

inequality **desigualdad** *f.* (14)

inexpensive **barato/a** (5)

inexperienced **inocente** (9)

infancy **infancia** (9)

influence *n.* **influencia** (11); *v.* **influir (y) en** (13)

informal **informal** (4)

injustice **injusticia** (13)

inside (+ *noun*) **dentro (de** + *noun*) (2)

inspect **revisar** (11)

interest (*someone*) **interesarle** (9)

interested **interesado/a** (9)

interesting **interesante** (2)

interior **interior** *m.* (4)

international community **comunidad** (*f.*) **internacional** (13)

Internet **Internet** *m.* (13); Internet café **café** (*m.*) **cibernético** (13)

interstate **autopista** (10)

intimate relationship **relación íntima** (15)
intimidated **intimidado/a** (9)
irritate (*someone*) **irritarle** (9)
irritated **irritado/a** (9)
isolated **aislado/a** (15)
Italian *adj.* **italiano/a** (1)
itinerary **itinerario** (10)

J
jacket **chaqueta** (7)
January **enero** (6)
Japanese *adj.* **japonés, japonesa** (1)
jealous: to be jealous **tener** (*irreg.*) **celos** (15)
jeans **(pantalones) vaqueros** *pl.* (7)
jewelery **joyería** (7)
job **puesto** (12); job placement agency **agencia de colocaciones** (12)
July **julio** (6)
June **junio** (6)
jungle **selva** (10)
just in case **por si acaso** (11); just like **al igual que** (3)

K
kiosk **quiosco** (10)
kitchen **cocina** (4)
knit *v.* **tejer** (8)
know (*facts, information*) **saber** *irreg.* (6); to know (*someone, some place, something*) **conocer (zc)** (6); to know about **estar** (*irreg.*) **enterado/a de** (13); to know how to (*do something*) **saber** (*irreg.*) + *inf.* (6)
knowledge **conocimientos** *pl.* (12)

L
Labor Day (May 1) **Día** (*m.*) **del Trabajador** (9)
laboratory **laboratorio**; chemistry laboratory **laboratorio de química** (2); language laboratory **laboratorio de lenguas** (2)

lake **lago** (10)
lament **lamentar** (13)
lamentable **lamentable** (13)
lamp **lámpara** (4); (*overhead*) **luz** *f.* (4)
land: ancestral land **territorio ancestral** (14)
landscape **paisaje** *m.* (10)
large **grande** (1); to be too large **quedarle grande** (7)
late **tarde** (6)
laugh *v.* **reírse (i, i)** (9)
law **ley** *f.* (11)
lawyer **abogado/a** (12)
lazy **perezoso/a** (1)
learn **aprender** (11)
leather **cuero** (7)
leave *v.* **salir** *irreg.* (3)
legal **legal** (11)
lemon **limón** *m.* (5)
less **menos**; less + *adj.* + than **menos** + *adj.* + **que** (5); the least + *adj.* **el/la/los/las menos** + *adj.* (5)
letter **carta** (3); letter of recommendation **carta de recomendación** (12); to write letters **escribir cartas** (3)
lettuce **lechuga** (5)
level **nivel** *m.* (12); level of education **nivel** (*m.*) **de educación** (14)
librarian **bibliotecario/a** (12)
library **biblioteca** (2)
lie *n.* **mentira** (13); *v.* **mentir (ie, i)** (13)
lift weights **levantar pesas** (8)
light skin **piel** (*f.*) **clara** (1)
light(ing) **luz** *f.* (4)
like (*as*) *adv.* **como** (1)
like *v.* (*someone*) **caerle** (*irreg.*) **bien** (9); I (don't) like ____ **(no) me gusta(n)** ____ (2); I don't like it/them at all! **¡no me gusta(n) para nada!** (7); I would like ____ **me gustaría(n)** ____ (5); no, I wouldn't like that **no, no me gustaría eso** (8)
likewise **igualmente** (1)

link **enlace** *m.* (13)
listen (to) **escuchar** (2)
literature **literatura** (2)
little **poco/a**; a little of **un poco de** (5); little **pequeño/a** (1)
live **vivir** (3); to live with uncertainty **vivir con la incertidumbre** (11)
living room **salón** (4)
loan *v.* **prestar** (15)
lobster **langosta** (5)
long hair **pelo largo** (1)
look for **buscar (qu)** (11); I'm looking for ____ **busco** ____ (7)
lose **perder (ie)** (8)
love *n.* **amor** *m.* (15); *v.* to love (*someone*) **querer (ie)** (7); to love (*thing*) **encantarle** (7); to love each other **quererse (ie)** (15)
lucky: to be lucky **tener** (*irreg.*) **suerte** (11)
luxurious **lujoso/a** (4)
luxury **lujo** (4)

M
made by hand **estar** (*irreg.*) **hecho/a a mano** (7); to be well/poorly made **estar** (*irreg.*) **hecho/a bien/mal** (7)
main course **plato principal** (5); as a main course **de plato principal** (5)
maintain **mantener** (*like* **tener**); **preservar** (11); to maintain a fixed (*regular*) routine **mantener** (*like* **tener**) **una rutina fija** (6); to maintain distance between the two **mantener** (*like* **tener**) **la distancia entre los dos** (15); to maintain traditional values **mantener** (*like* **tener**) **los valores tradicionales** (14)
major **carrera** (2)
majority **mayoría** (14)
make **hacer** *irreg.* (3); to make someone feel + *adj.* **ponerle** + *adj.* **a alguien** (9)

mall **centro comercial** (7)
many **muchos/as** (2)
March **marzo** (6)
marginalized **marginado/a** (14)
market *n.* **mercado** (5)
married: to be married **estar** (*irreg.*) **casado/a** (3)
marry **casarse** (15)
marvelous **maravilloso** *adv.* (9)
match (*game*) **partido** (8)
mate **pareja** (15)
maternal **materno/a** (3)
mathematics **matemáticas** (2)
matter to (*someone*) **importarle** (9)
May **mayo** (6)
means of transport **medios de transporte** (10)
measure *v.* **medir (i, i)** (5)
meat **carne** *f.* (5)
mechanic **mecánico/a** (12)
medicine **medicina** (6)
meet new/other people **conocer (zc) a otras personas** (8)
member **miembro** (3)
mental health **salud** (*f.*) **mental** (6)
message **mensaje** *m.* (13)
metro station **estación** (*f.*) **del metro** (10)
Mexican *adj.* **mexicano/a** (1)
middle class **clase** (*f.*) **media** (14)
milk **leche** *f.* (5)
mineral water **agua** (*f.* [*but* **el agua**]) **mineral** (5)
minimum experience **experiencia mínima** (12); minimum salary **sueldo mínimo** (12)
minority *n.* **minoría** (14); *adj.* **minoritario/a** (14)
minute **minuto;** it's _____ minute(s) till _____ **son la(s) _____ menos _____;** it's _____ minutes to _____ **falta(n) _____ minuto(s) para la(s) _____** (6)
Miss (*unmarried woman*) **señorita** (1)

miss a bus (ship, train, flight) **perder (ie) un autobús (barco, tren, vuelo)** (10)
mixed-race (*person*) **mestizo/a** *n.* (14)
mixture **mezcla** (11)
modern **moderno/a** (4)
Monday **lunes** (1)
month **mes** *m.* (6)
monument **monumento** (10)
mood: to be in the mood **encontrarse (ue) en ambiente** (8)
more **más;** more + *adj.* + than **más** + *adj.* + **que** (5); the most + *adj.* **el/la/los/las más** + *adj.* (5)
mother **madre** *f.* (3)
mount(ain) **cerro** (10)
mountain peak **pico** (10); mountain range **cordillera** (10), **sierra** (10)
moved (*emotionally*) **emocionado/a** (9)
movie theater **cine** (13)
movies **cine** (13)
Mr. **señor** (1)
Mrs. (*married woman*) **señora** (1)
Ms. (*unmarried woman*) **señorita** (1)
much; *pl.* many **mucho/a** (2)
multilingual **multilingüe** (12)
museum **museo** (10)
mushroom **champiñón** *m.* (5)
music **música** (2)
must: you (*form. s.*) must get more rest **debe descansar más** (6)

N

naive **inocente** (9)
name **nombre;** my name is **me llamo _____** (1)
nationality **nacionalidad** *f.* (1)
native **indígena** (13); native language **lengua nativa** (11)
natural disaster **desastre** (*m.*) **natural** (13)
necessary **necesario/a** (2); it's

necessary to (*do something*) **es necesario** + *inf.* (6)
necessity **necesidad** (4)
necklace **collar** *m.* (7)
need to (*do something*) **necesitar** + *inf.* (6)
neighbor **vecino/a** (4)
neighborhood **barrio** (4); neighborhood market **mercado del barrio** (5)
neither **tampoco** (8); neither _____ nor _____ **ni _____ ni _____** (8)
nephew **sobrino** (3)
nervous **nervioso/a** (9)
never **jamás** (8); **nunca** (8); never ever **nunca jamás** (8)
news **noticias** (13)
newscast **noticiero** (13)
Nicaraguan **nicaragüense** *n.* (13)
nice (pleasure) to meet you **encantado/a** (1), **mucho gusto** (1)
niece **sobrina** (3)
night table **mesilla de noche** (4)
nine **nueve** (1)
nine hundred **novecientos/as** (7)
nineteen **diecinueve** (1)
ninety **noventa** (3)
no **no** (2); **nada de** (5); *adj.* **ningún, ninguna** (5); no one **nadie** (8)
Nobel Peace Prize **Premio Nobel de la Paz** (13)
nobody **nadie** (8)
noise **ruido** (8)
none *pron.* **ninguno/a** (8)
not **no** (2); not any **nada de** (5); **ningún, ninguna** (5); *pron.* **ninguno/a** (8); not anybody **nadie** (8); not either **tampoco** (8); not ever **jamás** (8); **nunca** (8); not to be pleasing (*to someone*) **disgustarle** (9)
notebook **cuaderno** (2)
nothing **nada** (5)
November **noviembre** (6)
number **número** (1)
numerous **numeroso/a** (14)
nurse *n.* **enfermero/a** (12)

O

o'clock: it's _____ o'clock **es la / son las** _____ (6)
obituary **obituario** (13)
objective **objetivo** (12)
obtain **conseguir (i, i) (g)** (5)
occupation **oficio** (12)
ocean **océano** (10)
October **octubre** (6)
of/from the **del** (_contraction of_ **de + el**) (2)
offer _n._ **oferta** (12); _v._ **ofrecer (zc)** (12)
OK **regular** (1); OK, I'll take it/them **bueno, me lo/la/los/las llevo** (7)
old **viejo/a** (5); old age **vejez** (9)
older (than) **mayor (que)** (3); older person **persona mayor** (9)
olive oil **aceite** (_m._) **de oliva** (5)
on a walk **de paseo** (15); on one hand _____ on the other (hand) _____ **por un lado** _____ **por otro (lado)** _____ (10); on the dot **en punto** (6); on the inside **por dentro** (4); on the outside **por fuera** (4); on the right/left (hand side) **a mano derecha/izquierda** (10); on time **a tiempo** (6)
one **uno** (1)
one hundred, a hundred **cien(to)** (3)
one hundred five **ciento cinco** (3)
one thousand **mil** (7)
one-way **de ida** (10)
onion **cebolla** (5)
online newspaper **periódico en línea** (13)
only **solamente** (11), **sólo** (11); only child **hijo/a único/a** (3)
open your (_form. s._) mouth **abra la boca** (6)
opportunity for advancement **oportunidad** (_f._) **de avanzar** (12)

optimistic **optimista** _m., f._ (9)
optional **optativo/a** (2)
orange (_color_) _adj._ **anaranjado/a** (7); (_fruit_) _n._ **naranja** (5)
origin **origen** _m._ (_pl._ **orígenes**) (1)
other **otro/a** (3); _pl._ **los/las demás** (15)
ought to (_do something_) **deber + inf.** (6)
outskirts **afueras** (4)
oven **horno** (4)
overcoat **abrigo** (7)
overcome economic barriers **superar las barreras económicas** (14)
overwhelming **abrumador(a)** (13)

P

pact **pacto** (13)
paint **pintar** (8)
painting **cuadra** (4)
pants **pantalones** _m. pl._ (7)
parents **padres** (3)
part **parte** _f._ (11)
part-time job **trabajo de tiempo parcial** (12)
participate **participar** (2)
partner **pareja** (15)
party **fiesta** (8)
pass (free time) **pasar (el tiempo libre)** (3)
Passover **Pesaj** _m._ (9)
pastimes **pasatiempos** (8)
pastry **pastel** _m._ (5)
paternal **paterno/a** (3)
patio **patio** (4)
pay **pagar (gu)** (7)
pencil **lápiz** (_pl._ **lápices**) _m._ (2)
pendant **pendiente** _m._ (7)
pepper (black) **pimienta** (5); bell pepper (red, green) **pimiento (rojo/verde)** (5)
percent **por ciento** (11)
perhaps **quizá(s)** (11)
Peruvian _n., adj._ **peruano/a** (14)
pessimistic **pesimista** _m., f._ (9)
philosophy **filosofía** (2)
photographer **fotógrafo/a** (12)

physical health **salud** (_f._) **física** (6); physical strength **fuerza física** (12)
picture _n._ **cuadro** (4)
pie **pastel** _m._ (5)
piece of news **noticia** (13)
pilot **piloto/a** (12)
pineapple **piña** (5)
pink **rosado/a** (7)
plain (high) **altiplano** (14)
plateau **altiplano** (14)
play (_a game_) **jugar (ue) (gu) a** (4); to play baseball **jugar (ue) (gu) al béisbol** (4); to play basketball **jugar (ue) (gu) al baloncesto** (_Sp._) (4); to play billiards (pool) **jugar (ue) (gu) al billar** (8); to play cards **jugar (ue) (gu) a los naipes** (8); to play chess **jugar (ue) (gu) al ajedrez** (8); to play music **tocar (qu) música** (8); to play soccer **jugar (ue) (gu) al fútbol** (4); to play video games **jugar (ue) (gu) a los videojuegos** (8)
player **jugador(a)** (8)
plaza **plaza** (10)
pleasing: to be pleasing to (_someone_) **gustarle** (9)
political party **partido político** (13)
politician **político/a** (12)
poor **pobre** (14)
pork **carne** (_f._) **de cerdo** (5)
port **puerto** (10)
position (_job_) **puesto** (12)
possession **posesión** (3)
post office **oficina de correos** (10)
poster **cuartel** _m._ (4)
potato **papa** (_Lat. Am._) (5)
poverty **pobreza** (11)
powerless **impotente** (14)
practical **práctico/a** (2)
practice **practicar (qu)** (2); to practice a sport **practicar (qu) un deporte** (8); to practice martial arts **hacer** (_irreg._) **artes marciales** (8)

prairie **llanura** (10)

prefer **preferir (ie, i)** (4)

prepare the meal/food **preparar la comida** (4)

preserve **preservar** (11)

press *n.* **prensa** (13)

prestige **prestigio** (12)

pretty **bonito/a** (1); **guapo/a** (1)

price **precio** (7)

profession **profesión** *f.* (12)

program **programa** *m.* (13)

promising future **futuro prometedor** (12)

pronoun **pronombre** (1)

prosperous: to be prosperous **ser** *(irreg.)* **próspero/a** (11)

protect (the rights of) workers **proteger (j) a los obreros** (14)

proud **orgulloso/a** (9)

psychology **psicología** (2)

publish **publicar (qu)** (13)

Puerto Rican *adj.* **puertorriqueño/a** (1)

purple **morado/a** (7)

purse **bolsa** (7)

put on *(clothing)* **ponerse** *irreg.* (7)

Q

quality **calidad** *f.* (7)

quantity **cantidad** *f.* (5)

quarter **cuarto;** quarter past *(time)* **y cuarto** (6); quarter to *(hour)* **menos cuarto** (6)

R

raincoat **impermeable** *m.* (7)

raining: it's raining **llueve** (6)

rarely **raras veces** (9)

rather, *adv.* **bastante** (11)

raw **crudo/a** (5)

read **leer (y)** (3); to read magazines **leer (y) revistas** (3); to read novels **leer (y) novelas** (3); to read the newspaper **leer (y) el periódico** (3)

reader **lector(a)** (13)

reason **razón** *f.* (11)

rebellious **rebelde** (9)

recommend **recomendar (ie)** (5)

reconfirm **reconfirmar** (10)

red (bell) pepper **pimiento rojo** (5)

reduction **rebaja** (7)

refrigerator **refrigerador** *m.* (4)

refugee **refugiado/a** *n.* (13)

region **región** *f.* (14)

regret **lamentar** (13)

regretful **lamentable** (13)

rejected **rechazado/a** (14)

relaxation **relajación** *f.* (6)

relaxed: to be relaxed **estar** *(irreg.)* **relajado/a** (8)

religion **religión** (14)

remain (in bed, at home) **quedarse (en cama, en casa)** (6)

remedy **remedio** (6)

remember **recordar (ue)** (9)

renew **renovar (ue)** (11)

report *n.* **reportaje** *m.* (13); *v.* report *(expose)* **exponer** *irreg.* (13)

reporter **reportero/a** (13)

request **pedir (i, i)** (5)

require **requerir (ie, i)** (12)

required **obligatorio/a** (2)

requirement **requisito** (12)

resemble **parecerse (zc) a** (10)

resentment **resentimiento** (14)

residence hall **residencia estudiantil** (2)

residential street **calle** *(f.)* **residencial** (4); residential zone/area **zona residencial** (4)

resolve **resolver (ue)** (13)

respectful **respetuoso/a** (9)

responsibility **responsabilidad** *f.* (12)

rest *v.* **descansar** (3)

résumé **currículum (vitae)** (12)

retired: to be retired **estar** *(irreg.)* **jubilado/a** (3)

return *(something)* **devolver (ue)** (7); to return *(go back)* **regresar** (2); to return *(to a place)* **volver (ue)** (4)

reveal one's secrets **revelar los secretos** (15)

review *n.* **reseña** (13)

revolution **revolución** *f.* (13)

rice **arroz** *m.* (5)

rich **rico/a** (14)

ride a bicycle **andar (irreg.) en bicicleta** (8)

ridiculous **ridículo/a** (13)

rights **derechos** *pl.* (13)

ring **anillo** (7)

ripe **maduro/a** (5)

risk-taking **arriesgado/a** (12)

river **río** (10)

rob **robar** (14)

romantic film **película de amor** (13)

romanticism **romanticismo** (15)

room **cuarto** (4), **habitación** *f.* (4)

root **raíz** *f.* *(pl.* **raíces)** (11)

round-trip **de ida y vuelta** (10)

rug **alfombra** (4)

run **correr** (8); run the risk **correr el riesgo** (11)

S

sad: to be sad **estar** *(irreg.)* **triste** (6)

saint's day **día** *(m.)* **del santo** (9)

salad **ensalada** (5)

salesperson **dependiente/a** (7)

salt **sal** *f.* (5)

salty **salado/a** (5)

Salvadoran **salvadoreño/a** *n.* (13)

same here **igualmente** (1)

sandwich **sándwich** *m.* (5)

satellite TV **televisión** *(f.)* **de antena parabólica** (13)

Saturday **sábado** (1)

save *(money)* **ahorrar** (11)

savory **sabroso/a** (5)

say **decir** *irreg.* (5); say *(form. s.)* "ahhh" **diga «aaaa»** (6)

scandalous **escandaloso/a** (13)

schedule **horario** (2)

school **facultad** (2); School of Education **Facultad de Educación** (2); School of Liberal Arts (Humanities) **Facultad de Letras** (2); School of Sciences **Facultad de Ciencias** (2)

science **ciencia** (2)

scientist **científico/a** (12)

season (*of the year*) **estación** *f.* (6)
secretary **secretario/a** (12)
see **ver** *irreg.* (3); let's see **vamos a ver** (6); see (one's) the relatives **ver** (*irreg.*) **a los parientes** (3); see you around **nos vemos** (1)
seem: it seems to me **se me hace** (*Mex.*) (11)
sell **vender** (7)
send back **mandar de regreso** (11)
sensible **sensato/a** (9)
sensitive **sensible** (9)
separate **separarse** (15)
September **septiembre** (6)
serve **servir** (i, i) (5)
set up **fijar** (12)
seven **siete** (1)
seven hundred **setecientos/as** (7)
seventeen **diecisiete** (1)
seventy **setenta** (3)
sew **coser** (8)
share **compartir** (4)
shave **afeitarse** (6)
she **ella** (1)
shellfish **marisco** (5)
shelving **estantería** (4)
ship *n.* **barco** (10)
shirt **camisa** (7)
shocking **chocante** (13)
shoes **zapatos** *pl.* (7)
shop *n.* **tienda** (7)
shopping: to do the shopping **hacer** (*irreg.*) **la compra** (5); to go shopping **ir** (*irreg.*) **de compras** (3)
shopping center **centro comercial** (7)
short **bajo/a** (1); short hair **pelo corto** (1)
shorts **pantalones cortos** (7)
should (*do something*) **deber** + *inf.* (6)
show (*something to someone*) **mostrarle (ue)** (7); to show affection in public **mostrar (ue) cariño en público** (15)
shower *n.* **ducha** (4); *v.* **ducharse** (6)

shrimp **camarón** (5)
shy **tímido/a** (9)
siblings **hermanos** (3)
siblings-in-law **cuñados** (3)
sick: to be sick **estar** (*irreg.*) **enfermo/a** (6)
silk **seda** (7)
silver necklace **collar de plata** (7)
similar (to) **parecido/a (a)** (1); **similar (a)** (1)
simple **sencillo/a** (4)
sing **cantar** (8)
single **soltero/a** (3)
sink (*bathroom*) **lavabo** (4); (*kitchen*) **fregadero** (4)
sister **hermana** (3)
sister-in-law **cuñada** (3)
six **seis** (1)
six hundred **seiscientos/as** (7)
sixteen **dieciséis** (1)
sixty **sesenta** (3)
size (*clothing*) **talla**; (*shoes*) **número**; what size (*clothing*) do you (*form. s.*) wear? **¿qué talla lleva?** (7); what size (*shoes*) do you (*form. s.*) wear? **¿qué número lleva?** (7)
skate **patinar** (8)
ski *n.* **esquí** *m.* (8); *v.* **esquiar (esquío)** (8); to water ski **esquiar en el agua** (8)
skiing **esquí** *m.* (8)
skill **competencia** (12)
skin **piel** *f.* (1); brown skin **piel** (*f.*) **morena** (1); dark skin **piel** (*f.*) **oscura** (1); light skin **piel** (*f.*) **clara** (1)
skirt **falda** (7)
sleep **dormir** (ue, u) (4)
small **pequeño/a** (1); to be too small **quedarle pequeño/a** (7)
smile *v.* **sonreír** (i, i) (9)
smoke **fumar** (8)
smuggler of illegal immigrants **coyote** *m., f.* (11)
snack (*afternoon*) *n.* **merienda** (5); *v.* **merendar (ie)** (4)
snorkle **bucear** (8)
snowing: it's snowing **nieva** (6)

so that **para que** (14)
soap opera **telenovela** (13)
social problem **problema** (*m.*) **social** (14); social sciences **ciencias sociales** (2); social worker **asistente social** (12)
sociology **sociología** (2)
socks **calcetines** *pl.* (7)
sofa **sofá** *m.* (4)
soft drink **refresco** (3)
some **algo de** (5); *adj.* **algún, alguna/os/as** (5); *adj.* **unos/as** (1)
something **algo** (5)
sometimes **a veces** (9)
son **hijo** (3)
so-so **más o menos** (1)
soup **sopa** (5)
sour **agrio/a** (5)
Spanish (*language*) **español** *m.* (2); *n., adj.* **español(a)** (1)
speak **hablar** (2)
specialty store **tienda especializada** (7)
speech **habla** *f.* (*but* **el habla**) (14)
spell: it's spelled _____ **se escribe** _____ (1)
spend (*free time*) **pasar (el tiempo libre)** (3); spend time with the (one's) children **pasar tiempo con los hijos** (3)
spicy **picante** (5)
spite: in spite of **a pesar de** (15)
sportsperson **deportista** (8)
spouses **esposos** (3)
spring **primavera** (6)
square (*plaza*) **plaza** (10)
stability **estabilidad** *f.* (13)
stadium **estadio** (2)
stage **etapa** (9)
stale **viejo/a** (5)
stare (deeply) into each other's eyes **mirarse (profundamente) a los ojos** (15)
stay (in bed, at home) **quedarse (en cama, en casa)** (6); to stay informed **mantenerse** (*irreg.*) **informado/a** (13)

steak **bistec** *m.* (5)
steal **robar** (14)
stepbrother **hermanastro** (3)
stepfather **padrastro** (3)
stepmother **madrastra** (3)
stepsiblings **hermanastros** (3)
stepsister **hermanastra** (3)
stick out your (*form. s.*) tongue **saque la lengua** (6)
stockings **medias** (7)
stop **detener** *irreg.* (11); to stop (over) in **parar en** (10)
store (specialty) **tienda (especializada)** (7)
stove: (electric/gas) stove unit **cocina eléctrica / de gas** (4)
street **calle** *f.* (4)
stress **estrés** *m.* (6)
stressed **tenso/a** (9)
student **estudiante** *m., f.* (2)
studies **estudios** (2)
study *v.* **estudiar** (2)
stupendous **estupendo** *adv.* (9)
subscribe **abonarse** (13)
suburbs **afueras** (4)
subway **metro** (10); subway station **estación** (*f.*) **del metro** (10)
successful: to be successful **tener** (*irreg.*) **éxito** (11)
suffer from anxiety (stress, insomnia) **sufrir de ansiedad (estrés, insomnio)** (6)
sufficient **suficiente** (11)
sugar **azúcar** *m.* (5)
suit **traje** *m.* (7)
suitcase **maleta** (10)
summer **verano** (6)
Sunday **domingo** (1)
sunny: it's sunny (*weather*) **hace sol** (6)
super *adv.* **súper** (11)
superhighway **autopista** (10)
supermarket **supermercado** (5)
surf *v.* **surfear** (8); surf (*the Internet*) **navegar (gu)** (13)
surgeon **cirujano/a** (12)
suspend **suspender** (13)
sweater **suéter** *m.* (7)
sweet **dulce** (5)

swim **nadar** (8)
swimming **natación** *f.* (8); swimming pool **piscina** (4)
swindle **engañar** (14)

T
table **mesa** (4)
take (*a class*) **llevar** (2); to take a bath **bañarse** (6); to take a shower **ducharse** (6); to take a siesta (nap) **dormir (ue, u) la siesta** (4), **echar una siesta** (3), **tomar una siesta** (6); to take a trip **hacer** (*irreg.*) **un viaje** (10); to take a walk **pasear** (3); to take off **quitarse** (7)
tall **alto/a** (1)
taxi **taxi** *m.* (10); taxi stand **parada de taxis** (10)
tea **té** *m.* (5)
teach **enseñar** (2)
teacher **profesor(a)** (2)
team **equipo** (8)
teenager **adolescente** (9)
telephone **teléfono** (4); telephone company office **telefónica** (10)
television *adj.* **televisivo/a** (13); television channel **canal** *m.* (13); television viewer **televidente** (13)
tell **decir** *irreg.* (5); to tell jokes **contar (ue) chistes** (8)
ten **diez** (1)
tender **tierno/a** (5)
tennis **tenis** *m.* (8); tennis shoes **zapatos de tenis** (7)
terrace **terraza** (4)
terrible **horrible** (9)
testimony **testimonio** (13)
textbook **libro de texto** (2)
thank you for + *noun or inf.* **gracias por** + *noun or inf.* (11)
Thanksgiving **Día** (*m.*) **de (Acción de) Gracias** (9)
that **ese/a** *adj.* (4); that _____ over there **aquel, aquella** _____ *adj.* (4); that (stuff) *neut. pron.* **eso** (4); that (stuff) over there *neut. pron.* **aquello** (4); that one *pron.* **ése/a** (4); that

one over there *pron.* **aquél, aquélla** (4); that seems (doesn't seem) very interesting **(no) me parece muy interesante** (8); that's why **por eso** (11)
the **el** (*m. s.*), **la** (*f. s.*), **los** (*m. pl.*), **las** (*f. pl.*) (1)
theater **teatro** (10)
there **ahí** (4); (way) over there **allá, allí** (4)
there is/are (not) **(no) hay** (2)
these **estos/as** *adj.* (4); these ones *pron.* **éstos/as** (4)
they *f. pl.* **ellas** (1); *m. pl.* **ellos** (1)
thin **delgado/a** (1)
think (of, about) **pensar (ie) (de/en)** (4)
thirteen **trece** (1)
thirty **treinta** (1)
thirty-eight **treinta y ocho** (3)
thirty-five **treinta y cinco** (3)
thirty-four **treinta y cuatro** (3)
thirty-nine **treinta y nueve** (3)
thirty-one **treinta y uno** (1)
thirty-seven **treinta y siete** (3)
thirty-six **treinta y seis** (3)
thirty-three **treinta y tres** (3)
thirty-two **treinta y dos** (3)
this **este/a** *adj.* (4); this one *pron.* **éste/a** (4); this (stuff) *neut. pron.* **esto** (4)
those **esos/as** *adj.* (4); those _____ over there *adj.* **aquellos/as** (4); those ones *pron.* **ésos/as** (4); those ones over there *pron.* **aquéllos/as** (4)
three **tres** (1)
three hundred **trescientos/as** (7)
throat **garganta** (6)
through **por** (11)
Thursday **jueves** (1)
ticket **billete** *m.* (*Sp.*) (10); **boleto** *m.* (*Lat. Am.*) (10)
tie *n.* **corbata** (7)
time **hora** (6); what time is it? **¿qué hora es?** (6)
tired: to be tired **estar** (*irreg.*) **cansado/a** (6)
to **a** (2)

to the **al** (*contraction of* **a** + **el**)
(2); to the left (of + *noun*) **a
la izquierda** (**de** + *noun*) (2);
to the north (south, east,
west) **hacia el norte (sur,
este, oeste)** (10); to the right
(of + *noun*) **a la derecha**
(**de** + *noun*) (2)

toast **tostada** (5)
together **junto/a** (3)
toilet **retrete** *m.* (4)
tomato **tomate** *m.* (5)
too **también** (1); too (much)
demasiado *adv.* (11)
toward **para** (11)
town **pueblo** (4); town hall
ayuntamiento (10)
tradition **tradición** *f.* (14)
traditional **tradicional** (4);
traditional belief **creencia
tradicional** (14); traditional
workday **jornada
tradicional** (12)
train **tren** *m.* (10); train station
estación (*f.*) **de trenes** (10)
trainer: (personal) trainer
entrenador(a) (personal) (12)
translator **traductor(a)** (12)
travel **viajar** (10); travel agency
agencia de viajes (10); travel
agent **agente de viajes** (10)
trick *v.* **engañar** (14)
trip: to be on a trip **estar** (*irreg.*)
de viaje (10)
truce **pacto** (13)
trusting **confiado/a** (9)
truth **verdad** (13)
try: to try on **probarse (ue)** (7);
to try to maintain one's
customs **tratar de mantener
las costumbres** (11)
T-shirt **camiseta** (7)
Tuesday **martes** (1)
turn right/left **doblar a la
derecha/izquierda** (10)
twelve **doce** (1)
twenty **veinte** (1)
twenty-eight **veintiocho** (1)
twenty-five **veinticinco** (1)
twenty-four **veinticuatro** (1)

twenty-nine **veintinueve** (1)
twenty-one **veintiuno** (1)
twenty-seven **veintisiete** (1)
twenty-six **veintiséis** (1)
twenty-three **veintitrés** (1)
twenty-two **veintidós** (1)
twin **gemelo/a** (3)
two **dos** (1)
two hundred **doscientos/as** (7)
two thousand **dos mil** (7)

U
ugly **feo/a** (1)
uh . . . (*pause sound*) **este...** (8)
uncle **tío** (3)
underdeveloped
subdesarrollado/a (14)
understand **entender (ie)** (4)
underwear **ropa interior** (7)
undocumented person
indocumentado/a (11)
unfriendly **antipático/a** (1)
unhappy **infeliz**
(*pl.* **infelices**) (9)
uninformed: to be
uninformed **estar** (*irreg.*)
desinformado/a (13)
university **universidad** (2)
unlike **a diferencia de** (3)
unmarried **soltero/a** (3)
unripe **verde** (5)
until (see you) later **hasta luego**
(1); see you soon **hasta pronto**
(1); until (see you) tomorrow
hasta mañana (1)
up-to-date: to be up-to-date **estar**
(*irreg.*) **al corriente** (13)
use *v.* **usar** (2)
useful **útil** (2)

V
vacation: to be on vacation **estar**
(*irreg.*) **de vacaciones** (10)
valley **valle** *m.* (14)
value **valor** *m.* (11)
VCR **video** (13)
vegetable **vegetal** *m.* (5),
verdura (5); vegetable
store **verdulería** (5)
very (*adv.*) **bastante** (11)

veterinarian **veterinario/a** (12)
video **video** (13); to play video
games **jugar (ue) (gu) a los
videojuegos** (8)
visit the (one's) relatives **visitar
a los parientes** (3)
volcano **volcán** *m.* (10)
volleyball **voleibol** *m.* (8)

W
waiter **mesero** (5)
waitress **mesera** (5)
wake up **despertarse (ie)** (6)
walk **caminar** (10)
wallet **cartera** (7)
want **querer (ie)** (4); **desear** (5)
wash one's face (back, hands)
**lavarse la cara (la espalda,
las manos)** (6)
washing machine **lavadora** (4)
watch *n.* **reloj** *m.* (7); *v.* to
watch **mirar**; to watch a film
ver (*irreg.*) **una película** (8);
to watch TV **mirar la
televisión** (3), **ver** (*irreg.*)
la televisión (3)
waterfall **salto** (10); *pl.*
cataratas (10)
we **nosotros/as** (1)
wealthy **rico/a** (14)
wear (*clothing*) **llevar** (7); **ponerse**
irreg. (7)
weather: it's good/bad weather
hace buen/mal tiempo (6)
wedding **boda** (15)
Wednesday **miércoles** (1)
weight: to lift weights **levantar
pesas** (8)
welcoming **acogedor(a)** (4)
well, actually _____ **pues, la
verdad es que** _____ (8)
well-being: emotional
well-being **bienestar
emocional** (15)
what? **¿qué?** (2); **¿cómo?**;
(*which?*) **¿cuál(es)?** (2); what
about this (one) / these
(ones) here? **¿qué tal
éste/a/os/as aquí?** (7); what
are _____ like? **¿cómo son**

_____? (1); what can I bring you as/for _____? **¿qué le(s) traigo _____?** (5); what do you (_form. s._) recommend? **¿qué recomienda (usted)?** (5); what is _____ like? **¿cómo es _____?** (1); what is/are _____ 's/s' (national) origin(s)? **¿de qué origen es/son _____?** (1); what time is it? **¿qué hora es?** (6); what would you (_form. s., pl._) like (to eat)? **¿qué desea(n) (de comer)?** (5); what's the weather like? **¿qué tiempo hace?** (6); what's up? **¿qué tal?** (7); what's wrong? **¿qué le pasa?** (6), **¿qué tiene hoy?** (6); what's your (_form. s._) name? **¿cómo se llama usted?** (1); what's your (_fam. s._) name? **¿cómo te llamas?** (1)

what a + _adj._! **¡qué + _adj._!** (13); what a/an + _adj._ + _noun_! **¡qué + _noun_ + más/tan + _adj._!** (13); what a good idea! **¡qué buena idea!** (8); what a scandal! **¡qué escándalo!** (13)

when? **¿cuándo?** (2)

where? **¿dónde?;** to where **¿adónde?** (2); where are you (_form. s._) from? **¿de dónde es usted?** (1); where are you (_fam. s._) from? **¿de dónde eres (tú)?** (1); where is he/she from? **¿de dónde es el/ella?** (1); where is it (located)? **¿dónde está?** (2)

which? **¿cuál(es)?** (2)

while **mientras que** (10)

white **blanco/a** (7)

who? **¿quíen(es)?** (2)

why? **¿por qué?** why don't (_we do something_)? **¿por qué no (nosotros/as) _____?** (8)

wife **esposa** (3)

win **ganar** (8)

window **ventana** (4)

windy: it's windy (_weather_) **hace viento** (6)

wine **vino** (3); a glass of wine **una copa de vino** (5)

winter **invierno** (6)

wise **sabio/a** (9)

with **con** (2)

within (+ _noun_) **dentro (de + _noun_)** (2)

without hesitation **sin dudar** (15)

wool **lana** (7)

work _v._ **trabajar** (2)

working conditions **condiciones (_f._) de trabajo** (12)

worse than **peor(es) que** (5)

would you (_fam. s._) like to (_do something_)? **¿te gustaría + _inf._?** (8)

write **escribir;** to write letters **escribir cartas** (3); to write stories/poetry **escribir cuentos/poesía** (8)

writer **escritor(a)** (12)

Y

years: to be _____ (and a half) years old **tener (_irreg._) _____ años (y medio)** (3)

yellow **amarillo/a** (7)

yes **sí** (1); yes, of course **sí, por supuesto** (7)

you (_fam. s._) **tú** (1); (_form. s._) **usted** (1); (_fam. pl._) **vosotros/as** (1); (_form. pl._) **ustedes** (1); and you (_fam., form. s._)? **¿y tú? ¿y usted?** (1); you (_fam. s._) (don't) like _____ **(no) te gusta(n) _____** (2); you (one) must (_do something_) **hay que + _inf._** (6); you say _____ **se dice _____** (1); you (_form. s._) should get more rest **tiene que descansar más** (6)

young person **joven** (_pl._ **los jóvenes**) (9)

younger (than) **menor (que)** (3)

your (_form. s._) throat is inflamed **tiene la garganta inflamada** (6)

Index

GRAMMAR AND VOCABULARY INDEX

Note: The use of *n* after a page number indicates that the information is found in the notes at the foot of that page.

A
a + el, 51
a mí, 197
a personal, 80, 144, 162, 197, 410
accent marks
    esdrújula, 259, 447
    indirect object pronouns, 197
    preterit, 202
    written accents, 78, 168, 202, 259, 447
adjectives
    agreement of, 25–26
    demonstrative, 101–102
    descriptive, 20–21, 33, 36, 53, 125, 126
    emotions and behavior, 90, 273
    gender of, 21*n*, 21
    possessive, 75
adverbs, 332–333
ago, 317
agreement, expressing, 21, 24–26
alguno/a, 137*n*, 137
alphabet, Spanish, 8–9
anciano/a, 250*n*
andar, 225
aquellos/as, 101–102
-ar verbs
    conditional, 439
    future, 421
    imperfect, 255
    imperfect subjunctive, 443
    infinitive, 44
    negative commands, 358–359
    present perfect, 298–299
    present tense, 44
    subjunctive, 377

B
borrowed words, 312
bueno/a, 21*n*, 21, 26, 412

C
caer, 267*n*
capitalization
    days of week and months, 19
    nationality, 10*n*
cognates, 29, 66*n*, 250*n*
comer, 298
commands
    formal, 114–115
    formal **(usted/es),** 347–349
    informal, 114–115
    negative, 348, 358–359
    vosotros/as, 115
¿cómo?, 46, 49
comparisons, 23, 83, 294–295

equal, 412
    unequal, 411–412
complemento directo, 142
compound tenses. *see* progressive tenses
conditional tense, 439–440
conducir, 276*n*
conjunctions, 423, 431
conocer
    imperfect, 255
    saber and, 165
contar, 228
contractions, 51, 73*n*
contrasts, making, 23, 83, 294–295
creer que, 391*n*, 391–392
¿cuáles? and **¿qué?,** 46
¿cuánto?, 46

D
dar, 84, 225, 348*n*
days of the week, listed, 19
de + el, 51, 73*n*
¿de quién es/son...?, 73
decir, 141*n*
definite articles, 24–25
    contractions, 51
demonstrative adjectives, 101–102
describing, 20–21, 33, 63, 372
devolver (ue), 194
diphthongs, 168
direct object pronouns, 142–143
    double, 237–238
-do form, 177*n*
¿dónde?, 49
dormir, 104
dormir (ue, e), 228

E
-er verbs
    conditional, 439
    future, 421
    imperfect, 255
    imperfect subjunctive, 443
    negative commands, 358–359
    present perfect, 298
    present tense, 84
    subjunctive, 377
[-]ería (suffix), 123, 189
[-]ero/a (suffix), 253
escuchar, 38*n*, 38
estar
    + adjective, 177
    food and dishes, 125
    + **ndo,** 112
    present tense, 57
    quedar versus, 210

ser versus, 57, 177–178, 179
    uses of, 57, 177
estos/as and **aquellos/as,** 101–102
everyday behavior, emotions and
    behavior, 262–263
everyday language
    classroom expressions, 47
    emotions and behavior, 172, 173, 182–183, 250, 311, 394
    health and illness, 172*n*, 172, 173, 174, 184
    home activities, 97

F
family names, 12, 67
feminine forms
    compound words, 333
    foto and **moto,** 291*n*
    greetings, 6, 9*n*
    nouns, 24
    occupations, 343
    plural pronouns, 14*n*, 14
formal commands, 114–115, 347–349
    formation of, 347
    politeness formulas versus, 349
frequency, expressions of, 248
functional language
    a personal, 80
    agreement, expressing, 21
    combining ideas, 322
    comparing and contrasting, 23, 33, 83
    contractions, 51
    directions, giving, 293
    doctor's office, 174
    job interview, 355
    obligations, 154
    ongoing actions, 299
    para + *infinitive,* 52
    reactions and comments, 374, 401
future
    forms, 421–422
    ir + a + *infinitive,* 55
    uses of, 422

G
gender. *see* feminine forms; masculine forms
gustar
    with actions (verbs), 266
    expressions with, 222
    like versus, 209
    likes and dislikes, 37
    other verbs like, 267
    preferences, 208
    with things (nouns), 266

H

ha habido, 299
haber
    imperfect subjunctive, 443
    + past participle, 298–299
hablar, 255, 299
hace que
    past tense, 317
    present tense, 299, 317
hacer, 84, 225
    idioms with, 299, 317
hay/no hay, 50
    conditional, 439
    future, 422
hypothetical actions, 440

I

idioms, with **hacer,** 299, 317
if... then patterns, 442–443
imperfect
    conditional versus, 440
    describing time and age, 256
    irregular verbs, 255
    preterit versus, 194, 255–256, 283–285
    regular verbs, 255
    uses of, 255–256
imperfect subjunctive, 442–443
impersonal expressions
    infinitives with, 320
    using **se,** 129
impersonal **se,** 129
indefinite articles, 24–25
    + occupation, 178*n*
indirect object pronouns, 197–198
    double, 237–238
    gustar with, 208
    unexpected or unplanned actions,
        330–331
infinitive
    prepositions before, 322
    as subject, 288
informal (**tú**) commands, 114–115, 358–360
informal (**vosotros/as**) commands, 360
interrogative, question words, 41, 49,
    55, 62
ir
    imperfect, 255
    present tense, 55
    preterit, 225
    uses of, 55
ir + **a** + *infinitive,* 55, 422
-ir verbs
    conditional, 439
    future, 421
    imperfect, 255
    imperfect subjunctive, 443
    negative commands, 358–359
    present perfect, 298
    present tense, 84
    stem-changing, 141
    subjunctive, 377
irregular verbs
    formal commands, 348
    preterit, 225–226
    subjunctive, 379

J

jamás, 236
jugar, 104*n*

L

likes and dislikes, expressing, 37, 209, 267
llevar, 44, 194
lo + adjective, 300–301

M

malo/a, 21*n*, 21, 26, 412
mantener, 158*n*
más/menos... que, 50, 411–412
masculine forms, 24*n*, 24, 144
mayor/menor que, 70, 412
-mente (suffix), 333
mirarse, 162
months, 169
motives versus purposes, 320
mucho/a, 50

N

nada (de), 137, 236
nadie, 236
nationality, 9–10, 15–16, 27*n*
-ndo form, 112, 287–288
    conjugated verbs with, 322
    indirect object pronouns, 197
    two object pronouns with, 238
negative
    double, 137
    sentences, 44–45
    words in sentences, 236–237
ni... ni, 236
ninguno/a, 137*n*, 137, 236–237
numbers
    cardinal, 19*n*, 19
    listed, 19, 68, 203*n*, 203
    mayor/menor de, 70*n*, 70
nunca, 236

O

o to **u,** 158*n*
obligations, expressing, 154, 440

P

para and **por,** 130–131, 318–320
past, narrating in, 284
past participle, 177*n*
    haber +, 298–299
pedir, 141
pensar que, 391*n*, 391–392
poder, 225
politeness formulas, 366, 459
    commands versus, 349
    conditional form, 439–440, 459
    with *will,* 422
poner, 225
por and **para,** 130–131, 318–320
porque, 320
possession, expressing, 73
    possessive adjectives, 75
preferences, expressing, 37, 208, 209, 222
preferir, 141

prepositional phrases, 332
prepositions
    of location, 52
    para and **por,** 130–131, 318–320
    position of, 46
    with **ser,** 15–16
present participle, 287–288
    indirect object pronouns, 197
present perfect, 298–299
    word order, 333
present progressive, 112
present subjunctive, 377–379
    basic uses of, 380–382
    cues for, 380–381
    expressing doubt or uncertainty, 391–392
    expressing emotion, 394–395
    forms of, 377–379
    with future actions, 423–424
    with noun antecedent, 409–410
    uses of, 377
present tense
    irregular verbs, 84
    preterit versus, 194
    regular verbs, 84
preterit
    foreground actions in past, 256
    imperfect versus, 194, 255–256, 283–285
    irregular verbs, 225–226
    regular verbs, 194–195
    special translations, 284–285
    stem-changing verbs, 226
    uses of, 194–195
primero/a, 45*n*
progressive tense, present, 112
pronouns
    direct and indirect together, 237–238
    direct object, 142–144
    formal commands, 348–349
    indirect object, 197–198
    informal commands, 359–360
    reflexive, 162–163
    subject, 14
pronunciation and spelling
    b and **v,** as consonant sounds, 290
    d and **g,** as consonants, 324
    consonant + vowel combinations, 202
    consonants, 18
    [g] sound, 134
    intonation in questions, 49
    jota sound, 134
    [k] sound, 134
    l, as consonant, 231
    ll, y and **z,** 107
    m, n, and **ñ,** as nasal sounds, 416
    p, t, and **c/qu,** as consonants, 385
    r and **rr,** as consonant sounds, 231
    [s] sound, 352
    special letter combinations, 134
    spelling conventions in questions, 49
    vowels, 18

Q

¿qué? and **¿cuáles?,** 46
quedar
    estar versus, 210
    uses, 210

querer, preterit, 226
question words, 41, 46, 49, 55, 62, 73
questions
    formation of, 46–47
    intonation, 49
    job interview, 355
    restaurant, 138
    spelling conventions, 49
    yes/no questions, 46–47

R
reactions, expressing, 222, 374, 401
    positive and negative, 267
recibir, 194
reciprocal actions, 361
recomendar (ie), 382*n*
reducir, 165*n*, 225
reflexive pronouns, 162–163
    differences in usage, 163
    reciprocal actions, 361
reírse (i, i), 262*n*
restaurant questions, 138

S
saber, 225, 226
    conocer and, 165
salir, 84
se
    impersonal, 129
    le and **les** to, 238
    reflexive, 162–163
    two object pronouns, 238
    unexpected or unplanned actions,
        330–331
seasons, 169
self/selves, 162
ser
    + adjective, 178
    estar versus, 57, 177–178, 179
    events, 57*n*
    food and dishes, 125
    present, 15–16
    preterit, 225
    uses of, 178
servir, 228
si (*if*) clause, 442–443
sizes (shopping), 191*n*
soñar, 104
spelling changes, preterit, 202
stem-changing verbs
    conditional, 439
    conocer, 165
    formal commands, 347–348
    future, 421
    (i), 141
    (ie, ue), 103–104
    imperfect subjunctive, 442
    preterit, 226
    subjunctive, 378–379
subject pronouns, 14
    emphasis or clarification, 16*n*
subjunctive
    cases that do not take subjunctive, 452
    cases that take subjunctive, 452–453
    cues for, 380–381

expressing doubt or
    uncertainty, 391–392
expressing emotion, 394–395
expressing will, volition, or influence,
    381–382
with future actions, 423–424
imperfect, 442–443
indicative versus, 453
with noun antecedent, 409–410
present, 377–379
sugerir, 382*n*
su(s), 75

T
tampoco, 236
tanto/a/os/as... como, 412
telling time, 39, 62–63, 154
tener
    idioms with, 313
    present tense, 73
    stem-changing, 104
    + **un(a),** 75*n*
traer, 136*n*
transition words, 195
tú
    commands, 114–115
    versus **usted,** 14
    versus **vos,** 14, 286, 399

U
u from **o,** 158n
unexpected or unplanned actions, 330–331
un(o), 68*n*
usted
    commands, 114–115
    versus **tú,** 14

V
variar, 159*n*
ver, 84, 255
verbs
    cooking and eating, 151
    daily routines, 38, 97, 119, 156, 157
    emotions and behavior, 172, 173,
        273, 311
    family activities, 80, 90–91
    obligations, 154, 183
    pastimes, 220
    present tense, 84
    preterit, 194–195
    shopping, 189, 198
    stem-changing (i), 141
    stem-changing (ie, ue), 103–104
    travel, 276, 277, 306–307
    university studies, 63
viejo/a, 250*n*
vivir, 298
    imperfect, 255
vocabulary
    adjectives, 20–21, 151
    age, telling, 69, 90
    biculturalism, 325, 329, 339
    border regions, 310–311, 325, 327
    borrowed words, 219

celebrations, 260–261, 264, 273
city life, 291, 294–295, 307
classroom expressions, 50, 62
clothing, 186–187, 215
colors, 187, 215
computing vocabulary, 388
craft markets, 203
cultural influences, 386, 389,
    400–401, 407
daily routines, 38, 97, 156, 157, 160, 183
dates, 19
days of the week, 19, 33
degree programs, 40, 42
demonstrative adjectives, 101–102, 119
descriptions, 33, 63, 273
electronics terms, 371, 388
emotions and behavior, 172, 173,
    183–184, 250, 262–263, 311, 394
ethnic groups, 404–405, 407,
    427–428, 430
family and relatives, 66–67, 68, 71, 79,
    82, 88, 90–91, 435
food and meals, 122, 123, 125, 126, 127,
    138, 139, 145, 150–151, 248
frequency, expressions of, 248, 272
friendship, 434, 437, 458
furnishings, 108, 119
gifts, 188, 198–199, 210
greetings and leave-takings, 6–7, 32
groups, 105
health and illness, 171, 172*n*, 173, 174,
    175, 184
housing, 94, 95, 98, 109, 110, 118–119
immigration, 310–311, 314, 338–339
indiscreet questions, 75
introductions, 6–7
jewelry, 187, 215
life stages, 250, 273
mass media, 375, 400–401
memories, 253
months, 169, 183
movies, 372–373, 400–401
national origins, 9–10, 12, 32
national symbols, 295, 297
newspapers, 370–371, 400, 401
numbers, 19*n*, 19, 33, 68, 91, 203*n*,
    203, 215
obligations, 183
occupations, 342–343
partying, 232, 244
pastimes, 31, 220, 232, 234, 244
politeness formulas, 366
politics, 401
quantities, 151
reactions, 222, 245
regions, 22
relationships, 434–435, 448, 450,
    458–459
restaurants, 135, 136–137, 138, 151
seasons, 169, 183
shopping, 186–187, 191, 192, 198, 206,
    215–216
social life, 244
social problems, 417, 419, 431
sports, 218–219, 223
stress and relaxation, 158, 183–184

subjects and fields of study, 36, 37, 38
television, 372–373
temperature, 20, 171
tianguis, 192
time of day, 38, 39, 62, 154, 183
transportation, 276, 306
travel, 276, 277, 281, 306–307
university studies, 40, 42, 51, 53, 56, 63
weather, 169–170, 171, 183
work and professions, 342–343, 345,
    353, 356, 364–365, 366–367
vos, versus **tú,** 14, 286, 399
voseo, 286, 437*n*
vosotros/as, 84*n*
    commands, 115, 360

W
weather, 169–170
will/shall, 421–422
word order, 143
    adverbs, 333
would/wouldn't, 440
written accents, 78, 168, 202, 259, 447
    compound words, 332

Y
yes/no questions, 46–47

TOPIC INDEX

Culture, general
    age, telling, 68
    anthropology museum, 205
    archeological sites, 414
    bargaining, 200–201
    baseball, 230
    biodiversity, 61
    Bolívar, Simón, 149
    border regions, 323
    Buenos Aires, 289
    celebrations, 260–261
    ch and **ll,** 9
    Clemente, Roberto, 243
    clothing, 186–187
    Colombian pledge of allegiance, 28
    concept of, 2–3
    daily routines, 156, 157
    dates, 19
    days of the week, 19
    dialects, 106, 124
    Easter Island, 362
    egalitarianism, 48
    electronics terms, 371
    equator, 86
    ethnic groups, 404–405, 426–428
    family names, 12, 67
    family and relatives, 66–67, 68, 77,
        79, 82
    fast food, 133
    food and meals, 122, 123, 125, 133
    frontier Spanish, 312
    furnishings, 108
    generational conflicts, 336
    greetings, 7, 17

Hispanic TV channels, 373
housing, 94, 98, 106
immigrants, 258, 321
legends, 302
Mafalda cartoons, 286
marriage, 435, 441
Mexican border visas **(visa láser),** 321
Mitiendita.mx, 212–214
music, 182, 303–304, 305–306, 327,
    363–364
New Years' resolutions, 241
newspapers in Nicaragua, 370, 384
numbers, 19*n,* 19
online auction sites, 213
pastimes, 220
picadillo, recipe for, 272
professions, feminine variants, 343
racial attitudes, 415
relationships, 448
restaurants, 135, 136–137
Shining Path guerrillas, 420
shopping, 200–201
soap operas, 397–398
social problems, 417
sports, 219, 230, 243
stereotypes, 3, 406
temperatures (Celsius and
    Fahrenheit), 171
tianguis markets, 192, 200
time of day, 167
typical weavings, 396
university studies, 36, 37
vos form, 14, 437*n*
womens' rights, 351
yerba mate (tea), 436

Latin America
    Argentina, 274–275, 278, 286, 289,
        294–295, 303–304, 305–306
    Bolivia, 152–153, 167, 181, 182
    Chile, 340–341, 351, 362
    Colombia, 4–5, 17, 28
    Costa Rica, 34–35, 48, 61
    Cuba, 230, 246–247, 258, 260
    Dominican Republic, 120–121, 146–147
    Ecuador, 64–65, 86
    Guatemala, 368–369, 385
    Honduras, 368–369
    Mexico, 184–185, 200–201, 205, 206, 213
    Nicaragua, 368–369, 370, 384
    Panama, 368–369
    Paraguay, 432–433, 436, 445
    Peru, 402–403, 414, 415, 420
    Puerto Rico, 216–217, 230, 241, 243
    El Salvador, 368–369
    Uruguay, 432–433, 446, 448
    Venezuela, 120–121, 133, 135, 149

Lecturas (readings)
    "Citas en el ciberespacio," 456
    "Clasificados: Pisos," 116–117
    "¿Cómo son las carreras que prefieren
        los jóvenes?," 59–60
    "Cultura y generaciones," 336
    dance poster, 30

"La calidad de vida (adaptación)"
    (Lupe Andrade Salmón), 180–181
"La cocina en la República
    Dominicana," 146–147
"La guitarra," 303–304
"La madre, la cocina, la abuelita y los
    chicos," 270
"Las familias en tiempo de crisis," 88
"Mitiendita.mx," 212–214
"Para formar pareja," 448
"Resoluciones para el año
    nuevo," 241
"Sexto sentido," 398
"Testimonio de una mujer shipiba,"
    427–428

Maps
    Argentina, 274
    Bolivia, 152
    Chile, 340
    Colombia, 4
    Costa Rica, 34
    Cuba, 246
    Dominican Republic, 120
    Ecuador, 64
    Guatemala, 368
    Honduras, 368
    Mexico, 184
    Nicaragua, 368
    Panama, 368
    Paraguay, 432
    Peru, 402
    Puerto Rico, 216
    El Salvador, 368
    Spain, 92
    Uruguay, 432
    U.S.-Mexico border, 308
    Venezuela, 120

Spain, 92–93, 106, 116–117

Timelines
    Argentina, 274–275
    Bolivia, 152–153
    Chile, 340–341
    Colombia, 4–5
    Costa Rica, 34–35
    Cuba, 246–247
    Dominican Republic, 120–121
    Ecuador, 64–65
    Guatemala, 368–369
    Honduras, 368–369
    Mexico, 184–185
    Nicaragua, 368–369
    Panama, 368–369
    Paraguay, 432–433
    Peru, 402–403
    Puerto Rico, 216–217
    El Salvador, 368–369
    Spain, 92–93
    Uruguay, 432–433
    Venezuela, 120–121

United States-Mexico border region,
    308–309

Credits

Photos *Page 1 upper left* © Michael Okoniewski/The Image Works; *1 upper right, middle, lower right* © Robert Frerck/Odyssey/Chicago; *1 lower left* © John Maier Jr./The Image Works; *5* © Fernando Botero, The Street, 1995. Oil on Canvas. 58" x 44 1/8". Courtesy of Marlborough Gallery; *11* Marcelo Salinas/Latin Focus; *28 left* © Robert Frerck/Odyssey/Chicago; *28 middle* © Bruce Ayers/Tony Stone/Getty; *28 right* © Tony Freeman/Photo Edit; *35* Crisanto Badilla, Aterdecer Heredia. 1987. Oil on canvas, 90 X 126 cm; *49* © Ulrike Welsch; *52* © Ulrike Welsch; *58* © Ulrike Welsch; *61 upper left* © Darrell Jones/The Stock Market/Corbis; *61 lower right* © Michael Fogden/ DRK Photo; *65* El Matrimonio by Daniel Chasen Vega. Courtesy of Arts of Tigua; *70 left* David Young-Wolff/Photo Edit; *70 right* © Ulrike Welsch; *70 middle* © Ronnie Kauffman/The Stock Market/Corbis; *76* © Owen Franken/Corbis; *86* © DDB Stock Photo; *93* © Corbis; *96 left* © Craig Lovell; *96 middle* © Ric Ergenbright; *96 right* © Yves Gellie Gamma; *100* © Mcduff Everton/The Image Works; *121* El Mercado by Celeste Wos y Gil. Courtesy of Museum of Modern Art y Dominican Republic; *128* © Ricardo Barbato/Latin Focus; *132* Dominic Arizona Bonuccelli/pPotographersdirect.com; *134* © Ricardo Barbato/Latin Focus; *145* © Pablo Corral/Corbis; *147* © Beryl Goldberg; *149 upper left* © Robert Frerck/Odyssey; *149 lower right* © Galyn Hammond; *153* © Craig Duncan/DDB Stock Photo; *159* © Toni Morrison/South American Pictures; *181* © Halaska / age Fotostock; *185* The Flower Carrier (formerly The Flower Vendor); 1935, Diego Rivera © Estate of Diego Rivera, Courtesy Banco de Mexico; *188 left* © Jeff Greenberg/Peter Arnold, Inc.; *188 middle* © Bob Daemmrich/The Image Works; *188 right* © Chip and Rosa Maria de la Cueva Peterson; *193* © Spencer Grant/PhotoEdit; *201* © Chip and Rosa Maria de la Cueva Peterson; *203* © Robert Frerck/Odyssey; *205* © Robert Frerck/Odyssey; *217* © Jose Jimenez-Tirano/Liaison Agency/Getty; *222* © Larry Mayer; *245* © Rolando Pujol/South American Pictures; *252* © Martha Cooper/Viesti Associates; *259* © Paul Conklin/PhotoEdit; *262 left* © Robert Frerck/Odyssey/Chicago; *262 right* © Bob Daemmrich; *263* © Robert Frerck/Odyssey/Chicago; *270* © Jerry Alexander/Lonely Planet Images; *275* Alejandro Xul Soler. Otro puerto. Acuarela, 27.5 x 37 cm. Colección: Amalia Lacroze de Fortabat. Copyright Fundación Pan Klub, Museo Xul Solar; *278 upper* © D. Donne Bryant; *278 middle* © Eric L. Ergenbright; *278 lower* © Norman Benton/Peter Arnold Inc.; *293 left* © Bill Bachmann/The Image Works; *293 right* © Chad Ehlers/Stone/Getty; *302* Zurbaran Galeria, Buenos Aires/SuperStock; *303* © North Wind Picture Archives; *305* © Corbis; *309* © Robert Fried; *311* © Jimmy Dorantes/Latin Focus; *325 left* © Bob Daemmrich/The Image Works; *295 right* © T&D McCarthy/The Stock Market/Corbis; *326* © Charles Gupton; *334* © Steven Rubin/The Image Works; *336* © Bob Daemmrich/The Image Works; *341* © Schapowalow / Atlantide / Fotofinder.net; *344* © Larry Dale Gordon; *350* © Jason P. Howe/South American Pictures; *352* © Beryl Goldberg; *362* © Jack S. Grove/Tom Stack & Associates; *364* © HO/Reuters; *373* © Susan Greenwood/Liaison Agency/Getty; *385* © Rob Cousins/Panos Pictures; *386* © Cindy Karp/Black Star; *396* © D. Donne Bryant; *403* © Alejandro Balaguer/Tony Stone/Getty; *408* © John Maier Jr./The Image Works; *414* © Boyd Norton/The Image Works; *417 left, middle left* © Fran Antmann; *417 middle right* © Don Mason/The Stock Market/Corbis; *417 right* © Ulrike Welsch; *433* © Francis E. Caldwell/DDB Stock Photo; *435* © Rodrigo Guillenea/Latin Focus; *445* © Gerard Loucel; *448* © Kevin Dodge/Masterfile.

Readings *Page 17* Excerpts from copyrighted material by Terri Morrison, President, Getting Through Customs, http://www.getcustoms.com, (610) 725.1040,

About the Authors

Robert L. Davis is Associate Professor and the Director of the Spanish Language Program at the University of Oregon. He teaches courses in Spanish language, historical linguistics, and teaching methodology. His interests include language pedagogy and materials development, in particular the development of language skills within content-based instruction. He has written an advanced oral skills textbook and articles on language pedagogy, materials development, and language program direction.

H. Jay Siskin received his Ph.D. from Cornell University in Romance and French linguistics. He is Director of the Language Lab at Cabrillo College. Dr. Siskin has written numerous articles and reviews that have appeared in such journals as *Foreign Language Annals, The French Review, The Canadian Review of Modern Languages,* the *ADFL Bulletin,* and the *Modern Language Journal.* His research interests include autobiographical narrative and the teaching of culture.

Alicia Ramos is Associate Professor of Spanish and Coordinator of the basic language program in French, Italian, and Spanish at Hunter College (CUNY) in New York. She received her Ph.D. from the University of Pennsylvania, has served on the faculties of Barnard College and Indiana University of Pennsylvania, and as Assistant Director of the Spanish School at Middlebury College. Dr. Ramos' interests include methodology and materials development for courses from the elementary through advanced levels, including courses for Spanish speakers. Dr. Ramos has published in the field of Hispanic literature and has co-authored intermediate- and advanced-level textbooks including *Cofre literario* (McGraw-Hill), a literary reader for the intermediate and advanced levels.